Handbook of Business Planning and Budgeting for Executives with Profit Responsibility

Handbook of Business Planning and Budgeting for Executives with Profit Responsibility

Thomas S. Dudick

Editor-in-Chief

Robert V. Gorski

Associate Editor

 VAN NOSTRAND REINHOLD COMPANY
NEW YORK   CINCINNATI   TORONTO   LONDON   MELBOURNE

Copyright © 1983 by Van Nostrand Reinhold Company Inc.

Library of Congress Catalog Card Number: 82-8341
ISBN: 0-442-22188-6

Manufactured in the United States of America

Published by Van Nostrand Reinhold Company Inc.
135 West 50th Street, New York, N.Y. 10020

Van Nostrand Reinhold Publishing
1410 Birchmount Road
Scarborough, Ontario M1P 2E7, Canada

Van Nostrand Reinhold
480 Latrobe Street
Melbourne, Victoria 3000, Australia

Van Nostrand Reinhold Company Limited
Molly Millars Lane
Wokingham, Berkshire, England

15 14 13 12 11 10 9 8 7 6 5 4 3 2 1

Library of Congress Cataloging in Publication Data
Handbook of business planning and budgeting for
  executives with profit responsibility.

  Bibliography: p.
  Includes index.
  1. Planning. 2. Corporate planning. 3. Budget in
business. I. Dudick, Thomas S. II. Gorski, Robert V.
HD30.28.H364 1983   658.4'102   82-8341
ISBN 0-422-22188-6   AACR2

Editorial Advisory Board

Preface

Executives with profit responsibility, whether engaged in marketing, research, production, or finance, are faced with increasingly complex and difficult problems in managing the businesses for which they are responsible. The technical competence of these executives within their own disciplines is without question. However, the ability of this assortment of disciplines to work together as a coordinated team is subject to question in many companies. It is the purpose of this book to discuss the key disciplines in a manner that will make the problems of each discipline clear to executives in the other disciplines. The book also discusses solutions to these problems for the purpose of improving interdisciplinary understanding and cooperation.

This handbook is broken down into nine sections. The first of these is an overview of business planning and budgeting. In the first chapter of this section, William Agee, chairman, president, and chief executive officer of the Bendix Corporation, emphasizes the importance of early warning systems through monitoring and forecasting—to continually highlight major risks and soft spots that could defer the attainment of company goals.

David N. Judelson, president of Gulf + Western Industries, explains how he achieved good control in his company through the use of the flash forecast and flash actual. In his chapter, he walks the reader through the early warning procedures and the steps that he follows in assuring effective controls as well as achieving better interdisciplinary coordination.

The debilitating effect of inflation on profitability prompted four executives from Main Hurdman & Cranstoun to write a chapter explaining how business performance can be improved during inflationary times.

C. Gadzinski, president of Capital Management Corporation, tells executives with profit responsibility how they can avoid pitfalls in business planning, while James W. Taylor, management consultant, lists the ten commandments for realistic planning.

Section II, dealing with strategies in business planning, lays the groundwork for discussing product planning and new markets. One of the characteristics of American business in past decades has been a pattern of unrelenting growth, achieved by acquisitions as well as internal expansion. In the early years of this century, some 125 individual automobile companies have 'shaken out' to only four. The same trend occurred with other products—radios, television sets, and cameras, to name a few. Included in this section is a chapter by Andrew Clapp of Arthur D. Little, Inc., in which he emphasizes the need for inclusion of diversification as part of the strategy for effective planning.

Professor Philip Kotler discusses market strategy from the point of view of the market leader, the challenger, and the follower. He discusses such strategies as "head-on," "back door," and "guppy."

Peter Lorange, Associate Professor of Management of the Wharton School, outlines the need for effective regeneration of optimum allocation of funds, people, and technology in designing a strategic planning system.

Cortlandt Cammann, of the Institute for Social Research, concentrates on strategies for control. In his chapter, he deplores the fact that subordinates frequently do not contribute to organizational goals as expected. He also points out that conflicts among these subordinates waste substantial amounts of energy and resources, and describes the elements of the control strategy that should be developed.

Section III, Planning for Products and New Markets, is devoted to the importance of changing trends and the need for increasing the productivity of new-product research as well as the marketing organization.

Charles Reed, a retired senior vice-president of General Electric Company, discusses the wide variety of trends, crises, and concerns that have combined to make the process of national planning an active issue on the political agenda of the United States. Mr. Reed explores the adequacy of our response to this challenge.

Carl Barnes, Vice-President 3M Company (Ret.), an expert in new-product research, discusses the reduced productivity of product research in our country while such countries as Japan and Germany continue to outpace us in new products and new technology.

James Hind, vice-president of planning at R. J. Reynolds Tobacco Company, compares the intuitive approach to the market place versus the disciplined, deliberate approach of examining the facts, considering the alternatives, and determining the best strategy.

The product life cycle is well understood by many, but Sonia Yuspeh, senior vice-president of J. Walter Thompson Company, points out the fallacy in the common belief that all products follow a regular life-cycle pattern in its familiar four predictable stages.

J. Herbert Holloman, director, MIT Center for Policy Alternatives, explains the social and political changes now taking place that provide opportunities and what these changes portend.

Porter Henry, of Porter Henry & Company, Inc., deals with problems of selling. In his first of two chapters in this section, he demonstrates the various yardsticks that can be used for measuring and improving productivity of the sales force. In the second, he discusses methods for scheduling sales calls for products and customers to produce the maximum profit per call.

Dr. Sam R. Goodman, executive vice-president of Magnuson Computer Systems, proposes mathematical models for use in eliminating much of the wasteful expenditure of money in new-product strategy.

Section IV supplements the previous section with two case examples. The first of these examples demonstrates a well-structured approach to making up a marketing plan for a new consumer product. The second case example outlines the steps of a marketing plan for a new business.

Emphasis on the need for good control of assets is the subject of Section V. The better the controls, the lower the assets and therefore the higher the return on these assets.

Purchasing is no longer a stocking function to assure that the company would not run short of material. With material making up 50% or more of the manufacturing cost in many companies, purchasing is an important source of improved profits.

Inventory control policy and the forecasting of inventory are the topics of the next two chapters in this section. Sound inventory policies are an important prerequisite to good purchasing policy.

Jacob Brooks, vice-president, and Breaux Castleman, vice-president, of Booz Allen & Hamilton, discuss materials management problems in widely distributed operations in hostile environments.

Paul Maranka, director of materials management at Incom, International, Inc., explains the master schedule and its importance in the manufacturing business plan.

Earl Corriveau, manufacturing accounting manager at Wang Laboratories, explains the various steps in the implementation of a sound capital expenditures control program—using actual examples.

John T. Hagan, director of quality management at ITT, explains that the most important goal of quality management is to assure that quality standards not be eroded each time there are excessive pressures. He believes in the old adage "Tell it like it is"—and he tells it in Section VI.

In our highly competitive business community, it behooves the executive with profit responsibility to be aware of what competitors are doing. This is discussed in two chapters making up Section VII. The first of these is titled "Industry Statistics as a Management Tool." Analysis of Company Weaknesses, the second chapter in this section, demonstrates how a group of key executives can review the operating statement, make comparisons with industry statistics, and determine the reasons for their company's shortfall in profits.

Section VIII deals with Product Costing and Pricing. It is a logical follow-up to the previous section, in which it has been determined where the company's excessive costs are occurring.

Phillip J. Wingate, retired vice-president of E. I. DuPont de Nemours & Company, discusses pricing in a free economy. In his down-to-earth chapter, he points out that pricing decisions are made in relatively narrow limits. He discusses the factors that cause variations in these limits and provides illustrations.

In recognition of the fact that unit costs of products are greatly influenced by the capacity level at which the company is operating, the next chapter in this section discusses five methods for arriving at capacities and demonstrates the impact on unit costs for each of the methods.

Raymond B. Jordan, retired administrator—cost systems and studies for General Electric, explains the concept of the learning curve, an important and sometimes overlooked tool for reducing costs.

The final section, Section IX deals in methods for improving profit performance.

William T. O'Neill, executive vice-president of Newport News Shipbuilding and Dry Dock Company, points out how the success or failure of a company depends on how well the manufacturing operation manages the resources under its scope of responsibility. He further points out that this is dependent upon the degree of coordination between manufacturing and the various support functions within the company.

Hugo Swan, vice-president of operations, Clausing Corporation, cautions against using budgetary controls as a substitute for other operational controls. He describes the steps required in an intelligently prepared budget.

Thomas G. Hardy of McKinsey & Company and John E. Neuman of Dewey, Ballantine, Bushby, Palmer & Wood discuss the wastefulness of providing overhead services without regard to the cost involved in creating them.

In the selection of contributing authors for this handbook, we recognized that every executive has his or her special field of expertise—a field that comes naturally to him or her. We also recognized that no single author could possibly write authoritatively on the range of topics covered in the book. For these reasons, we recognized that the selection of the authors was crucial in the development of recommended techniques for improving the performance of a company. It is the opinion of the editors that the authors have done their work well.

Thomas S. Dudick
Editor-in-Chief

Robert V. Gorski
Associate Editor

Contents

Handbook of
Business Planning
and Budgeting
for Executives
with Profit
Responsibility

SECTION I
OVERVIEW OF BUSINESS
PLANNING AND BUDGETING

1
Futurism—A Lesson From The Private Sector

William M. Agee

Chairman, President, and Chief Executive Officer
The Bendix Corporation

Mr. Agee urges that executives recognize the need for early warning systems through continuous monitoring and forecasting in order to highlight major risks and soft spots that could defer the attainment of goals.

It is axiomatic that all human beings get a delayed report card. Indeed, it is biblical. As Paul said, "...whatsoever a man soweth, that shall he also reap." I'm also partial to Satchel Paige's wisdom: "Never look back. Something might be gaining on you."

Both of these lessons apply to corporate managers, who take charge of an ongoing business knowing that the first few annual reports they sign will be the results of what their predecessors did and did not do. Luckily for me, Mike Blumenthal left the Bendix Corporation in splendid shape. But the outcome of the 1980s is mostly up to those he left behind when he moved up to bigger budgets. The dim shape of the 1980s is what I spend most of my time thinking about.

I think the first point is that what will happen to business in the 1980s will be even less divorceable from what happens to the rest of the country than it is now. I make this statement because of a common tendency to talk about the American economy as a collection of sectors, separate and discrete. Examples are business, labor, government, and in recent decades, an independent sector, composed of foundations, charities, and voluntary organizations. These categories have their uses as catch phrases or verbal shorthand, but we must keep in mind that they are just that.

GOVERNMENT'S PAPERWORK DEMANDS ON MODERN BUSINESS

The world may well have looked so organized to the entrepreneur Vincent Bendix when he launched his company. It was his, or largely his, and he ran it in the manner of his day. He was tough, authoritarian, and he had no trouble living with decisions as long as they were his. His job, as he saw it, was to see the demands of the market economy and satisfy them. And he was good at it. His company was renamed Bendix Aviation at a time when only 8% of the company's business had anything to do with the promising new machine called the airplane. He saw the future coming, a theme upon which I want to elaborate.

I believe that Vincent Bendix would find the present unthinkable. He would find *his company* living with reams of paper to be filled out daily because the government needs them, regulated by a blizzard of laws on such issues as the environment, safety, pricing, taxation, and equal opportunity, perceived as a public institution responsible not only for profit and shareholder value, but for a subtle list of obligations that have more to do with sociology than economics, and doing well in an age when you need more than a quick look to find out who *owns* it.

The complicated fact is that the climate in which business now operates has little to do with the world Vincent Bendix knew. That is not to confess Mr. Bendix's shortcomings. He was very right for his time. The question before the managers of the 1980s is: Will they be right for theirs?

Vincent Bendix died in 1945, just as the pent-up demand of the war years began to create the consumer society we know today. So he missed the soaring economy of the late 1940s and early 1950s, and the relative quiet of the Eisenhower years. He missed the time when the business sector shriveled in the public mind from being the cornerstone of our economic well-being to an object of ridicule and suspicion. He did not see Rosa Parks refuse to turn her seat on the bus over to a white man, and he missed the nonviolent dream of Martin Luther King. He might have applauded John Kennedy's decision to skirt Keynesian dogma and try a tax cut that *did* get this country moving again. He did not hear the first shots in the war on poverty, or see the trickle of advisors to Vietnam grow to the size of an army. He probably would have liked Lyndon Johnson, but still would have told him that it was a mistake to think an already overheated economy could generate guns, butter, and rapid social change without producing an intractable kind of inflation.

Well, it is human to define your own glimpses of public events as the broad sweep of history. The environment in which business goes about the business of business will never be the same. There has been a generalized failure of the belief of Americans in our institutions, and business is not alone in that. If it makes us feel any better, the press may also be included.

CYNICISM OF THE 1960s AND 1970s

We have lived through the early 1970s in self-criticism, self-hatred, and cynicism. The 1960s and 1970s were the time in which it became fashionable to question everything—every value we previously held, every perception of what it takes to be a responsible citizen, every ethic of work and reward. There emerged what social scientist Daniel Yankelovich named *the psychology of entitlement*. As belief in institutions—government, business, labor, and the rest—dove downward, our citizens turned to themselves as the place to find trust and happiness. Now, I believe strongly that the road to personal happiness lies in conscious control of your own life. That idea squares with my values. Self-reliance, hard work—you can fill in the rest. But what seemed too different about this turning to the self—if Yankelovich's formulation is right—was the vague, individual feeling that somehow the good things in life are *owed*, and are a birthright. You would see social science surveys in which people would say that their city, state, or even the whole country was heading for economic, nuclear, or environmental disaster. And they would go right on, in the same survey, to report that their own futures were right on track, with more money, more promotions, more leisure time just about assured. Well, this is where I get off that train of thought. What happens to all of us happens to each of us.

ARE AMERICANS DOOMED TO CONSTANT TURMOIL?

I sometimes think we Americans are doomed to turmoil because we take on so much. It seems to be downright American to figure that every domestic problem we face can be taken on and solved. We are doers. And that is, or certainly has been, the source of our greatness. We can focus, if we wish, on how various dreams of social change are less than fully realized. But for myself, I am more struck by how much we do get done. There is not another government on the face of this earth, for instance, that could have survived the anguish of Watergate. As Gerald Ford said, "The system works." The Congress and the Supreme Court lived up to their responsibilities. It was a painful triumph, one I wish we had never experienced, but it *was* a triumph.

I hope that we Americans never give up trying to make our lives better. But I think there is a huge amount of room for change in the way we do it. Just about every time we embark to change our laws to improve matters, we do it in an atmosphere of crisis.

It doesn't take much to start a crisis. A Gallup Poll will do it, especially one that says 67% of the American people are worried about a problem. Our communications media roll the drums with headlines, interviews, and rapid-fire analysis. Congress and the Administration respond with legislation. I would laugh—if it didn't hurt so much—over the charges of the radicals of the 1960s that our government is not responsive. It responds, my friends, with fury.

I doubt there is a person who is willing to advocate a dirty environment, dangerous factories, or cheating consumers. But the crisis orientation of our legislative process means that we approach social problems as if we are at war. And a war, we understand, is for winning. It is a poor patriot who stops to count the cost, or who asks what else winning that war will mean.

Garret Hardin, a biologist and human ecologist, offers an elegant statement: "You can never do merely one thing." And there is the rub. For instance, American industry is currently producing well below its capacity, yet we do not see the elimination of inflation we could hope for and expect. I believe that an important reason can be found in the new costs levied on business by such regulatory efforts as the Environmental Protection Act and the Occupational Safety and Health Act. It has been estimated that "the cost of capital investment for all pollution control requirements of the Environmental Protection Agency will reach over \$100 billion." That is \$100 billion that will not go for research and development or for increases in productivity. It is quite clear to me now. In a few years, it will definitely be apparent to all that we started on a project that was manifestly worth doing, and then let our crisis orientation make us overspend grossly.

AMERICAN BUSINESS MUST RECLAIM SELF-RESPECT

Now, it is usual to stand in forums and *fulminate* about the government. It is an infuriatingly large target. But the managers of the 1980s will have to do more than that. They will have to be politically involved people, as aware of social currents as of output on the production line, as well-read as the academician testifying before Congress.

I believe that just about now, American business has the beginnings of a chance to reclaim its position as a respected American institution. For years now, we have been losing the rhetorical battles with our critics, and part of the reason lies in our own behavior. We must not only *appear* to be credible when we take part in talking about upcoming legislation, we must *be* credible. It does little good, for instance, to swear that we cannot live with a given piece of legislation—cannot accomplish it physically—if we then magically pull off what the law demands after the President signs it.

Take the matter of equal opportunity. It is the law that there be no discrimination about race or sex, and all of us can give a glib speech about how we believe in the law. But too many businessmen have failed to express the next obvious thought about righting these social wrongs. It is that aggressive, ambitious people of any color or either sex are priceless assets. We do not say often enough that bigotry and sexism are expensive. We do not speak loudly enough to say that there is no conflict between our moral sense and our economic sense.

We have to take those next logical steps in

the direction of social change; it would be far better if we took them on our own. It is now Bendix policy that when it comes time to award financial incentives to our managers, we look not only at bottom-line results, but also at the manager's record of success in affirmative action, management development, and safety.

That is only one example of social responsibility that makes good business sense—along with being the right thing to do. I think it is a particularly good point that economic and social interest will often marry, if we stop grousing and convincing each other that change should not be brought up in the first place.

We have no time for merely complaining about the social and political forces that make such an impact on our businesses. We have to use the thought processes and analytical tools—the ones we know how to use better than anyone else—to help with solving public problems and to reeducate our crisis-bent legislators on how this system really works.

LEGISLATING IN CRISIS AND REGRETTING AT LEISURE

I sometimes think that we need a "Secretary of the Future" in government, as an antidote to our current practice of legislating in crisis and regretting at leisure. It is certainly true that businessmen are the natural futurists in this country. If we ran our businesses the way government makes laws, there would be a lot of resumes flying through the mails. I see this Secretary of the Future as being responsible for weighing *all* the implications of a particular piece of legislation, so that Congress makes an informed decision instead of a hasty one. The additional responsibility would be to announce—well in advance—that there's a problem on the way.

Does anyone doubt that there was plenty of time to see the energy crisis coming? And yet, the program to deal with it had to be originated when Americans found themselves lined up in their cars at gas stations. In a re-

sult typical of crisis reaction, we are worse off for our efforts. If you will recall, after the Arab embargo of 1973, this nation proclaimed its intention to become energy independent. The program was launched with predictable hullabaloo, tied to the patriotism of the Bicentennial celebration and named, appropriately, Project Independence. Without detailing all that happened, let me point out that before we embarked on this program, we imported 35% of our oil. Shortly thereafter, we imported about 50% of the oil we use—and sent $45 billion to other countries to pay for it. If we had been as successful when we launched the first Project Independence in 1776, we'd still be paying taxes to the King of England.

THE COMING PENSION CRISIS

There is another crisis on the way, and it will impact the 1980s in a way that will get our full attention. I'm talking about pension funding, particularly about Social Security. Congress passed a $227 billion Social Security tax increase, which was the largest peacetime tax increase bill in American history. Once more, it was done in haste, and I will bet that many or most Americans think that bill solved the problem. True, there has been a great deal of feedback to Congress that the voters aren't thrilled with the tax increase. But their annoyance now won't be a patch on the public rage that will rise if and when the system stops issuing the pensioners' checks. The beneficiaries will rage because a promise has been broken. Those active in the work force will rage because it will be their job to pay the new taxes. Consider that the unfunded liabilities of the Social Security system total about *$2 trillion.* Social Security may well face bankuptcy before the end of the 1980s because the new legislation is based on some assumptions that are, in my opinion, too optimistic. Social Security is only one part of the pension-funding pyramid. The unfunded liabilities of government pension plans—on the local, state, and federal levels—are in similar financial straits.

FREE ENTERPRISE IS NOT DEAD

I have dealt at some length with the political atmosphere in which our businesses operate because I am convinced that there will be little change in the future—in the direction of less regulation or less public expectation that business has a social role to play. The free enterprise that we speak of so fondly is not dead, but is a mutation of the type of free enterprise practiced before the Depression. Because I see no practical possibility of revising the rules of this society so that we would return to those simpler days, I think businessmen have no choice but to take full and vigorous part in the affairs of the larger society. They want to participate. They have much to contribute. They must, in their own self-interest.

MANAGING IN THE COMING YEARS

I will be surprised if the manager of the 1980s is confronted with the sweet but *disconcerting* problem of enormous growth. The managers of the 1960s had plenty of chances at that giddy experience, and there was a time when it was hard to find an investment manager who didn't look pretty smart on paper. But recessions have a way of letting the water down from the ships of our industry so that all can see the barnacles.

I think the 1980s, as never before, will be a rich opportunity for managers who are sophisticated in their use of financial planning and control techniques. It is one thing—and a pleasant one—to manage a business that is rocketing ahead in all measures of growth. It is another to be able, as Vincent Bendix so often was, to see the future coming and react before it arrives.

At Bendix, our planning and control mechanism includes what we call the "early warning system." Principally, we get an early warning of future conditions through monitoring and forecasting, on a monthly basis, key balance sheet and income statement data as compared to the yearly financial plan and five-year, long-range plan and the previous forecast.

Aside from the quantitative tools of business, there remains the question of leadership and what sorts of people the managers of the 1980s will be trying to lead and how they will try to do it.

I noted earlier the cynicism about everything—not just business—that has been a fact of American social life for the last decade or better. What strikes me is that it comes most vividly from those who have benefited most from the truly astonishing performance of the American economic system over the last 100 years. The challenge to our economic system does not come from what the nineteenth-century Marxists called "the wretched of the earth," but rather from those who were moving up, the middle classes, the intellectuals, the professional people—and many of their children.

We should not be surprised by this. Cynicism is a luxurious commodity. It cannot flourish beside gut-level despair and desperation. In any case, I think we have seen the worst manifestations of it. There is strong evidence for instance, that our young people are moving strongly into quite traditional and reassuring courses of study at the college level. But let's not be fooled into thinking that the political turbulence of the 1960s didn't change anything. It changed any number of values—toward sex, marriage, the role of America as a world power, and what it means to be a complete human being. Allow me the oversimplification of thinking that, as with previous radical movements, our society took some of the better ideas from this last one, and dropped the chaff by the wayside.

If I am right about that, it means the people that managers will be leading in the next ten years will be quite insistent that the jobs they do have personal meaning to them, and that the businesses they work for act in ways commonly called moral. There will be very little gratitude simply because they were hired. They will expect personal growth and a sense of power and achievement in their jobs.

They will respect power wisely used, but they won't fear or follow a traditional authoritarian.

PARTICIPATING MANAGEMENT

At Bendix, we talk about "participatory management," and sometimes we observe the ideals of it in the breach. Put baldly, our tendency is toward getting more and more people into the act when we are planning or thinking about general policies. We try to draw into the process all those who have something to contribute and most assuredly those who will be responsible for doing what we decide.

I am not suggesting that there is a huge room at Bendix where hundreds of managers collect to vote corporate policies up or down. Our top executives are paid to decide, and they do. I feel that a greater degree of participation in decision making is the right way to go.

Most of us are already at the point where the easy jobs are no longer available. By easy jobs, I mean those that you can do yourself. The tougher ones are those that others must do for you and with you.

Our fiction is full of corporate leaders who seem to have gotten by on being glib, telling lies, and manipulating other people. I am glad those stories are much more often fiction than fact. There are at least two reasons you cannot base a career in management on the idea that you can manipulate other people:

1. All people, and particularly the young ones coming along, are too smart. They will catch you at it. They feel your contemptuous disrespect, and your battle to lead is lost.

2. Time is too short to make an enterprise—of whatever size—operate on deceit.

Notice that I have given pragmatic reasons for being honest with people. There is a third reason: You won't sleep very well if you do otherwise.

I am glad there is not a dirty little secret or a trick to bounding up the corporate ladder. I'm glad there is not a particular way of acting, or seeming to be, that is rewarded in the long run.

Finally, I suppose, it comes to this: from the viewpoint of human relationships and leadership, you will get from your organization and your people just about what you expect from yourself.

The coming years will be the time when wise managers can win back for business the reputation that was tarnished in the 1960s and 1970s. We can do that if we see that the interests of business and the larger society are very often convergent. We can do it even though the prospect is for more legislation and regulation—if we use our skills as futurists to take vigorous part in debates over the nation's future. We can do it if we will drop the defensive tone that makes us sound unprogressive. We are so much better than that, and have too much to be proud of.

Within our companies, the successful managers of the 1980s will be those who can manage a slower rate of growth and react very quickly to changing opportunities. Pinpoint control and forecasting will be the key. And although the discipline of profit will still govern, the leadership of our businesses will depend to a greater extent on the informed consent of those we lead, and how well employee aspirations for personal fulfillment and growth fit corporate goals. The day of the autocratic taskmaster is over.

2
Monitoring Progress Against the Business Plan

David N. Judelson

President

Gulf + Western Industries, Inc.

Mr. Judelson explains how good monitoring and control can be achieved through the *Flash Forecast* and the *Flash Actual*.

Talk about the great growth record at Gulf + Western Industries, Inc. sometimes bothers me. What concerns me is the idea of runaway growth implied in much of the talk about the company. The headline about Gulf + Western *is* its meteoric growth since the late 1950s. But the fact is that Gulf + Western is a very well controlled company.

CONTROLLED INTERNAL GROWTH THROUGH BUSINESS PLANNING

Controlled internal growth might well be called the name of the game at G + W these days. We have gone into business planning and management controls with the same enthusiasm as our growth-by-acquisition drive of past years. Largely homegrown, management controls were launched in 1967 and have been refined intensely since that time.

It takes sound planning and controls to guide a company as large and diverse as G + W on a growth path. The company, with annual sales running about $4.3 billion, has eight operating groups covering widely divergent products and services ranging from manufacturing, including energy products and capital goods, to food and agricultural products, natural resources, and movie producing. (See Table 1.) Still, both the corporate and group operating managements find the controls very workable and effective.

In October, 1980, G + W, through its eight groups, projected what its operating income would be at the end of July, 1981. The business plan held up in a wildly hectic year. We didn't miss it by 2%. That's a fact!

NEED FOR FULL AND FREE COMMUNICATIONS

The management controls at G + W feature full and free communications between group and corporate management. The timeliness of the controls spotlights problems as they occur, not, as controls often do, sometime after problems have been either solved or turned into real crises.

Before detailing of G + W's system of business planning, management controls, and reports, I feel it is necessary to understand the corporate setting and underlying philosophy of G + W as being a highly centralized *decentralized* company. This means it is highly

9

Table 1. Gulf + Western at a glance

The company's products and services include:

1. Manufacturing (including energy products and capital equipment)
2. Financial services
3. Paper and building products
4. Leisuretime (including movies and television products)
5. Automotive replacement parts
6. Consumer and agricultural products
7. Natural resources
8. Apparel products

The fiscal year ends July 31.

FINANCIAL DATA IN THOUSANDS		
	19X2	19X1
Sales	$4,311,956	$3,647,517
Income before taxes	257,916	205,927
Net earnings	180,516	150,327
*Return on sales	4.2%	4.1%
*Return on stockholders' equity	13.1%	12.2%

GULF + WESTERN OPERATING GROUPS

	19X2 IN MILLIONS		OPERATING INCOME % CHANGE FROM 19X1
	SALES	OPERATING INCOME	
Manufacturing	$1,097	$72.6	−22%
Financial services	985	93.7	+104
Paper and building products	492	17.6	+14
Leisure time	802	84.1	+136
Automotive replacement parts	350	28.3	+8
Consumer and agricultural products	440	76.4	+69
Natural resources	414	5.3	−88
Apparel products	725	54.8	+23

centralized through the reporting system between group and corporate levels. However, on a day-to-day operational basis, we rely completely on the people who run our groups—those who make the day-to-day decisions. These are the decisions on what orders to take, what inventory levels to maintain, what prices to put on products, and so on.

Field managers cannot undertake major variations from the normal course of business. No group head, for example, can commit the company to a multimillion dollar capital project not authorized in the business plan. In the same vein, one person cannot make an acquisition without verification from corporate.

The reasoning behind these exceptions is clear enough. If each of our eight groups thought a given $20 million expenditure made sense, this would add up to $160 million.

EFFECTIVE CONTROLS REQUIRE PARTICIPATION

However, company controls and reporting systems were developed with the complete agreement of the people who have to use the system. If we didn't have their agreement, it would all be meaningless. The reports, controls, and figures would have no meaning. This is why our controls are so good: They are accepted by the people who use them as tools to run their own businesses, a most important requirement.

HOW G + W PLANNING DEVELOPED

G + W started in 1967 on its program of business planning and controls. At first, there were the standard one- and five-year plans. Next, planning was put on a continuous quarterly basis—managers forecast in one quarter for the same quarter in the following year, and dropped a quarter. This gave a rolling one-year forecast. One of the improvements was that operating managers were dealing with the quarterly problems that were taking place when they made their forecasts. The same quarters in different years usually include patterns that are similar. These patterns include such elements as number of work days and seasonal sales characteristics. This move improved the credibility of our forecasting greatly, but there still remained a problem of timeliness.

When the annual business plan was presented sometime in the first quarter of the year, we were at the point in a discussion about the upcoming year. But in many cases the first two months had already ended. This meant deviations from the plan could already be strongly underway, leading top management to the conclusion that timeliness in business plan projections is an essential factor. Our business planning resulted in a month-to-month plan. The plan covered the entire year, as it always did. Then, for each quarter, we assembled and projected sales, earnings, inventories, return on investment—the whole gamut—on a month-to-month basis.

MONITORING PROGRESS AGAINST THE PLAN

I can now pull out a book for each of our groups, consolidated and consolidating, by entities within the groups, to show month-to-month projections of the indices we look at in our business planning. But even the month-to-month plan had too long a time lag to please management.

Our first month was over by August 31. By the time I had the information on my desk, it was the end of September or the first week in October. That was the report for the month of August. I wasn't happy about asking field managers questions on events that happened five or six weeks previously. I would ask, "Why are your sales down in August?" The manager would answer, "Well, I just finished September and my sales are up and that made up for the August shortfall."

THE FLASH FORECAST

What came out of our dissatisfaction with this month-to-month plan is possibly unique in management controls. G + W managers refer to it as the *Flash Forecast*. Under the Flash Forecast approach, each of the top group managers telephones me on the fifteenth of every month. At the time of the call, I have in front of me the monthly report book. In it, entries are broken down by groups and meaningful divisions within each group. This book includes the group's business plan for the year, prior year's results, a space for the monthly forecast, a space for variances from the Flash Forecast, and a column for a *Flash Actual* (explained later) that comes at the end of each month.

The basis of reporting by any group head at this point is the business plan made before the end of the previous year and updated at year-end for the coming year. This overall plan is then updated at the end of each quarter. At the end of the third quarter, I receive a fourth update. This gives the group head next year's total plan. Updates include the year-to-date plan and forecasts for the balance of the year plus the next quarter. Included are any adjustments for the month.

All this allows us, as the year goes on, to focus on our year-end figures. The main advantage of the Flash Forecast is that it provides the basis for communication with group heads. More important is the fact that the group manager, to be able to describe for me the group's activities for that month, must be in turn talking to each division manager. And each division manager must be talking to those who report to him. This process goes on right down to the plant level.

In the Flash Forecast, we are not only talking about the forecast for that month, but we are talking about problems as they happen. The dialog is fresh.

THE FLASH ACTUAL

The telephone becomes a vital instrument in management controls on the sixth day of each month. On that day, the eight top group managers call me with what is called a *Flash Actual*. This is a follow-up of the Flash Forecast telephoned in on the fifteenth of the previous month. Both reports, of course, cover the same month of operations. The Flash Actual call is a dialog between each group manager and myself on how the Flash Forecast turned out—and "why or why not."

At the time of the Flash Forecast, a group manager may have told me, for example, that earnings would be up 10% over the plan for the month. I enter that number. On the sixth of the next month, in the Flash Actual, he tells me exactly what happened. At that point, he might be up only 5%. Or he might be over his forecast. We then have another dialog about what actually happened last month. Again, each group head receives information so that he is right on top of his operations. To answer his questions, the group head asks questions of his division managers, and so on down the line.

One of the important by-products of these flash reports is that both corporate and field people are kept wideawake as to what is happening as it happens. Another important by-product is that we can project accurately what our earnings will be on a quarterly and yearly basis. This gives us a sound basis for long-term planning. I credit the soundness and the thoroughness of the short-term planning for

the good results experienced with the company's five-year planning.

DISCIPLINE IN GOOD BUSINESS PLANNING

Our controls and business planning serve as a real discipline. They make operating managers read their businesses well. It upgrades their knowledge about their own business when they have to think five years out.

There is a third telephone-speeded approach at G + W that aids in planning and control. This is a weekly forecast on cash. Every Friday, the treasurer telephones the financial heads of all the operating groups and gets from them a cash forecast for the next week and the next two weeks. He also gets the acutal cash figures for the previous week.

These reports are appraised and a cash forecast is made for the next three weeks. Any major variations from cash forecasts goes immediately to the controller's office. This office investigates to find out why variations occur. These checkups uncover such deviation causes as sales slides, lagging collections on receivables, and the need for additional inventory.

Any critical matters in the cash reports are passed quickly to me, and I contact the group managers involved. These cash matters, controlled on a weekly basis, tie in with our Flash Forecast approach. The ability to get an almost instantaneous warning system on your operational projections comes out of these reports. After all, if cash is off, you will get into discussions on such things as receivables, payables, inventory levels, working capital ratios, sales, capital spending program delays, and so on.

The timeliness that has been built into the business planning and controls system has enhanced the discipline and quality of all managers. Those involved in any meaningful way with the direction and destiny of the company are kept on their toes at all times as to what's happening, why it is happening, and what is being done about it. As good as the business planning and controls are, as shown by their great success record, I give the real credit to the people who work with them.

When I said earlier that our business plan projections last year were off by less than 2%, that doesn't mean we are good at corporate headquarters. It means our operating managers have become excellent in their ability to "read" their businesses and come up with accurate projections. We have something that works. I can't say that the system will work for any other company. On the other hand, I can say with certainty that parts of what we have could work elsewhere. It is purely a case of how much top management wants to become involved, how much responsibility they want to assume, and how much motivation they have.

STAYING ON TOP OF BUSINESS PLANNING IS HARD WORK

It has taken a lot of hard work to stay on top of G + W business planning and controls, to police them and to make sure that all the people responsible for the actual reporting of the figures feel the same commitment that corporate management does. The idea of "policing" is not to infer that corporate management puts so great a priority on plans and controls and reports that operating management initiative is stifled or frustrated. This is not the case at G + W. Planning and controls are put in overall perspective in running the company.

INNOVATION IN GOOD PLANNING

The basic point of our management style involves the type of people we employ. The ideal G + W man is an innovator. He is creative. He is the type of man who can realize professional fulfillment only in a fast-paced, highly structured business environment such as we maintain. He raises the question, "What do we do with these creative innovators once they are on board?" We give them substantial creative and operational freedom within the framework of our overall objectives. With the challenge goes the responsibility that hard-charging professionals demand.

This approach results in a voluntary and spirited collaboration among all levels of management. It is easy to see how corporate planning and management controls fit in this context. Managment has been successful in handling these people because after we grant them responsibility, we set goals for them and we supervise their progress in attaining these goals. We delegate authority, but we do not abdicate responsibility.

In short, I stress the personal touch along with the reports and figures. Last year, for example, I made more than 75 visits to G + W facilities to fulfill this personal touch.

3
Improving Business Performance In Inflationary Times

Lavern O. Johnson, Partner
Richard D. Lehmbeck, Manager
Anthony Sullivan, Partner
John K. Wulff, Partner
Main, Hurdman & Cranstoun

Experience with inflation throughout the late 1960s and the 1970s, combined with the expectation that inflation will continue for the foreseeable future, highlights the need for deliberate business policies to counteract the debilitating effects on "real" profitability.

A popular indicator of the United States inflation rate, the *Consumer Price Index* (CPI), increased from 100% in 1967 to 217.4% in 1979. Most estimates for the 1980s are for continued inflation at rates averaging at least 6%. Performance of the CPI during the late 1960s and the 1970s highlights the need to consider inflation as an integral part of setting business policy, especially when expected inflation rates are contrasted with the relative price stability of the 1950s and early 1960s. Although the CPI is an indicator only of inflation rates in the United States, other Western industrialized countries have experienced the same phenomenon—some at higher and some at lower rates throughout recent history.

BUSINESSMEN'S PERCEPTION OF THE PROBLEM

Surveys of businessmen show clearly their concern about inflation. The following table ranks, by most important problem, responses to a regular survey carried out by the National Federation of Independent Business (NFIB) in early 1980. The survey covered respondents generally having sales of $3 million or less:

MOST IMPORTANT PROBLEM	RANK
Inflation	1
Taxation	2
Interest cost and financing	3

A survey of small- and medium-sized businesses entitled "Looking Toward the 80's," conducted in 1979 by Louis Harris and Associates, Inc., for the Chemical Bank of New York, produced similar responses. Companies covered by this survey had annual sales of $5 million to $105 million.

The Conference Board's study, *International Experiences in Managing Inflation,* published in 1977, said:

One major United States firm identified six major impacts on business firms resulting from inflation that it believed all its managers should understand. Effective ways of dealing with the six points became an important part of its internal training program.

1. It affects the financial accounts or "basic language" of the business;
2. It affects cash requirements of the firm by forcing an expansion of assets employed;
3. It results, in conjunction with tax law, in the taxation of real losses;
4. It leads to decapitalization of the firm if dividends are paid on illusory profits;
5. It limits the rate of real growth to be financed internally;
6. It increases the nominal cost of money, making the external financing of real growth more difficult.

FINANCIAL DISTORTION

There is no question that the inflation rate has had a severe impact on financial statements. Distortions of operating results have received the most attention. There is little wonder that many well-known companies have reported "record profits" year after year while some of these same companies have fallen into financial difficulties or even gone bankrupt. Traditionally, historical-cost-based financial statements have not reflected economic reality. The gap between reported profits and "real" profits has eroded the credibility and relevance of financial statements as a true measure of performance.

In 1979, the Financial Accounting Standards Board (FASB) adopted its Statement No. 33, *Financial Reporting and Changing Prices*, which may help to report the financial effects of inflation. However, the methods called for by that statement will be experimental for a number of years. In the meantime, businesses must wrestle with the problem of distorted financial statements.

EFFECT ON CASH REQUIREMENTS

Changing price levels, even at constant rates of change, causes pressure on cash flow as revenues lag expenses computed on the basis of replacement cost. In an environment characterized by fluctuating rates of change, the cash-flow problem is compounded by fluctuating borrowing costs.

Moreover, working capital requirements increase not only because of increased levels of receivables and inventory in line with inflationary sales and cost increases, but also because of delays in payments from customers resulting from their higher costs. Additionally, vendors may be expected to press for prompt payment of invoices to meet their increased cash needs. Finally, purchasing management may tend toward a policy of even higher inventories as a "hedge" against anticipated price increases.

While the impact of inflation may be obscured in most historical-cost-based financial statements, the impact on cash flow over time is often dramatic. On one hand, cash flow from operations tends to deteriorate as costs rise faster than revenues. On the other hand, cash-flow requirements expand because of increased fixed-asset replacement costs, working capital requirements, and dividends.

To compound matters, outside capital may be available in only limited amounts, and even then, at prohibitive rates. In an inflationary environment, strict cash management becomes critical; failure to reconsider approaches to minimize working capital requirements, to reduce delays in adjusting selling prices for cost increases, to evaluate investment alternatives, to identify and evaluate technological advances and otherwise to minimize the cost of replacing productive capacity, and to forecast future cash flows under varying assumptions very likely result in deteriorating profitability and cash flow.

Enterprises that simply continue "business as usual" in the face of continuing fluctuation in price levels may risk serious liquidity problems even as they continue to report relatively healthy shareholders' equity and net income on a historical cost basis. At the very least, these businesses may be required to forego investment opportunities. More significantly, some may be required to curtail operations.

TAXATION

Surveys have ranked taxes as the second most important problem (after inflation) facing business. Profit retention has been substantially reduced as a result of inflation increasing taxable profits while "real" profits (i.e., profits without inflation) may be decreasing. Income taxes continue to take larger shares of real profits while inflation continues. The following example illustrates the effects of corporate tax rates on real profits:

Sales	$2,000
Cost and expenses	1,600
Taxable income	400
Less	
Additional cost required to replace inventory sold and existing productive assets	120
	280
Income tax (46%)	184
"Real" net income	$ 96
Effective tax rate	66%

DECAPITALIZATION

"Some businesses are actually paying dividends out of capital," said Harold Williams, chairman of the Securities and Exchange Commission in his article, "Financial Reporting in a Changing Economic Environment" (included in *Financial Reporting and Changing Prices: The Conference*, published by the Financial Accounting Standards Board in 1979). His statement was amply supported by many companies' 1979 annual reports showing the information required by the FASB's Statement No. 33. In fact, this condition was generally true for the retailing and public utilities industries.

INTERNAL FINANCING

The combined effects of the foregoing factors result in smaller amounts of internally generated capital available to finance operations. First, there is a need for increasing amounts of cash merely to maintain existing capacity. Second, there is the confiscatory effect of tax laws. Third, there is the effect of dividend pay-out from the smaller "real" net income. In 1960, approximately 90% of capital expenditures were financed by internally generated capital. In 1979, this amount was about 60%.

EXTERNAL FINANCING

With inflation and high tax rates draining business profits, it is not surprising to see interest rates and financing ranked as the third most important problem. Because of limited equity financing, particularly with respect to smaller companies, shortfalls in profit retention tend to be financed by corporate borrowing.

The Harris and Chemical Bank survey showed that half of the businesses that raise outside financing plan to use borrowed funds for working capital. Unfortunately, some of these companies who plan to use financing for working capital purposes already may be experiencing the effects of decapitalization.

Other uses of financing are more predictable:

Financing growth	26%
Expand facilities	20%
Purchase capital equipment	17%
Acquisition or merger	16%

Inflation has caused interest rates and borrowing costs to increase. In early 1980, the prime interest rate hit a record high of 20%, making borrowing costs for those who could obtain loans prohibitive, and causing others to press hard to reduce outstanding loan balances.

It is only speculative to assess the full effect of the difficulty in capital formation on business decisions, because that involves estimating effects of business decisions not to build new plant facilities, develop new products, or begin new businesses. However, the overall adverse effect it has had on the United States productive capacity during the 1970s has been well publicized.

WAYS OF DEALING WITH INFLATION

Respondents to the Harris and Chemical Bank survey were asked to indicate the main ways that their companies would deal with inflation in the 1980s. Among the eight items offered, four were selected by at least one-fifth of those interviewed. Heading the list, not unexpectedly, is raising prices; six in ten companies would try to pass the costs of inflation further down the line. However, many companies also indicated they will contend with inflation by increasing efficiency and cost control:

   Nearly one-half (45%) plan to become more efficient.
   Nearly two-fifths (36%) will scrutinize costs more closely.
   One-fifth (21%) will invest in improvements to promote efficiency.

Accepting lower profits (11%), streamlining production facilities (6%), and cutting back on staff (5%) to fight inflation were received unenthusiastically by most of these companies. The only notable exception was the manufacturing sector. Not surprisingly, it is substantially more interested (12%) in streamlining facilities. In last place was delaying capital improvements. only 4% of all companies indicated that approach to fighting inflation.

CORPORATE LIQUIDITY AND THE CASH-FLOW CYCLE

Peter Drucker, in *Managing in Turbulent Times*, writes:

In turbulent times, liquidity is more important than earnings, and liquidity, unlike reported earnings, is a reasonably reliable measure even in inflationary times.

In any economic environment, maintenance of liquidity is a prerequisite to survival. Either a business pays its bills or it goes out of business. During inflationary times, the problem of maintaining liquidity becomes more onerous. Enterprises must be positioned to withstand dramatic, often unforeseen, changes in the business environment, which means that businesses must maintain a higher level of liquidity than would otherwise be required: a cushion to meet periodic recession and unanticipated developments.

Cash Flow as a Measure of Performance

Unlike other measures of financial performance, cash flow remains meaningful as a guide in periods of changing price levels. In contrast to the historical-cost-based statement, cash flow does reflect the current cost of maintaining productive capacity, the current cost of inventories, and other assets required to continue operations.

The cash-flow cycle provides a logical yet simple way to conceptualize an enterprise's operations. After all, the essence of any business is the conversion of cash—to product, to accounts receivable, and back to cash—hopefully in an amount greater than the initial investment.

In Figure 1, a hypothetical company starts with $1,000 in cash together with fixed, productive assets. The cash is used for payroll, material, and other operating expenses required to produce a product, such as goods or services. (In the case of a service organization, "inventory" may be viewed as unbilled work in progress.) Cash invested in inventory will be reduced so that payment of vendor invoices is deferred. The inventory in Figure 1 is sold for $1,600 and converted to accounts

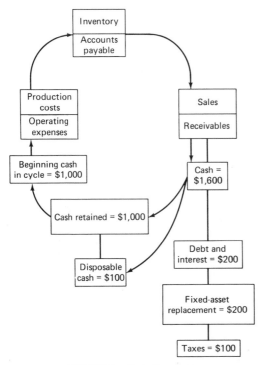

FIGURE 1.   Cash flow cycle.

receivable. Finally, the accounts receivable are collected and the business is left with $1,600 in cash. From this amount, interest charges and fixed-asset replacement costs of $400 are paid, taxes of $100 are due, and $1,000 is set aside to fund another cycle. The business is left with $100—referred to as disposable cash—that can be used for distribution to shareholders or for business expansion without adversely impacting existing operations. Disposable cash can be viewed as one true measure of an enterprise's financial performance.

The original $1,000 will be retained in the business to continue the same capacity in the next cash-flow cycle. No additional money is required because Figure 1 assumes zero inflation and no change in the cycle timing or flow.

Disposable cash generated in a given period of time can be increased by accelerating the cash-flow cycle. An increase from one to two cycles per year will, at a minimum, double the annual disposable cash. In fact, dis-

posable cash will more than double because certain expenditures, such as interest on debt, vary with the passage of time and not with the number of cycles. In Figure 2, an increase of between one and two cycles per year will increase disposable cash flow from $100 to at least $300 because no additional interest costs will result from cycle acceleration. To the extent that fixed-asset replacement costs are a function of time rather than usage, disposable cash may be increased further.

Alternately, the original return of $100 disposable cash could be obtained from smaller cash investments as cycle completion is accelerated. An increase of between one and two cycles per year will enable an enterprise to generate $100 of annual disposable cash flow from employing considerably less than $1,000.

Impact of Inflation on the Cash-Flow Cycle

To see the impact of inflation, assume the same facts as in the preceding example but add a 10% inflation assumption. Two major consequences are noticeable immediately.

First, because of inflated product costs, an additional $100 is required in the succeeding cycle just to maintain the present level of operations. This cash requirement completely eliminates all disposable cash. Second, fixed-asset replacement costs have risen by $20. An inflation rate of 10% more than eliminates all disposable cash flow.

Some may assert that Figure 2 is biased by assuming no change in the $1,600 selling price. Logic would have it that selling prices should also increase by 10% or $160. This may or may not be reasonable depending upon the characteristics of the enterprise's market and the company's awareness of the need to increase prices. In fact, many businesses are not able to raise selling prices in line with increased costs. But note that even if one assumes a 10% higher selling price, the company still fails to maintain its original disposable cash flow of $100. After taxes at

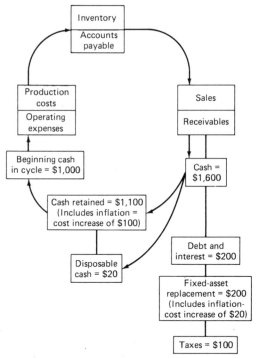

FIGURE 2. Cash flow cycle with inflation.

cash-flow cycle. If the cycle can be accelerated, the historic return will be maintained without the need to increase cash employed in the business.

The theory is simple, but the real challenge is to know how to effect cycle acceleration. In this regard, what does cash cycle acceleration really mean? If each box in the exhibits is viewed as a potential cash bottleneck, then the problem becomes one of identifying where cash flow is being hindered unnecessarily and developing a plan to eliminate the bottleneck.

For example, accounts receivable turnover may be slowed because of a high frequency of errors in invoice preparation. The cause may be inadequate familiarity with invoicing procedures on the part of billing department personnel. Perhaps the bottleneck could be eliminated through the use of training programs.

50%, the increased revenues contribute additional cash flow of only $80, or $40 less than the incremental amounts, aggregating $120, needed to replace fixed assets and fund next year's inflated production costs.

To maintain disposable cash flow at the original level of $100, a company has the two following alternatives:

1. It might defer the replacement of fixed assets or reduce the level of future production activity. In either case, business capacity is reduced. This alternative amounts to decapitalization of the business.
2. It might obtain additional outside financing. In the long term, this approach only aggravates the problem by either increasing future debt service costs or diluting owners' equity. Moreover, the availability of outside financing is not unlimited.

A solution far more positive than either of these alternatives is the acceleration of the

Disposable Cash Flow

Before delving into the development and implementation of corrective plans, it might be useful to take a closer look at the concept of disposable cash flow.

Table 1 shows a disposable cash calculation. Starting with net profits, depreciation and other noncash charges are added. Estimated expenditures required to maintain fixed assets and the working capital needed to support current sales volume are deducted. Maintenance of business capacity encompasses the

Table 1. Disposable Cash Calculation

Sales	$100,000
Cost and expenses, including $10,000 depreciation	90,000
Taxable profit	10,000
Taxes	5,000
Net income	5,000
Add depreciation	10,000
Less additional funds needed to maintain business capacity (more working capital, asset replacement, and so on)	(12,000)
Disposable cash	$ 3,000

replacement of fixed assets and working capital. Working capital represents a drain on cash-flow, a drain that will be aggravated as inflation pushes up production costs.

In the absence of inflation, disposable cash flow generally is equivalent to net income, unless major technological changes or other external developments alter the productive capacity of fixed assets. In a noninflationary environment, net income should represent funds available for distribution to owners or for business expansion. In fact, this is a time-honored concept of what net income should portray. Inflation has distorted the concept by creating illusory profits that are not represented by disposable cash. As a result, a calculation is necessary to estimate disposable cash flow.

The calculation involves subjective estimates of working capital and capital expenditures that are needed to maintain operating levels. Such estimates may be based on budgets, sales projections, and other operating plans. For example:

1. Inventory cost increases should be based on planned purchases using industry indices or anticipated supplier increases. The extent to which increased inventory costs can be financed through accounts payable must be considered.
2. Increases in accounts receivable carrying costs should be based on recent company and industry aging trends and anticipated changes in financing costs.
3. Annual fixed-asset replacement cost should be developed from a three- to five-year plan that spreads the replacement burden equitably.

Clearly, the calculation of disposable cash lacks the precision associated with historical-cost-based statements. But isn't it better to be approximately right than exactly wrong?

Negative disposable cash requires analysis to determine the reasons. For example, negative cash flow resulting from major fixed-asset replacement generally can be financed. How-ever, negative cash arising from a permanent working capital need (not seasonal) to maintain business capacity may not be. The plan should consider such factors.

A survey of small- and medium-sized businesses entitled "Looking Toward the 80's," conducted in 1979 by Louis Harris and Associates, Inc., for the Chemical Bank of New York, produced similar responses. Companies covered by this survey had annual sales of $5 million to $105 million.

Improving Liquidity and Cash Flow

As discussed previously, the first step in dealing with the problem is to calculate and review the company's disposable cash position—the objective being to learn where it stands and to identify the magnitude of the problem. Diversified enterprises should perform such a review on a product line or component basis. In general, the more detailed the computational level, the easier it is to zero in on problem areas.

The second step is to perform a preliminary review of each cash-flow cycle for which a disposable cash analysis was performed. The preliminary review should be directed to identifying areas in which the greatest potential pay-off can be obtained from elimination of bottlenecks. A fundamental aspect of the preliminary review is computation of the cycle length.

Calculation of cycle length involves such steps as computing average days to produce inventory, average number of days that inventory is held, and accounts receivable turnover. Such information is a key factor in identifying cash-flow bottlenecks.

For example, if a company produces a product in 20 days, holds it in inventory for 120 days and the sales remain as accounts receivable for 90 days, then a priority may be to reduce the apparent 120-day bottleneck in inventory. If the inventory holding period were reduced to a level in line with production time, say 30 days, then the cash-flow cycle could be shortened by 40%.

In addition to computing the cycle length, general explanations of the cause of apparent bottlenecks should be obtained. The goal is to form a subjective idea of the degree of difficulty associated with eliminating bottlenecks. If in the preceding example, the apparent inventory bottleneck is the result of customer demands to maintain specified finished goods inventory levels, it may be that the bottleneck can only be eliminated through drawn-out contract renegotiations. In that event, top priority perhaps should be given to another area such as accelerating accounts receivable turnover. Thus the preliminary review is intended to be a method of focusing first on those areas with the best cost/benefit potential.

Once having identified those areas, the third and most important step is to address the cash-flow problem—namely, the development of specific plans for improving cash flow.

The object of a plan is to identify opportunities that improve cash flow. Finding such opportunities requires a return to the basics of operating a company. This involves focusing on those practices that made the company successful. A plan should not be based on the assumption that cash-flow improvements result only from new investment. Cash flow usually can be increased without substantial new investment.

The most important ingredient in a plan is commitment. Such a commitment requires a change in attitude about how the business is run. Daily routines should be questioned from a systematic "fresh-look attitude" about "How can we make the most of what we have?"

Successful plans include three basic characteristics. First, a specific individual should be assigned the clear responsibility for implementing the plan. That person must, of course, have the authority necessary to carry out this responsibility.

Second, a "critical path" of due dates leading to a successful completion date is important in obtaining timely feedback on the plan's progress. This approach provides a basis for evaluating the soundness of the plan prior to the completion date and allows for timely correction of problems encountered along the way.

Finally, it is important that a plan for an area have measurable objectives. The best proof of a successful plan is the achievement of measurable improvements.

A company will harvest many other significant advantages when implementing plans to improve cash flow. Some are:

1. Renewed emphasis on cash retention
2. A heightened awareness of cash needs and current working position
3. Increased focus on immediate cash consequences of daily business activities and decisions
4. A simple concept that can be related to every employees' actions or inactions
5. A common goal for all employees.

Improving cash-flow management practices is key to success during inflationary times. Stronger corporate liquidity, which will result from such practices, can position a business to take advantage of growth opportunities that it may otherwise have to forego.

THE INFORMATION SYSTEM—A FIRST LINE OF SAVINGS FOR BUSINESS

Accurate financial data are critical to the implementation of plans to improve cash flow. An information system is required to collect, analyze, interpret, and report business transactions on a timely basis to permit corrective management action. Therefore, some modification to a company's information system may be part of an overall plan. The modifications may involve both changes to accelerate the reporting of cash-flow information and the elimination of unnecessary reports and procedures. For example, use of the same reports for operating and accounting purposes frequently is possible.

A complete understanding of information needs is an important prerequisite for modification. However, an initial focus should be on the following:

1. Budget management practices
2. The appropriateness of responsibility reporting
3. The key internal controls.

Budget Management Practices

Budgets essentially serve two control functions:

1. An aid to hold costs to a budgeted level.
2. A focal point for the reduction or elimination of costs.

A budget can highlight large cost items that should be reconsidered. For example, a large expense for repair of a fleet of trucks may trigger changes to standardize vehicles in a fleet; a large expense for production facilities could trigger a search for less costly places of doing business. Even "fixed" expenses are not necessarily unchangeable.

One company that controlled its costs through budgets asked each department to be responsible to achieve some reduction by reconsidering the need for each budget item. While some departments did more and others did less, the overall result was a 10% cut in budgeted costs.

Improving budget management practices can produce quick pay-offs. Some examples of typical business policies include:

1. Watching budgets by top management and adjusting them quickly to changing circumstances.
2. Holding budgets to short-time periods. For example, some companies have found it desirable to commit to a budget for no longer than six months.
3. Cultivating employee awareness and cooperation to achieve budgeted objectives. Employees can be instrumental in eliminating internally generated costs, such as through waste reduction.

4. Challenging major costs with the objective of reducing costs by substitution. An example is the review of all insurance coverage (both corporate and employee benefits) for lower bids, different coverage options, and plan administration.
5. Highlighting important budget items that are particularly sensitive to price change (such as commodities) and closely following such items to enable management to react quickly to changes.

Responsibility Reporting

Internal financial reports should follow management's lines of responsibility. Careful evaluation is necessary to determine whether present financial reports "track" the results that are controllable by the individual held responsible for them.

Internal Controls

Regardless of what modifications are made to the information system, reasonable assurance should exist that reported information is reliable, that transactions are recorded appropriately, and that corporate assets are safeguarded. Modifications that might reduce this reasonable assurance should be evaluated carefully not only from a cost/benefit point of view, but also based on the minimum control needs unique to the company.

CASH

The objectives of cash management are relatively straightforward. Do everything possible to maximize the available cash balance by accelerating cash receipts and delaying disbursements.

Cash Receipts

Procedures with respect to cash receipts include accelerating credits to the bank account—making sure not only that remittances are deposited as quickly as possible but also that the bank provides maximum cash availability. One company increased its average cash balance by 65% by adopting a nation-wide lock box system. Another business surveyed the deposit clearance procedures of several local banks. Based upon the survey, the company selected a bank willing to guarantee 24-hour clearance of at least 80% of deposits. As a result, available cash balances were substantially increased. Other companies have established bank accounts regionally— near major customers or groups of customers, and so on.

Simply accelerating credits to bank accounts is not particularly useful unless the company is aware, at all times, of the available cash position. This is the available cash shown by the bank's records, not the "book" cash balance. Thus there is a need to accelerate the accounting recognition of receipts through current daily reports of receipts, disbursements, and most important, available cash as per the bank's records.

Establish minimum daily cash receipts budgets. To utilize available cash effectively, it is necessary to have at least a rough idea of average daily receipts. Companies with relatively predictable cash receipt patterns may be able to accelerate the transfer of receipts from remote depository locations to the central bank based upon anticipated deposits. One company, for example, became dissatisfied with delays in wire transfers from remote depositories to the main bank. To improve cash flow, a procedure was instituted whereby automatic transfers were made daily based upon anticipated deposits.

Cash Disbursements

Delaying cash disbursements involves such factors as the maximization of float. Some companies utilize weekends and grace periods to delay clearance. Some adopt policies of making payment only on designated days. As in cash receipts, it is important to "track" the checks paid by the bank. Many companies have consolidated their disbursement functions as a means to control the timing of disbursements better. Other companies, whenever possible, encourage their employees to use credit cards to minimize employee expense advances.

Cash Balances

Simply maximizing available cash, of course, is not an end in itself. The objective is to use the cash to meet operating needs. Any excess available cash shown by bank balances, rather than "book" cash balances, should be invested. Assuming that in effect receipts are being accelerated and disbursements are being delayed, the available cash according to the bank's records may exceed the book balance by a substantial margin.

To maximize yield on cash balances, operating cash should be consolidated whenever possible. Not only does this improve control, but it may enable small organizations to take advantage of short-term investment opportunities not otherwise available. In general, relatively small cash balances spread throughout various locations cannot be invested effectively. Similarly, cashier locations and functions should be reduced or eliminated wherever possible. Funds left in cashier's safes are nonproductive.

Other actions to consider are to "cash in" miscellaneous assets by following up and collecting security deposits no longer required, borrowing the maximum amount allowable against the cash surrender value of insurance policies held by the company, and similar actions.

Once having consolidated funds, an estimate should be made of the minimum required available cash based upon anticipated daily receipts and disbursements. Any excess cash should be invested routinely. With the advent of money market funds, even small amounts of cash can be put to work. Moreover, the establishment of overdraft facilities or line-of-credit arrangements can eliminate the risks associated with temporary cash shortfalls from budget.

Cash may be invested overnight and on weekends. As little as $100,000 invested overnight and on weekends may earn $4,000 to $5,000 over the course of the year.

PRODUCTION AND OPERATING EXPENSES

Conceptually, the approach to control costs and expenses is to review each cost area and challenge whether the organization is getting benefit for the expenditure as compared to alternative approaches that may change the structure of the costs and improve overall profitability.

All parts of the business are involved and might include, for example, each of the following areas:

1. Purchasing procedures
2. The selling function
3. The production function
4. Work schedules
5. Payroll
6. Inventory holding, storage, and handling costs.

Purchasing Procedures

Purchasing is an important factor in the success of retail and wholesale companies and most types of manufacturing companies. By streamlining procedures, many of these organizations have been able not only to reduce purchasing costs but also to improve controls through more attention to truly important areas.

A summary of typical successful practices adopted by many organizations follows:

1. Selecting vendors based on product quality, past performance, pricing policies, financial stability, capacity to fill purchase commitments, and lack of dependency on the company.
2. Coordinating multiple purchasing locations to avoid overstocking and take advantage of volume discounts.

3. Obtaining routine competitive bidding requests from vendors only for defined items of significance.
4. Using multiple vendors to assure vendor competition and alternate sources (e.g., protection against cost increases and shortages resulting from strikes)
5. Negotiating longer, or installment payment terms when favorable (e.g., insurance premiums)
6. Using blanket orders to fix purchase prices and allow delivery (and payment) in installments (i.e., use vendors' inventories to save holding costs)
7. Designating line personnel who have authorized purchasing responsibilities (e.g., to avoid backlogs)
8. Reducing the purchase approvals on materials purchased regularly and controlled by reorder point systems
9. Evaluating reorder points and make-or-buy calculations regularly to reflect changes in interest rates and other current economic conditions
10. Designing purchase order forms for clarity and simplicity.
11. Using purchase order forms that require vendor confirmation and advance notification of cost increases
12. Using purchase order forms that provide for automatic cancellation after designated dates.
13. A regular follow-up of open purchase orders to avoid shortages
14. Updating new purchase costs continuously for the sales pricing function.

The Selling Function

A cost-effective selling function is vital to most profit-oriented companies. A summary of frequently successful approaches to achieve results in line with costs is as follows:

1. Designing financial reports to highlight profit contributions by territory, product line, customers and warehouses

2. Evaluating commission, travel, and payroll expenses in relation to profit contribution
3. Evaluating the merits of multiple selling locations.
4. Using sales representatives instead of an inhouse sales force for some areas
5. Establishing a program of regular customer visits based on customer needs.

The Production Function

Control of the production function—from product design and quality through production scheduling and the manufacturing process to labor and manufacturing costs—is key to the success of manufacturing companies.

Following are examples of approaches by successful manufacturers in this area:

1. Scheduling production based on machine and labor capacity in coordination with delivery dates, production time, and planned inventory levels
2. A program of regular "audits" of production to identify reasons for bottlenecks, production overruns, quality control problems, down time, high scrap rate, equipment breakdowns, and high skilled-worker turnover
3. Periodic "energy audits" to identify potential savings
4. Establishing accountability for each cost center (e.g., small enough to be manageable by the responsible supervisor)
5. Developing a continuous awareness by production personnel of cost-saving measures (e.g., through education programs, energy-saving campaigns, awards for suggestions)
6. Updating standard costs continuously for the sales pricing function.

Work Schedules

Many organizations have been successful in reaching higher levels of profitability through innovative and flexible approaches to work scheduling. In some instances, entirely new cost structures result.

In several cases, companies were able to pare costs by changing the work week. For example, an iron foundry in a rural area cut costs of both energy and maintenance by going to a ten-hour shift and a four-day week. In addition, the change effectively increased pay for employees who gained from reduced commuting costs and four-day weekends twice a month.

Some other examples follow:

1. Using multiple work shifts (e.g., daytime-production with nighttime-equipment maintenance, set-up and clean-up)
2. Lengthening production runs or schedules to reduce set-up and clean-up time
3. Running high energy-consuming equipment during "off-peak" hours for lower rates
4. Running equipment that requires fixed rates of energy for longer periods and shutting it down when not in use
5. Using variable work hours for plant and office employees to increase productivity
6. Work weeks of three 12-hour days or four ten-hour days for possible cost savings or increased productivity
7. Using unskilled or part-time help for certain jobs to reduce cost and increase scheduling flexibility
8. Eliminating overtime through improved scheduling, a second shift, or part-time help.

Payroll

Cost and the quality of personal services often is the single most important cost to many business. Careful attention to this area has large potential for improved profitability. Following are examples of successful approaches:

1. Separating incentive pay increases from cost of living adjustments to encourage productivity

2. Union agreements tied to productivity increases when possible
3. Management compensation based on inflation adjusted financial results.

Inventory Holding, Storing, and Handling Costs

For many businesses, the largest single asset is inventory. It is a major or secondary factor in the success of most retail, wholesale, and manufacturing entities. Control of inventory costs can usually be improved. Examples of practical approaches to control of this area are:

1. Coordinating inventories at all locations to increase turnover
2. Varying inventory levels based on seasonal or cyclical sales
3. Inspecting inventories routinely to maintain saleable quality
4. A regular review of slow-moving products for liquidation
5. Selecting inventory accounting methods that reduce taxes
6. Using warehouses in "free port" states to save on property taxes
7. Storing imported components in bonded warehouses to delay payment of duty until inventory is used
8. Planning warehouse layouts to minimize handling costs
9. Choosing warehouse locations to reduce customer delivery time and transportation costs
10. Selling underutilized warehouse space
11. Establishing cost-effective controls over freight:
    a. Development of routing guides for incoming and outgoing freight
    b. Utilizing a freight audit agency
    c. Billing vendors for freight on rejected shipments
    d. Recording freight claims for accounting control
    e. Selling "deadhead" truck space
    f. Closer attention to freight that can be billed to customers.

Inventory

In most companies, cash flow can be improved by tighter control over inventory levels. Because conditions change constantly, optimal inventories are rare. Nearly always, more improvements can be made.

Pressure for High Inventories. Most pressures within an organization are for higher inventories:

1. Purchasing is able to obtain the lowest unit costs with volume purchasing.
2. Sales personnel want high inventories to assure prompt shipment of orders.
3. Customer service personnel want large inventories of spare parts.
4. Production wants large inventories to assure that materials are available for long production runs.

The only counterbalance comes from financial and top management, who must address the question "How much inventory is enough?" This is a question of deliberate business policy.

The goal is fast turnover of inventory. This suggests that inventory should only meet the planned level of customer service. A company rarely should be out of stock on items with high turnover, but may plan deliberately to be out of stock on some items with little demand.

Cost-Effective Inventories. An objective is to order or produce the most cost-effective quantities. This should include costs that are frequently overlooked—interest, taxes, handling, and storage.

For example, one manufacturing company had its engineers compute the most economical size for production orders. Usually these were large production runs because of the labor savings. However, the calculations did not include the considerable financing costs to carry inventories. When the engineers' calculations were modified to take interest into account, it became apparent that reduced order quantities were most economical and inventories should be reduced.

Reducing Inventories. Most companies probably can achieve at least some inventory reduction without reducing customer service levels. Basically, there are two steps:

1. To measure existing excesses
2. To identify why the excesses occurred in order to eliminate recurrences.

The first step requires a system of sales forecasting in relation to the lead time needed to order or produce the items. The second step to reduce recurrences of excess inventory requires some monitoring system. That system may be as simple as stepping into the stockroom to "eyeball" the shelves for small businesses. Or it may be a sophisticated reorder point system based on equations that consider dozens of variables tailored for the specific company.

For example, a large wholesale company had a reorder point system based on the past 12 months' sales with a formula to consider recent trends, so that order sizes increased when sales grew and decreased when sale declined. This worked well for most items but was counter productive for a number of seasonal inventory items (e.g., small orders for sunglasses in February when stocks should have been up and large orders in May when the sales season was over). Once that problem was corrected, half of both the company's out-of-stock problems and its excess inventory problems were solved.

A summary of successful approaches by many companies to managing inventory levels follows:

1. Using sales forecasts to define inventory levels needed to meet the planned level of service:
   a. Levels based on historical sales records when available (e.g., averages, moving averages, weighted averages, trend fitting, other regression analyses)
   b. Levels based on subjective methods when historical records are not available (e.g., individual or collective executive opinion, sales force composite forecast, customer poll, market research studies)
2. Determining when and how much to order (or produce) through one or more of the following systems:
   a. Physical counts or visual inspection, which may be cost-effective when the cost of inventory is low and the cost of control needs to be minimized
3. Two-bin system, in which orders are placed when the first of two bins are exhausted, may be cost-effective for high volume, low-cost items
4. Material requirements planning (MRP), which may be cost-effective when there are accurate bills of material and there is reliable knowledge of when each component is required.
5. Reorder point systems, in which orders are placed when quantities on hand equal the forecast of demand during the period of time required to place and receive the order, plus a safety stock factor:
   a. Economic order quantity (EOQ), a system in which the optimum order lot size is determined by a formula that considers both unit price and selected variable cost factors including costs to carry (e.g., interest, cost of order placement, freight, materials handling)
   b. Minimax system, in which minimum quantities are the safety stock factor and maximum quantities are the minimum plus the optimum order lot size
   c. Reservation system, a modification of any reorder point system so that "available" inventory quantities are used as a basis for reorder points. Available inventory represents quantities on hand less quantities "reserved" to meet existing material requirements.

d. ABC system, in which inventory records and controls are applied to "critical" inventory items, normally those of high usage or high unit value or both. Less costly records and controls are applied to less important items, categorized B and C.

ACCOUNTS PAYABLE

From the perspective of cash-flow management, controlled levels of accounts payable are an integral part of calculating total cash invested in inventory and other components of working capital.

A set of policies are needed to make the best use of cash in light of current investment alternatives together with managment controls. This entails ongoing evaluation and review of supplier terms because of interest rates and other current economic conditions. Prompt revision of policies as conditions and investment alternatives may change.

Supplier terms of 2%, 10 days or net, 30 days, results in a 36% annual rate for 20 days and might suggest added borrowing. One retailer was able to obtain "anticipation" of a 10% discount from suppliers by paying each invoice within one week of its receipt.

In another case, a candy manufacturer convinced its supplier of sweetener to build a bulk distribution facility adjacent to the plant on surplus land leased from the candy manufacturer at favorable terms. The candy manufacturer metered the sweetener supplied to the candy kitchens. Generally the candy inventory was less than a week's supply. The supplier's invoices, based on meter readings, were payable in 30 days with a cash discount offered for payment within ten days. Even when cash discount was taken, the candy maker frequently had collected for candy sold before paying the vendor—certainly an effective way to manage the cash invested in that inventory.

Sales and Accounts Receivable

Improving cash flow from sales and accounts receivable requires attention to the following matters:

1. Pricing
2. Fast receipt and processing of sales orders
3. Fast shipping and invoicing
4. Control over collections.

Pricing

Surveys show that raising prices is a principal way business plans to deal with inflation. Developing pricing strategies to pass along increasing costs is an important part of business policy to improve cash flow during inflationary times.

An effective pricing strategy can maintain or improve gross margin, in spite of escalating costs. Some important factors in developing pricing strategy include:

1. *Knowledge of the company's market.* This means an awareness of why the company's products sell, what its competition is doing, and the industry's total production capacity.
2. *Knowledge of profit contribution by each product or product line.* This provides insight about prices that should be considered for increase or, if increases are not possible, what marginal products should be discontinued.
3. *Knowledge of fixed and variable costs and breakeven points.* This assists companies to determine when prices should be increased.
4. *Knowledge of replacement costs.* Whenever possible, pricing decisions should be based on next-in, first-out costs (NIFO). To retain gross margin levels, it is necessary to adopt selling prices that anticipate the next round of cost increases.
5. *Avoidance of long-term sales commitments at fixed prices.* During inflationary times, successful companies avoid long-term sales commitments that do not include escalator clauses.

The goal is to develop a pricing strategy that results in selling price increases as the costs increase for a gross margin that is a constant percentage, regardless of inflation.

Fast Receipt and Processing of Sales Orders

Cash flow may be accelerated by getting sales orders in house quickly. Some companies have installed computer terminals in sales offices to eliminate mailing delays. Others have adopted techniques such as telephoning orders, instituting messenger services, and other devices to reduce transit time. In one instance, a company reduced order processing time a full day by changing mail room procedures to provide immediate delivery of apparent sales orders.

Once the order is in house, ways to speed processing need to be considered. Examples of successful policies include approval of credit and preparation of shipping documents and invoices as integral, "parallel" steps in sales order processing. Some companies have shortened the credit approval process by programming credit approval procedures into the computers. Routine changes in individual customer credit limits are automated by programming flexible credit limits based on the customer's recent payment history. This substantially reduces bottlenecks caused by routine changes in credit limits and permits management to focus more effort on true problem accounts.

The final step in improving order processing techniques is the prioritization of "best" orders. Orders that are large, or from best-paying customers, or for goods in stock deserve particular attention.

Fast Shipping and Invoicing

Fast order processing should be matched with fast shipping and invoicing. Shipping may be speeded by preparing packing lists that are in the same sequence as the goods are stored in the warehouse. An efficient warehouse layout and logical inventory storage also speeds shipping time. One technique is to locate high turnover items nearest the shipping point.

Invoice preparation in advance of shipment frequently can facilitate mailing the invoice immediately upon shipment. Many companies have lost advantages gained from quick processing and shipping of orders by the delays experienced in subsequent preparation and mailing of invoices.

Control Over Collections

Control over collections is the final step in improving cash flow from sales and accounts receivable. Payment policies need to be reviewed regularly to determine whether they provide adequate incentive for customers to pay promptly. Regular reviews are especially needed in times of changing interest rates and investment alternatives.

Many companies have found that simplified remittance procedures either improve collection or, as a minimum, assure that the payment is mailed to the right location.

Others have found that programs to reduce or eliminate shipping and invoice errors have improved their collections. Many companies have found that backlogs in their billing adjustment department represent a bottleneck to cash flow because customers tend to delay payments pending receipt of the adjustments.

Prompt follow-up of past due accounts is important to improved collections as well as to control of credit losses. In this respect, it is critical that timely access to collection information be available.

Enforcement of late payment charges may be the incentive necessasry to cause some customers to pay promptly. Some companies have experienced a reasonably high rate of success with this practice.

DEBT AND INTEREST

Debt and interest frequently require significant amounts of cash flow. Corporate profits and liquidity often may be enhanced by improving management practices in this area.

Objectives of debt management are to adopt a debt structure that develops and maintains the ability to pay in the face of uncertainty, develops and maintains available borrowing capacity to take advantage of business opportunities, and controls interest costs.

Ability to Pay in the Face of Uncertainty

Many companies find it useful to plan worst-case scenarios based on past experience or industry and regional trends. Such plans, of course, require regular review for continued appropriateness.

Borrowing practices, which during inflationary times are based merely on the concept of paying debt with tomorrow's "cheap" dollars, begs the real question of whether the debt payments terms are favorable in relation to expected returns from the asset to be financed, taking associated risk into account. Therefore, a debt management practice with general applicability is "matching" assets and liabilities.

The concept of matching assets and liabilities means identifying specific assets that are financed by debt. This is key both to evaluating the risk of additional borrowing being considered and to evaluating actual results from assets that are currently financed by debt.

For example, assume that a company finances an inventory build-up. It should first evaluate the investment returns expected from that action. Subsequent management of the inventory should be closely pegged to changes in the associated debt level. As the inventory build-up is liquidated, the debt should be liquidated in proportionatal amounts. Further, if financial results from the inventory build-up are not as great as expected and do not justify the financing costs, that knowledge should trigger liquidation of both the inventory and the debt.

Available Borrowing Capacity

There is truth to the old adage that the worst time to ask for a loan is when one needs it. Establishing lines of credit (and terms of re-lated compensating balance requirements) and sound banking relationships well in advance of need are important components of effective business policy. Many businesses find it advantageous to send their financial statements to the bank's loan officer even when no loans are outstanding.

Control of Interest Costs

High inflation rates, particularly fluctuating rates, also require increased attention to controlling interest costs. Interest rates are usually made up of three separate rates—the expected inflation rate, a "pure" interest rate for the use of money, and a "risk" rate.

The risk rate can be a few percentage points added to the prime rate. Regular presentations of financial performance and plans to lenders and credit rating agencies can improve the lenders' risk evaluation of the company as well as improve communication and display management's talents.

Interest rate futures contracts are a relatively recent development that may enable companies to reduce exposure to fluctuations in variable interest costs. Alternatively, futures contracts may be used in connection with the management of short-term investments to "hedge" against market value fluctuations during times of high interest rate volatility. Because the purchase and sale of futures contracts involves substantial risk, however, companies are well advised to seek expert counsel before entering into futures transactions.

The conversion of short-term debt to a long-term lease can have the advantage of "locking-in" a fixed interest rate, thereby removing uncertainty about possible cash drains caused by fluctuating interest rates associated with short-term borrowing. Similarly, sale and leaseback transactions, carefully timed, can enhance liquidity and fix favorable interest rates.

An industrial revenue bond issue is another possibility for control of interest costs. One company was able to issue industrial revenue bonds at an interest rate 7% below the lending rate otherwise available from its bank. Of equal importance, the bond rate was fixed while the bank rate was pegged to prime.

Other alternatives include:

1. Small Business Administration (SBA) loans may be offered at lower interest rates. This is particularly true if a business has been designated for special loans because of hardship (i.e., high unemployment, flood, fire, and so on).
2. Economic Development Authority (EDA) loans are available through state agencies. Initial funding is provided through a federal umbrella program of the same name. Generally, the purpose of the loans is to maintain or increase employment. As a result, it may be possible to secure a loan for working capital purposes rather than for the purchase of specific assets, as is ususally required for an industrial revenue bond issue or an SBA loan.

FIXED ASSETS

The Harris and Chemical Bank survey found that one of the ways business plans to deal with inflation is by improving efficiency. Careful planning is key to maximizing returns on equipment. Many companies find that making the best of what they have often is the best way to improve their cash flow.

Efficiency also can be improved through replacing fixed assets; however, fixed asset purchases may involve a substantial cash-flow commitment. A first priority, then, is the evaluation of the extent to which cash flow can be improved from existing assets.

Improving Efficiency of Existing Assets

Production managers generally have a high interest in upgrading fixed assets. That interest may be at odds with corporate objectives of improving cash flow. For example, one company was able to reduce fixed asset pur-

chases without affecting productive capacity by elevating the level of management authorization necessary to purchase new assets. This change not only improved cash flow but increased investment return from existing assets.

Improving cash flow from existing fixed asset management generally requires some combination of the following practices:

1. Periodic tests of equipment productivity to identify reasons for changes in efficiency. Low efficiency may be a result of poor operating techniques rather than poor equipment performance.
2. Equipment service programs to minimize equipment breakdown. Even when new equipment is purchased, breakdowns may occur if maintenance programs are missing.

Replacement of Fixed Assets

When fixed assets replacement is indicated, coordinated replacement programs are necessary to assure a reasonable level of integration between new and existing equipment. Fixed asset replacements that are not coordinated properly can have an adverse effect on cash flow. Isolated asset purchases may be disruptive to existing productive efficiency and may be more costly than the existing equipment. The cash drain caused by asset purchases may not result in improved cash flow to pay for the asset, but many increase the cash flow to a level that justifies acquisition.

A comprehensive asset purchase analysis should be made to evaluate the cash-flow trade-offs. Many companies evalute prospective fixed asset purchases based on projected future cash flows discounted to present value. It is important that this discount rate embodies a factor for future inflation to measure expected returns in future inflated dollars. Alternately, the expected inflation rate can be ignored if the projected future cash flows are stated only in terms of current dollars.

TAXES

Federal and state income taxes usually require a significant part of a company's cash flow, and, during inflationary times, the significance of income taxes is magnified.

Advance tax planning can reduce the company's cash outlays for taxes. Whether the reduction is permanent or merely a deferral depends upon the tax planning techniques available to the business and the potential for similar tax planning in subsequent years. In any event, the cash generated by the planned tax reduction will be available for business requirements or disposition to shareholders.

Objectives of tax planning may be summarized as follows:

1. Cash-flow conservation
2. Financing fixed asset purchase and expansion
3. Distribution of cash to owners.

Cash-Flow Conservation

Cash flow from operations may be conserved through a delay of tax payments made possible by selecting alternatives in the following areas:

1. Accounting methods
2. Fiscal year
3. State and local taxes
4. Estimated tax payments.

Accounting Methods

At least the following items should be considered during an evaluation of the tax deferral potential of tax accounting methods:

1. Cash receipts and disbursement versus accrual methods
2. Last-in, first-out (LIFO) inventory method
3. Bad debt reserve method
4. Long-term contract method
5. Installment sales method
6. Vacation pay accrual
7. Fiscal year change.

Cash Receipts and Disbursement Versus Accrual Methods. A company may adopt cash receipts and disbursements or the accrual method, or a hybrid method. However, when inventory is a material income-producing item, the accrual method must be used both for trade receivables and payables. Hence, any service organization should consider adopting the cash method as a means of deferring recognition of income for tax purposes even though the accrual method is used for financial reporting purposes. An organization that both manufactures a product and sells a service should consider placing the service operation in a separate tax entity that could adopt the cash method.

LIFO. The last-in, first-out method of inventory valuation assumes that the most recently purchased merchandise is sold first. Thus LIFO eliminates some profit arising solely from inflation. This accounting technique essentially "freezes" the cost of the opening inventory in the year LIFO is adopted. This is one of the easier changes in tax accounting methods because it does not require the advance permission of the IRS.

In the year of change, any increase in the volume of the ending inventory over the opening inventory is priced at current costs. Hence, the lower costs of the opening inventory are preserved and some inflationary costs become tax deductible.

There are some drawbacks to adopting LIFO:

1. There is an increase in clerical effort because most companies using LIFO for tax purposes continue to keep certain records of inventory costs using first-in, first-out or average costs for interim periods. However, with the availability of computers and sampling techniques, this problem can be reduced significantly.
2. There is a requirement that companies use LIFO for financial statements issued to stockholders, and creditors. However, this problem has been reduced through more liberalized rules that per-

mit disclosure of supplemental information as to financial results from another inventory accounting method.

3. Inventories must be stated at cost with no reserves for obsolescence or other write-down. When there is such a reverse in the opening inventory, it must be eliminated through filing an amended return for the previous year. However, in light of the Supreme Court decision in the Thor Power Tool case, such reserves are generally not deductible whether or not companies have adopted LIFO.

Bad Debt Reserve Method. For tax purposes, a company may choose to recognize its bad debts either when they actually become worthless or when the company establishes a reserve. During inflationary time, establishment of a reserve is the preferred method because it accelerates a company's tax deductions. The reserve is usually determined using the Black Motor Formula, which is based on a ratio of bad debt experience for the current and five previous years.

Long-Term Contract Methods. Construction companies and certain manufacturers may adopt either of two methods of reporting income:

1. The *percentage-of-completion method* requires the contractor to recognize as gross income that portion of the gross contract price corresponding to the percentage of the contract completed for that year. All expenditures incurred during the year in connection with the contract are deducted.
2. The *completed-contract method* requires the contractor to report the gross income from the contract and deduct all applicable expenses in the year of completion and acceptance. In inflationary times, this is the preferred method. When price disputes are involved, income recognition may be deferred for a considerable time.

The following kinds of companies may use either of these long-term contract methods.

1. Producers of unique items that are not normally carried in finished goods inventory
2. Producers of items that normally require more than 12 calendar months to complete (regardless of the duration of the actual contract).

There is no requirement that tax and financial reporting be the same. However, a change to one of these methods does require advance permission of the IRS; the effect of a change is recognized in taxable income over ten years.

A change to the completed-contract method is accomplished in three steps.

1. Contracts completed in the year of change are reported as income in that year even though some of the income may have been reported in previous years. Hence, there is a "doubling" effect.
2. The doubling effect is mitigated through deduction of the income previously reported over the following ten years.
3. Income earned on contracts not completed in the year of change is deferred.

As a general rule, these steps can defer taxes for a company that is growing or experiencing rising contract prices because of inflation.

Installment Sales Method. A dealer in personal property may elect to pay no tax on gross profits from installment sales until payments are collected. This deferral is permitted even when the method of accounting is the accrual method, regardless of what method is used for financial statement purposes.

In view of the cash-flow benefits from deferral of tax payments on profits until they are realized in cash, a company whose accounts are paid either slowly or in installments should consider whether it can qualify for this accounting method. Not only will the benefit of substantial tax deferrals be obtained, but also it may give the company an opportunity to charge interest to customers' who are slow payers.

Adoption of the installment method does not require advance permission by the IRS. A company needs only to make the election on the return for the year of adoption, which can be filed up to nine and one half months after year end.

Vacation Pay Accrual. Normally, a company may deduct an accrual at year end for vacation pay only if the employee's rights to the vacation are *vested* i.e., if the employee quit on the last day of the year, he would be entitled to payment for the vacation accrual. Under a special provision in the Code, a company may elect to accrue contingent, nonvested vacation pay. The election does not require advance approval and can be made upon filing the tax return for the year of change. While there are limitations on the amount of the deduction, adoption of the accrual method is generally advantageous when the amount of the vacation accrual increases from year to year.

Fiscal Year Change. Careful choice of the fiscal year of a corporation, partnership, or Subchapter S corporation frequently can defer tax payments. For example, if a partnership or a Subchapter S corporation elects a January 31 year end, the income for that 12-month period is not reported by the partner or shareholder until the following year. The tax on 11 months' income is thereby deferred for a year.

There are some limitations to the partnership year end. Normally, a partnership must adopt a year end that coincides with the year end of its principal partners. However, an important exception is when there is a sufficient business purpose for selecting a different year end—such as to follow the company's natural business cycle.

Another example of planning the year end involves a company starting up new opera-

tions. Closing the year just prior to the busy season may result in reporting loss or reduced profits in the initial year. Paying tax on the profitable busy period is deferred for another 12 months. Additionally, an allowable method for determining estimated tax payments is to base them on the income for the immediate preceding year, thereby deferring tax payments for almost two full years.

State and local taxes

Although there are other business factors, the location of a company's offices and plants in states with low taxes can reduce state and local taxes substantially. This will not inhibit the business from engaging in interstate commerce.

Federal legislation (Public Law 86-272) prohibits a state from imposing a tax on income derived by a foreign corporation from interstate commerce, provided that the business activities within the state are limited to the solicitation of orders for sales of tangible personal property by the corporation's representatives, and orders are filled by shipment or delivery from outside the state.

Sometimes, doing business in at least two states can reduce the tax burden as compared to doing business in only one state. This results from the method of sales allocation used by many states. For example, sales may be allocated to the taxing state only when shipments are made to points within that state. Accordingly, doing business in two states that have this method of allocation will exempt from state taxation some of the income attributable to sales outside both states.

A review also should be made of personal property tax, being careful to store inventory or equipment in states that have no or low property taxes when possible. There are over 30 states that have "trade-free zones" or what are commonly referred to as "free port" laws. Business can keep inventory in these zones and be free from personal property taxes and sometimes state income taxes.

Estimated Tax Payments

In times of high interest rates and inflation, planning estimated tax payments can be critical.

Estimated payments can be based on the lowest quantity:

1. The prior year's tax
2. The tax computed on the prior year's income
3. Exactly 80% of the current year's tax on income determined quarterly.

There are a number of ways of determining the current quarter's income:

1. The first quarter is equal to three months.
2. The second quarter is equal to three to five months.
3. The third quarter is equal to six or nine months.
4. The fourth quarter is equal to nine or 11 months.

One company that earned most of its income during the last six months of the year, was able to defer its estimated tax payments for several months. Based on Revenue Ruling 76-563, no payments were required during the first two quarters because there was little or no income; in the third quarter, the company based the payment on the first six months results, again requiring no payment. In the fourth quarter the company paid one-quarter of 80% of the tax liability for the year. Hence, by careful planning, only 20% of the total tax for the year had to be prepaid.

Selecting the Taxable Entity

Selecting the best taxable entity for a business is a major consideration in tax planning. In addition to the corporate entity, partnerships and Subchapter S corporations should be considered together with the Domestic International Sales Corporation (DISC) for businesses that have export sales.

Partnerships and Subchapter S corporations are useful to avoid double taxation; anticipated losses (such as in a start-up situation) can be utilized against the shareholder's other income. In addition, these entities can be used to shift income to family members who are in lower tax brackets.

The DISC is a useful tax planning tool even though there are some limitations. DISCs are tax-exempt and permit a company to defer the tax on 50% of the income earned on qualified export sales. However, rules limit the DISC deferral to the increase in export sales over an average of four previous years. In the case of a new DISC, there is a $100,000 floor before this limitation comes into effect.

FINANCING FIXED ASSET PURCHASE AND EXPANSION

The acquisition of fixed assets frequently causes a cash drain either in the year of purchase or in subsequent years as interest and principal on debt are paid. This cash drain may be alleviated by tax reductions available through leasing, utilization of investment tax credits, and rapid depreciation methods.

Leasing

The leasing alternative has the following advantages:

1. It avoids risk of loss on sale or obsolescence.
2. Cash is available for other needs.
3. The lessor may "pass-through" the investment tax credit.
4. It may provide "off balance sheet financing."
5. The early lease payments (and tax deductions) may exceed depreciation and interest.

Investment Tax Credits

The investment tax credit affords business taxpayers an opportunity to reduce income tax liability when buying or constructing equipment and other qualified property such as elevators, escalators, and other tangible, depreciable property having a useful life of at least three years. No credit is permitted for buildings or their structural components. A lessor of qualified new property may elect to pass the credit through to the lessee.

The investment credit rate is 10% of the qualified investment in property placed in service during the year. An additional credit of 1% to 1.5% is available to corporations that have investment credit employee stock option plans for their employees. Following is a schedule of the qualified investment in property as a percentage of the cost:

YEARS	PERCENTAGE OF COST
7 or more	100%
5 to 7	66.7%
3 to 5	33.3%

The maximum credit allowable for any year is the tax liability for the year or $25,000, whichever is less, plus a percentage of the excess over $25,000. For 1980, the percentage is 70%, in 1981, the percentage is 80%; in 1982 and thereafter, the percentage is 90%.

The unused portion of the investment credit in any year is carried back three years and forward seven years. The unused credit for the current year is carried back for use in the earliest carryback year and any remaining unused credit is then applied to each succeeding year in chronological order. A credit of 10% is also allowed for rehabilitation expenditures.

Rapid Depreciation Methods

If the fixed asset is purchased, both ADR class lives and accelerated methods of depreciation should be considered to defer the tax burden. The adoption of ADR allows the company to adopt a useful life that can be as low as 80% of the IRS's published life for the asset. The use of "one-half year conventions" also is helpful. In addition, component depreciation can increase the depreciation deduction.

DISTRIBUTION OF CASH TO OWNERS

Tax planning can enhance the after-tax cash available for pay-out to owners. Some of the principal techniques include:

1. Deferred compensation plans
2. Split-dollar life insurance
3. Buy-sell agreements
4. Employee stock ownership plans (ESOP)
5. Family trusts
6. Freezing estate values.

Deferred Compensation Plans

After an employee's current cash needs are satisfied, both funded and unfunded deferred compensation plans offer numerous advantages. In the funded pension or profit-sharing plans, the employer's contribution to the fund is deductible currently; the trust fund income is tax-exempt and the employees are not taxed on the compensation until receipt after retirement. The unfunded plans defer the company's cash outlay, defer the employee's tax payment until receipt in lower income years, and they accumulate interest on pre-tax compensation.

Split-Dollar Life Insurance

Split-dollar life insurance plans are a way to offer life insurance protection to employees at costs comparable to term insurance without the disadvantage of the usual declining protection available from term insurance. The company owns the cash surrender value of the life insurance, but the cash value can be borrowed under most policy provisions.

Buy-Sell Agreements

A buy-sell agreement may be the best means of distributing cash to retiring shareholders or survivors. Usually, the desire to avoid an excessive estate tax valuation for a business interest, whether corporation, partnership, or sole proprietorship, is a reason for entering into a buy-sell agreement. Securing the continuity of the concern with experienced management and preventing excessive claims by family members are also motivating factors for entering into an agreement.

Under the typical buy-sell agreement, a corporation or individual (usually a co-stockholder) promises to buy, and the stockholder promises to sell stock at a specified price upon the happening of a defined contingency, usually the stockholder's retirement or death. Usually, this is funded with life insurance.

Employee Stock Ownership Plans (ESOPs)

An employee stock ownership plan is a defined contribution plan that invests primarily in employer stock to provide significant cash-flow benefits. An ESOP may utilize either a profit-sharing or stock-bonus format. The profit-sharing format has two limitations:

1. Employer contributions to the ESOP trust may come only from current and accumulated profits.
2. The plan may not borrow funds on the basis of guarantees by corporate or majority stockholders to purchase employer stock.

The major advantage of the profit-sharing format is that it allows distribution of benefits to employees not only in the form of cash or securities, but also in the form of employer stock—an important consideration when the employer stock is not publicly traded or otherwise readily marketable. An important advantage of either type of ESOP is that the employer's contribution can be made in employer stock as well as cash. Accordingly, an ESOP offers an employer a deduction without the payment of cash. However, the contribution of stock to an ESOP may not be a significant consideration when stockholders participate in the ESOP as employees.

Family Trusts

The creation of trusts for the benefit of members of the family is a common means of splitting income among family members. A taxpayer wanting to split his income with children for college education or with elderly parents for support may do so by conveying the property in trust for the family member. The taxpayer may thereby avoid tax on part of the income, subject to the general requirement that he must in fact transfer income-producing property rather than the income alone. The trust can be a party to various methods of shifting income such as lease of property, stocks, bonds, partnership interest, or interest-free loans.

The trust may also be used as a means of retaining management control of stock or partnership interests. As long as management does not exercise a veiled control over the beneficial interest, management control may be exercised by the creator or an agent of the creator.

To the extent that the trust income is distributed or distributable, it is taxable to the beneficiaries. However, if the income is accumulated, it is taxable to the trust as a separate entity.

A transfer to a trust involves a gift, and therefore may subject the donor to the gift tax. A taxpayer is entitled to a $3,000 gift exclusion per year per donee. In the case of a transfer to a trust, it is the trust beneficiaries and not the trust itself that is the donee; therefore, the taxpayer is entitled to as many exclusions as there are beneficiaries. This annual exclusion is not available except for gifts of present interest. It may not be used for a gift of an income interest in trust unless the trust requires the income of the trust to be distributed at least annually.

Freezing Estate Values

The transfer of either limited partnership interests or nonvoting common stock to family members, or trusts for the benefit of family members, results in numerous tax advantages without the loss of voting or management control.

First, the gift or estate tax on the post-transfer appreciation in the value of the transferred assets is avoided by the donor. In the case of a recapitalization, the donor generally retains voting preferred stock with liquidation values equal to nearly the entire value of the corporation at the time of the recapitalization. Any increase in the corporate value then accrues solely to the nonvoting common stock. Second, the transfer tax may be reduced further by subsequent gifts of preferred stock qualifying for the $3,000 per donee annual exclusion. A third advantage is the taxation of dividends or partnership income at the lower tax brackets available to family members. The last significant tax advantage is the elimination of any gift tax paid on the transfers from the donor's taxable estate.

CONCLUSION

Experience with inflation throughout the late 1960s and the 1970s, combined with the expectation that inflation will continue for the foreseeable future, highlights the need for deliberate business policies to counteract the debilitating effects on cash flow and "real" profitability.

The Conference Board's study ". . .found no magic remedies. Most [companies]. . .found the solution in better management across the board—from large matters such as planning, to smaller ones, such as product designing. . . .Better information, faster, is clearly necessary. So are better cost control, and better correlation between real costs and pricing mechanisms. . . ."

A structured approach to improving the cash-flow cycle of each business—from accelerating the completion of the cycle to reducing the cash required by the cycle—clearly can yield lasting benefits and go far to reducing the impact of inflation. All parts of the cycle—from cash balances required for operations to the taxes payable from profits—should be considered.

REFERENCES

1. Peter F. Drucker, *Managing in Turbulent Times*, Haper and Row, 1980, New York, N.Y.
2. Thomas Dudick and Ross Cornell, *Inventory Control for the Financial Executive*, John Wiley and Sons, 1979, New York.
3. Financial Accounting Standards Board, *Statement of Financial Accounting Standards No. 33: Financial Reporting and Changing Prices*, September 1979, Stamford, Connecticut.
4. James Greene, *International Experiences in Managing Inflation*, The Conference Board, Inc., 1977, New York.
5. Paul A. Griffin (ed.), *Financial Reporting and Changing Prices: The Conference*, Financial Accounting Standards Board, 1979, Stamford, Connecticut.
6. Louis Harris and Associates, Inc., *Looking Toward The 80's–A Chemical Bank Survey of Small and Medium Sized Business in New York*, November 1979, New York.
7. Alan M. Loosigian, *Interest Rate Futures*, Dow Jones Books, 1980, Princeton, N.J., pp. 315–347.
8. Alfred Rappaport, "Measuring Company Growth Capacity During Inflation," *Harvard Business Review*, January–February, 1979.
9. James McNeill Stancil, "Getting the Most From Your Banking Relationship" *Harvard Business Review*, March–April 1980.

4
Avoiding Pitfalls In Business Planning

C. Gadzinski
President
Capital Management Corporation

Using real-world examples, Mr. Gadzinski points out the most common pitfalls that are made in business planning—and how to avoid them.

Planning is a continuing, systematic, and formalized means of determining

1. Where we are
2. Where we want to go
3. How we can get there.

WHERE WE ARE

This might be referred to as the situation analysis. The purpose of this analysis is to identify the company's internal and external strengths and weaknesses.

One example of internal strength is know-how. The company may have skills in a particular manufacturing process or it may have superior expertise in developing new products. An illustration of a weakness would be a multilevel factory building with equipment that has outlived its usefulness.

In the matter of external strengths and weaknesses, the company may be in a strong competitive position because of a well-developed marketing organization that assures a good share of the market. It may be weak with respect to its ability to cope with government regulations such as OSHA because it does not have water treatment facilities that may require more capital than the company can spare.

WHERE WE WANT TO GO

The second step concerns itself with the economic environment in which the company will be operating during the planning period. Will it be a "shake-out" period in the industry? If so, prices are likely to be highly depressed. Management must then gear its goals and expectations at levels lower than normal.

HOW WE GET THERE

The third step in the planning process concerns itself with the denominators for measuring our objectives. These include such factors as utilization of facilities, profit on sales, return on investment, level of inventory, and so on. These must not only be specific and quantifiable; there must be a regular, ongoing feedback to permit management to compare its actual performance continually with the plan.

PITFALLS IN PLANNING

Now that we have stated and illustrated the three basic steps in the planning process, let us categorize the pitfalls into the following:

1. All levels of management must get involved.
2. The plan must paint a realistic picture.
3. A bottom-up approach must be integratable with top-down measurements to assure achievement of objectives.

Total Involvement

The business plan, to be carried out successfully, should not be written by the general manager, an outside consultant, or an internal staff consultant. It must be put together through the combined efforts of the entire organization. Failure to get the entire organization involved will result in failure to get the enitre organization committed; the plan will become "their plan," not "our plan."

I recall one incident when I visisted a company to review its business plan. One section of the plan included a cost reduction of $250,000, without giving the specifics as to how the reduction would be achieved. Without the specifics, there could be no meaningful "feedback" to monitor progress—to determine "how we get there."

When I asked the plant manager how he would achieve the $250,000 cost reduction, he had a quizzical look on his face—which told me that he knew nothing about this cost reduction objective. It became obvious that the business plan had been put together entirely by the general manager with no other involvement.

In some companies, in which total involvement is lacking, the business plan is prepared for the "corporate staff guys." A plan developed by edict can be self-defeating because it contains what "they want to hear"—it is prepared for "them," not for "us."

Realism in Planning

There are occasions when a sincere attempt is made to develop a plan with full involvement but the plan lacks realism. I recall a situation in which the general manager of a company attended a seminar on business planning. He was very enthusiastic in his desire to have such a program in his company. Accordingly, he called his key managers together and requested them to start work on a plan for their activity. Unfortunately, the final product listed some conflicting factors:

1. *Engineering.* In the narrative of this executive's plan, he did not indicate a strong effort to develop new products. In fact, he challenged the numerous marketing department requests for new products by pointing out that the products that had been developed never achieved the sales volume forecasted by the marketing group.
2. *Marketing.* The marketing executive included in his part of the plan a strong bid for larger inventories so that he could provide better service to his customers.
3. *Finance.* The finance department, in its coverage of inventory investment, showed a projected 30% reduction of inventories.

These three executives were all strong men who spoke bluntly. Unfortunately, the general manager vacillated. To appease the conflicting forces, he soft-pedalled the business plan, causing it to become a statistical exercise based on unrealistic and conflicting viewpoints.

Things continued along as they had before the idea of business planning had been suggested to his staff. Had this general manager exercised true leadership qualities, he would have asked some probing questions.

1. *Engineering.* Because the engineering manager indicated very little new product development work in his plan, the general manager could have asked him what he intended to do with his staff, which represented an annual payroll cost of $850,000. Was he planning to make some cuts?

2. *Marketing*. The general manager could have pointed out to the marketing executive that his field intelligence was unrealistic because half of the new products he had been requesting from the engineering department were in the "twilight" stages of their life cycles— competitors were beginning to phase them out.

3. *Finance*. To the finance group, he might have suggested that they stop looking at broad mathematical measurements of inventory turns and begin to look at inventory investment by major product lines, thus avoiding the need to bury problem areas and making unrealistic forecasts.

A business plan will expose interdepartmental conflicts quickly. This is a sure sign that some unrealistic thinking exists—a clue to top management that there is a problem. Although this is the "back-door" approach to evaluating realism, there is a more positive approach. Following are illustrations of the more positive method.

1. *Marketing*. A good area to explore is the size of the market, the company's share, and opportunities that exist for increasing this share. One company had a total potential market of $200,000,000 in one of its divisions, but enjoyed only 2% of this market, or $4,-000,000. The business plan continually showed how a larger share of the market would be captured, but only increased the 2% share a few tenths of a percent. Closer scrutiny revealed that the company's product line really only addressed itself to $20,000,000 of the $200,000,000 market. Furthermore, there were 11 companies competing for this $20,-000,000 portion of the $200,000,000 market. The company, with $4,000,000 of the $200,-000,000 was a "big gun" in the market, so increased penetration was difficult. Wild dreams written into plans just wouldn't make it happen. In another industry, three companies dominated the market. One had 65%, another 25%, a third had 9% and Company X

had 1%. Company X did not have the know-how that was required to get beyond its 1% share—it had no business being in that market. A realistic plan would have made this obvious.

2. *Field Sales*. The effectiveness of the field sales force is not as easy to evaluate as a function that is concentrated in a single location. But difficult as it may be to monitor an activity that may be spread out over many territories within a region—or across the country—it must be done by a direct review other than statistical measurements that can be highly deceptive.

A good case in point is the example of a salesman who continually met or exceeded his sales quota. He was considered to be an outstanding salesman because the statistical formula did not take into account all the facts. Of the 15 potential customers in the territory, this salesman was covering five. He had developed a "milk route" that permitted him to meet his objectives, but not those of the company.

3. *Advertising*. In developing the advertising budget, one cannot merely base it on an approximation of the dollars spent in the preceding year with adjustments for inflation. It is necessary to determine what the dollars will buy. Nor does it make sense to advertise nationally when the company is regional.

4. *Product Line*. In taking a realistic approach, we must determine which new products are going to be introduced and which old products will be purged from the line. Peter Drucker noted that various products or product lines can be categorized in four ways:

- Yesterday's breadwinner
- Today's breadwinner
- Tomorrow's breadwinner
- Investment in management ego

In reviewing product line performance, we must be mindful of these categories. As we introduce new products, we should be taking a hard look at those products that never made it or are not making it today.

5. *Engineering*. No new product plan should be permitted to start without a product

plan that spells out the potential costs and benefits.

The policy of writing off all development costs, as incurred, precludes the possibility of waking up one day to find that there is a million-dollar investment in "management ego" that will have to be written off. A realistic approach to controlling engineering costs is to require that every development program over $25,000 be budgeted with milestones so that progress can be monitored.

Assignment of engineering department personnel to projects is as important as budgeting the dollars. There should be a balanced allocation of resources to assure that the same engineer is not assigned at the same time to, say, ten separate projects. To assure a realistic balance in making assignments, it would be helpful to create a matrix that shows the types of engineering skills available. These would include mechanical engineers, mechanical designers, draftsmen, stress analysts, thermodynamic analysts, electrical engineers, component designers, and systems engineers. The number of each type of engineer and amount of available time is determined. This is then balanced against the schedules.

In determining what projects are needed, we must decide on the proper balance between new products and cost-reducing old products. There are too many cases where engineering is so involved with new products and new product development that little or nothing is done to achieve current product cost reduction.

Integrating the Bottom-Up and the Top-Down Plans

Some companies use the bottom-up approach to arrive at the projected financial statements and then make modifications without actually comparing the bottom-up approach with a carefully conceived overall objective. Other companies think out the overall objective carefully to arrive at the desired profit. They then allocate to the various functions the allowed cost that will assure attainment of the profit objective.

Bottom-Up Emphasis. When the company gives the main emphasis to the bottom-up approach, it is depriving itself of one of the major benefits of planning. The top-down methods provides an opportunity to establish such goals as what the desired return on investment and investment turnover should be. Such evaluations as the following would be made:

- If the average return on investment for other companies in the same industry is 12%, the company would know that 9.5%, indicated by the bottom-up approach, is unacceptable. This would provide the logic for taking a closer look at volume, labor efficiencies, and production losses.
- If the average industry turnover of inventory is 5.2 times per year and the bottom-up approach shows only 3.8, this is indicative of possible noncompetitiveness on the part of the company. The company will then know that it must look at inventory levels more closely.

Top-Down Emphasis. Some companies that emphasize the top-down approach, in arriving at the desired profit, determine the difference between net revenues from shipments or services rendered and the desired profit. This difference between revenues and profit becomes the allowable cost that is distributed among the various functions. While this is a pragmatic approach, it could work to the detriment of the plan for two reasons:

- The functional managers will feel that they were not participants in the planning function. In short, it's the general manager's plan.
- Proper consideration may not be given to company requirements to become truly competitive. Take the case of a company that has fallen behind its competitors in its quality of products. It may be necessary to "beef up" the engineering and the quality control functions to

catch up. A blind allocation of resources to achieve the profit objective could be self-defeating.

WISDOM IN PLANNING

As we grow older, we develop additional "mental spotlights" that add to the number of such lights that focus on problems. The more light that is played, the better the understanding. This is referred to as wisdom.

The same applies to business planning. The bottom-up view provides one insight, the top-down approach, another. The two together contribute to greater wisdom in planning.

5
Ten Commandments For Realistic Planning

James W. Taylor
Management Consultant

Mr. Taylor responds to the thought-provoking question, "Who would accept a plan that showed losses?". The ten commandments included in this chapter summarize the key factors that must be considered in the process of business planning.

All too often, companies that believe they have adopted and are practicing strategic business planning find that the results are less than satisfactory. They can point to stacks of attractively bound reports and cite hundreds of man-hours of work on planning, but cannot seem to identify clearly the results of this effort. Sometimes, it is even worse. They find that planning seems to cause resentment among managers. Or, planning is said to have interfered with accomplishing quarterly or annual goals.

When planning seems to be ineffective or disruptive, it is usually a sign that the management has not been realistic about implementing planning activities. Because the theory of planning is fundamentally very simple, it is easy to fail to understand that putting planning into action is quite difficult. Planning theory says that corporate weaknesses should be identified and that they should be replaced with new opportunities that are more profitable than the current weaknesses. There are two significant problems that arise when real people set out to accomplish these goals. One problem is that planning deals with the future, and the future is increasingly difficult

to forecast. The second problem is that many business plans end up being only pages of numbers representing financial "wishful thinking."

THE FORECASTING PROBLEM

Corporate weaknesses are usually found in markets that are expected to slow down in rate of growth or to decline in size. Corporate opportunities are almost always found in markets that are expected to grow rapidly. Thus the key elements of planning deal with expectations about the future. Such expectations are presented formally as forecasts. Realistic planning requires that management acknowledge constantly that it is virtually impossible to forecast the future with any degree of accuracy.

Nevertheless, forecasts must be made. Planning is about the future and there can be no escaping the fact that assumptions must be made. The important point is if forecasts are viewed as accurate and clear representations of a world yet to come, there will be a great temptation to commit corporate resources in ways that can become irreparable mistakes.

As the necessary planning horizon becomes longer and longer, this problem becomes increasingly acute. One has only to look at what the commitment to jumbo jets in the late 1960s did to commercial airline profits in the early 1970s. Decisions were made based on a future that never came to pass.

While there is probably no final solution to the forecasting problem, there are definite steps that management can take to minimize, or at least control, this problem.

THE "NICE NUMBERS" PROBLEM

The final product of planning must be presented in the form of financial numbers. When forecasts of market growth, company sales, and costs are pulled together, they represent the financial impact that planning is expected to have on the company. They express the bottom-line impact in dollars and cents.

Because all of these numbers are written in a form that is all but indistinguishable from similar reports of *past* company performance, e.g., annual reports, there is a great temptation to view them as "chickens already hatched." Further, because these numbers are always positive (who would accept a plan that showed losses?), a great pressure is generated to make sure that these numbers come true. They become the board of directors' commitment to the stockholders. They become the president's commitment to the board. In turn, they become the vice-presidents' commitments to the president and the division managers' commitments to their respective vice-presidents.

The problem is that all of these numbers are presented in an inflexible time frame. They become the yardstick for measuring actual performance at annual, semiannual, and quarterly reviews. Managers are judged on their ability to make the planning numbers happen. Unfortunately, future events, which the plan assumes, are extremely resistant to inflexible time frames. New product development does not occur on a neat, regular schedule. Acquisitions rarely appear on schedule,

let alone consummate in a predictable manner. Thus individual managers find themselves in the position of having to achieve numbers based on events over which they have no control. This is the "management dilemma of planning" and its implications are serious. Managers repeatedly take short-term actions to meet the plan that may have disastrous long-term effects. Premium priced products have been subjected to such frequent and deep price dealing that, in order to meet plan numbers, their margins have eroded permanently.

Because the "nice numbers" problem is so firmly related to the forecasting problem, there is no single, final solution to this problem either. There are, however, ways for management to approach the problem to soften the potential disruptiveness and counterproductivity. Such approaches are found in the Ten Commandments For Realistic Planning.

Commandment No. 1
Place the major emphasis on the *process* of planning.

The literature on planning contains considerable discussion of whether planning should be "bottom-up" or "top-down." That is, should planning be conducted by having the lowest levels prepare plans that are then integrated with other groups' plans, moving to higher and higher levels in the organization, or should planning begin with the president and be delegated down throughout the organization? While this may be an interesting theoretical question, it has absolutely no relevance in realistic planning. Planning must begin with the president. Anything else is a waste of time and money.

The reason that realistic planning must begin with the president is simple. Planning is hard work and subordinates will devote their efforts to it in exactly the proportion that they perceive their superiors place importance on it. If planning is seen as something that is delegated to somebody else, the results will never have value because they will always be superficial. This fact is so firmly grounded in actual practice the corollary is that if the president is not deeply committed to planning, it will fail.

If, however, the president and the top officers of the company are deeply involved in the planning process, they cannot help but be aware of the fragile nature of the forecasts underlying the plan. This alone will minimize the use of the plan numbers as a control device. The best results come from planning when top management concentrates actively on the assumptions and trends on which the plan is based rather than passively demanding "how much" and "by when."

Commandment No. 2

Distinguish those financial commitments that represent a risk to the balance sheet from those that represent a risk to the profit and loss statement.

The point of planning is to allocate corporate resources today to produce the greatest return tomorrow. The resources that are allocated are almost always financial. Because the future is always unpredictable, some number of the allocation decisions will be erroneous. While planning is intended to reduce the number of mistakes, it is unavoidable that some will be made over any course of time. Management should never lose sight of that fact.

Some of those allocation decisions will involve risks to the balance sheet. An unsuccessful balance sheet risk is one that can produce a negative impact on stockholder equity. Other allocation decisions will involve only risk to the profit and loss statement. In other words, P & L risks, if unsuccessful, can usually be covered out of annual profits.

A bad decision concerning a balance sheet risk almost always results in wholesale replacement of top management. Thus the company suffers not only the financial loss but significant personnel disruption as well. On the other hand, a bad decision about a P & L risk can usually be handled by a promise to do better in the future. While such a result is

not a happy one for dividends and profit sharing, it is of considerably smaller impact than a balance sheet error.

For example, the Arden Group is a Los Angeles–based supermarket chain with sales in the $500 million range. Between 1972 and 1977, the company recorded losses of $19.3 million and profits of $1.6 million (losses in four out of six years). During that period, the per share book value fell from $9.06 to $2.08. Yet the management group, none of whom are important stockholders in the company, have not only been able to hold on to their jobs, but they have been able to fight off two takeover attempts by promising to do better next quarter and next year. The Arden Group committed only P & L mistakes.

By way of contrast, Food Fair, Inc., a Philadelphia-based supermarket chain, committed balance sheet errors, during approximately the same time period, through their acquisition and rapid expansion of the J. M. Fields discount operations, In the same six-year period, Food Fair posted profits in five out of six years and per share book value rose from $14.09 in 1972 to $18.58 in 1977. Nevertheless, in 1978 virtually the entire management group was fired. The company is currently in Chapter XI bankruptcy proceedings.*

When a balance sheet risk is encountered, and after management is completely familiar with all of the uncertainties involved, the final decision should be as broadly based as possible. The board of directors and major shareholders should be briefed on the reasons for the decision, its possible implications, and their endorsement of the decision. If that endorsement is not forthcoming, the decision should be abandoned. Approaching decisions in this manner substantially reduces the pressure to "make the plan happen" on a rigid and arbitrary time schedule.

*With thanks to Howard Dawson and Louis Zitnik, Wagenseller & Durst, Inc., Laguna Beach, California for suggesting these two perfect examples of the different types of risk and their consequences.

Commandment No. 3

The total market and the shares of the major competitors must be measured as accurately as possible.

The absolute minimum data that must be available for realistic planning are historical trends for 1) the total market, 2) the company's products, and 3) competing products. Without these, it is impossible for a company to understand its industry and its own position within the industry. A clear understanding of the company's present and past position in the market is essential for predicting possible future positions.

Sometimes, these data are not easily obtainable. Such difficulty, however, must not be accepted as an excuse for not obtaining them. These data are the most critical inputs to planning. When these data are not easily obtainable, as is frequently the case with service companies and industrial manufacturers, there seems to be a temptation to let the difficulty in reading the future extend to reading the past. This temptation must be resisted at all costs.

Not only must these data be accurate, they must also be the *right* data. The classic example is confusing the number of quarter-inch drill bits sold with the number of quarter-inch holes that customers need and want. This, in turn, means that the company must have a clear answer to the question, "What business are we in?" before these data can be specified and collected. The fact that this commandment demands such definition makes it one of the most powerful for realistic planning.

Commandment No. 4

Make the plan "event dependent."

Because all planning must be summarized eventually in financial numbers, the plan must be cast against some time frame. This was discussed under the "Nice Numbers" problem. The danger that can arise, unless the company is doing realistic planning, is that dollars that the company can control get treated the same as the dollars that cannot be controlled. For example, the plan will specify plant expenditure dollars, which can be controlled, and sales dollars, which cannot be controlled. When middle-level managers are confronted with both controllable and uncontrollable dollars, they usually spend the controllable dollars, almost as a hedge against achieving the uncontrollable dollars.

Because the plan calls for spending a certain amount in dollars this year, another amount the next year, and still another amount the next, the momentum of this planned commitment of resources tends to sweep management past caution and stop signals. To minimize this method of spending controllable dollars, they should be identified in the plan and their expenditure made "event-dependent." Some examples of event-dependent expenditures are:

1. Authorize R & D expenditures only on projects that have a minimum potential market of $50 million.
2. Authorize test marketing only when 80% of all target customers rate the new product superior to competition in blind in-home tests.
3. Authorize new equipment expenditure only after pilot plant operations confirm a minimum of savings of 10% in overall cost of goods.
4. Authorize regional roll-out of the new product only after it has achieved sales of $150 or more, per million dollars of retail sales for six consecutive months.
5. Authorize warehouse expansion at any location only after stock-outs exceed 5% for six successive months.

In this way, automatic restraints are built into the plan, making it much more difficult for internal events to outpace external events.

Commandment No. 5

Reduce controllable dollar expenditures to the smallest possible units and authorize step by step.

This commandment is closely related to Commandment No. 4. Once expenditure dollars are identified in the plan, not only is there pressure to spend them, there is also pressure to spend the maximum amount. Manufacturing will prepare numbers to show that a maximum size plant will be most efficient and most profitable. The financial department will show that inflation trends and projections make this the best time to build the maximum size plant.

Of course, given their assumptions, they are right. The difficulty is that the assumptions are not firm enough to guarantee their arguments. Their assumptions are derived from the "Nice Numbers." If top management has been deeply involved in the planning process (Commandment No. 1), there will be an acute awareness of the "softness" of the forecasts of market growth and sales growth. Top management therefore needs a method to trade off the requirements of growth and the likelihood of errors in the forecasts. Authorizing controllable dollar expenditures step by step provides the ability to match resource dollar commitments to the actual occurrence of the anticipated events.

The idea is that pilot plants, test programs, regional roll-outs, and so on, are always going to be better management decisions over time and over a number of decisions. The final argument supporting step-by-step expenditures is that these decisions are most often balance sheet risk decisions (Commandment No. 2) and that the down-side risk of such decisions must always be minimized because of the difficulty of forecasting the future accurately. Smaller scale operations that can be expanded after expectations have been proven true are always preferred by management.

Commandment No. 6
Set advance criteria for abandoning planned projects.

One of the most troublesome kinds of growth projects are those that never quite meet planned goals but are never quite obvious failures. Such projects tend to take on a life of their own because they have, by this time, developed "champions" who see the fate of the project associated with their own careers. They argue that just one more year, or just one more change, or just one more something, will get the project on target. Besides, they say, "we've already invested so much money in the project it would be a mistake to walk away from it now." All of this often makes it difficult for top management to say "no."

The fundamental error in these arguments is that they assume that all of the growth projects undertaken by the company will be successes. Unfortunately, the facts of life are that this is just not so. Every company is going to be dealt bad hands and marginal hands. Good management folds the bad and marginal hands as early as possible so that they may maximize the returns from backing good hands.

This commandment is designed to minimize the disruption and personnel problems involved with marginal projects. Abandonment criteria that are determined in advance puts everyone involved with the project on notice of what to expect concerning top management's commitment to the project. Some examples are:

1. Stop development of a new product if less than 60% of all target customers rate the product superior to competition in blind in-home use tests.
2. Abandon pilot plant operations if a minimum savings of 7.5% in overall cost of goods has not been achieved after eight months of operation.
3. Withdraw from test market if the new product is not selling at the rate of $65 per million dollars of retail sales six months after introduction.

Note the similarities and the differences between these examples and those shown for making plans "event dependent" (Commandment No. 4). The differences are important. Event criteria are designed to control the rate at which resources are devoted to the project while abandonment criteria determine whether resources will be devoted at all.

Commandment No. 7
Construct an alternate plan with time as the primary dimension.

When the basic business plan is completed, it will specify certain dollars of sales, profits, and other figures during period one, another set of amounts during period two, and so on. While this format is unavoidable, it does lead to the "management dilemma of planning" discussed earlier. One very useful way to deal with this dilemma is to build a second plan around the same forecasts by using time as the primary variable.

This second plan indicates that satisfactory performance will be accomplished if certain dollars of sales, profits, and so on are achieved between Time X and Time Y. These intervals should reflect reasonable judgments about the time it may take to complete various phases of each project rather than tying everything to an arbitrary calendar year. For example, If sales of the newly acquired company reach $1,000,000 between 18 and 36 months, and if profits reach $150,000 between 24 and 45 months after acquisition, this project will be satisfactory.

A second plan provides a valuable tool for evaluating the company's overall progress towards meeting its goals and gives individual managers a controlled amount of latitude.

Commandment No. 8
Start a monitoring system.

The purpose of planning is to help manage the transition from today's business to tomorrow's business. In order to know whether this transition is being made successfully requires more than simply evaluating the company's own financial statements. It requires an evaluation against external benchmarks. The question is "Where is the information about external events to come from?"

Most companies have a source of external information that is relevant to today's business that they use to manage today's operations. The difficulty is that the external information required to manage tomorrow's business is seldom the same as that required for today's business. In turn, this means that the company must set up a new system to monitor those external events that are relevant to tomorrow's business.

For example, consider a major pharmaceutical firm that decides it wants to become a leader in delivering health care in order to lessen its reliance on the discovery of new drugs. It manages today's business by monitoring its share of antibiotic prescription sales, but the external information about the total prescription sales of antibiotics is only marginally relevant to the company's business tomorrow. What is required is a system that monitors the sources of health care, its costs, and its quality—quite a different information set.

If top management has been deeply involved in the planning process (Commandment No. 1), it has defined the crucial assumptions underlying the business plan. These assumptions provide the focus for developing a new monitoring system that is relevant to tomorrow's business. The extensiveness and accuracy required of these monitoring systems will vary from company to company, depending upon the number of assumptions underlying their plan and how directly these assumptions impact the projects and plans.

Commandment No. 9
Review and revise the plan on a regular basis.

Realistic planning is difficult, time-consuming work. All too often, when the initial plan is completed, reviewed, and communicated to all interested parties, the temptation is to put it on the shelf and sit back with a sigh of relief. If that temptation is followed, the main value of planning will be lost. After all, the reason to adopt planning in the first place was to assist in managing change. Because change is continual and ongoing, so must planning be continual and ongoing.

The only way that planning will ever become continual and ongoing is when it is scheduled regularly. At an absolute minimum, top management must do the following, at least on an annual basis:

1. Examine the assumptions underlying the plan to ensure that they are still relevant to the success of the planned activities.
2. Compare trends in assumptions about external events with the data supplied by the monitoring system.
3. Identify the reasons for differences between expectations and actual occurrences. Evaluate the impact of these reasons on the plan.
4. Review the company's interim progress toward its planned goals.
5. Identify the reaons for overperformance and underperformance on individual projects.

This is the bare minimum required for successful, realistic planning on an ongoing basis. More frequent and more in-depth reviews increase the benefits to be gained from planning. There is absolutely no danger of anyone doing too much planning. It's simply too much hard work for that to happen. The real danger is not doing enough planning!

Commandment No. 10

Keep long-term financial goals private.

When a planning cycle is completed, there is an understandable but undesirable urge among many companies to rush out and proclaim to the financial community, the public at large, or just about anyone who will listen, that "By 19XX, we are going to be an $X million (billion?) company and that we are going to be in the Y business." This urge is understandable because realistic planning is hard work. When it is done well, it is only human to look for admiration and applause. Such publicity is, however, undesirable. Here are some of the reasons it should be avoided:

1. It's probably inaccurate! Nobody can forecast that well and if Commandment No. 1 has been observed, top management is all too well aware of just how shaky that announcement really is.
2. Even if the dollars are accurate, it's unlikely that the time frame is accurate. If a second plan has been made (Commandment No. 7), top management is also aware of that.
3. It is going to change within a year anyway. (Commandment No. 9 will see to it.)
4. It gives unnecessary assistance to the competition. (Commandment No. 11 says that is not smart.)

With apologies to a famous American, the best practice for management is "Walk softly and carry a big (planning) stick."

SECTION II
STRATEGIES IN BUSINESS
PLANNING

6
Considering Diversification as Part of the Strategy

Andrew D. Clapp

Senior Staff Consultant Arthur D. Little, Inc.

Because of weakened market positions, dated technology, and increased foreign competition, many managements looking for new products, new markets, and entirely new businesses have turned to diversification.

There is enormous pressure on corporations to extract maximum earnings from their businesses, as well as to maintain positive growth rates in sales and earnings. This worked well during the 1970s, and shareholders were generally pleased with the almost uninterrupted series of quarterly sales and earnings increases generated by so many United States companies.

Maintaining this steady trend has had its problems, however. Many companies that deferred capital investment during the 1970s for the sake of earnings growth find themselves with weakened market positions, dated technology, and increased competition because of foreign entrants that have literally burst their way into the United States marketplace. For some companies (and even entire industries), it is too late to regain their former position of prominence. Managements are looking anxiously for new products, markets, and entirely new businesses to make up for difficulties within their own industries, hence the quest for diversification.

Unlike the late 1960s, free-form diversification is acknowledged to be risky and expensive, particularly without high-multiple stock with which to buy into new businesses. The task has become one of acknowledging the state of the business and industry, rather than accepting the fact that it will be difficult to find a new industry at a price you'd be willing to pay.

Is it too late to rededicate oneself to one's own business? We think not. One purpose of profiling a business and installing a strategic planning system is to determine which businesses are suitable for rededication and which should be divested or abandoned.

Diversification includes entering businesses and markets that may be quite close to those currently being pursued by a business unit. It also includes free-form diversification into totally unrelated areas. However, the key to selecting the most appropriate diversification strategy begins with an evaluation of the strengths and concerns of each business unit within the corporation. This opens up a number of diversification directions that a business unit could pursue, based on its strengths and concerns, given the financial and managerial resources of the firm or its parent.

The corporate diversification strategy should reflect the sum of diversification strategies developed for each business unit, to the extent that the parent management group can weigh, prioritize, and select those diversification strategies that meet the stockholder and corporate goals and objectives, within the limits of the firm's resources. Free-form diversification then becomes a radical departure from business areas in which the corporation is currently active, and as such, entails a higher degree of risk and often a higher cost of entry. Today, given the fact that many shareholders of public companies are disappointed with the stock's price performance relative to earnings, free-form diversification may be too costly, as it frequently leads into industries that have higher growth rates, hence higher entry costs, such as a high price/earnings multiple. In those few instances where management and shareholders are willing to pay the comparatively high price required to enter a new, faster growing business, free-form diversification can be a realistic long-term strategy for improving a company's stock performance. But for most corporations that are unwilling to pay such high premiums, related diversification may be a more satisfying and acceptable route to follow.

PROFILING STRENGTHS AND WEAKNESSES AT THE PLANT OR BUSINESS UNIT LEVEL

For purposes of developing strategy, profiling is conducted at the strategic business unit (SBU) level. Strategies resulting from the installation of such a planning system may include marketing, manufacturing, distribution, and perhaps diversification strategies at the SBU level. Historically, most companies think of diversification being decided and implemented at the corporate or divisional level. For example, they often consider what characteristics a diversification candidate ought to possess, such as minimum/maximum sales volume, minimum earnings level, the number

of experienced management personnel willing to remain, in-place sales and distribution systems, and so forth. The difficulty is that given such a set of acquisition/diversification criteria, scores of industries and hundreds of companies qualify. The matrix of opportunities then becomes unmanageably large and collapses into an opportunistic process.

Continuing this scenario, acquisition candidates are submitted by intermediaries, with most being rejected on the basis of a "poor fit" with existing operations, or simply a "low comfort level" as perceived by the would-be acquirer. So why not begin by looking at the resources, strengths, and weaknesses of the acquirer, and developing a diversification strategy that seeks to identify a business or industry that "fits," takes advantage of existing strengths and know-how, and offsets known weaknesses or concerns.

Evaluating the strengths and weaknesses of a corporation is accomplished by "profiling" each business unit as is normally done during strategic planning, or in a condensed form specifically designed to generate a set of diversification strategies. So that this process can be differentiated from the conventional profiling technique, we call this diversification profiling.

DIVERSIFICATION PROFILING—WHO SHOULD PARTICIPATE

The characteristics and measures of an operating business that form the basis of strength upon which to build a diversification program can be divided into six functional areas:

1. Products and technology (Table 1)
2. Marketing and sales (Table 2)
3. Manufacturing (Table 3)
4. Distribution and service (Table 4)
5. Profit management (Table 5)
6. Asset management (Table 6)

It is desirable to have key management personnel representing each of these areas, although the titles of these people may not co-

Table 1. Products and technology evaluation worksheet.

EXAMINE	CONCERNS/ STRENGTHS	WEIGHT	BECAUSE OF. . .	S	C	STRATEGIC OPPORTUNITIES
Compare $ R&D with $ sales	R&D, new product development capability					Acquire technology; transfer technology
	Product design and engineering		Know-how			Apply/acquire
Compare with competitors	Product image; style					Apply/acquire; exploit halo effect
Changes in design, style, technology	Product vulnerability					
Compare to competition	Breadth of line insufficient					Acquire
Evaluate return/line	Excessive breadth of line					Analyze, divest
Examine new entrants/exits	Barrier to product entry		Technology, know-how			Exploit; acquire
Compare to competition	Product/customer fit					
Perceived value	Product quality					Enhance "perceived value"
	Product pricing					

Table 2. Marketing and sales evaluation worksheet.

EXAMINE	CONCERNS/ STRENGTHS	WEIGHT	BECAUSE OF . . .	S	C	STRATEGIC OPPORTUNITIES
Past cycles	Cyclical approaches Seasonal approaches Economic swings					Seek counter cyclicality Seek counter seasonality Seek recession resistance
Recent new entrants, other comparable industries	Potential entry: By foreigners		Growth market			Rededicate efforts; invest
	By "biggies" By opportunists		Volume attractiveness Low barriers to entry			Divest
	Commitment by competitors					Avoid confrontation Leapfrog
Compare promo with $ sales for industry	Advertising and promotional capability					Apply/acquire; add new methods Consolidate promo efforts Product extension
	Selling organization					
Compare to competition	Strength/weakness within selected markets; channels					Market extension (by segment, geography) Integrate forward
	Customer concentration		Dependency of few customer segment of market			Enter/acquire new segment
Turnover	Customer loyalty					Exploit
Basis of competition	Customer acceptance					Address needs; perceptions
Market shares; trends	Competitive position		Market share vs. maturity			Select appropriate strategy

Table 3. Manufacturing evaluation worksheet.

EXAMINE	CONCERNS/ STRENGTHS	WEIGHT	BECAUSE OF. . .	S	C	STRATEGIC OPPORTUNITIES
Economic outlook Industry outlook	Raw materials Sources of supply		Dependence/concentration suppliers			Integrate backwards Consolidate buying needs
Energy outlook (by industry)	Energy		Impact dependence on energy			Seek lower energy usage situations
Regional characteristics of current and other geographic areas	Labor		Costs Skills Supply			Shift to/from labor intensive to more automated Enter lower cost or more plentiful labor markets
Other geographic areas and other industries	Unionization					Avoid union conflicts
Competitors	Ingenuity		Manufacturing and engineering			Seek out complementary strength
Industries of your suppliers, customers	Added value					Integrate forward or backward into higher value added industries
Competitors and industry	Productivity					Introduce incentives Shift production to other or new units
Competitors and industry	Cost position					Upgraded plant and equipment; methods engineering Divest, close
Adequacy; state-of-art today and in future	Production facilities					Reinvest Divest
Current and anticipated industry needs vs. projected capacity	Plant capacity					
Competitors; customer need	Manufacturing quality					Seek complement

Table 4. Distribution and service evaluation worksheet.

EXAMINE	CONCERNS/ STRENGTHS	WEIGHT	BECAUSE OF. . .	S	C	STRATEGIC OPPORTUNITIES
	Proximity to customers					Improve current system
Basis of competition within industry	Delivery: speed and cost Service: speed and cost Service quality					Acquire companies with complementary capabilities Integrate forward, acquire
Geographic relationship of customer, plants and related costs; trends	Warehousing/distribution		Cost/logistics			Optimize by consolidating, expanding
	Transportation fleet		Utilization, handbacks			
Growth, profitability, loyalty, and so on	Channels of distribution					Enter/expand other channels Acquire complementary companies

Table 5. Profit management evaluation worksheet.

EXAMINE	CONCERNS/ STRENGTHS	WEIGHT	BECAUSE OF. . .	S	C	STRATEGIC OPPORTUNITIES
Earnings/sales	Profitability					
Examine other industries	Growth rate of profits					Enter industries with higher profit growth rates
	Inflation		Inability to pass through inflationary cost increases			
	Line management					Diversify into related/ unrelated businesses
Factors/competitors, known emphasis on planning	Ability to forecast performance; corporate planning					
How this has affected company's position vis-à-vis competitors.	Risk aversion					
Performance strategies of other regulated industries	Government regulation					Seek/avoid regulated industries
	Environmental or circumstantial conditions, issues					Avoid, withdraw Rededicate

Table 6. Asset management evaluation worksheet.

EXAMINE	CONCERNS/ STRENGTHS	WEIGHT	BECAUSE OF...	S	C	STRATEGIC OPPORTUNITIES
	Balance sheet performance: • • • Return on equity • Return on net assets (RONA)					
Examine funds generation and deployment	Cash generator/user: Outlook: Anticipated capital needs: • • • • • •					
Compare with industry	Debt/equity balance					
Costs of capital and sources (now and projected)	Sources of debt capital Sources of equity capital Staff management					Diversify into unrelated businesses
Shareholder expectations vs. those of comparable companies in other industries	Dividend payout ratio Stock P/E ratio					Diversify/acquire where enhancement results
Board of director's expectations	Stock dilution					Diversify/acquire low P/E businesses, or pay cash

incide with the above six categories. For example, asset management and profit management are measures of financial performance, and while the chief financial officer may be most knowledgeable of the sources for good and bad financial performance of the business unit, it is the president and various other managers who may know the reasons for such performance. In the area of products and technology, a research and development manager may know what technology is within the firm's grasp. However, the manager of sales and marketing may better understand what the marketplace seeks as well as the current basis of competition that the firm's products should seek to satisfy. In the area of distribution and service, there may be no single senior level individual who is responsible for this function, although the head of sales and marketing may be the person best qualified to comment on them. His perception of the company's reputation as well as his ability to deliver is important. Ideally, the participants at this session should include the firm's president, R&D and/or engineering manager, marketing and sales manager, and the manager of manufacturing. The most senior individuals responsible for these functions should be included. Where these are particularly important functions to the company, it may be appropriate to include other persons within the organization.

PROFILING THE DIVERSIFICATION STRENGTHS AND WEAKNESSES

There are six tabular worksheets to be used, one for each of the six functional areas just described.

On each sheet, the key strengths or concerns of the business unit are listed, with space to add appropriate additional ones. In the beginning, it is important to weigh each of these strengths and concerns in terms of their significance or importance. For example, a scale of one to ten can be used, in which "10" indicates greatest importance. They should also be noted as "S" for strengths or "C" for concerns. A strength could be quite

significant and merit a score of "9", and another aspect of the unit could be described as a serious concern, and also be scored with a "9".

As each of the six tables are completed, the values assigned in weighting may shift, as the group gains experience. Therefore it is important at the conclusion of the exercise to review the tables to adjust any numbers necessary for consistency.

As each strength or concern is listed, a brief explanation for each should be noted in the "Because of. . ." column.

Each of these strengths or concerns should have a measurable benchmark against which the firm or industry can be compared. It is important to identify these as they will provide a basis for screening diversification opportunities. It also suggests how candidates, once found, can be evaluated to assure that they meet the desired profiles. This should be entered in the "Examine" column.

MATCHING DIVERSIFICATION OPPORTUNITIES WITH STRENGTHS/ CONCERNS

As the various strengths and concerns and their related rationales are listed, directions in which the firm could diversify begin to emerge. For some strengths or weaknesses, no diversification opportunities emerge, but perhaps a strategic action could be undertaken. For nearly all of the business unit's strengths or concerns one or more appropriate strategies or diversification opportunities identified that correct a weakness or take advantage of a particular strength. Thus it is important to identify each diversification or strategic opportunity as its corresponding concern or strength is listed. This exercise builds an acceptance of diversifying on the basis of existing strengths and concerns, not on financial criteria alone.

Now it is appropriate to think about prioritizing each diversification opportunity. They should be listed on a flip chart as they are developed, and given a weighting that corresponds to the assigned to the corresponding strength or concern. Other nondiversification strategies should be similarly listed and weighted on another flip chart.

In some instances, the same diversification strategy may occur more than once. For example, vertically integrating forward may appear as a marketing and sales diversification strategy as well as a manufacturing, asset management, and profit management diversification strategy. Accordingly, the weighting assigned to each diversification strategy should be the cumulative total each time it is used.

By the time the exercise has been completed, a set of weighted diversification strategies appropriate for the business unit will have been listed on one flip chart, and a set of nondiversification strategies, also weighted, on a second flip chart. At any time, but particularly now, the application of "judgment" and experience helps refine the list further to produce a final list of prioritized diversification strategies. These are sound, bottom-up diversification strategies that the business unit can rightfully and reasonably consider. It is entirely possible that the strategies that are scored highest appear on the nondiversification list, in which case the particular business unit might be better off focusing its attention on its current business needs rather than diversification. For certain businesses, the foregoing exercise may show that a particular unit brings few strengths to a diversification undertaking. Instead, it faces more in the way of long-term weaknesses. The decision to divest or abandon that unit should then be studied. Interrelationships between it and other business units of the corporation must be examined. Divestment of a unit with little promise or opportunity is not easy. But when the high cost of continued ownership is considered, even when a low price might be realized from its sale, the choice should be clear.

COSTING AND DIVERSIFICATION STRATEGIES

Heretofore, the development of diversification strategies was based upon the business unit's strengths and concerns, not on the reality of financial aspects. While it is fairly easy to estimate the approximate cost and likely return for each strategy, it may be more useful to look at some actual cases. For example, past acquisitions can be studied as cases. Where actual examples of each diversification strategy cannot be found, public companies in the business that fits the diversification strategy should be studied. A third approach would be to hear from a person who is knowledgeable with the industry or functional area suggested by the strategy. His experience and background can enable a company to "see" into another business area before any investment is made.

At this point, the cost for each diversification strategy should be calculated, with a projected return. The cost of a diversification program may be integrated with other corporate undertakings to determine what the demand on the corporation's resources will be. The overall planning activity of the corporation should reflect the normal demands of the various business units along with those caused by diversificaion.

DIVERSIFICATION STRATEGIES AND BUSINESS MATURITY

A key step in strategic planning is determining the maturity of a business unit's industry. It has been fairly well determined that the available strategic alternatives are limited to a large extent by the maturity of the particular industry. Using the four basic classifications of maturity, embryonic, growth, mature and aging, most industries can be categorized without difficulty. A company seeking to improve its competitive position in its industry may do so fairly easily in an embryonic or growth industry, but not without considerable difficulty and high cost in a mature or aging industry. Take the example of the telephone interconnect market, which is a growth industry. The growth rate is high, and the opportunity to increase shares exists through a number of strategic options, including geographical expansion, introducing new products within existing markets, and so on. However, in a mature industry such as the appliance industry, there are relatively few competitors, and the cost of entry or geographical expansion can be more costly and risky.

On the other hand, diversification by a company in a mature or aging business permits it to transcend some of these strategic limitations, which is why it is so appealing. Take for example a textile company, which is a very mature industry. Diversification into another industry with a higher growth rate than its own industry possesses offers the promise of balance and renewal. However, a well-intended diversification effort can run awry when a mature company embarks upon a growth-oriented diversification strategy without considering the different characteristics of the business it seeks to enter. So it is useful to look at each of the diversification strategies developed previously and place them on a maturity spectrum. A horizontal line should be drawn across the appropriate maturity for each strategy. The completed chart, entitled "Natural Period of Strategy Execution," will be referred to when entry strategies are considered.

After each diversification strategy posted on the chart, a vertical red line should be drawn through the chart to show the maturity of the diversifier. Those strategies that intersect with the vertical red line probably can be undertaken by the diversifier without a great deal of difficulty. Those strategies that do not intersect with the line may be less familiar territories, and hence entail a higher level of risk. By carefully selecting the entry strategy, risk can be reduced. For example, let's consider a mature company entering an early growth industry by acquiring a medical electronics company. Attractive as it may seem, this acquisition might bring management, marketing, and cash-flow problems that the acquirer may not be equipped to handle. However, as volume production and large-scale distribution and service is well understood by a mature organization, these skills could be brought to the younger company. Still, outright acquisition as a means of entering that industry may be too risky for the diversifier. Other entry strategies may be

more satisfactory to both. These could include a minority investment, joint venture, a subcontracting or marketing relationship, a loan with options or warrants convertible to equity, or a combination of these.

CORPORATE/DIVISIONAL GOALS AND OBJECTIVES

So far, we have focused on the strengths and concerns that management may have towards the strategic business unit levels and the diversification options they suggest. Now it is time to return to the corporate level and consider what basic goals and objectives a parent company may have for each business unit as well as for the parent corporation as a whole. These goals and objectives at the parent company level may include:

1. Achieving and maintaining a certain growth rate in sales and earnings
2. Improving profitability as a percentage of sales and as a return on assets or equity
3. Improving the price/earnings ratio (P/E) of the firm's common stock
4. Balancing the corporation's businesses by adding new ones of a different maturity
5. Reducing cyclical or seasonal approaches by entering businesses with offsetting or more moderate cycles
6. Where a number of business units are involved, it becomes a portfolio management issue

There has been much written on this subject, from many points of view, in which management is seen as a hero, balancing disparate businesses and achieving stockholder's expectations, to the other extreme where management is accused of building an empire that carries with it greater "perks" and assurances of job longevity.

Goals and objectives developed at the corporate level frequently do not coincide with those developed at the divisional or strategic business unit level. While they may be settled at the corporate level, it is important that they be generated at both levels if the opportunities within sight of a business unit, but out of the corporate view, are going to be pursued.

Setting goals and objectives may create gaps in sales, profitability, and other areas that may be filled through diversification. For example, with a corporate five-year sales objective of $700 million and a projected sales volume of $500 million by that year from the existing businesses, a $200 million gap must be filled through diversification. Discounting that $200 million per year gap in the fifth year back to the present yields a need for a $100 to 150 million per year business today, depending on the business' growth rate and the assumed inflation rate.

To capture the $110 million in revenue, any number of corporations with annual sales of $110 to $150 million, as well as many companies with annual sales of $20 to $50 million in sales, could be acquired. Affordability may constrain a would-be acquirer severely, given that companies today are selling for between five and 40 times earnings, with the average running at 12 to 13 times earnings. If there are certain constraints placed upon the diversifier, such as no dilution of earnings or no good will, the population of companies that could fill this gap is reduced to a handful, consisting mostly of aging, commodity-type businesses that often sell for four to six times earnings and below book value. The best-laid diversification plans are frustrated by the natural pricing process, in which companies with relatively high P/Es and aggressive acquisition policies can do the acquiring, while mature companies with low P/Es suffer in silence, as each attractive but too costly opportunity passes them by.

Perhaps the whole issue of the cost of entering a new business should be examined carefully to see what it means to the diversifier. There is a net cost of making an acquisition or an investment, for which there is a reasonably predictable stream of earnings and dividends. In addition, one can forecast the cost of capital with reasonable accuracy. It is on these two elements that many diversification decisions are made.

During the last decade, primary emphasis has been placed on quarterly increases in sales and earnings. As a result, investment in plant and equipment, new technology, and new markets has decreased. As we entered the 1980s, we found that a number of Japanese companies have taken advantage of our position by "investing" heavily in their own technology, plants, and equipment, as well as our market. It is believed that they have done so at the expense of profits for a number of years, as a part of a long-term strategy to gain a significant market and technological position here in the United States.

We see that this strategy has worked. In a number of industries, including some which are as American as apple pie, machine tools for example, the Japaneses have taken a large share of the market. Their cumulative market share exceeds that of any United States company within the lathe market. As they behave much as one company, they are the leading competitors to reckon with today.

How should management deal with the question of sacrificing short-term earnings to gain a long-term market position? Who wants to face the shareholders at the next annual meeting to explain this strategy in light of a first decline in earnings for eight years, and no increases in a dividend likely for the next three or four years? For some companies, this is exactly what may be needed. Without this, these companies remain locked into their respective industry, with a steadily weakening competitive position.

The other cost associated with diversification may in fact be an "opportunity lost" cost, which is difficult to measure and more difficult to explain to the shareholders. In most cases, the strategy embarked upon will go unexplained or couched in terms that will not incur the wrath of shareholders, particularly orphans and widows.

Again, let's look at our Far Eastern neighbors, where we see a few examples of Japanese firms acquiring minority positions in United States firms, in some cases accompanied by a joint venture of technology exchange agreement. This type of entry strategy has been avoided by United States businesses as it not only leaves control in the hands of the recipient of the funds, but yields little enhancement to the earnings of the investor, with no points for management for scoring another consecutive increase in earnings. Often, the most productive diversification strategies of those listed in the previous exercise involve a maturity level different from that of the diversifier, with a higher level of risk. For example, one of the best strategies might be to enter a product area that is late embryonic to early growth. Conceivably, an outright acquisition could threaten the management and the incentives of that organization, whereas an investment with options to acquire control under certain conditions could leave management with incentives as well as autonomy. For the diversifier, it gives them a "window" on a technology or market, and the opportunity four or five years hence to acquire control. Do this every year or two, and by the fifth or sixth year, those minority investments will begin to roll over into control or 100% ownership. The accounting benefits of control replace the disadvantages suffered through minority ownership. The cost of an entry strategy other than majority acquisition can be considerably less, as only a premium is paid for control. Retention of autonomy with the opportunity to cash in the remaining stock at a higher value later on is often sufficient incentive for management to set a much lower offer than an outright sale of the company would generate. The risk of losing management following an acquisition is practically eliminated where they are still equity owners, thus reducing one of the greatest risks of diversification where little is known of the business being bought.

By combining alternative entry strategies to diversification, with selection of strategies that relate to a firm's present strengths or concerns, the net cost of a diversification can be reduced to an acceptable level and a commensurate level of risk.

7
Market Challenger Strategies

Philip Kotler

The Harold T. Martin Professor of Marketing
Northwestern University

Professor Kotler views the market structure as being made up of the leader, challengers, and followers. This chapter examines three ways in which the market challengers can improve their position.

Every market is occupied by one or more firms that play different competitive roles in meeting demand in that market. Up to four roles can be distinguished, as shown in Figure 1. In this hypothetical market, 40% of the sales is in the hands of one firm called the market leader. Another 30% is in the hands of a *market challenger,* a runner-up firm that seeks to maintain its market share without rocking the boat. Twenty percent can be categorized as imitators or followers. The remaining 10% is in the hands of several small firms called *market nichers*, firms that serve small market segments that they hope will not attract the interest of the larger firms.

Here we will concentrate on firms that choose to play the role of market challengers or aggressors. They differ from market followers in not being content to "play ball" and

not "rock the boat." We want to examine the strategies that are available to market challengers to aggrandize their position.

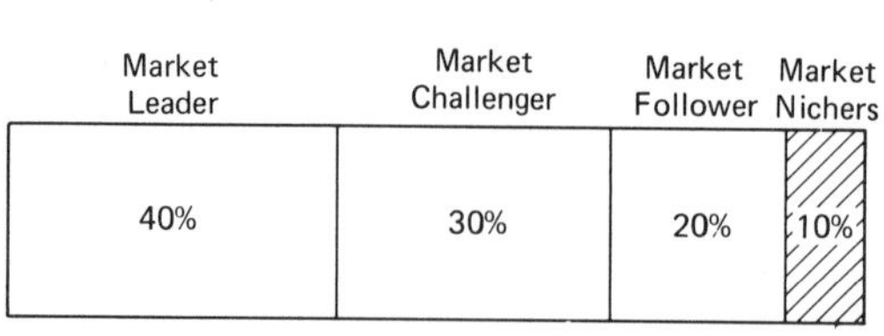

Market challengers can attempt to gain market share in three ways. The first is through a *direct attack strategy* (also called "head-on" strategy), in which a challenger tries to best the market leader through sheer doggedness. For years, Colgate launched direct attacks on Proctor and Gamble but without much success.[1] The second is through a *"backdoor" strategy* (also called "end-run" or "blindside") in which the challenger runs *around* the dominant firm rather than *into* it. Timex gained its leadership in the low-price watch market by selling its watches through mass-merchandise outlets rather than through conventional jewelry stores that were locked up by the major watch manufacturers. The third is through a *"guppy" strategy* of attacking smaller competitors rather than the market leader. Many major beer companies owe their growth not to taking share from the leader or each other but through gobbling up small regional and local beer companies in the process of competition.

Market Leader	Market Challenger	Market Follower	Market Nichers
40%	30%	20%	10%

FIGURE 1. Hypothetical market structure.

Basically, the market challenger has to decide whether to aggress against the leader, other runner-ups, or smaller firms based on discovered weaknesses. They then build a strategy to take advantage of the weakness. Yet challengers are found from time to time going after competitors with nothing more than a strong determination to win. Recently, the second-place razor blade manufacturer in Brazil decided to go after Gillette, the market leader. Management was asked if they were offering the consumer a better blade. "No," was the reply. "A lower price?" "No." "A better package?" "No." "A cleverer advertising campaign?" "No." "Better allowances to the trade?" "No." "Then how do you expect to take share away from Gillette?" they were asked. "Will power," was the reply. Needless to say, their offensive failed.[2]

In fact, several strategies are available to the market challenger who is seeking an advantage vis á vis competition.

1. *Price discount strategy.* A major attack strategy for challengers is to offer buyers a comparable quality to the leader's at a lower price. This strategy can be illustrated using the price/quality matrix shown in Figure 2. We will assume that the leader follows the premium strategy shown in cell 1. The challenger in turn decides to attack the leader by offering a comparable product at a lower price, as illustrated by cell 2. The Fuji Company used this strategy to attack Kodak's preeminence in the photographic paper field by introducing paper of comparable quality priced 10% lower than Kodak's. Kodak chose not to lower its price, with the result that Fuji made strong gains in market share. Bristol-Myers adopted a price discount strategy in launching its new aspirinlike product called Datril against Johnson & Johnson's leading brand, Tylenol.[3] It budgeted a heavy advertising campaign to announce its lower price and to convince consumers that all the new aspirinlike products are identical. Johnson & Johnson, however, countered by lowering its price and Bristol Meyers' brand never achieved the expected market share. Texas Instruments is perhaps the prime practitioner of price cutting. It will enter a market by offering a comparable quality product that is successively lowered in price to gain market share and lower costs. Texas Instruments is willing to forego profits in the first few years in order to gain unchallenged market leadership. They did this with transistors and hand calculators and now seem bent on doing this in the low-price watch market.[4]

		Price		
		High	Medium	Low
Product quality	High	1. Premium strategy	2. Penetration strategy	3. Superbargain strategy
	Medium	4. Overpricing strategy	5. Average-quality strategy	6. Bargain strategy
	Low	7. Hit-and-run strategy	8. Shoddy-goods strategy	9. Cheap-goods strategy

FIGURE 2. Nine competitive positioning strategies on price/quality.

For a price discount strategy to work, three assumptions must be fulfilled. First, the challenger must be able to convince buyers that its product and service are of comparable quality to the leader's. Second, the buyers must be sensitive to the price difference and feel comfortable about turning their back on existing suppliers. Third, the market leader must stubbornly stick to its price despite the competitor's attack.

2. *Cheaper goods strategy.* Another strategy to gain market position is to offer the market an average or low quality product at a much lower price. The market challenger could, in other words, offer a product in cell 5 or 9. This works when there is a sufficient segment of price-conscious buyers. Firms that get established through this strategy, however, are vulnerable to attack by still "cheaper goods" firms. In defense, they try to upgrade their quality gradually to the level of the market leader.

3. *Prestige goods strategy.* A market challenger can attempt to get around the market leader by launching a higher quality product and charging a higher price. In this case, the challenger offers a product that is an extension of cell 1. Mercedes gained on Cadillac in the American market by offering the American public a car that was of even higher quality and higher price. Some attackers, after gaining market acceptance for its premier product, later roll out lower priced products.

4. *Product proliferation strategy.* The challenger can go after the leader by launching a large number of product variants. Hunts went after Heinz's leadership in the ketchup market by creating several new ketchup flavors and bottle sizes, in contrast to Heinz's reliance on one flavor of ketchup, sold in a limited number of bottled sizes. The success of this strategy depends upon the new product managing to attract and hold customers and the leader failing to react fast enough with its own product variants.

5. *Product innovation strategy.* The challenger may pursue the path of product innovation to attack the leader's position. Polaroid and Xerox are two examples of companies whose success is based on continuously introducing outstanding innovations in the camera and copying fields, respectively. Miller recently took over second place in the beer industry because of its successful development of Lite beer and its introduction of "pony-sized" bottles for Lite beer drinkers. In many ways, the public gains most from challenger strategies oriented toward product innovation.

6. *Improved services strategy.* The challenger may attack the leader by finding ways to offer new services or better service. IBM achieved its success in the computer market by recognizing that customers were more interested in the quality of software and service than in the hardware. Avis' famous attack on Hertz, "We're only second; We try harder," was based on promising and delivering cleaner cars and faster service than Hertz.

7. *Distribution innovation strategy.* A challenger should examine the possibility of expanding its market share through developing a new channel of distribution. Avon became one of the largest and most profitable cosmetics companies by perfecting the ancient method of door-to-door selling instead of battling other cosmetic firms in conventional store outlets. Timex decided to sell its low-price watches through mass merchandise channels, thus bypassing the jewelry stores.

8. *Manufacturing cost reduction strategy.* Some companies see the key to building market share in achieving lower manufacturing costs than their competitors. The lower manufacturing costs can be achieved by more efficient purchase of materials, lower labor costs, and more modern production equipment. The company could use its lower costs to price more aggressively to gain market share. This has been the key to the successful Japanese invasion of various world markets. A company like Texas Instruments reverses the process by first lowering its prices aggressively, then winning market share, and then finding its costs falling through the "experience curve."[5] As it captures more volume, its costs continue to fall, thus providing a basis for further price cutting or profit taking.

9. *Intensive advertising promotion.* Some

challengers seek to gain on the leader by increasing the quantity and/or quality of their advertising and promotion. When Hunts went after Heinz in the ketchup market, it built its annual spending level to $6.4 million as against Heinz's $3.4 million. Miller has similarly been outspending Budweiser in its attempt to achieve first place in the United States beer market. Substantial promotional spending, however, is usually not a sensible strategy unless the challenger's product or advertising message exhibits some superiority over competition.

A challenger rarely succeeds in improving its market share by relying on only one strategy element. Its success depends on designing a total strategy that will improve its position over time. This is shown in the following examples.

Pepsi-Cola vs. Coca-Cola. Before World War II, Coca-Cola dominated the American soft-drink industry. There was no really second-place firm worth mentioning. "Pepsi raised hardly a flicker of recognition in Coke's consciousness."[6] Pepsi-Cola was a newer drink that cost less to manufacture and whose taste was generally thought to be less satisfying than Coke's. Its major selling point was that it offered more drink for the same price. Pepsi exploited this difference by advertising "Twice as much for a nickel too." Pepsi bottles carried a plain paper label that often got dirty in transit, thereby adding to the general impression that it was a second-class soft drink.

During World War II, Pepsi and Coke both enjoyed increased sales as they followed the flag around the world. After the war ended, Pepsi's sales started to fall relative to Coke's. A number of factors contributed to Pepsi's problems, including its poor image, taste, packaging, and quality control. Furthermore, Pepsi had to raise its prices to cover increased costs, and this made it less of a bargain than before. Morale was quite low at Pepsi toward the end of the 1940s.

At this point, Alfred N. Steele came to the presidency of Pepsi-Cola with a great reputation for merchandising. He and his staff recognized that the main hope lay in transforming Pepsi into a first-class soft drink, not a cheap imitation of Coke. They recognized that this turnaround would take several years. They conceived a *grand offensive* against Coke that would take place in two phases. In the first phase, which lasted from 1950 to 1955, the following steps were taken. First, the taste of Pepsi was improved. Second, the bottle and other corporate symbols were redesigned and unified. Third, the advertising campaign was redesigned to upgrade Pepsi's image. Fourth, Steele decided to concentrate on hitting the take-home market that Coke had relatively neglected. Finally Steele singled out 25 cities for a special push for market share.

By 1955, all of Pepsi's major weaknesses were overcome, sales had climbed substantially, and Steele was ready for the next phase. The second phase consisted of mounting a direct attack on Coke's on-premise market, particularly the fast-growing vending-machine and cold-bottle segments. Another decisions was to introduce new bottle sizes that offered convenience to customers in the take-home and cold-bottle market. Finally, Pepsi offered to finance its bottlers who were willing to buy and install Pepsi vending machines. These various steps, running from 1955 to 1960, again led to considerable sales growth for Pepsi. Within one decade, Pepsi's sales had grown fourfold.

Yamaha v. Honda. In the early 1960s, Honda had established itself as the top motorcycle brand in the United States. Its lightweight machines with great eye appeal, the slogan "You meet the nicest people on a Honda," and an aggressive sales organization and distribution network all combined to expand the market for motocycles greatly. Yamaha, another Japanese manufacturer, decided to enter the market against Honda. Its first step was to study the leader's major weaknesses, which included several dealers who had grown rich and lazy, abrupt management changes, discouragement of franchise-seeking dealers, and a neglect of promoting the mechanical aspects of their motorcycles.

Yamaha offered franchises to the best of the Honda-rejected franchisees and built an enthusiastic sales team to train and motivate their dealers. They improved their motorcycle to the point that they could claim and demonstrate its mechanical superiority. They spent liberally on advertising and sales promotion programs to build buyer awareness and dealer enthusiasm. When motorcycle safety became a big issue, they designed superior safety features and advertised extensively. The sum of these strategies propelled Yamaha into a clear second position in an industry of over 50 manufacturers.

CONCLUSION

A market challenger deliberately chooses to play a dangerous game, taking on the possible glory and the certain risks of a David attacking a Goliath. Many challengers have spent countless funds trying to become number one but never made it. The outcome of the contest depends on two things. One is the response of the market leader who might make mistakes or fail to take the threat seriously enough until it is too late. An ineffective leader increases the chances of successful aggression greatly. The other is the quality of the challenger's

strategy. The challenger who develops a preemptive strike in the form of a new technology, distribution channel, or service management system may gain a lasting advantage over the market leader and thereby displace him. On the other hand, a strategy of head-on competition unaccompanied by any decisive advantage is likely only to generate higher costs to both competitors and the public.

REFERENCES

1. "How to be Happy Though No. 2," *Forbes*, July 15, 1976, pp. 36, 38.
2. See also William E. Fruham, Jr., "Pyrrhic Victories in Fights for Market Share," *Harvard Business Review*, September–October 1972, pp. 100–107.
3. See "A Painful Headache for Bristol-Myers?" *Business Week*, October 6, 1975, pp. 78–80.
4. See "The Great Digital Watch Shake-Out," *Business Week*, May 2, 1977, pp. 78–80.
5. See "Selling Business a Theory of Economics," *Business Week*, September 8, 1973, pp. 86–88.
6. Alvin Toffler, "The Competition that Refreshes," *Fortune*, May 1961. See also "Pepsi Takes on the Champ," *Business Week*, June 12, 1978, pp. 88–97.

8
Designing a Strategic Planning System

Peter Lorange
Associate Professor of Management
The Wharton School, University of Pennsylvania

Good business planning facilitates optimal allocation of funds, people, and technology. The company's success is dependent on the degree of effectiveness in the regeneration of these three resources.

INTRODUCTION

This chapter discusses an approach to the design and implementation of strategic planning systems.[1] The key premise is that a strategic planning system is a decision-making tool, assisting senior management in the allocation of a company's scarce strategic resources. Thus we shall not see planning as an end in itself but as a means of improving management by having the abililty to make decisions. Many planning systems in the past have focused almost exclusively on financial variables, notably funds. We contend that a broader view of strategic resources to be taken, which includes critical managerial capabilities as well as technological knowhow. Our view is that the planning process should facilitate the allocation of funds, people, and technology. Accordingly, the criterion for a firm's success is the degree to which its strategic resources (funds, people, and technology) are regenerated at a satisfactory rate, not only so the firm can avoid depleting its strategic resources, but

also so it can maintain its options for future expansion and development.

First, we discuss types of strategic planning tasks, recognizing that the task of planning at the corporate level typically is different than planning within the various business elements of a corporation. We then outline several critical steps in a planning process, thereby clarifying the various planning tasks. Next, we discuss the issue of tailoring the design of a planning process to a given company, reflecting this company's particular situational setting and strategic challenges. In our opinion, there is no one general planning systems approach that is appropriate for every company; a careful tailoring of the design is necessary to reflect each company's unique needs. This chapter also deals with issues of managing the evolution of an effective planning process, so that it can maintain its effectiveness despite significant changes in a firm's situation and its corresponding planning needs. The roles of various executives usually involved in planning—notably the corporate planner, the chief executive officer, and division managers—is discussed, followed by a set of brief conclusions about designing and implementing a strategic planning system. Finally, we provide in an appendix a checklist

*I am indebted to Martin Dalgleish, Pascal Tone, and Michael Treacy for commenting on an earlier draft of this chapter.

for avoiding pitfalls when designing a planning system or for identifying potential weaknesses in an existing system.

LEVEL OF STRATEGIC PLANNING

In delineating what might be a useful set of strategy levels or building blocks for developing a strategic plan, consider Figure 1. We see from this simplified organization chart of a typical diversified corporation that there are several organizational levels—in this case, five. However, we contend that even though a real organization might have a quite complex formal organizational structure, it can usually be decomposed into three strategic levels for planning purposes. At the corporate level, we call the planning task *portfolio planning*. Here, a chief executive will attempt to strike a reasonable balance among the various types of business involvements that his company is in or attempts to get into. The focus, therefore, is one of balance in the allocation of strategic resources, so that the overall pattern

of expected returns, adjusted for the relevant risks, seems reasonable. It is normally useful to view the group vice-presidents as being part of the corporate office's portfolio strategic task to avoid the creation of a suboptimal overall corporate strategy. Normally, groups should not be considered a separate strategic level; as extensions of the corporate office they should facilitate an overall, unified corporate strategic portfolio planning approach. If seen as a separate strategic level, the groups are, in essence, chartered to develop their own "mini-portfolio strategies." The group level's major role is in relieving the corporate level in the execution of plans and at the operations end. This role should not become a set of filters preventing the corporate level from seeing the overall pattern of the firm's business exposures.

Let us now turn to the next level of planning, to be called *business planning*. Looking again at Figure 1, we see that there are several so-called business elements reporting to a division. The business elements and the division together are responsible for planning the business family. The focus is to come up with a strategy for succeeding relative to competition within this business area. Products and markets are normally somewhat defined and the competitive challenges relatively clear. Consequently, planning at this level is fundamentally different from planning at the corporate level. It consists of the generation of strategic resources through specific instances of competitive success rather than balancing the commitment of strategic resources to the various business strategy involvements.

As implied in Figure 1, a division, while chartered to operate in one business area, can typically be seen as consisting of several business elements, i.e, different, but related product/market involvements. It is thus necessary to develop separate subplans for each product/market element. However, this sharpened competitive focus should not be allowed to blur the fact that the business elements are more or less interrelated, thus also calling for the development of an overall divisional or

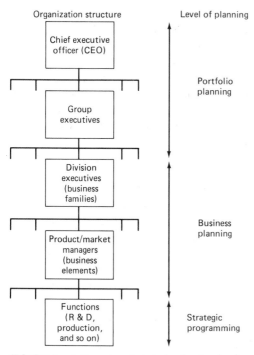

FIGURE 1. A hierarchy of strategic planning levels

business family plan. In summary, then, the second level of strategic planning, *business planning*, is carried out by the division and its business elements, allowing for focused product/market analysis as well as "pulling together" interrelated elements into one coordinated plan.

Consider the functional departments and their involvements in planning. The functional elements within an organization are critical to strategy formulation and implementation in that most of the specialized human and technological resources rest with these functions. Paradoxically, however, we state that there is little room for functional plans per se. The reason is that the functions' strategic roles should be to support and facilitate the implementation of business plans. An organization does not achieve strategic success by having excellent functional departments per se; it is the interaction among the various functions in carrying out new strategic programs which brings strategic success. Thus the third level of planning should be called *strategic programming*. Given that the functions' strategic tasks are, in effect, derived from the role they play as part of a given business strategy, we should be careful to acknowledge that when notions such as "marketing plans," "production plans," "R&D plans," and so on, are being used, they are, in fact, a summary of the functions' roles in business strategy implementations, and *not* independent functional baronial plans.

PROCESS STEPS

We delineated three distinctive types of strategic planning, each associated with different organizational levels. In this section, we discuss further the nature of these planning tasks, i.e., what steps are found in a planning process. Figure 2 outlines the critical steps in the planning process. Before discussing each step in more detail, it should be pointed out that we view planning as an integrated, comprehensive process for setting and reinforcing strategic direction. Excessive segmentation into long-term planning, budgeting, monitoring, and incentives is less useful, unless we recognize that all are aspects of the overall strategic directing-setting task.

The purpose of the first step (see Figure 2), labelled "objectives setting," is to determine strategic direction. This implies reconciliation of questions such as Where to go? What is the rationale for the business? What are one's own strengths and weaknesses? What is the attractiveness of the business? In short, the task is to develop one's competitive niche in operational terms.

It is important to approach the objectives setting task in such a manner that a sense of creative, opportunistic thinking is instilled, in contrast to merely an extrapolation of past trends, mentally and/or in numbers. A more systematic and open-ended reassessment of one's strategic environment should facilitate the delineation of opportunities that one might

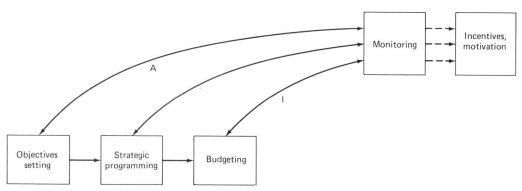

FIGURE 2.   Stages in the planning process

expect to remain attractive over a period of time, thereby being worth committing strategic resources.

The next step, labeled strategic programming, focuses on identifying a useful way of implementing the strategic direction through delineation of specific and typically cross-functional programs. Such programs might include a wide variety of types. They may, for instance, be concerned with the development of new products, penetration of new markets, modification of existing production processes, efficiency improvements, and so on. Again, we see that while the strategic programs have to be conceived and carried out by the functional resources of the company, the key to strategic programming is its cross-functional nature, implying, for example, that R&D, manufacturing, and marketing should cooperate in developing a new product program, and so on.

When corporate management agrees on what constitutes the most desirable set of strategic programs that the organization as a whole should pursue, the broad allocation pattern for strategic resources has, in fact, been decided. As a consequence, the role of the traditional capital- and expense-budgeting procedures is changed somewhat. In situations without prior planning, the financial resources (traditionally seen as the major strategic resource) tended to be allocated through those procedures. We now see that the allocation has been pushed forward into the planning process and that it encompasses the allocaton of human, technological, and financial resources. Capital budgeting and strategic expenditure procedures now serve as vehicles for fine-tuning and consistency checking of the broad resource allocation pattern.

The third step, budgeting or action programs, consists of the near-term implementation of the strategic thrust. Here we are dealing with the tip of the iceberg of the strategic direction. While budgeting needs no further comments here, it is necessary to stress that a budget should be reconcilable with the long-term strategic direction. If it becomes difficult to see what a budget contributes towards the implementation of the long-term strategic direction, then this might be symptomatic of too weak a linkage between the budget and the strategic programs.

While the three steps discussed so far deal with the *prior* setting of strategic direction, the next step, monitoring or control, deals with the *posterior* assessment of the progress towards achieving this strategic direction. It is important to distinguish this step (as well as the next step—management incentives) from the three steps just discussed. We now deal with a more or less continuous follow-up process. In contrast, setting strategic direction is a discrete activity, taking place once or several times a year.

Most of the classical control we find in corporate practice today is based on budgetary control, i.e., comparing the actual performance with a preset standard given by the budget. Given the typically short time span involved between the comparison of actual against standard (one year, a quarter, or a month), the budgetary control approach is a feasible and natural one.

Unfortunately, the classical monitoring approach seems less applicable when it comes to strategic programs and objectives. Given that the actual achievement of an objective is typically expected to come through far into the future, a comparison of whether we made it or not ten years out becomes more or less an academic exercise of little practical managerial value. Consequently, monitoring of progress towards these more strategic goals is often lacking, or, at best, done quite informally. A serious implication is the resulting lack of interpretation of budgetary performance data within the context of changes in prior strategic positons.

There are, however, ways of monitoring progress towards objectives and strategic programs fulfillment not dependent on the classical monitoring approach. This approach starts out by isolating the critical factors upon which a particular objective rests. These factors are typically environmental in nature and could, for instance, include specific economic trend developments, competitive changes in situations, technological developments, legal and legislative actions, and so on. A critical factor might have positive as well as negative effects. Experience shows that executives frequently tend to be better at identifying negative rather than positive factors. For this reason, particular emphasis should be placed on seeking out positive environmental leverage opportunities. Factors must also be carefully ranked to insure that only the more important ones are being considered. Each of the critical underlying factors has a certain value or position attached to it at the time of agreement on an objective. We can therefore monitor the evolution of each of these factors relative to the initial or base value. If our monitoring indicates that the competitive situation has deteriorated significantly, this might prompt us to go back and reassess the objective. We may or may not conclude that the objective is still valid. Thus indirect monitoring through focusing on developments of the critical underlying assumptions is an operational way of adding control relative to objectives.

In monitoring strategic programs, we should again make use of the indirect approach of focusing on the critical environmental assumptions behind a program. For instance, the technological rationale behind a strategic program that consists of building a new plant may significantly change during the building period. If we monitor this carefully, we may still have time to modify the program so that the plant does not become obsolete. In this case, we can also establish milestones or checkpoints for the completion of critical phases or segments of a given program. Here too is a useful monitoring vehicle, in seeing to what extent a strategic program is slipping from schedule as well as whether the expenditure of resources is as intended.

As indicated, it is often difficult to interpret traditional budgetary control signals without simultaneously taking into account changes that may have shown up with respect to one's objectives and/or strategic problems. For example, a particular business unit might show extremely good profits in a given year, significantly exceeding the budget. However, in examining the strategic position of the business, it may turn out that the competitive strength has been allowed to deteriorate through loss of market share. Also, the basic market may have decreased beyond expectation. The management may have attempted to cut down on expenditures such as market promotion, R&D, and so on, with the effect that profits in the near-term increase while the strategic position has been weakened. It is impossible to determine whether the budgetary performance in this case is good or bad. Management's interpretation of control data therefore, must be three-dimensional, as implied by Figure 2. Whenever a deviation is to be interpreted, signals from all these monitoring modes must be considered together, in order to draw the appropriate conclusions.

The last process step, as indicated in Figure 2, is management motivation or incentives. It is difficult to see how management pursues the fulfillment of strategic objectives and programs aggressively, if their incentives happen to be based solely on achieving the near-term budget. This is the way incentives schemes are often structured in corporations today. We might even expect that such incentive schemes might actively bias management behavior against strategic performance. It is important to coordinate management incentives with the rest of the planning process, so that the implementation of strategic process can be reinforced, not frustrated.

In the present context, we are considering motivation and incentives in a broader sense than payment bonus schemes. Factors such as promotion, being entrusted with more discretionary authority and resources, fringe benefits, praise and prestigious exposure, and so on, naturally are important, in addition to the more classical bonus schemes. Just as for the control task, a three-dimensional view must be taken in interpreting actual performance against prior set standards for objectives, strategic programs, and budgets.

INFORMATION FLOWS

In this section, we discuss the information flow for connecting the strategic levels and the process steps. We shall also highlight several common pitfalls that might tend to obstruct a useful information flow when implementing this conceptual scheme.

Consider for now the objectives setting task. We need top-down/bottom-up interaction as well as a vehicle for iteration of preliminary statements in order to identify a good set of objectives alternatives and to reach agreement on a set of objectives. This must incorporate the various business objectives of each of the divisional units into an overall corporate objective by fitting the various inputs together in a portfolio sense. Analogous top-down/bottom-up interactions have to take place when it comes to the delineation of the strategic programs and budgets. Figure 3 outlines the general shape of the information flow within what might now be seen as a conceptual scheme for strategic planning.

Figure 3 does not portray an entirely clearcut exposition of the conceptual planning schemes on two accounts. First, the information pattern flow diagrammed in Figure 3 does not convey clearly the fact that the process usually is iterative. Although difficult to illustrate, information typically goes back and forth between the levels several times at each stage before actual agreement has been reached on a set of consistent objectives, programs, or budgets. Second, the two final steps of the process, control and incentives, have not been included, in order to preserve simplicity. These steps are of course, connected to the rest of the process through information channels. One set of channels connects monitoring and incentives with the outputs of each of the three direction setting stages, so as to establish information links that compare actual developments to the relevant aspects of the plans. Another set of channels links the strategic levels so that relevant monitoring information can be transmitted in a bottom-up/top-down manner for analysis and deliberation on eventual corrective action. In terms of potential pitfalls when implementing the conceptual framework for strategic planning system portrayed in Figure 3, there are several problems that tend to frustrate the intended flow of information exchange.

The first potential pitfall relates to the role of the chief executive officer. As seen in Figure 3, it is assumed that the CEO initiates the process. While it is commonly agreed that the

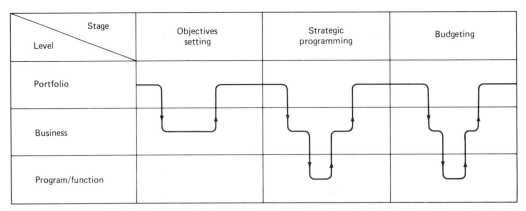

FIGURE 3.   The information flow pattern in the conceptual framework for strategic planning. (Source: Vancil, Richard F. and Peter Lorange, "Strategic Planning in Diversified Companies," *Harvard Business Review,* January–February, 1975)

strategic planning cannot work unless the CEO endorses the process, we require a more definite involvement of the CEO rather than mere tacit support. Specifically, the CEO should be involved by giving three types of inputs: brief (but tentative) statement of his overall strategic intentions for the company; a (tentative) delineation of the discretionary strategic resources that he reckons will be available; and a brief detailing of common underlying assumptions, such as interest rates, inflation rates, economic outlook, and so on, to facilitate consistency in the planning work ahead. An open-ended lack of realism should be avoided. On the other hand, too much specificity during this opening phase might stifle creativity by giving the organization a sense of false relief from having to examine the critical issues.

A second potential pitfall issue relates to the business level executives' mode of examination of their competitive environments during the objective setting phase. There might easily be an element of mental (and/or numerical) extrapolation when it comes to reassessing their business directions. If things are going well, there might be a tendency to pretend that the successful mode of the past can continue in the future. What is necessary at this stage is a deliberate and forceful attempt to end any reliance on the past. Only after an objective assessment of opportunities and threats in the environment should one reconcile these with one's internal strengths and weaknesses relative to competitors. Unless at this point realistic and insightful reassessments are done at the business level, the strategic planning process might run the danger of suffering from "garbage in, garbage out" throughout the rest of the stages.

A third potential pitfall relates to the corporate review of the divisional objectives inputs. It is important that divisional inputs should be evaluated on an overall basis, as elements of a corporate portfolio, as opposed to being reviewed in a one-to-one sequential mode. In the latter case, the resulting overall balance of the portfolio strategy would be more or less incidental, arrived at as the sum of the results of individual approvals. Instead, it is necessary that each business element be reviewed contingent upon the rest of the portfolio. Thus it makes little sense to attempt to judge in isolation whether a particular business is attractive or not. This depends entirely on a business element's fit within the overall portfolio.

A fourth pitfall issue relates to the role of the functions during the objectives setting stage. As we see in Figure 3, the information flow pattern does not include the functions formally during this first stage. The focus here is to deal with the general management task of adapting to new business directions, and not functional adaptation tasks per se. Too much emphasis on the latter might result in weak adaptation because of the functions' natural emphasis on protection of the status quo. Thus the top-down/bottom-up interaction during the objectives setting stage should be focused at a higher level in the organization than is the case during the other stages of the planning process.

This brings us to the final pitfall issue, dealing with the role of the functions during the strategic programming stage. At this stage, the functions are critical for the development of imaginative, creative strategic programs for implementing the objectives. As we have seen, the fundamental nature of strategic programs is typicaly cross-functional. Thus, a key issue is to insure that the functions work together in order to develop meaningful programs.

Given that functional departments, to a large extent, are busy with day-to-day operational tasks, it is important to make a clearcut delineation between resources needed by the functional department to apply towards the implementation of strategic programs and resources to be applied toward operations. Unless this distinction is stated, it frequently becomes difficult for the functions to carry out their strategic programming tasks in a satisfactory manner. Operating pressures tend to drive out strategic considerations. Further-

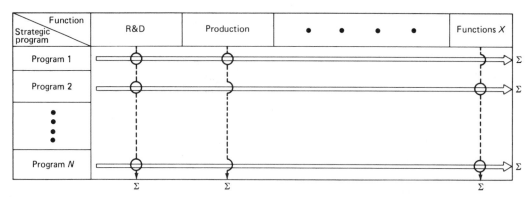

FIGURE 4. Interrelationship between strategic mode programming and operating mode budgeting. (Adapted from: Vancil, Richard F., "Better Management of Corporate Development," *Harvard Business Review*, September–October, 1972)

more, it is important to make a clear-cut delineation as to the specific responsibility of each function for each particular strategic program. Given the cross-functional nature of most strategic programming, we are in essence dealing with a matrix where the programs can be laid out along one dimension and the resulting consequence in terms of program involvement for each function can be seen along the other dimension. This pattern has to be made explicit in terms of roles and resource requirements in order for strategic programming to function properly.

Figure 4 outlines how the functions' roles in the strategic programming phase and in the budgeting phase might be delineated, with the various strategic programs along the horizontal dimension and each function's consequential role in each program along the vertical dimension. This provides an unambiguous strategic budget for each function, i.e., what strategic resources are needed by the function to carry out its contributions to the strategic programming tasks. In addition a separate budget should be established for the operating activities of the function. In this manner, a functional manager is less able to manipulate his own two resource pools.

Unexpected resource adjustments or cuts that must be made during the year can be done by eliminating the least critical strategic programs and, thereby, also indirectly reducing the strategic components of the functions'

budgets consistent with each function's intended involvement in the program that was eliminated. Thus the trimming of the budget is done from a strategic priority viewpoint, avoiding the unplanned disturbance to most of the strategic programming activities that would result from an equal across-the-board percentage cut of each functional strategic budget.

There are always a number of other pitfall issues, pursue this discussion further at this point. The issues discussed in this section are particularly relevant, we think, given their dysfunctional effects on the adaptive capabilities of the planning process.

TAILORED SYSTEMS DESIGN[2]

The issue of implementing a strategic planning system is complicated by the fact that all corporations are more or less different, in their strategic competitive settings, in their management styles and philosophies, in the availability of discretionary strategic resources, and so on. Consequently, it is pertinent to address the issue of how to tailor the design and implementation of a planning system to the particular situation at hand. Our approach is to attempt to match the capabilities that we intend to build into its planning process with the needs for planning of a given organization stemming from its strategic setting. Figure 5 addresses this task. In the upper box of Figure 5, it is stated that the needs for planning are functions of the strategic setting of the organization. For instance, an embryonic business that is attempting to establish itself in a high growth area typically faces highly adaptive planning needs stemming from pressures to establish appropriate product design and provide new marketing and distribution channels while under strict time constraints. Adaptation here means the recognition of and adjustment to environmental threats and opportunities. A mature business, on the other hand, facing slower growth and more established competition, has more integrative planning needs. Integration in this context means the pursuance of developing one's own internal competitive strengths and ameliorating one's weaknesses.

Thus, we can identify the planning needs in terms of adaptive as well as integrative components, or, stated in different but analogous wording, effectiveness and efficiency pressures. The adaptive needs for a business might stem from changes in the attractiveness of the business' environment that may be caused by facing a rapid growth rate, being in an industry that is experiencing a high rate of technological breakthroughs, facing large structural changes in production, distribution, or competitive situation, and so on. Integrative planning needs, on the other hand, typically stem from changes in an internal competitive strength situation. If in a high market share position, for instance, it is necessary to pursue actively the internal efficiency opportunities created, in terms of internal cost advantages.

In the middle of Figure 5, it is indicated that the capabilities of the planning process are a function of the design of the planning process. Thus the issue is to choose the design of the process in such a way that the planning capabilities are being created to meet the needs that have been identified through the needs analysis (the upper box). A useful measure of planning effectiveness, therefore, is the extent to which the needs and the capabilities match. In the bottom box of Figure 3, we have indicated that the decision-making impacts from the strategic planning process change the firm's situation. Strategic resources are allocated in the pursuance of particular strategic programs, say, to establish a new plant, to acquire a new subsidiary, to develop a new product, to break into a new market, and so on. An important consequence follows from the fact that the strategic setting thereby changes through planning: the needs for planning change. Because of this change, and the fact that environmental factors also change the needs for planning, there will be a more or less continuous challenge to update the design of the planning system so that its effectiveness can be maintained.

The match between the needs and the capabilities must be kept. No planning system is perfect over the longer run. On the contrary, the system is, in essence, self-destructive, as illustrated by the arrow that connects the bottom box and the top box in Figure 5. This implies that the process of managing the updating and evolution of the planning efforts is critical.

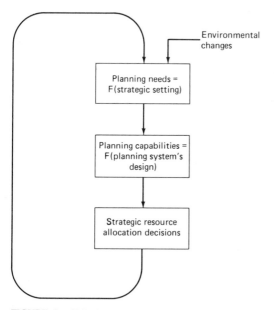

FIGURE 5.   Tailoring and updating a strategic planning system's design.

We shall return to the issue of managing the evolution of planning shortly. However, first we need to discuss the various systems design elements that we might use to tailor the capabilities of our planning process to meet its needs. We shall discuss five major design options, the "tools" in our "systems design kit."

An important design issue relates to the format of the planning documentation that the corporate planning department may specify for the various operating divisions. The formats can be tailored in two important aspects. First, when it comes to the description of the documentation, it is important to give format guidelines that are relevant for the business at hand. Thus an embryonic growth division should receive guidelines that can help it to pursue adaptation through entry and growth. A more mature business, on the other hand, should receive guidelines that facilitate more integration orientation. When it comes to format guidelines for strategic programs, these too should typically be different because they apply to adaptive entry and growth settings rather than more integrative situations. Thus different formats should be given to different divisions to facilitate a more relevant focus on their objectives and strategic programs. The degree of financial detail to be prescribed in the business plans should also be different, with relatively less financial detail to be requested from embryonic start-up businesses than from mature, well-established businesses. Efficiency considerations call for a more detailed documentation of the internal operating aspects of the plan, not only because of the maturity of the business, but also often as a consequence of the typically larger size of such organizational units.

A second systems design issue deals with the choice of review style of corporate management in interacting with the divisions regarding the discussions of their plans. For a business in a highly adaptive mode, it seems appropriate that corporate management spend relatively more time reviewing the front-end objectives setting part of this division's plans.

Similarly, it seems appropriate that this interaction allow for a relatively heavy bottom-up divisional initiative, where the corporate level's role is primarily one of reasoning and discussing with the division. A stronger set of top-down directives, on the other hand, might curtail the creative front-end inputs needed from the manager's being closer to the business. For a more mature business, the opposite review style would be the case. Here the issue is one of a more heavy management involvement towards the latter stages of the process, particularly emphasizing a detailed budget review. In general, corporate management should be more top-down oriented in its interaction with these divisions in order to encourage that efficiency-inspired integrative moves are, in fact, being carried out. A strong bottom-up level adaptive initiative would be unnecessary and distracting.

A third planning systems design consideration relates to the linkage of the monitoring and incentives cycles to the three direction setting cycles—objectives setting, strategic programming, and budgeting (see Figure 2). There are several ways to link the phases together, all impacting the information flow pattern. The most apparent one is what we might label *content linkage*. This refers to the extent to which the planning content dealt with during a particular direction setting stage is being closely resembled or not in terms of the content of what is being monitored. With respect to budgeting, we usually monitor rather closely the same variables that have been established in the budget; therefore, there is a tight content linkage, in this case. This would tend to increase the integrative capabilities of the planning system. Tight objectives-related content linkage, on the other hand, enhances adaptation.

Another type of linkage relates to the time being spent on the various monitoring activities, i.e., how much on budget monitoring versus objectives related monitoring. Significant time spent on the former indicates tight budgetary time linkage, which tends to enhance the integrative planning capabilities.

Conversely, tight objectives-related time linkage enhances adaptation capabilities. A final linkage type, which we shall label *organizational linkage*, focuses on the degree of fragmentation among management staff groups responsible for design, implementation, and management of the strategic planning process. A typical pattern is to have the planning department responsible for objectives setting and strategic programming, the controller's department in charge of budgeting and monitoring, and a human resource department administering the incentives scheme. This rather high degree of fragmentation of responsibilities implies a loose organizational linkage, with relatively little explicit adaptive or integrative effects. If, for instance, the planning department were in charge of the entire process, with the other staff departments being subordinated to the planning staff, then we have a tight organizational linkage design intended to enhance the adaptive planning capability. Conversely, with the controller's department in charge of the overall process, the integrative side of planning is strengthened.

The feedback nodes on Figure 2 indicate these different types of planning capabilities resulting from different linkage designs. When we have a tight linkage to the objectives-setting stage, by choosing the content, time, and organizational linkage designs accordingly, then we are reinforcing the adaptive abilities of planning (see the node marked A on Figure 2). On the other hand, when there is a tight linkage to the budget stage, then we are reinforcing the integrative planning capabilities (see node I). In our experience, the set of linkage design characteristics is both powerful and easily implemented for tailoring the planning approach. Unfortunately, corporate planning practices often tend to overlook this factor. Implicitly, linkage practices are often such that they have a tendency to reinforce a bias in the planning process towards more integration.

A fourth design issue relates to how the planning calendar has been laid out in order to provide enough time for adaptive and inte-grative planning tasks. If, for instance, an organization is facing relatively high adaptive pressures, then the planning calendar should allocate enough time towards the front end of the process to objectives setting. If, on the other hand, a strong integrative need prevails, then relatively more time should be spent on the budgeting side. It is useful to develop individual timetables for the various divisions, reflecting the different needs among the divisions for adaptation and integration. For example, a highly adaptive growth division needs to spend more time on objectives setting than a highly integrated mature division. In addition, it is necessary to make sure that the objectives-setting cycles of all divisions culminate at a given time so that the corporate level is in a position to review all the divisional inputs in a portfolio mode. Similarly, with strategic programming and budgeting cycles, all divisions must have these completed by a common date. Within the confines of these broad deadlines, there should, nevertheless, be enough flexibility to allocate relatively more or less time towards the front end or the back end of the process.

A final planning system design tailoring item is the following. When monitoring the critical environmental assumptions underlying an objective or a strategic program (see process steps), the mode of monitoring should be tailored so as to reflect the different natures of the various environmental tasks that are being faced. It is worthwhile to distinguish environmental tasks along two dimensions. First, we should assess to what extent we can actually foresee the movement of an environmental factor through trend analysis, lead indicator analysis, or plain expert judgment and insight. Second, an additional assessment should consider to what extent we might have options to take corrective measures to counteract a particular factor's development.

When facing an environmental factor with relatively high predictability as well as relatively high response potential, it would be appropriate to use a mode of control that calls for intensive and frequent monitoring and frequent but relatively small incremental responses. This might be called *steering control*. If, on the other hand, we are facing a factor that has relatively low predictability, but still offers several response options, then it might be appropriate to use a mode of control that might be labeled *contingency control*. This would call for the preparation of several contingency plans, one of which would be put into effect if a particular critical environmental factor develops in a particular way.

Third, we may be dealing with a critical environmental factor that has relatively high predictability but low response potential associated with it. The issue then is to sensitize ourselves to facing the decision of whether it would be appropriate to continue to stay in the business or withdraw, in light of a particular development of the environmental factor. We call this *anticipative go/no-go control*. It is essential that such judgments are made as early as possible. Lost time often makes it much more expensive to withdraw from a business, or, conversely, may lead to significant opportunity loss because of a delayed business entry. Experience has shown that psychological factors often frustrate decisions of this type. Hence an important aspect of the anticipative go/no-go control consists of establishing relatively clear-cut rules of thumb ahead of time for entry or withdrawal moves.

Finally, we may be facing a situation with environmental factors that can be neither predicted nor answered. The control mode in this instance is, of course, less critical, in that there is very little we can do to ameliorate a particular development. We shall label this *post facto go/no-go control*.

Before completing our discussion, one important observation should be made. Corporations generally have become more aware of the need for individually designed planning systems from one company to another, realizing that it is difficult or even impossible to expect a planning process that works well in one company to work well in another company. However, there still seems to be relatively less recognition of the need to tailor the planning process further to meet the various divisions' needs *within* a given company. Highly standardized planning approaches still tend to prevail within particular companies, thereby weakening planning's effectiveness. More emphasis should be put on tailoring the planning process so as to serve the individual businesses better within the firm.

EXECUTIVES' ROLES IN PLANNING

Let us now turn to a final set of issues that deal with the roles of various groups of executives participating in the planning process and being responsible for the implementation of effective planning system. Given the focus of this chapter, the center of the discussion is on the corporate planner, with other executives' roles to be delineated relative to his.[3]

A fundamental issue when it comes to the role of the corporate planner is the importance of seeing him as a guardian of the planning process; he should be concerned with maintaning and improving the process. Such a task can be contrasted with the issue of contributing to the substantive strategic issue developments and choices that are being dealt with in the plans. These latter issues should be seen as the primary responsibilities of line management. Thus the planner's role can be seen as that of a catalyst, to be contrasted with the line managers' roles as strategists. Stated differently, the planners' role can be seen as one of "providing the rules of the game," while the role of the line managers can be seen as that of "playing the game."

If the planner attempts to combine the above two roles by also becoming heavily involved in substantive planning issues, then there is a danger that the effectiveness of the planning process might deteriorate. A reason for this is the risk that the planner runs in losing credibility among the line managers. They might easily become distrusting and perceive him as manipulative, i.e., as one who simultaneously controls the rules of the game and also attempts to play the game. Second, weakened credibility on the part of the planner creates lack of proper management attendance to important planning process issues. The task of further refinement and management of the planning process might easily suffer.

Of initial issues that need to be kept in mind by the corporate planner when planning is in its infancy, we mention three. First, it is important that a relatively complete strategic planing system is installed early. Thus the entire five steps of planning should be dealt with and all three strategic levels should be involved. In this respect, it is of course legitimate that the degree of initial detail and refinement might be sparse. Conversely, if only one or a few of the stages and/or levels are part of the planning system during the initiation phase, we run into the problem of an unrealistic planning approach. Above all, the decision-making focus that makes planning real is likely to suffer. Despite our intent to expand the initial planning activity gradually to more levels and/or stages, line managers might quickly see this "planning as a learning exercise only" as a more or less esoteric activity. Unless they become relatively quickly convinced that planning is a useful tool in their strategic decision-making deliberations, line managers might easily discard the approach as another wasteful activity imposed by the staff. It subsequently becomes difficult to change the line's initial disappointment into a more meaningful decision-oriented commitment.

An implication of the approach that line managers should live with their plans is that the plans themselves might be revised quite frequently. One should never hesitate to make revisions in plans that make sense from a strategic point of view. Whether or not the entire set of plans should be formally redrafted and resubmitted, during a mid-year update, for instance, is less relevant. By putting too much emphasis on formal requirements for redrafting and resubmitting the entire planning documentation, time-consuming logistics might drive out creative thinking

and divert management's attention away from modifying strategic business decisions.

It is important to instill from the very beginning an emphasis on good working habits among management with regard to planning activities. In this respect, line managers should be exposed to the concepts of planning so as to be given clear understanding of what the overall strategic planning process is all about. Maybe the most easily abused working habit trait relates to the portfolio review concept. For example, if a particular business should face some sort of strategic crisis during the year, it is necessary to maintain that ameliorating actions relating to modifying the strategic plan must be seen within the context of and with respect to the effect on the overall corporate portfolio plan. By requiring portfolio thinking, not sequential or partial thinking, another good habit issue is also raised, namely, that managers must be expected to manage with an added sense of discipline that reflects their commitment to the plan. A plan is a contract and should not easily be allowed to be discarded, compromised, or altered by individual managers. Sloppy and unrealistic planning from one business not only has adverse effects on the business itself, but affects all other businesses, too, though the resulting portfolio level plan repercussions.

In terms of managerial roles in the implementation of planning beyond the initial start-up, we have already discussed the critical challenge to the corporate planner for monitoring the evolution of the planning process, so that the evolving needs for planning can be met through a corresponding evolution of the strategic planning system's design. The planning process is probably going to be an increasingly powerful management tool. By managing the evolution of this process, the corporate planner probably becomes an exceedingly important executive within many corporations, not by virtue of any direct decision-making authority, but by virtue of his indirect impact on strategic choices by manipulating the process. Although not exercising direct decision-making responsibility on strategic choices, he has a strong indirect impact on the strategic direction of the firm. (The Appendix provides a checklist of useful questions that should be addressed at certain intervals when it comes to managing the evolution of the planning process.) Thereby, the corporate planner, in effect, can administer a self-assessment check-up on his corporation when it comes to the continued appropriateness of its planning practices.

A large, complex organization cannot be easily managed from the CEOs office by virtue of his brilliance and persuasiveness alone. Except in very rare situations, a leader needs help from his strategic planning processes to instill a common sense of direction in a company. It is much more likely for him to have an impact if he attempts to influence his organization indirectly through tailoring the strategic processes. The emergence of comprehensive, operational strategic planning approaches thus provides a vehicle that has the potential for better corporate-wide strategic management. It might be argued that the hand of the CEO is thus being strengthened. This added power in the hands of devoted and competent senior executives opens up exciting perspectives. There is also a danger that the process might be misused. For this reason, the responsibility of the CEO is to insure that the strategic management challenge be channeled in an ethically proper direction. The board of directors may also be faced with a responsibility in this respect.

CONCLUSION

We have concluded our discussion on the design and implementation of strategic planning systems. The approach that we have taken has been based on several premises. First, we have stressed that strategic planning is a decision-making process focused around the allocation of the strategic resources of people, technology, and funds. Second, our conceptual approach serves the dual purpose of setting an adaptive and opportunistic direction for the firm while ensuring efficient operating

performance. It is important that strategic planning be seen as a creative, imaginative process, not as an extrapolative, overly formalized, often uninspired process. It is also important that planning integrate the internal efforts of a corporation, so that opportunities are not pursued in so many directions that the competitive edge of the company is being weakened.

We have stressed that a strategic planning approach should fit within the context of the organization in order to be useful. In this regard, it may facilitate the development of a shared sense of strategic direction among the various organizational subunits and managers. This is best accomplished through an interactive as well as iterative information-handling approach such as the one outlined in this chapter. We also suggested that learning should be seen as a major aspect of sound strategic planning. By providing a vehicle for systematic experience building among the managers of the corporation, which in turn improves their understanding of strategic challenges, this difficult task can be achieved. Thus planning also becomes an important element of management development, attempting to build one of the most difficult management skills.

The strategic planning system approach developed in this chapter is not new. Experiences from several corporate applications have shown the basics of the approach to provide a reasonable and operational set of guidelines for more effective strategic management. As a rapidly increasing number of corporations gain experience with strategic planning systems, it is indeed becoming a competitive tool. This tool has the definite potential to provide a competitive advantage to those who are able to make meaningful use of it. In light of this development, it might become exceedingly risky to take a wait-and-see attitude to planning at this stage. We suggest, therefore, that an increasingly critical management task should be to focus on the design, improvement, and evolution of its strategic planning system.

APPENDIX: STEPS IN AUDITING THE STRATEGIC PLANNING SYSTEM

A. Strategic Structure

1. Are business (i.e., product/market) elements clearly delineated?
   — unambiguous product/market delineation?
   — is there an explicit adaptive dimension? a clear integrative dimension?
   — is the size manageable, not too big, not too small?
2. Is there a useful grouping of business (product/markets) into divisions (business families)?
   — coherent business families, meaningfully pulled together?
   — efficient, operational synergy?
3. Is there a clear delineation between strategic structure and operating structure in terms of:
   — spelling out and responsibility for strategic programs, reconcilable with functional budget responsibilities?
   — unambiguous distinction among resources (people, funds, technologies) to be used for strategic purposes versus for operating purposes?
4. Is there adequate ability to define new businesses at early stages in terms of:
   — adaptive flexibility?
   — strategic resource mobility (funds, people, technology)?

B. Strategic Pressures and Planning Needs

1. For each of the business elements:
   — what is the nature of the adaptive needs?
   — what is the nature of the integrative needs?
   — what is the relative adaptation/integration need balance?

2. For each division:
   — what is the nature of the adaptive needs?
   — what is the nature of the integrative needs?
   — what is the nature of the (integrative) needs stemming from consolidation of business elements?
   — what is the relative adaptation/integration need balance?
3. For the corporate portfolio level:
   — what are the (integrative) planning needs stemming from strategic resource generation/utilization imbalances?
   — what are the (adaptive) planning needs stemming from portfolio structure imbalances?
   — what is the relative adaptation (integration need balance)?

C. Planning Process: Is the Process Functioning without Major Pitfalls?

1. During the objectives-setting stage:
   — is the CEO's initiation and involvement adequate?
   — is the business environment seen through opportunism, not extrapolation?
   — is there a portfolio mode of corporate level planning review, not a sequential review?
   — is the organizational focus proper, particularly when it comes to objectives setting?
2. During the strategic programming stage:
   — are the strategic programs sufficiently cross-functional in nature?
   — are they adequately consolidated into overall business element and/or family strategies?
   — is there an overall allocation and commitment of resources (people, funds, technologies) to the strategic programs?

3. During the budgeting stage:
   — are the strategic programs and the budget adequately reconciled?
   — does the budget, in fact, reflect the strategic direction?
4. General:
   — is there sufficient consistency between the outputs from the various cycles (objectives setting–strategic programming–budgeting)?

D. Planning Calendar

1. For each business element:
   — is the time pattern allotted to objectives setting, strategic programming, and budgeting adequate, given the particular strategic needs (adaptive, integrative) at hand?
2. For each division (business family):
   — is the allocated time pattern adequate, given the particular strategic needs, in terms of:
   a. overall divisional adaptive and integrative pressures?
   b. allowing for the reconciliation of all the business elements?
3. For the corporate level:
   — is the allocated time pattern adequate, given:
   a. the overall corporate need for redirecting the portfolio balance to respond to adaptive and/or integrative imbalances?
   b. the time required for a portfolio mode reconciliation of the divisions' plans?

E. Planning Review

1. Division manager's review of each business element:
   — is the top-down/bottom-up focus and review style appropriate, given the particular strategic needs at hand?
   — is the front-end/back-end focus and review style similarly appropriate?

2. Corporate manager's review of each division
   — is the top-down/bottom-up focus review style appropriate, given the particular strategic needs at hand?
   — front-end/back-end focus and review style similarly appropriate?
   — is there a clearly articulated portfolio focus in the corporate review style, as opposed to sequential and incremental review?

F. Business Plan Format

1. For each business element as well as division:
   — do planning formal guidelines satisfy the particular need for adaptive and for integrative strategic focus at hand?
   — do planning format guidelines provoke consistency between objectives setting, strategic programming and budgeting?
   — do planning format guidelines enhance relevant strategic focus, not add unnecessary paper flow, workload, and distraction?

G. Linkages (control, incentives)

1. Relative to each business element:
   — is the control process linkage balance appropriate against objectives, strategic programs as well as budgets?
   — is the incentives process linkage balance appropriate against objectives, strategic programs as well as budgets?
2. Relative to each division:
   — is the control process linkage balance appropriate against objectives, strategic programs as well as budgets?
   — is the incentives process linkage balance appropriate against objectives, strategic programs as well as budgets?

3. Relative to the corporate portfolio level:
   — is the control process linkage balance appropriate against objectives, strategic programs as well as budgets?
   — is the incentives process linkage balance appropriate against objectives, strategic programs as well as budgets?

H. Plan for Planning

1. Based on the assessments made in Sections A and B, what is the pattern in terms of needs for planning (adaptive, integrative):
   — for each business element?
   — for each division?
   — for the corporate portfolio?
2. Based on the assessments made in Sections C, D, E, F, and G, what is the pattern in terms of the planning process' ability to provide relevant support capabilities:
   — for each business element?
   — for each division?
   — for the corporate portfolio?
3. Based on the emerging patterns of needs for planning versus capabilities for planning, what are the types and nature of lacks of adequate planning support:
   — for each business element?
   — for each division?
   — for the corporate portfolio?
4. What are the specific modifications that should be made in the planning process so as to ameliorate need-capability discrepancies:
   — for each business element?
   — for each division?
   — for the corporate portfolio?

This is the resulting PLAN FOR PLANNING!

REFERENCES

1. For an elaboration of the issues discussed in this chapter, see Peter Lorange, *Corporate Planning: An Executive Viewpoint,* 1980, Prentice-Hall.
2. For an extensive discussion of implementation issues, see Peter Lorange (ed.), *Implementation of Strategic Planning,* 1980, Prentice-Hall.
3. See John Ackerman, "Role of the Corporate Planning Executive," in *Strategic Planning Systems,* Peter Lorange and Richard F. Vaneil, 1980, Prentice-Hall.

9
Strategies for Control

Cortlandt Cammann
Institute for Social Research
University of Michigan

Frequently, executives find that many of their subordinates do not contribute to organizational goals as expected; that conflicts among their subordinates waste substantial amounts of energy and resources; and that problems often get hidden until they are too big to solve easily. This chapter describes the elements of control strategy that executives can develop to increase the effectiveness of control processes in their organiation.

Some of the most difficult problems experienced by executives involve the motivation and control of the people in their organizations. They are responsible for the actions of subordinates with widely differing skills, needs, and personal aspirations and they must somehow find a way to make sure that the activities of these diverse individuals fit together into an integrated pattern of action that achieves their organization's objectives. Frequently, executives find that many of their subordinates do not contribute to organizational goals as expected, that conflicts among their subordinates waste substantial amounts of the energy and resources, and that problems often get hidden until they are too big to solve easily. Developing an organization that can solve these problems and can motivate organization members to work together represents one of the most challenging aspects of most executive positions.

How can executives develop organizations that will motivate their members to work together? Unfortunately, there does not appear to be any single right answer. Research and theory in the behavioral sciences indicates that the methods that work in one setting are not successful in another,[1] and that there is generally more than one method that can work in any particular setting.[2]

While the behavioral sciences do not provide a simple formula for controlling the behavior of subordinates effectively, they have developed a number of theories to help executives deal with control problems. This chapter examines some of these theories and explores their implications for the design of an organizational control strategy. The chapter first examines models of *individual motivation* and *control processes* that provide a picture of the dynamics of control within organizational settings. Then it explores the factors that can influence the effectiveness of control processes in an organization and develop a *congruence model* of effective control. The chapter concludes by describing the elements of *control strategy* that executives can develop to increase the effectiveness of control processes in their organizations.

THEORIES OF MOTIVATION AND CONTROL PROCESSES

Behavioral scientists have developed a number of theories that are useful in understanding how organizations can control the behavior of their members. Two sets of theories are particularly helpful. The first are theories of individual motivation, particularly expectancy theory,[3] which describes the factors influencing the way individuals choose to act. The second are theories of control processes, which describe the activities involved in directing organization members to achieve specific objectives.[4]

Expectancy Theories of Motivation

Expectancy theories of motivation have been developed by behavioral scientists to describe the factors that influence the way people make choices. These theories have proven particularly useful in identifying aspects of working environments that influence individual performance and in guiding the development of organizational policies and systems to motivate people to perform well.[5]

Expectancy theory is based on three simple ideas:

1. People have needs and desires.

One fundamental assumption of expectancy theory is that people have needs and desires that they wish to satisfy. These needs and desires may be for extrinsic rewards such as food, shelter, or money; they may be for social rewards such as respect and love; or they may be for intrinsic rewards such as a feeling of competence or accomplishment.[6] Further, these needs and desires are the result of each individual's particular history of development. As a result, the personal goals of each individual are different.

2. People act to achieve outcomes that they believe help them meet their needs.

The second fundamental assumption of expectancy theory is that people choose to act in ways that help them satisfy their needs and achieve their personal goals. In the context of organizational behavior, this implies that organization members behave differently depending on personal goals and the reward structure that exists in an organization. If they feel that they can best meet their needs by performing as certain other organization members expect (either peers or superiors), they will try to meet these expectations. If they think that their needs will be met if they perform well in terms of organizational measurement systems, they will try to look good on these measures (even if this means reducing overall effectiveness or, in extreme cases, directly manipulating the measures themselves). If they believe that their needs will be met by doing a good job and accomplishing specific objectives, they will work hard to accomplish the objectives and perform the job well.[7] In short, their behavior will be determined by their expectations about the types of activities that allow them to meet their needs.

3. People behave in ways that they expect allow them to succeed in achieving valued outcomes.

The third fundamental assumption of expectancy theory is that when people choose among many courses of action, they choose a course of action that they expect to accomplish successfully. Thus if they have been told that they will be richly rewarded for accomplishing specific goals, but do not see any way to achieve them, they will probably try to accomplish some other set of objectives instead.[8] It also follows that if organization members do not know what actions will be rewarded, they will not be motivated to perform well. Instead, they will probably try to act in ways that are designed primarily to protect themselves from penalties and criticism.

These three simple assumptions have proven useful in predicting the ways in which individuals behave, and have a number of important implications for the design of control strategies in organizations. First, they imply that people can be expected to behave in ways that are dysfunctional for the organization if the organization's control processes motivate them to do so. Thus if organization members find that valued rewards such as pay are contingent on achieving specific goals, they can be expected to try to achieve these goals even when doing so makes the organization less effective overall.

A second implication is that the organization members are not motivated by rewards that they do not want, or by rewards that are not contingent on their actions. Thus job security will not work as a motivator if employees can easily get other jobs, if they don't need to work, or if they can't be fired. Similarly, pay does not motivate people to perform well if they do not see any connection between their performance and the level of pay they receive. Control strategies that rely on the use of rewards people do not want or that the organization cannot control fail to achieve their objectives.

A third implication is that people cannot be expected to accomplish tasks that they do not understand and do not accept. If people are told to achieve specific goals, but not why the goals are important, or what consequences will follow, they cannot be expected to work hard to accomplish them. Further, if people don't know how to accomplish the tasks, they are unlikely to accept the task personally as a goal and thus are unlikely to succeed in achieving it. Rather, they probably become motivated to show why they could not succeed and to develop excuses explaining why the failure was not their fault.

Taken together, these implications suggest that when organizations experience problems coordinating and controlling the behavior of their members, they need to alter the way in which their members experience their work environment. It may be that organization members are not motivated to achieve organizational objectives because they do not feel that they are able to accomplish them with the available skills and resources, or because they don't feel that they can best achieve their personal goals by achieving the organization's objectives. Alternatively, it may be that they

are motivated to achieve the goals as they perceive them, but that the goals they are trying to achieve conflict in some way with the organization's intended objectives. In either case, some aspect of their work environment needs to be changed so that they can meet their personal goals while achieving objectives desired by the organization.

THE NATURE OF CONTROL PROCESSES

Theories of individual motivation are very useful for understanding how individuals behave, but they are only helpful indirectly for examining the way in which organizations coordinate the behavior of their members to achieve organizational objectives. More useful for this purpose are theories of control processes. According to these theories, intentionally achieving any objective involves three different processes or sets of activities: 1) planning a course of action to achieve the objectives and setting specific goals and responsibilities for organization members to carry out in the context of the plan; 2) monitoring the consequences of activities under the plan and feeding back progress information to people responsible for seeing that the plan succeeds; and 3) solving problems that are indicated by feedback so that the plan can be altered when the results are not as expected or when the plan did not specify completely how goals should be achiveed.[9]

Planning and Goal Setting

One of the principal determinants of an organization's effectiveness in achieving goals is the quality of its planning and goal-setting processes. To be successful, the organization must be able to develop a broad plan for allocating goals and resources to its members. It must also get the commitment of its members to put energy and resources into accomplishing the tasks. Without an integrated plan, the behavior of organization members is likely to be extremely variable, producing conflicts in some cases, and nonperformance of critical tasks in others.[10] Either situation produces problems of control. Furthermore, if the planning process produces a well-integrated plan of action, but does not create conditions where organization members are motivated to carry out their goals, the required actions will not be carried out and the objectives will not be achieved.[11]

There is no single, best method of planning in organizations. It can be done by a central planning group that develops a comprehensive schedule of activities and gives instructions to people in the rest of the organization about what they are to do and when it is to be done. Alternatively, a general objective can be established and then subdivided into sets of goals that need to be accomplished for the objective to be achieved. These goals are then assigned to organization members who have the responsibility for developing action plans to achieve them. Another possibility is for goals to be set by organizational subunits who decide what they can do to help the organization achieve its broad objectives. If there are necessary tasks that no group volunteers to accomplish, managers negotiate with each other to decide how they will get them accomplished. Any of these planning processes, and many others, can work if they suit the needs of the particular organization that is using them. The crucial test is whether they produce an integrated plan of action and a commitment by organization members to carry it out.

A number of factors appear to influence the effectiveness of the planning process. The first is the existence of some form of systematic planning. When organizations are small, all organization members are likely to know what the organization is trying to achieve. In this case, their activities can be coordinated effectively through an informal process of discussion and agreement. As they get larger, however, organization members cannot keep as well informed about what is going on. Unless a systematic planning process is developed, individuals lose touch with the current

objectives and their activities are not likely to fit with those of others. Some systematic process is required to insure that organization members find out regularly what goals have current priority, and what they have to do if the goals are to be accomplished successfully.

A second factor is the degree of participation of organization members in the planning and goal-setting process. When organization members participate in planning and goal setting, they get enough information about organizational objectives to understand how their own goals relate to broader organizational performance, and they can add enough information to the planning process to insure that their goals are reasonable and achievable. As a result, they are likely to accept their goals and work hard to achieve them. At the same time, however, participation takes time and can make it difficult to reach agreement on a plan that requires personal sacrifice by some organization members.[12] Further, if organization members are not committed to achieving broad organizational objectives, allowing them to participate in planning simply gives them an opportunity to set easy goals and to find ways of meeting their own needs at the expense of the broader organization.[13]

A third dimension of the planning processes is the nature of the goals that are set for organization members. Two aspects of the goals seem particularly important: difficulty and form. Difficulty refers to the extent that they stretch the organization members' capacity to perform. In general, more difficult goals result in higher levels of performance, as long as the organization members believe that the goals can be achieved. If the goals are too difficult, however, organization members do not try to achieve them and performance suffers.[14] Form refers to the nature of the goals. In particular, the goals can be set in terms of activities (the way in which organization members are expected to behave) or in terms of outcomes (the results that organization members are expected to achieve). Setting goals in terms of activities is more important when there is clearly one best way for goals to be achieved and when the way in which one person performs depends on the way others perform their tasks. Outcome goals are more appropriate when there are many ways that the goals can be achieved and the appropriate actions differ from situation to situation.[15]

Finally, the method used to motivate organization members to achieve their goals influences the effectiveness of the planning process. Methods of obtaining commitment can be divided into two sets that can be used separately or together. The first set involves the creation of intrinsic motivation to achieve the goals. Intrinsic motivation results when organization members accept the goals because they want to contribute to overall organizational performance or because they feel that the goals give them a sense of personal satisfaction from accomlishing them. In either case, achieving the goal becomes a personally desired objective and the organization member is motivated to succeed. This form of motivation is most likely to occur when employees understand and accept broader organizational objectives and when they participate in the process of setting their personal work goals.

The second approach to gaining commitment relies on extrinsic rewards. In this case, rewards such as pay, promotion, security, or respect are made contingent on goal achievement, and employees are motivated to achieve the goals in order to achieve the rewards. This form of motivation can prove quite reliable[16] and if done correctly can be used simultaneously with more intrinsically oriented methods.[17] The problem with overreliance on extrinsic methods of motivation is that they motivate employees to achieve the specified goals. If the goals are for any reason inappropriate, organization members will work hard to achieve the wrong goals and will resist altering their activity for fear of reducing the rewards they receive.

Monitoring and Feedback Processes

Organizations and individuals can never be certain that their plans and actions produce the intended results. Their activities are based on assumptions that may prove wrong. As a result, people require information about the actual consequences of their actions. Without it, plans are not changed to deal with unanticipated results and performance is likely to deteriorate.

There are two sets of activities involved in finding the consequences of actions: monitoring and feedback. Monitoring activities focus on collecting information about the effects of activities and can be accomplished either directly by the actors involved or indirectly by monitors (e.g., inspectors) or monitoring systems (e.g., accounting systems that record expenditures). Feedback activities provide people with the results of monitoring activities. When the monitoring is done directly by the people who are to receive the information, feedback happens automatically. When the monitoring is indirect, however, feedback is required for the information to get to the people who can use it. This feedback can be through some form of interpersonal communication in which a monitor talks directly to the person receiving the information, or it can be through a formal communication system such as a regular report.

Research has demonstrated that monitoring and feedback processes can have a number of effects on individual and organizational performance. Perhaps the most significant finding, however, is that monitoring and feedback processes do *not* alter behavior or performance directly.[18] Rather, they serve as a stimulus for setting new goals and developing new plans and these goals and plans alter behavior. The importance of this finding is that feedback that is not accompanied by problem solving and goal setting does not influence performance directly.

Monitoring and feedback can influence performance indirectly in a number of ways. First, monitoring and feedback activities focus attention on some areas and not others, and tend to focus the attention of organization members on performance in monitored areas. If the information does not cover all relevant aspects of performance, important problems may be ignored and overall performance may suffer.[19] This result is especially likely when individual goals are set in terms of monitored performance areas and personal rewards are contingent upon high measured performance.[20]

In addition to influencing performance by focusing attention on some areas and not others, monitoring and feedback systems can influence the relationships among organization members indirectly. Two effects in particular seem important. The first is that they can create defensiveness and conflict. When employees feel that monitoring and feedback systems exist to spy on them and inform their superiors about their mistakes, they tend to view the system and the people who run them as enemies. This can lead them to play games with the systems, even to the point of actually falsifying data so that they can look good.[21] On the other hand, monitoring and feedback systems can provide organization members with information they need about other people's performance. This can reduce the need for direct personal observation and therefore reduce the closeness of supervision and the likelihood of interpersonal conflict. When used for constructive purposes, monitoring and feedback systems can increase participation and trust within an organization and improve the relationships among organization members.

Problem Solving

Problem-solving processes refer to the development and execution of action plans in the course of trying to accomplish the goals set during planning. They may occur either in response to feedback, indicating that plans are not producing intended results, or in response to the recognition that plans did not specify fully the activities required in order to meet the goals. Problem solving involves a number of steps: 1) diagnosing the nature of the problems to be solved; 2) identifying the factors that can influence the effectiveness of different solutions; 3) developing alternative action

plans that might solve the problem; 4) choosing a solution and implementing it; and 5) evaluating the adequacy of the solution as it is implemented. In many ways, problem solving is key to effective control. Given the uncertainties involved in setting goals, it is virtually certain that errors and omissions occur. Effective control is largely a matter of successfully detecting and correcting these problems.

Two aspects of problem solving in particular appear to have an important effect on an organization's effectiveness. The first involves access to information. In order to facilitate effective organizational action, problem-solving processes must generate appropriate information about the causes of problems and the nature of alternative actions that can solve them. If problem solvers cannot get accurate information in a timely manner, their effectiveness will be reduced. The second involves the motivation of organization members to implement the solutions. Solutions to problems are useless if the organization cannot motivate organization members to accept them and alter their behavior to make them work.

A number of factors can influence an organization's ability to solve problems effectively. One of these is the skill of organization members in problem-solving activities. As in any activity, the experience and skill of the people involved can make a difference. For example, some organizations would not benefit directly from involving assembly workers in designing their work stations because the workers do not have the knowledge to analyze alternative approaches to doing the job. Instead, this type of analysis is left to engineers. In some cases, however, managements have provided workers with basic training in industrial engineering concepts and have found that the workers can then participate constructively in developing simplified work procedures.[22] When the people involved in problem solving have the appropriate technical and interpersonal skills, constructive solutions are likely to result. When they do not, problem solving is likely to create as many problems as it solves.

A second factor influencing problem solving effectiveness is the climate of the organization. If people in the organization generally trust each other[23] and exchange information freely, it will be easier for organization members to get information they need and to implement solutions they develop. By contrast, if organization members are afraid to try new things because they expect that failure will be punished, and if they only share information when they see that it is directly to their advantage, problem solvers are likely to find it difficult to diagnose problems, and even more difficult to get solutions implemented.

A third factor influencing problem-solving effectiveness is the distribution of information and authority within the organization. If organization members do not have access to information or the authority they need to develop and implement solutions to problems, they are unlikely to solve problems effectively. It is worth noting, however, that organization members need not have information or authority personally. They simply need to be able to involve the people who do.

Finally, problem-solving effectiveness is affected directly by the way in which organization members define their responsibilities for problem solving. If organization members define their goals and responsibilities narrowly in terms of specific outcomes and actions, they will be likely to limit their activities to problems that are clearly within their defined areas. It may be difficult to involve them in developing and executing solutions to problems that are outside the scope of their authority, because these problems are not their responsibility. For example, problems of relationships among organization members and problems involving the distribution of goals and authority are likely to be difficult because the people who experience these problems cannot solve them within the scope of their delegated authority. In contrast, organization members can define their responsibility more broadly in terms of contributing to the overall objectives of the organizations and solving any problems that influence their ability to accomplish their goals. This concept of responsibility makes it easy to involve organization members in solving problems outside of their immediate areas of authority, but it can also lead to conflict if people feel that others are making decisions that affect them without getting them involved.

Summary

Behavioral scientists studying motivation and control in organizations have developed a number of theories that are useful in understanding organizational dynamics. Unfortunately, these theories do not lead to simple prescriptions of how control should be exercised. Rather, they highlight the variability of individual goals, the complexity of organizational settings, and the variety of factors that can influence the organizational dynamics that result.

However, some conclusions do emerge. First, organizations coordinate the activities of their members through a series of control processes: planning and goal setting, monitoring and feedback, and problem solving. While these activities can be accomplished in many different ways, unless they are carried out in some specific manner, the behavior of organization members cannot fit into a flexible pattern that can achieve objectives desired by the organization. Second, people tend to respond to situations as they experience them and try to achieve their personal goals in the best way that they can discover. To work effectively, control processes must create situations where individuals believe that they can achieve their personal goals by working for the organization, not by behaving dysfunctionally.

These conclusions do not, however, answer the more critical question of how control processes should function in order to produce coordinated action. While the answer to this question is not simple, research has provided some indications of the factors that determine the effectiveness of organizational control.

THE NATURE OF EFFECTIVE CONTROL

Based on existing research, it appears that effective organizational control depends primarily on two factors: the adequacy of the level of control processes and the congruence of the control processes with each other and with the broader organizational situation. The issue of the level of control process refers to the fact that overall organizational control is impossible if the activities of planning, goal setting, monitoring, feedback, and problem solving do not occur. Unless people in the organization devote sufficient time and energy to exercising control, the actions of organizations members become disorganized and organizational objectives are not achieved.[24]

The second major factor of the effectiveness of organizational control is the congruence of the existing control processes with each other and with other aspects of the organizational situation. The idea of congruence[25] refers to the extent that the control processes are complementary in facilitating the development and execution of a single pattern of organizational action, and to the extent that they fit well with the environment, roles, and formal systems of the organization. When congruence is high, the control processes reinforce each other in helping the organization achieve its objectives within its external environment. They complement and are complemented by the roles and formal systems. When congruence is low, different control processes and other aspects of the organization conflict with each other and with demands placed on the organization by its environment, resulting in confusion and poor organizational performance.

It is easier to specify the importance of congruence than it is to describe how it can be created. In most settings, a large number of factors are involved. To some extent, congruent control processes always have to be unique to fit the contingencies of a particular organization at a specific point in time. It is possible, however, to describe some of the critical determinants of fit to illustrate some of the conditions that determine when a fit occurs.

Congruence Among Control Processes

One important type of fit involves the control processes themselves. The way in which each control process is carried out must be generally congruent with the others or ineffectiveness will result. Three dimensions in particular appear to be important here: the nature of the activities being controlled, the role of organization members in exercising control, and the methods used to motivate organization members to accomplish their goals. In terms of the activities being controlled, it is important that planning and goal setting, monitoring and feedback, and problem-solving activities all relate to the same sets of activities and outcomes. If organization members have goals that focus on one area, receive feedback information about their performance in a second, and involve in problem solving in a third, they are likely to be confused. They will not understand whether they should give priority to achieving their goals, responding to feedback, or solving problems. It may seem unlikely that organization members would find themselves in this position, yet researchers and consultants observe managers who receive feedback information that relates primarily to financial resource utilization (through budgets), and who spend most of their time solving day-to-day personnel and production problems. In such circumstances, it is not surprising that people become confused, frustrated, and defensive or that organizational objectives are not achieved.

The role of organization members in exercising control refers primarily to the extent that they participate in making decisions. If control processes are generally participative, organization members will have a say over goals and plans, will have significant responsibility for monitoring and feedback, and will be involved personally in solving problems that affect their goal achievement. If control processes are generally autocratic, their goals will be set for them, monitoring and feedback systems will be set up to give their superiors information about their performance, and their superiors will be heavily involved in problem-solving activities. Either of these approaches can be used successfully. It is problematic, however, when some control processes are autocratic and others are participative. Hopwood[26] describes a case where managers participated in goal setting but not in other aspects of exercising control. In order to protect themselves, the managers used their participation in goal setting to insure that they had easy goals to achieve. This result was dysfunctional for the organization.

Finally, the nature of the control processes and the methods of motivation used by the organization must be consistent. If the organization is attempting to motivate people using intrinsic methods, they need to be involved in decision making and problem solving, they need to receive feedback on their performance, and they need to have clear, challenging tasks that they are responsible for performing. If the organization is attempting to motivate organization members by making extrinsic rewards contingent on performance, the rewards should be made contingent on achieving difficult goals and goal-setting processes should be designed to make these contingencies as clear as possible. Further, the organization should assume that the organization members are tempted to play games with their performance measures. Monitoring systems should be set up that are not easy to manipulate, goals should be set carefully so that if they are achieved organizational objectives will be accomplished, and feedback procedures should be set up so that superiors can keep track of how well the organization members are performing. When goal achievement is difficult to measure, when contingencies between performance and rewards are difficult to establish, or when clear goals are difficult to set, the use of extrinsic methods of motivation is problematic and reliance on these methods is likely to produce failures of control.[27]

Congruence with the Environmental Context

As second aspect of fit is that the organization's control processes must be congruent with the environmental context in which the organization is operating. Two aspects of the environment appear to be critical: the predictability of task demands and the speed of change in external domains that affect organizational functioning. When organizational tasks are highly predictable and rapid changes are not likely, control processes can be extensive and detailed. The organization has the time and knowledge to develop extensive plans, very specific goals, and elaborate monitoring and feedback systems. When problems do arise, they can be isolated and given to experts or high-level managers to solve. In short, when stability is high, organizational activities can be controlled closely and, if appropriate, decision making can be centralized effectively.[28]

When task demands are unpredictable and change is rapid, quite a different type of control process is necessary. Organization members must be able to adjust rapidly to changing conditions and to coordinate their activities with others on an ongoing basis. Goals and plans have to be flexible and general in nature. Monitoring and feedback systems have to provide information rapidly, and organization members have to be able to solve problems directly. Decision making must be decentralized and people have to be able to communicate information to others rapidly about changes that affect them. Generally speaking, participative processes and the use of intrinsic methods of motivation are appropriate under these circumstances.[29]

Congruence with Managerial Roles

Managers play a key role in the development of control processes in any organization. The way in which they behave has a strong influence on the way in which organization members react to goal setting, feedback and problem solving, and on the effectiveness of control processes in coordinating and controlling the behavior of people. To a large extent, managerial behavior and its effects depend on the roles managers· are expected to perform in monitoring the effectiveness of the organization. A variety of different roles are possible. The effectiveness of control processes varies depending on which are used.

Decision-Making Roles. In some organizations, managers are viewed primarily as decision makers within specific areas.[30] They are given specific goals to achieve by using resources that they are allocated. They are expected to form the plans required to achieve the goals, allocate appropriate responsibilities to their subordinates, monitor subordinates' activities, and make key decisions to solve problems that develop. The managers are viewed as leaders and controllers within the organization.

This broad definition of managerial role is congruent with traditional conceptions of control processes. Goal setting is top down in nature, with each manager developing goals for each subordinate that, if all achieved, allow the manager to meet the goals that have been set for them. Every attempt is made to match formal authority to areas of responsibility, and goals are set, whenever possible, in concrete, measurable terms so that managers can receive regular reports on how well their subordinates are doing in achieving goals.

The monitoring, feedback, and problem-solving processes most consistent with this role definition are hierarchical in nature. Each manager needs to receive regular information about the progress that is being made in achieving goals so that he can detect any deviations from plans rapidly and get involved in developing actions to resolve problems. Information needs to flow freely up and down the chain of command, and problems need to be communicated rapidly up the hierarchy to the managers with the authority to resolve them.

Motivation can be problematic in situations where this definition of managerial roles exists. Subordinates must be willing to take orders and carry out decisions made by their superiors. This implies that the organization will have to rely on extrinsic methods of motivation, and that superiors must be able to make rewards subordinates value directly contingent on goal achievement. As a number of behavioral scientists have observed, this can be problematic in today's organizational environments where many basic needs are largely satisfied and where institutional constraints (such as union contracts and organizational policies) make it difficult to establish clear contingencies between rewards and performance.[31]

Linking-pin roles. Likert[32] has described a variation on the traditional decision making conception of the managerial role. He describes managers as linking pins between their superiors and their subordinates. In dealing with their superiors, they are responsible for providing information about the capacity and activities of their work units. In dealing with their subordinates, managers are responsible for describing broad organizational goals and making decisions about work to be done.

As in the case with the decision making role conception, control processes that complement the linking pin model will be hierarchical in nature. They should facilitate the process of superior-subordinate negotiations in goal setting and the flow of information and decision making up and down the hierarchy. The major difference is that the control processes should be participative in nature and ought to utilize intrinsic methods of motivation. The linking pin conception is based on the assumption that all organization members are interested in contributing to the organization if they are given a chance, and the control processes need to reflect this assumption.

To be congruent with the linking pin model, planning and goal setting should be done jointly between superiors and subordinates with the intent of jointly agreeing what each will do to help the organization achieve its broader objectives. Monitoring and feedback systems need to be designed to provide both superiors and subordinates with enough information about work unit and organizational performance so that they can work together in decision making. Problem solving should, to the extent possible, involve all who are affected by solutions, and the focus of problem-solving activities should be on achieving broad organizational objectives, not on helping specific organization members achieve the specific goals that they have been assigned.

Boundary Management Roles. A third conception of managerial roles has been described by Rice.[33] In this model, managers are viewed as responsible for managing relationships with other units in the organization and for designing the structures and relationships that guide the behavior of their subordinates. This means that the managers are responsible for accomplishing a number of tasks. They must make sure that the task objectives of their unit are clear and that each of their subordinates has a clear image of how they are to contribute to the accomplishment of these objectives. They are responsible for making sure that their subordinates have the resources (capital, personnel, information, and materials) they need in order to accomplish their tasks. They must also insure that their subordinates have constructive working relationships with each other and that internal support structures (pay systems, performance evaluation systems, information systems, training programs, and so on) facilitate task performance.

This role conception differs from the others in two main respects. First, in terms of external relations, the responsibilities of managers are very broad and not limited to areas where they have direct authority. They must negotiate with representatives of other units to clarify task requirements and acquire resources in situations where they do not generally have the authority to mandate outcomes unilaterally. Second, their role inside their work units is to facilitate action rather than to act. Thus they are primarily responsible for creating conditions that allow others to accomplish tasks, and only secondarily to make decisions and accomplish tasks themselves.

In large organizations, this conception of managerial roles results in a need for complex and formalized control processes. Each manager is, to some extent, an entrepreneur. Coordinated action does not result unless the planning and control processes result in clear agreements about who is accomplishing which tasks. All such agreements are transitory, but their link to broader organizational objectives should be clear, and once made, managers need to be able to rely on them. Further, managers fulfilling this type of role require large amounts of information about the performance of their own units in meeting the agreements that have been made and about the activities of other units whose behavior affects their ability to perform. Thus, monitoring and feedback systems need to be extensive and reliable. Finally, organizations wih this type of managerial role require extensive, decentralized problem solving. Organization members in work units should be able to solve their own problems, and managers must be able to work effectively with managers in other units to resolve day-to-day problems that interfere with task accomplishment. Because most problem solving is likely to occur among peers, organization members must be skilled in developing solutions without the reliance on authority to decide who is right.[34]

Congruence with Formal Systems

Finally, most organizations develop a variety of formal systems to facilitate organizational functioning and control. These systems are tools to help organization members perform their roles. The control processes must be congruent with the way they are designed. If not, formal systems tend to impede the actual exercise of control and reduce organizational effectiveness. There are a number of key systems that most organizations develop that are particularly important.

Authority Distribution. An organization's system for distributing authority represents one of the most important determinants of control process effectiveness. The authority system specifies the formal relationship of organization members to decision processes in various domains. It describes the extent to which each organization member has a legitimate right to participate in making different types of decisions. Although rare in practice, the formal authority systems could be specified for every decision that has to be made within the organization. The most important domains are likely to be covered. Generally, these include specification of authority to participate in policy decisions regarding the overall objectives of the organization, resource allocation decisions regarding the use of financial materials and human resources, personnel decisions regarding employment conditions of individual organization members, and task decisions regarding the execution of day-to-day activities. They way in which authority is allocated in these domains is an important determinant of the power relationships in the organization and each individual's ability to meet their personal needs.

When the distribution of authority is not consistent with the control processes that exist, coordination is likely to suffer. Planning and goal setting will be of little use, for example, if organization members cannot get the resources they need to carry out the plans which are developed, and problem solving will do little good if problem solvers cannot implement their solutions. It is not critical that the people involved in control processes directly have the authority to set goals and solve problems, but they must be able to get the support of people who do. If the authority distribution is too inconsistent with the control processes that exist, appropriate plans will not be developed and problems will not get solved.

Personnel Systems. Most organizations develop extensive policies and procedures to handle personnel. These includes methods of compensation, evaluation, job placement, and career management among others. They affect the organization members' motivation to perform directly and ability to achieve personal goals. These systems need to be congruent with control processes in two different ways. First, because personnel systems involve decisions about an individual's job, career, and compensation, they give the people who control personnel decisions the capacity to make rewards contingent on specific actions. Thus the personnel systems can affect the distribution of influence within the organization markedly, and if inconsistent, with the influence needs required by the control processes, can interfere with the organization's ability to control behavior.[35]

Second, the personnel systems can create contingencias between patterns of individual action and rewards that are allocated. Pay systems can, for example, reward performance in some areas and not others, and layoff policies can reward seniority of different types. If these contingencies are inconsistent with the requirements of existing control processes, individuals are likely to be faced with conflicting goals. The performance the pay system rewards may be inconsistent with the actions required to solve problems that come up, or the layoff policies may reduce people's willingness to switch jobs as work loads shift. This type of conflict can reduce the effectiveness of control processes directly unless the personnel systems can somehow be changed.

Control Systems. Organizations usually set up a variety of formal control systems to facilitate control processes. Accounting systems, budgets, schedules, management information systems, and other similar tools serve to monitor organizational performance in various domains and to distribute information about performance to a network of organization members. They also provide a language for goal setting and performance monitoring that is relatively unambiguous and concrete.

A number of key aspects of control systems must be congruent with control processes if the control processes are to be effective. First, patterns of information distribution must be congruent with the control processes. Control systems are useful only if they provide information to the people who are going to use it for problem solving and can be harmful if they waste resources providing people with information they don't need. Second, the domains of action covered by the control systems should be congruent with the control processes. If the organization relies on extrinsic methods of motivation and ties rewards to control system measures, the measures should be comprehensive. Otherwise, organization members concentrate on measured performance to the detriment of performance in other areas. If intrinsic methods of motivation are used, the specific domains are less likely to be crucial. Finally, all control systems have some mechanism for collecting information about organizational activities. These mechanisms must provide an accurate representation of the activities being measured for the system to be useful. If the control system is to be used to motivate subordinates through extrinsic means, these mechanisms must be relatively difficult to allow tampering by organization members.

Congruence and Effective Control

In order for control processes to work, they must be congruent with each other, with the organization's context, with the managerial roles that exist, and with the formal systems in play. When all of these elements are congruent, planning and goal setting provide overall direction to activities, feedback processes insure that problems are identified, and problem-solving activities are activated to solve problems that develop. When these aspects of the organization are incongruent with existing control processes, or, for that matter, with each other, conflicts and inconsistencies reduce the coordination among organization members. The greater the incongruence, the higher the likelihood that organization members find their activities in conflict with those of others, and that organizational objectives are not achieved.

DEVELOPING A CONTROL STRATEGY

From the perspective of top executives, the goal of a control strategy is to produce effective control processes within their organizational units. The problem they face is that they cannot determine the nature of the control processes directly. While executives may want to have effective planning and goal-setting processes in their organizations, lower-level managers may not plan effectively or set clear goals. While they may set up monitoring systems, organization members may ignore them. While they may try to stimulate effective problem solving, their subordinates may attempt to avoid responsibility for implementing solutions. Thus, the problem facing executives is to develop a plan of action to influence others to utilize effective control processes.

Before examining some of the characteristics such a plan of action might have, it seems worthwhile to point out some strategies that will probably cannot work. First, simply telling subordinates to develop better control processes is unlikely to produce any constructive results. If organization members are not effectively controlling performance, it is probably because there is an incongruence between the existing control processes and the current state of the organization. Unless the incongruencies are recognized and resolved, improvement in control is unlikely.

Second, developing a new set of procedures for coordinating and controlling performance and ordering people to follow them probably cannot work either. In the first place, subordinates may well lack the skills to carry out the procedures and as a result are likely to fail. Further, it is very likely that any problems with control processes have roots in the behavior of the executives themselves. Any changes that are not accompanied by changes in the way the executives themselves manage their organizations are unlikely to succeed unless the executives demonstrate the new ways of behaving.

What then can executives do? They can begin a process of change that results in a new, more effecive process of control. Such a strategy for creating change is likely to involve four different stages: diagnosis, objectives setting, change programs, and ongoing problem solving.

Diagnosis

The first step in creating more effective control is diagnosing the current state of the control processes within the organization. It is difficult to develop a strategy for improvement without an accurate understanding of the existing problems that need to be solved. The objective of such a diagnosis would be to develop an accurate description of the nature of the control processes that exist, the methods of motivation that are being used, and the congruence of these processes with the organization's external environment, the nature of managerial roles, and the formal systems within the organization.[36]

A diagnosis of this type can be conducted in a variety of different ways. It can be done by the executives themselves, by external consultants, by organizational staff members, or by a task force with representatives of different levels and functions within the organization.[37] Each of these approaches has characteristic advantages and disadvantages. In general, the more people who are involved in the diagnosis, and the more functions they represent, the more likely that all relevant information surfaces, but also the more time it takes and the more complicated it is to coordinate the diagnostic activities. If control problems are severe, it is probably worth the time and trouble of using a representative group. The expense of using an external facilitator (either an outside or an internal consultant) probably can be justified. If only fine tuning is necessary, then a diagnosis by a single person is probably sufficient.

Objectives Setting

Based on the diagnosis, a set of objectives should be established. These objectives should describe the type of control processes that should exist. Many organizations have found it useful to develop a written philosophy of control that is adopted as policy for the organization. Such a statement of philosophy can begin with a description of the major tasks the organization is trying to accomplish and the nature of the external environment it faces. It then states assumptions about the nature of the people, resources, and technology available to the organization for use in achieving the objectives. The nature of the ideal control processes are then described and linked to the assumptions that have been made.

This statement serves a number of broad purposes in the development of an overall control strategy. First, it provides a clear statement of how control processes should function for all organization members. This helps them to understand what the overall control strategy is designed to accomplish. Second, it provides a rationale for the control strategy that helps organization members understand why it is being adopted, and may reduce resistance to changes. Third, the philosophy statement provides a standard against which all organization members can test their own behavior, and, if necessary, a general goal for change.

Once the general philosophy of control is completed, a plan of action must be created to make it operational. This plan varies widely from organization to organization, but it generally involves five components. First, it includes some mechanism for communicating the control philosophy to organization members and for helping them to explore what it means in terms of their jobs and behavior. This step is critical because people are unlikely to learn to behave in new ways if they do not know that changes are expected.

Second, the plan must provide programs to teach organization members any new skills required by the control philosophy. It is unreasonable to expect that all managers have the skills to behave in new ways if this is required by the new control philosophy. To implement the new processes successfully, they must have an opportunity to learn the appropriate skills.

Third, programs have to be developed to teach managers the role expectations required by the new approach. These programs should provide a clear statement of how they are expected to behave and to give them a chance to practice acting appropriately in a setting where they can get feedback on the adequacy of their new role performance. Further, these programs must concentrate on integrating the new role conceptions into the ongoing process of planning and goal setting. In this way, the organization establishes tasks that become congruent with the new role expectations.

Fourth, change programs must be developed to alter any of the formal organizational systems that are inconsistent with the control processes. Inconsistent formal systems are barriers to the change and signal organization members that the changes are not real. Programs for altering them are essential to successful implementation of the new control processes.

Finally, some type of monitoring mechanism must be developed to keep track of changes and to resolve problems. In any complex change program, mistakes can be made. Some mechanism needs to be created to identify problems when they arise and to alter the change programs appropriately to solve them. This mechanism could be an individual who has overall coordinating responsibility for the change projects, or it could be a group of people who oversee the change process. Without it, however, the change programs themselves run the risk of getting out of control.

Change Programs

Once the objectives have been set and the plans for implementing the new control strategy have been developed, the change programs that have been developed must be implemented. Two factors are likely to be

critical at this stage. The first is the timing of the implementation of different programs. If changes are minor, this is not crucial. If not, the organization may not have the time and resources to accomplish all the changes at once. When this happens, it is important that the plan include some communication to organization members concerning the sequence of change activities so that they know when to expect action in different areas. If, for example, the pay system has been identified as a barrier to effective control, it is not necessary that it be changed immediately but it is important that the people know that it will be changed and have some idea about when the changes will occur. Otherwise, they may view the lack of change in the pay system as an indication that the organization is not serious about following its new control philosophy.

Further, the order of programs may make a difference. It is unreasonable to expect, for example, that changes will be successful if they require skills that have not yet been taught in training programs. In addition, some programs may deal with particularly critical organizational systems, procedures, or role expectations, while others may focus on other less central areas. If the critical areas are not addressed first, the programs in other areas may fail because organization members are not convinced that top management is committed to the objectives of the change.

The second factor is the congruence of the change programs and the new control philosophy. The programs represent concrete evidence about what the new control philosophy means, and if they are not implemented in a way that is consistent with the philosophy, the implementation procedures reduce the likelihood that the new control strategy is effective. If, for example, the control philosophy states that organization members should have clear objectives, and the change programs do not provide any, then people are likely to feel that the program is all words and no substance. Similarly, if the control philosophy states that organization members should participate in decision making and the change programs do not involve people in designing change, distrust is likely to result.

In practice, designing change with appropriate timing and consistent procedures can be a difficult task, but an executive's success in these two areas is likely to be an important determinant of the effectiveness of the control strategy that has been developed.

Problem Solving

The first aspect of the change strategy is to solve the problems that arise as the change programs are implemented. As in the case of the implementation of the change programs, the problem-solving activities should be congruent with the control philosophy being implemented so that they reinforce, not contradict, the new programs. Further, it is important that the executives designing the program allocate sufficient time, energy, and resources so that the problems can be solved. The fact that they develop is a virtual certainty and unless people are prepared to deal with them, problems can sabotage even well designed change programs.

Finally, some problem-solving and evaluation mechanisms should remain in place even after the control strategy has been implemented successfully. As time goes on, conditions change both inside and outside the organization. To remain effective, the control processes in the organization must change to meet changing conditions, and a complete control strategy insures the mechanisms are available to create the changes that are necessary. At a minimum, these mechanisms should include a regular diagnosis of the nature of control activities and the formation of groups that can design new change programs to remove new barriers to control. Further, these should probably be, at intervals, a review of the adequacy of the control philosophy itself. Without these evaluation and problem-solving mechanisms, even the best control strategy becomes obsolete and new failures of control begin to emerge.

CONCLUSIONS

Developing a control strategy for an organization can be a complex undertaking. Control processes are influenced by almost every aspect of the organization's context and structure, and developing effective control involves designing systems, procedures, and roles that complement each other in motivating organization members to work together to meet the organization's objectives. If these systems, procedures, and roles have gotten seriously out of alignment, getting them back into balance can be a difficult task. On the other hand, the costs of incongruence can be high and show up in rigidity, conflict, and failure. Executives responsible for an organization that is out of control face a difficult task in developing a control strategy that will solve their problems, but while the costs of change are likely to be high, the costs of not changing are likely to be higher.

REFERENCES

1. Burns and Stalker (1961), Lawrence and Lorsch (1967), and Woodward (1965) are among the social scientists that have demonstrated that the most effective organizations have developed internal procedures and policies for controlling the behavior of their members. These are appropriate for the technology the organization is using and the type of environment in which it is operating.

2. This point has been made most clearly by systems theorists such as Katz and Kahn (1978) who have stressed the importance of *equifinality*, the concept that more than one set of organizational relationships can produce the same levels of organizational performance.

3. Expectancy theories include a variety of different theoretical formulations. Lawler's (1973) review of motivation theory provides a useful introduction into this work.

4. Control theories have been developed separately by theorists as divergent as engineers and systems theorists. Lawler and Rhode (1976) provide a useful summary of these

theories and their implications for designing control systems in organizations.

5. Vroom (1964) and Lawler (1973) provide good examples of the use of expectancy theory for understanding work behavior. Lawler (1971), Lawler and Rhode (1976), and Hackman and Lawler (1971) provide examples of the use of the theory in designing pay systems, control systems, and jobs, respectively.

6. This typology of needs has been developed by Alderfer (1972). Other typologies have been developed by Maslow (1943), Lawler (1973), McClelland (1962), Litwin and Stringer (1968), and others. These theorists differ in the specific configurations of needs that they believe to exist, but all agree on the basic idea that needs exist and that people try to satisfy them.

7. Behavioral scientists have paid considerable attention to the nature of jobs that create an intrinsic motivation to perform well. Hackman and his colleagues (Hackman and Lawler, 1971; Hackman and Oldham, 1980) have concluded that people work hard to perform well for intrinsic reasons when their jobs are defined clearly as important, when they have the autonomy to make the crucial decisions that determine the quality of performance, and when they get feedback on how well they are performing. Hackman (1977) has extended this work to apply to work groups as well as individuals.

8. This aspect of expectancy theory is also included in many learning theories that argue that people do not learn new behaviors that are too difficult and require too much change.

9. This model of control processes has been proposed by Nadler, Cammann, and Mirvis (1980), among others.

10. Recent work by Alderfer and his colleagues (Alderfer, 1976) on underbounded systems and the characteristics of organizations without adequate planning processes demonstrates the fact that organizations cannot effectively coordinate the activities of their members unless there is some form of planning.

11. There is evidence that organization members frequently do not fully accept the goals that are set for them. Onsi (1973) found,

for example, that over 80% of the managers he interviewed said that they built slack into their budgets. Hofstede (1967) found considerable variations in the extent to which lower level managers actually intended to achieve the goals that were set for them.

12. It is possible for organization members to participate in developing plans to cope with difficult problems such as lay-offs, budget reductions, etc. However, not many organizations have developed a strong enough climate of trust to use participative methods under these circumstances, and other methods of planning.

13. Hopwood (1973) provides a nice illustration of this defensive use of participation. He found that subordinates with generally autocratic managers would use participation in goal setting to reduce the difficulty of the goals they were expected to achieve so that they could insure adequate performance and keep their loss for bothering them.

14. Lawler and Rhode (1976) review the relevant literature on goal setting and provide the rationale for this conclusion.

15. Ouchi and colleagues (Ouchi and McGuire, 1975) and Thompson (1967) have explored this issue.

16. Pay, in particular, is frequently used for this purpose and can be a very successful motivator if the contingencies are clear (Lawler, 1971).

17. Scanlon plans provide a useful model for integrating intrinsic and extrinsic motivation into a single motivational scheme (Frost, Wakeley, and Ruh, 1974). Some theorists have argued that intrinsic and extrinsic motivation are mutually exclusive (Deci, 1975) but Staw (1976) has demonstrated that for most organizational situations this is unlikely to be the case.

18. Nadler (1977) provides an overview of the ways in which feedback can influence behavior. Locke et al. (1968) provide a clear demonstration that it is goal setting and not feedback that directly influences behavior.

19. Argyris (1964) and Likert (1967) have both made strong arguments demonstrating that financial measurement systems in particular focus managerial attention on financial performance to the exclusion of performance in other areas. The result can be deteriora-

tion in the organization's capacity to perform that is not noticed or attended to because it is not measured by the financial indicators.

20. Jasinski (1956) and Lawler and Rhode (1976), among others, have provided clear descriptions of the dysfunctional effects that can result when goals are set and performance rewarded based on an inadequate set of feedback measures.

21. A number of researchers have observed this phenomenon (Argyris, 1952; Cammann, 1976; Hofstede, 1967; Hopwood, 1973; Jasinski, 1956; Lawler and Rhode, 1976). The phenomenon is clearly widespread, at least for minor forms of information distortion. Onsi (1973) found that 80% of the managers he interviewed built slack into budgets. It can reduce the value of information systems as a tool in controlling individual performance markedly.

22. Vough (1975) provides an interesting description of a program designed to accomplish this objective.

23. Golembiewski and McConkie (1975) provide a review of the research on trust and its effect on interpersonal relations.

24. The idea that some organizations may evidence inadequate levels of control is related closely to Alderfer's (1976) concept of underbounded systems. An underbounded system in his terminology results in part from inadequate levels of control processes and produces ineffective organizational performance because the organization is unable to utilize its resources effectivelly in accomplishing tasks.

25. Nadler and Tushman (1979, 1981) provide a useful description of the importance of congruence in determining organizational effectiveness.

26. Hopwood (1973).

27. Cammann and Nadler (1976) provide a more complete exploration of the relationship between the methods of motivation used and the appropriate measurement system requirements.

28. Galbraith (1973) has argued that when predictability is high and the speed of change is low, the organization can use hierarchical, mechanistic methods of control because the organization does not have to process information rapidly and can afford to con-

centrate on the efficient coordination of resources in task performance. Participative methods can be used under these circumstances, but they are not required by the task demands.

29. Burns and Stalker (1961) have examined the nature of appropriate coordination and control under conditions of uncertainty and concluded that organic, flexible methods are most appropriate for creating effective response to problems under these conditions. A number of other researchers (Thompson, 1967; Perrow, 1967) have confirmed and extended these findings.

30. This is the traditional concept that underlies bureaucratic hierarchies of control and serves as the foundation for a traditional, pyramidal design of responsibilities.

31. Argyris (1976), Herrick and Maccoby (1975), and Hackman and Oldham (1980) are among the social scientists who have discussed this agreement. Hackman and Oldham in particular point out that developing motivation by using extrinsic rewards can be difficult in many existing situations.

32. Likert (1961, 1967).

33. Rice (1965).

34. The actual control systems that develop in organizations using this conception of roles tend to be complex and somewhat unique to the organization. Davis and Lawrence (1977) have described the evaluation of matrix organizations and the different types of control processes that can evolve in this context. Texas Instruments' OST control system represents another example of a complex control system that complements this type of managerial role (*Business Week*, 1978). One of the few things these different systems have in common is that they take a long time to develop and require skillful, highly motivated managers for success.

35. French and Raven (1959) have provided a useful description of bases of power and their importance in determining influence relations in organizations. Most formal organizational systems alter the bases of power the individuals can exploit, thereby altering the influence structure. Personnel systems can be important in this regard particularly because they determine who can reward and punish individuals by giv-

ing or withholding important personal rewards such as pay, promotion, security,
and so on.

36. Nadler (1977) provides a clear, comprehensive analysis of the use of information in
creating organizational change. He gives a
detailed description of many of the available options for conducting a diagnosis and
highlights some of the pitfalls to be
avoided.

37. Alderfer and Smith (1980) in an un-
published manuscript provide a useful
model for how this type of diagnosis can be
accomplished and what results it can generate.

SECTION III.
PLANNING FOR PRODUCTS AND NEW MARKETS

10
Market Planning:
National Versus Corporate Planning

Charles E. Reed
Senior Vice-President (ret.)
General Electric Company

A wide variety of trends, crises, and concerns have combined to make national planning an active issue on the political agenda in the United States. Charles Reed discusses the adequacy of our response to this challenge.

Our societies, our institutions, and our business planners face a challenge of historic proportions because of momentous economic, social, and technological forces of our time. How adequate is our response to this challenge depends in part on the clarity with which we perceive the issues and the options before us.

Nowhere is this observation more true than with the issue of national economic planning. The issue is truly the crux of future business–government relationships. Depending on how this issue is resolved, we can have either a tightly controlled economy and society, or one in which there is still a reasonable prospect for an active market of choice and flexibility.

NATIONAL PLANNING—AN ACTIVE ISSUE IN THE UNITED STATES

A wide variety of trends, crises, and concerns have combined to make national planning an active issue on the political agenda in the United States. We have experienced a widespread feeling of drift and powerlessness, high rates of inflation coupled with persistent high unemployment, the crises and trade-offs in energy and the environment, and a desire by some to reorder our national priorities. For these reasons, among others, a wide variety of proposals have been made to introduce some form of economic planning at the national level. The best-known proposal is advanced by the Initiative Committee for National Economic Planning, which includes in its membership Leonard Woodcock of the United Automobile Workers, Wassily Leontief of Harvard University, and Robert Roosa of Brown Brothers, Harriman. This proposal formed the basis for the bill sponsored by the late Senator Hubert Humphrey and former Senator Jacob Javits. But there have been other proposals, and we must expect many more as the debate unfolds.

PROPONENTS OF NATIONAL PLANNING—DIFFERING VIEWS

Not surprisingly, proponents of national economic planning hold differing views of its meaning, of the ends to be served, and the means to be employed. Opponents, by contrast, are almost monolithic in their flat rejection of any further governmental planning, insisting that it already does too much badly.

Those who oppose planning at the national level categorically attack the idea of the tightly controlled economy that they believe will follow. But you can have planning without controls, just as you can have controls without planning. On the other hand, those who advocate national planning by government share the conviction that rational anticipation of problems is infinitely preferable to what they perceive as irrational improvisation in response to crises. Clearly, improving government's planning capability does not necessarily mean that we must have detailed planning of the economy by government.

The diversity of proposals, the uncertainty of definitions, opponents and proponents talking past each other—these are the hallmarks of an issue still in its formative stage. The issue, as I see it, is not whether we should have planning or no planning. Rather, it is the role that planning should play in our society.

Our aim should be, not the planned society, but a "planful society"—a society in which planning is diffused throughout the system, decentralized to improve its relevance and flexibility, but sharing some common perceptions about the ends toward which our plans and actions should be directed.

The crucial question in such a society, as in a corporation, is how to agree on some integrating goals without becoming coercive as to the means for attaining them. There is constant tension between the desire for purposeful coordination and the need for flexible diversity.

One way of drawing the needed distinction between the planned society and the planful society is to look at pairs of contrasting terms, for instance:

1. Centralized vs. decentralized
2. Fixed vs. flexible
3. Limited options vs. multiple alternatives
4. Promulgation of plans vs. diffusion of information.

The contrast, then, is between detailed prescriptive planning by a central government and articulated adaptive planning by a network of institutions, large and small, public and private.

To get a better fix on what such a society might be, what it might require and how it might evolve, I suggest that we use three vectors:

1. The lessons to be learned from countries with planning experience
2. The lessons to be learned from corporate planning experience
3. The areas of agreement between proponents and opponents.

Applying Lessons for Other Countries

We in the United States can benefit from the experience of those countries that have engaged in some form of national planning. Certainly the roster of such countries is impressively long, ranging through a spectrum from the limited industrial planning in West Germany, through the business–government consensus planning of Japan and indicative planning exemplified by France and Brazil, to the tight, centralized control of the Soviet Union and the Communist bloc.

The dissimilarities among these countries and planning systems may seem to preclude any transference of experience. However, it is not the specific forms and institutions of planning that I am considering. Rather, I am looking for lessons in the contexts, objectives, and consequences of these planning efforts. Here, I think, we may pick up some clues.

First, nearly all the planning efforts outside the Communist bloc were initiated in the post–World War II recovery period by countries trying to recover from the ravages of the war. These efforts have subsequently been reinforced by regional planning moves as, for example, in the European Economic Community.

Second, all planning efforts have the common theme of directing economic activity toward growth and full employment of resources. Possibly the greatest benefit of planning has come through the conscious stimulation of selected industries or economic sectors.

Third, all efforts in sector and industry planning involve close government-business-labor cooperation (again, excepting most Communist bloc countries, where there is little or no "business" sector).

Fourth, despite planning, all planned economies have experienced discontinuities and setbacks in the past three years. Even the Soviet Union has not been able to avoid poor harvests through its planning, and as a result may have been forced to recognize that planning has to allow for uncertainties. Clearly, planning is no panacea for achieving economic stability.

Indeed, the limitations of broad attempts to plan a whole economy seem to be becoming apparent to most European planners. Jean Ross-Skinner, European correspondent for *Dun's Review*, quoted a veteran French planning expert as saying:

I think Europeans accept now that, with the grand plans the effort is very thinly spread and they usually aren't properly carried through. The new attitude is to single out the problem areas for concentrated effort.

This, in effect, is what the French have done in focusing their efforts on nuclear energy, on regional plans and on restructuring industries (such as the computer industry) to deal with competition in the Common Market.

Finally, all planning systems reflect the economic and cultural traditions of the individual countries.

The last point is, I believe, especially important. Any planning system, corporate or governmental, must be compatible with the dominant culture of the organization it serves. Otherwise, it will be rejected, as transplanted organs can be rejected by the body. In the United States, for instance, we have to accept the fact that we are, by and large, not a society of consensus as, for instance, Japan is.

Our nation is dominated by a culture of individualism, decentralization, competition, and confrontation.

Further, we have to accept and deal with the political facts of a two-party system, the constitutional separation of powers, states' rights, and two-, four-, and six-year changeovers in the institutions of our national government. These factors are deeply embedded in history and culture, and are likely to change slowly, if at all. We would do well, therefore, to design our approach to planning around them.

Applying Lessons from Corporate Planning Experience

Some proponents of national economic planning argue that it is analogous to an extended form of corporate planning. If planning works well for corporations, they reason, why should it not work well also for nations? However, a simplistic analogy between corporate and government planning is inaccurate. We must not allow the similarity of the terms to hide the very real differences between these two forms of planning.

Corporate planning is responsive to market forces and is subject to many constraints external to the corporation (including customers, competitors, and government). Government planning, on the other hand, is by its very nature responsive to political forces, and can (at least in the near term) ignore or override market forces. Corporate planning must be highly flexible and responsive to rapid, unforeseen changes in the market. Government planning is relatively inflexible because the momentum of large-scale government activity is extremely difficult to halt or reverse. Within the overall economy, corporate planning is decentralized to each company, and is competitive with planning by many other companies: this is the ultimate discipline and corrective. Planning of the economy by government is centralized and noncompetitive: in effect, we would "bet the country" on a single set of plans.

Another fundamental difference lies in the goal-setting process. At the national government level, goal setting is democratic and diffuse: the resultant goals are piecemeal and often conflicting statements of aspirations. At the corporate level, the process is more tightly structured: the resultant goals are better integrated, measurable, and more precisely stated. Governmental or national goals are dictated by social and political aspirations, frequently unconstrained by economic realities. Corporate goals are dictated primarily by economic opportunities and constrained by social and political factors.

However, having pointed out the differences between corporate and government planning, I want now to stress some of the similarities in the challenges confronting both. Obviously, in these remarks, I am drawing primarily on our experience in General Electric in implementing our strategic business planning approach. Both the challenges we faced and the approaches we have taken to them have something to say about the situation facing government for many years.

Forces Shaping General Electric's Corporate Planning   Four forces shaped corporate strategic planning in General Electric Company during the early 1970s:

1. *Expanding complexity.* A key need in improving our business planning was to make the company's growing complexity more manageable. (Quite often, planning systems do just the opposite.) Government faces a growth in complexity many times greater than any business. It is the failure to control this complexity by planning that leads to the duplication, contradiction, and runaway cost of government.

2. *Growing appetite for resources.* In the 1960s, we invested for growth faster than we generated internal funds, and had used debt leverage to the point that,

in 1970, our debt reached an effective limit, consistent with our desire to maintain an AAA credit rating. Many governments found themselves with the challenge of trying to meet a wide range of social expectations without further deficit spending and inflation. Some have reached their debt limit; witness Britain, Italy, and New York City. Allocating scarce resources among proliferating demands is, perhaps, one of the most critical problems facing government planners today.

3. *Increasing competition.* The breadth and strength of the competition we faced was increased by our growing diversity, and could only intensify as markets saturated, growth slowed, and international competition became more prevalent. The analogous situation facing government is the growth of international interdependence and competition. Nations have become tied together, economically and politically, as world trade and investment have surged. As governments become ever more involved in international trade and monetary negotiations, both their sovereignty and their international strategies become increasingly constrained by the realities of their competitive position.

4. *Rapidly changing environment.* Our planning had to anticipate and respond to structural changes that were becoming more significant in most markets. We were impacted by almost every major economic and technological development; social and political influences were an increasingly important factor in business performance. Government faces the same challenge of a changing environment, and it is here that its planning failure is perhaps most conspicuous. Discontinuities such as the energy crisis and runaway inflation have exposed serious gaps in government foresight and policies. Much of the recent

dramatic increase in regulation stems from a crisis reaction to such problems.

Confronted with these four challenging forces, we developed a planning structure and process that sought to decentralize plan formulation without abdicating control of the enterprises's overall direction. The key feature of our decentralized planning is the development of business strategies at the level of the strategic business unit (SBU), each a complete business, responsible for formulating its own business strategy. We have long since found that basic business strategy is best carried out on a decentralized basis. In as large and diverse an organization as General Electric, a centralized planning organization cannot be sufficiently knowledgeable to carry out strategy formulation successfully. In those cases where it was tried, we found that centralized planning negated many of the benefits of scale and diversity.

However, we have also found that it is essential at the corporate level to develop a strategic planning framework that emphasizes overall goals and permits a more rational allocation of resources. In this way, we seek to improve the "planfulness" of the total organization.

We have sought to define very carefully what the corporate (or policy) level in a large, diverse organization should do to complement decentralized strategy formulation, and to avoid, for example, the profitless "diseconomies" of diversification. Without going into details, here are the four tasks that our experience shows should be performed at the corporate level:

1. Shaping the corporte business scope and diversification thrust
2. Setting objectives and priorities for the corporation as a whole and for each SBU
3. Estimating and allocating corporate resources
4. Designing corporate management sys-

tems, including compensation and promotion systems.

Each of these corporate planning activities complements, rather than duplicates, the development of decentralized business strategies. All these actions provide the right environment for decentralized business planning without usurping the creative task of strategy formulation. We hope that this approach adds up to strategic leadership without dictatorship.

Our corporate experience suggests, therefore, a careful pondering of the following implications for government planning:

1. The more comprehensive type of centralized government planning proves to be unwieldy and unworkable. It presupposes a planning elite and a central store of knowledge that is not feasible, in practice.
2. A strong case can be made that the need to articulate goals and priorities is a large part of the battle in any planning system. At the national government level, when such goals can be articulated by the President and generally endorsed by the electorate, they can serve as the "strategic context" within which the decentralized planning of public and private organizations can be executed.
3. There is a need for an improved resource allocation capability in the public sector. This is asking a great deal of the federal government, given its huge array of programs. However, this is one of the major purposes of planning.
4. There is a need to coordinate and integrate the federal planning system.

These four lessons from our General Electric experience lead into a discussion of the third vector on the planful society, namely, building on the areas of agreement between proponents and opponents of national economic planning.

Areas of Agreement Between Proponents and Opponents

Whatever their differences, proponents and opponents seem to agree on three points:

1. The need to improve coordination and foresight in public sector planning
2. The need to develop better information and clearer national goals
3. The need to focus on specific problems in an effort to improve our economic problem-solving capability.

Each of these areas of agreement can be translated into actionable proposals that would help to make our system more planful, more farsighted, more self-consciously aware of the alternatives and the need for critical choices.

Improved Coordination of Public Sector Planning. Planning is not, of course, a new function in government—virtually every agency of the federal government houses some form of planning component in its organization—but it is imperfectly coordinated and generally focuses on a narrow time horizon. A common theme emerging from the discussion about national planning is the need for the federal government, both Congress and the administration, to take better integrated, more farsighted action.

While individual agency planning is commonplace, the overall coordinating and integrating function is presently weak in government planning. This deficiency contributes in a major way to the difficulties in arranging (and adhering to) priorities, in anticipating (and resolving) trade-off decisions among goals and policies, and in developing synergy (rather than conflict) in government programs.

The other major planning deficiency in government—a too narrow planning horizon—is largely a reflection of the election timetable in our political system. Budgets and goal setting are still geared to an annual cy-

cle, and the limits to political futurity are set by the lowest common denominator in the election timetable—the two-year life of a Congress.

Fortunately, the organizational structure for increased coordination and improved longer term forecasting is already in place in the form of:

1. The Office of Management and Budget
2. The Council of Economic Advisors
3. The Office of Technology Assessment
4. The Congressional budgetary process, comprising the Congressional Budget Office and the Budget Committees of the House and Senate.

The Office of Management and Budget already has responsibility for the coordinated development of the President's budget proposals, and so becomes involved in the establishment of the administration's priorities, at least on a year-to-year basis. It has also, in recent years, commenced work on "social indicators," i.e., the evaluation and measurement of progress toward what might be termed national goals.

OMB would also seem to be the logical agency within the executive branch to perform the basic policy function of developing the planning framework within which individual agency planning, short and long term, should take place. Such a unifying framework, with a five-year planning horizon, would go a long way toward integrating (at an early stage) governmental goals, policies and programs, and facilitating necessary trade-off decisions (again, at an early stage) regarding goals and impacts as well as costs.

From its inception, the Council of Economic Advisors has contributed its economic forecasting capability to governmental planning. Until recently, this forecast has been short term. However, starting in 1975, the horizon was extended to five years. Clearly such an extension was desirable, even essential, prerequisite to longer term planning by the government, and should be continued.

The Office of Technology Assessment was established to give Congress a better analytical and forecasting capability for legislative decisions on technological matters. In view of the increasing scale, complexity, and lead time for modern technology, OTA was a necessary social invention, as a result of which we may reasonably hope that political decisions in technical areas will be taken with a better sense of their long-term and varied consequences.

The Congressional budgetary process is a relatively recent addition, only becoming fully operative with the FY 1977 budget. As an essential mechanism for forcing Congressional decisions on spending priorities, the work of the House and Senate Budget Committees and the Congressional Budget Office is to be applauded. This forms a necessary counterpoint to improvement and strengthening of executive branch planning. But these are new institutions in Congress, as indeed is the "foresight" provision, adopted by the House in 1974, that requires that each Committee "shall on a continuing basis undertake futures research and forecasting" on matters within its jurisdiction. These institutions need to be encouraged, strengthened, and given a chance to work, for they are addressing the right problems in the right way.

Even more recently, the decision to reinstate the Office of Science and Technology Policy to the White House is a most welcome one. As Congress needs OTA, so the executive branch requires, as part of its planning effort, a foresight capability in technical matters.

In sum, these various moves are all designed to strengthen the planning function in both the executive and legislative branches of government. If planning becomes more a part of our political culture, not only will coordination in the federal sector improve, but (to use the corporate analogy) there is a better prospect of developing the "strategic context" within which the decentralized planning of other public and private organizations can be strengthened.

Developing Better Information and Clearer Goals. A second point on which there is widespread agreement is the need to develop better information and clearer goals in order to preserve the vitality of our decentralized, democratic system.

In recent years, we have faced the grave threat of an effective disenfranchisement of large segments of the public through uncertainty and lack of information on the complex, highly technical issues that cry out for decisions. On energy, resources, the environment, land use, capital formation, and many more, the situation is the same. The experts are divided. The public is confused and frustrated. Congress and the administration, sensing this, tend to procrastinate on the needed decisions. Corporations, trying to chart their own course, are blown about by the shifting winds of uncertainty.

Obviously, there are no easy ways out of this dilemma. However, it is clear that one need—required by citizens, corporations, and governments alike—is for more and better information on the key problems confronting us. You cannot have an active electorate, you cannot have a planful society, you cannot develop intelligent alternatives in the absence of adequate, relevant information. Information, widely disseminated and fully credible, is one of the keys to improved goal setting and to the diffusion of planning throughout our system.

We do not lack for organizations that devote themselves to policy analysis in one form or another. Think, for instance, of the Brookings Institution, the National Planning Association, the Urban Institute, the Institute for the Future and a whole range of university policy centers. In addition, there is a plethora of public-interest groups, each promoting its own set of preferred policies and demanding participation in the decision-making process. The trouble is that there are very real limitations to all of these organizations. Many of them are limited in scope, and none of them has truly national organization and widespread acceptance.

This suggests the possibility of a new institutional arrangement, at the national level, in which both the public and private sectors might participate. Canada has established an Institute for Research on Public Policy, and proposals have been circulating in this country for an Institute for Analyses of Public Choices. Whatever the title might be, such an institute should derive its finances and its governing body from both the public and private sectors and should be an independent entity, answerable to the public at large rather than to Congress or the executive branch. (Certainly the Watergate episode has demonstrated very clearly the advisability of keeping such an important information-gathering and disseminating function separate from the other government branches that might be tempted to suppress or distort data for their own ends.)

The purposes of this institute would be to identify critical national issues, examine the policy options, disseminate information on the alternatives, and catalyze debates. By focusing on forward-looking analyses, clarifying the relationships between ends and means, and examining the trade-offs involved, it could do much to help our society clarify its goals and priorities and make both public policies and private plans better informed and more in harmony with these goals.

Improved Economic Problem Solving. The third point on which agreement focuses is the need for improved economic problem solving. The performance of our economy has left much to be desired. Proponents of national economic planning cite our economic problems as the reasons why national planning should be introduced. Opponents, on the other hand, reject this line of reasoning, while conceding the poor performance of the economy (for which they find other explanations, including deficiencies in public policies and governmental actions).

The closer one looks at the arguments, however, the more obvious it becomes that both sides are pointing to specific economic problems as the cause of our trouble. For the most part, they are not making blanket statements about an overall, inevitable malfunctioning of the market system or the political system. It makes sense, therefore, to suggest that we should focus our data gathering, analyses, and action programs on specific problems rather than diffuse our efforts over the whole field. This, after all, is a conclusion that European planners seem to be finding.

Certainly, we have no lack of agenda items. The nation is faced with severe problems in a number of key economic sectors, including energy, utilities, health care, and construction, as well as in a number of issues that cut across industry sectors, such as inflation, capital formation, employment policy, and urban revitalization. Each one of these problem areas calls for aggressive, joint business, labor, and government action—to define the basic difficulties, to examine alternative futures and strategies, to develop possible programs, to inform the electorate, and to promote constructive action.

A model for such joint action is provided by the private labor-management group that meets under the chairmanship of former Secretary of Labor John Dunlop. This group owes its origins to the former Presidential Labor-Management Committee that, also under Mr. Dunlop's chairmanship, was described by A.H. Raskin of *The New York Times* as "the most effective instrument ever formed for improved understanding between the ranking leaders of American industry and labor."

However, the institutional format, though important, is secondary to the basic idea of agreement to pursue solutions to our problems on an incremental, problem-by-problem basis. Certainly we should not expect complete consensus or instant solutions, but focusing on specific problems in a coordinated and cooperative manner can surely improve our problem-solving capabilities.

THREE PLANNING TARGETS

The approach I have taken here will not, of course, resolve all disagreements on the issue. However, I do believe that the three vectors I have used focus on a program that is needed, feasible, and legitimate.

It is needed, for it focuses on three target areas in which improved performance is crit-ical—coordination of public-sector planning, national goals clarifications, and joint economic problem solving. It is feasible, because it adheres to an incremental, "walk-before-you-run" approach. And it is legitimate in the sense that it is more likely to earn legitimacy through public support than proposals for comprehensive economic planning.

11
Improving Productivity of New Product Research

Carl E. Barnes
Vice President (ret.)
3M Company

In years gone by, progressive companies rid themselves of maturing products and replaced them with new products that would command higher profits. With the reduced productivity of research, many companies concluded that the "research pond" was all fished out, even though the Japanese and Germans continue to develop new products and new technology. Carl Barnes addresses the question: "Have we lost our skill as fishermen?"

This chapter presents some of the principles of managing a productive industrial research organization. But first, upon observing the status of research in most United States companies, I feel called upon to restate the need for the industrial research laboratory.

AN AMERICAN INNOVATION: RECESSION

There is increasing concern today about what *Time* (October 2, 1978) has termed the "Innovation Recession" in the United States. Japan and West Germany are forging ahead of us in the introduction of new products and processes. An example is the currently popular home video recorder. Although this was an American invention, not a single one is now made in this country. All are made in Japan.

Lagging R&D has affected the balance of trade to the point where United States exports of high-technology items have fallen so low that they no longer offset our imports of low-technology items such as shoes and clothing. This fact simply reflects the national need for

such high-technology products in the individual companies that make up the national production.

WHAT HAPPENED TO INDUSTRIAL RESEARCH?

What has happened to the once-productive industrial research laboratory? Have American inventors become less creative or has top management lost its nerve at risk taking? Has present-day management become more interested in preserving investment in existing plant and equipment than in replacing mature products made on such equipment with newer and more profitable ones?

I suggest that what may be needed is a re-education of top management, many of whom have come into power since the era of plentiful new products from their research laboratories. Like many "third-generation rich," their philosophy may be influenced by the "keep what you have" theory of economics rather than maintaining the philosophies that create wealth in the first place. But keeping what you have may be difficult in the face of foreign appetites for the United States market.

The chief executive officer of a rapidly growing and highly profitable company I worked for some 20 years ago used to stress the point that if one of our company's products could be replaced with a better one, our company must be the one to do it. This company also prided itself in the fact that better than 50% of its products were unknown ten years before, an important factor in its excellent earnings record. This philosophy prevailed in the growth companies of the 1960s. Now, the managements of too many companies act as though they believe "the public will buy what we give them"—a philosophy that appears to be valid only in a totalitarian economy.

DESIRE TO PROTECT EXISTING INVESTMENT

I can appreciate the tremendous urge to protect heavy investment in plant and equipment, but in a free economy, it is an ostrichlike philosophy. Beyond this, however, the kind of products in which plant investment is heaviest are nearly always mature commodities with correspondingly low profits.

There was a time when progressive companies would rid themselves of a maturing product by selling it to some less enterprising company and replacing it with a new product that commands higher profits. In this way, the company remains in a proprietary, noncompetitive business, thus avoiding the vagaries of the commodity market.

Lacking a ready supply of such new products from the research department in later years, some companies had to continue with maturing products even if it led to a commodity business. It may not have occurred to management that something could be done to restore the productivity of their research. Other companies were having the same trouble and many concluded that the "research pond" was all fished out.

I cannot buy this explanation. I do not believe that there are no new inventions to be made. The Japanese and the Germans seem to be developing new products and new technology—and we are all fishing in the same pond, the pond of fundamental knowledge.

Could it be that we have lost our skill as fishermen? Perhaps the answer is yes. I believe that we were hooking them a few years ago but we failed to pull them in. Potential new products and processes were being discovered a decade ago even in the "unproductive" laboratories. They germinated but died in this unfavorable climate.

RESEARCH REDUCED TO SERVICE

But now we have quit fishing altogether. With few exceptions, the so-called research laboratories of most large companies today serve as little more than technical service laboratories or, most likely, aimed at either reducing the production cost of a mature product or satisfying some requirement of the Environmental Protection Agency (EPA).

I might observe that the EPA, together with OSHA, the Delaney amendment, and to some extent the Food and Drug Administration, impose regulations on American industry that act as strong deterrents to innovation. In many instances, before a product, if it is a chemical, can be registered for sale under these regulations, any patent thereon may have come close to expiration, thus leaving little opportunity for building a business on a proprietary product.

With the hope that some of these problems can be solved, let us return to our study of the lack of productivity in industrial research laboratories aside from the effects of government regulation. My garden guide, in referring to perennials, has this to say: "It is advisable to entirely remake the garden every five or six years since it tends to become unproductive." I think it may be necessary to do the same with research laboratories, although they may last somewhat longer. Why should this be so? What sort of change brings about a lack of productivity?

CAUSE OF POOR RESEARCH PRODUCTIVITY

It has been my good fortune to have studied some of these mature industrial research laboratories and observe firsthand the factors that make them unproductive. In these laboratories, a bureaucracy comprising various levels of research management between the scientist at the bench and the decision-making personnel has developed. Promotions to middle-management positions had nearly always been given to people who had made no mistakes. The promotion of a new research development that did not make the grade is an example of a serious mistake that would prohibit upward movement.

Because the way to the top was clearly a matter of "playing it safe," it is rather easy to predict what kind of decisions will be reached by such managers regarding the risky matter of recommending emerging new products for further development. Such managers are always looking for a good reason to shelve development rather than to advance it. They point out things that may be wrong with a product and often expect "brownie points" for recognizing these deficiencies at an early stage, thus saving costly development expenditures. For what?—a new product which doesn't have anything wrong with it? I have yet to see one.

NEW PRODUCTS, LIKE THE OLD, HAVE DEFICIENCIES

Actually, there is something wrong with everything, even mature products. Iron rusts, plexiglas scratches, penicillin has side effects, the jet engine is noisy, office copiers are always out of order, and so on. Yet all these products have been successful because there is something *right* about them. I once made the comment that it is a good thing that glass was developed before the era of the modern indus-

trial research laboratory. It would have never made it through. Not only does it break, but the broken pieces can cut people!

The new product that can be potentially successful is usually not very spectacular when first observed. Thus the first "reduction to practice," to use a patent term, of what is now the Xerox process was only a faintly discernible image. It was not until some $5 million had been spent on its development that it became the near-perfect process it is today.

NEW PRODUCTS ARE FREQUENTLY ACCIDENTS

Nylon, the first manmade fiber, evolved from an observation made by Dr. J. W. Hill who, while removing a sample of one of Dr. W. H. Carothers' molten polymers from a vessel, noted that it formed a string that, when cooled, could be extended by drawing to form a fiber. This observation, along with some $6 million in development work, led to a commercial fiber. Other synthetic fibers soon followed.

And when Alexander Flemming noticed that bacteria did not grow around a spore of mold that had accidentally fallen onto one of his cultures, it was not apparent that this observation would lead to the discovery of penicillin. Fortunately he did not require the approval of anyone else to do the work necessary to satisfy his curiosity.

BUREAUCRACY IN RESEARCH

One wonders how many useful new products may have been lost by failure to follow through on similar observations. And if one of these observations is made in a laboratory where an established bureaucracy exists, it is very unlikely that funds will be authorized for further exploration. This is an important reason why many of the older research laboratories have such a poor record of turning out really new products.

I have known research directors who honestly believe their primary duty is to ferret out the flaws in products or processes being recommended for further development. The expression "I caught that one in time" sums up their concept of responsibility.

Of course, the great majority of potential new products are doomed to failure, because of prohibitive cost, existence of a competitive product, marginal properties, or whatever. Less than 1% make the grade; this figure would be considered high in most laboratories. Certainly it is the duty of research management to cull out such projects when recognized. But this is a chore, not the main objective.

The charter of the research laboratory is to discover and develop new products. To this end, a good research director should endeavor to instill enthusiasm, optimism, and confidence in the research staff—particularly confidence that management is behind their efforts. Rather than point out what may be wrong with a new idea, the director should give it the benefit of the doubt. Whatever he may think personally, he should say, "Sounds like a good idea to me—go ahead and try it!" I must confess I have said this several times when I really didn't mean it, only to find out later that it really was a good idea. And I was thankful that I hadn't killed the idea by being negative.

The research director cannot be up to date in every field under his direction (if he can be up to date in *any* one field, for he has too many other duties). Accordingly, he usually does not have sufficient background with which to judge the idea critically. In order to keep enthusiasm and morale high, the research director must be very careful not to appear negative; even a frown may discourage the timid scientist. It has been my experience that you take very little chance in encouraging him. For if his idea turns out to be a poor one, he will kill it himself.

RESEARCH DIRECTORS MUST BE OPEN-MINDED

This discussion is not theoretical. I once headed a very productive industrial research laboratory. Visitors could feel the enthusiasm that prevailed. Management really wanted new products and everyone knew it. The result was that nearly everyone, including some of the technicians, was constantly on the lookout for a possible new product.

As an example, a laboratory employee who was not a technician said that he understood the company was interested in any new idea, even if it didn't come from a member of the technical staff. I assured him that it was true and listened to his idea. It sounded like a good one to me and I helped him sell it to the division best suited to handle it. The product is still on the market today. I wonder if such an employee could have even gotten in to see the research director in some of the present-day bureaucratic research organizations.

GRANTING OF PATENT DOESN'T END NEED FOR FURTHER PRODUCT DEVELOPMENT

There is only one satisfactory yardstick to measure the productivity of a research organization. It is not the number of patents obtained, a quantity used frequently for this purpose. The yardstick must be the number of *profitable* new products stemming from research.

I was once associated with a research laboratory that had been very productive in terms of patents granted, but no new products were ever introduced to the market. Upon investigation, it was found that the research management had a purely academic background and regarded the granting of a patent as the end of its responsibilities. There seemed to be some vague idea that the marketing people in the company would select patents that were of interest and commercialize the products. Certainly, this is not the way it works.

If the number of successful new products stemming from the research organization is to be the measure of productivity, then it is clear that, in order to score, a decision has to be made to attempt the commercialization of a promising new development. Usually, this is a decision that the research director cannot make alone. If a decision is made not to commercialize, the research department will ordinarily not be able to cite the new development as one of its successful projects. I do know of an instance in which a decision was made not to attempt commercialization of a research development. Somewhat later, however, another company did introduce essentially the same product successfully. Productive research is not the sole responsibility of the research department, and one wonders if there might not be other cases where a research development might have proved fruitful if commercialization had been attempted. There is little I can suggest to avoid such a situation except to observe that the research director must be a good salesman. Management must have confidence in him and be prepared to take some risk if the research effort is to pay off.

PRODUCTIVE RESEARCH GENERATES COMMERCIALLY SUCCESSFUL PRODUCTS

Because the productivity of the research department depends on generating commercially successful products, the organization should be set up to identify promising candidates as early as possible. How is such a candidate to be recognized?

The first indication will be the discovery of at least one unique feature. This feature at the very least must be one that can compete with a similar product already on the market. It should be unique and superior in some way, i.e., either perform better or be cheaper to manufacture. In this case, it will have to be determined whether a market exists or can be created for it.

SUCCESSFUL RESEARCH CALLS FOR A TEAM EFFORT

In any event, an experienced market development person is required to define the nature and extent of the market as well as the prob-

able price that the product could command. It is important to determine the ultimate market potential as soon as possible. I have seen more than one project that was allowed to accumulate costs higher than the market could justify before being terminated. At an early date, the probable selling price should be compared with the estimated production cost in order to determine whether the project should continue or be dropped. The great majority of research developments fail because although the novel features may be very attractive, production costs are higher than the price that the customer will pay.

Returning for a moment to the research laboratory that generated only patents, an applied research group examined the patented materials for unique properties. These were found. One of these materials passed the cost versus selling price test and is now a commercial product. I would like to note, though, that this product would not have made it through the various decision-making levels to the market without the dedicated help of the person who discovered the unique property. I have termed such people "product champions." It is generally true that few products reach the marketplace without the help of a person such as this.

There was a time when it was popular to allow considerable freedom in research. Senior scientists could work in virtually any field they chose. When this was found not to be very productive, the pendulum swung to the extreme opposite position. I believe both extremes are bad. The trouble with research directed toward practical goals is that the management people who decide what is practical are really not qualified to make this judgment in the research area. Likewise, the research scientists usually do not have enough commercial experience or contact with the market to make intelligent selections.

The solution, I believe, is to create strong applied research and market development groups staffed with technically trained people who can evaluate current market needs and trends and suggest areas of research that might be profitable. At the same time, these groups can interact with the research staff who are probably the only people up to date with the frontiers of science and who are therefore best qualified to select promising new areas. Such relatively unexplored areas, are more likely to be productive than the older areas of science. Together they can develop research programs based on up-to-date science that relates to market opportunities as well as the company's place in the market.

THE FINANCIAL EXECUTIVE—
BUSINESS PLANNER OR FINANCIAL
HISTORIAN?

I would like to point out the role that accountants can play in improving the productivity of industrial research. This might sound strange, for often financial executives are the bane of a research scientist's existence. Research is unpredictable, and accountants who want everything to go as planned are often quite disturbed at even relatively minor departures from the budget. The research scientist, however, is apt to regard a budget as something planned before he knew what he now knows.

Many financial executives act like historians. They present you with an accurate record of what you have done, but without much in the way of constructive suggestions as to how you might do better in the future, except "Try to stay closer to the budget!"

By way of contrast, let me cite an incident that occurred when I was the director of a company's central research laboratory. One day, the controller of the division asked me to accompany him to an internal divisional research budget review. "I want you to make recommendations as to what areas of research might be better directed or intensified," he said. "This division is in trouble profit-wise and the manager is recommending cuts in the R & D budget, probably in an attempt to show better profits. In my opinion, this is not what should be done for what he needs are new and more profitable products." Later on, when I became vise president for research, this became standard operating procedure. I attended all the informal divisional budget reviews and I found the opinions of the accounting department very helpful.

The financial executive is the best position to know the broad, in-depth picture of the whole company. If he understands the role of research, he can be of great help in keeping research expenditures in balance and placed where they will do the most good.

Perhaps accountants are being trained in research philosophy in some companies as part of their responsibility in helping to maintain profits. I suspect more and more that research management is beginning to appreciate how helpful these watchdogs can be. If this is not the case, I highly recommend that it be tried.

12
The Six-Step Planning Process

James F. Hind
Vice-President of Planning
R. J. Reynolds Tobacco Company

James Hind asserts that in almost all marketing departments there are two approaches to planning. One is based on an intuitive feel for the marketplace. The other is based on a disciplined, deliberate approach of examining the facts, considering the alternatives, and determining the best strategy.

In almost all marketing departments there are two approaches to planning, the clairvoyant approach and the systematic one.

The clairvoyant planner believes he can cut to the heart of the problem with creativity and experience. He often rushes to conclusions based on his intuitive "feel" for the marketplace.

The systematic marketing planner, on the other hand, knows how to use a disciplined, deliberate approach of examining the facts, considering the alternatives, and determining the best strategy. This planner's approach is based not only on experience and an innovative mind, but also on a thorough understanding of data and alternatives.

The following is a case study in the tobacco industry that uses the deliberate approach successfully. It demonstrates the use of long-range planning in developing strategies for consumer marketing.

In this particular instance, the planning process guided the new products development group of our marketing department by identifying consumer needs and matching them with company needs, forming the basis for a new product concept.

THE PLANNING PROCESS

In order to follow our planning process through the case study, I describe briefly the six steps in the process.

Our first step is to conduct *environmental analyses*. Here we identify major trends, issues, events outside the company. We want to project the environment or marketplace for the coming five years.

The sources are varied, including both formal analyses by our marketing research department or outside firms and a survey of the trade literature or personal interviews with individuals and organizations outside the company. An additional valuable source is line management's own qualitative judgments.

The second step is development if an *external forecast* from these environmental analyses. This forecast "paints the scene" down the road. It identifies the implications of major trends or events, their timing, and the extent of their impact on our company. It thus uncovers critical problems and opportunities.

The third step in our long-range marketing planning is *identification of internal strengths and weaknesses* of each of our brands and our company cigarette line in total.

Fourth, we *extrapolate key marketing issues* based on our external forecasts and our analyses of our product line. We define key issues as significant problems or opportunities that could affect our marketing department's ability to accomplish corporate goals.

At this point, the fifth step, we *develop objectives and strategies* that correspond to these key issues.

Objectives are specific results to be achieved. A strategy describes qualitatively what must be done to accomplish the objective. Emphasis is on the course of action, timing, and the direction in which we allocate resources—not the specific tactics used to implement the strategy.

The last step in our marketing planning process involves *tactics*, or *specific action programs*, used to implement the strategy.

In examining the case study, only those points relevant to this particular example are covered.

ENVIRONMENTAL ANALYSES

The first step began nearly five years ago and covered four areas: economic factors, cigarette categories, consumer values/lifestyles, and demographics.

EXTERNAL FORECAST

Forecasted economic factors that were felt to have a major influence in the future were increasing retail cigarette prices and decreasing consumer purchasing power.

In the area of cigarette categories, we saw three growth segments: menthol, low-tar, and extra-long (100-millimeter) cigarettes.

In consumer values and lifestyles, we saw two trends. First, there was a continued increase in the number of working women, which meant a different set of values and aspirations for women revolving around a career and a strong desire for independence.

Second, there was a significant trend toward new values in both sexes. These new values focused strongly on self-realization and physical enhancement—individualism, if you will, as opposed to the more traditional values centered on the family, community, and nation. These new values had a direct bearing on the consumer's product needs and preferences. Physical enhancement among men had already resulted in several new products and market segments.

Increased fashion consciousness in men led to a market for less conservative business clothing. For example, the John Weitz Palm Beach line combines style with function, offering more alternatives in sportswear. This fashion awareness also carried over to accessories; men's jewelry, watches, and scents have blossomed into lucrative businesses. Who would ever have thought there would be a Chanel for men? Markets for products and services ranging from hairpieces and hair transplants to physical fitness apparatus and clubs have grown tremendously as a direct result of this physical awareness.

Consumer values, then, have a most important influence on consumer needs and preferences that, in turn, indicate directions for the marketing planner. This area must be an important part of external forecasting for any consumer product, because the key to defining real opportunity in the marketplace is seeing people's needs through *their* own eyes.

Another important area in our external forecast was demographics. Here, we noted that the 18 to 34-year-old population "bubble"—a result of the post-war baby boom—was moving through the marketplace. Additionally, our survey data showed quite clearly that more women were smoking more cigarettes.

INTERNAL STRENGTHS AND WEAKNESSES

Our next step was to identify the internal strengths and weaknesses of our total cigarette line. We found that our product line, relative to the population, was:

1. Strongest in the over-35 age group; weakest under 35, particularly among males
2. Strongest among smokers having the older or more traditional values; weakest among those with newer or more contemporary values
3. Strongest in low tar and methols; weakest in the growing, extra-long 100-millimeter cigarette category
4. Strongest in the South and in middle-to-small-population cities; weakest in the Northeast, the West, and large metropolitan areas (such as New York, Los Angeles, San Francisco, Detroit, and so on).

KEY MARKETING ISSUES

Key issues, based on the external forecast and our product line evaluation, were divided into problems and opportunities.

Problems were company line weaknesses in:

1. The growing extra-long cigarette category
2. Smokers having the "new values"
3. The under-35 age group, particularly among males
4. Large urban markets.

Our opportunities were:

1. A strong trend toward increasing retail cigarette prices and decreasing consumer purchasing power, which suggested that extra value (more puffs per cigarette) could be a meaningful benefit.
2. A strong trend among men toward new values—individualism and physical enhancement—suggesting that fashion and style in a cigarette targeted at men would be a meaningful benefit heretofore limited mainly to women.

Additionally, the strong desire of women for independence suggested a new, bolder receptivity on their part to new, adventurous lifestyles and products.

These key issues gave direction to a new cigarette concept at R. J. Reynolds. Through a thorough consumer testing program, a strong new brand concept evolved.

OBJECTIVES AND STRATEGIES

Our objectives for this new brand were:

1. To achieve an incremental 0.8 share of the market in one year
2. To help overcome existing product line demographic and geographic weaknesses.

The result was MORE, a cigarette longer than the extralongs and unique in appearance by virtue of its length (120 millimeters) and its brown cover. Advertising was aimed at positioning MORE in a niche, as yet unoccupied by other cigarette companies, with appeals to style, value (more puffs per cigarette), and self-enhancement.

MORE's advertising is simple and direct, built around the brand name in clever, easy-to-remember headlines noting the benefits it gives to the consumer. For example: "What's MORE. It's longer. It's leaner. It's slower. It's easy drawing. It's a cigarette." The closing copy points out MORE's value: "Over 50% more puffs than a 100 mm cigarette, yet MORE doesn't cost more."

Word play on the name MORE, in fact, was the basis for all the new cigarette's advertising. The value story was pointed out at the point of sale in window posters and counter displays.

MORE quickly achieved close to a 1% share of the market, worth $72 million in annual sales to R. J. Reynolds. In its third year, it continued to grow in sales at a rate approaching 10%, versus a 1% growth rate for the cigarette industry as a whole.

"Cannibalization" is estimated at 20% to 25% of our company line. Our geographic and demographic targets were met.

EPILOGUE

The accelerating changes in our society—in demographics and consumer values and lifestyles—makes development of new products increasingly complex. These changes have to be fully analyzed, understood, and addressed in the planning and product development process if success is to be achieved in today's marketplace.

The cigarette case study is but one example in one industry. There are numerous others that prove the point.

1. *Fragrance industry*. Companies here have demonstrated clearly that they understand and address changing demographics and consumer lifestyles in their marketing efforts. With the United States population slowly approaching zero growth, it is most important to focus on the changing composition of the United States population and identify the rapidly changing age groups and their changing needs.

Charlie perfume recognized the 18 to 34-year-old population "bubble" noted previously and captured the new, young, and more assertive, career-minded woman. Jontue is equally successful in projecting the classical and more old-fashioned feminity, innocence, and romance.

Because women were working, heading families, and being soft and sexy all at the same time, there became an opportunity to market fragrances. Enjoli is the new perfume aimed at this more complex, contradictory woman. Its strategy is to market to the total woman, indicating the acceptance and vitality of her new lifestyle by demonstrating the "attractiveness" of being the working/housewife/sexy woman. Enjoli appeals to the complete woman who can "bring home the bacon, fry it up, and still make him feel like a man."

With the lifestyle change in women, came a similar change in the habits of men. Individuality became most important in the "Me Decade." Whereas women wanted to project a tougher, more career-minded image, men were toning down their tough image and grooming themselves differently to look and smell good to women.

Aramis picked up on this trend and demonstrated itself as a means of establishing that identity with the appeal, "the masculine fragrance *your* woman likes."

2. *Watch industry*. The success of Timex further demonstrates the importance of marketing to emerging trends, specifically individualism and style consciousness.

This brand gained a major share of the watch market by providing a wide range of watch styles to suit individual tastes at inexpensive prices.

3. *Food and Drink industries*. Products here play to the physical fitness and health concerns of Americans and to the increasing number of singles and smaller households.

Dannon demonstrates the goodness of yogurt by noting it is both nutritious and low in fat content. It further demonstrates the product's benefits in today's lifestyle: mobile (carry it anywhere) and single serving (for singles and smaller households).

Perrier makes consumers aware of its naturalness (comes naturally sparkling from Mother Earth) and its French origin, thus appealing to both health concerns and status.

It is surprising enough to see white wine served in place of the martini at lunch, but who would have ever thought you would see bottled water replacing white wine?

13
Pitfalls In The Product Life Cycle

Sonia Yuspeh
Senior Vice-President
J. Walter Thompson Company

Sonia Yuspeh points out the fallacy in the common belief that all products follow a regular life-cycle pattern—usually described in four predictable stages.

The concept of a product life cycle has had wide currency for many years. A review of the extensive literature on this subject indicates that the concept is typcially treated as a useful one, providing practical guidance in the marketing of products.

SHOULD THE PRODUCT LIFE CYCLE BE CHALLENGED?

In view of the widespread treatment of this subject, one might expect that the company which is generally acknowledged to be the leading marketer of consumer packaged goods, Procter and Gamble would be a believer in the concept. Yet such is not the case. In a rare speech by a Procter and Gamble executive, the chief executive officer stated the following view publicly:

In marketing circles, it is popular to talk about the life cycle of products. I am sometimes asked what is our theory on the life cycle of products and my answer is very simple. We don't believe in it.

These are very strong words, but from my vantage point as an advertising researcher,

they appear to be well justified. It is my intention to demonstrate that there are persuasive reasons for questioning the utility of the product life-cycle concept. There is a strong belief, almost to the point of religious fervor by some advocates, that products follow a life cycle and are subject to inevitable mortality after a lapse of a limited number of years. Like so many fascinating but untested theories in economics, the life cycle concept has proved to be remarkably durable and has been expounded eloquently in numerous publications. In fact, its use in professional discussions almost seems to add luster and believability to the insistent claim that marketing is close to becoming a science.

DEFINING THE PRODUCT LIFE CYCLE

Normally, the way to begin discussion of a subject is to start with a definition. But one of the most troublesome aspects of the product life-cycle concept is its difficulty to define. The concept has been borrowed from the biological sciences. It is an attempt to describe the stages that a product goes through from birth to death. In its most generalized form, the life cycle is most typically shown to con-

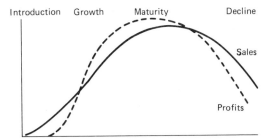

FIGURE 1. Generalized product life-cycle pattern.

sist of the four stages shown in Figure 1.

Looking at the sales curve first (solid line), in the introductory stage, sales are low. They spurt upward during the growth period. There is a leveling off in the maturity stage and finally, the decline stage begins. What about profits (broken line)? Given the investment costs of launching a product, the introductory period yields no profits. During the growth stage, unit profit margins soar. There is downturn in profits during maturity as sales continue to expand. In the decline stage, both volume and profits fall off.

There is considerable appeal in thinking about products in terms borrowed from the biological sciences. But the world of biology and the world of product marketing are vastly different—far too different to draw easy parallels.

Fundamentally, the life cycle of living organisms are characterized by two conditions:

1. The *length* of each stage is fixed in fairly precise terms.
2. The *sequence* of each stage is fixed: each stage follows the next in an immutable, irreversible sequence.

VARIATIONS IN THE LENGTH OF THE PRODUCT LIFE CYCLE

Clearly, neither of these conditions is characteristic of the marketing world. The *length* of the so-called life-cycle stages can vary enormously from one product to the next. Examples come readily to mind. Compare the development and marketing of hair coloring with that of color television. Hair-coloring

products have been available for many generations, but only in recent years have they developed a substantial level of consumer acceptance. And there's still ample room for growth, especially among men. In contrast, the pattern for color television is radically different. The product is an infant compared to hair coloring. It has only been available since the early 1960s and despite initial technical problems and high unit pricing, the acceptance of the product far exceeds that for hair coloring in a far shorter period of time. This is a dramatic contrast used simply to make a point, but if you look over the vast array of marketing case histories, you will find it impossible to make any generalizations about the length of the different stages in the purported life cycle of products.

SEQUENCE OF STAGES

What about the *sequence* of the stages? Here too it is impossible to make generalizations. There is no reversal of direction or skipping of stages in nature, but not so in the world of marketing. The patterns are enormously variable. One life-cycle advocate attempts to put this maze of variability into some semblance of order by postulating six different life-cycle curves. Another authority has developed as many as nine variants. The nine curves (noted by a broken line) and a brief description of each are shown in Figures 2 through 10. Each curve varies in a different way from the generalized pattern (noted by a solid line).

Even without defining these nine patterns of sales performance fully, they are generally recognizable. This seems to be an exercise in semantics. Certainly, it amounts to an admission that the generalized life-cycle model—which covers the four stages of introduction, growth, maturity, and decline—is an inadequate and misleading representation of the marketing of products.

You may have noticed that I haven't defined the term "product" yet. In reviewing the literature on the product life-cycle concept, not only is the "life-cycle" part highly variable, but the same can be said for the term "product." The concept has been applied to product *classes* (for example, cigarettes), to product *forms* (for example, filter cigarettes) and to specific *brands* (for example, Winston filter cigarettes). But whatever the level of aggregation—whether class, form or brand—the utility of the life-cycle concept is questionable.

BROADNESS OF CLASS OF PRODUCTS DETERMINES STABILITY

Although marketers may differ in their definitions of what constitutes a *class* of products,

it is generally recognized that the broader the classification, the more stable it is. Many product classes have enjoyed and probably will continue to enjoy a long and prosperous maturity stage, far more than the human life expectancy of three score years and ten. Good examples are Scotch whiskey and French perfume. Their life span can be measured not in decades but in centuries. Almost as durable are such other product classes as cigarettes, automobiles, radios, mouthwash, soft drinks, cough remedies, face cream, and so on. In fact, broad product classes can be expected to maintain a healthy, vigorous life so long as they continue to satisfy some basic human

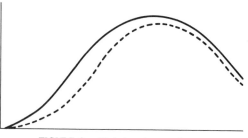

FIGURE 2.   High learning products.

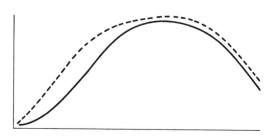

FIGURE 3.   Low learning products.

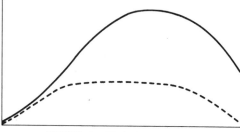

FIGURE 4.   Marketing specialties.

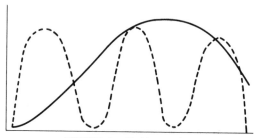

FIGURE 5.   Fashion cycles.

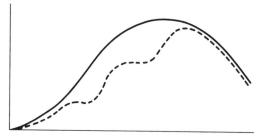

FIGURE 6.   Pyramided cycles.

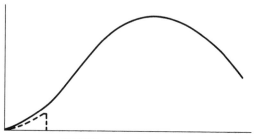

FIGURE 7.   Instant busts.

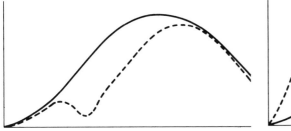

FIGURE 8. Abortive introductions.

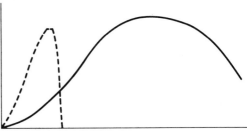

FIGURE 9. Straight fads.

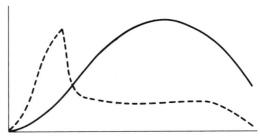

FIGURE 10. Fads with significant market residual.

need such as transportation, entertainment, health, nourishment, or the desire to be attractive.

What about product *form*? Certainly, product forms exhibit less stability than product classes. Form is what many authorities have in mind when they speak of a generalized life-cycle pattern for a "product." Here too the model is not subject to precise formulation. Presumably, there should be some guidelines indicating the movement of a product form from one stage to another. However, exceptions to generalized guidelines are not

hard to find. One example is toilet tissue forms. Figure 11 shows the sales patterns for one-ply and two-ply toilet tissues since 1960. The sales have adjusted to a common base in order to remove such extraneous forces as population growth and inflationary pressures.

Looking at the one-ply pattern, believers of the product life-cycle concept would certainly have concluded by 1965 that one plies were entering a decline stage. But true to their disbelief in the product life-cycle concept, Procter and Gamble did not view the decline as inevitable. They gave strong support to a one-

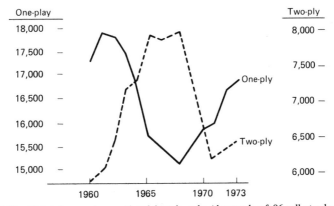

FIGURE 11. Toilet tissue sales—national brands only (thousands of 96-roll standard cased).

ply brand (Charmin), imbued it with a two-ply image (softness), and within a few years, sales for one plies bounced back dramatically. Figure 12 tracks the sales performance for the two leading one-ply brands over this same period of time. Looking at the pattern for Brand A and Brand B, it is not difficult to figure out which one is Charmin.

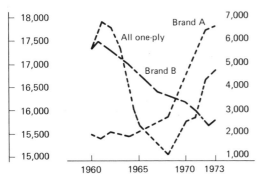

FIGURE 12. One-ply toilet tissue sales (thousands of cases).

ASSOCIATION OF LIFE CYCLE WITH BRANDS

When it comes to *brands*, the concept of a product life cycle is all but meaningless. Yet there are marketing people who guide their management of brands based on a belief in the product life cycle. In cases where they believe their brand is in a decline stage, they pull out all support for the brand. Then, when the brand's sales plummet further for lack of support, they nod with satisfaction about how right they were. They are, in effect, making self-fulfilling prophecies.

One of the most thorough attempts to validate the product life-cycle concept was carried out a few years ago by the Marketing Science Institute. The authors examined over 100 product categories in the food, health, and personal-care fields. They measured the number of observations that did not follow the theorized sequence of introduction, growth, maturity, and decline. They compared these actual observations with simulated sequences

of equal length generated with the aid of random numbers, their purpose being to see whether the product life-cycle model could explain sales behavior better than a chance model could.

We must register strong reservations about the general validity of the product life cycle model, even stated in its weakest, most flexible form. In our tests of the model against real sales data, it has not performed uniformly well against objective standards across a wide range of frequently purchased consumer products nor has it performed equally well at different levels of product sales aggregation.

Some supporters of the product life-cycle contend that its main value is not as a predictive tool. Instead, they focus on a set of marketing guidelines that are considered to be appropriate for each stage of the cycle. Table 1 represents a summary of the types of marketing actions that, according to proponents of the product life-cycle concept, are appropriate for each stage of the cycle. While there is not total unanimity among advocates of the concept on the details of this summary, the basic relationship has been described repeatedly by authorities. In reviewing the guidelines for each of the marketing elements, one can easily find exceptions to the recommended actions.

Camel and Pall Mall cigarettes. Even in a case where a product form has had a prolonged and severe decline (such as nonfiltered cigarettes), it is questionable as to whether a brand should follow the recommended guidelines for the decline stage. Although all the nonfilter brands have had drastic sales losses in the past 20 years, such brands as Camel and Pall Mall continue to be profitable because of their appeal to a hard-core group of committed users. Had the retail price been lowered as advised by the guidelines, the brands would obviously not have been as profitable.

Budweiser beer. This brand has been in a

Table 1. Marketing actions suggested for each stage of the product life cycle

	INTRODUCTION	GROWTH	MATURITY	DECLINE
Competitive Picture	None of importance	Some emulators	Many competing for a small piece of the pie	Few in number with a rapid shakeout of weak members
Overall Strategy	Market establishment; persuade early adopters to try the product	Market penetration; persuade mass market to prefer the brand	Defense of brand position; check inroads of competition	Preparations for removal; milk the brand dry of all possible benefits
Profits	Negligible, because of high production and marketing costs	Reach peak levels at a result of high prices and growing demand	Increasing competition cuts into profit margins and total profits	Declining volume pushes costs up to levels that eliminate profits entirely
Retail Prices	High, to recover some of the excessive costs of launching	High, to take advantage of heavy consumer demand	What the traffic will bear; need to avoid price wars	Low enough to permit quick liquidation of inventory
Distribution	Selective, as distribution is built up slowly	Intensive; employ small trade discounts because dealers are eager to store	Intensive; heavy trade allowances to retain shelf space	Selective; unprofitable outlets slowly phased out
Advertising Strategy	Aim at the needs of early adopters	Make the mass market aware of brand benefits	Use advertising as a vehicle for differentiation among otherwise similar brands	Emphasize low price to reduce stock
Advertising Weight	High, to generate awareness and interest among early adopters; persuade dealers to stock the brand	Moderate, to let sales rise on momentum of word-of-mouth recommendations	Moderate, because most buyers are aware of brand characteristics	Minimum expenditures required to phase out the product
Consumer Sales and Promotion Expenditures	Heavy, to entice target groups with samples, coupons, and other inducements	Moderate, to create brand preference (advertising better suited to do this job)	Heavy, to encourage brand switching, hoping to convert some buyers into loyal users	Minimal, to let the brand coast by itself

maturity stage for many years. According to the guidelines for this stage, its advertising weight should be moderate because most buyers are aware of the brand's characteristics. Indeed, a widely heralded experimental program undertaken by Anheuser-Busch in the 1960s demonstrated that the brand was heavily overspending in advertising—that it could halve its advertising budget without any loss in sales. In recent years, however, Budweiser has dramatically escalated its advertising weight because of the aggressive marketing of Miller Highlife and Miller Lite. Had it maintained the moderate spending levels recommended by the product life-cycle proponents, it is highly doubtful that it could have retained its leading share position.

Considering the many pitfalls of the product life-cycle concept, one could well ask why it has appeal in some circles. Perhaps the answer lies, in part, with the "romance" of new products.

In the rush to enter the new products arena that characterized the 1960s, there was a tendency in some companies to ignore the old standby brands and lavish time and money on the "new babies" in the house. How comforting it is in such cases to find a rationale for doing this by citing the product life-cycle concept.

But the demise of old brands is by no means inevitable. It is easy enough to cite many examples of old brands that have retained their vitality. Here are some so-called old brands that readily spring to mind: Anacin, Budweiser, Bufferin, Coca-Cola, Camel, Colgate, Crisco, Drano, Dristan, Geritol, Ivory, Jell-O, Kelloggs, Kleenex, Kodak, Kraft, Listerine, Maxwell House, Planters, Tide, Windex.

In contrast to these thriving old brands, the annals of business are full of records of once strong and prosperous brands that have died because of neglect and diversion of attention to new brands. A good example is the case of Ipana. This toothpaste was marketed by a leading packaged goods company until 1968 when it was abandoned in favor of launching

new brands. In 1969, two Minnesota businessmen picked up the Ipana name, developed a new formula, but left the package unchanged. With hardly any promotion, the petrified demand for Ipana turned out to be $250,000 in the first seven months of operation. In 1973, a survey conducted by Target Group Index showed that, despite poor distribution, this toothpaste was still being used by 1,520,000 adults. Considering the limited resources of the current owners, the brand would probably have been in an even stronger position had it been retained and given appropriate marketing support by its original parent company.

The experience of many companies demonstrates that attention to new products need not be at the expense of the old. Clairol, for example, has introduced a steady stream of new hair coloring products, yet it has continued to provide support to one of its initial entries, Loving Care. In the same vein, Procter and Gamble has launched many detergent products over the years, yet Tide, the first detergent they launched, continues to dominate the market thanks to steady marketing support and constant product improvements—altogether a remarkable total of 55 significant product changes in its 29-year history, according to a Procter and Gamble spokesman.

All the evidence we have seen clearly indicates that a product's life cycle is a *dependent* variable that can be influenced by marketing actions; it is *not* an *independent* variable to which companies should adapt their marketing programs. It is useful, in this regard, to examine the varying fortunes of brands that at one point in their histories had roughly equal share levels. Using a 15-year time frame from 1961 to 1976, four such cases are noted in the following.

Deodorants. In 1961, Secret and Five Day had roughly equal shares. By 1976, Secret's share had zoomed to about six times that of Five Day.

Fragrances. In the perfume/cologne category, Arpege had a slight edge on Chanel 15 years ago. Now Arpege's share is only a fourth as large as Chanel's.

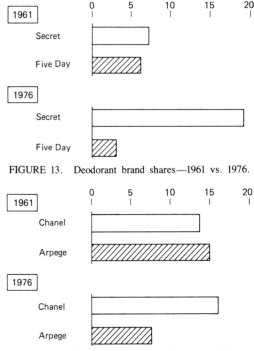

FIGURE 13.　Deodorant brand shares—1961 vs. 1976.

FIGURE 14.　Perfume/cologne brand shares—1961 vs. 1977.

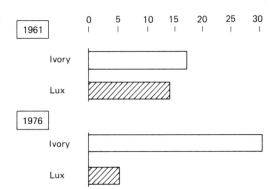

FIGURE 16.　Soap brand shares—1961 vs. 1976.

of how it is the marketing effort of the manufacturer—not some inherent life-cycle factor—that explains why one brand fared well and another fared poorly. For example, in the case of Ivory and Lux, each brand took a different approach to the marketplace. Through the years, Ivory continues to talk to the consumer through advertising. Lux did not. Here are the figures:

Advertising Expenditures (000)

	1961	1966	1971	1975
Ivory	$800.5	$820.9	$4,443.6	$5,830.4
Lux	195.9	420.0	0.8	0.4

Lux did not withdraw support from the brand. What they chose to do was to spend their money almost exclusively on trade and consumer promotions. Following these policies over a 15-year period, Ivory's share had almost doubled. In contrast, Lux had less than half the share it did previously. Obviously, it was not some magical product life cycle that made the difference; it was the marketing policies of the two brands.

Lux had virtually stopped advertising and this was the major difference. But what actually happened? If you stop advertising, do consumers forget about you? The answer is no, according to some recent consumer research.

We found that women today are just as aware of Lux as they are of Ivory. In fact, everyone has heard of both brands. Yet despite the fact that women are well aware of

Shampoos. Lustre Creme had a respectable share in 1961, not far behind Prell. By 1976, Lustre Creme's share had dwindled to less than a tenth of Prell's.

Bar Soaps. In 1961, Lux was trailing Ivory but only a few share points. Fifteen years later, Ivory's share was about five times greater than Lux.

It is instructive to examine the variations in marketing efforts put behind brands such as those mentioned to provide an understanding

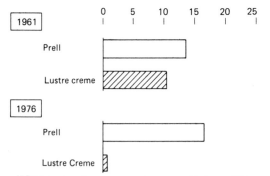

FIGURE 15.　Shampoo brand shares—1961 vs. 1976.

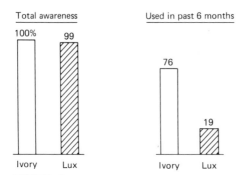

FIGURE 17.   Awareness and use of soap brands.

both brands, they buy Ivory. As shown above, 76% of all women have used Ivory in the last six months, but only 19% of all women have used Lux. Why? If women are just as aware of both brands, what makes them choose Ivory over Lux?

It is not that Lux is not well thought of—even today. We checked among people who *used* to use Lux to find out what they thought of the product.

As shown in Figure 18, nearly 42% of the past users think it is a good brand and they might buy it again sometime. But it is unlikely that they will buy the product again unless Lux gives them a reason to do so.

FIGURE 18.   Soap brand impressions among past users.

EFFECT OF ADVERTISING ON LIFE CYCLE

If Lux does not start communicating with these people, they may continue to have good thoughts about Lux, but they probably won't do anything about it. Their good thoughts about Lux are not being reinforced, whereas their good thoughts about Ivory and other leading brands are continually being reinforced through advertising.

The vitality of Lux in Europe, where it is a leading brand, suggests that the brand could have maintained its franchise in the United States had advertising support not been withdrawn. This is not meant to imply that promotion does not have an important role. It can be a necessary defensive tool and a tiebreaker in highly competitive markets. But it cannot, by itself, compete with another brand's advertising.

The Lux and Ivory comparisons and the varying fortunes of Lux in the United States and Europe demonstrate that a product's life cycle is not an independent variable. It is dependent upon the marketing actions taken on behalf of the brand. Being in advertising, I chose a case demonstrating the value of a particular marketing action—advertising—to prolong the life of a brand. Obviously, there are other marketing actions that can maintain and expand a brand's franchise:

1. Successive *product reformulations* of Tide to keep pace with detergent improvements
2. *Repositioning* of Johnson's baby shampoo as a product for adults
3. Addition of new *forms* for Ban Deodorant
4. Broadened *distribution* of Revlon cosmetics
5. Continued *recipe variations* for Jell-O puddings and gelatin.

FACTORS AFFECTING LIFE CYCLE

Admittedly, there are cases where no amount of marketing genius can salvage a declining sales picture. Here are some obvious examples:

1. *Technological changes.* As soon as refrigerators hit the marketplace, ice boxes were doomed.
2. *Changing consumer perceptions.* Once the hazards of smoking became known, all nonfilter brands were in deep trouble.
3. *Adverse brand publicity.* With the devastating publicity stemming from a case of botulism poisoning, Bon Vivant soups were not able to survive.

Short of dramatic cases such as these, *if* a product can offer benefits to consumers, *if* it has not been outdated by technological improvements, *if* consumers continue to value its benefits, and *if* consumer confidence has not been shaken by adverse publicity, then it should be possible for a brand to retain its vitality.

It would be an exaggeration to say that one of the greatest disservices of the product life-cycle concept to marketing is that it has caused top executives to overemphasize new product introduction, although this route is fraught with innumerable perils. Experience has shown clearly that nothing seems to take more time, cost more money, involve more pitfalls, or cause more anguish than new product programs.

Actual statistics are hard to obtain, but it is generally believed in business circles that the odds are four to one against emerging with a winner. Yet, like a new baby in the house, the new product too often gets all the attention, while the older brands are pretty much neglected.

This is in no way intended to suggest that new product introduction should come to an abrupt halt. But one should not regard this avenue as the only insurance against the future. However vital tomorrow's products may be—and undoubtedly they are very important—it is today's products that are closest to the cash register and upon which the company's chance of generating more profit normally depends. It is unfortunate that corporations invest millions of dollars to build goodwill for a brand, then just walk away from it and spend additional millions all over again for a new brand name with no consumer franchise.

Admittedly, many large corporations can afford to have both new and old products on their roster. But even their resources are not unlimited, with the result that the marketing budget for each brand gets progressively smaller as the number of items expands. No wonder then that the brand death rate is on the increase. Obviously, this mortality is because of lack of sufficient nourishment to survive, and has nothing to do with the blind operation of the life-cycle forces.

To sum up, the product life-cycle theory has little validity at any level of aggregation, be it product class, product form, or brand. Advocates of this concept specify certain marketing strategies for the brand at each stage of the cycle. Some of the recommendations are misleading, while others are based strictly on common sense and do not suggest anything different from what would have been carried out in normal circumstances. In some respects, the concept has done more harm than good by persuading top executives to neglect existing brands and place undue emphasis on new products.

The 1960s were a period of growing affluence, cheap energy, limitless supplies, and rising public expectations. This brought about brand proliferation, product parity, and market segmentation to an extreme. The scenario has now changed considerably.

SOARING BRAND PROLIFERATION

Inflation, shortages, and slow economic growth are the new by-lines. As a result, soaring brand proliferation no longer makes sense. The emphasis should shift from spouting out new "me-too" products to prolonging the productive life of existing brands through sound and solid marketing support.

The key to product vitality lies with the basic marketing concept—satisfying consumer needs. So long as a product class or form or brand continues to be relevant to consumer needs, it should prosper in the marketplace whether it is two, 20, or 50 years.

As the head of Procter and Gamble has observed, "In our experience, it isn't enough to invent a new product and to introduce it in the market. The real payoff is to manage that brand in such a way that it continues to flourish year after year in a changing and competitive marketplace."

14
Potential Markets in Coming Years*

J. Herbert Holloman
Director
MIT Center for Policy Alternatives

Anyone interested in organizing or investing in a new business must know what changes are taking place in the market and what the potential of that market is. The author discusses the social and political changes that are now taking place and the opportunities that these changes present.

Adult education, hospital management, pollution control, mass transportation, day-care centers—these are only a few of the areas that will provide vast new markets for the resourceful entrepreneur in the coming years.

This may seem to you a basic transformation of the relationship between business and the society that supports it. To a certain extent, this is right. This transformation is already taking place. Yet, in another sense, the change has its roots in the same business strategy and tactics that helped American industry to achieve the position it now holds.

Anyone who was ever interested in organizing or investing in a new business had to be aware of two factors for success. First, he had to know what changes in the market might alter its future character radically. Second, even when he had identified a future need, he had to be sure that a market actually existed.

THE POST-INDUSTRIAL SOCIETY

These two conditions are as valid today as they were 50 years ago. What has changed is the environment. No longer is it enough to evaluate economic and technical factors. Key events that now determine the ultimate acceptability of technology and its timing are often social and political.

You can experience such an environment today if you take a drive in certain sections of Maine. You might go on for ten miles and not see another car. There is no continual interaction. Traffic safety, for example, is less of a problem. If there are only a few automobiles on the road, they don't pollute the atmosphere and they don't run into each other.

Let me return to the example of traffic safety. The more cars on the road, the more safety becomes a problem. Yet, it is obviously not an individual problem. There is no sense in my paying $15,000 for a safe, nonpolluting automobile if no one else invests in antipollution devices and if there is no overall safety system that insures that someone will not demolish my expensive car.

*Chapter 14 was adapted from the September, 1970 issue of *Innovation*.

The problem of safety then becomes a collective community problem. The new markets will be such community markets. The social and environmental effects of technology have created urgent needs. Most of these needs have yet to be integrated into a real and profitable market, but the opportunity is there.

GROWTH MARKETS IN THE SERVICE INDUSTRY

As I remarked earlier, business in the past tended to deal with the individual, primarily to provide him with material things. However, as our society grows more affluent, the market for material things will decrease slowly. A need (consequently a possible market) for services that increase the quality of life will rapidly take its place.

This tendency is already evident in our young people. Looking at the most vocal group, there are now more than seven and a half million young men and women in American colleges. They form a vast new class of people. This new group is fundamentally different from that which we have experienced before.

They are children of the middle class and have reached a higher level of need than just for material things. Their prime interest is not a house, a car, and a color television. Most are interested in creating situations that bring joy and spontaneity, and permit freedom and self-expression. They envision their work in these terms and are determined to make the business world serve the needs of society.

If existing businesses (and those being contemplated) fail to acknowledge such a radical cultural change, they will cut themselves off from many new market opportunities and, in certain instances, find themselves in a totally hostile environment.

GOVERNMENT LEGISLATION—CLUE TO POTENTIAL MARKETS

The third factor that influences the new markets and that the entrepreneur can use to his own advantage is government legislation.

For example, the Traffic Safety Act created a vast new market for safety devices. Yet, almost without exception, the American auto industry fought this legislation. Their short-sightedness worked against their long-term best interests. The legislation opened the industry for a great deal of innovation in the way automobiles are designed and built. You no longer have to depend on style to sell a car, but can point to its increased safety. It has been estimated that a very significant portion of auto sales was a result of the safety devices. An example is the bumper that can absorb collision impacts at low speeds with no damage to the body of the car. Although power brakes were not included in the legislation, note how large a segment of car buyers want cars with power brakes.

However, the point is that such legislation will be necessary in many other areas if we are going to create new social markets and thus foster innovation and deal with our community needs.

Take the obvious case of water and air pollution. Paper companies seldom adopt an expensive program of antipollution voluntarily. This increases their costs. If a competitor in a different section of the country decides not to bear these costs, the first company is at a serious disadvantage in the marketplace.

Our free market system causes neither manufacturer to install antipollution devices. In a free market system based on profit making alone, there is little incentive to do it. The company hurts its stockholders and jeopardizes its own existence because it just isn't profitable. A company cannot "do good for society" if it isn't profitable. It would cease to exist.

The way to solve such problems is to make uniform rules for all companies in the same business or general region. Every competitor will have to use such-and-such antipollution devices. Besides solving an environmental problem, legislation would open up new markets and provide incentives for people to develop the cheapest and most effective antipollution devices. Such legislation is definitely on the way, and a smart businessman will begin now to take advantage of it and encourage it.

For example, the sulfur dioxide put into the air by coal-burning electric plants must be reduced. In the future, we will need more and more electric power; there is just not enough low-sulfur coal or oil. The person who can develop a way to get the sulfur out before it leaves the smokestack is going to make a good deal of money someday.

MAKE PLANS EARLY—DON'T WAIT FOR LEGISLATION

There is no need, however, to sit back and wait for the legislation. If I were in such a situation, I would work as hard as I could to get federal or state laws requiring standard safety rules. This is the prime tool at my disposal for creating the market for my product.

A friend of mine in California used just such a tactic. The state legislature allocated $5 to 6 million for research on highway safety. He happened to be experimenting with the automatic control of vehicles entering the roadway at different points. The allocation, when spread around, was not large enough to make for a profitable market, nor did it give a company much play to develop new devices.

Eventually the legislature increased the appropriation and my friend was able to increase the size of the market and consequently build a bigger company.

THE JUNIOR COLLEGE MARKET

The junior college could easily be operated by private contractors to the municipality. The ideal would be to operate a chain of such colleges. If there were companies that had 40 or 50 schools of the same general character, they could afford to develop or purchase expensive technology.

The thing we must remember when engaging in this type of speculation is that a company can earn a great deal of money in any of

these fields if it can do a better job than existing institutions. Serving the needs of society and achieving a good return on your investment are not mutually exclusive goals.

THE MARKET FOR PRIVATE HOSPITALS AND DAY-CARE CENTERS

In this vein, another institution that could be vastly improved and turned into a profit-making operation is the private hospital. There have always been some profit-making hospitals, but what few there are cater solely to the very wealthy. But if someone were to join a string of private hospitals into a chain, similar to many hotel chains, he could afford to offer the service to middle-income groups. He would get the advantage of consistent management, record keeping, accounting services—with a central office handling all the administrative problems for the whole chain as well as centralization (or regionalization) of such services as purchasing, laundry, and food services.

This would cut the cost of running hospitals to the degree that they could become profit-making businesses.

The cost of getting sick is rising much faster than people are willing to pay. If you can reduce the cost, you are most certainly going to have a market. Stopping short of a chain of hospitals, there are many other ways to cut costs.

For instance, everyone is aware of the rapidly rising cost per day of staying at a hospital. Almost 75% of this cost is a result of the constant availability and service rendered by nurses and doctors, and everything else that goes with intensive care. Now, a significant fraction of the people in hospitals don't need this kind of service. In a few places I know, motel type businesses are being built next to hospitals. They handle people who are semi-outpatients and provide a modest amount of service. They can do this for approximately 60% of the daily cost of staying at a hospital. This is a way of substantially cutting hospital costs and still making a profit.

Along this same line, very few institutions have done anything at all about setting up day-care centers. With the advent of the women's liberation movement and the push to reduce the welfare rolls, this could become an enormous market.

THE MARKET FOR MORE EFFICIENT FIRE PROTECTION

There are many other societal markets in which the ability to cut costs could be the basis for a profitable business. Fire protection is one of them. In this country, we have one of the highest rates of serious fires, both loss of life and property damage, of any country in the world. Japan, for example, is better than we are by a factor of six or eight.

The only way we are going to solve this problem is through uniform fire-protection systems required by legislation. As Assistant Secretary of Commerce for Science and Technology, I helped introduce some modest legislation along this line. Yet the people selling fire protection devices never really saw the necessity for legislation to guarantee them a large and growing market. The Fire Safety Act was passed but there were never any funds made available for research and development and field testing. Note, however, how the use of smoke alarms has increased in popularity.

It must be obvious by now that the attitude of business towards government legislation must change. Until now, the free enterprise system has in the main resisted government regulation or interference. Yet the opposite has to be true. The free enterprise system does not operate where the costs or benefits are to the whole community and not to the individual buyer.

An individual company, as in the fire-protection business, should press for legislation. This would be in their own interest. They should lobby for R&D funds in the same way that the DOD (Department of Defense) and its subcontractors obtain their allocation.

However, at this point, going beyond the necessity of legislation, you might be asking yourself "How do I gain entrance into these markets to know what they really need and to find out how to market the product once it's developed?"

Let's return to the fire-protection business. One man I know from the Rand Corporation didn't do anything for a year except gain the confidence of the men in the fire department of New York City. He spent most of his time with the firemen, riding on trucks, in the station house, or at lunch.

It dawned on him that the department wasn't organized around the statistical facts of where and when most fires occur. It turned out that most fires happened between 7:00 P.M. and 2:00 A.M. Immediately, this pattern should tell you something about how to distribute your men.

Further, most fires took place in ghetto and slum areas of the city. This should indicate where to concentrate your men and equipment. Such data are also an indicator of which houses are going downhill, a source that can aid fire departments in prevention efforts by instructing them where to concentrate inspections and repairs.

It would not be very difficult for a company representative to learn, in this manner, about the disposition of fire stations, most efficient size of engines, information systems, means of anticipation, and early warning.

For example, New York City spends hundreds of millions of dollars a year on men and equipment for fire fighting. And this has been increasing at the rate of 15% a year. If a company could do something about reducing the amount of equipment needed, or its operating and replacement costs, they might capture an enormous market. Everyone knows how effective it would be to add a wetting agent to the stream of water coming from the hose. Yet no one has as yet developed the little gadget necessary to do this. If it were done, you could reduce the size of the hose from 2-½ inches to 1-½ inches. Then only one man is needed to carry the hose instead of two.

There are other questions a company can ask itself. What size ought fire equipment to be? Is it better that the engine stay in one place and wait for fires, or should they be cruising like police cars? What does this tell us about how to change the equipment we manufacture?

I know of a man who received a contract from a Southwestern city to run a fire department. He designed and built a special fleet of smaller trucks. He says that big trucks are ridiculous. It is too hard to cruise in them, you can't get the trucks you need for the money that you have to spend, and they're too cumbersome to get to a fire as quickly as they should. This is the kind of innovative thinking that can help the fire-protection business.

MASS TRANSPORTATION

Fire departments are not the only market in need of speed amnd efficiency. If you add convenience and comfort, you have the four demands people are making of mass transportation. How do you begin to think about this market? First of all, you have to realize that transportation in and out of the city has become much more efficient and easier in the last 20 years. If this was not so, there would be less movement to the suburbs. The trip time has decreased regularly in every city in the United States except New York and San Francisco. This is because one is an island and the other a peninsula, so there are fewer points of entrance and exit. Too many people trying to squeeze through small pipes: that is a problem not found in the rest of the country.

Given the fact that transportation has steadily improved, how do you make it better? If you don't, it is obviously liable to get worse. I don't think the best solution involves subway and bus systems. All the evidence shows that as soon as you get wealthy enough you buy a car and ride in it. You want the convenience of getting into your own car and ending up exactly where you want to be.

For example, during the six years I was in Washington I never rode a bus. Not even

once. They never went where I wanted to go. The only people who ever ride the bus in Washington are those who can't afford any other means of transportation. If you want to reduce the amount of money spent on highways to and from the city, maintenance, congestion, smog, and every other source of expense, you have to reduce the number of cars on the road. (This would free a great deal of money that could then be plowed back into inner-city mass transportation.)

What you obviously need is the convenience of an automobile and efficiency of a bus. If I wanted to go to National Airport, I would pick up my phone and say "I need transportation within the next ten minutes to the airport." This can be done today.

A company can have vehicles of the proper size, holding eight to ten people, which are nonrouted and hooked up to a central computer. Such systems are now large enough to handle this kind of load. The computer then assigns the vehicle to pick up so many people along a convenient path. They get their individual transportation, conveniently and efficiently, and they don't have to find a parking space or pay the costly fare of an ordinary taxi ride. They ride a "taxi-bus." This is already being done in some suburban communities, but on a far too limited basis.

COPING WITH THE VESTED INTERESTS

Now the difficulty is, how does a company get started in this type of endeavor. The bus manufacturers don't want to do it because they have vested interests in big buses. Taxi companies won't do it for the same reason. There are only two answers—either get the needed legislation or corner a monopoly on ground transportation from one point to another. In Washington, one bus company has now become large enough to deal with the problem and has a franchise for all airport services.

It seems to me that this is one of the major ways to deal with our transportation problems immediately. We can't put subways where everyone wants to go. We can't put enough buses in a city or suburb to satisfy everyone. In my view, the market for a taxi-bus system seems so enormous and so predetermined that I am genuinely surprised that no one has attempted to develop such a system on a large scale.

DEALING WITH THE POLITICIANS

I suppose that some disgruntled innovator (or, conversely, a put-upon status-quo executive) would react to my surprise with another question. "How can I deal with politicians who, as the case may be, either understand or don't understand, and who are either for me or against me?

I have often heard scientists and engineers say that more of our politicians ought to have technical backgrounds, implying that they would then understand the problems of engineering and science and thus not expect too much or too little.

In response I would say that I have never had a problem with lawmakers failing to understand the consequences of technology. And that is all they need to understand. It isn't necessary that they know what goes on inside the black box. It is definitely wise for a politician to have some trust and appreciation for people who work inside the black box, but I think it is also very unlikely that someone trained in science and engineering will make a good politician.

I think we ought to turn the statement around. It is the technical people who ought to learn how to speak the politician's language and understand how the political process actually works.

The politician is a catalyst trying to balance a system that encourages private enterprise to innovate and be profitable, but which also protects the public. He is the embodiment of Woodrow Wilson's political theory— a mediator between public and private interests. Yet, if approached properly, he is still interested in creating new markets for business. He can do this through legislation.

An example of doomed and misguided opposition can be found in the drug industry's fight against federal control. Politically (if not morally), it is wrong to fight such supervision. The government, having stepped into the field of regulation, is responsible in the eyes of the public for any ill effects that may result from the use of certain drugs. On this score, each politician has to answer to his constituency.

The Puritan ethic of hard work and free enterprise must somehow combine with the necessity of protecting the public. This requires a fundamental change in attitude on the part of businessmen toward legislation. In the past, the general reaction has been that legislation is restrictive. Yet, even his own self-interest should prompt the businessman to say "I'm in favor of legislation that opens my business to new possibilities."

MONITORING THE POLITICAL ENVIRONMENT

In order to catch wind of such legislation, an executive has to monitor the political environment and evaluate the signals of social change. Government actions that underwrite some new technology or finance a certain study ought to be watched very closely and evaluted in their particular context.

Occasionally, we can pick up a strong signal in the appointment of a specially talented man to a government department or bureau. Knowing his goals, interests, and opinions can often help a company to determine what markets it can open up through legislation and which markets will be closed for the next four years.

I have already mentioned one signal of social change—the culture of the young—but others are not hard to come by. Use of leisure time, occupational interests, the growth of poverty, crime, drug addiction, pollution, or a shift in the winds of political opinion—all these are valid indications of social change.

Anyone trying to sustain a present business, or start a new one, must have his ear to the ground. He must identify social needs and use the same expertise to meet them as he used to sell his products to individual buyers. He ought to be able, with a little insight, to serve the community and make a profit at the same time.

The principles discussed in this chapter refer to profit-making hospitals, day-care centers, pollution control, fire prevention, mass transportation, adult education, and junior colleges. In all these areas, I indicated large and potentially profitable markets. But what about crime prevention and detection, constructing schools from modular units so they can easily change with the child population, running effective prisons and drug addiction centers, providing services for the aged? You take it from here.

15
Improving Sales Force Productivity

Porter Henry
Porter Henry & Company, Inc.

Porter Henry explains the various yardsticks that can be used for measuring and improving productivity of the sales force.

A necessary first step in any program designed to increase sales force productivity is to determine how to measure productivity. The nature of the improvement effort, its chances of success, and indeed the behavior of the sales force are influenced by the measurements selected.

MEASUREMENTS OF PRODUCTIVITY

Much has been written about methods of measuring the productivity of the total sales force and the individual salesperson, yet there can be no universal method.

The best advice is for the sales manager to measure his salesmen by whatever yardstick his management measures him. If the top brass is gung-ho for a bigger share of market, then that becomes the key measurement applied to each salesman. If, as in most companies, the top executive primarily looks to the sales force for its profit contribution, then profit contribution becomes the measurement the sales manager will try to improve.

Sales Volume—Least Useful Measure

Total dollar sales, by the entire force and each individual, is the most widely used measurement, and at the same time the one that is least useful as a guide to sales force productivity.

Top management's most frequent criticism of sales managers is that they pursue volume without regard for profits. Profitless volume is no way to make the board of directors and stockholders happy. Similarly, where two salesmen turn in identical sales dollars, one may be making a handsome contribution to profit and the other operating at a loss, when total costs and expenses are considered.

Another difficulty with total sales volume as a yardstick of productivity is that it is the one measurement most subject to fluctuations for reasons beyond the control of the sales force: prices, competitive activity, economic conditions, product quality, advertising effectiveness, and so on.

A sales force might increase its effectiveness by every other measure, and still show a decrease in dollar volume if competition comes up with a better and less expensive product.

We all have to live with sales volume figures because they are the basis for forecasting, budgeting, and analysis. But how effectively the sales force is performing, or which individuals are doing the best job, is

145

not disclosed by dollar volume figures, an extremely fuzzy measurment.

Sales vs. Quota or Potential

If sales quotas are set with realism and judgment, or if sales potentials can be measured accurately, then each salesman's performance against quota or potential is a valid measurement of how well he is doing or where he needs to improve. Similarly, achievement of quota or of some sales objective based on market potential is a good indicator of whether the total sales force is fulfilling its responsibilities.

Sales-Producing Activities

When it is difficult to measure the salesman's direct effect upon sales, as in the case of a "merchandiser" for advertised consumer goods, the salesman is often measured in terms of activities that are presumed to influence sales, such as number of displays built, amount of shelf space obtained, and so on.

Profit Contribution

Another type of measurement is the contribution to profit and overhead made by the sales force, or by the individual salesperson. This figure is obtained by totaling the margin or markup on all products sold, and subtracting direct costs such as salesmen's compensation, travel and entertainment expenses, and communications costs.

Using ROAM

Top executives evaluate a potential investment in terms of its projected return on investment. Why not measure a sales force in terms of the return on capital invested in it?

This relatively sophisticated measurement is obtained by taking the profit contribution (described above) and dividing it by the capital tied up in the sales force, primarily accounts receivable, warehouse inventories, autos, and other equipment provided to the salesmen.

Instead of the cumbersome phrase "return on assets invested in the sales force," Doctors Michael and Jack Schiff call it *return on assets managed* by the sales force, shortened to the acronym ROAM.

Quantifying ROAM

Figure 1 illustrates the various steps in the selling process that culminate in the return on assets managed. Each step in this chain can serve to some degree as a measure of sales force productivity, with the accuracy of the measurement increasing as one moves along the chart from left to right.

Starting at the left, the sales dollars produced by the sales force result from the number of calls made, the quality or effectiveness of the calls, and the allocation of sales effort among the various types and sizes of customers and prospects. The quality of calls has an effect on a salesman's ability to hold the price line or at least get the maximum possible prices.

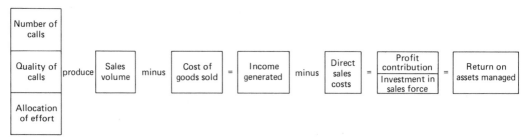

Figure 1.   Return on asset management (ROAM).

If we subtract the cost of goods sold from total sales volume, we get a measure of the gross income generated by the sales force. If we subtract from this direct sales cost, we have a measure of profit contribution. Dividing this measure by assets invested in or managed by the sales force gives us ROAM—return on assets managed.

Many companies simply keep track of the number of sales calls as indicated by daily or weekly sales reports and total sales dollars.

The quality of calls can be monitored in a number of ways, especially if a computer is available. Possible measurement ratios are average dollar sales per call, gross profit dollars per call, number of calls per order written, or number of items sold per order.

WHY IS PRODUCTIVITY BELOW PAR?

Before launching any effort to improve productivity, it is important to ascertain the probable causes of any lower-than-targeted productivity level. Figure 1 can serve as a framework.

Is the sales force making too few calls? If so, should the size of the force be increased, or should the existing salesmen be shown how to route themselves more effectively and to handle nonselling chores in less time?

Here, as in every aspect of improving sales performance, an important question is "Can I improve this aspect of sales performance by training salesmen in this skill, or can I more easily provide some type of SOP (standard operating procedure) that would improve performance automatically? For example, should I train salesmen in the skills of classifying customers, establishing call frequencies, and routing themselves effectively, or should we develop a standard 'cookbook' procedure for covering the territory?"

If the number of calls seems adequate but results are not, one suspects that the quality of the calls is not what it should be. But here again, it pays to do a bit of analysis before rushing into a sales training program.

1. Do the salesmen have the *information* they need? Are they adequately informed about the product or service and its application, maintenance, or usage? Do they know all they should know about the customer's problems and objectives—collectively and as applied to the individual customer?

2. Do they have the ability to *communicate* the sales message effectively? Do they know how to plan the call? Have they been drilled to talk in terms of customer benefits rather than product features? Do they realize that questioning and listening are as important as talking? Would some type of visual aid help them tell a better organized story?

3. How well do they relate to *people*? Are they sensitive to the buyer's reactions? How well do they handle complaints? Can they say no in a diplomatic way?

The third input item is a key one for many companies: how well is the salesman allocating his efforts? Is he working hard to sell more of the profitable specialty products or is he devoting too much time to the low-profit commodity types? Is he spending too much or too little time on nonbuying prospects? Is he spending too much time with small or unprofitable accounts?

Answers to these questions enable the sales manager to determine where he can most profitably invest time and money in upgrading the performance of the sales force.

METHODS OF INFORMING AND TRAINING THE SALES FORCE

There are basically three methods of imparting knowledge or skills to the sales force: (1) self-study materials, such as literature, tapes or other materials sent directly to the individual salesperson; (2) sales meetings, national or local; and (3) on-the-job coaching by the salesman's immediate manager or by a special trainer.

In general, information—on products, prices, market conditions—can be transmitted directly to the sales force. Skill training, however, is more effective at meetings and most effective in the form of field coaching.

Individual Study Materials

Material sent to salesmen can be classified as semi-permanent, like sales manuals, or current, such as periodic bulletins.

On the permanent side, a good sales manual can be valuable in breaking in new salesmen and can serve as a reference book to experienced salesmen. A good sales manual includes company and industry background, complete product and application information, definition of all relevant company policies, instructions on all forms and reports from salesman to company and from company to salesman, a clear description of compensation plans, and even some practical pointers on how to cover a territory and how to sell the products.

Monthly bulletins or newsletters are prized by salesmen if they are concise and contain useful information and sales tips.

Some companies equip their salesmen with cassette tape recorders so that salesmen can listen to company news bulletins or training programs while driving or during evenings in motel rooms.

Ready-made training programs on scores of subjects, in the form of texts, correspondence courses, programmed instruction, and tapes are also available.

Sales Meetings

The annual sales meeting, in addition to splashy introductions of new products and inspiring speeches by the brass, can also be a vehicle for some good solid sales training. If the audience is too large for participative types of training, it can be subdivided into smaller groups.

Role playing or simulated practice of sales calls is often resented by salesmen as being embarrassing. Yet, if handled right, it can be the most effective form of training.

Rather than subject a salesman to possible humiliation by asking him to role-play a sales call in front of a large group, we at Porter Henry & Company often send salesmen off to separate rooms in groups of five.

Each salesman is given background information on a hypothetical customer or prospect and is given 15 minutes to prepare the call. One person makes the call on a second group member acting as the customer, while a third member acts as conference leader and the remaining two serve as observers. After each call has been made and analyzed, using a scorecard as a guideline, roles rotate. No executive or trainer is present except by invitation.

Even the most hard-bitten veteran salesmen find it interesting to see how four other salesmen make calls. They do not resent taking their turn as salesman in such a small and relaxed group.

For companies that expect their district or regional managers to conduct sales meetings, training for those managers in how to plan and conduct a meeting can pay off handsomely. Even if company headquarters provides meeting aids, the materials need to be tailored to local circumstances and the manager should be able to identify and handle training opportunities that apply to his area alone.

Field Coaching

One-on-one training, in which the local manager or a trainer observes a salesman's performance in the field and coaches him in specific areas where he needs improvement, is undoubtedly the most effective way of improving the productivity of the individual salesman. Yet this function is neglected completely in some companies and handled poorly in others.

Regardless of the nature of the product or service, regardless of the type of selling, first-line managers must be convinced that field coaching is an important part of their function. They must be trained to handle this function well. Even in companies that have a supervisor or nonmanagement trainer, it is advisable for the manager to spend time in the field with his men to evaluate their individual strengths and weaknesses.

It is also important to distinguish between calls made by the manager to help close an important sale and calls made by the manager to observe and coach the salesman.

When the objective is to close the "big one" or handle a sticky situation, the manager is likely to do most of the talking; in any event, he concentrates more on the customer than on the salesman.

If he wishes to observe the salesman, the manager should accompany him on calls where the outcome is not crucial. In this way, the manager can concentrate on the salesman's performance without interfering in the process.

The groundrules for effective field coaching are:

1. Before each call, agree on the roles of the manager and salesman. If the manager wishes only to observe, he makes it clear that the salesman is to carry the ball.
2. The salesman takes center stage by introducing the manager—by name only, not title—taking the seat at the buyer's desk while the manager sits off to the side, generally managing the conversation.
3. The manager observes and keeps his mouth shut. Because the sales outcome of a coaching call is not crucial, the manager does not jump in to rescue a floundering salesman. If he does, any advice he offers the salesman afterwards will be ineffective; the salesman will be thinking, "I would have done that if you hadn't interfered."
4. In the post-call discussion—the curbstone conference—it is as important for the manager to reinforce what the sales-

man did well as it is to offer constructive suggestions in areas where the salesman was weak.
5. The manager makes only two or three major suggestions and makes sure the salesman understands them by doing a bit of role-playing if necessary. Too many suggestions merely confuse the salesman.

INCENTIVE COMPENSATION AND PRODUCTIVITY

One method of increasing sales productivity that is often overlooked or misused is the provision of some type of incentive compensation plan for the sales force.

A straight commission plan or a draw against commission is the purest form of monetary reward for increased productivity. Yet the mere possibility of larger commissions cannot motivate a salesman to plan well, allocate his time wisely, and make effecitve sales calls if he does not know how to do it. Even commission salesmen, in short, can usually benefit by effective guidance, training, and supervision.

A more common compensation plan is one in which the salesman gets a base salary large enough to cover the necessities, plus an additional bonus, commission, override, or other form of incentive to spur him to greater achievements.

Such plans can be effective if designed well but useless if conceived poorly. In the author's judgment, about half of all existing compensation plans either don't motivate the salesman at all, motivate him to do the wrong things, or demotivate him by causing resentment and frustration.

The Ideal Incentive Plan

Ideally, the incentive plan should meet these criteria:

1. *The amount of the incentive payment should be substantial*. Few salesmen will put in a lot of extra effort and overtime work for

a measly $75 or $100 a quarter. Experience indicates that to provide a motivating force, the salesman should be able to earn up to 30% or 35% of his basic salary in incentive payments.

Inflation has made it necessary for many companies to revise their compensation plan in the last year or two. If the cost of living has gone up 50% over a period of time, and a salesman's base salary and incentive dollars have both increased 50%, the salesman is a loser. He is now in a higher tax bracket, which means that a bigger percentage of his incentive dollars are taxed away from him and the purchasing power of his incentive earnings has actually decreased.

2. *The plan should motivate the salesman to seek profit, not dollars.* This is perhaps the most frequent weakness of ineffective plans. In any product mix, there are usually a few specialty products that are more difficult to sell but carry a much higher gross profit margin for the company. At the lower end, there are usually some commodity products in which there is a great deal of competition and margins are low.

Because the salesman can generate more sales dollars per hour or per call in the lower-profit lines, any incentive program that rewards him on the basis of dollar volume will encourage him to neglect the hard-to-sell high-profit items and concentrate on the dogs.

To illustrate, assume a company has a new noncompetitive specialty product on which it grosses 30%, a so-so product with a 20% gross, and a highly competitive product on which it grosses 10%. The salesman gets a base salary, plus 1% of all sales over $800,000. The present situation is the following:

PRODUCT	GROSS PROFIT PERCENTAGE	SALES VOLUME (THOUSANDS)	GROSS PROFIT DOLLARS (THOUSANDS)
X	30%	$ 150	$ 45
Y	20%	350	70
Z	10%	500	50
Totals		$1000	$165

On his $1 million of sales, the salesman earns his base salary plus a bonus of 1% of $200,000 ($1,000,000 − $800,000), or $2,000.

Being a conscientious and profit-minded salesman, he redoubles his missionary efforts on Product X and increases its volume by $100,000. As a result, he has less time to devote to Product Z, on which volume drops by $200,000. The new results are:

PRODUCT	GROSS PROFIT PERCENTAGE	SALES VOLUME (THOUSANDS)	GROSS PROFIT DOLLARS (THOUSANDS)
X	30%	$250	$ 75
Y	20%	350	70
Z	10%	300	30
Totals		$900	$175

He now earns a base salary plus 1% of $100,000 ($900,000 − $800,000), or $1,000. He has increased his contribution to company profit by $10,000 and is rewarded by having his bonus cut in half.

The example, of course, is simplified and exaggerated, but it illustrates the basic truth that incentives based on dollar sales volume have a built-in motivation to chase the easier, and often less profitable, sales dollars.

The solution is to base the incentive upon gross profit dollars or to separate the products into categories, some of which carry more weight or win more points toward the bonus than others.

It is this emphasis on profit production that makes the incentive program profitable to the company. The company is not sharing existing profits with the sales force; it is giving them a share of additional profits they generate. A good plan gives the company $3 or $4 in extra profit for every dollar paid out in incentives.

3. *The incentive payoff should be as frequent as practical.* A salesman slogging through the snows of February is not motivated by the thought of an annual bonus he may receive a year in the future. Quarterly

payments are desirable; they can be made even more frequently if the resulting amounts are not too small and the extra administrative costs not too great.

One company that offered a rather small bonus seemed to contradict the frequency principle by getting good results with a bonus paid annually, just before Christmas. Reason: every month the salesman received a statement showing his bonus for the past month and the amount he had accumulated year-to-date. While he might not have been very motivated by a $50 check at the end of the month, he was more motivated to learn that he was building up a $600 Christmas bonus.

4. *The incentive plan should award the salesman for his own efforts.* In general—though there are many exceptions to this generality—plans that pay off for individual achievement are more successful than those in which sales results are pooled and everyone shares in the pool.

The obverse of this is that the salesman should not be penalized for actions beyond his control. If the company is frequently the higher bidder, the salesman should be re-warded for bird-dogging the opportunities to bid, rather than being rewarded or penalized for the winning or losing of contracts for reasons beyond his control.

5. And finally, it's desirable but not mandatory that the plan be *easy to understand and simple to administer*. This is a desirable goal, but if the product line is complicated, if profitability varies widely by product, if sales credit must be divided between the salesman who calls on headquarters and those who call on field locations—when such conditions prevail, it is more important to have a plan tailored to these complications than to have a simple plan that doesn't work.

In summary, to increase sales productivity, it is necessary to (1) establish the best possible measurements of productivity; (2) analyze the causes for any inadequacies in productivity; (3) take specific and practical steps, via training or procedures, to correct the weaknesses; and (4) measure the improvement. The salesman will work harder to achieve this improvement if he is highly motivated. Substantial cash incentives are still a pretty good motivator.

16
Scheduling Sales Calls for Maximum Profitability

Porter Henry
Porter Henry & Company, Inc.

Recognizing that sales calls are expensive, Porter Henry discusses methods for scheduling these calls among products and customers to produce the maximum profit per call.

For a company selling more than one product, some products are more profitable than others; for any company, some types of customers are more profitable than others; in many types of selling, some sales activities are more immediately conducive to profits than others.

Each individual sales call is a scarce and expensive commodity; the challenging task of the sales manager is to allocate these sales calls among products and customers to produce the maximum profit per call.

A basic formula is:

$$R \propto N \times Q \times A$$

which means that sales results (R), however measured, are proportional to the number of sales calls (N) times the quality of sales calls (Q) times the effectiveness with which they are allocated (A) among big customers versus small ones, existing customers versus prospects, profitable speciality products versus "me-too" commodities.

Many companies monitor the number of calls a salesman makes. Targets are often set as to the number of calls per day or week without making similar efforts to measure the quality and allocation of calls.

This numbers game tends to irritate salesmen who realize that a few really effective calls are more productive than a flock of calls made primarily to fill out the daily call quota.

Quality of calls can be monitored by using ratios such as number of calls per order, number of items on each order, average dollars per order, average dollars per call, and so on.

The optimum allocation of sales calls or sales effort can be developed following the principles described in this chapter and then monitored by analyzing salesmen's call reports.

KNOWING WHERE THE PROFITS ARE

Before a company can allocate sales effort to maximize profits, it must know which products and which customers are the most profitable. Yet a surprisingly large proportion of North American companies have not analyzed the relative profitability of their product lines carefully.

This is a standard procedure called *distribution cost analysis* or *product line profitability analysis*. For the company that has not tried it, the results can be surprising.

Table 1. Sales of a company with four product lines (in thousands)

	W	X	Y	Z	TOTAL
Sales volume	$4,000	$5,000	$6,000	$3,000	$18,000
Percentage of sales volume	22.4%	27.8%	33.3%	16.7%	100%
Manufacturing costs	2,400	3,000	4,200	1,800	11,400
Gross profit	1,600	2,000	1,800	1,200	6,600
All other costs					−4,800
Net profit					$ 1,800

Consider a hypothetical company (Table 1) with four product lines. Products W and X are established products; Product Z is a new product requiring missionary selling. Product Y is a highly competitive product; manufacturing costs on Y are 70% of the sales price, compared with 60% on the other three products. Product Y also takes a good bit of sales time in negotiating prices. The company nets $1.8 million on sales of $18 million.

How should sales effort be allocated among the four products? The company decides to analyze the true profitability of each product. It does this by allocating only the direct costs—that is, costs that can be directly attributed to the individual product lines. Corporate overhead is ignored for the moment.

Sales costs are allocated by taking the total cost of the sales operation (salesmen's income and expenses, managerial salaries, fringe benefits, office rentals, secretarial expenses, and so on) and dividing them among product lines in proportion to the amount of sales time each product absorbs.

It is not necessary to make a complicated time-and-motion study of the sales force to obtain this allocation; estimates from first-line managers or analysis of a month's sales call reports is sufficient. Hairline accuracy is not needed; reasonable guesstimates can yield valuable information, and refined data can be sought later if necessary. Table 2 shows that the new product and the price-negotiated Product Y were absorbing more than their share of sales time.

Most advertising and promotion costs can be allocated directly to the products being advertised; costs of institutional or corporate image advertising can be allocated on the basis of the sales volume in each line or simply left in corporate overhead.

Warehousing costs can be allocated on the basis of the square feet or cubic feet each product line normally requires. Inventory costs, such as insurance and property taxes, can be based upon the manufactured costs of the products in inventory. (Interest on capital invested in inventory is probably included in corporate overhead.)

Billing costs can be allocated in proportion to the number of invoice lines devoted to each product line. Other direct costs, such as credit losses, costs of carrying accounts receivable, customer service, and so on, can usually be allocated in some logical manner.

When these direct costs had been allocated to product lines, the company learned this about their relative profitability (see Table 2 on page 154).

By subtracting each product's direct costs from its gross profits, you come up with its "contribution"—that is, the number of dollars that product contributed to corporate overhead and profits.

In our hypothetical case, Product W, with 22.4% of sales volume, was producing 33.1% of the total contribution. Product X, with 27.8% of sales, was accounting for 45.2% of contribution. As might be expected, the new Product Z was making a contribution somewhat less than its proportion of total sales volume, while the footballed product Y, with

Table 2. Profit contribution in four product lines (in thousands)

	W	X	Y	Z	TOTAL
Sales volume	$4,000	$5,000	$6,000	$3,000	$18,000
Percentage of sales volume	22.4%	27.8%	33.3%	16.7%	100%
Manufacturing costs	2,400	3,000	4,200	1,800	11,400
Gross profit	1,600	2,000	1,800	1,200	6,600
Direct costs:					
Sales	150	150	600	300	1,200
Advertising and promotion	100	100	200	200	600
Warehousing and inventory	200	200	500	100	1,000
Shipping	75	75	100	50	300
Billing	25	50	100	25	200
Other direct costs	25	25	75	75	200
Total direct costs	575	600	1,575	750	3,500
"Contribution"					
(Gross profit minus direct costs)	1,025	1,400	225	450	3,100
Percentage of contribution	33.1%	45.2%	7.2%	14.5%	100%
Overhead costs					1,300
Net profit					$1,800

33.3% of the company's sales volume, absorbing half of the sales force's time, was contributing only $225,000, or 7.2% of the amount available for overhead and profits.

Obviously, that sales force should reduce the time spent on Product Y drastically and generate more sales in the other three more profitable products.

Note that we did not allocate corporate overhead to product lines. Such an allocation would be largely hypothetical: should overhead be allocated on the basis of sales dollars, gross profit dollars, units shipped, tons shipped, or some other factor?

However, if one insists on coming up with a somewhat fictitious "net net" by product lines, one can allocate overhead in some arbitrary way. In our hypothetical case, if we allocate overhead in proportion to sales dollars, the bottom of Table 2 would look like below.

Now Product Y actually shows a loss. This does not mean that Product Y should be dropped; after all, we assigned $433,000 in overhead to it. If it were dropped, the other three lines would have to absorb this.

But we now know that Y is losing money primarily because of high costs in sales, advertising, and warehousing. It may be possible to cut this loss by spending less sales time on Y, reducing inventories, establishing a minimum order size, or even raising prices and settling for a smaller share of market.

The importance of this type of analysis in the allocation of sales effort is obvious. In our hypothetical case, we would want the salesmen to spend more time exploiting the potential of the new product Z, to spend as little time as possible on Product Y, and to devote most of their time to increasing the sales of the profitable products, W and X.

It is true that this would allocate more sales costs to these products, but the increased volume might well reduce sales cost as a percentage of sales and would also reduce the

Table 3. Overhead allocated in proportion to sales (in thousands)

	W	X	Y	Z	TOTAL
Contribution	$1,025	$1,400	$225	$450	$3,100
Overhead allocation	288.9	361.1	433.3	216.7	1,300
"Net net"	736.1	1,038.9	−208.3	233.2	1,800

ratio of costs of advertising, inventory, and other direct expenses.

The same type of analysis can be made of the relative profitability of types and/or sizes of customers. It is not unusual to find that customers below a certain size make a negative contribution to profit when all direct costs are allocated to them, and that sales effort should not be expended upon them unless justified by future potential.

THE THREE VARIABLES IN ALLOCATION

There are three variables in the allocation problem; when two are given, the third can be determined.

These variables are: (1) the number of customers, usually grouped by type and/or size; (2) the call frequency required for each category of customer; and (3) the number of salesmen (or sales calls) available.

A new company building a sales force could determine, from the number of potential customers and the desired call frequency, how many salesmen it needed.

If a company has a given number of salesmen and a determined call frequency, it can determine how many customers it can call upon regularly.

In the more frequent case, the number of salesmen and customers is relatively fixed. The variable to be calculated is how frequently the salesmen should call on each category of customers.

OPTIMUM CALL FREQUENCY

Underlying the sales allocation procedure is the concept that for each customer, there is some frequency of calls that maximizes the return per sales call.

The top portion of Figure 1 represents the total volume of sales a company might expect to get from one company in one year, if the salesman called the number of times indicated on the bottom line.

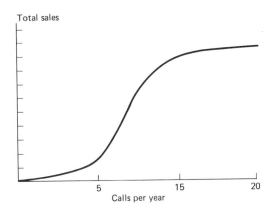

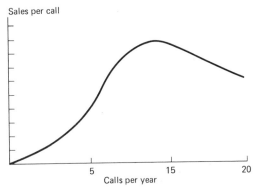

FIGURE 1. Optimum call frequency.

(To illustrate the method, we use sales volume figures. In light of the preceding discussion, that company should allow for the varying profitability of product lines, usually by working with "gross profit" or "contribution" figures rather than sales dollars.)

If the salesman makes only one or two calls per year, for example, he is likely to get little or no business. If he calls ten or 12 times, his efforts will usually result in more orders. But if he calls more frequently than that, the volume of additional business will decrease; he has reached a point of diminishing returns.

If we divide the total expected sales at each level by the number of projected calls to obtain that sales volume, we get the average dollar volume per call, charted on the lower half of Figure 1.

To maximize the return per call on this particular customer, the salesman will want to call on him about 12 to 14 times per year.

Theoretically, there is a different "expectancy curve" for every customer and prospect. But because it would be confusing and impractical for a salesman to establish a different call frequency for every customer, we group customers by call frequencies—those to be seen once a month, twice a month, once a week, and so on.

ESTABLISHING CUSTOMER CATEGORIES

As a start, we make a preliminary grouping of customers on the assumption that the bigger the customer, the more frequently he should be called upon. There are some exceptions to this—the largest customer may have an automated reorder system and not want to see us too frequently—but we make adjustments for these exceptions later.

In making this grouping, we have to take into account not only the customer's present level of sales volume, but also the potential additional sales that might be obtained by cultivating the customer more intensively.

A customer currently buying $5,000 a year from us but with no potential at all for any larger sales volume is not called upon as frequently as a prospect who is not now buying anything from us, but who could conceivably buy $100,000 a year.

To determine the "call value" of every customer and prospect, we need to consider his present purchases plus the probable value of any potential additional purchases.

To analyze the customers in one territory, it is useful to print up a number of index cards like this:

ACCOUNT ANALYSIS

Name of co. or person _____

(1) Present annualized sales to them .... $ _____

(2) Potential additional volume .... $ _____

(3) Chances of getting it .... _____

(4) "Expected value" of future business (2) × (3) .... $ _____

(5) Estimated present and future value of
    this account—(1) + (4) ("call value") .... $ _____

For example, the "call value" of a customer with $5,000 in present sales and no potential additional sales would look like this.

ACCOUNT ANALYSIS

Name of co. or person ____*John Jones*____

(1) Present annualized sales to them .... $ _*5,000*_

(2) Potential additional volume .... $ _____

(3) Chances of getting it .... _____

(4) "Expected value" of future business (2) × (3) .... $ _____

(5) Estimated present and future value of
    this account—(1) + (4) ("call value") .... $ _*5,000*_

ACCOUNT ANALYSIS

Name of co. or person __*GEORGE SMITH*__

(1) Present annualized sales to them .... $ _____

(2) Potential additional volume .... $ _50,000_

(3) Chances of getting it .... _25%_

(4) "Expected value" of future business (2) × (3) .... $ _12,500_

(5) Estimated present and future value of
    this account—(1) + (4) ("call value") .... $ _12,500_

On the other hand, if a prospect is now buying nothing from us, but his potential purchases are $50,000 and we estimate that we have a 25% chance of getting them, his call value would look like above.

The next step is to list all customers and prospects in the order of the total expected value or "call value" of the account.

GROUPING CUSTOMERS

We now employ the principle of the "important few and the unimportant many." As

analysis, a salesman allocated his available calls by seeing the A accounts twice as often as the B's, and the B's twice as often as the C's.

He might, for example, see each A account once a week, each B account every two weeks, and each C account every four weeks. Or it might be twice a week for the A's, once a week for B's, and once every two weeks for C's.

To determine how frequently he can call on each category of customer, the salesman estimates the total number of calls he can make

Table 4. Two ways of grouping customers

PARETO METHOD			JURAN METHOD		
CUSTOMERS RANKED BY VOLUME		SALES DOLLARS	CUSTOMERS RANKED BY VOLUME		SALES DOLLARS
25%	A items	75%	15%	A items	65%
75	B items	25	20	B items	20
100%		100%	65	C items	15
			100%		100%

indicated in Table 4, we will find that the top 25% of the customers will give us about 75% of total projected sales or, to use a refinement developed by Juran—the top 15% will give us 65% of sales, the next 20% will give 20%, and the smallest 65% of all customers altogether will yield only 15% of total sales volume. The salesman makes a preliminary grouping of his customers using these percentages.

Using Juran's more sensitive 15-20-65

per year and multiplies that by 0.36.* This is the total number of calls on A accounts. By

*This factor is determined via the following table:

ITEM CLASS	CALLS/ CUSTOMER	NO. OF CUSTOMERS	TOTAL CALLS	%
A	4	15	60	36%
B	2	20	40	24
C	1	65	65	40
			165	100%

dividing that total by the number of A accounts, he can determine the number of calls per year to be made on each A account.

On each trip through his territory, he calls on all the A's, half the B's, and about one-fourth of the C's. Next time around, he calls on all the A's again, the other half of the B's, and a new one-fourth of the C's.

For each four cycles, through his territory, he will thus call on each A four times, each B twice, and each C once.

If the salesman uses the simpler 75-25 division into A's and B's, and if he calls on A's twice as often as B's, he will be making 40% of his calls on A accounts and 60% on B's.

To obtain his call frequency with the 75-25 distribution, he estimates the total number of calls he can make in a year, multiplies that by 0.4 to get the total number of calls on A customers, and divides that by his number of A customers to determine the number of calls per year on each.

Earlier, we referred to this as a "preliminary" grouping of customers and prospects. The salesman now makes any necessary common-sense adjustments by asking, "Does this call frequency make sense for this customer?"

He may have a large customer in the A category who simply does not want to see him that often; in this case, the customer is reclassified as a B—from the standpoint of call frequency, not importance.

Or a customer in the B category may insist on more frequent service. If the salesman might lose the account by calling less frequently, he may decide to upgrade this customer into the A frequency.

The procedure outlined above is only a basic framework that any company can modify to fit its needs. It may be, for example, that each salesman selects a handful of key accounts—Super A's, so to speak—that he will call on much more frequently than the rest of the A's. Within a key account, various executives who influence purchases might be divided into A, B, and C categories for frequency of contact.

ASSIGNING CALL FREQUENCIES

A more important refinement, for companies having multiple product lines, is to take relative profitability into account in assigning call frequencies. This can be done in two ways:

1. The account analysis index cards can be based upon gross margin, or profit contribution, instead of sales dollars.

2. The sales dollars obtained on line 5 of the account analysis index card can be weighted according to the product mix the customer buys or might buy, so that customers for the more profitable products rank higher on the "call value" scale.

3. The salesman can first allocate his total time among product lines roughly in proportion to their profitability. Table 5 shows, for our hypothetical company, how he might apportion his time among the four product lines.

Table 5. Allocation of time by product lines

PRODUCT / CUSTOMER	W	X	Y	Z	TOTAL
A					
B					
C					
Total	30%	40%	10%	20%	

The A-B-C system described above results in his spending approximately 36% of his calls with A customers, 24% with B's, and 40% with C's, so the salesman enters these in the right-hand column as shown in Table 6.

Table 6. Allocation of time by customer categories

PRODUCT / CUSTOMER	W	X	Y	Z	TOTAL
A					36%
B					24%
C					40%
Total	30%	40%	10%	20%	100%

The next step is to subdivide each *customer* allocation in proportion to the *product* allocations. For example, of the 35% of his calls he plans to invest in A customers, he will make 30% of those, or 10.8% on Product W, 14.4% on Product X, and so on. Table 7 shows the semi-final result.

Table 7. Allocation of effort by customer and product

PRODUCT / CUSTOMER	W	X	Y	Z	TOTAL
A	10.8%	14.4%	3.6%	7.2%	36%
B	7.2%	9.6%	2.4%	4.8%	24%
C	12.0%	16.0%	4.0%	8.0%	40%
Total	30%	40%	10%	20%	100%

This means, for example, that 14.4% of his calls will be spent in selling Product X to large A accounts, 4% of his time in selling Product Y to smaller C accounts, and so on.

This was called the semi-final result because an arbitrary allocation like this needs to be modified to fit the facts of life. If, for example, the smaller C customers cannot use Product W, the 12% of his calls tentatively assigned to that pigeonhole would be transferred to the sale of Product W to A and B accounts. If he wishes to maintain the 40% allocation to C accounts, he will spend a bit more time selling Products X, Y, and Z to them, reducing the time originally scheduled to sell those products to A or B customers.

SOME VARIATIONS

The principles described above apply primarily to the salesman spending most of his time making repeat calls on regular customers, with some percentage of effort invested in converting nonbuying prospects into customers.

But there are other patterns of sales coverage. To allocate sales energy in those circumstances requires some modification in the basic ideas of investing the most time where the most profits are.

An interesting application of time allocation arises when the salesman sells only through distributors and may have a relatively small number of distributors—anywhere from 10 to 25 in his territory.

In this case, he can estimate the "call value" of each distributor, using the formula of present sales plus expected value of potential additional sales volume.

He then calculates what percentage of his total sales each distributor will be expected to contribute, and allocates his time to distributors in that proportion. A distributor who is expected to generate 10% of the salesman's total volume will get 10% of his time, a distributor whose present and potential sales represent only 5% of the territory total will get 5% of the salesman's time, and so on.

Because this salesman will be allocating large chunks of time to each distributor—10% of 225 working days per year is 22.5 days to be spent with that distributor—it is advisable to make a further allocation of that time among the various functions the salesman can perform when with that distributor.

For example, the salesman who plans to spend 22 days with a distributor would fill out a plan like this:

_____5 days working in the field making calls with the distributor's salesman

_____1 days planning and conducting sales meetings for distributor salesmen

_____2 days counseling the distributor management on inventory, reorder levels, and promotions

_____3 days conducting open houses or demonstrations for the distributor's customers

_____11 days calling, by himself, on key accounts to generate sales volume through the distributor

_____22 total days with this distributor

A different type of energy allocation problem is faced by the salesman selling a once-only, high-ticket item, such as an executive airplane or a turnkey construction contract.

A time boobytrap facing this salesman is the possibility of getting so involved in a few current negotiations that he neglects lead-generating and opportunity bird-dogging activities. Then, when the hot current sales have been made or lost, he suddenly finds himself with a dearth of immediate prospects, and it may take months to fill up the pipeline of prospects.

The answer is to set aside time for, and give first priority to, those activities that uncover prospects and create opportunities to bid. These lead-generating activities might include speeches at association meetings, direct mailings, public relations work, market studies, and similar means of getting exposure.

As for the time he spends with active prospects and "suspects," the salesman will often benefit by budgeting his time. Most of us tend to spend too much time doing the things we like to do, too little time doing the things we find distasteful.

The salesman selling executive airplanes may be a flying fanatic himself, and tend to spend too many hours making repeat calls on a similar flying enthusiast in a prospect company. On the other hand, if the salesman dislikes writing proposals or planning sales calls, he is likely to neglect those chores. The budget of his time, by functions, enables him to invest his total time for maximum payoff.

As much as most salesmen dislike mathematics and paperwork, a few hours once every quarter carefully allocating sales effort can pay off as handsomely as anything else they can do to improve performance.

Instead of the old barroom exhortation to "put your money where your mouth is," the wise salesman knows that it's profitable to do his talking where the money is.

17
Mathematical Models for Marketing

Dr. Sam R. Goodman
Executive Vice-President
Finance & Administration
Magnuson Computer Systems

The author proposes mathematical models for use in eliminating much of the wasteful expenditures of money in new product strategy. He describes several models that can be utilized for various situations.

I am appalled at the tremendous waste that takes place because of a new product strategy that has been traditionally careless. Like many other consumer industries, we tend to view the individual who will buy our products as essentially irrational. Thus our pursuit of him has become a kind of game in which various producers compete to gain his attention. Not only is our advertising directed increasingly toward television, including spot commercials and network programs, but vast amounts of promotional funds are being spent either in the form of virtual bribes to storekeepers to carry the product on the shelf or as direct remittances to the consumer in the form of ostensible price reductions. Literally billions of dollars have been spent in an almost blind manner by many firms to establish, protect, and enhance their franchises.

INTEREST IN MATHEMATICAL MODELS

The growing concern over this situation has led quite a few executives to explore the possibilities of using mathematical models as aides to market analysis and decision making.

This interest has generated a good deal of enthusiasm and a few notable success stories. Yet there remains considerable confusion—as well as skepticism—about the function of such models, how people should use them, and what effect they will have on the firm's marketing strategy and organizational patterns.

THE EXTREMES

At one extreme, people predict that marketing decisions will become automated and that computer programs, based on mathematical models, will arrive at policy decisions with little or no need for an executive's intuition.

On the other hand, many executives hold that the marketing environment is much too complex to be represented adequately by an abstract model, and that consumer behavior is random and chaotic. They believe that whatever a computerized model can do, they can do cheaper.

In my opinion, neither of these viewpoints is correct—for reasons I hope to make clear in the body of this chapter. However, at this point, the need for more inclusive and accurate techniques of processing information and more reliable decision guides in the formation of marketing policy is evident to everyone.

SURVIVAL RATE OF NEW PRODUCT IDEAS

For example, the figure commonly used in industry is that for every 20 new product ideas that are initiated, only one survives to become a profitable product. Yet in the food industry, the ratio is nearer 60 to 1! Moreover, it has recently been estimated that the number of consumer products carried by the average supermarket will increase from the current 7,500 items to more than 10,000 products. It is probable that new products will compose about one-third of this amount. This means that 3,300 items on supermarket shelves will be new products and that 200,000 ideas will have been produced in order to generate them.

There are many reasons for this high mortality rate. Yet it seems to me that one of the most important defects in our present system of new product development is the lack of any adequate means for predicting the real market for a product and for adopting the optimal strategy in approaching that market at each stage of the product's life cycle.

Consider for a moment the company trying to sell a product. It has been developed and cost and profit constraints have been set. Now, management must decide precisely to whom they will sell the product. To a specific segment of the market? In a certain geographic location? To middlemen or directly to the consumer?

Then they must establish a pricing policy. Decide how to package the product. Calculate its effect on the total sales of the company's other products. They must decide on a strategy for advertising.

But consider just advertising alone. With some 4,000 radio stations and 1,800 newspapers available, the number of possible combinations runs into the billions. Further, if we compound these alternatives by forming a different appeal for each age group and each section of the country, the number of decisions facing a marketing executive becomes astronomical. As a result, he must limit the number of alternatives drastically, or he will remain in a state of indecision. Even of the ten or 12 alternatives he can handle, the executive will probably not be able to evaluate more than three or four adequately. He simply does not have the means at his disposal to hit upon the optimal media combination in his marketing strategy.

DETERMINATION OF OPTIMUM MEDIA COMBINATION

I see this problem getting worse because the average age of managers is dropping.

In the past, managers were exposed to marketing problems for many years before they received decision-making power. During that time, they developed an intuition that helped them cope with its complexity. Even though their decisions were often not the best, they were able to keep the company alive and—in most cases—expanding.

The younger man who has not had this exposure needs a substitute for the intuition he has not had time to develop. (I'm not saying that the older man doesn't need such an aid, too.)

THREE MAJOR MATHEMATICAL MODELS

Three major mathematical models have been developed specifically for new product marketing, and serve as precisely this sort of crutch. These models have been given the acronyms of DEMON, SPRINTER, and NSPM.

Before comparing the advantages and disadvantages of these models, it is necessary to describe what they attempt to do in a general way.

First, they are a means of structuring the marketing environment to focus upon those factors and relationships that have a bearing on sales and profits and exclude those which do not.

Second, they enable the executive to predict—within limits I will explain later—the outcome of each possible decision, screen out those not worth considering, and highlight the few altèrnatives that promise maximum profitability.

Third, they constitute a control device that permits him to vary his strategy in advance for each stage of the product's life cycle, dictating, for example, a specific plan for advertising at each stage, even selecting which magazines or newspapers to use.

Suppose that you were faced with introducing a new brand of detergent. How would you go about developing a model to aid you in your marketing decisions?

Essentially, mathematical model building consists of a four-stage process. First, we identify all those factors that might have a bearing upon future sales, and then attempt to discover any interrelationships that might exist among those variables.

Next, a flowchart is created to mirror the interrelated variables. A generalized model is built, based upon the qualitative representation shown in the flowchart.

To take an almost trivial example, assume you want to test the effectiveness of your advertising campaign for a certain type of detergent. You gather your data concerning sales, money spent on advertising and promotion, information regarding your share of the market, studies of brand awareness among consumers, and so on. You measure each variable's relationship to sales by plotting the data on a simple form of flowchart, using sales as the horizontal axis, and brand awareness or the promotion budget as the vertical axis. If there is an upward trend to the line, you know that there is some degree of correlation between the two factors.

The third step involves deciding whether to go ahead and market the product, abandon it as too risky, or, if enough promise still exists though the evidence is inconclusive, decide to conduct further research. If such an On decision is made, the model will select the areas that demand more information and, when it is received, will alter the marketing plan so as to improve the chances of a Go decision. This is the fourth step.

When and if a Go decision is reached, the fifth step involves whatever revision of the marketing plan may be required by new data until management is satisfied that it has achieved the optimal marketing mix.

DEMON

At this point, the two basic advantages of DE-MON must be apparent. If the product is good and DEMON establishes a satisfactory marketing plan, you simply market the product nationally and expect maximal profits. If the product is unacceptable to the market or the risk involved too great, DEMON scraps it quickly, thus minimizing losses by eliminating the chance of failure at an early stage of development.

DEMON, though it represents a tremendous advance in the art of model building, still has one major defect. In the course of my research, I interviewed personnel at one company that had used DEMON with unsuccessful results. They attributed their failure to the model's lack of flexibility. As dynamic a model as DEMON is, it was not sufficiently flexible to compete with the even more rapid dynamics of the marketplace.

In other words, the one factor that DEMON is unable to handle is the problem of product interaction. Just as the Monte Carlo simulation looks at marketing variables in isolation, DEMON looks at products in isolation.

For example, to the company that markets six different brands of soap, DEMON would be of little help. The model would calculate the profits derived from introducing a new brand of soap, but would not take into account the effect that the new brand would have upon the already existing products produced by the company. Profits resulting from the introduction of brand number 7 may be wiped out by the losses incurred because a drop in sales of the other six brands.

DEMON is also not able to calculate the effects of competition entering the field. Once a company has successfully proved that it can market a product, other firms will attempt to cut a piece of the cake for themselves, the sort of thing that happened to General Electric after it introduced the electric toothbrush.

SPRINTER

SPRINTER, a more complex model developed by Glen Urban of M.I.T., is oriented, like DEMON, toward yielding a Go, On, or No decision. However, SPRINTER gives explicit consideration to the effect of the new product upon existing ones and to the variations in competitive response over the life cycle of the product.

For example, the SPRINTER model was run for a large chemical company that had developed a new nylon compound that carried both cost and performance advantages in several significant markets. The company also marketed several other nylon products, and management worried about the loss of sales for these products because of the introduction of the new compound.

SPRINTER was supplied with the price, advertising and distribution plans for both the old and the new product and the competitive strategies for these products over a proposed ten-year period.

The initial plan stipulated that the new product would sell for $350 a carton for the first three years, and $200 a carton for the remaining seven years. When the program was evaluted without considering any other product, it was predicted that the new item would generate a profit of $8.5 million.

However, the product was in fact not independent; it had a high degree of interaction with other products already in the line. Therefore, SPRINTER revealed that the incremental profit (new profit minus loss of profit because a drop in sales of other products) was actually only $6 million.

Because the total investment necessary to produce the product was more than $7 million, SPRINTER rejected the original marketing plan.

In the course of an hour and a half, SPRINTER evaluated more than two million other possible marketing programs. It finally recommended one in which each carton would sell for $250 for the first three years and $200 per carton for the next seven years. On the basis of that price, and a slight alteration in the plans for already existing products, the incremental profit would amount to almost $9 million. After some further calculations, which increased the profit somewhat and notably reduced the risk, the decision was made to add the product to the present line.

Even though SPRINTER has improved upon DEMON in several significant respects, both continue to share one major limitation. They both assume that new product ideas are proposed and analyzed one at a time. This is often not the case. General Foods, for example, recently experienced the overwhelming success of one of its products that had been on the market for almost two years, and at the same time, a growing demand for a brand new product just introduced. This has caused a delay in the introductory timetable for a third and very promising product.

Further, although SPRINTER can supply the differential profit and uncertainty information for each new product, it is unable to perform this same function for a whole group of new product ideas. In other words, SPRINTER cannot select the one that is most promising out of even a small group of possible new products. The only way the model can handle such a situation, and not very adequately, is to run each idea separately and then compare the results, a slow and expensive affair.

NSPM

NSPM is another planning model that has been used frequently by clients of Young & Rubicam. The initials stand for *natural sales projection model*. In 1959, Young & Rubicam became convinced that the major fluctuations in the sales curve of a new product are the result of a combination of predictable consumer activities. The major inputs to the model involve the rate at which new purchasers enter the marketplace, the proportion of repeat purchasers, the time lag between purchases, and the quantity purchased at each transaction. The major advantage of this model—which has been used with varying degrees of success and has gone through several transformations—is that it allows planning and timing marketing activities to compensate for a predictable lag in consumer interest. An executive can thus determine very specifically the amount and frequency of advertising needed in each stage of the product's life cycle and can predict the long-term effects of any changes in advertising allocations.

In recent years, two interestingly different approaches to models have emerged, one from the academic arena and the other from an advertising agency research arm.

At the University of Michigan, Paul Root has amplified upon an earlier model conceived by Ed Pessemier. This new model has an interesting approach that directs its efforts not so much towards quantifying a go or no-go decision but rather with the difficulties of implementation when surrounded by interdependent inputs (for example, the elasticity of demand implies that unit sales are interdependent upon unit pricing). The model provides for two other pragmatic requirements, i.e., ranges of input weighted by probabilities (expressed in percentiles) and the impact of product cannibalization within the same firm (unlike SPRINTER, expressed as negative profit).

The model was configured as a risk analysis model, which implies that rather than dealing inputs of single estimates various financial criteria were presented as ranges of probabilities. The model is geared to answer questions such as: What are the chances that RO1 will be less than 20 percent? What is the RO1 that has a 50/50 chance of ocurring?

The model assumes a simulation of three distinct plans: marketing, manufacturing, and financial. The marketing plan module requires as its first input a product and/or product line definition. For example, a basic camera may add film, paper, and developing equipment to the line definition.

A single strategy is developed for each iteration of the model. The presumption is that each strategy requires different unit volume information. Output reports provide ancillary information ranging from dollar sales aggregates for the product line, average unit prices, and the percentage each product bears to the total line (product mix). Estimators (inputters) use the model to simulate cannibalism by defining a component of the product line as an existing product employing negative unit prices.

ONE MARKETING PLAN FOR SEVERAL MANUFACTURING PLANS

Any given marketing plan may encompass one or more manufacturing plans to be evaluated. Each manufacturing plan requires assumptions about the amount and timing of capital expenditures so that cash flow from depreciation and capacities can be simulated. Capacities are matched in an output report with ninetieth percentile unit sales estimates in order to quantify list sales because of capacity shortfalls. Fixed cost estimates are a referred input as well as variable manufacturing costs. The resultant variable manufacturing profit (sales minus variable manufacturing costs) forms the basis for break-even analysis (fixed costs divided by variable profit). The model can also handle varying input for the variable cost component of manufacturing costs simulating learning curve experience.

When the marketing and manufacturing plans have been formulated sequentially (200 simulations each), further financial estimates are required to study the economics of the strategy. The RO1, expressed in discounted cash flow terms as well as present value, permits a view of its impact on divisional (or unit) and total corporate financial statements. Working capital requirements and ratios and tax credit considerations round out the financial module and form the basis for probability estimates of results.

While I do not wish to minimize the importance of the model or question its utility (CPC International uses it) I do question whether it is really a model or merely a sequence of statistical calculations. A model is a representation of reality; this sequence permits no loops backwards to the initial plan requirement (marketing) following completion. In real life, financial considerations often dictate the formulation of the marketing plan.

PREDICTIONS OF SUCCESS AS GOOD AS ASSUMPTIONS

Predictions of success for any product are only as good as the basic underlying assumptions. In the risk analysis model, input is largely a factor of subjective probabilities. A different attempt to correlate various new product success factors was made by the advertising firm of Leo Burnett Co., Inc. and has resulted in an interesting model called TRACKER.

The model is designed for use by account executives or corporate brand managers and is primarily designed to evaluate marketing plans and analyze test market data. Secondarily, it diagnoses problems in an ongoing mode. Unlike many other models, TRACKER uses survey data to predict year-end test market sales from early test market results. TRACKER commonly uses test market data of three months duration; most other models use longer time periods, i.e., 12 months.

Diagnostically, the model relates advertising expenditures, price, and brand satisfaction to sales and indicates strategic or physical product weaknesses prior to larger scale introduction.

TRACKER

Although readily understandable in concept, TRACKER employs a wealth of statistical relationships involving least squares and econometric adjustments necessary to accommodate various errors for categories that may lack sufficient observations. The model uses one or

two variables at each stage of calculation and is designed for ease of understanding by users.

The underlying theory of the models assumes the interdependence of three submodules:

1. Awareness model
2. Trial model
3. Projection model.

In terms of sequence, the model assumes that advertising (to be defined) creates product awareness. A quasi-decision tree relationship emerges separating those who are aware of the product from the "non aware." In turn the "aware" class becomes triers or nontriers of the product. Triers, in turn, develop attitudes about product quality and satisfaction from trial experience. Repurchase rates are derived and correlated with nonrepeat user classes. The model cycle accommodates continued repurchases or even a nonrepeat user becoming a repurchaser.

TRACKER input derives from questionnaires filled out by potential product users. Three waves of 500 to 1,000 questionnaires are collected for each new product introduction. Each wave is administered about every four weeks after introduction depending on the duration of the purchase cycle for a product.

The *awareness model* concentrates on two essential variables, total brand awareness and advertising weight, which is measured by gross rating points (GRPs). A GRP measures the percentage of TV households reached at least once with an advertiser's message multiplied by the number of times that household is exposed to the message. The dependent variable, total brand awareness, is measured against the independent variable, GRP.

Brand awareness may be affected by any one of the following variables that the model can accommodate:

1. Media plan
2. Advertising memorability
3. Brand name memorability
4. In-Store awareness
5. Product category.

Subset variables of each of the above are definable.

The *trial model* follows on the theory that those who are aware will choose to try or not to try the product. Mathematically, the model first expresses the triers as a percentage of those who are aware of the new product. Aware customers are defined by the model as those who have become aware in the present period and those who become aware in prior periods but who have not yet chosen to try the product. These two groups form the universe of potential triers. The model design does not ignore the real possibility that trial may be dependent on a number of factors including:

1. Product concept
2. advertising copy (persuasiveness)
3. Price
4. Promotion
5. Distribution
6. Store visibility on shelf
7. Product category.

The *projection model* forecasts year-end market shares using inputs of trial rates, repeat usage rates, repeat purchase proportions, and trial usage rates. Of the above, repeat purchase rates present some difficulty because such rates may be a function of the time since a consumer first purchased a new brand. Data collection procedures for this submodel break respondents down into five categories in order to establish how various repurchase rates are dependent on a consumer's past experiences:

1. Nonproduct category users
2. Potential triers
3. Triers
4. Users
5. Nonusers.

Each is defined relative to time periods in order to be both mutually exclusive and yet encompass previous respondent behavior. Awareness and trial figures are correlated with buying rates. The resulting estimate of units purchased by the sample in the first year is extrapolated to estimate the total number of units sold in the test market.

The validation of any model is its real life utility. The model has been used in evaluation of 18 new products introduced since 1978. TRACKER has thus far had a "usefulness" record that far exceeds its predecessors. Its major contribution is to *timeliness*, the creation of an early warning system. It does not merely ring whistles and bells or raise red flags. The flags are pointed in the direction requiring remedial action. In this respect, the model is unique.

It seems to me that TRACKER demonstrates that analysis of a total process is best digested in chewable pieces, i.e., test marketing rather than the whole, which contains an infinite number of interdependent variables. The attempt to explain the whole in one large gulp has too often proven to be the graveyard of model elephants. In this respect, TRACKER is a first strike into a new direction.

Most of the new models being developed today are of this same nature. They are aimed at predicting consumer behavior rather than delineating a total marketing plan.

Model building is an expensive proposition. The fact that so many people do not understand models means that you need a group of specialists—sometimes a whole department—who are able to act, in effect, as translators between your marketing people and the computer programmers.

Furthermore, if you are going to use models, you must have fairly free access to a computer and probably one at least as large as the IBM 360 if you are to derive maximum benefit from the models. Thus a small program could cost a company up to $300,000 or $400,000 a year unless it is willing to have work done by an outside firm such as an advertising agency.

Is it all worth it? Does an expensive model actually produce enough net gains in profit to justify the expense?

I think the answer to this question is rooted in two considerations: the caliber of people within the company and the number of new products being marketed by the company.

The entire success of a marketing program based on a mathematical model depends upon the willingness of management to accept and understand the concept and actual performance of a model. Often, the greatest limitation of a model is that people do not understand its limitations, as for example when it yields a range of answers that is considered too broad to be useful.

In most cases, it is extremely difficult to establish an effective relationship between model builders and "conventional" marketing executives. Most marketing people regard model building with suspicion or open hostility. Even when some cooperation is achieved, marketing managers often continue to resent operations researchers as potential competitors for funds and organizational status.

The point I wish to make here is that if your firm has the type of executive who is able to adapt to new techniques and see a model as a tool he can fashion and use to his advantage, then you stand a good chance of cutting your losses and maximizing your profits.

In my opinion, two kinds of companies can benefit most from new product simulations: the high-technology companies, because the basic training of most of their personnel makes them uniquely suited to utilize a mathematical approach to decision making, and the company in a highly competitive consumer market that is saddled with the burden of multiple product introductions at frequent intervals. Though the difficulty of educating executives to use modeling may seem great to the latter firm and the initial cost of an advanced model quite large, these obstacles disappear when compared to the possible cost of making a wrong decision.

RISK OF PREMATURE OR INCORRECT USE

While mathematical models offer significant opportunities for improved marketing, there is a real risk of premature or incorrect use. A model can be constructed out of false assumptions, inadequate knowledge, or incomplete conceptions of management problems. Often, its results will be faulty because the original inputs were distorted by biased sampling methods. It is the responsibility of line executives to define their objectives clearly and to decide when, where, and how to use mathematical models in the solution of marketing problems. But to decide intelligently, an executive must understand models and the process of model building, forcing him to become more conscious of the need for continuing reeducation.

I also believe the introduction of marketing models will force the executive to modify his self-image. Rather than seeing himself as a kingpin, as one who hands down a decision, he will have to adopt the role of a mediator or an overseer. The marketing world is becoming so complex and the alternatives so vast that the executive is now in the position of having to choose the best possible decision among many provided by a model, as opposed to making one "right" decision.

He will have to become a mediator because no longer will the different departments in a company resemble isolated kingdoms. No longer will the marketing department make marketing decisions, the accounting department make accounting decisions, and so on. Marketing models cut across departmental lines and demand a great degree of cooperation and interaction. This might possibly dictate a change in the organizational philosophy of many firms and force people to admit, maybe for the first time, that they are all actually working for the same company.

SECTION IV
CASE EXAMPLES OF STRATEGIC
MARKET PLANNING

18
Strategic Market Planning for a New Consumer Product (A Case Example)

G. David Hughes
Burlington Industries Professor of Business Administration
University of North Carolina

Phillip E. Downs
Associate Professor of Marketing
Florida State University

Persons who have not made a marketing plan for a new product can be overwhelmed by the complexity and amount of information required in developing such a plan. The authors demonstrate, through a set of worksheets, the organization of the relevant information. This approach points out missing information and illogical thinking as well as facilitating a creative overview.

The strategic marketing plan is part of all business plans. In companies that are largely marketing organizations, the strategic marketing plan is the major part of the business plan. Persons who have not made a marketing plan can become overwhelmed by the complexity and amount of information in such a plan. This chapter illustrates how a set of worksheets can be used to organize the relevant information. Once the information is organized, the creative process of strategy development begins.

THE WORKSHEET APPROACH

The worksheet approach to planning includes two worksheets: the environmental worksheet and the strategy worksheet. The environmental worksheet examines the market environment for the business or the brand. It begins with an examination of the values, policies, and goals of the chief administrators, because these provide direction for marketing efforts and limit the strategic alternatives that may be considered. The marketing organization is examined to determine if the company has outgrown its old organization or if the present organization limits a company's ability to implement a plan. The total industry demand for a product or service is examined in great detail. The demand for the company's brand is studied. Present and potential competitors are considered. The effect of government regulations must be evaluated. The distillation of this environmental analysis is a statement of market opportunities and problems. We may think of this as an audit of the environment in which the brand or business operates.

The strategy worksheet begins with a ranking of the opportunities and problems that were identified during the analysis of the environment. It then states the present goals (financial and marketing) and summarizes the present marketing mix strategies: product, price, channel, advertising, personal selling, and research. Systems for evaluation and control are noted during the examination of the current strategy.

With the rank order of the opportunities and problems and the current strategy laid out in a logical format, the planner can decide whether the current strategy will tap the opportunities, solve the problems, and reach the target goals, or whether there is a *planning gap*. Rarely will it be necessary to develop a completely new strategy for the entire marketing mix, except when a new product is introduced.

The planner must identify new alternative strategies for each of the elements in the marketing mix. This is a creative and difficult step. He or she will recommend one of these strategies based on its ability to tap opportunities and to solve problems and on its net favorable effects on the income statement and balance sheet. The latter information is translated into a profit plan and a statement of resources required to implement the plan.

The final output of this analysis is a clearly written marketing plan that summarizes the current position of the brand, the goals for the planning period, and the marketing mix strategies that will be used to reach these goals. Frequently, the plan is only four pages in length with accompanying exhibits giving some details and time schedules for activities such as advertising or sales promotion.

To understand the marketing planning process, we need to walk through an example. For illustrative purposes, it will be clearer if we examine a new product. More detailed discussions of the marketing planning process may be found in the senior author's textbook.[1]

Crystal, a New Entry in the Sparkling Water Market

In early 1978, Jimmy Sturgel, associate product manager at Starlite, Inc., became intrigued by the meteoric sales rise of Perrier sparkling bottled water. While Sturgel's product (which was a hangover reliever) was not even distantly related to the sparkling water market, Sturgel began accumulating information about the sparkling water market and Perrier's marketing strategy (see Appendix A).

Sturgel began discussing with his product manager Robert Trent the possibility of mounting a competitive challenge to Perrier. They quickly agreed that a direct competitor with no real distinguishing characteristics could conceivably be marginally profitable. But to make significant profit, a competitor would have to offer at least one distinct benefit not offered by Perrier.

After a few weeks of thought, Sturgel came up with the idea of a tablet that, when mixed with tap water, would produce the rough equivalent of Perrier water. Sturgel went directly to Dwight Alamar, vice-president of R&D at Starlite, to discuss the feasibility of developing such a product.

In a previous job, Alamar had spent time developing a tablet soft drink. The product that resulted from his efforts was not well received by consumers. Alamar felt that demand for the tablet soft drink was not large because the flavor and carbonation were not commensurate with the quality of regular soft drinks. Doubtful but still wanting to benefit from his previous work, Alamar began to work diligently on formulating a "sparkling water" tablet.

A few months passed before Alamar contacted Sturgel. Alamar was simply ecstatic. His latest formulation, when mixed with water, could not be differentiated by the R&D staff from Perrier water. Sturgel and several other employees tasted the mixture and none could differentiate it from Perrier.

Sturgel and Alamar next met with J. T. Browning, the vice-president of production, to discuss the feasibility of producing these tablets on a wide-scale basis. The formulation that Alamar developed was very stable and presented no major difficulties to Browning. By October 1978, Browning indicated that production could start by November.

Sturgel, who by this time had been elevated to product manager of this new test product, developed a test market strategy for the new tablet. It was decided that the product would be tested in Richmond, Virginia and Indianapolis, Indiana. Before testing the product, much work was required in developing specific marketing strategies. From December through February, advertising strategies, trade strategies, distribution strategies, and pricing strategies were perfected. Finally, the name Crystal was chosen.

Test Market

By May 1979, testing of Crystal in the two test market areas began. Rather than examining the relationship between different levels of marketing variables and consumer demand, management decided to use the same marketing strategy in both test markets. Crystal was packaged in 2-, 6-, 12-, and 24- tablet packages with the following prices:

> 2 tablets: $0.69 (retail)
> 6 tablets: $1.89
> 12 tablets: $3.49
> 24 tablets: $6.59

Advertising expenditures were set at a level that management felt could be sustained if the product went national. Starlite's distribution structure of drug and grocery stores was used in the test market.

Crystal remained in the test markets until the end of November. At that point, management began to consider a go/no-go decision on the basis of data collected throughout the test period. The following tables summarize information collected during the test market period. Individuals fitting target market characteristics were randomly selected to be interviewed.

Sales and Market Share/Test Market
(May to November 1979)

	UNIT SALES	DOLLAR SALES	MARKET SHARE
Crystal	100,000 tablets (12 oz)	33,400 (retail)	17%
Perrier	178,005 bottles (23 oz)	131,725 (retail)	58%
Others	76,726 bottles (23 oz)	55,240 (retail)	25%

Awareness Test
(%age having heard of the brand, August 79)

Crystal	60%
Perrier	93%
Saratoga	74%
Montclair	38%
Deer Park	34%
Poland Spring	29%

Trial and Repurchase Rates
(October 1979)

	CRYSTAL	PERRIER	SARATOGA
Have heard of the brand	60%	93%	74%
Have tried the brand	16.8%	38%	21%
Have purchased the brand repeatedly	4.2%	19%	8%

Reason for Selecting Crystal
(October 1979)

Because of Crystal advertising	28%
Looking for alternative to soft drinks	31%
Looking for alternative to alcohol	18%
Unhappy with other brands	29%
Just wanted to try a change	35%
Because a friend recommended it	32%
Saw it in the store and decided to try it	17%
Other	12%

Blind Taste Tests
(July 1979)

	PREFERRED CRYSTAL	PREFERRED OTHER	NO PREFERENCE
Perrier vs. Crystal	21%	28%	51%
Crystal vs. Saratoga	25%	26%	49%
Crystal vs. Montclair	20%	31%	49%

APPENDIX A

The sparkling, bottled water market in the United States has grown dramatically in the past few years. In 1978, United States sales for sparkling, bottled water totaled $225 million. Of this amount, Perrier accounted for $30 million, with sales of 90 million bottles. Perrier's unit sales growth in the United States has been fantastic, starting with 3.5 million bottles in 1976, while estimating 180 million bottles for 1979. Sparkling bottled water sales on a worldwide basis have been much more stable over time, both for Perrier and for the industry as a whole.

Perrier's dramatic sales increase in the United States was a result of an ingenious marketing strategy representing a drastic change from previous strategies. In 1976, Perrier was sold primarily at specialty food outlets and fine restaurants. By mid-1979, supermarkets accounted for 70% of Perrier's distribution, up from only 10% two years ago. Contribution to total sales from gourmet shops had shrunk to 5% by 1979. Over 80% of the sales by 1979 were for home consumption. This dramatic change was brought about by switching from store-door delivery to centralized distribution through soft drink bottlers and beer wholesalers.

Another significant change involved a price cut by nearly a third to around 69¢ to 79¢ for a 23-ounce bottle at retail. At this price, Perrier was still roughly 50% above the average soft drink price. Positioning strategy underwent considerable transformation from a snob-appeal product to a noncaloric, chic alternative to soft drinks and alcoholic beverages.

Perrier hit the United States market in 1977 with an advertising budget, heavy by industry standards, of $2 million. By 1979, Perrier's advertising expenditures had been increased to $9 million. In the words of one analyst, "Perrier's success rests on a meticulously orchestrated marketing campaign that draws heavily on the Procter and Gamble Company formula of market segmentation and heavy advertising. Previously, there has been very little attempt to segment the soft drink market on a price basis or to significantly tap the adult-user market."

Bottled Water Industry

By some estimates, there are 500 brands of bottled water in the United States. Nearly all of these producers are small, regional firms. Bottled water has no calories, no impurities, and no preservatives. Sparkling bottled water is all of the above, with varying degrees of natural or artificially derived carbonation. Bottled water contains no chlorine because it is purified by ozone, which is tasteless, colorless, and odorless.

Market

A study done by a leading marketing research firm indicates that heavy users of sparkling bottled water are athletically and socially active. Most are health conscious and concerned about staying in shape. Product usage is heavier in larger metropolitan areas and in the northeastern and far western parts of the United States. Unmarrieds and marrieds with no children represent heavy users. Generally, heavy users report incomes higher than the median income in the United States.

Table 1. Environmental worksheet

ENVIRONMENTAL ELEMENTS	CURRENT FACTS	ASSUMPTIONS/RESEARCH NEEDED	CONCLUSIONS
Values, objectives, and policies	To become the dominant force in the sparkling water industry	Based on current information, it is assumed that the goal is profit and market-share oriented. Assume also that quality is a prerequisite to becoming a "dominant" force.	Strategies must generate profit and market share levels, while maintaining quality image.
Organizational design	Product manager system	Assume product manager for Crystal has enough persuasive ability to garner his share of time and man-power from supporting staff areas, such as marketing research and advertising.	Product manager has authority to implement marketing strategy, thus the marketing plan is the document for allocating the marketing effort.
Situation analysis generic demand	Mineral water—over $225 million annually in U.S. (1978)	Assume soft-drink market will expand slowly, while mineral water market will expand rapidly, but face considerably more variability in the long run.	How generic market is defined will have significant effect on formulation of marketing strategy and subsequent success of such a strategy.
Time patterns	Perrier—35 million bottles in U.S. (1976) Perrier—375 million bottles worldwide (1976) Perrier—90 million bottles in U.S. (1978) (estimated 180 million for 1979)	Assumed worldwide market for mineral water will show a moderate growth, while U.S. demand will continue to grow at a dynamic rate.	Marketing efforts should be focused on the U.S. market.
Consumer profile	Traditional market (mineral water) consists of those interested in health and/or snob appeal. Heavy users are active, health conscious; upscale economically and socially; singles and childless couples; metropolitan areas in northeastern and western U.S.	Research needed to determine if Crystal will appeal to the "new" mineral water market.	If Crystal can appeal to the "new" mineral water market, then future success is highly probable. If not, alternate markets must be explored or the product idea dropped.

ENVIRONMENTAL ELEMENTS	CURRENT FACTS	ASSUMPTIONS/RESEARCH NEEDED	CONCLUSIONS
Brand demand Crystal	1979 test market, 100,000 tablets. Predict nationwide for 1980, 200 million tablets. Crystal achieved a 17% share in the test market area.	Assume distribution in 50 largest U.S. markets can be achieved in 1980. Assume consumer acceptance nationwide will parallel acceptance in test markets.	Crystal retail dollar sales for 1980 = 24 Size: 20 million = 0.84 m boxes $\times$ 6.59/box = 5.54 m 12 Size: 30 million = 2.50 m boxes $\times$ 3.49/box = 8.72 m 6 Size: 70 million = 11.6 m boxes $\times$ 1.89/box = 21.92 m 2 Size: 80 million = 40 m boxes $\times$ 0.69/box = 27.6 m 200 million tablets Retail sales = $63.78 m Wholesale = $38.04 m Manufacturer = $34.24
Crystal market share in dollars	Estimated mineral water sales $375 million (1980). Estimated soft drink sales $13 billion (1980).		34.24/375 = 9.13% share of dollars
Determinants of share			Distribution in top 50 market by the end of 1980. Heavy advertising to educate and inform users.
Brand position	Low cost; "as good as imported mineral water."		Emphasize lower price; ease of fixing; domestic production.
Awareness	60% of target market after three months in test market.		Advertising strategy in test market adequate in achieving awareness.
Trial rate	28% of those aware of Crystal purchased it; 17% purchased on an impulse without prior awareness.		Advertising must achieve awareness and trial. Special consumer deals will be needed to stimulate trial.
Repurchase rate	In blind taste tests, only 28% claimed that Crystal was inferior to Perrier. In test market, only 25% of triers repurchased.	Need to discover consumers' motivation for lack of repurchasing Crystal	Product has adequate "real" taste, but perceived taste is lacking. This negative perception must be corrected.

Distribution rate	Distribution for Crystal limited to the test market areas. However, the Starlite Company has a national distribution structure (grocery and drug stores and night clubs) for its hangover cure.		Starlite's national distribution structure will be necessary to insure product profitability.
Competitive national advertising	Perrier spent $2 million in 1977 and $9 million in 1979.	Assume all other mineral water marketers have a low level of advertising, based on the history of the industry.	Will have to at least match Perrier's expenditures in order to make significant increases in the market.
Competition— Market structure	Most mineral water marketers are small regional water bottlers. Most add carbonation to the water. There are roughly 500 regional bottlers.	Need to determine the probability that a major soft-drink producer will enter the mineral water market.	Starlite's major competitor at present will be Perrier. Future competitors might include a major soft-drink producer.
Industry success factors	Perrier has succeeded by using a non-traditional distribution structure, premium (but not exclusive) pricing, and heavy advertising. Positioning success based on positioning Perrier as a non-caloric, chic alternative to soft drinks and alcohol.		Crystal must achieve adequate national distribution and receive heavy advertising support. A unique positioning strategy needs to be created.
Industry capacity	Current capacity is sufficient.		Given the sudden, explosive growth of the U.S. market, short-term capacity deficiencies may result.
Public Policy Considerations:			
Antitrust	No antitrust issues currently relevant in mineral water.		Antitrust problems not of immediate or intermediate range concern.
Regulatory agencies	Crystal must meet EPA standards. No new chemicals or substances used in Crystal.		FDA approval is not required since all substances in Crystal presently meet FDA standards.

ENVIRONMENTAL ELEMENTS	CURRENT FACTS	ASSUMPTIONS/RESEARCH NEEDED	CONCLUSIONS
Consumerism	No consumerism activity generated toward existing mineral water marketers. Soft-drink industry faces pressure from medical and parent groups.		Crystal does not contain artificial sweeteners or sugar. Therefore consumerism pressure should be nonexistent.
Environmental	Energy saved because Crystal tablets do not require refrigeration. Production of Crystal is practically pollution free.		Environmental concerns are almost nonexistent. Can use energy saving as a promotional tool.

OPPORTUNITIES

1. Growing demand for mineral water in the U.S.
2. Opportunity for a lower-priced mineral water.
3. Crystal is more easily stored and transported than existing mineral water.
4. Crystal requires less retail shelf space than existing mineral water.
5. Crystal can be distributed via Starlite's existing distribution structure.
6. Favorable test market results.
7. Only a few nationally known competitors currently exist.
8. Crystal creates no major public policy concerns.

PROBLEMS

1. Crystal must overcome Perrier's terrific head start in the market.
2. Consumers must accept the do-it-yourself concept, i.e., they must be willing to exert a little effort and be convinced that a make-at-home carbonated beverage will taste as good as a naturally carbonated or factory-carbonated beverage.
3. A high, national distribution rate will be required to compete with Perrier.
4. Crystal may not be perceived as "natural" because it is a tablet.
5. The high level of marketing expenditures necessary to compete with Perrier will make it difficult to derive a profit.
6. Taste of Crystal will be dependent upon tap water if bottled water is not used.

Table 2. Strategy worksheet

DECISION AREAS	RECOMMENDED STRATEGY	ESTIMATED EFFECT ON PROFIT PLAN
Generic	Define generic market as mineral water market. Too much marketing expenditure will be necessry to compete in the soft-drink market. Take advantage of Perrier's marketing attempts to compete with the soft-drink market. Use own marketing to compete with Perrier and other mineral water producers.	By defining market generically as mineral water, Crystal's marketing expenditures will help expand generic market, while capturing a significant share of the market.
Brand	Position Crystal as an economical, quality mineral water that can be ready whenever you are. Positioning emphasis will also be focused on Crystal as a diet alternative to soft drinks.	Combination of price appeal, quality assurance, and zero calories should enable Crystal to achieve brand success.
Strategic Goals:		
Financial	Because of the high level of marketing effort, the goal is to reach break-even sales level by the end of the first year.	See profit plan.
Marketing	To achieve a 9% unit market share in the U.S. sparkling water market by the end of the next 12 months.	See profit plan.
Marketing Mix Strategies:		
Product	Product is a diamond-shaped tablet that dissolves in five seconds when placed in tap or distilled water. Tablets will come in "natural," lemon, and mint flavors.	Three flavors give Crystal a competitive edge over current sparkling water. Tablets enable user to prepare only as much as is desired, i.e., the problem of losing carbonation from a half-used container is eliminated.
Package	Each tablet will be individually wrapped in a "water-blue" colored foil. A package of 2, 6, 12 or 24 tablets will be enclosed in a rectangular box made of emerald green mock felt cardboard.	Packaging is coordinated with the positioning concept and to overcome any preconceived quality deficiency resulting from a lower price, the emerald-green mock felt will symbolize quality. Imagery of the product will be enhanced with the "water-blue" foil. Package sizes (6, 12, and 24) correspond to six-pack and case sizes of small Perrier bottles, and the two-tablet size corresponds roughly to the quart-size bottles.

DECISION AREAS	RECOMMENDED STRATEGY	ESTIMATED EFFECT ON PROFIT PLAN
Price	Crystal will retail at the following prices: 2 tablets (24 ounces) $0.69 6 tablets $1.89 12 tablets $3.45 24 tablets $6.59	Retail price will vary (depending upon the size of the package) from 69¢ to 79¢ per 24-ounce serving. This compares favorably with a retail price of Perrier at 73¢ to $1.09 per 23-ounce bottle. Retail markup will be 40% and wholesale markup will be 10%.
Channels	Crystal will be distributed primarily through grocery stores and drug stores, i.e., the distribution structure presently being utilized by Starlite's hangover cure. In one year, plan to achieve distribution in 60% of the outlets currently being used to distribute the hangover cure. Achieve 90% distribution in two years. 8% off-invoice allowance for the first six months. A display allowance to each direct-buying retail customer of 50¢ for each counter display and $1.25 for each floor display.	Starlite's successful hangover cure has paved the way for additional products. A successful track record with a previous product, plus an introductory bonus mark-up percentage and display money should ensure distribution goals. Cost of additional off invoice for six months: 100,000 tablets, (six-month supply) at wholesale equal 19.02 m less 10% mark-up = 17.12 m. Less 18% mark-up = 15.60 m. Cost of additional 8% mark-up = 17.12 − 15.60 = 1.52 m.
Advertising:		
Promotion	Use sampling and coupons to get trial and repeat use. Samples will be distributed to one million individuals in metropolitan areas in the northeast and the west coast. Use POP (point of purchase) displays to increase awareness and to encourage impulse buying. Secure Olympic Games affiliation.	Two million two-tablet packages will be distributed to randomly selected individuals (fitting target market characteristics) in the top 50 metro areas. Total cost = $778,000 $340,000 production costs — 4 m tablets 82,000 packaging and distribution 300,000 postage 56,000 overhead $778,000 Total cost of sampling Coupons will be for 20¢ off the 69¢, two-tablet package. Retailer will be reimbursed for the 20¢ coupon, plus a 5¢ handling fee. It is estimated that 1,000,000 coupons will be redeemed. $250,000 Total cost of coupons POP displays $300,000 Olympic affiliation: $100,000 Total cost of Olympic affiliation Total promotional costs = $1,428,000

Advertising copy

—Make it at home and save money.
—Your friends will never know if it's Crystal or one of its higher priced imitations.
—Save refrigerator and cabinet space.
—The sparkling taste now comes in three flavors.
—Diet alternative to soft drinks.
—Official drink of the U.S. Olympic team.

It is felt that the appeals made are sufficiently different from traditional sparkling mineral water ads that Crystal will create its own niche in the rapidly expanding sparkling mineral water market. Advertising expenditures = 15% of sales = $5.3m.

Target audience

Aiming for audience which is a notch below upscale market reached by Perrier and other sparkling, bottled water producers. Middle income market in Northwest, west coast, and midwest areas. Active individuals.

Crystal is attempting to open up the sparkling mineral water market to not only the masses of upscale individuals, but also to the masses of middle-class individuals.

Media and weight

Heavy TV to 1) reach large middle income market and to 2) show preparation of product. 250 GRP's (gross rating points) for first month of product and during Thanksgiving-Christmas period. 100 GRP's for remainder of time. Use magazines to reach diet-conscious and active individuals (e.g., Glamour, Family Circle, Sports Illustrated, Ziff-Davis Network).

GRP achieved will accomplish awareness of product and implant the major product attributes in the minds of the target market.

Continuity

Alternate network daytime and prime time TV throughout April to September and during Thanksgiving-Christmas period. Maintain magazine coverage throughout the year.

Periodic and saturation advertising will result in high recall of product name and attributes.

Personal Selling

Have salespeople call on major retailers to help set up counter and floor displays and to work for prime shelf positioning. Salespeople will be responsible for coordinating store inventory levels with heavy introductory advertising.

Salespeople have already been calling on the retailers in distributing the hangover cure. No lag time needed to sell retailers on the company or the salesperson.

Research

Do research to reveal problems encountered by requiring consumer to mix his own drink (eight focus group interviews).

Eight interviews at $2,500/interview = $20,000.

Industry Sales

$ value (1978) $225,000,000 (U.S.)
$ value (1979) $275,000,000 (U.S.)
$ value (1980) est. $375,000,000 (U.S.)
Perrier (1978) $30,000 (U.S.)
Perrier (1979) est. $60,000,000 (U.S.)
Perrier (1980) est. $90,000,000 (U.S.)
Crystal (1980) est. $34,240,000 (U.S.)

DECISION AREAS	RECOMMENDED STRATEGY	ESTIMATED EFFECT ON PROFIT PLAN
Profit Plan:		
Brand Sales	34.24 m	100.0%
Cost of goods sold		
Fixed cost	9.0 m	26.3
Variable cost	8.0 m	23.4
Total CGS	17.0 m	49.7%
Gross margin	17.24 m	50.4%*
Marketing Expenses		
Promotion		
Media/production	5.3 m	15.5%
Sampling/couponing	1.03 m	3.0
Trade allowance	1.52 m	4.4
Other promotion	0.4 m	1.2
Total promotion	8.25 m	24.1%
Sales force	2.4 m	7.0
Distribution	1.5 m	4.4
Administration	0.9 m	2.6
Total Expenses	13.05 m	38.1%
Contribution to profit and overhead	4.19 m	12.2%

*Percentages are off slightly because of rounding errors.

DECISION AREAS	RECOMMENDED STRATEGY	ESTIMATED EFFECT ON PROFIT PLAN
Evaluation and control:		
Product tests	Do blind taste tests to compare Crystal with Perrier among users and nonusers of Crystal.	$10,000
Channel studies	Monitor Nielsen Retail Index (of products sold through retail outlets) and examine warehouse withdrawals to food stores (provided by Selling Areas—Marketing, Inc.).	$25,000
Price	Have sales force monitor retail prices of major sparkling bottled water producers.	$5,000
Advertising	Utilize Daniel Starch & Associates for magazine advertising effectiveness. Use Gallup-Robinson service to monitor television advertising effectiveness.	$25,000

CRYSTAL'S 1980 MARKETING PLAN

I. Brand's Current Performance

In the Richmond and Indianapolis test markets, Crystal achieved a 17% market share. This exceeds the 9% market share objective. Marketing expenditures in the test market were commensurate with projected national expenditures for 1980.

II. Recommendations

Sales for 1980 are projected to be 200,000,000 tablets, resulting in $34,240,000 in sales. To achieve this objective, Crystal will be priced slightly below Perrier, and supported by $8.32 million in advertising and in other promotion. Distribution will be through already established grocery and drug retailers.

III. Effect of the Recommendation on Income

Sales	34.24 m
Share est.	9.13%
Cost of goods	17.0 (49.7%)
Adv/Promotion	8.25 (24.1%)
Other costs	4.8 (14.0%)
Pretax profits	4.19 (12.2%)

IV. Situation Analysis

A. The market

1. *Size*. The total United States market for mineral water in 1978 was $225 million. The market is growing rapidly and is expected to reach $275 million in 1979 and $375 million by 1980. This market is served by roughly 500 bottlers, most of which are regional.
2. *Consumer*. The greatest demand for beer and soft drinks has traditionally been the under-35 group. However, mineral water has appealed to upscale individuals, aged 25 to 44. Crystal will broaden this market (18–54) and also focus on the vast middle class in terms of income and lifestyle. Two major segments will be active: athletically and

socially active individuals and calorie-conscious individuals.

3. *Pricing*. Crystal will be priced marginally below Perrier. While Perrier is priced from 73¢ to $1.09 for a 23-ounce bottle, Crystal will vary between 69¢ and 79¢.
4. *Seasonality*. As a refresher for athletically active individuals, Crystal will be consumed more during the April-September period. As a social drink, consumption will increase during holiday periods.

B. Crystal

1. *The product*. Crystal is a tablet which, when mixed with tap or distilled water, produces a light, sparkling water. The product comes in lemon, mint, and "natural" flavors.
2. *Manufacturing*. Meeting production schedules for the estimated 200 million tablets for 1980 will present no burden to existing plant capacity.

V. Opportunities and Problems

A. Opportunities
Success is anticipated for the following reasons:

1. Skyrocketing demand for bottled mineral water in the United States.
2. Market opening for a low-price mineral water.
3. Crystal is more easily stored and transported than existing mineral water.
4. Crystal requires less retail shelf space than existing mineral water.
5. Crystal can be distributed via Starlite's existing distribution structure.
6. Favorable test market results.
7. Only a few nationally known competitors exist.
8. Production and marketing of Crystal creates no major public policy concerns.

B. Problems

1. Crystal must compete with Perrier,

which has a very strong market position.

2. Consumers must accept the do-it-yourself concept. This presents two basic problems. 1) projecting a quality image, and 2) inconvenience of mixing the drink.

3. A high national distribution rate will be required to compete with Perrier.

4. Crystal may not be perceived as a "natural" product because it is a tablet.

5. The high level of marketing expenditures necessary to compete with Perrier will make it difficult to derive a profit.

VI. Strategies

A. Marketing

The objective of the Crystal strategy is to attain a 9% market share in dollar volume. To achieve this objective, the following strategy will be implemented:

1. Low cost, high quality positioning strategy. Diet appeal will also be emphasized.

2. Promotion will be established at 24.1% of the sales level to achieve awareness and trial.

3. Promotion will be stepped up during the warmer months and during holiday period.

4. Crystal's retail price will be marginally lower than Perrier's. Also, the trade discount will be increased during the first six months.

B. Copy

The objective of the copy is to establish the following attributes:

1. *Economy.* "make it at home and save money.'

2. *High quality.* "your friends will never know if it's Crystal or one of its higher priced imitators."

3. *No calories.* "a spritely refresher or a perfect mixer—there are still no calories."

4. *Several flavors.* "the sparkling refresher comes in three flavors."

5. Minor emphasis will be given to the space-saving benefits and the Olympic affiliation.

C. Media

Crystal's media objective is to reach athletically and socially active adults (18–54) as frequently as possible.

1. 250 GRPs will be generated during the first month of introduction and during the holiday period, with 125 GRPs generated during the remainder of the year.

2. Magazines whose target markets are socially and athletically active individuals and magazines that appeal to diet-conscious individuals will be utilized.

D. Promotion

Crystal's promotion is designed to achieve the following objectives:

1. Heavy trial accomplished by distributing 2 million two-tablet packages to individuals in the top 50 metro areas.

2. High trial and repurchase rates by featuring 20¢ off coupons in local retailers' advertisements.

3. High impulse buying by establishing floor and counter displays in retail outlets.

4. Product legitimacy by being the "official Olympic sparkling water."

VII. Test/Research

	Estimated Costs
1. Blind taste tests to compare Crystal with Perrier among users and nonusers of Crystal.	$10,000
2. Nielsen retail index and SAMI warehouse shipments.	25,000
3. Monitor competitors' retail prices.	5,000
4. Monitor magazine and TV advertising effectiveness through Starch and Gallup-Robinson.	25,000
	$65,000

EXPANDING THE MARKETING PLAN

The example illustrates how marketing and accounting information comes together to develop a final plan. The estimated effect of the plan on the profit plan was kept simple for the sake of a clear illustration. The "Estimated Effects on Profit Plan" column could be expanded to include the effect on the income statement, the balance sheet, and personnel utilization. By including these additional effects, we could easily expand the marketing plan into a business plan. We could then examine how the proposed plan would affect corporate productivity measures. For example, capital utilization measures would include ratios such as asset turnover, inventory turnover, production capacity utilization, and investment required per dollar of sales. The productivity of personnel could be measured by ratios such as sales per employee, employee compensation per dollar of sales, and value added per employee. These ratios are critical in diagnosing problem areas in the company.

THE ADVANTAGES OF THE WORKSHEET APPROACH

There are many advantages to a worksheet approach when one develops marketing plan. The following are just a few of the advantages that have been noted by those who have used this approach.

1. It forces the planner to be complete and logical. Holes in information and illogical thinking are identified quickly.
2. All of the relevant information can be spread out in front of the planner so that important strategic links may be seen in a creative, nonlinear process.
3. Planners, group product managers, and top executives use a common language, which makes it easier to communicate and evaluate a plan.
4. Key assumptions are identified, so that they can be accepted or challenged at each step in the planning process.
5. Completion of the worksheets forces an audit of the present environment and strategy of a brand.

In conclusion, marketing planning is becoming more complex because products are more complex, buyers are more demanding, domestic and foreign competition is greater, and sophisticated research has increased the quantity and quality of the data that are available. This increased complexity requires an organized approach, such as that provided by the worksheets described in this chapter.

REFERENCE

1. Hughes, G. David, *Marketing Management: A Planning Approach*, Addison-Wesley, 1978.

19
Strategic Market Planning for a New Business (A Case Example)

Thomas S. Dudick

The author breaks this case example down into two parts. The first deals with the various indicators required to measure the market potential and the characteristics of the market. The second deals with profitability and financial requirements.

When capital is being sought for a new venture, the demands for proper business planning are quite stringent. The lending institution and underwriters are demanding in the amount and type of information that is required to support all phases of the new business.

The quality of business planning in an ongoing company varies with the management. Some managements demand definitive planning for all functions within the company; others are quite lax, particularly when the income statement shows reasonably acceptable results.

Planning in business is somewhat like a flight plan that must be prepared before take-off. In our highly competitive economic society, as in the preparation of a flight plan, there can be no laxity in the planning process—one of the prime responsibilities of management.

Because business plans in evaluating new ventures are usually more fully developed, such a plan would provide a good case study.

This chapter follows the steps developed for a planned cable television operation, sometimes referred to as *subscription television*. This type of business was selected because it is relatively new and has problems that should be fairly easy to visualize and understand.

Our investigations concern themselves with the selection of indicators that measure market potential and the characteristics of this market, while the second part of the chapter addresses itself to the determination of profit opportunities and capital requirements.

MEASURING MARKET POTENTIAL AND CHARACTERISTICS

Probably the most important indicator of the market potential of subscribers to pay television is an analysis of income stratification. Such an analysis gives a clue as to the portion of the area population that can afford to pay for television services. It also gives some rough indication as to tastes, which are helpful in programming. While an important indicator, income by itself is not sufficiently comprehensive. It is therefore necessary to take into account such other indicators as education, occupation, age of the potential viewing audience, and family makeup.

Analysis of Income.

The median (most frequently occurring) annual income in the population area selected for study was found to be $16,600 per year— compared with $12,470 five years previously. The increase over the five-year period represents a larger percentage than the corresponding increase shown by the national average. This is attributable to the influx of business and professional people attracted by several new residential areas. The income range breakdown for five levels is summarized in Table 1. It is evident from a brief review of Table 1 that the first two ranges—under $6,000 and between $6001 and $12,000— have decreased, while the remaining three levels have increased. Because the shift into the higher ranges is in excess of existing inflationary increases, it may be concluded that the residents of this area are increasing their affluency at a greater rate than the nation as a whole.

Table 1. Analysis of income

INCOME RANGE	THIS YEAR (%)	FIVE YEARS AGO (%)
Under $6,000	1.2	3.7
$6,001 to $12,000	19.8	26.3
$12,001 to $20,000	62.0	58.8
$20,001 to $40,000	13.3	10.0
Over $40,000	3.7	1.2
	100.0	100.0

Scholastic (Educational) Profile

The scholastic profile was determined through an analysis of the breadwinner member of each of the households in the area being stud-

Table 2. Scholastic profile

SCHOLASTIC LEVEL	%
No high school	5.5
Some high school	22.1
High school graduate	35.4
Some college	16.6
Undergradute degree	15.8
Graduate work	4.6
	100.0

ied. The median level of scholastic attainment falls within the high school graduate category. The breakdown of breadwinners falling in the various categories is shown in Table 2.

The analysis shows a fairly high educational attainment. This correlates with the relatively high income status reflected in Table 1. Both are important factors in the marketability of subscription television. The scholastic level is also important in determining the types of programs that would be in demand.

Analysis of Occupations

The occupational specialty can also be helpful in determining the subscriber's program pref-

Table 3. Analysis of Occupations

OCCUPATION CATEGORY	%
Executive and junior executive	27.5
Professional	21.2
Skilled labor	16.0
White collar	11.5
Salesmen or business owners	10.3
Service	7.3
Retired	6.2
	100.0

Table 4. Age profile of breadwinners

AGE	%
Below 20	0.7
Between 20 and 29	11.1
Between 30 and 39	22.1
Between 40 and 49	36.4
Between 50 and 59	13.2
Over 60	16.5
	100.0

erences. The analysis of occupations, shown as Table 3, indicates that more than half of the surveyed population is made up of the executive and professional categories, certainly a good guide as to tastes in programs viewed.

Age Profile of Breadwinners

Tastes and interests in programming are also influenced by age, by family makeup, and by the number and age of children in the household. These are dealt with next.

The median age of the head of the household was found to be about 43 years of age. See Table 4 for breakdown by age groups.

The age of the breadwinner is a fairly good indicator of the age of the balance of the family. However, because an age breakdown of the children is important to determination of programming, a survey of the ages of the children was considered to be important. This is shown in Table 5.

The average number of children found per household was 2.2. More than half of the households had two children of which the average age was found to be 13. Table 5 shows the breakdown by five age categories. Because the average age of children in the surveyed area is greater than the adjacent cable television area used for comparison, (13 versus 11.9 years), programming for children will most likely be affected by this average age difference.

This survey provides additional figures that show 63.5% of breadwinners living with their spouses, 16.3 widowed, and 20.2% single or living separately from their mates.

Table 5. Age breakdown of children

AGE OF CHILDREN	%
Below 6 years	17.3
6 through 10 years	17.6
11 through 15 years	25.6
16 through 20 years	28.2
21 years and over	11.3
	100.0

Modifying the Statistics with Judgment.

Judgments on the potential profitability of a business should not be determined through use of raw statistics without the application of a large dose of common business sense. The factors that cause people to be subscribers must be carefully considered. For example:

1. Do the potential subscribers expect that the program content is superior to conventional television? Do they then drop out when they find that they were overrating the program quality they expected?
2. Did they become subscribers because of impulse as a result of high pressure selling by a door-to-door sales effort?
3. Has the subscriber lost interest in home entertainment in favor of seeking amusements outside the home? Tastes do tend to swing in cycles.
4. Was the disenchanted subscriber dissatisfied with the quality of the films? Are the so-called good movies so loaded with sex and violence that subscribers fear that their children will be exposed to them?

It is important in a survey of this type to know the principal reasons that subscribers drop out. If this is not taken into account, the market survey may leave an overoptimistic picture of the true revenue potential. In addition to a probing analysis to seek out such answers, a good idea of customer preferences can be obtained from questionnaires that have been carefully prepared to determine people's preferences for programs and their willingness to pay for them.

Survey of Programs Watched

Such a survey was made by obtaining information from a neighboring subscription television area. The operators of the system agreed to furnish the names and addresses of their subscribers in return for a copy of the results.

The high percentage of time spent watching sports events was quite unexpected. (See Table 6.) Another unexpected finding not included in the summary in Table 6 was that almost half the films watched were of the B type, as distinguished from first-rate.

Table 6. Programs watched in an adjacent neighborhood

TYPES OF PROGRAMS	%
Films	34.2
Sports events	39.0
Children's films	9.8
Night club acts	10.2
Broadway stage plays	6.8
	100.0

In making evaluations of any type, it must be rememberd that programs watched are a function of programs that are available to watch. Availability can affect viewing to a certain degree.

A survey of viewers in an existing subscription television area is likely to be more reliable than one conducted among prospects who have never experienced this type of programming. Nonetheless, the more information that can be gathered about the prospective subscribers, the better. The process of questioning serves an important ancillary purpose—advertising and developing interest in the new venture.

The questionnaires must be worded carefully to assure that questions arising from the previous survey are answered. The questions covered should include an expression of preference for various types of programs, requesting specific examples of the types of movies, stage plays, sporting events, and other types of entertainment.

Willingness to pay certain amounts for the various types of programs should also be ascertained, as should be the attitude toward installation charges of various amounts.

Once viewer preferences are known, and the schedule of fees has been determined, we are ready to summarize the data relating to the total potential market.

The Potential Market

The area selected for the new venture covers about 29 square miles and is located about 30 miles from a major city that transmits programs from three channels. Because of the surrounding hills, only about half of the residents receive all three channels. The other half receive two channels with varying degrees of quality.

Interest in receiving better reception and more programs is high. This is reflected by the fact that there are more than 2,700 television homes per square mile—a total of 75,600 for the selected area (2,700 per square mile × 28 square miles).

Sampling surveys (both by telephone and by mail) of these 75,600 television homes show that 47.5% expressed interest in becoming subscribers. This compares with an actual percentage of installations in the neighboring area of 42%, despite a lower density of television homes amounting to only 2,300 per square mile.

Applying the 47.5% to the total television homes in the area shows a potential of 35,910 subscribers. In evaluating the time requirements for completing approximately 36,000 hookups, it was estimated that an average of slightly more than 3.5 subscribers could be tied into the system per workday. This includes stringing a cable as well as making the actual hookup to the subscriber's television.

This estimate allows for delays resulting from the more difficult terrain through which the telephone company would have to install additional poles leading from the transmitting unit on top of one of the hills. It also takes into account that construction of new residential areas is not to be started for at least another year.

With the number of subscribers and time-phasing of the hookups established, the next step is to project the revenues and to match them against costs of programming, rental of telephone company facilities, startup, operating, subscriber units, and transmission center equipment. These are covered in the second section of the chapter.

DETERMINATION OF PROFITABILITY AND FINANCIAL REQUIREMENTS

The second part of this chapter deals with the projection of revenues, expenses, capital requirements, profits, and cash flow.

Income (Revenues) from Subscribers

It was determined from a study of the experience of other pay television operations that the annual income from subscribers should be at least $180. The test surveys indicated that subscribers would not be reluctant to pay this amount.

For purposes of projecting periods of less than a year, subscriber income was adjusted seasonally to reflect the deviations in television viewing throughout the various months. Table 7 breaks down the $180 annual charge by months through the application of a monthly viewing index.

Table 7. Estimated subscriber income by months

MONTH	VIEWING INDEX	MONTHLY INCOME PER SUBSCRIBER
January	1.2	$18.00
February	1.1	16.50
March	1.1	16.50
April	1.1	16.50
May	0.9	13.50
June	0.9	13.50
July	0.8	12.00
August	0.8	12.00
September	0.9	13.50
October	1.0	15.00
November	1.1	16.50
December	1.1	16.50
		$180.00

Income from Installations

It was determined from a rough time study that the cost per installation should be $16 per subscriber. Field surveys did not reveal any objection to the payment of this charge.

Expenses

The items categorized as expenses in the income and cash-flow projections include:

1. Programming
2. Rental of telephone company facilities
3. Depreciation
4. General and administrative expenses

Programming

The nearby cable television company had no objections to revealing its programming figures because there was little risk that another company could use this information competitively. Programming costs for this company averaged just over 40% of revenues. On a per subscriber basis, the revenues averaged $162, which was $18 per year less than was planned for the new venture. This meant that the percentage of programming cost on a base of $180 would be 37%. Because it was planned to keep programming at a high quality level (in terms of demand by subscribers), with additional emphasis on championship sporting events, the decision was made to allot 40% of revenues for programming costs.

Rental of Telephone Company Facilities

Arrangements with the telephone company provide that it will furnish a transmission cable, run it over their telephone poles, and make hookups to the subscribers' sets. The cost for providing the cable and maintaining service will be $2,550,000, payable according to the following schedule:

1. Start-up period: $510,000
2. Six months after start: $510,000
3. Annually thereafter until completion: $510,000

For purposes of projecting the operating results, rental of telephone facilities including hookups was estimated at $1 per month per subscriber.

Depreciation and Amortization

Costs covered in the depreciation expense and the period over which these are taken are shown in Table 8. The operating statement reflects depreciation expense on a straight-line basis.

Table 8. Depreciation and amortization

	TOTAL COST	USEFUL LIFE
Transmission cable	$2,550,000	10
Hookups	2,048,000	4
Transmission center equipment	680,000	10
Hookup units	6,604,000	10
	$11,882,000	

General and Administrative Expenses

This category of cost includes promotional expenses, engineering, administration, and costs associated with making collections from subscribers.

Promotional Expenses. The sales manager, salesmen, automobile rental costs, publicity material, and a television program booklet are included in this category of expense. The breakdown is shown in Table 9. In

Table 9. Promotional expenses

	FIRST YEAR	STARTUP COST
Sales manager	$20,000	$10,000
Salesmen	162,000	40,500
Automobile expense	37,600	9,400
Payroll-related costs	25,500	7,100
Publicity material	3,600	98,000
Television program booklet	1,200	600
	$249,900	$165,600

the third quarter of the fourth year, it has been estimated that only eight salesmen would be required because the saturation point would have been reached. The sales effort would at that time be concentrated on replacement of subscribers lost through turnover.

Engineering. This group of expenses is related to the operation of the transmission center. The breakdown is shown in Table 10. Although one electronic maintenance man is included in the annual cost, this covers only the first year. As installations increase, two more will be added as the requirement is perceived. As the facilities become older, it may be necessary to add still another electronic maintenance man.

Table 10. Transmission central payroll

	FIRST YEAR	STARTUP COST
Engineers	$45,500	$18,000
Projectionists and camera-men	34,000	8,500
Maintenance technician	12,000	2,000
Electronic maintenance man	11,000	3,800
Payroll-related expenses	14,350	4,500
	$116,850	$36,800

Transmission Center Expenses. Automobile expense was based on the anticipated miles of travel. Such items as video and audio tape, as well as replacement parts, were projected on the basis of $1,000 the first year, $2,000 the second, $3,000 the third, and $4,000 the fourth. A summary of the non-labor expenses for the first year and for the startup period is shown in Table 11.

Table 11. Transmission center expenses

	FIRST YEAR	STARTUP COST
Automobile expenses	$4,000	$1,000
Tapes and replacement parts	1,000	500
Supplies	200	100
	$5,200	$1,600

Table 12. Administrative cost breakdown

	FIRST YEAR	STARTUP COST
General Manager	$30,000	$18,750
Program director	23,000	15,000
Secretary	12,000	6,000
Accountant	15,000	9,000
Bookkeeper	10,000	2,000
Switchboard operator	9,000	3,000
Clerks	18,000	6,000
Service bureau charges	114,000	
Payroll-related expenses	15,000	8,400
Route manager	15,000	
Routemen	24,000	
Automobile expenses	6,000	
Unanticipated contingencies	65,000	32,500
	$356,100	$100,650

Administration. The office building and personnel performing administrative duties characteristic of a headquarters are to be located in the business section rather than at the transmission center. The functions considered to be administrative in nature include the general manager, program director, accounting personnel, and the collection function. While the administrative costs—other than the collection function—are expected to be fairly stable during the four-year period, the number of routemen responsible for making the collections will increase as the number of subscribers grows. Collection consists of the emptying of coin boxes at the individual homes. (These payroll and nonpayroll expenses for the first year and the startup period are shown in Table 12.)

Subscriber viewing statistics will be supplied by the local service bureau. Reports will be issued weekly showing the time each program was viewed and the revenue by subscriber for each program. This type of report not only provides viewing statistics, but it also serves as an audit check of collections.

Projected Income and Cash Flow

The projected income, expenses, and cash flow covered a four-year period, over which it

was anticipated that the installations would be completed. The figures by quarters for the four years are shown in Tables 13, 14, 15, and 16.

The revenues (income) from subscribers, although fixed at $15 per month, have been adjusted to reflect seasonal viewing habits.

Startup costs are not included in the statements. They are shown separately in Table 17.

Projected Capital Requirements

Table 17, in addition to showing the startup costs, also summarizes all the capital needs over the four-year period—which includes the startup period as well. Note that although the total cumulative capital requirement is $7,908,788, the peak is reached in the third quarter of the fourth year. The peak amount is shown as $8,116,573.

Although the data in Tables 13 through 17 are important in evaluating the profit potential of this cable television operation, a more probing analysis is needed. The information for such an analysis is provided through determination of the breakeven point.

Determination of the Breakeven point

In calculating a breakeven point, it is important that the time period used represents reasonably normal operations. In this venture, which represents a programmed growth, in which the system is being installed over a four-year period, no one of these four years represents a normal period in which all installations of an ongoing operation are present. For purposes of developing the breakeven point shown in Table 18, the assumption was made that all 35, 910 hookups had been completed except for normal turnover and population growth.

An important requirement, before the breakeven calculation can be made, is to identify those costs that are variable and those that are fixed (relatively speaking).

Those items that were considered to be variable are programming costs, rental of telephone facilities, and the expenses associated with the routemen. These include salaries, payroll-related costs, and automobile expenses.

The fixed costs include promotional expenses, depreciation, engineering, and the headquarters expenses—exclusive of the collection function. Promotional expenses include the payroll of only the salesmen needed when the 35,910 subscribers have been hooked up. The related payroll expenses and automobile costs were adjusted accordingly.

Variable expenses amount to 48.7% of the subscriber income—leaving 51.3% of the income to cover fixed costs and profits. By dividing 51.3% into the fixed expenses of $2,145,650, we arrive at the breakeven point of $4,181,738 in revenues, which is equivalent to 23,232 subscribers.

The pretax profits on all the income above the breakeven level is 51.3% of such additional revenues. Conversely, the loss would be 51.3% of every dollar by which revenues fall below breakeven level. If any additional sales above breakeven apply to subscribers outside the existing system, then the need for additional fixed costs must be taken into account. This would change the breakeven point and the profit calculations.

With these basic facts available, various assumptions can be made. Should revenues per subscriber be lower than $180 per year, for example, the new breakeven point could easily be recalculated to reveal the effect on profitability. If programming costs should be higher (or lower), this adjustment can also be made.

Table 13. Income and cash-flow projection: first year

	FIRST QUARTER	SECOND QUARTER	THIRD QUARTER	FOURTH QUARTER	TOTAL YEAR
Number of subscribers	2,244	4,488	6,732	8,976	8,976
Income					
From subscribers	$ 75,200	$160,400	$231,100	$396,100	$ 862,800
From installations	1,700	3,800	6,000	8,200	19,700
Total income	$ 76,900	$164,200	$237,100	$404,300	$ 882,500
Expenses					
Programming	$ 30,100	$ 64,200	$ 92,400	$ 158,400	$ 345,100
Rental, telephone company facilities	4,500	11,200	18,000	24,700	58,400
	34,600	75,400	110,400	183,100	403,500
Depreciation					
Transmission cable	2,700	6,700	10,800	14,800	35,000
Hookups	5,400	13,500	21,500	29,600	70,000
Hookup units	6,800	17,200	27,500	37,800	89,300
Transmission center equipment	17,000	17,000	17,000	17,000	68,000
	31,900	54,400	76,800	99,200	262,300
General and administrative					
Promotional expenses	62,500	62,500	62,400	62,500	249,900
Engineering	30,500	30,500	30,500	30,500	122,000
Administration	89,000	89,000	89,100	89,000	356,100
	182,000	182,000	182,000	182,000	728,000
Total expenses	$248,500	$311,800	$369,200	$464,300	$1,393,800
Pretax profit (loss)	($171,600)	($147,600)	($132,100)	($ 60,000)	($ 511,300)
Provision for federal and state taxes					
Net profit or (loss)	($171,600)	($147,600)	($132,100)	($ 60,000)	($ 511,300)
Cash flow					
Net profit or (loss) from above	(171,600)	(147,600)	(132,100)	(60,000)	(511,300)
Add:					
Depreciation	31,900	54,400	76,800	99,200	262,300
Deferred receipts from installations	34,200	32,200	29,900	27,700	124,000
Cash flow	($105,500)	($ 61,000)	($ 25,400)	$ 66,900	($ 125,000)

Table 14. Income and cash-flow projection: second year

	FIRST QUARTER	SECOND QUARTER	THIRD QUARTER	FOURTH QUARTER	TOTAL YEAR
Number of subscribers	11,220	13,464	15,708	17,952	17,952
Income					
From subscribers	$532,900	$550,900	$576,800	$826,900	$2,487,500
From installations	10,500	12,700	14,900	17,200	55,300
Total income	$543,400	$563,600	$591,700	$844,100	$2,542,800
Expenses					
Programming	$213,200	$220,300	$230,700	$330,800	$ 995,000
Rental, telephone company facilities	31,400	38,200	44,800	51,600	166,000
	244,600	258,500	275,500	382,400	1,161,000
Depreciation					
Transmission cable	18,900	22,900	26,900	30,900	99,600
Hookups	37,600	45,700	53,900	62,100	199,300
Hookup units	48,100	58,400	68,700	78,900	254,100
Transmission center equipment	17,000	17,000	17,000	17,000	68,000
	121,600	144,000	166,500	188,900	621,000
General and administrative					
Promotional expenses	62,500	62,500	62,500	62,400	249,900
Engineering	38,600	38,700	38,700	38,700	154,700
Administration	97,400	97,300	97,300	97,400	389,400
	198,500	198,500	198,500	198,500	794,000
Total expenses	$564,700	$601,000	$640,500	$769,800	$2,576,000
Pretax profit (loss)	($ 21,300)	($ 37,400)	($ 48,800)	($ 74,300)	($ 33,200)
Provision for federal and state taxes					
Net profit or (loss)	($ 21,300)	($ 37,400)	($ 48,800)	($ 74,300)	($ 33,200)
Cash flow					
Net profit or (loss) from above	($ 21,300)	($ 37,400)	($ 48,800)	($ 74,300)	($ 33,200)
Add:					
Depreciation	121,600	144,000	166,500	188,900	621,000
Deferred receipts from installations	25,400	23,200	20,900	18,700	88,200
Cash flow	$125,700	$129,800	$138,600	$281,900	$ 676,000

Table 15. Income and cash-flow projection: third year

	FIRST QUARTER	SECOND QUARTER	THIRD QUARTER	FOURTH QUARTER	TOTAL YEAR
Number of subscribers	20,196	22,440	24,684	26,928	26,928
Income					
From subscribers	$ 990,700	$945,000	$922,300	$1,257,800	$4,115,800
From installations	19,500	21,700	23,900	26,100	91,200
Total income	$1,010,200	$966,700	$946,200	$1,283,900	$4,207,000
Expenses					
Programming	$ 396,300	$378,000	$368,900	$ 503,100	$1,646,300
Rental, telephone company facilities	58,300	65,100	71,800	78,600	273,800
	454,600	443,100	440,700	581,700	1,920,100
Depreciation					
Transmission cable	35,000	39,000	43,100	47,100	164,200
Hookups	70,000	78,100	86,200	94,200	328,500
Hookup units	89,400	99,600	109,800	120,200	419,000
Transmission center equipment	17,000	17,000	17,000	17,000	68,000
	211,400	233,700	256,100	278,500	979,700
General and administrative					
Promotional expenses	62,500	62,500	62,500	62,400	249,900
Engineering	46,800	46,800	46,900	46,900	187,400
Administration	105,700	105,700	105,700	105,700	422,800
	215,000	215,000	215,000	215,000	860,100
Total expenses	$ 881,000	$891,800	$911,900	$1,075,200	$3,759,900
Pretax profit (loss)	$ 129,200	$ 74,900	$ 34,300	$ 208,700	$ 447,100
Provision for federal and state taxes					
Net profit or (loss)	$ 129,200	$ 74,900	$ 34,300	$ 208,700	$ 447,100
Cash flow					
Net profit or (loss) from above	129,200	74,900	34,300	208,700	447,100
Add:					
Depreciation	211,400	233,700	256,100	278,500	979,700
Deferred receipts from installations	16,400	14,200	12,000	9,800	52,400
Cash flow	$ 357,000	$322,800	$302,400	$ 497,000	$1,479,200

Table 16. Income and cash-flow projection: fourth year

	FIRST QUARTER	SECOND QUARTER	THIRD QUARTER	FOURTH QUARTER	TOTAL YEAR
Number of subscribers	29,172	31,416	33,660	35,910	35,910
Income					
From subscribers	$1,448,500	$1,331,800	$1,267,900	$1,688,600	$5,736,800
From installations	28,400	30,700	32,900	35,900	127,900
Total income	$1,476,900	$1,362,500	$1,300,800	$1,724,500	$5,864,700
Expenses					
Programming	$ 579,400	$ 532,700	$ 507,200	$ 675,400	$2,294,700
Rental, telephone company facilities	85,300	92,000	98,700	105,500	381,500
	664,700	624,700	605,900	780,900	2,676,200
Depreciation					
Transmission cable	51,200	55,200	59,200	63,300	228,900
Hookups	102,300	110,400	118,500	126,500	457,700
Hookup units	130,400	140,800	151,100	161,400	583,700
Transmission center equipment	17,000	17,000	17,000	17,000	68,000
	300,900	323,400	345,800	368,200	1,338,300
General and administrative					
Promotional expenses	62,500	62,500	62,400	28,800	216,200
Engineering	52,300	52,300	52,400	52,400	209,400
Administration	114,100	114,100	114,000	114,000	456,200
	228,900	228,900	228,800	195,200	881,800
Total expenses	$1,194,500	$1,177,000	$1,180,500	$1,344,300	$4,896,300
Pretax profit (loss)	$ 282,400	$ 185,500	$ 120,300	$ 380,200	$ 968,400
Provision for federal and state taxes		39,500	72,200	228,100	339,800
Net profit or (loss)	$ 282,400	$ 146,000	$ 48,100	$ 152,100	$ 628,600
Cash flow					
Profit or (loss) from above	$ 282,400	$ 146,000	$ 48,100	$ 152,100	$ 628,600
Add:					
Provision for tax		39,600	72,100	228,100	339,800
Depreciation	300,900	323,400	345,800	368,200	1,338,300
Deferred receipts from installations	7,500	5,200	3,100	100	15,900
Cash flow	$ 590,800	$ 514,200	$ 469,100	$ 748,500	$2,322,600

Table 17. Projection of capital requirements

	PAYMENTS TO TELEPHONE COMPANY	HOOKUPS	HOOKUP UNITS	TRANSMISSION CENTER	WORKING CAPITAL	TOTAL REQUIREMENTS	CASH FROM OPERATIONS	NET CAPITAL REQUIREMENTS PERIOD	NET CAPITAL REQUIREMENTS CUMULATIVE
Startup period	$ 510,000			$680,000	$75,000	$ 1,265,000	$ (304,650)	1,569,650	1,569,650
First year									
First quarter		128,000	412,750			540,750	(105,492)	646,242	2,215,892
Second quarter	510,000	128,000	412,750			1,050,750	(61,061)	1,111,811	3,327,703
Third quarter		128,000	412,750			540,750	(25,380)	566,130	3,893,833
Fourth quarter		$ 128,000	412,750			540,750	66,847	473,903	4,367,736
Total first year	$1,020,000	$ 512,000	$1,651,000	$680,000	$75,000	$ 3,938,000	$ (429,736)	$4,367,736	
Second year									
First quarter		128,000	412,750			540,750	125,756	414,994	4,782,730
Second quarter	510,000	128,000	412,750			1,050,750	129,794	920,956	5,703,686
Third quarter		128,000	412,750			540,750	138,547	402,203	6,105,889
Fourth quarter		$ 128,000	412,750			540,750	281,938	258,812	6,364,701
Total second year	$ 510,000	$ 512,000	$1,651,000			$ 2,673,000	$ 676,035	$1,996,965	
Third year									
First quarter		128,000	412,750			540,750	356,978	183,772	6,548,473
Second quarter	510,000	128,000	412,750			1,050,750	322,814	727,936	7,276,409
Third quarter		128,000	412,750			540,750	302,449	238,301	7,514,710
Fourth quarter		$ 128,000	412,750			540,750	497,003	43,747	7,558,457
Total third year	$ 510,000	$ 512,000	$1,651,000			$ 2,673,000	$1,479,244	$1,193,756	
Fourth year									
First quarter		128,000	412,750			540,750	590,876	(50,126)	7,508,331
Second quarter	510,000	128,000	412,750			1,050,750	514,132	536,618	8,044,949
Third quarter		128,000	412,750			540,750	469,126	71,624	8,116,573[a]
Fourth quarter		$ 128,000	412,750			540,750	748,535	(207,785)	7,908,788
Total fourth year	$ 510,000	$ 512,000	$1,651,000			$ 2,673,000	$2,322,669	$ 350,331	
	$2,550,000	$2,048,000	$6,604,000	$680,000	$75,000	$11,957,000	$4,048,212	$7,908,788	

[a]Peak capital requirements.

Table 18. Breakeven analysis

	TOTAL BASED ON COMPLETED SYSTEM	BREAKEVEN	EXCESS ABOVE BREAKEVEN
Number of subscribers	35,910	23,232	12,678
Income from subscribers	$6,463,800	$4,181,738	$2,282,062
Variable expenses			
Programming	2,585,520	1,672,695	912,825
Rental of telephone facilities	430,920	279,006	151,914
Routemen	130,500	84,387	46,113
Total	$3,146,940	$2,036,088	$1,110,852
Contribution to profit	3,316,860	2,145,650	1,171,210
Fixed expenses			
Promotional expenses	115,200	115,200	
Depreciation	1,495,400	1,495,400	
Engineering	209,350	209,350	
General and administrative	325,700	325,700	
	$2,145,650	$2,145,650	
Pretax profit	$1,171,210		$1,171,210

Table 19. Profit potential

| | NUMBER OF SUBSCRIBERS | THOUSAND DOLLARS | | | PERCENT RETURN ON | | TURNOVER OF CAPITAL (TIMES) |
		INCOME FROM SUBSCRIBERS	CUMULATIVE CAPITAL REQUIREMENTS	PRETAX PROFIT	INCOME FROM SUBSCRIBERS	CAPITAL	
First year	8,976	863	4,368	(511)	(59.7)	(11.7)	5.1
Second year	17,952	2,487	6,365	(33)	(1.3)	(.5)	2.6
Third year	26,928	4,116	7,558	447	10.7	5.9	1.8
Fourth year	35,910	5,737	8,117	968	16.8	11.9	1.4
Completed installation	35,910	6,464	8,117	1,171	18.7	14.4	1.3

Note: Because the full complement of installations was not completed until the end of the fourth year, the completed installation figures were shown to provide information for a full year's results.

Summary of Key Financial Data

The key financial informational data needed to make an appraisal of the profit potential of this new venture is summarized in Table 19.

With the availability of this type of information, the management of the proposed venture has the basic financial data it needs to make a management decision as to whether it should invest in the proposed venture or not. There is no generally established rule as to what the return on a business should be. This is a management decision based on management goals. It must evaluate market potentialities, competitive forces, and the problems that can be expected to be encountered—not to mention coming trends.

In subscription television, uncertainties have existed with respect to the question of copyrights on programs that are rebroadcast. Also, strong resistance has been shown by free television and theaters. All such factors must be appraised and carefully weighed before a decision is made. Then, even if the unexpected problem arises, the new company will be prepared to cope with it.

SECTION V
CONTROLLING THE TWO LARGEST ASSETS: INVENTORY AND FIXED ASSETS

20
Greater Profits Through More Effective Purchasing

Robert L. Janson
Manager
Ernst & Whinney

In the old days, purchasing was considered to be a stocking function with the mission of assuring that the company would not run out of inventory. Today, purchasing is looked upon as an important contribution to profits. The author explains how.

When one thinks about the procurement function, it is significant to say that many opportunities to achieve profits are lost in numerous companies. This chapter explains the methodology, policies, and procedures necessary to achieve greater profits through better purchasing.

Times have really changed for this function. In the old days, purchasing was measured by a "do not run out of inventory" standard that, in reality, was an inventory control measurement not suitable for purchasing. Today, purchasing is looked upon as a profit contributor to the company and concurrently as a public relations function.

OPPORTUNITIES IN PURCHASING

Progressive management now realizes the responsibility in terms of the money handled by the procurement function. As illustrated in the following list, the "responsibility index" of the buyer is several times that of the company production and sales employee.

1. A typical production employee may handle $50,000 worth of goods annually.
2. The average sales person might handle $600,000 in a year's time.
3. The average buyer usually handles as much as $1,500,000 annually.

Thus it is submitted that the buyer can and should contribute greatly to his company's profitability. In truth, if a purchasing department saves $100, the contribution to gross profits is approximately $50, assuming a 50% tax rate. In contrast, to achieve the same profit increase, the sales department would have to increase sales by over $800. Thus the worth of purchasing should be clear.

MANAGEMENT SUPPORT THROUGH A POLICY STATEMENT

One of the major difficulties in purchasing is that the specific objectives of the company for the procurement function are often not clearly delineated and communicated. This problem can be solved easily through the issuance of a policy statement that clearly defines why the department exists, what it should achieve, and how it should report its activities. A typical statement for purchasing policies in a company might be as follows:

Recently the market in which we operate has become highly competitive. In addition to the increase in raw material prices, we have also had to raise the cost of our product due to costs of buying component parts. We must meet this market with its attendant profit challenge by directing our purchasing efforts to improve our ability to serve the needs of our customers but at reduced total procurement costs.

Therefore, the following specific policies are directed towards the procurement function and should be implemented by the management of that department:

1. Maximize the use of the buyer's time for negotiations and procurement planning.
2. Select vendors that have adequate capacity on a continuing basis to provide the material needs of the company.
3. Study the market, analyze prices, and determine how materials can be purchased at a lower price than paid in the past.
4. Investigate and select alternate sources of supply to minimize our dependence on any single supplier.
5. Assist the engineering department in a value analysis program to determine cheaper methods and materials for purchasing parts.
6. Maintain information on open purchase orders and, through routine expediting, obtain delivery as required.
7. Document the prices paid, service rendered, and delivery received from suppliers and report this information to the better and the poorer vendors.
8. Train department employees on purchasing techniques and negotiation methods

so as to improve their assistance to our company.
9. Conduct all activities in a highly ethical manner treating vendors cordially on a completely objective basis.

ETHICAL PRACTICE WITH EIGHT OPERATING CONTROLS

Management places a high trust in purchasing. In the course of purchasing activities, many opportunities do arise for impropriety. To minimize the possibility of irregularities and to assure the procurement of materials in the best possible manner for the company, eight operating controls should be instituted. The procurement manager and his superiors should carefully determine and insist on the following items.

1. *Authorized vendors list.* This precludes buying from any poor credit risk and even possibly a false vendor. No activities should be permitted with any vendor not on this list. The vendors that purchasing wishes placed on the list should be recommended by procurement and approved by another department (such as accounting) prior to acceptance.
2. *Requisitions.* These are the authorizations to procure all goods and services. Each and every purchase order should be supported by a requisition and keyed to this document.
3. *Request for quotations.* RFQs are the primary working tool in competitive negotiations, evidence that a thorough buying job has been done.
4. *Prenumbered purchase orders.* This entails using a log or other control mechanism that accounts for all purchase order numbers, even those that have been voided.
5. *Dollar signature levels.* A buyer can only sign a purchase order to a specific total value. All higher buys should be approved by his superior and others in

the company chain of command, depending on the total purchase order value.

6. *Authorized receiving signatures.* This limits the official receipt of goods to a few specific individuals in the receiving department.

7. *Invoice processing.* Invoice processing entails using the purchase order contents as a legal document, matching with an authorized receiver, and paying the invoice based on the purchase order contents.

8. *Performance reports.* A monthly quantitative report of purchasing activities that includes cost savings and cost avoidance is generated to provide an incentive for the lowest possible price consistent with the quality required.

The ethical possibilities in purchasing should be handled by a specially worded ethical statement that carefully explains the ground rules under which purchasing personnel operate in the function of their job. The following statement is a good example of an ethical policy. Note that specific limits are identified in this statement.

BUSINESS ETHICS POLICY

All company employees are expected to use sound business judgment and to maintain high ethical and moral standards in their business conduct. Honesty, confidences, and avoidance of inproper situations are to be part of our business operations.

All employees are to comply with all ethical practices, laws, and regulations that may be applicable to our business. No situations should occur whereby an employee would develop a conflict with company responsibilities.

Employees should not purchase material from any company in which they have a financial interest which exceeds 2% of the company assets.

Employees are not to solicit or suggest any gifts, entertainment, or loans from suppliers.

Lunches and occasional dinners with sales representatives for the purpose of business discussions are permitted provided that they are done on a reciprocal basis. The company will reimburse its employees for such expenses.

Visits by company employees to vendor plants, field operations, demonstrations, or open houses are permitted provided these visits serve the interests of our company. Any expenses will be paid by our company.

Any exceptions to this policy must be authorized by an officer of the company. If the question involves an officer, the immediate superior will review the situation.

LINKAGE TO THE REQUISITIONER

As indicated by one of the major controls, all procurement must be the result of an independent request for materials or services. This request comes from an inventory control function for production plus miscellaneous stores or special purchase need for nonproduction items. Normally, three different requisitions should be used to communicate the requisitioners' needs to the purchasing department.

1. *General-purpose requisition.* This document should be used for more infrequent purchases, those which happen less than three times a year. This form should be fairly detailed to communicate the purchased item specifications clearly.

2. *Travel requisition.* This form so called because it "travels" from the requisitioner to the purchasing department for action and back to the requisitioner for filling. The document is prepared on the first buying requirement. All repetitive (fixed) information is typed or clearly written on the form, usually of cardboard stock. Then all variable (specific)

buying information is placed on this form and is sent to purchasing. The purchasng department makes the procurement decision and notes the purchase order number, vendor, and so on, and then returns this travel requisition to the requisitioner. The next time an item is needed, the form is used again. Thus the form provides a history of usage, prices paid, and vendors selected over a period of time.

3. *Capital equipment requisition.* Larger procurement buys such as capital equipment should be communicated on a more complicated form with carefully worded specifications. This form should provide space to give the justification and rationale for requesting the capital items.

LEAD TIMES

One of the problems encountered in purchasing is lack of adequate time to select the proper vendor, place the purchase order, and get the desired materials when the requisitioner requires them. This "lead time" is a combination of the company's paperwork time, the vendor's paperwork time, and the vendor's production time to prepare and ship the materials.

Purchasing's responsibility is to determine the correct and most recent lead time by type of item and communicate this information to the requisitioner. The requisitioner is responsible to give purchasing the total lead time necessary for its activities. The best method to determine the vendor's lead time is to analyze recent performance history with your company. This could be done through the use of a computerized vendor delivery analysis report. If such equipment is not available, then analyze each completed purchase order and determine the time necessary by type of commodity (groups of material).

Another method to minimize the effect of lead time is to have the requisitioners forecast their needs for purchased items on a routine basis. This procedure can be simplified by stressing the need for a forecast of the "A" classification or high-volume parts. When this information is obtained, it is forwarded to the vendor on a noncommittal basis. Usually, the vendor is most pleased to get this kind of data and will respond by anticipating your needs in a better manner.

SPECIFICATIONS

Another problem is obtaining the correct specifications for more complicated items necessary to support the company activities. The target for purchasng is to buy as many standard parts as possible because these usually are more inexpensive and have shorter lead time for delivery to your company. While it is always difficult to prepare specifications, purchasing can do much to assure that the specifications for standard materials are required. A six-step procedure should be followed to perform this function. These include:

1. The requisitioner should develop a general specification or statement of the items or material required.
2. The requisitioner should use the purchasing catalog library as a reference guide to determine what standard items are available.
3. A list of similar parts already being utilized in the system should be developed so that design personnel can see what standard items already exist.
4. Purchasing should utilize the vendor's technical personnel as well as salesmen to communicate to the design function standard vendor items.
5. The requisitioner should finalize the specifications and send them to purchasing.
6. Purchasing should review these specifications and complete the procurement cycle.

THE QUOTATION AND NEGOTIATION CYCLE

Good purchasing follows a series of distinct steps in selecting the vendor to give a specific procurement order. True effective cost savings and cost avoidance procurement results from a series of six steps as illustrated in the vendor selection funnel in Figure 1.

The first step utilizes the purchasing library, which consists of a collection of vendor catalogs, price lists, brochures, and so on from which the more likely vendor candidates are selected. In step two, the more likely candidates are sent a form letter that requests

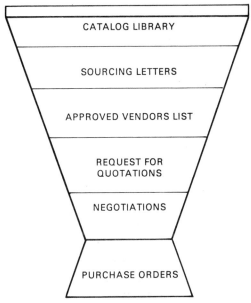

FIGURE 1. Vendor selection funnel.

specific information about the company such as their credit rating, references, products, detailed price information, and so on. These "sourcing letters" should be marked such that "salesmen are not to call unless requested," so as to minimize the influx of salesmen resulting from this letter. For those companies that appear to be potential candidates, their names should be submitted to the accounting

department who, after review, will include them on an "approved vendors list."

Upon the placement of a vendor on the authorized vendor list, requests for quotations should be submitted to these vendors that appear to be better candidates for subsequent purchasing activities. When the answers are received from the request for quotation, the better two or three vendors, when possible, should be selected for face-to-face, private negotiations. In the negotiations, the request for quotation price should not be considered as the lowest possible price from the vendor but should be used as a point of departure to determine the final price, conditions, and delivery required. The last step in this cycle is the issuance of the purchase order to the one or two suppliers with which the company wishes to do business. In this entire six-step cycle, one might look at 15 companies in the library, send sourcing letters to ten, put five on the approved list, send quotations to four, pick the better answers from two for negotiations, and then send the purchase order to the best one selected through this process.

REQUEST FOR QUOTATION

The key document in this selection process is the request for quotation, a classical design which is shown in Figure 2. Most office supply houses offer a printed form or a company can design its own specific one as necessary. The purpose of this document is to communicate to multiple vendors, normally three for each form, the basic information concerning a desired procurement. Each vendor knows that others are quoting, but through the use of blank-out carbons, does not know their actual names. When the answers are received, the "summary of quotations block" should be utilized as a comparison device to select the best supplier. When the supplier has been selected, especially if the lowest price offered was not picked, the buyer should note in the section marked "reason order placed with vendor"

REQUEST FOR QUOTATION

| NUMBER | DATE |

THE ABOVE NUMBER MUST APPEAR ON ALL QUOTATIONS AND RELATED CORRESPONDENCE. **THIS IS NOT AN ORDER**

DATE	ADDRESS YOUR REPLY TO	REQUISITION NO. OR REQUESTED BY	SUMMARY OF QUOTATIONS
			VENDOR / QUANTITY/PRICE

NO. 1

	1
	2
	3

NO. 2

| | FOB POINT |
| | TOOL COST |

NO. 3

	DELIVERY
	FREIGHT ALLOW.
	PAYMENT TERMS

REASON ORDER PLACED WITH VENDOR

| BEST DEL'Y. | LOWEST PRICE | LIKE ITEM | PAYMENT TERMS | SERVICE QUALITY PAST PERF. | FREIGHT ALLOWED | ONLY SOURCE | OTHER REASONS |

This order placed with Vendor _____ on P.O. _____   SELECTED BY _____

TERMS	F.O.B. POINT	SHIPMENT VIA	SHIPPING WT.	DEL'Y. LEAD TIME

ITEM	QUANTITY	U/M	DESCRIPTION/B.P. NUMBER	INV. CL.	COM. CODE	UNIT LIST PRICE	% DISC.	UNIT NET PRICE	TOTAL PRICE

PLEASE CHECK THE FOLLOWING:

- WARRANTY
- FREIGHT CHARGES, IF NOT FOR DESTINATION
- DIFFERENCE IN SPECIFICATIONS
- SHIPMENT CAN BE MADE IN _____ DAYS FROM RECEIPT OF ORDER.
- SUGGEST ALTERNATE MATERIALS OR TOLERANCES.
- TO BE CONSIDERED. QUOTATION MUST REACH US BY
- DELIVERY DATE REQUIRED
- YOUR QUOTATION NO.

WE QUOTE YOU AS ABOVE

This price quotation is valid for_____ days.

BY (SIGNATURE)_____

OFFICIAL TITLE_____ DATE _____

FIGURE 2.   Request for quotation.

the reasons for the selection. The section marked "we quote you as above" should be completed by the supplier because this makes the price valid for a specific time period.

Once the quotations have been received, the buyer should review all quotes and look at what history is available about this vendor. Often the lowest quoted price vendor is not the best vendor. The concept of "least pur-chase cost" is followed by progressive companies who consider not only price but quality, on-time delivery, lack of partial or unauthorized split shipments, overall vendor performance, and technical assistance.

Sometimes the vendor request for quotation answers are not clear. When this occurs, all vendors should be permitted to redo this so as not to play favorites. In addition, it is considered poor purchasing practice to give out the prices quoted in confidence by a supplier. This point is not germaine in public bid contracts where all quotes are opened at one time and a formal selection made.

Sometimes a vendor is able to communicate via the request for quotations a suggested change in the design of the part or a quantity price break that could lessen the unit cost. When this occurs, it is purchasing's responsibility to go to the requisitioner and ascertain if different material, specifications, or a larger purchase quantity could be obtained.

NEGOTIATIONS

Negotiation requires special skill, a skill learned and improved only with experience. Most persons who are analytically minded and enjoy the give-and-take of negotiations become superior buyers. There are certain ground rules that should be followed in negotiations. These include the following:

1. Develop a negotiation checklist of points to be considered in the discussions, such as freight, delivery, inventory stocking, special packaging, and so on.
2. Practice negotiating with others in a series of training sessions.
3. Remember that a major part of the negotiation is the difference between the price you wish to pay and the price at which the seller wishes to sell. These prices should be anticipated in advance.
4. Prepare well in advance the analytical aspects, because more often than not the better prepared person wins.
5. Conduct negotiations in a calm, unemotional, unhurried manner and do not be pressured to complete the negotiation.
6. Remember the salesman is usually more anxious to conclude than you, so take your time.
7. Select the best negotiater within your company and use whenever possible.
8. Do not negotiate alone. It often helps to

have a technical person or someone else from the company, using the theory that two heads are often better than one.
9. If all things are equal, ask for a 2% tenday prompt payment discount.

Requisition purchase orders may be prepared by the requisitioner and sent to purchasing. The vendor name, purchase order number, and other data are entered, a photocopy made, sent to receiving, and the original sent to the vendor. (See Figure 3.)

Telephone log purchase orders utilize a log that lists the salient points of the order. Upon receipt of the goods, the vendor's packing slip is compared to the log.

Check attached orders are orders designed with a check as part of the form. They can be a blank check with a maximum price (usually $100) that is filled in by the supplier or the buyer.

A computer printed purchase order has the same basic design as the standard document. However, this order is produced by a computer, responding to a manual or an automatic ordering requisition.

CAPITAL EQUIPMENT

More money is wasted in purchasing capital equipment than in any other commodity group. The reason is that numerous capital equipment buying decisions are made before the purchasing department is aware of the plan. Success in capital equipment purchasing can be assured by following a seven-step capital equipment purchasing program.

1. Include in your company purchasing policy statement the requirement that purchasing is to get involved right from the start.
2. Require that all capital equipment vendor contacts, including the request for quotation, are coordinated and mailed through purchasing.
3. Request that a complete request for quotation document be filled in.

COMPANY CONFIDENTIAL INFORMATION SECTION

- FOR CUSTOMER NAME:_____   SALES ORDER NO: _____
- SUGGESTED VENDOR(S):_____   ESTIMATED VALUE: _____
- SPECIAL INSTRUCTIONS: _____   APPROVED BY: _____

	REQUISITION, PURCHASE ORDER AND BLANKET ORDER RELEASE	Req'n. No. _____ Date _____

Dept.	Requested By	To Be Used For	Required By
Acc't. No.	Cost Center No.	Appro. No.	Deliver Att. of

SPECIAL INSTRUCTIONS _____   Approved By: _____

Quantity	Part No.	Description	Unit Price

BLANKET ORDER RELEASE:
Last Shipment Considered
Was:_____ (quantity)
Dated:_____

_____
Inventory Control Authorization

MONTH						
FIRM						
TENTATIVE						
RAW MAT'L.						

Vendor Name and Address

_____

_____

_____

_____

TAXABLE☐   EXEMPT☐   OUR PURCHASE
Vendor No. _____   ORDER NUMBER

Confirming To:_____ Date: _____

Terms and   FOB_____   Payment Disc. _____
Conditions   Other _____

Buyer Authorization: _____
                        (Must be signed to be valid)

Vendor Please Note: Unless you provide us written expressed exception to the contents of this order, we will assume you agree and pay your invoice accordingly.

FIGURE 3. Combination requisition, purchase order and blanket order release.

4. Calculate the equipment repair or replace cost including the justification for the capital addition.
5. Issue a purchase order that carefully communicates the terms and conditions, specifications, and other salient points in the offer to buy.
6. Monitor the vendor's progress in manufacturing the capital item.

7. Perform, one year after receipt of the equipment, an evaluation of the equipment justification accuracy.

Another point of concern is the potential product liability in procurement. Today's regulations require the salesman and the buyer to communicate clearly and understand the need of the item being ordered. If not, the buyer may be liable for misleading the vendor. Therefore, the responsibility is on the buyer to communicate carefully to the potential vendor the possible uses of the item being purchased.

MAKING THE PURCHASING FUNCTION MORE PRODUCTIVE

Statistics show that the average sales call by a supplier's salesman requires 40 minutes—20 minutes waiting to see the buyer and 20 minutes for making the sale. The progressive buyer can put these 40 minutes to work and can achieve greater productivity by following some simple guidelines.

Updating Catalogs

A bookcase conveniently located in the purchasing reception area for storage of all vendor catalogs will provide two benefits at little cost:

1. It would centralize the filing of vendor catalogs.
2. During the time the salesman is waiting to see the buyer, he could be requested to update his company's literature. At the outset of the interview, the buyer could spend a few minutes becoming familiar with the catalog changes and asking the salesman questions related to these changes.

Value Analysis Assistance by the Salesman

In addition to a centralized file of up-to-date catalogs, the company should provide a display case of all its products and components. While the various salesmen are waiting for their appointment with the buyer, they could be requested to come up with suggestions for redesign of parts and possible substitute materials. In some instances, when a part is troublesome to make or assemble, the salesman could be given a sample to take back with him to discuss with his technical people.

Many companies use a welcoming booklet that is placed in the reception room. The purpose of this booklet is to list various ways a salesman can help the company. In addition, more important company purchasing policies can be included, such as: "We wish to have three vendors quoting whenever possible," and "Kindly refrain from giving any gratuities, favors or material items to our buyers." This approach specifies to the vendor's representatives clearly the ground rules by which the company wishes to operate.

Expediting Open Orders

To facilitate action on open orders, particularly those that are late, it would be helpful to provide public telephones in the reception area to make it convenient for the salesmen to call their factories.

The use of techniques such as the above, not only makes the salesman more productive—it will make the purchasing function more efficient and will reduce purchasing costs.

UNIQUE PURCHASING REQUIREMENTS

Certain organizations have distinct problems that should be kept in mind.

Hospital purchasing often includes the materials management concept wherein the purchasing and the inventory control functions are under the same manager—often called a materials manager. This is frequently true in manufacturing companies. The interrelationship of the two departments is advantageous since the person who is responsible for the inventory investment also has to decide how long the goods will be inventoried at their actual carrying cost. Another characteristic is the *prudent buyer concept*, a method utilized by the government to insure that the lowest possible price is paid for the items purchased. Because the lowest purchase price is not always the best price, a vendor performance analysis (discussed later) should be followed in a four-point program: (1) All vendors should be rated; (2) substandard performers should be notified; (3) buying decisions should be documented if the lowest price is not accepted; and (4) the hospital group purchasing organization should be used whenever possible. Hospitals have another concept called the *prime vendor*, in which a prime or major vendor acts as a stocking center and provides prompt, off-the-shelf delivery of the goods ordered. The concept is good but one should be careful not to give one prime vendor too high a percentage of the hospital needs. It is suggested that one vendor be given 80% and another vendor 20% as an example to keep one vendor price competitive. Naturally, the other is interested in getting more of the business.

The retail purchasing environment uses two special procedures. The first is often called a *deal sheet* wherein the sales person specifies, before the sales call, the ingredients of the sale such as special allowance for advertising, number of items available for promotion, and trade discounts for this particular offer. The second is called the *open-to-buy* system. In this, the buyer is given a total figure of the number of items at inventory value one can have at any given time—both on hand and on order. Thus the buyer can only make purchasing commitments (inventory on hand plus on order) that do not exceed this total amount. It is somewhat akin to a manufacturing plant's machine loading where the new input (buys) must be equal with the output (sales) to keep the desired maximum inventory level.

Government purchasing also has certain characteristics that must be considered. Bidding on a sealed bid public opening basis is the normal routine for all buys over a certain dollar figure—often $1,000 or $2,000. The second special characteristic is the use of comprehensive proposals for all buys subject to many regulations. The range of buying duties is also more broad because it often includes many service items and contracts. A special problem in government purchasing is receiving because the goods may come to many different receiving departments within the government organization. This places spe-

cial need on getting accurate and timely receiving documents.

Lastly, banking has some special problems. In this purchasing environment, many of the items are forms and paper supplies with numerous, often hundreds, of different size envelopes and even thousands of different forms. Standardizing banking forms is essential because better prices can be obtained by increases in the volume for each item used. Thus the number of forms should be standardized and minimized; a form control procedure should be established and stockless purchasing, contract buying, automatic reordering and similar techniques sould be carefully considered.

VALUE ANALYSIS, A NECESSITY

All purchasing departments, no matter how large or how small, should have a value analysis program. This program combines the talents of the purchasing individual with that of the designer, such as an engineer, assisted by others in manufacturing, to determine the best value possible of the items purchased. The concept includes breaking apart the ingredients of the item purchased such as a component part or the materials specification to ascertain where improvements can be made in design, materials, manufacturing tolerances, and so on.

A good value analysis (VA) program starts with sending a letter to suppliers informing them of this program saying: "We are extending to you this opportunity to participate in our value analysis program." The letter should continue stressing the contributions possible by the vendor and the fact that he can gain by increased business and often lowered manufacturing costs. Once this announcement letter has been developed, the value analysis individual should be designated in the purchasing department. In a large company, this could be a full-time employee. In a smaller company, it should be the partial duties of one of the buyers. The assistance in the program such as engineers, manufacturing personnel, and quality control should also be designated and put on a value analysis committee. Cost-saving objectives should be established and a value analysis display placed in the lobby (as discussed previously). Supplier qualifications should be checked and subjected to subsequent reporting of activities.

A key ingredient in value analysis is the participation of the technical representatives of the vendor. Their advice should be sought regarding materials, standardization, and so on. Sometimes a value analysis technique can result in a whole new item being developed, such as a new assembly product or a new capital equipment item. The controlling document is the value analysis work sheet shown in Figure 4.

DEPARTMENT: _____   PROJECT NUMBER: _____

PROJECT TITLE:_____   DATE:_____

LEADER:_____   APPROVED BY: _____

POINTS TO CONSIDER   Outline the problem stating the needs that exist, the objective of the project and the relative importance of this project. What are the major steps that must be completed to ensure reaching the objective? Estimated cost and target date. How will this project improve our profit? Will this project provide a new or improved product? What marketing efforts are necessary to success? Can this project be brought to a successful conclusion?

OBJECTIVE

PROJECT PLAN

TARGET DATE:	ACTION TO BE TAKEN:	ASSIGNED TO:

ESTIMATED COSTS & SAVINGS

COSTS TO BE INCURRED:

_____ Date: _____   _____ NATURE OF EXPENSE _____   _____ Amount: _____

ESTIMATED NET SAVINGS:

CURRENT YEAR $ _____   EACH FUTURE YEAR $ _____

ADDITIONAL COMMENTS

FIGURE 4.   Profit improvement program worksheet.

INVOICE PROCESSING DECISION RULES

The responsibility of the purchasing function does not end until an approved invoice has been processed for payment. The match of the invoice to the receiving report and the purchase order must not be done in the purchasing department as one of the basic controls mentioned previously. The invoice should be received and then reviewed by the accounting department. In making this review, the contents of the purchase order should be matched to the receiving report and the invoice using certain ground rules called *decision rules*. These decision rules, which are listed in Figure 5, give an indication of the decisions necessary in the processing. If the match of the invoice, purchase order, and receiving report does not fit within these decision rules, then the invoice should be returned to purchasing for resolution. The terms, conditions, and especially the price on the purchase order as acknowledged by the vendor are the guiding criteria. Implicit in these instructions is the fact that purchasing must negotiate carefully with the supplier to determine the price. If the vendor and purchasing agree on a different price, the changes should be communicated to accounting for invoice processing.

However, it is not always necessary to get exact prices on small purchasing commitments. If the value of the order is less than $50, estimated prices can be used and certain actions followed as shown in the decision rule. By following these rules, the processing of invoice can be accomplished more efficiently. At the same time, the purchase order contents can be enforced and money saved for the company by not overpaying when the invoice differs from the purchasing contract.

VENDOR PERFORMANCE ANALYSIS

One of the more difficult tasks in purchasing is to ascertain how well the vendor is serving your company. This determination can easily be done on a judgmental (subjective) basis, but often these ratings are inaccurate because

NO.	CONDITION	ACTION
1.	NO PRICE ON PURCHASE ORDER	WRITE INVOICE REVIEW SLIP
2.	"WILL ADVISE" PURCHASE ORDER	WRITE REVIEW SLIP
3.	INVOICE PRICE MORE THAN PURCHASE ORDER PRICE BUT TOTAL INVOICE DIFFERENCE LESS THAN $50	DISCOUNT INVOICE AND PAY ACCORDING TO PURCHASE ORDER
4.	SAME AS #3 BUT DIFFERENCE GREATER THAN $50	WRITE INVOICE REVIEW SLIP
5.	PROMPT PAYMENT DISCOUNT ON PURCHASE ORDER BUT NOT ON INVOICE	DISCOUNT INVOICE AND PAY ACCORDING TO PURCHASE ORDER, IF WITHIN TIME PERIOD ALLOWED
6.	INVOICE PRICE LESS THAN PURCHASE ORDER PRICE BUT TOTAL INVOICE DIFFERENCE LESS THAN $50	PAY INVOICE
7.	SAME AS #6 BUT DIFFERENCE GREATER THAN $50	WRITE INVOICE REVIEW SLIP
8.	TIME PERIOD TO COUNT FROM FOR PROMPT PAYMENT DISCOUNT CALCULATION.	USE DATE INVOICE OR GOODS WERE RECEIVED; WHICHEVER IS THE LATEST TO COUNT FROM

FIGURE 5. Accounts payable department decision table.

they are usually predicted on the more recent performance by the vendor and not on service over a longer period of time. Companies should continually evaluate the performance of the vendor in deciding whether or not they wish to deal with certain suppliers in the future based on their performance in the past. This review, called *vendor performance analysis*, includes a study of how well the vendor has served you on delivery, quality, and price over a recent period of time. A convenient way to do this analysis consists of these five steps:

1. Rate each vendor's performance on each purchase as it is completed using the vendor rating stamp shown in Figure 6. This stamp permits a indication by the buyer when each purchase order is completed.
2. Place the completed purchase orders in the closed vendor file.
3. Remove whenever desired, often quarterly, the completed orders from the file and summarize the various ratings indicated on the stamp.
4. Communicate to the vendor this summary by preparing two copies of a form letter about the vendor's performance. One copy is mailed to the home office of the vendor.
5. Present to the salesman at the next call a copy of the recent performance, to provide an indication as to how well the vendor is serving or not serving the company. Because often service is less

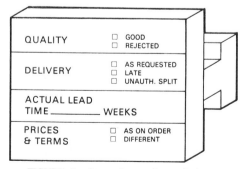

FIGURE 6.   Stamp for vendor analysis.

than desired, the resulting bad news to the salesman tends to put him more on the defensive and aids the buyer in future negotiations.

PROCEDURE MANUAL

As much as any other function, purchasing seems to have informal procedures and never enough time to do the work. Therefore, organizing the documents and defining the procedures clearly for ease of understanding greatly hastens the speed by which the department functions. An important tool to accomplish this is a purchasing manual. Normally, preparation of a complete manual takes a long time and considerable effort. A purchasing manual can be developed in one of two ways. The more traditional manner is to establish the table of contents and then write each chapter. This can be time consuming. Often, a shortcut can be tried. Many companies over the years have written many policy statements, memorandums, and instructions regarding the procedures they wish to use in purchasing. It is possible to create a purchasing department manual using these existing documents by following these ten steps:

1. Collect all memorandums, instructions, reports, and forms on purchasing subjects written over the past years.
2. Sort all the material, culling out the duplicate memorandums used on title and contents.
3. Establish a tentative table of contents.
4. Extract from these existing documents all unnecessary information, colloquialisms, and other unneeded notes.
5. Break apart this material in a cut-and-paste fashion, reorganizing it based on the table of contents.
6. Review these edited materials with selected people within the company, get their comments, and start rewriting.
7. Type up the information in rough draft form and have the same selected indi-

viduals (step 5) and reedit the material.

8. Add certain segments to the manual that you wish to have in the final manual.
9. Finalize the manual, once more giving it a last critique.
10. Distribute the manual to those concerned.

Once a manual has been developed, it will be accurate for a few months, maybe a year. Then changes will begin to be received because purchasing is a dynamic system. Updating can be performed by using a page change transmittal form that indicates what was revised and requests that the now out-of-date pages be returned so they can be destroyed. Next, a record of the changes on a kind of "add on to" record should be made using a master copy. Then, a responsibility list should be provided to the users as a reference tool that defines who is responsible for certain aspects of the manual. Lastly, an alphabetical keyword index should be used as a reference for all sections including forms in the manual. This index, placed at the end of the manual, should guide readers in using the sections that are applicable to their responsibility and areas of interest.

COMPUTER-ASSISTED PURCHASING

The purchasing deartment handles extensive amounts of paperwork. Not only are many purchase orders issued but the supporting documents can be extensive in the form of price history records, requests for quotations, correspondence, and requisitions. This paperwork can be so extensive that as little as 5% of a buyer's time is spent in negotiating. The majority of the work is spent performing a clerical function and expediting. One way to minimize this clerical time is to use a computer that can perform much of the routine work, saving time for the buyer negotiations and obtaining the maximum dollar benefits possible from the procurement activities.

An initial step is to determine which of the

purchasing functions are laborious and extensively clerical. Although the possibilities are almost unlimited, there are commonly used computer purchasing reports (as listed below). One should review this list and select those that may be more appropriate to their environment. From this, certain specifications can be developed to communicate to computer personnel the type of assistance that might be necessary.

1. *Inventory History.* This computer report provides a tabulation of the more recent usage by part number, along with commodity code number, buyer, standard cost, and vendor part number.
2. *Part requirements; scheduled and forecast.* A key summary by part number shows the balance on hand, available for new orders, reorder point as well as anticipated requirements by month for the vendor lead time.
3. *Price and quotation history.* A buyer needs to know, by part number, the price in the past few years paid for the item along with the better, more recent quotation by vendor.
4. *Ordered and released.* This report shows the current open order by vendor along with the quantity to be released; it is a type of forecast.
5. *Open purchase order status, expedite and commitment.* This is a key working report that shows by buyer name, then by vendor the open orders, number of vendor delivery promises and expected receipts by month for cash-flow projection.
6. *Expedite letter.* An expedite letter is a form letter sent to vendors that lists open orders and asks for current delivery promises. This is a first-level followup effort.
7. *Receiving and inspection report.* This report shows by vendor the current receipts, inspection action, and indicates if order is complete.
8. *Invoice, receiving, and purchase order match.* This program performs the time-consuming match of these three

documents and indicates where differences occur.

9. *Purchases by vendor, commodity code, and part number*. Several sorts can be used to provide an activity history for negotiation reference purposes.

10. *Purchase price and index variation*. This report gives an indication by part number of the buyer's ability to purchase effectively by comparing the prices paid, by part number, against the standard purchase price. It also measures, by commodity, the price trend compared with the government purchasers' price index.

11. *Vendor rating*. The vendor performance rating for price, delivery and quality is then compared with other vendors' ratings within the same commodity code.

12. *Buyer rating*. A buyer rating determines the amount and dollar value of purchase orders placed, the total variation to standard price, and to government index and also lists the percentage of orders received late based on vendor's acknowledgment or quoted lead time.

EVALUATING THE FUNCTION

This chapter has concentrated on the policy, procedures, and techniques in effective purchasing activities. However, management should evaluate as objectively as possible the activities of their purchasing department to ascertain if it is meeting previously established standards.

This review can be done provided the purchasing head can be objective enough to analyze the function and determine what can be improved. The purchasing management and controls review that follows is a self-rating checklist that can be used in determining the effectiveness of the function.

To make this initial check, complete each of the 15 questions below, then compare your answer value with the standard and add up the ratings. If your score is above 90, your department is in excellent shape; if between 75 and 90 in good condition. However, if your score is below 75 points you had best do a full-scale evaluation. For Question 2, score one point for each 5% of multiple quotations.

Once this checklist is completed, then items that score below the indicated level

QUESTION	STANDARD	YOUR ANSWER	SCORE VALUE
1. Has purchasing system been reviewed in past five years?	Yes	_____	7
2. What percentage of all purchases (in dollars) have been obtained through multiple vendor quotations and/or negotiations?	70%	_____	16
3. What percentage of annual purchases (in dollars) were cost savings?	3%	_____	7
4. How many different departments actually buy (select vendors)?	1	_____	5
5. What is the average number of line items purchased each day per buyer?	40	_____	5
6. Are all purchase order numbers controlled and accounted for?	Yes	_____	5
7. Does an approved vendor master list exist?	Yes	_____	9
8. What is the average number of vendors quoting per request?	3.0	_____	5
9. Are formal vendor performance analyses regarding price adherence, quality, and delivery made and reported to vendors?	Yes	_____	6
10. Is a policy statement such as a welcoming booklet given to vendor representatives?	Yes	_____	6
11. Are invoices checked to purchase order and receiving report in accounting?	Yes	_____	3
12. Do buyers change commodity assignments every three years?	Yes	_____	7
13. What percent of items purchased are priced?	95%	_____	4
14. Is a price history record maintained by part number indicating recent price quotations?	Yes	_____	8
15. Does the purchase order contain a statement that the vendor must agree to all information on the front of the order or "clearly express any exception"?	Yes	_____	7
TOTAL	Your Score_____		100

should be seriously considered for improvement possibilities. The typical purchasing problems noted in review and from other information about the department should be listed. When this list is completed, then certain major areas should be studied to ascertain where improvements can be made. The analysis would be of little value if a program were not established to improve the department and increase its effectiveness in the future. Thus for each low rating characteristic and problem identified a specific improvement plan should be created and used to upgrade the function.

MANAGING THE FUNCTION USING THE KEY INDICATOR REPORT

Often management does not have a satisfactory method to monitor the purchasing department. It has been found that one of two conditions usually exist; too many items of little and confusing value are reported to management about the department activities or nothing is sent forward for review and understanding. What results is often a lopsided view of the department. The many fine contributions and also the problems are not known by management. Buyers often feel they are measured on a "don't run out of material" standard that, as indicated earlier, is an inventory control measure.

The *key indicator report* is a control document for the purchasing environment in the form of a monthly report that consists of statistical information measured against previously established targets. Figure 7 provides an example of this summary of activities of the department as a whole giving an indication of such things as the trend, the type of documents processed, and productivity of individuals. While it is often desirable to supplement the statistical reports with a narrative portion, the key indicator report gives perspective to the overall purpose of the department giving clear, concise information and trend indication.

The target or goals should be established using historical knowledge about the company. When this is not available, then a target should be established on a judgment basis and modified over a period of time. In a narrative portion, certain commentaries should be provided regarding trends, problems, and other nonstatistical information. These qualitative data are of importance because they add to management's perspective about the department. Note the emphasis on cost savings as well as cost avoidance information. This is a key need of the department and should be communicated to management. Often management does not converse with the department and because it tends to leave the department alone, is neither supportive nor critical of the department's operations. A key indicator report gives this information with a minimum amount of time both in preparation and in use.

FUTURE OF THE FUNCTION

A constructive yet critical perspective of the purchasing function leads to the conclusion of almost mandatory requirements for the future.

1. Increased emphasis on professional conduct with higher ethical performance than some other functions.
2. Improved training and productivity of individuals in the arts of purchasing including negotiations, computerization, community relations, and motivation
3. Additional demands on profit contribution through a "least total purchasing cost" approach
4. Monitors on performance using measurements against previously set targets
5. Substantial awareness by executive management on the value of successful purchasing.

REFERENCES

1. Robert L. Janson, *Production Control Desk Book*, Prentice Hall, 1975.
2. Robert L. Janson, *Purchasing Agents Desk Book*, Prentice Hall, 1980.

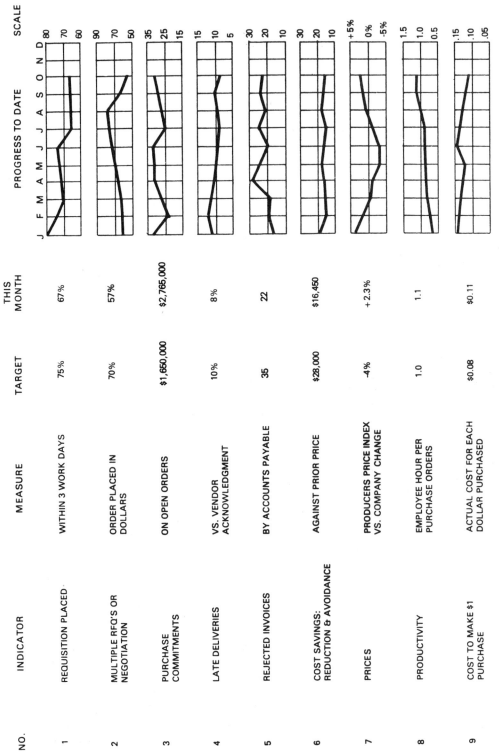

NO.	INDICATOR	MEASURE	TARGET	THIS MONTH
1	REQUISITION PLACED	WITHIN 3 WORK DAYS	75%	67%
2	MULTIPLE RFQ'S OR NEGOTIATION	ORDER PLACED IN DOLLARS	70%	57%
3	PURCHASE COMMITMENTS	ON OPEN ORDERS	$1,650,000	$2,765,000
4	LATE DELIVERIES	VS. VENDOR ACKNOWLEDGMENT	10%	8%
5	REJECTED INVOICES	BY ACCOUNTS PAYABLE	35	22
6	COST SAVINGS: REDUCTION & AVOIDANCE	AGAINST PRIOR PRICE	$28,000	$16,450
7	PRICES	PRODUCERS PRICE INDEX VS. COMPANY CHANGE	-4%	+2.3%
8	PRODUCTIVITY	EMPLOYEE HOUR PER PURCHASE ORDERS	1.0	1.1
9	COST TO MAKE $1 PURCHASE	ACTUAL COST FOR EACH DOLLAR PURCHASED	$0.08	$0.11

FIGURE 7. Purchasing key indicator report month of October.

21
Inventory Control Policy

Ross H. Cornell, Ph.D.
Yale Law School

Inventory control policy is a set of executive level directives that establishes guidelines for inventory management. The author distinguishes between inventory control policies and day-to-day management of inventories. He also discusses the development of inventory control policy in some detail.

The business executive is responsible for managing the firm's assets. For firms that manufacture and sell products, inventories constitute a major asset. Unfortunately, executive control over inventories is not easily achieved. The reason for this lies in the nature of inventories. Inventories are constantly changing when being renewed. In contrast to capital expenditure planning, which occurs periodically, inventory planning must be carried on continuously. Inventories are the economic buffers intended to absorb the impact of many small changes in business environment and the nature and quantity of these many small changes shifts from day to day. Inventory control is affected at the SKU* level through many small daily decisions.

Executive control of inventories is carried out through inventory policy. Inventory control policy is the set of executive level directives that establishes guidelines for inventory management. Day-to-day management of inventories, on the other hand, consists of the many small decisions made by many inventory controllers. These controllers are usually supervisory or clerical employees reporting to the production control department or its equivalent. The decisions of the controllers are subject to a variety of pressures made under continually changing conditions. The level of detail is too small to justify executive review of the individual decisions. Thus control is exercised by setting performance standards and monitoring actual performance against the standards. This chapter deals with techniques for setting performance standards and monitoring actual performance against the standards.

The alternative—no policy—is equivalent to no executive control over inventories. In the absence of inventory policy, inventory control by default falls to the inventory controllers acting independently, each in his own way to his own pressures. For example, suppose that the president of the company desired to have the inventory investment reduced from $10,000,000 to $6,000,000 by year end in order to comply with a restriction in the indenture of the company's new debt issue. Without policy/policy monitoring procedures as a tool

---

*SKU = stock keeping unit, a specific item of inventory at a specific location.

to effect the reduction, the president would be reduced to jawboning in the hope that some ad hoc solution would be devised. Inventory management of this quality can do a great deal of harm.

Vague, intangible, or highly subjective inventory policy is also equivalent to no executive control over inventories. Policy must be thought out carefully and stated in quantitative denominators such as "95% of the line item orders will be shipped within two days," "inventory turns will be six times per year or better," and "machine delays due to parts shortages will be less than 2,000 hours annually." To the extent that analysis is required to determine the proper course, it is best done as part of setting policy. This approach puts analysis "up front" at the planning stage—before procedures are firmed up and personnel trained. To barge ahead without considering the "up front" requirements could require complete revision of procedures, and lead to administrative problems in reorganizing and retraining personnel. Company resources would be wasted.

Once policy has been formulated, those responsible for planning the inventory procedures have the required knowledge of overall objectives. If the inventory system performs as well as or better than expectations, then the systems plan has fulfilled management's expectations. However, should the reverse occur—bad performance through too much inventory, excessive stockout rates, late deliveries, and so on—then either the systems planning or operating performance is at fault.

CUSTOMERS ARE PART OF INVENTORY POLICY

At a meeting of executives at one company, the sales vice-president said: "There's no loyalty in this business; whenever our competitor gives a 10% price cut, we lose the customer. I wish I knew how to overcome this kind of a temperament."

Studies by marketing research groups relating the company's sales to its own price discounts support the vice-president's view that sales of their products are very sensitive to pricing. While the importance of pricing is obvious to most persons, the advantages of good service may not be recognized so clearly. One district sales manager, puzzled by the loss of an important customer, said: "We've always met competitive prices and even undercut our competitors when necessary." A review of correspondence from various customers reveals numerous complaints about broken delivery promises. Recent examples are:

1. Delivery scheduled to arrive on November 7 and arrived November 22.
2. Delivery scheduled to arrive on January 8 was rescheduled for January 12. Half the shipment arrived on January 14 and the customer was notified that the balance could not be delivered until January 21.

Consequently, the customer had to alter production schedules as well as delay deliveries to his customers. These examples represent the negative costs of poor service.

In addition to the obvious positive side of good service, a benefit that can be even greater to the customer than price discount is the reduced amount of inventory that he has to carry. With inventory carrying costs approximating 25% of the value of the inventory, good service permits the customer to reduce inventories to a minimum and thus avoid excess carrying charges.

SUPPLIERS ARE PART OF INVENTORY POLICY

The ability of suppliers to meet shipping schedules influences the buyer's material and work-in-process inventories. Inventory policy should take into account company purchasing efficiency as well as supplier performance. A supplier's difficulty in meeting shipping schedules is not always caused by his low level of inventory. More often than not, he has too many of the wrong items in inventory and not enough of those needed by the buyer. Frequent calls by the company's salesmen relaying customer complaints interrupt schedules and are costly. Accelerating customer complaints can snowball rescheduling causing failure to meet schedules. The increased cost results from numerous production interruptions and changeovers. Part of the problem may be a result of confusion because the buyer does not provide the supplier with accurate forecasts of requirements.

Inventory policy should address the relationship between the company's purchasing function and the company's suppliers. Although materials, quality, and price are important, consistency of supplier service is also important. It is that consistency that affects the size of the company's materials and stores inventories. Inventory policy needs to consider performance standards for its purchasing function as well as for the suppliers. The purchasing function must not be permitted to cause supplier delays.

CASE HISTORY OF NO INVENTORY POLICY

This company, let's call it the XYZ Paper Products Company, produces about 300 items. These include napkins, towels, industrial cleaning tissues, and personal and facial tissues. The manufacturing operations are located in the northwest and in the south with the warehouses centered in major metropolitan areas. For the most part, public warehouses under short-term lease arrangements are used. Generally, the products can be shipped from any mill to any warehouse. There are a few exceptions, however. As an example, the products made of coarser wood from the northwest are not readily saleable in the central and eastern states because of their roughness.

Sales Characteristics

Sales are made primarily to industrial customers and such institutions as schools, hospitals, and government agencies. Large quantities are also sold to food chains for resale in their retail outlets. Paper jobbers are not used. Food chains and large industrial customers order on a national basis with shipments throughout the country. The orders, which are triggered by favorable prices, are usually large and frequently call for delivery on a release basis (that is, the company has annual contracts with the customer, and shipments are made at specified intervals and quantities).

The pattern of sales reflects little in the way of seasonal fluctuations. Periodic purchases because of favorable pricing result in greater fluctuations than does seasonal buying. Thus the leveling of production to maintain a constant work force could be controlled by staging promotions at strategic times.

Usually consumer products are promoted, not industrial items. The consumer products are promoted regionally rather than nationally.

Inventory Control

Work-in-process inventories, consisting of cut logs, pulp, and roll paper, are relatively small. Most of the inventory dollars represent finished goods stored at the various warehouse locations. Such inventory amounts overall to a three-month supply. There is some concern about the management of inventories, as depicted in Figure 1. The item shown, which is typical of the other items in inventory, reflects the end-of-week balance at the New York warehouse.

During January, the warehouse ordered large stocks from the manufacturing plants. These arrived during February and exceeded that month's sales, with the result that the inventory balance increased. In late March and April, the balance was at a satisfactory level for filling orders on an ongoing basis. Restocking orders were placed, but because of overstock in February, small quantities were ordered. Because these orders were small in relation to the shipments, the inventory balance was reduced. In May, the item was out of stock. Throughout the summer, the warehouse was periodically out of stock of the

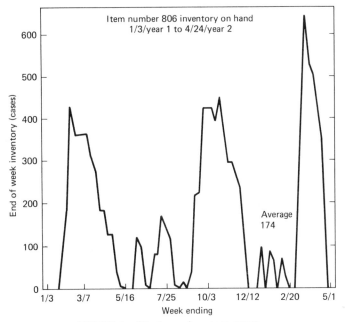

FIGURE 1. Warehouse inventory report.

item. Orders continued to be placed according to the pattern set in March and April when inventory was being worked down; stocks were therefore insufficient for the conditions in May, June, and July.

Under existing procedures, this situation prevails until lobbying by the regional sales manager results in executive awareness of the out-of-stock situation. Then, another surge of orders for the item leads to the increase in inventory shown on October 3. This sequence of "feast or famine" has been repeated over and over for almost every item in inventory.

To correct the situation, management has formed a committee to develop scientific techniques for managing inventory. Discussions held with representatives of production, sales, and finance have not come up with any important conclusions except agreement that service is important. This is the extent of inventory policy. Because no performance standard has ever been set and no method of service measurement has been agreed upon, all participants are left with their own ideas of what constitutes sound inventory control. The "feast or famine" inventory performance continues.

To compound the problem, inventory decisions are dominated more and more by the sales department with production and finance continually on the defensive. Although it is bad management for a sales group to take over control of inventory, it is equally reprehensible for other groups to do such a poor job that such action is considered necessary.

WHY SET POLICY?

The situation of the paper products company is not unusual. Because the marketing organization is pressured to bring in sales, it wants products available for immediate shipment irrespective of the resulting high levels of inventory. The production executive finds that he cannot produce a product efficiently when there are frequent changes to satisfy an immediate sales need. The financial executive, on the other hand, wants to conserve capital by holding inventories at an optimum level.

If inventory policy is not defined clearly, these conflicting interests cause frustration and discord. Frequently, one of these interests prevails because of a dominating personality.

Dominance by any faction is never in the best interests of a company.

A vague inventory policy can be as bad as no policy. In both cases, middle management and operating supervisors are left to their own devices with no clear understanding of what is required. Policies must provide meaningful guidelines such as: "98% of all units of catalog items ordered will be shipped from stock within three days."

The percentage established, such as the 98%, could apply to the company as a whole; it could vary by warehouse, by nature of the product, or by customer grouping. Stating the policy in specific terms provides all segments of the company with guidelines that should minimize the conflicting interests and foster more cooperation among the departments. Equally important is the articulation of a specific service policy that can become part of the company's selling aid to reassure the customer that delivery promises will be honored.

INVENTORY POLICY AND THE COMPUTER

It is not unusual for a company to have 15,000 to 20,000 or more items in inventory. There are not only finished products but manufactured components, purchased parts, and raw materials. To keep a record of the quantities in the various stockrooms, the movements in and out of each stockroom and work-in-process area, as well as the many analytical and control factors, is a tremendous job. The computer takes over a burdensome and costly manual task.

When use of the computer in inventory accountability became practical, many writers described how computers should take over inventory management as follows: Translate all conflicting inventory objectives into cost denominators. In particular, program the computer to interpret customer service in terms of cost of stockout, back orders, split shipments, delayed shipments, and other related factors. Then express production service in terms of setup cost, size of run, and so on. After this

has been translated into inventory unit cost, develop a formula that ties all these costs together to arrive at an overall cost of inventory. This formula applies the cost factors of stockout rate, order size, and cost of capital. Then it calculates the minimum inventory cost which results from taking these factors into account. The result is considered to be inventory policy. Then, according to the policy, production is run in two shifts, say 258 days a year; the distribution group obtains a new warehouse in, say Miami, and the company rejects those orders that do not fit in with the policy prescribed by the computer.

Although textbooks continue to teach these procedures, few companies follow them because they recognize that inventory policy requires judgmental considerations. The lack of formal analysis or decision rules means that the computer cannot be programmed to formulate inventory policy.

Today, many companies consider their inventory management automated even though the automation may apply to little more than record keeping and reporting. Inventory stock status reports are maintained and management is provided with current exception data to monitor inventory performance. At the policy level, the computer has little to do with inventory management.

For many companies, the limitations of automated inventory management with respect to policy surfaced during the 1974–1975 recession. The energy crisis, high inflation, and recession changed business conditions so rapidly that many time-honored inventory policies became obsolete overnight. Many executives whose inventory records were automated discovered that their company had no mechanism, automated or otherwise, for setting policy—and therefore no control over inventory.

DEFICIENCIES OF THE COST FORMULA APPROACH

The failure of the "all cost" approach to inventory policy has left a gap in automated inventory management as practiced in most companies. The starting point in filling this gap through a comprehensive inventory management program is to examine the reasons for the failure and then to determine practical methods to overcome the difficulties.

Failure of the "textbook" approach to setting inventory policy can be attributed to one or more of the following:

1. The textbook procedures for determining policy are not adaptive to dynamic business conditions.
2. Certain assumptions are not realistic.
3. Cost information is not available.

Typically, management pursues textbook inventory control by assigning the task to a staff team in the systems group. This group collects and analyzes data, interviews the appropriate operating personnel, and finally presents recommendations for executive review and approval.

Executives studying the recommendations became dissatisfied because the recommendations contain some or all of the faults mentioned above. But because executives are usually not specialists in inventory management, they cannot explain their dissatisfaction. Therefore, they either recommend further study or accept the proposal reluctantly with the hope that the problem areas will be worked out in use. Usually the objections are forgotten, leaving things much the way they were before.

The paper products company described earlier provides an example of what does not work in setting inventory policy.

The problems of too much inventory of some items and too little of others, too much inventory at one time and too little at another time, have existed for some time. The sales and production departments have squared off, each blaming the other for the problems plaguing the company. The systems department has been instructed to study the problem and to suggest an inventory policy and how to implement it. After extensive studies and interviews at the plants and warehouses, the group has issued a report explaining the causes of the inventory problems and recommending improvements. The following are some key points in the report:

1. There is too much inventory and too little customer service (a reiteration of a well-known fact).
2. Causes include bad product delivery to warehouses, incorrect lot sizes, poor forecasts, too frequent product changes, and generally poor factory performance.
3. Recommendations include the following: Calculate the cost of a stockout, cost of carrying inventories, and overall percentage of stockouts. Determine the overall inventory level that would minimize all costs. Then maintain the overall stockout rate and the overall inventory investment at the levels determined by the analysis.
4. Determine the overall inventory level. Then allocate inventory to individual items based on average sales. Stock each item at the warehouses with a two-month supply. The following is a statement of policy: The production department maintains that level for all items at all times.
5. Assign a task force to improve forecasting procedures. Base production scheduling on the average projected demand.
6. Improve the scheduling of deliveries from plants to warehouses so that warehouse orders arrive on schedule.

Management has reviewed the report and recommendations without enthusiasm but has approved a study that should improve forecasting procedures. The attempt to determine overall inventory cost minimization, as recommended, has been seriously delayed because the controller's department cannot provide information on costs of carrying inventory—a task that has been started a number of times but not completed during the time period in which it was needed. It has also been difficult to elicit the kind of creative thinking that would provide information on the cost of stockouts in order to determine inventory levels.

Weaknesses of this Cost Formula Solution

The recommendations to allocate an acceptable overall level of inventory to individual items based on average sales contains a basic weakness. The assumption that a fixed number of months' requirement is a suitable method for determining inventory needs of the various items overlooks the following facts:

1. Many warehouses are stocked from more than one location. Items shipped from the east coast and from the northwest require different lengths of time in transportation. Obviously, the amount of allowed inventory must take into account the longer pipelines that must be kept filled.
2. For some items, the demand patterns are fairly stable while for others they are somewhat erratic. The level of inventory for stable items would therefore differ from that for the erratic.
3. Certain items are produced constantly, others intermittently, with lot size considerations. Here again the amount of inventory differs for these different production patterns.
4. Promotions affect demand; inventory stocking rules should account for this.
5. Items sold to large chains must take such demand factors into account: Items not sold to chains require a different level of stocking.

Any recommendation suggesting a two-month average inventory for all items must be erroneous. Because the marketplace changes

rapidly, the system for inventorying has to be flexible and dynamic rather than rigid across the board. Flexibility should allow the company to provide for advance orders, consignment stock, product substitution, product life cycles, discounts, customer returns, slow-moving items, obsolete stock, preferential customers, tax rates, warehouse costs, manufacturing efficiency, automation, production capacity, and transportation availability.

Also to be considered are the following questions: 1) What would policy be with respect to the introduction of new items into inventory? 2) How can the system provide for a possible rail strike, a strike at one of the manufacturing facilities, or some other exigency that affects demand? The executive knows instinctively that recommendations for control of inventory have to be flexible, allowing for unexpected and expected changes.

The study at the paper products company did not consider inventory policy sufficiently. A cost formula was developed, based purely on analysis of company data. Where data were missing, the systems personnel made assumptions without the benefit of experience. The formula developed was based on erroneous assumptions and was so inflexible that half of the items would have insufficient inventory to meet customer service requirements while the other half would be in excess of needs. Thus excess inventory was built into the system at the start, and additional crash scheduling would be needed to satisfy customer needs for the items that would be in short supply.

WHAT DOES WORK?

The following are six steps for developing sound inventory policies. Not all of these are suitable for every company but those that are serve as a good reference point.

1. Identify the relevant areas to be included in the policy.
2. Determine the basis of measuring performance in the relevant areas.

3. Establish standards for acceptable performance. If possible, specify upper and lower limits for compliance.
4. Identify the executive point of control to assure that policies are being properly carried out.
5. Define the changes in business conditions that will trigger a reevaluation of inventory policy.
6. Design a mechanism to act as a test of the effect of policy changes on operations.

Discussing and Applying Policy Steps

The first step in developing a sound inventory policy is to identify the areas to be incorporated into the policy. The areas affecting customer service such as stockout rates and order processing time are generally high on the priority list for wholesalers and certan manufacturers. Downtime is high on the list for companies in the processing industry. A checklist of areas that should be considered in the development of policy is included in Table 1. This list has been compiled from a number of inventory projects for companies in a wide variety of businesses.

Table 1. Checklist: areas that should be covered by inventory policy

Inventory turnover	Setup time
Inventory values	Expediting
Stockout rates	Overtime
Order processing time	Intercompany transfers
Delivery time	Intercompany transfers
Back orders	Obsolete inventory
Order frequency	Slow-moving inventory
Split orders	Cancellations
Lead times	Inventory location
Returns	Product changes
Substitutions	Production run size
Hedge inventory	Quality rejection criteria
Consignment stock	Certified vendors
Process downtime	Incoming inspection
Routing	Cycle counting
Bills of material	Engineering changes
Requirements forecasting	Assignment of respon-
Machine downtime	sibility

Each area in the checklist should be reviewed, first to identify applicability and then in light of current inventory performance, to establish priorities. Certain areas warrant a policy statement—some will be categorized as actionable, while others will have low priority, depending on the company.

The following case study demonstrates a high priority area:

A new president of a gear manufacturing company has given top priority to assessing inventory problems. He has concluded that work-in-process is far too large and that much work is required to improve inventory management. Guidelines are needed. In discussions with plant personnel, problems have been raised. Because foremen in various departments schedule their own production, inprocess inventory components have become unbalanced and the overall inventory is almost twice as great as necessary. Sales forecasts are inaccurate, vendor deliveries are poor, and expediting procedures are disorganized.

However, careful review shows that the lack of policies relating to production scheduling has resulted in independent scheduling by a number of supervisors on an ad hoc basis. None has guidelines nor understands the overall situation in the plant. Wanting to help other departmental supervisors and to spare themselves the criticism that goes with stockouts, they have created excess inventories. The solution is to give high priority to establishing inventory policy in the areas affecting production schedules—overtime, machine downtime, production run sizes, and so on.

In some instances where a review or revision of an existing policy is indicated, immediate change may not be practical. For example, if changes in customer service are contemplated, proposed alternatives could be checked out with selected customers. Before determining what changes to make in inventory policy, the company has to complete investigatory work.

In a program for developing inventory policy, all executives and other key personnel affected by such policy should be parties to discussions that affect their areas of responsibility. Many individual areas representing segments of inventory policy are governed by overall inventory policy guidelines. The chief financial executive may, for example, establish that inventory must not exceed a total company value of $18 million and it must turn over at least five times a year.

Frequently, policy is confused by differences of opinion between production and sales. In such instances, a staff team should investigate the issues and recommend a policy that satisfies both. If differences cannot be reconciled through this approach, a higher level executive should settle the issues. Fortunately, such disputes are in the minority. In most instances, accord is reached without exhaustive analysis and arbitration.

Policy must be formulated in quantifiable terms whenever possible. Because this aspect of measureability might be useful to the financial group, they should also be involved. The limits within which measurement of acceptable performance is determined should be spelled out in the policy furnished to this group.

Policy must be stated in specific terms that are easy to apply. A statement such as "5% stockout rate" may appear definitive enough. However, it can be interpreted in many ways. Is the rate measured in dollars? In boxes? Line items? Number of orders? Or some other denominator? Often, orders containing many line items are received. Because one or two of the items are sometimes back ordered, service performance may be penalized even though overall performance may be excellent.

In one of the companies whose procedures were studied, the inventory policy required that 95% of customer orders be shipped within five days. The new report showing shipping performance indicated performance as being 65%. Upon investigation, it was found that the orders that contributed to this low performance were those received in advance. Orders shipped on schedule were being recorded as late in terms of the date the order was received. Performance looked bad but was actually good. The problem was quickly corrected by changing the date from which performance was measured.

The foregoing illustrations emphasize the need for specificity in developing policy. In the more complex cases, it would be well to present illustrative examples under various situations that might occur, particularly in exceptional cases.

Most companies evaluate inventory turnover on an overall basis, calculating turns on the total value carried on the balance sheet. For purposes of control, the policy should provide for more definitive measurements. To illustrate, two companies may both have five inventory turns per year. If one has little in-process inventory and the other has a substantial portion of its total inventory in manufactured parts, five turns per year may not reflect comparable performance attainments. Because the "flowthrough" of work-in-process is normally more rapid than that of finished products, the latter company with its predominance of work-in-process may not actually perform as well as the former company.

This example illustrates the desirability of basing measurements on meaningful segments for purposes of control. In line with accountability by responsibility, control should be segmented further so that the performance of supervisors responsible for smaller segments of the inventory can also be measured. Because the whole is a sum of its parts, good performance in the segments of inventory assures good overall performance.

Flexibility of Policy

The policy that works well in a seller's market may become an albatross when a buyer's market prevails. As an example, customer returns during a seller's market, when demand is greater than supply, may allow return of only defective goods or goods shipped in error. During a buyer's market, these allowances are frequently loosened. It is also possible that other allowances, such as acceptance of smaller size orders, may be made without the penalty of setup charges. For this reason, persons who establish policy must provide the mechanics for changing policy when circumstances so dictate. They must also define which policies are subject to change. Failure to provide for such changes in advance could burden the company with a rigidity that will not permit even the simplest of changes.

Implementing the Six-Step Inventory Policy

For companies starting with no inventory policy at all, implementing the six-step inventory policy requires much detailed work particularly if the company is in a variety of businesses. Fortunately, the inventory policy program can be implemented piecemeal.

The inventory committee of the XYZ Paper Products Company is in this situation and is finally getting on with it. The resources required for a comprehensive review of policy have not been made available in full measure. The program, therefore, has to be implemented piecemeal. When the obsolete inventory segment was being evaluated, the committee considered whether the obsolescence was potentially related to several other areas such as slow-moving stock, product changes, and production run sizes.

Discussions with the operating personnel indicate that obsolete inventory in the company is related primarily to product changes. Therefore, the committee has decided to address the problem of defining inventory policy for obsolete inventory and for product changes as they relate to obsolete inventory. By comparison with the

other areas on the checklist in Table 1, obsolete inventory is judged to be of prime importance.

The second step involves determining the basis of measuring performance. Those responsible for the program raised the question What constitutes obsolescence? Does an item become obsolete when it is dropped from the catalog? What happens when it was dropped from the national catalog but is still selling in some areas of the country? What happens when production resumes after an item has been declared obsolete? Frequently, the obsolete product and its replacement differ merely in decorative features. Should the old product be sold at a discount or should it be scrapped? Answers to these questions are worked out as part of determining the definitions of obsolescence. The unit of measurement adopted for the new definition of "obsolete" is dollar value, rather than weight or units. Implementation of this step—getting a clear definition and assignment of a dollar value to obsolescence—leads to the next step, which is setting standards that assign responsibility for such losses. This responsibility has been placed with the sales department. Because new product introduction is the responsibility of product managers and obsolete inventory is created primarily as a result of introducing replacement products, assigning the responsibility of the obsolete inventory to the appropriate product managers combines the responsibility with those executives exercising effective authority over the size of the obsolete inventories. Because responsibility is assigned to product managers, they are consulted to determine appropriate standards to use in gauging obsolete inventory performance. Several important facts of the business are brought out by these interviews. The first fact is that product improvements (replacements) are usually in response to market pressures such as competitors' new product introductions. Under these conditions, the timing of replacement introduction is dictated by the marketplace and not by the size of inventory in stock. The second fact is that the secondary market for replaced (obsolete) product declines as time passes. The obsolete product can be sold for a number of months after its replacement, but as time passes the possibilities of a sale become less and less.

After considering these facts, the XYZ company decides to set obsolete inventory standards in terms of time rather than amount. A good performance is one in which the obsolete inventory is sold through secondary markets within six months, and a poor performance is one in which the dispositon of obsolete inventory is not so rapid. These standards are in contrast to the usual practice of defining a good performance in terms of a small dollar level of obsolete inventory. In terms of management motivation, the distinction is significant. By selecting the correct standard, product managers are not inhibited from making the product changes dictated by the marketplace. At the same time they are motivated to clean out the obsolete inventory in a cost-effective way.

The policy standards for disposing of obsolete inventory are based on the opinion that the replaced product can be sold for only a short period of time after obsolescence. The company recognizes the need to reevaluate inventory policy should this condition change. The product managers are free to discount the price of the obsolete product in order to clean it out by the end of the six months, and management examines the amount of these discounts together with product movement to determine whether business conditions are changing. If, for example, the obsolete product continues to sell at only a small discount up until the end of the six-month period, then the period may be too short. Management alerts the systems personnel implementing the policy to the possibility of changes in policy so that the necessary flexibility can be incorporated in the procedures.

Finally, in order to test the effect of the policy changes, the company implements the changes on a limited basis and plans for management reports to monitor the effect of the changes.

Achieving good executive control over inventory is probably one of the most difficult tasks encountered in asset management. One reason for the difficulty is the tendency to try to control on an overall basis without first developing step-by-step guidelines. The XYZ Company successfully solved its obsolete inventory problem before moving on to other inventory considerations. Inventory policy was developed for this one step by addressing the limited question—how to clean out obsolete inventory—and by considering only those factors important to a resolution of that issue. Other considerations, such as how to prevent obsolete inventory, were addressed at later steps. The interaction of several issues need not preclude their being addressed as separate steps. For the XYZ Company, the procedures for disposing of obsolete inventory worked so well that the need to prevent obsolete inventory became a low priority. The journey of a thousand miles is taken one step at a time.

MEASURING PERFORMANCE

The procedures relating to measuring performance are important in inventory system planning and should be distinguished from the operating procedures related directly with procurement, maintenance, and use of inventory. The operating procedures are carried out by operating personnel; the procedures relating to measuring and reporting on the operating performance, by contrast, may involve accounting, financial, and staff personnel. Inventory controllers are subject to such day-to-day pressures that they cannot be expected to implement inventory policy without the assistance of executive reports spotlighting their performance and supporting their claim that they are doing the job right.

The starting point for designing performance measurement is the inventory policy. The importance of measuring performance against inventory policy cannot be overstressed. This is illustrated in the case study that follows:

The inventories in question are the manufacturer's finished goods of heavily promoted, high-volume, low-cost household consumer goods. Obsolescence is a serious problem with such inventories because of packaging and promotional changes—as well as minor product changes. Every year, a "new and improved" version is put out, even if new and improved means only that the color is changed and the price increased.

In a company in which production is king and the consumers willing, the solution is relatively simple. The sales manager must move all the "old and unimproved" product before they can sell the new product. However, when marketing policies reign supreme and heavy outlays are made for advertising campaigns beginning at a predetermined date, then at dawn on the first day of the campaign, the "old and unimproved" is effectively obsolete. The production managers must arrange to shut

off production of the old product in time. This is not to make a case for either production or marketing predominance in formulating policy relative to obsolescence. Irrespective of which policy rules, old stocks must be worked down as quickly as possible to minimize obsolescence. This calls for careful planning.

Figure 2 shows the company's obsolete buildup over a three-year period. Even though product life cycles for the company's products have been well known, the obsolete inventory has been trending upward rather than downward. The deficiency in this company is that obsolete stock has not been reported effectively. Although the on-hand figures for the various items have been available, there has been no attempt to discern trends, as has been done in Figure 2.

The company depicted in Figure 2 did not use the available figures effectively. The company procedure was to work down the obsolete items in its stockrooms spasmodically with a flurry of effort when time allowed. This approach was ineffective because the obsolete inventory increased further, during periods when interest waned. The company finally solved this inventory problem by instituting an obsolete inven

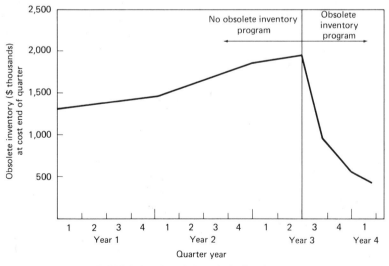

FIGURE 2. Cumulation of obsolete inventory.

tory program that was essentially a performance measuring program.

By implementing the obsolete inventory program, the company benefited in three ways:

1. Obsolete inventory was prevented from accumulating without notice for months at a time by monitoring performance on a monthly basis.
2. Efficient procedures for selling obsolete items were provided. Monthly reports listed the obsolete inventory by location and provided this information to the sales department for disposition.
3. Standard procedures were substituted for what had been an undirected and intermittent flurry of activity, thus reducing the management effort required to deal with the problem.

The results obtained from the program can be seen in Figure 2. The program was inagurated in July of the year, by which time the obsolete inventory had grown to about $2,000,000 at cost. Within a period of seven months, the obsolete inventory had been reduced to a level of about $500,000.

The key to the success of the program was a performance measurement report that, with appropriate modification, could be effective for many companies. The report, shown in Table 2, was prepared monthly by computerized procedures and distributed to the field automatically. Note that the report shows the stock status history of the various items making up the obsolete inventory. One can tell at a glance the makeup of the items and whether the problem is growing worse or getting better. The report also provides selling instructions.

Item 12-100-M5, for example, includes a total of 936 cases that have been obsolete for six months. Of this total, six cases are located in the Boston warehouse, 653 in New York, and 277 in Cleveland. At the extreme right of the report, the selling instructions specify that these items are available at 40% off inventory cost.

This inventory report (for November 1) also shows items 12-100A-30Z and 24-100F-30Z in the three-month obsolete column. When the salesman receives this report, he has in a single report information he could get previously only by making lengthy phone calls and searching through inventory records.

Because the format of the inventory information in Table 2 is somewhat unusual, an explanation is in order. An item officially declared obsolete is added to the obsolete inventory report. The inventory so declared is recorded as one month obsolete. At the end of the next month, the remaining part of the one month obsolete inventory becomes two months obsolete and is so recorded. At the end of six months, every effort is made to dispose of remaining items on hand. This kind of inventory history allows management to judge how fast the obsolete inventory is being worked down. If the particular product classified as obsolete is not selling, the selling instructions section can be altered to increase the discount or otherwise make the product more readily disposable.

If the planned disposal discount is expected to work in one location but not in another, the inventory can be transferred to the most saleable location, as was done for 12-100-M5 between months one and two and again between months two and three in the example. Customers in New York were willing to make purchases at the 40% discount off cost so transfers were made to New York from Philadelphia.

Under the new procedures, an item is officially classified as obsolete through an authorization form. The product manager responsible for the new replacement product is one of the signators. At the end of the month, the obsolete inventory for that period becomes his responsibility. He can set the selling terms as he sees fit within

Table 2. Obsolete inventory report (figures in cases) November 1, 19XX

| | | | STOCK STATUS MONTHS AFTER OBSOLETE DATA | | | | | | SELLING |
ITEM	OBS.	LOCATION	1	2	3	4	5	6	INSTRUCTIONS
12-100-M5	4/XX	BO	1,459	945	551	6	6	6	Available 40% off cost
		NY	1,343	233	2,594	2,115	962	653	Available 40% off cost
		PH	4,649	2,101	160	0	0	0	Available 40% off cost
		CL	2,181	2,378	2,121	1,669	1,424	277	Available 40% off cost
			9,632	5,657	5,426	3,790	2,392	936	
12-100A-30Z	7/XX	NY	214	204	204				Scrap
24-100F-30Z	7/XX	BO	1,092	492	492				Special price refer—
		NY	2,569	2,569	2				ence sales release
		PH	4,118	4,068	4,068				no. 132
		CL	875	875	575				
		CH	2,893	1	1				
			11,547	8,005	5,138				

certain guidelines. Along with this, the formula for determining his bonus has been revised to encourage him to work down inventories before bringing new products on board. At the end of the six-month period, the remaining product is automatically scrapped if no markets remain and the loss is reflected in the bonus. This bonus system motivates managers to dispose of obsolete inventory. However, the kind of control measurement available in Table 2 is an integral part of the system. Without the report showing the current status of the obsolete items and measuring the impact of sales disposal efforts, the managers would not be able to deal intelligently with the problem.

MONITORING INVENTORIES

Monitoring inventory performance is simplified because only two things can go wrong: too little or too much inventory. The objective of effective monitoring is first to identify where and when either of these situations ex-

ists and then to trace back through the procedures to identify the factor or factors contributing to the out-of-balance condition. This monitoring should usually start at the SKU level and only rarely should aggregates of items be the lowest level monitored. A limited number of factors causes the inventory imbalance.

Consider an item that is consistently in short supply. The cause is frequently traced to one of the following:

1. The product is not available from the source (vendor, work station, and so on).
2. Orders are not placed on a timely basis.
3. Quantities ordered are too small.
4. Deliveries are erratic.

The first factor refers to disruptions such as strikes, fires at supplier plants, and so on. It is questionable whether companies should carry inventories routinely to guard against such contingencies. However, special hedge inventories can be considered to guard against a known probability such as an impending vendor strike or plant move.

The second item—orders not placed on a timely basis—is indicative of failure to attend to business. This is a common fault with manual systems when it is just impossible for the inventory controller to keep on top of several thousand items. The most widely used monitoring technique for this is the *red line* or *warning line*. When inventory on hand plus on order falls below the warning level, the item is listed on a warning report. One company uses two warning lines. If inventory on hand and on order falls below the first warning line and nothing is done, the level eventually falls below a second warning line. The item is then listed on a separate report. Although the doubling up of warnings seems redundant, the company finds it effective. The method triggers two actions. The level 1 warning says "Order immediately" while the level 2 warning says "Check on the inventory controller." The level 1 warning relates to daily operations whereas the level 2 warning relates to procedures.

The third problem—order amounts too small—is the most difficult to monitor. Usually, the root cause is changing business conditions. Balancing demand and lead time will give the proper order size for an item but last week's order size may not do this week. Further, the change may be difficult to detect. An increase in demand this month may be a permanent increase or it may be a random fluctuation. This is the one point in inventory management where mathematical methods have been most helpful. A good way to monitor order sizes is by using the appropriate statistics and playing the favorable odds.

Another area worth exploring is erratic delivery times. Erratic rather than long delivery times cause inventory problems. If a vendor had long but predictable lead times, a pipeline inventory can be set up so that inventory stocks on hand are relatively low. With erratic deliveries, one can never know what action to take. One approach, and probably the most effective, is for the purchasing department to

maintain a record of the number of days that orders are open before the vendor makes delivery. If there is a history of erratic delivery patterns, then the vendor should be contacted. If he cannot correct the condition, it may be possible to find another vendor who will follow more orderly delivery patterns.

When companies have problems of too little inventory under the conditions described earlier, some measure of too little is required. Some frequently used measures are:

1. Stockout rate computed as units ordered (but not shipped) divided by units ordered
2. Stockout rate computed as: the number of order entry line items ordered (but not completely shipped) divided by the number of order entry line items ordered.
3. Stockout rate computed as the number of items with zero inventory at month-end divided by the number of items.
4. Units backordered divided by units ordered.
5. Order entry line items backordered divided by order entry line items ordered.
6. Items back ordered divided by items in stock.

Variations of the above can be employed. As an example, the denominator in most of the above might substitute shipments for orders.

The stockout rate (or back order rate) should not be defined and monitored entirely by the inventory supervisors. Top and middle management must assure that the calculations are correct and consistent, and even more important, that proper corrective action is taken when inventories become unbalanced. The proper corrective action cannot be left to inventory controllers. In such matters, profit margins must be considered. When some items are highly profitable and others only marginally profitable, the stockout measure should be weighted; the more profitable the item, the more strict the followup.

A more common error is to select out-of-stock measures on the basis of number of items rather than on the basis of the relative volume. By doing this, low volume items are kept in excessive supply in order to achieve a low stockout rate while the high volume best-sellers are not given their due weighting according to the sales volume they represent. Out-of-stock measures are suitable when the sales of most items are about equal in volume.

Table 3 illustrates a unit-based stockout measure, which does not require much effort. The clerk who maintains the inventory records fills in preprinted worksheets. The average daily sales figures in units are updated semi-annually. At the end of the month, the clerk reviews the inventory records and determines the number of days out-of-stock for each applicable item. These figures are entered in the second column from the right. The days out-of-stock are then extended by the average daily sales to obtain an estimate of lost sales. Finally, the stockout rate is computed as the quotient of lost sales divided by the sum of sales and lost sales (5.3% in Table 3).

Table 3. Stockout rate for July

ITEM NO.	AVERAGE DAILY SALES IN UNITS	DAYS OUT-OF-STOCK	LOST SALES IN UNITS
5165	1.2		
5170	3.0		
5171	14.6		
5172	8.1		
5200	.2	8	1.6
5205	.7	8	5.6
5230	11.5	2	23.0
5260	2.2		
5265	1.8		
5270	5.1		
.	.	.	.
.	.	.	.
.	.	.	.

Total lost sales: 1,672.5

Total sales: 29,671

Stockout rates: $\dfrac{1,672.5}{29,671 + 1,672.5} = 5.3\%$

Because the number of items out-of-stock in a given month was rarely more than 15, the entire process required less than two hours a month.

The advatages of this type of calculation became obvious. The inventory supervisor soon realized that he would look worse if a high-volume item ran out of stock than a low-volume item. This encouraged a tendency to pay closer attention to the high sellers. Further, the supervisor realized that a ten-day stockout made him look worse than a one-day stockout. As a result, he moved quickly to correct out-of-stock situations. This example demonstrates the advantage of changing the stockout measure from a product number item to a SKU basis.

As in all reporting, tricks of the trade can be introduced so that an inventory controller's performance will not look so bad. As an example, the inventory controller in Table 5 may retain one unit in stock even though he had demand for that unit and more. The system would then record no out-of-stock when the item is in fact out-of-stock. In such a circumstance, cross checks should be prepared with sales or order entry records. The sales department could be asked to report all items that were not shipped completely during the month and the sales out-of-stock list compared with the warehouse stockout report. Such cross checks, through management involvement, assure proper reporting. Such checks could be applied on either a regular or an exception basis.

It is important to monitor excessive inventories as well as insufficient inventories. This is rarely done, even in companies that prepare back order reports. Probably one of the reasons is the uncertainty as to what is excessive. Excess inventory means inventory that is not needed to meet the objectives set by policy. Slow-moving stock need not be excessive although many persons would define it as such. Some of the inventory in the highest usage items could be excess. In fact, a product could be a star performer with rapidly expanding sales and a healthy profit margin yet part of its inventory could be classified as excessive.

If a basic reorder system is used, excess can be defined partly from the reorder rules. For example, with the order-point/order-quantity (OP-OQ) system, inventory on hand and on order should not exceed the sum of the order point plus the order quantity. Allowing some margin, say 10%, for leveling out quantities provides a basis for the excess. Any inventory above the level of the order point plus order quantity plus 10% is excessive. If, typically, two orders are outstanding at the same time, then excess might more appropriately be defined as any inventory on hand above the level of the order point plus 10%. Similarly, for a mini-max system, inventory in excess of maximum plus 10% might be classified as excess. If inventory policy is set by turnover rates, then those rates can be used to define excess inventory. If the required turnover for an item is four times a year, then that translates into a three-month stock on the average. Allowing a margin for small deviations, we could define excess as any stock above three and a half months' supply.

Excess inventory, as just defined, can arise in several ways. A common method is through overordering. Inventory supervisors frequently order in excess of the rules to provide a cushion against complaints from the sales department in the event of stockouts. Overordering may also reduce the number of times they have to review and/or reorder the items. In the absence of an excess inventory report, who will notice?

If in systems where the excess inventory is defined in part by reference to order points, maximum, order levels, and so on, these quantities are revised, inventory may become excessive. If the inventory of an item is at its maximum when its maximum is adjusted downward, some of the inventory may be reclassified as excess even though the amount in stock has not changed. This does not mean that the classification is incorrect. It only means that excess inventory can result even when everyone is following the rules.

Obsolete and damaged inventory certainly could be classified as excess. However, if proper reporting exists for these classes of inventory, it is best to leave them out of the excess report. This restricts excess to "good saleable product" and simplifies the design of special procedures to deal with the excess amounts. Another type of inventory that may be included in excess is a product soon to be discontinued from stock at a certain location. It may be advantageous to subject such stock to the special attention devoted to excess inventory and to classify all the inventory of the item at the particular location as excess.

Excess inventory should be monitored by aggregation starting at the SKU level. Excess should be calculated for each SKU and then summarized according to the responsibility for the inventory. If the inventory at a plant is the responsibility of one supervisor, then a plant excess report would be desirable. However, if the responsibility for the plant inventory is divided, say by product line, then product line excess inventory reports would be indicated.

Figure 3 illustrates aggregation of excess inventory for the finished product inventories of a division. The report is denominated in dollars because it is part of an executive sum-

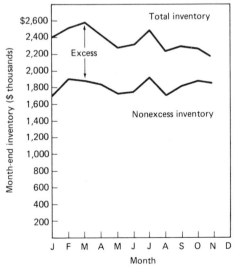

FIGURE 3.   Excess inventory report finished product inventories.

mary report. The excess portion is a good product that previously sold quite well at the location represented by these figures. Now, sales have fallen off so that inventory requirements are less.

Note that the gap between total inventory and nonexcess inventory narrows in the latter months. This is a result of a program to transfer some of the slow-moving items to locations where sales of these items are strong. The program was instituted as a consequence of executive review of the report. Without the report, it is unlikely that anything would have been done.

EMPIRICAL INVENTORY CONTROL

Businessmen with engineering or science backgrounds are familiar with control through feedback. Feedback controls are used extensively in process industries, in computer-controlled manufacturing processes, and in many other types of production processes. The concept is simple and practical. A good illustration is the thermostat. If the thermostat is set for 68°, when room temperature drops below 68° the furnace starts automatically. If the system is tied into central air-conditioning, the temperature is controlled on the top side as well.

The following steps in feedback control can be applied to inventories:

1. Set a standard in measurable terms. The standard may be a range.
2. Regularly monitor activity against the standard.
3. If activity is below standard, initiate actions to raise it; if above standard, initiate actions to lower it.

Figure 4 illustrates the effect of feedback controls on a chemical process. Note that the fluctuations in temperature are not random. As the temperature falls at the beginning of the graph, the feedback control senses the drop and initiates countermeasures. The coun-

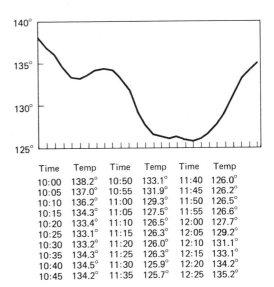

Time	Temp	Time	Temp	Time	Temp
10:00	138.2°	10:50	133.1°	11:40	126.0°
10:05	137.0°	10:55	131.9°	11:45	126.2°
10:10	136.2°	11:00	129.3°	11:50	126.5°
10:15	134.3°	11:05	127.5°	11:55	126.6°
10:20	133.4°	11:10	126.5°	12:00	127.7°
10:25	133.1°	11:15	126.3°	12:05	129.2°
10:30	133.2°	11:20	126.0°	12:10	131.1°
10:35	134.3°	11:25	126.3°	12:15	133.1°
10:40	134.5°	11:30	125.9°	12:20	134.2°
10:45	134.2°	11:35	125.7°	12:25	135.2°

FIGURE 4. Chemical process: temperature readings.

termeasures at first should be small or moderate. The feedback control continues to monitor the temperature. The countermeasures should gradually bring the slide in temperature to a halt. If it continues to drop, the reversng action may be increased.

As can be seen in Figure 4, the temperature seems to be steadying at about 133 degrees on the sixth reading. After that, it drops again. Finally, it is stabilized again. When temperatures fall below the desirable range, countermeasures are increased in order to raise it.

Inventory level is maintained by feedback controls much like the temperature in the preceding illustration. A standard range is set for the desired level of inventory and the inventory is controlled to that level. The standard range consists of an upper and lower limit. If the level rises above the upper limit, countermeasures bring the inventory down. If the inventory falls below the lower limit, similar measures increase the level. As discussed previously, the control should be developed at the SKU level.

Fifty years ago, when business was less complex and less competitive, the inventory control manager, upon discovering an unexpected increase in inventory, would try to determine whether the situation was temporary or permanent. If he discovered, for example, that the sudden drop in sales corresponded with a competitor's special promotion, he might consider the situation temporary and do nothing to correct it. But a feedback control does not think about the nature of the drop. It reacts like an automaton. Although this automatic approach appears to be acting in ignorance, it is this ignorance that makes the system effective.

It is difficult to pin down the cause of increased inventory. Marketing blames sales; sales blames materials management; materials management blames production; production blames purchasing—and so on in circles. Explanations are plentiful. Some sound valid, but a determined effort to assess the impact of each reason given may take several man-weeks of effort.

Feedback controls eliminate the need for analysis. As a result, the job gets done in less time than would be required in probing the reasons why the inventory deviates from the standard range. Even if probing were followed, the casual factors may never be known completely. The result of such uncertainty is frequently a "play-it-safe" strategy.

Conditions for Empirical Controls

Empirical inventory control is based on automated feedback techniques. It also includes a mechanism for keeping the controls tuned. It may include a time-series forecast of demand to adjust the upper and lower inventory level limits (standard). This empirical approach has proved successful in many different industries but it is not applicable to all inventories. Applicability requires:

1. Predictability of demand or usage
2. Availability of product
3. Reasonably short lead times for replenishment
4. High-volume products with few product modifications.

To summarize, the first requirement assumes the need is known, while the second and third requirements allow the need to be fulfilled. The advantage of high volume is that by the law of averages changes cancel each other out.

Forecasting has had an important impact on the number of products with predictable demand. When the forecasting is restricted to annual budget preparation and thereafter plays only a minor role in operations, the items with predictable demand are the items with stable sales patterns. In a department store, sales of such items as children's underwear, kitchen utensils, buttons, and linens are fairly constant and therefore predictable. Note in Figure 5 that the upper portion, depicting sale of children's underwear, is fairly flat with minor deviations above and below the straight line representing the average. The lower portion shows sales of sporting goods that reflect a seasonal line. Sales of items such as the latter may vary markedly from their averages. Basing inventory on the average sales could lead to difficulties in meeting demand.

In Figure 6, we see the effect of a sporting goods forecast. In the upper portion, the fore-

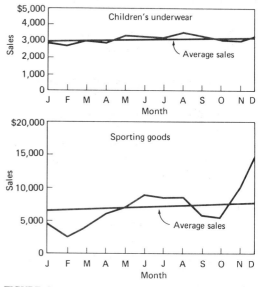

FIGURE 5.   Monthly variation of sales from average.

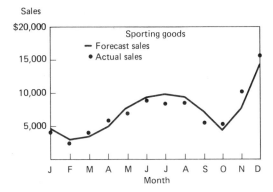

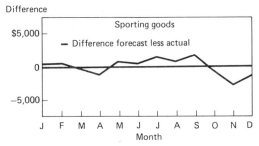

FIGURE 6. Monthly variation of sales from forecast.

cast is compared with actual data. If the inventory were based on the forecasted level rather than on the average, we would have difficulty only if the actual sales showed marked deviations from the forecast. In the lower portion of Figure 6, the forecast is taken as the straight line with the actual showing the amount of deviation from the forecast. This illustrates how the forecast in effect changes the seasonal product line into one of relative stability and thus permits the application of empirical control procedures.

An unpredictable item is not suited to empirical control. If a good forecast cannot be obtained, whether or not the demand is cyclical, then control should not be left to an automatic system. Women's fashion items are an example. With heavy durable goods such as aircraft and atomic power plants, sales may be large in dollars but they depend on a few decisions made by a relatively few buyers. Demand for such items can be highly unpredictable because the law of averages is not useful when the universe is small.

When applied to sales of such items as children's underwear, the feedback controls are relatively simple to implement. At the end of each month, the store is provided with a sales-by-item report that serves as the basis for the following month's orders. The previous month's sales are compared with orders for the month. The difference is added to or subtracted from the forecast for the following month's sales to arrive at the orders for the following month. If orders for an item exceed sales in the previous month, then inventory would be increased by an equivalent amount. Consequently, the orders for the following month could be reduced by that amount. If these rules are used, the inventory at the end of the month equals standard inventory plus or minus the variation between actual and expected sales for the month.

Table 4 illustrates the mechanics of this simple feedback mechanism. Because most of these items were ordered from a company's central warehouse, delivery was always possible within two weeks—provided the item was available at the central warehouse. Thus the

Table 4. Feedback controls for men's T-shirts

	T-SHIRTS (H) SIZE		
	34–36	38–40	40–42
		•	
		•	
		•	
July			
May sales		26	
May orders		12	
Differences		14	
July forecast		12	
July orders		26	
		•	
		•	
		•	

	MAY	JUNE	JULY	AUGUST
Beginning inventory	17	3	6	16
Receipts	12	12	26	12
Sales	26	9	16	17
Ending inventory	3	6	16	11

conditions—short lead times and availabilty of product—are important to the success of the controls.

An example of slightly more elaborate feedback controls is shown in Table 5. The item is a cam made by sintering powdered metal. The production machine operates on a high-volume basis but is used to make a number of sizes. The parts are stocked in an in-process stockroom and are used in a variety of products. As in the previous example, the objective of the feedback mechanism is to replenish the in-stock inventory to a predetermined level.

Two factors complicate the mechanism, however. The requirement for the parts depend on the sales of the finished products containing these parts. Estimates of sales of finished products must first be prepared. Then these estimates are processed through a bill of material explosion to determine the requirements for the cams. The second difficulty encountered is scheduling the machine. Backing out the requirements plan based on standard lead times for assembly of finished goods may lead to requirements in a given week in excess of the machine's capacity. In this case, the requirements are scheduled ahead, taking into account:

1. The inventory level of each item produced on the machine.
2. Standard production lot sizes.
3. A priority for work-in-process items.
4. Rules governing the use of overtime and the permissibility of downtime.

Because of those scheduling rules, the inventory level might not be completely restored at the end of each week. Inventory for a part might rise above standard and still additional production would be scheduled to avoid downtime on the machine. On the other hand, the inventory might be below the standard range without production being scheduled because of requirements for higher priority items. Of course, as the situation worsens, the counterpressures are bound to increase. Thus when the inventory level of a part greatly exceeds the standard, downtime would be accepted rather than further increases in inventory. As a result, inventories are always pushed back to the standard althouh the correction could be sluggish at times.

Table 5 helps to explain how the controls work. The inventory standard (maximum) for the item is 600. At the end of week 12, the inventory is 462 units. Because the BOM sys-

Table 5. Feedback controls for engine parts

Part number: 16-1732C
Inventory limit: 600

WEEK	BEGINNING INVENTORY	DELIVERIES	USAGE	ENDING INVENTORY	REQUIREMENTS	INVENTORY SHORT
•	•	•	•	•	•	•
•	•	•	•	•	•	•
•	•	•	•	•	•	•
12	472	202	212	462		318
13	462	0	185	277	180	553
14	277	206	231	252	230	528
15	252	201	246	207	180	683
16	207	413	290	330	290	•
•	•	•	•	•	•	•
•	•	•	•	•	•	•
•	•	•	•	•	•	•

tem projects requirements of 180 units in week 13, the total needed to satisfy this requirement and return inventory to standard is $600 + 180 - 462 = 318$ units. This last number appears in the Inventory Short column. Because of the scheduling rules, however, no production is scheduled for week 13. As a result, the end-of-week inventory drops to 277 units and the inventory shortage becomes $600 + 230 - 277 = 553$. Again, because of scheduling priorities, the full amount of the shortage is not scheduled for week 14. The item continues to qualify for "maintenance" level production until the end of week 15. At this time, the inventory shortage increases above 600. Thus the week-end inventory is not expected to provide the re-quirements for week 16. Because of the high overall requirements for the machine, the full production returning the inventory to standard is not scheduled.

The final element of the feedback control is a semi-annual measure of the standards to test the correctness of the inventory standards for each item made by the machine. The test is run to determine the minimum inventory levels during the period and the incidence of production delays caused by shortages of items. From the results of these tests, the company determines whether to raise or lower the inventory standards for the next six-month period. In special situations, the standards could be adjusted throughout the six-month period, but these were rarely required.

22
Forecasting Inventory Requirements

Ross H. Cornell, Ph.D.
Yale Law School

With service in mind, the author discusses the various methods of forecasting inventory needs as well as the advantages and disadvantages of each.

In businesses that manufacture or distribute goods, inventory is one of the largest controllable assets. In extraction, conversion, processing, manufacturing, wholesaling, retailing, and import/export, major capital commitments are made to maintaining finished goods, work-in-process, stores and/or materials inventories. These businesses must meet the competitive service requirements of their industries in order to prepare and deliver their goods to customers. Competitive service requirements necessitate inventory.

The retailer is required by competition to maintain inventories of finished goods. Consider the buying habits for consumer goods such as food, clothing, and household appliances. For most products, if the item is not in stock, the customer will make his purchase elsewhere. How many color television sets would be sold, if the sale required a production order to be placed for future manufacture and delivery? Service to the consumer, in the form of ready availability, forces retailers to maintain finished goods inventories.

Service in the form of ready availability of goods also forces the wholesaler to maintain inventory of finished goods to supply the retail outlets. Competitive service requirements force the manufacturer to maintain finished goods inventories to supply the wholesalers.

Except in the unusual cases where technology or other circumstances create a local monopoly, the competition for sales forces the vendor to maintain finished goods inventories in anticipation of future demand.

The manufacturer is required by competition to produce his goods cheaply. In order to attain high plant utilization and economic production runs, the manufacturer is forced to maintain work-in-process inventories. Such inventories provide a buffer between the various production stages, and contribute to improved operations of the following stages in the production or assembly process. Purchased component and other materials inventories likewise service the early stages in the production process. It is true that materials inventories may be built up occasionally as a hedge against a price rise or transportation strike. However, the principal concern of purchasing is to provide service to the plant, to keep the plant running efficiently by anticipating future requirements.

To the extent that inventories are maintained in anticipation of future requirements, forecasting is important for inventory management. Both the level of inventory and the product mix depend on future demand at the stock keeping unit (SKU) level. The retailer stocks an item so that when the future customer comes in, he will be able to purchase the item. The purchasing agent stocks a raw material item so that the process using that material will operate for a certain period in the future. The stores manager maintains spare fan belts so that if a fan belt breaks in the future, he will be able to replace it immediately and keep the engine running. Like it or not, businesses have to carry inventories to service future requirements and such inventories require forecasting.

NO FORECAST IS A FORECAST

No forecast is a forecast, and usually not a very good one. In a horse race, the spectator can bet on a nag (forecasting it to win) or he can elect not to bet (no forecast). This is not the case with inventories. Competition will not permit the business to elect no inventories. Some level of inventories will be maintained, whether inventory requirements are forecast or not. Thus the business question is not whether to forecast, but how to forecast.

Consider the work-in-process inventory of a manufacturer of business machines. Much of the company's inventory value consists of parts and subassemblies, many of which are common to a line of products. Company policy is to maintain only a small finished (totally assembled) goods inventory and to satisfy customer demand by the rapid final assembly of the subassemblies available in inventory.

When asked about this method of forecasting, the manager of production scheduling responds that none is used. The industrial engineering department has tried to develop a forecast that has never been used because its projections are off. The inventory rules used to determine the inventory levels of the subassemblies are order-point/order-quantity rules. When the inventory level of a subassembly item falls to a certain point, a work order is issued to prepare a number of subassemblies equal to the order quantity. The work order calls for

completion of subassemblies in two weeks. This timetable is almost always met.

One item in the subassembly category is a feed arm assembly. The order point for this item is 400 and the order quantity is 300. Let us suppose that a forecast has been prepared to project usage of arm assemblies of 400 units per month. Suppose further that the variability in usage has been measured, and in order to satisfy company service policy a safety stock of 300 units for one month's time is required.

Because the objective of the work-in-process inventory is to provide the units needed for assembly during the lead time of two weeks, the inventory requirements are about equal to two weeks' usage plus safety stock for two weeks. This comes out to $200 + 200 = 400$ units. (The 300 monthly safety stock adjusts to about 200 units for two weeks.) Thus the inventory rule would be to prepare a work order when the inventory level falls to 400 units. That is precisely what was being done. In short, the procedure being followed—with no forecast—is equivalent to a forecast of 400 units per month for the feed arm assembly.

This illustrates that "no forecast" is really equivalent to some forecast because some type of forecast is inherently built into the operating strategy. It is not a question of to forecast or not to forecast; the question is, Will a formal quantitative approach yield better results than forecasting by default?

The default forecast in the case of the feed arm assembly is 400 units a month. Because average monthly usage is only 250, the work-in-process inventory is too high. This is true of many of the items in inventory, with the result that millions of dollars are needlessly tied up in inventory. A formal forecast, even one with a sizable error, would give better results than those results obtained by using a "no forecast" forecast.

DETERMINISTIC CONDITIONS AND PROBABILITY CONDITIONS

When it is possible to predict with 100% certainty exactly what will happen, we are dealing with deterministic conditions. Under such conditions, it is possible to determine the future by reference to the current state of events and the past state of events. If, for example, when releasing a weight from the top of the Tower of Pisa, we are certain that it will fall to the ground, we are dealing with deterministic conditions (gravity). Some business phenomena may be deterministic, or at least appear to be so for all practical purposes, and some business phenomena may not be deterministic.

Business conditions may be deterministic even though it is extremely difficult to project exactly what will happen. To say that it is possible to predict precisely what will happen is not to say that it is easy to predict. For example, it may be possible to project a bank's increase in after-tax revenue that will result from reinvesting its bonds. If the bank's inventory of bond investments is managed properly, the bank should determine periodically the effect of selling the bonds for a current loss (or gain) and reinvesting the proceeds at higher (lower) rates. It may be possible to determine the impact of making all currently profitable reinvestments since the information needed for the determination—bank investments, yields, applicable tax laws—is known. However, to examine the hundreds of investments and solve the simultaneous equations resulting from the interrelationship of federal income, state income, and bad debt regulations would be a difficult and time-consuming task. However, if it can be done, the impact on income resulting from currently optimizing the portfolio should be considered a deterministic event.

Phenomena governed by the laws of probability are impossible to predict precisely. If gravitation were a probabilistic phenomenon, we could not predict when a falling object would hit the ground, even with all the factors known. The time the object takes to reach the ground would be a random variable; any number of different times would be possible. Although prediction of the fall time of an object may be "deterministic," some natural phenomena are clearly probabilistic.

Figure 1 illustrates a natural phenomenon that follows a probabilistic law. In their famous experiment, Rutherford, Chadwick, and Ellis[2] measured the number of α particles given off by a radioactive substance. A Geiger counter was set up to count the number of particles emitted during 7.5-second intervals. During some time intervals, no particles were emitted; during others, one particle; in others, two; and so on. In all, emission counts were taken for 2,608 intervals.

Figure 1 summarizes the results statistically and graphically. Of the 2,608 time intervals, 57 had no emissions at all, 203 had one particle emitted, and so on. If the radioactive emission were a deterministic phenomenon,

Count	Number of time intervals with given count	
0	57	
1	203	Total time intervals:
2	383	2,608
3	525	Total particles counted:
4	532	10,094
5	408	Average number of
6	273	particles per interval:
7	139	3,870
8	45	
9	27	
10 or more	16	

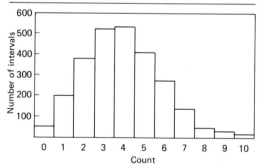

FIGURE 1. Radioactive emission: A probabilistic phenomenon. EXPERIMENT: During 7.5 second time intervals, count the number of α particles given off by a radioactive substance.

and the same number of particles were emitted during each 7.5-second time period (say four particles), then we could forecast this number for every interval.

Although this experiment did not follow a deterministic profile, it did follow a probabilistic pattern. The number of emissions in a given time interval is a random variable following the Poisson distribution. This distribution does not enable us to predict the exact number of emissions in the next 7.5-second interval, but it does enable us to make probability projections. Probability projections are usually qualified with such phrases as, "The chances are one in five that the number of emissions will be less than ten." Statistical expressions, such as average, median, and confidence interval are commonly used to describe probabilistic phenomena. We can never be more definite than this.

The distinction between deterministic and probabilistic conditions is important for forecasting. The forecasting techniques applied to deterministic phenomena differ substantially from those techniques applied to probabilistic phenomena. When dealing with deterministic conditions, the objective is to derive the formula that explains the phenomena. Algebra and functional analysis are important mathematical tools used to achieve this end. Probabilistic phenomena, on the other hand, are governed by laws that can only be explained by the application of probability theory and statistics.

A further distinction between the two types of conditions relates to business planning. Planning based on probabilistic conditions should take into account the uncertainty inherent in the conditions. If production requirements are known precisely, then materials inventories may be planned accordingly. However, if production requirements are probabilistic in nature, then inventory planning must take into account the fact that exact requirements cannot be known in advance. In such cases, planning should utilize statistical concepts, such as averages and confidence limits. Contingency plans should be developed to cover a range of reasonably likely outcomes. Because inventories are carried in order to provide a buffer against uncertainty, inventories are frequently governed by probability laws. Managers responsible for inventory planning should become familiar with the statistical concepts needed for probability forecasting.

BUSINESS CONDITIONS

The radioactive emission example illustrates the probabilistic pattern. Under these conditions, we cannot predict precisely the number of particles emitted during each interval. Trillions of atomic particles in the material were in random motion and not in precisely the same state at the beginning of each time period. Therefore, a random element was introduced to the number of emissions. In business, such randomness can be expected because many factors affecting business are changing continuously.

Sales of Cola

Figure 2 illustrates probability conditions graphically for 12-ounce cans of cola sold at several supermarket outlets. This item was selected because it exhibits a stable sales history and is sold in quantities that can provide ample statistics for study. During the test period represented by Figure 2, no promotions were conducted either for the cola or for competing products, nor were there price or packaging changes. The demand pattern did not indicate any pronounced seasonal effect during this period.

Although the underlying factors that would affect demand are stable, there are variations. Undoubtedly, these are caused by random purchase decisions. This randomness represents the background conditions underlying probability events. If the purchase variations could be identified and the impact readily measured, this would make the demand pattern more deterministic. If it is difficult to

Day/cases sold			
1/36	11/23	21/33	31/74
2/41	12/39	22/66	32/18
3/60	13/26	23/46	33/22
4/66	14/19	24/12	34/6
5/78	15/22	25/32	35/49
6/27	16/88	26/75	36/28
7/17	17/47	27/8	37/37
8/29	18/23	28/35	38/44
9/27	19/24	29/60	39/15
10/28	20/36	30/25	40/16

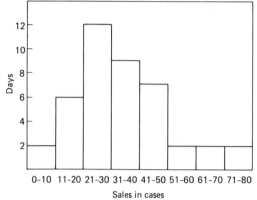

FIGURE 2.   Daily sales of cola (12-ounce cans) on supermarket routes

identify and measure the variations, the deterministic view is weakened, and the probabilist view prevails. Thus the probabilist view may prevail because of the nature of the phenomenon (e.g., radioactive emissions), or because of limitations in our ability to understand and measure.

Demand Data for Paper Plates

Figure 3 presents statistically and graphically the demand data for 10-inch white paper plates used for outdoor picnics. Although this product had a heavy seasonal demand because the consumer outlets stocked heavily in anticipation of filling summer needs, the histogram in Figure 3 is not designed to reflect seasonal patterns. Its purpose is to show the ranges of sales within certain parameters. The first range, for example, is 0 to 25 cases. Because four monthly periods had sales of 25 or fewer cases, the histogram shows four as the number of months' inventory for this range of

sales. Of the 60 sales figures, 40 fall between 25 to 100 cases (shown by the three highest bars).

Is the variability in the data a result of random fluctuations inherent in the sales, or do deterministic elements explain some of the variability? As noted, because there is a marked seasonality of the sales, the variability is not completely random, but is related to the month of sale.

This relationship is clear when the data is arranged by month as in Table 1. The pattern reflects light sales in January and February, which pick up in March. Sales become heavy in April, May, and June. Sales taper off in July and August and are light in September and the following months.

The second half of Table 1 shows each month's sales as a percentage of total sales for the year. The average percentages for each month are shown at the bottom of each column. We can use these average percentages to adjust the data in Table 1 to remove the seasonal effect, as presented in Figure 4. The adjusted sales for January of the first year is 85 cases. This means that sales for the month project into an annual average rate of 85 cases per month when the seasonal factor is considered. In this manner, the variability as a result of the seasonal effect is adjusted out of the data. Figure 4, then, reflects what the sales would be if the seasonal buying were leveled out. Clearly, this results in less variability in the data.

The histogram at the bottom of Figure 4 plots the seasonally adjusted data. Compare it to the histogram of the original data given in Figure 3. The adjusted data present a much tighter sales pattern. Now, 56 of the 60 monthly sales figures are in the three center ranges, 51–75, 76–100, and 101–125. There is much less variability and consequently the data lend themselves to more accurate forecasting. In this case the variability in the original data presented in Figure 3 is not a result of random fluctuations inherent in the business.

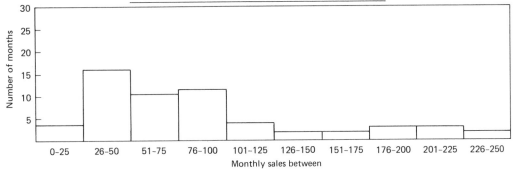

Paper plate monthly sales (no seasonal distinction).

81	35	90	58	231	36	25	35	80	165
72	106	85	25	92	191	36	54	121	32
126	179	42	54	40	164	113	51	222	39
242	63	57	71	59	54	94	79	54	38
78	12	31	212	43	40	130	209	41	86
87	41	120	27	28	25	86	45	190	92

FIGURE 3. Paper plate monthly sales (no seasonal distinction).

Table 1. Paper plate sales by month (in cases)

YEAR	JAN.	FEB.	MAR.	APR.	MAY	JUNE	JULY	AUG.	SEPT.	OCT.	NOV.	DEC.
1	40	35	87	121	90	130	86	58	38	12	41	54
2	27	28	80	106	165	126	85	86	39	25	32	41
3	43	45	92	231	242	179	113	92	42	25	35	54
4	59	71	120	191	164	190	94	81	54	36	57	79
5	31	36	78	212	222	209	72	63	40	25	54	51

Paper Plate Sales
Percentage of Annual Total by Month

YEAR	JAN.	FEB.	MAR.	APR.	MAY	JUNE	JULY	AUG.	SEPT.	OCT.	NOV.	DEC.	TOTAL
1	5.1%	4.4%	11.0%	15.3%	11.4%	16.3%	10.9%	7.3%	4.8%	1.5%	5.2%	6.8%	100%
2	3.2	3.3	9.5	12.6	19.7	15.1	10.1	10.2	4.6	3.0	3.8	4.9	100
3	3.6	3.8	7.7	19.4	20.3	15.0	9.5	7.7	3.5	2.1	2.9	4.5	100
4	4.9	5.9	10.0	16.0	13.7	15.9	7.9	6.8	4.5	3.0	4.8	6.6	100
5	2.8	3.3	7.1	19.4	20.3	19.1	6.6	5.8	3.7	2.3	4.9	4.7	100
Average percentage	3.9%	4.1%	9.1%	16.5%	17.1%	16.3%	9.0%	7.6%	4.2%	2.4%	4.3%	5.5%	100%

The next question relates to Figure 4. The figures still show a sizable range of 42–144. Is this variability a result of random fluctuations or some deterministic factor? And, if there is a deterministic explanation, is it worth the effort to find and measure the relationship?

Seasonal Patterns and the Business Cycle

In this case, another factor could easily be integrated into an explanation of the sales fluctuations—the business cycle. Sales were unusually low in year 1, a recession year, and picked up steadily after that until year 5.

As noted, the business cycle and seasonal patterns are major factors affecting the sales of paper plates. The question of whether to proceed further is treated as a practical problem. Even if there are other factors, would inventory performance be improved by integrating these factors into the forecasting procedures?

Impact of Pricing

Competitive prices are known to affect sales of paper plates but knowledge of competitive discounted prices has not always been available in time. Further, as a general policy, the company meets competing prices so that any competitive advantage gained by a discount is soon neutralized. The forecast prepared for the paper plates was analyzed to determine the effect of improved accuracy on inventory accountability. Clearly, the more accurate the forecast, the more clearly production and inventories can be tailored to the actual demand. However, the study indicated that the potential for inventory reduction, as a result of an improved forecast, was only 5%. That improvement appeared to be difficult to attain. Thus the remaining variability in demand was treated as random.

Importance of Lead Time

Figure 5 presents data measuring the lead time for delivery to a warehouse. The lead time is in days and is counted from the day

Year	J	F	M	A	M	J	J	A	S	O	N	D
1	85	71	80	61	44	57	80	64	75	42	79	82
2	58	57	73	54	80	55	79	94	77	87	62	62
3	92	91	84	117	118	78	105	101	83	87	68	82
4	126	144	110	96	80	83	87	89	107	125	110	120
5	66	73	71	107	108	91	67	69	79	87	105	77

Order number	Month ordered											
	J	F	M	A	M	J	J	A	S	O	N	D
1	12	22	16	30	24	39	14	16	14	18	18	17
2	20	19	15	31	21	28	20	12	20	11		20
3	12	14	14	18	16	38		14	20	20		18
4	14	22	15	26	21			22				4
5			32	20	22							20
6				29	21							28

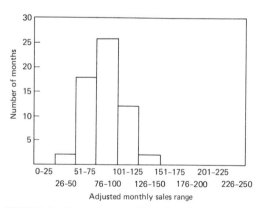

FIGURE 4. Paper plate monthly sales adjusted for seasonal effect.

FIGURE 5. Lead times in days for shipments to warehouse.

the order requisition is completed until the day the product is checked in at the receiving location. The warehouse in this instance is in San Francisco and the shipping plant is in Wisconsin. All shipments are by rail, except for the shipment of order number 4 in December. Because the warehouse operates seven days a week and has excellent unloading facilities, cars are unloaded almost immediately upon arrival. The loading at the plant is well run with sizable inventories maintained so that orders are processed promptly. The variability in lead times is attributable to the railroad—either delays in transit or delays in making cars available.

Lead time is important in inventory planning. Warehouse stocks are generally set to cover sales during the lead time period plus a suitable safety stock. Some software packages used for inventory control assume a constant lead time. A mere glance at Figure 5 shows how erroneous this assumption is. If this software package were actually adopted, what lead time would be used by it? Forty days would cover all items shown on Figure 5 but would require an excessively high inventory. Twenty days would be more reasonable but there would be trouble with 17 of the 46 shipments (excepting the item with the four-day lead time that was shipped by air freight). Even if inventory policy is defined clearly (favoring low inventory or good service), the only alternative is to play it by ear. If the variability in lead times is thought to be caused by some deterministic factors, then one could analyze those factors and use them to decide when the lead time would be 14 days, 21 days, 26 days, and so on.

Rail performance was analyzed for possible seasonal variations in lead time. The three long lead times shown in June are a clue to part of the difficulty: rail cars were in high demand in the farming communities.

The possibility that one railroad was more consistent than another was also investigated because consistency in lead times is more important than shorter lead times with less consistency. Using a railroad that delivers in 21 days consistently to a certain point would permit lower inventories than using a railroad that had variations running between 14 and 28 days. The results of this analysis did not provide a clear enough basis for definitely projecting the rail lead times. Hence they were considered to be essentially random.

The basic interpretation of inventory as a buffer between two points suggests that we need to project two quantities in order to determine what the inventory level should be. These two quantities relate to an input rate and an output rate. The output or demand for finished goods inventories is controlled by factors external to the company maintaining the inventory. Demand is thus the subject of considerable attention in forecasting.

The input into inventory raises similar questions. In the case of the distributor or retailer, the input may be variable because of fluctuations in lead times. In the case of the producer, the input may also be variable even though the process is under his control. This is especially true of process industries such as the chemical industry.

Figure 6, for example, shows a series of yields from a batch chemical process. The largest batch of 144 is more than three times as large as the smallest batch of 45. The daily yield is added to inventory and becomes material input for another process. Even though requirements are determined several days in advance so that outflow could be known exactly, the variability in the production process necessitates inventorying. Because the process cannot be controlled precisely, the yield could be insufficient for the next production step. To assure continuity of plant operation, it is necessary to maintain an inventory to make up the difference between an unusually low yield and the requirement for the next production step. If the process yield could be maintained at a nearly constant rate, the inventory would not be needed.

The variability of the process yield is depicted in the histogram in Figure 6. Ranges of yield are marked along the horizontal axis. The number of batches with yields within var-

Batch numbers				
1–5	6–10	11–15	16–20	21–25
115	99	81	90	100
128	67	103	135	70
99	133	90	80	102
63	92	81	92	69
144	103	45	77	83

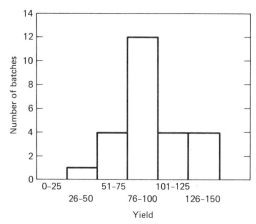

FIGURE 6. Yields from a batch chemical process.

ious ranges are shown vertically. Twelve of the 25 yields are in the range of 76–100.

Forecasting the Yield of a Process

Forecasting the yield of a process such as this is conceptually different from forecasting the sales of paper plates. The process is controlled by the company while the sales of paper plates, to a large extent, are not. Forecasting, in the case of the chemical process, means finding out the effect of certain factors in the process and then using these factors to regulate the output. The factors referred to are temperature, pressure, process time, and catalysts. Nevertheless all these examples—the demand for paper plates, the railroad lead times, and the output of the chemical process—have random elements. Forecasting for these factors themselves and for related inventory planning must take into account the random nature of these business conditions.

PROBABILITY FORECASTS

The data on production, sales, and lead times related to inventories show much variability. Rarely can we know in advance the precise inventory demand or time of product delivery. As discussed, if variability is inherent in the operation, it cannot be ignored or dismissed. We have covered the possibility of determining factors that explain this variability. However, the examples in the previous section do not explain all the variability. This also is typical of the data encountered in inventory control. For example, it is either inherently impossible to determine or it requires too much effort to determine demand lead times precisely.

Management, in using forecasts, must understand that uncertainty is unavoidable. Many executives today believe that with enough effort and thought it is possible to eliminate all variabilities, for example, in forecasting exact sales of paper plates for next month. This is unfortunate because 1) the wrong method of forecasting will be used and 2) any differences between the forecast and the actual results will be interpreted as an error.

Relate this to the earlier example of radioactive disintegration, clearly a probabilistic phenomenon. What is the projected count in the next 7.5-second period? Physicists tell us that it is impossible to know at the start of the period. It could be zero, one, two, three, four, five, six, or more. If four is picked—a good guess—the chances of being right are about one if five; if seven is picked, the chances of being right are about one in twenty. Any answer would most likely be incorrect.

Coming up with a specific number is the wrong way to forecast most business phenomena. The random element is usually present, meaning that a probability forecast is appropriate, which suggests a distribution, not a specific number. The distribution recognizes that a number of different things can happen and it determines the probability or chance of a range of possible outcomes.

Table 2 shows several distributions. The first is associated with rolling one die. Any number from 1 to 6 can come up, and all are equally probable. Thus the odds of rolling a particular number is one in six, or 16-⅔%. If both dice are rolled, the total could be any number from 2 to 12. In this case, the chances are not the same. Of the 36 possible permutations (6×6), two could only be obtained by rolling a 1 on each of the dice. The odds are one in 36, or 2.8%. A 3, however, could be rolled in two different ways: 1 and 2 or 2 and 1. The odds are then two in 36, or 5.6%.

A correct forecast of the outcome of rolling both dice is shown in Table 2. A table taken from the standard normal distribution is also shown. The outcome is stated in ranges above the below zero while the probability column shows the chances that the results will fall within each range. The rightmost table shows a 19.2% chance of an outcome between 0 and ½, while only a 2.2% chance that it will be greater than 2.

This is the probability forecast. Occasionally, the results are presented as a tabled distribution. More often the forecast is presented as a specified number together with confidence limits. The number is the average or expected value of the distribution. The confidence limits are a measure of the variability of the possible outcomes. The confidence limits consists of two values, an upper bound and a lower bound. If a 90% confidence limit is given, then the chances are nine in ten (90%) that the result will fall between the upper bound and the lower bound. The confidence limits are sometimes referred to as the confidence range or the margin of error. When using the latter terminology, keep in mind that "error" refers to unavoidable chance and does not connote a mistake. These two characteristics—the average or best estimate and a measure of the variability—provide most of what we need to know about a distribution for inventory purposes. When the distribution is presented in this manner, watch out for misinterpretation by deterministic-minded execu-

Table 2. Distributions

POSSIBLE OUTCOMES	PROBABILITY	OUTCOME RANGES	PROBABILITY
1 Die		Standard normal	
1	16-⅔%	less than 2	2.2%
2	16-⅔	−2 to −1	4.4
3	16-⅔	−1-½ to −1	9.2
4	16-⅔	−1 to −½	15.0
5	16-⅔	−½ to 0	19.2
6	16-⅔	0 to ½	19.2
	100.0%	½ to 1	15.0
		1 to 1-½	9.2
		1-½ to 2	4.4
2 Dice		greater than 2	2.2
2	2.8%		100.0%
3	5.6		
4	8.3		
5	11.1		
6	13.9		
7	16.6		
8	13.9		
9	11.1		
10	8.3		
11	5.6		
12	2.8		
	100.0%		

tives. They are predisposed to see the best estimate and not the confidence limits.

BUSINESS PROPERTIES OF FORECASTS

We have seen that inventory control relies heavily on either formal forecasts using mathematical methods or default forecasts inherent in the procedures used by purchasing or production control. The latter are usually based on "intuition" or "feel." Experience has confirmed that controlling inventories through subjective methods is not reliable.

The most common practice with these subjective methods is to use past averages instead of mathematical probabilities. By the very nature of past averages, the data will not be up to date. It will not reflect new trends that have crept in.

Suppose that we want to introduce more effective quantitative methods. What is the first step? Because some forecasting technology requires use of mathematics that call for years of graduate study, it would be unreasonable to expect the manager responsible for inventories to become proficient in forecasting technology. This area must be treated as a "black box"—with a technical specialist assigned to construct the formulas that are contained in the box. The manager responsible for the forecast provides the specialist with the forecasting specifications. The resulting forecast is used by the manager, not the technician. The manager should be judged on how well the forecast is used, the technician on how well the black box conforms to specifications.

Proper forecast specifications insure that when the forecast is developed, it will fit the needs of the business. Operating personnel should use a forecast when its specifications meet their needs. Although this point seems self-evident, it is frequently overlooked in practice.

For example, a manufacturer of high-quality brushes desired a demand forecast to use in scheduling production. The project was assigned to the data processing department without forecast specifications. The result was a monthly forecast by product group rather than by item. Obviously, the items that make up product groups need to be scheduled into production. The data processing department prepared projections by product group because such forecasts were more accurate. Although this was true, it did not help management's production scheduling needs.

Important elements to consider in developing the forecast are:

1. SKUs to be forecast
2. Levels of aggregation: stocking location, products, product groups, substitution items, customer groups, sales division groups, and so on
3. Units of measure: dollars, pounds, cases, and so on
4. Unit time of the forecast: weekly, monthly, and so on
5. Forecast horizon: how many weeks, months, and so on
6. Upside and downside error precision desired
7. Frequency of forecast update
8. Cost basis for items
9. Flexibility for item additions and deletions, change of units, level of aggregation, and so on
10. Item interchangeability and substitutability
11. Report formating and delivery time requirements.
12. Major business factors to be taken into account by the forecast
13. Exception reporting requirements.

As mentioned, these should not be left to the technician, nor should the specifications be developed through the give-and-take of consensus. The requirements of management are specific; accordingly, the specifications should be developed with these requirements in mind.

This responsibility of management to provide guidance in forecast preparation is a point that deserves emphasis. Because of the technical nature of forecasts, businessmen are tempted to leave forecasting entirely to the technician.

By way of further illustration, let us consider a forecast prepared for an oil drilling company to cover the requirements of such items as tubing, joints, and motors used in drilling and maintaining wells. Smaller items were purchased locally and were the responsibility of local personnel. For items forecasted on a corporate basis, the forecast had to come up with the quantities to be purchased, the delivery points, and the schedule for delivery. The forecast was left to a specialist in the data processing department.

How did the specialist know that an item purchased last year is no longer needed? How did he know that another item was being replaced by a technological improvement next month? How did he know that XB 10173 and XC 10173 were really the same item purchased from different vendors? How did he know that AT 20253 and LG 71112 were different items but interchangeable for the rigs in Alaska? Did he know that corporate purchasing ordered tools for the Midland fields even though the records were maintained at Midland rather than at corporate headquarters? Did he know that Houston's engineering department arranged purchases for the refinery parts even though the paperwork flowed through corporate purchasing? These are some of the pitfalls in "letting George do it."

Because management had not instructed the specialist in such operating considerations, the forecast had to be revised and rerevised. Each revision required a substantial data processing effort and each revision reduced management confidence in the forecasting system. To avoid these problems, operating consideration should be

factored into forecast specifications at the initial planning stage.

In addition to defining the items to be included in the forecast, management should also specify the units of measure and the stock keeping units (SKUs). An SKU is a particular item at a particular location. Three-inch copper tubing used at Midland would be the same item as three-inch copper tubing used at Hobbs, but they would be different SKUs.

Units of Measure

Most items have several different units of measure. Paint, for example, is measured in cans, cases, or gallons. Tubing may be measured in number of sections, linear meters, or linear feet. If purchasing personnel will be working with the forecast, the units used in the forecast should be familiar to the purchasing department. The same is true for other departments. It is the responsibility of management to specify these units to the forecasting specialist.

Such specifications are used in the output reports. The specialist can select several units of measure, for different purposes, provided that conversion factors are developed. Stocking locations and items to be stocked at each location (SKUs) should be defined by management, not by the specialist. For nationally purchased items to be delivered directly to field locations and inventories there, the vendor must be told the quantity to ship to each location. Such items should be forecast by SKUs.

In the case of the oil drilling company, the vendors carry in their inventory the more standard items that may be supplied to different oil companies working the same field. Because of competition among suppliers, these inventories are often maintained near the field. Items purchased from different vendors are planned according to total need by field regardless of the vendor. The breakdown by source is based on an allocation derived through use of a formula. For these items, the forecast should be prepared by aggregating all the SKUs for like items purchased from different vendors. Because the requirement for this accumulation is based on purchasing rather than technical considerations, the decision should be made by the purchasing department and given to the specialist as part of the forecast specifications.

After the items and SKUs to be forecast are listed, along with the units of measure, the next step is to analyze in greater depth how the forecast will be used. Forecast timing is an important business consideration and should be included in the forecast specifications.

Three aspects of timing must be considered in defining forecast specifications:

1. Units of time: weeks, months, quarters, and so on
2. Forecast horizon: six months out, 12 months, and so on
3. Frequency of forecast update: monthly, quarterly, semi-annually.

The major items handled by corporate purchasing at the oil company are covered by quarterly orders that include a monthly breakdown of requirements which the company is allowed to change during the quarter up to certain limits. Lead times vary considerably from item to item. Some items are ordered three or more quarters in advance. In effect, the company is placing orders on a monthly basis but reserving some flexibility to modify the orders for items with long lead times.

If forecasts using either weekly or monthly units of time would satisfy purchasing's requirements, the specifications should indicate either one as being acceptable. The final decision, within the specification constraints, is then based on systems considerations. If monthly forecasts are to be prepared, purchasing should specify whether calendar months are required or whether a combination of four, four, and five weeks for each quarter should be used.

Forecast Horizon

The forecast horizon depends on the vendor lead time and varies from one item to another. The specification should, therefore, be prepared in a manner that gives the minimum horizon for each item, and the maximum horizon likely to be needed now or in the future. A reasonable approach would be to divide the items into product classes and assign a forecast horizon to each class: for example, six months for paints and 18 months for tubing. The specialist can select horizons in preparing the forecast, subject to the constraints that the forecast for paints be prepared at least six months out and that the system contain the flexibility to expand that horizon up to the maximum.

The third aspect of timing, the frequency of updating the forecast, is primarily a technical problem, although purchasing management can provide helpful suggestions. It would be ideal if all businesses could prepare forecasts only once a year. However, because customers, vendors, and the economy are unpredictable, this would be hazardous. While some businesses can forecast quarterly periods that are updated quarterly, probably most businesses should be prepared at the outset to forecast weekly periods and update the forecast monthly. Once confident of this procedure, the company could forecast and update less frequently. In establishing the specifications for frequency of forecasting and updating, the company must carefully consider a policy that assures reasonable accuracy without "flying blind."

Margin of Error

Another area that warrants careful consideration in establishing forecast specifications is the margin of error. Figure 7 illustrates upside and downside errors. Error is an unfortunate word to use in describing the difference between the forecast and the actual because of the pejorative connotations. Upside and downside deviation would be better. However, deferring to convention, we use the term error.

The data in the Forecast column of Figure 7 is the forecasted usage in units. The forecast was prepared using monthly time periods with a one-year horizon. The forecast was updated monthly from February through June, then left fixed until the following February (note the highly seasonal usage). The forecast shown in Figure 7 was prepared during April, using data through the end of March.

When the forecast is too high, an upside error occurs; when it is too low, a downside error occurs. The error is the difference between the forecast and the actual amount. For example, the usage forecasted for June was 184 units. Because 167 units were actually used, the forecast was too high, resulting in

an upside error of 184 − 167 units, or 17 units. In July, however, the forecasted usage of 96 was lower than the actual usage of 120, giving rise to a downside error of 24.

In the case of a downside error, where usage exceeds estimates, the company risks a stockout. This could halt operations temporarily while the needed items are flown in from the vendor or from another location. Such out-of-stock situations could be expensive to the company. An overestimate, on the other hand, would result in extra inventory in the field. If the item is in continuous use, the excess can be adjusted in ensuing months. However, if the item usage is cyclical or if it is subject to obsolescence, the company risks becoming overstocked, with the resulting reduction in return on investment.

In dealing with the margin of error, there are two common alternatives:

Method 1. The precision requirement of the forecast is specified in terms of allowable error, say plus or minus 10%. The specification would call for the forecast to be within this range with, say 95% confidence. Because best-estimate forecasts tend to have symmetrical upside and downside errors, the specialist can concentrate on developing an estimate with enough of the variation accounted for to satisfy the precision requirement.

In a best-estimate forecast, there is about a 50% chance that it will be too large and a 50% chance that it will be too small. These risks of having too little or too much inventory are compensated for through the use of safety stock allowances. If the downside error is costly and the upside error less so, then a best-estimate forecast can be used with ample safety stock carried over and above the estimated usage.

Method 2. The forecast precision requirement could be stated in terms of an asymmetrical requirement. It might state, for example, that in 99 occurrences out of 100, the forecast must be greater than actual less

Month	Forecast	Actual	Upside error	Downside error
May	270	208	62	
June	184	167	17	
July	96	120		24
August	88	101		13
September	45	36	9	
October	25	19	6	
November	24	40		16
December	60	63		3
January	56	54	2	
February	57	55	2	
March	96	73	23	
April	209	198	11	

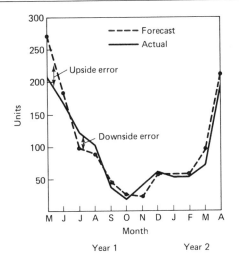

FIGURE 7. Forecast errors.

5%, but not greater than actual plus 15%. It pays to specify the forecast accuracy before development because it puts the forecast critics on notice that errors must be expected and that such errors do not mean that the forecast is valueless.

Reporting is clearly an area requiring management specification. If the forecast is to be incorporated into the planning efforts of a number of executives, each executive should be permitted to specify his own references for the layout of information, the level of aggregation, the level of detail, and other pertinent considerations. At a board meeting several years ago, a corporate president (and self-made millionaire) rejected a report showing percentages and demanded the figures used to compute the percentages. Report preparation had thought that by computing percentages, it was putting the data in a more useful form. Possibly? But useful to whom? The president didn't like percentages.

FORECAST CHARACTERISTICS

Once the specifications of the forecast have been drawn up, design can get under way. Several characteristics of the forecast bear on how effective it is as a tool for inventory management. A manager who understands these characteristics communicates better with the specialist during the forecast design and in the following implementation period. These characteristics include the following:

1. *The speed with which the forecast adjusts to fundamental changes in the business.* Working with inventories differs in an important respect from working with a natural phenomenon such as radioactive disintegration. The natural phenomenon remains unchanged in time while the business environment is continually changing. In all methods of forecasting, the past is studied in order to estimate the future. As long as the business environment remains unchanged, the forecast is likely to be reliable. Fundamental changes such as the oil embargo of 1973 can throw forecasts off by a considerable amount.

Some forecasting methods provide warning signals when fundamental changes have occurred. Others can make automatic adjustments when certain changes occur. During implementation, careful testing should be made to determine the answers to questions such as, If demand for the highest volume product were to be reduced 20% tomorrow, how quickly would the forecast react? What if demand tripled?

2. *The stability of the forecast with respect to oscillations.* Few conditions are as frustrating to the inventory manager as being continually "whipsawed" by an unstable forecast. "Zigzagged" might be a more appropriate word because the actuals to up when the forecast instructs the opposite.

Figure 8 demonstrates the whipsaw effect in forecasting. The forecast is applied to estimate the monthly sales of paper towels one month in advance. The forecast method determines first and second trends from recent history and projects this into the future. Note that when the stock price starts up, the forecast takes a while before it follows the same movement. When the forecast does go up, it overshoots and remains high while the stock price falls.

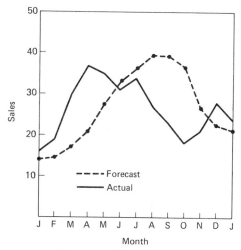

Paper towel sales in thousands of cases

FIGURE 8.   A whipsaw forecast.

To guard against this, the company should ask the EDP specialist to demonstrate how the forecast will perform in such cases. If the forecasting method cannot pick the turning points (where the value changes from increasing to decreasing and vice versa), then it should be damped (leveled) so it more nearly holds to an average value. Errors are inevitable, but they should be "inside" rather than "outside" errors. That is, there should be a downside error when the actual is high and an upside error when the actual is low. Note in Figure 8 that the forecast is higher than the actual high and lower than the actual low. Outside forecasts cause instability in operations.

3. *The ability of the forecast method to provide accurate error measurement.* Because the forecast specifications include precision, the specialist must have determined how to measure forecast error. How will actual forecast errors compare to specified margins of error? The specialist should demonstrate the expected pattern of errors when the forecast is used. A number of small errors may not be as much a problem as a few major ones. However, even worse than the random error problem is a forecast biased by unrealistic optimism.

4. *The reasonableness of the forecast in atypical situations.* Certain forecasting procedures can exhibit extreme behavior that can hurt the credibility of forecasting. A good example is a forecast based on an exponential function. Such a function may provide an excellent fit to historical data if the data reflect accelerated growth. However, if such growth has leveled off, use of the exponential function will provide results that might show such ridiculous sales forecast such as $5 trillion in 10 years. Management would question the sanity of persons responsible for such a forecast.

The key to reasonable forecasting is to temper forecasting procedures with a common-sense evaluation of the underlying trends. If the accelerating growth of the past, such as petroleum production in the United States, has obviously passed its peak, then the exponential method of forecasting should not be used.

Certain forecasting techniques give undue weight to extreme items at the ends of the range being analyzed. It is possible that only a few of these extreme items, perhaps only 2% of the total items, could produce unacceptably large errors in the forecast. The specialist should be asked to demonstrate the magnitude of the change in forecast when exceptional data patterns are encountered.

FORECASTING TECHNIQUES

The acceptability of the forecast with respect to these characteristics depends to a great degree on the technology employed. Several broad categories of techniques are employed in business forecasting.

Judgmental methods are based on the judgment of individuals qualified to render opinions. These estimates are then refined by using committee discussion, averaging methods, or more formal group consensus methods, such as the Delphi technique. Judgmental methods play an important role in inventory management and are used widely. When properly organized and interpreted, they can prove adaptable to fundamental changes.

This type of forecasting, however, does not provide for any error measurement. Studies show that businessmen are poor at estimating how good their forecasts are, perhaps because inventory managers tend to overreact to inventory problems when making forecasts, Assurance of better forecasts, then, is conditioned upon the ability to stem the tendency to overreact.

Formula fitting forecasting methods rely on formulating a relationship between the object to be forecast (e.g., sales) and other variables and/or past values. The formula is fit to historical data and used to project values. Statistical regression and econometric models are of this nature. These methods are very inflexible and unstable with respect to fundamental changes in business conditions. They are rarely of value in inventory management.

Time-series analysis is a branch of mathematical statistics that uses patterns in historical data to project the future. Examples of such methods are exponential smoothing, moving averages, Box-Jenkins, Wilson, and Shiskin methods. These methods are generally more flexible than other statistical methods and are widely used in connection with inventory management.

The more sophisticated types employing distribution filters adjust to fundamental changes in the business and, barring outright mistakes, all exhibit damping (leveling) behavior. They provide for measurement of error and usually also provide reasonable forecasts even in the presence of data errors. The drawback in using these is that the simpler models are slow to react to fundamental changes and provide good forecasts only in relatively stable environments and over short time horizons.

Simulation methods can formulate a model of the operation and then run data in one end and observe what comes out the other end. Simulation methods are rarely of value in forecasting inventory usage at the SKU level. The level of detail is so great that extremely complex stochastic models would be required. They are usually expensive in terms of data processing and human resource requirements. The desire of a specialist to use simulation techniques should be questioned.

The most effective forecasts employed to manage inventory are integrated forecasts that combine judgmental methods, time series, and, to a lesser degree, curve-fitting methods. Volume is important when using econometric or curve-fitting methods. To the extent that demand can be related to certain economic variables that serve as leading indicators, economic models can assist in inventory management. Generally, volume must be large for these methods to work.

Because most forecasts used in inventory management are at the SKU level with weekly or monthly time periods and short forecasting horizons, time-series methods are more widely applicable. These methods are intended to produce good forecasts over a time horizon short enough to exclude major shifts in business conditions—typically less than one year. They assume that conditions in the near future will be subject to trends but otherwise much the same as in the past. To provide for exceptional factors such as 1) additions and elimination of products and major customers or 2) productive capacity changes, judgmental methods should be integrated with the time-series methods.

REFERENCES

1. Rutherford, Chadwick, and Ellis, *Radiations from Radioactive Substances*, Cambridge, 1920.

23
Materials Management for Widely Distributed Operations in Hostile Environments

Jacob H. Brooks
Vice-President
Booz Allen & Hamilton, Inc.

Breaux B. Castleman
Vice-President
Booz Allen & Hamilton, Inc.

The authors point out that materials management is difficult and typically undermanaged. They cite a case in which the operating environment is particularly hostile—oil and gas operations in such locations as offshore Indonesia and the New Guinea jungle. Because of the complex and long logistical networks for moving equipment, supplies, and untrained personnel, one cannot expect highly sophisticated systems to succeed. The chapter identifies the difficulties and suggests guidelines to be followed in developing controls.

Effective materials management can make a significant contribution to corporate profitability. Yet where the relationship between materials management and overall company success is poorly understood, the function typically receives less than sufficient attention from top management.

This chapter examines the special materials management problems of a particular group of firms—companies such as oil, gas, and other natural-resource production and processing companies engaged in heavy operations in remote and often hostile environments.

In these businesses we have observed a dilemma: materials management is particularly difficult to manage, yet it is typically undermanaged. At worst, this leads to damaging writeoffs and avoidable downtime; at best it causes an unnecessary drain of top management time. In either event, it is clear that the strategic significance of materials management is poorly understood by many companies.

The group of companies described in this chapter share several characteristics that lead to a particularly difficult materials management environment. For example:

1. A remote, often hostile operating environment results from the need to operate where oil and gas are found, e.g., offshore Indonesia, New Guinea jungle, and so on. Imagine having to manage millions of dollars in inventory involving thousands of line items with untrained personnel, no covered storage, six-month lead times, and daily production of huge values at stake!

2. There are complex and long logistical networks (including customs clearance) for moving equipment, parts, and sup-

plies to operation sites. These often combine commercial with company-operated surface and air legs on one delivery. One or two transshipments may also be necessary. Document control problems are consequently compounded.

3. Equipment uptime is absolutely critical; malfunction of a $50 item can shut down a rig earning $30,000 per day or a chemical plant grossng millions.

4. There is a high emphasis on speed to bring production on stream, both initially and after "deadlined" or "turn-around" situations.

5. Operations are usually of a project nature, limiting complete development of materials management systems unless they are built up from other projects.

6. Finally, these issues are seldom fully appreciated or understood.

This chapter describes the nature and significance of these problems. Then, to help plan solutions, three stages in the evolution of materials management systems and related issues are described. This is important because there are two difficult transition points between stages, each leading to new, relatively permanent materials management capabilities; it is precisely at these points, where decisions are complex and relatively final, that top managers can become involved most productively by actively supporting and counseling with the materials manager.

The value of top management intervention in materials management strategy at the right time can be greater assurance of equipment uptime, lower operating costs, and generally smoother running operations.

AN UNUSUAL MATERIALS SUPPORT ENVIRONMENT

The subject matter is materials management for remote, capital-intensive operations. This chapter describes the special materials prob-

lems of such operations and the critical nature of material support.

For more capital-intensive industries, materials management priorities shift the focus to equipment uptime.

1. Provisioning of capital support-related materials, which we will refer to as operations, maintenance, and repair materials, becomes a more dominant aspect of materials management, often accomplished by a distinct organizational group.

2. The tendency to overstock operations, maintenance, and repair materials is greater because of the higher leverage of equipment uptime.

3. Assuring that maintenance and repair materials are on hand tends to be the dominant materials management objective, surpassing cost-effective purchasing, inventory cost optimization, or other criteria of effectiveness.

Our "special group" of companies beyond being capital intensive are further defined to be operators in remote, hostile locations. For example:

1. Oil and gas exploration and production companies operating in Indonesia or Peru.

2. Drilling contractors working for oil companies onshore or offshore

3. Mining companies opening or operating large mines in hostile areas

4. Engineering and construction companies building multimillion- or billion-dollar projects

5. Oil field services companies operating in support of drilling, such as seismic testing, formation treatment, and so on

6. Processing companies for refining, milling, or upgrading, fertilizer, cement, and liquified natural gas (LNG).

These companies purchase and often stock a variety of types of materials, many of which would not be stocked at all or in small quantities in well-developed areas. These "critical" materials include:

1. Equipment or project material production equipment, rolling stock, life support, and construction
2. Equipment spares that would normally be vendor stocked
3. Operation supplies, e.g., oil, mud, sand, cement, chemicals, inexpensive hardware, cleaning supplies, and so on
4. Stocked capital inventory, most peculiar to drilling or gathering type operations—including tubular goods and well head equipment.
5. Personnel support items, e.g., food, clothing, medical and recreational supplies.

These industries have several common weaknesses resulting from a casual approach to materials management functions. Of course, these findings are relative to other industries operating in advanced countries with shorter supply lines.

1. Relatively careless approach to requirements planning of stocked items, e.g., guessing what might be needed for one year and doubling it.
2. Lack of standardization of major equipment types, e.g., compressors, earth movers, trucks, and so on
3. Weak communication lines with operations limiting the ability to avoid "avoidable" emergencies.
4. Purchasing offices performing only "order taking" and expediting functions with relatively limited influence on sourcing and purchasing costs
5. Unclear organizational relationships and policies.

These industries also have particularly tough operating conditions that compound materials management problems. Faced with such difficulties, a *more* rigorous materials

management approach is required. For instance, consider these aspects of a typical petroleum exploration and production operation:

1. Operations often build up rapidly after the initial discovery. This is done under stress, so that emphasis is on speed rather than cost effecriveness.
2. The base of operations for a drilling contractor is likely to change locations frequently, sometimes changing continents. The supply lines must change too.
3. The materials management work force is most likely recruited on the site or consists of expatriates, and may be untrained and inexperienced.
4. Line operations often precede the support activities and do their own ordering and stockpiling without the benefit of materials management expertise. As a result, logistics networks and paper flow develop on a piecemeal basis.
5. There are complex consumption patterns on many thousands of line items.
6. Because of the nature of demand, consumption history is poor for many key items.
7. Highly decentralized decision making in such an environment is the norm. The expertise to specify and the knowledge of the degree of urgency are in the field.
8. For remote locations, management tends to change more frequently.
9. Equipment and parts that are used infrequently but are critical may corrode and be rendered useless by salt spray or jungle humidity.

SYMPTOMS OF UNDERLYING PROBLEMS

These materials management problems tend to be basic, yet can reach top management significance. Regardless of the reasons for the problems, companies that have a materials management philosophy that aggravates these problems tend to have certain consistent internal symptoms that should raise a red flag:

1. Purchasing (or some other corporate materials staff function) does not play an active role in sourcing materials or setting materials management policy.
2. Inventory and cost controls are weak, signaled by overstocking, stockouts, lost materials, excessive air freight, and fragmented purchasng patterns.
3. Organizational structures are unwieldy and mainifested in line/staff organizational conflict, causing frequent error.

Many companies conclude that downtime or shutdowns is the ultimate villain. They do not seek ways to improve effectiveness, assuming the cost of improving the materials management function will exceed the benefits. The next four points discuss more fully the symptoms of materials management weaknesses.

PURCHASING IS OFTEN LIMITED TO ORDER TAKING

Ideally, purchasing departments receive materials requisitions with a generic description (specification) and bid that item competitively to assure lowest cost to meet the specification. However, when equipment such as generating equipment, well heads, earth-moving equipment, mud pumps, and so on can be standardized, costs of repair, both maintenance materials and labor, are significantly reduced. Purchasing should encourage such standardization; it would be even better if they could monitor and enforce such standardization. However, purchasing usually defers to the field manager for selection and urgency. Field managers change frequently and like to purchase the equipment they are used to. As a consequence, standardization is difficult.

The true restriction to competitive buying, however, is that most companies are operating without specifications for almost all items. There is no indication of what is substitutable;

there are no performance specifications. There is no preestablished list of what is sole source and in what country to source it.

With such a shortage of predetermined sourcing guidelines and performance specifications, one would expect to find technical expertise in the purchasing offices, i.e., drilling specialist, instrumentation specialist, or parts specialist. Generally, this is not the case. The purchasing people can only try to fill the requisition as specified by the files.

A mistake caused by a poor specification on the requisition and a bad guess by a purchasing agent can be very costly and may take months to show up.

A further complication of the purchasing process is the dilution of purchasing power because of the multiple locations of purchasing offices. The reason is either convenience or necessity where certain items are required to be bought in the foreign markets of operations.

For example, a small oil exploration and production operation in Indonesia might have purchasing offices in Houston, Singapore, and Jakarta. With Mideast operations, the company might have other offices in Cairo, Abu Dhabi, and Kuwait. The Houston purchasing department in such an environment is pressed to be more than an order taker. What is called for is a set of strong corporate policies for purchasing to help guide sourcing, standardization, and cost control, thereby improving field decisions and optimizing corporate results.

INVENTORY AND COST CONTROLS ARE TYPICALLY WEAK

Several common characteristics of our group of companies make it difficult to control materials. First, because usage rates are very low, there is little history for estimating future requirements and planning stock levels. The companies are also normally stocking a high number of line items; 30,000 is not uncommon. These materials might be custom de-signed to a specific project, which compli-cates the requirements planning process.

Indications of a failure to manage these material control problems properly are:

1. No manuals or standardized forms
2. Poor data on usage and identification of critical materials
3. Stockouts and writeoffs because of mis-counts
4. Inventories increasing faster than infla-tion and activity levels.
5. High air freight bills
6. Projects awaiting material thought to be on hand
7. Excessive use of local purchasing vs. US purchasing for American-made items
8. Little standardization in equipment and parts.

More often than not, the material control systems have received little professional atten-tion. Often the system that controls materials was originally designed for cost-accounting purposes. If it has not patterned to field re-quirements, the system is usually unclear to field personnel, who are the ones who need workable procedures.

As a consequence of generally poor con-trols, inventories can be *double* what is re-quired, even though critical items are at or near stockout.

ORGANIZATION STRUCTURES ARE TYPICALLY UNWIELDY

The organizations we are describing, with their base of operations overseas, have corpo-rate offices with at least part of purchasing, accounting, and personnel support in the United States. But because the nature of the business necessarily located the technicians and the operating decision makers close to operations, the companies tend to be highly decentralized in the field.

Decentralization of decision making is rein-forced by the personalities involved in these businesses. They are by nature entrepreneurial and independent. Because of multiple remote locations, communications are often difficult and must be performed by telex or letter, rather than telephone or face to face. Further-more, the work force is largely made up of local nationals who lack training and proper attitudes toward work.

In addition, entrepreneurial field managers tend to operate independently, each ordering as it meets his needs. Such men bridle at head-office interference, particularly by staff types.

These attitudes and the poor communica-tions lead to organizational conflict. There are usually no clear policies or guidelines for re-solving differences. Top management ends up refereeing disputes.

ECONOMICS OF MATERIALS MANAGEMENT OFTEN OBSCURED

Because potential operating income from op-erations is usually very high in these field operations, the savings associated with im-proving control of materials appears to be insignificant. General managers tend to feel that their time should be devoted to reaching production objectives instead of performing staff functions.

The typical way to add material safety fac-tors, is to overstock, build in redundant sourc-ing, checkpoints, and transportation alterna-tives, and decentralize decision making. Under proper control and management, this is prudent; without proper controls it is wasteful and increases operating risk.

In the early stages of development, true economics are often masked because controls tend to focus on people cost. That happens to be the easiest thing to count and control. The type of management information that readily surfaces valuable tradeoffs, such as cost addi-tions for capable staff, is not available. The costs of poor performance in the materials management area can be hidden and fail to receive proper attention.

In fact, improvements can be made that not only reduce costs, but also improve the dependability of service.

FACTORS AFFECTING MATERIALS MANAGEMENT OBJECTIVES

The typically unstated objectives of materials management look something like this:

1. First, support operations and avoid a shutdown.
2. Second, improve and maintain control of materials.
3. Last, minimize related costs.

In almost all cases the first objective is, for the short term, reasonably satisfied. The other two objectives are much less satisfactorily achieved; there are deficiencies of three categories. Note that all relate in some way to poor requirements planning, which will be discussed later.

1. Excessive costs
2. Unnecessary operating and financial risks
3. Unnecessary drain of top management's time

Excessive Operating Costs Are a General Condition

Inventory of expensive, unnecessary stock takes up space, eats up capital, and gets lost or deteriorates. For example.

1. Unnecessary items such as a spare bucket for a dozer, or a spare prop and shaft for an offshore drilling rig, or complete spare power generating diesels can account for as much as 10–15% of total inventory dollars.

2. Those items that represent about 70% of inventory (called "A" items in an A, B, C classification scheme), often have a safety stock of two or three years consumption of safety spares. This can mean that as much as one-third of the inventory dollars is represented by unnecessary safety stock.
3. A redundant stock of parts occurs because the same item is designated by two different titles or part numbers. A similar category of unnecessary inventory is duplication of parts because of nonstandardization of equipment types. These categories can amount to as much as 20% of parts inventories.

Some of the above inventory categories overlap, but it is not uncommon to find 40–50% of inventory that could be eliminated without seriously reducing safety factors on critical items.

On the other hand, we normally find *some* critical items at a seriously low level, just because the system is too poor to pick up a run on a particular item in time to prevent a stockout. Also, no procedures exist to inspect for damage to critical spares.

So what one often finds is a poor apportionment of inventory dollars, some items high, some low, and others biased to the high side as a gross basis for improving safety factors.

1. Purchasing costs tend to run 5–10% higher than necessary for about 50% of purchases, because purchasing has limited priority and flexibility to purchase competitively.
2. In many cases, air freight is much higher than necessary with $2 items incurring $100 air freight bills. These occurrences are not closely monitored or planned. The limited systems cannot manage so many line items successfully.

Unnecessary Operating and Financial Risks are Introduced

Operating risks are introduced because stockouts of critical spares might occur. Perhaps more significant but very difficult to identify are the hidden costs of equipment nonstandardization. Ultimately, these manifest themselves in a poorly trained workforce, the appearance of a piecemeal approach to the business, and a general disorganization that creates a slow degradation of equipment utilization.

Financial risk is introduced in that major, unplanned inventory writeoffs may become necessary and because operating margins may slowly erode because of reasons cited above. Writeoffs occur because obsolete items are not routinely purged from files or records are inaccurate.

We have seen writeoffs of $100,000 to over $1,000,000 occur on an *unplanned* basis in a *single year* because material inventories were not well controlled.

Unnecessary Drain of Management Time

Unnecessary "fire fighting" and high-level involvement in emergency transactions on a one-at-a-time basis eat up management time. Questions like the following must often be answered in a near "panic" atmosphere:

1. Purchase vehicles from vendor X, Y, or Z in the United States, Britain, or Japan?
   a. One has a lower price
   b. One has better quality
   c. One will deliver faster
   d. One is now in most common use
   e. What to do *today*?
2. How large an order for drill pipe?
   a. Allocations are coming soon
   b. Prices are going up
   c. Annual requirements are unknown
   d. What to do *today*?

Organizational conflicts arising because of vague corporate policy tend to escalate the uncertainty of these questions:

1. Who selects vendor?
2. Who selects purchasing location and shipment methods?
3. Who plans requirements and inventory levels?
4. What is the corporate policy on these matters?

It is difficult to put a value on top management time, but look at it this way—how many managers see value in being able to concentrate their time on the more important issues facing their company? How many would like to spend less time on relatively trivial, day-to-day issues that should be handled by a system?

WHAT IS THE PRACTICAL WAY TO DEAL WITH THESE PROBLEMS?

The solutions to these problems are multidimensional and include personnel attitudes and capabilities, systems, and organization structure. It is our feeling, however, that the systems are the solution, leading naturally into other areas if that becomes necessry.

The problems discussed in the prior section result largely from poor requirements planning. This is a systems issue. Systems range from basic classifications of materials to highly sophisticated techniques for forecasting requirements and optimizing order quantities.

In any case, management must first identify where the company stands in selecting the systems most applicable to the company, now and in the future. From that point, a materials management strategy can be engineered to fit the company's current and long-term requirements.

THREE-STAGE EVOLUTION OF MATERIALS MANAGEMENT SYSTEMS

The companies referred to in this chapter tend to pass through three stages of evolution. Most companies can be categorized into one of these three stages with the majority falling into a middle ground.

The degree of materials management control and the effort required to provide that control must correspond to the magnitude and complexity of the problem. Our companies are unique in that they proceed through this evolution more often and more quickly than general industry. The rub is that many of the companies go through the process over and over without learning from prior experience.

Stage 1: Rapid Build-up Phase

This stage occurs after the discovery of oil or in the build-up stage of a mine opening or plant construction. Items to support operations are ordered in "guesstimate" quantities. Although they may begin with varying stages of urgency, they all tend to escalate to "urgent" status.

Typically, field control of materials is poor in this stage, ranging from nonexistent (stacks of crates with people sifting through them to find materials) to fairly simple locater systems. Material is often not even uncrated and binned according to material type, but instead is stored in shipping crates that contain different parts.

In this stage, control and planning varies from fair to very poor, largely because there is confusion and no history upon which to plan in this specific project. The controls at this stage are designed in broad parameters using dollar denominators. Materials requisition approvals are relatively uncontrolled with many order placers and often many purchasing points. Air frieght is virtually uncontrolled. Purchasing controls are limited, without the benefit of techniques such as bid sheets and competitive bidding.

Obviously, there should be advantages to developing beyond this stage. Management should learn from other projects, plan as much as they can, but recognize the urgent priorities of Stage 1 and go with them until Stage 2 is approached.

Stage 2: Development of Fundamental Controls

Preliminary steps to gain control of the materials function are taken in this stage. These involve building or expanding warehouse facilities and developing locater systems by line item. Better care is taken in developing nomenclature, including vendor numbers which purchasing offices can use to place orders correctly. A perpetual inventory is often installed to keep a record of line items by count, on something like a cardex system.

Communications between the field and warehouses begin to improve so that requirements can be better developed. This often involves warehouse stocking of maintenance and repair items based on "authorized stock lists."

Requirements for major items are planned periodically. Items might be classified by priority and dollar size in order to focus attention on the more important line items. Some thought is given to standardization of equipment types and parts.

Air freight is starting to be looked at and perhaps is allocated to cost centers or responsibility centers; reorder points are established based on better information concerning consumption and lead times; and order quantities, although not necessarily optimized, are given more thought.

The corporate policy on sourcing, inventory control, personnel policies, and so on, if not formally written, is at least discussed at operating levels. Quite often, this stage, usually found in the later stages of construction/development, is as far as a company needs to progress to optimize cost benefits of the materials management function.

Management should determine at this point if and when further system improvements are needed. To benefit future projects, this system should be heavily documented.

Stage 3: Refinement of Controls and Organization

Stage 3 begins with a commitment to achieve a higher level of sophistication in materials management. Investments in people, equipment, and procedures are increased. Some form of electronic data processing with a catalog often characterizes this stage. Many refinements through automation can follow, including:

1. Perpetual inventories
2. Order alerts
3. Economic order quantities
4. Statistically derived safety stock
5. Routinely purged catalogs with substitutes identified
6. A status reporting system on "A" items, e.g., those over $50 per piece or defined as critical
7. Management reports of costs, associated with responsibility centers:
   a. Inventory turns by line item
   b. Air freight costs by responsibility center
   c. Service levels by responsibility center.

The organization of staff functions in this stage typically begins to centralize somewhat; the need for higher levels of expertise can normally be achieved economically only by centralizing. Standardization becomes firmly instituted based on better usage records, leading to longer-term equipment planning. Suitable substitutes and competitive bidding are formalized.

MOVING FROM STAGE ONE TO TWO IS CRITICAL

Going from the rudimentary efforts to provide materials for the field to a stage of greater control is the most critical transition in the materials management functions. In the second stage, unsound procedures, organizational relationships, reliance on poor management information, and so on, can become entrenched to the point that revision at a later date is not economical.

As mentioned in the next section, the extent to which the new systems and controls are well planned also has a great impact on the ultimate economics of moving to Stage 3. In developing the first generation of controls, most personnel are not equipped to analyze needs far beyond their own, so that developing integrated, coherent systems normally requires input from a higher level. We have seen systems that support operations adequately but which have such an entangled, monstrous paper system that they could not be economically unraveled. Most stifling can be the absence of good information management, which usually means that serious management initiatives necessary to improve the system never transpire.

If your company faces this transition, every effort should be made to design and document a materials management system that will provide lasting and significant benefits.

SUCCESS IN STAGE 3 REQUIRES SOUND MANUAL SYSTEMS

Companies with inventories of a few million dollars and more than 10,000 to 15,000 line items should consider themselves candidates for eventual evolution through Stage 3, particularly if they have long-term growth prospects. The benefits to be derived through successful implementation of data automation are usually far beyond the more important cost reductions.

Such benefits include better overall control over the maintenance of capital equipment, upgrading of management capabilities, improved management information, impact on morale of having an up-to-date system, and the impression made on customers by modernization—all fringe benefits to go along with the basic economic justification. A necessary predecessor of the installation of a Stage 3 system, however, is a solid set of manual systems. The following requirements should be met:

1. A good stock record system, which means obsolete items have been cleaned out of the system, and small, trivial items are taken off the cards
2. A good catalog that has been worked over, backed up by authorized stock lists from each of the user groups
3. Some history by line item; characterization of demand patterns: random, project, or combined
4. Identification of critical items that will be given special planning attention.
5. Accounting interfaces defined
6. Personnel who understand the manual system.

Arriving at this level is a challenge in its own right, and practically infeasible if the evolution from Stage 1 to Stage 2 introduces clumsy, inefficient systems that tend to bog down and prevent progress.

SUPPORTING THE TRANSITION

Most top managers are unaware of the long-term significance of the design of their materials management systems and of the critical nature of timing transitions between stages. Compounding this is the lack of awareness of total costs of the materials management activities. There is a slot or "window" of time when moving into a new phase when you will be able to successfully influence the design of the systems.

The energy industries and most processing industries have spend very little time managing the total cost of operations maintenance and repair. Material projections are based on post experience because it is easier to review the familiar than to anticipate future needs. This is like other management responsibilties, however. If the responsibility is shifted and relegated to lower-level specialists with a narrow point of view, management will probably be dissatisfied with the ultimate performance.

Table 1 lists a few items that constitute early warning signals at each transition point and identifies the respective problems that should be evaluated and solved vigorously and methodically.

The role of the top-level manager, should be to assure that the correct resources are brought into play to:

1. Provide additional horsepower during the peak work period of the transition.
2. Assure practicality of solutions/systems.
3. Assure that a proper balance is struck between service and control.

The role of the materials manager is to project and manage the transition and to assure that organizational relationships and systems are designed in a thorough and professional manner.

1. To address both current and future materials management requirements.
2. To approach optimality in terms of cost and benefits.
3. To recognize the level of materials management professionalism required to succeed.

Table 1. Phase transitions in materials management

	FIRST TRANSITION MOVING FROM PHASE 1 TO PHASE 2 DEVELOPING MANUAL SYSTEMS	SECOND TRANSITIONS MOVING FROM PHASE 2 TO PHASE 3 DEVELOPING COMPUTER SYSTEMS

A Transition
In The Making
	1. Efforts to improve control are becoming visible.
	2. A patchwork of procedures is being written to cover a variety of document requirements:
	   a. Receiving reports
	   b. Requisitions
	   c. Issues
	   d. Logs
	3. Requests for clerical people are increasing.
	4. There is a notable increase in pieces of paper in the system.
	5. It is becoming more difficult to pinpoint problems.
	6. "Finger-pointing" and conflict is increasing.
		1. New terms are being used in general management discussions, such as:
		   a. Data fields
		   b. Time sharing
		   c. Partitions
		   d. Core, disk, tape
		   e. Hardware/software
		   f. Mini computers
		2. Small services are being performed by service bureaus.
		3. Computer hardware and software salesmen begin soliciting business.
		4. People with systems background being surfacing.
		5. Materials management staff begin agitating for more centralization to achieve real benefits.

Problem Areas	1. No consistent, long-term game plan for materials management. 2. No policy and procedures manual. 3. Insufficient management depth to design systems and organizational relationships.	1. Systems added piecemeal without sufficient planning or thought given to total cost, savings, and implementation. 2. Inadequate experience of technical staff on board. 3. Manual systems not cleaned up.

24
The Master Schedule—Implementing the Business Plan

Paul Maranka

Director, Materials Management
INCOM International, Inc.

Through the consolidation of the experience of design and user involvement in several different material requirements planning (MRP) systems, together with the master schedule philosophy, it has been possible to design computerized systems to relate the master schedule planning process to the realities of the manufacturing environment. Paul Maranka discusses the relevance of the master schedule in actualizing the business plan from the manufacturing viewpoint.

Business planning is the blueprint that allows individual functions in an organization to proceed in harmony toward achieving an established business goal. The plan generally has most credibility in the statement of the first year's objectives. Marketing's estimate of the marketplace is clearer, the short-term role of the business cycle can be predicted, and the company's own resources are known with relative certainty. In all likelihood, the business plan will be closely coordinated with the coming year's financial plan. As marketing projections extend beyond the next year, they tend to become more ambitious. The marketing executive who does not forecast growth (regardless of the state of the economy) frequently is looked upon as a *persona non grata*. If marketing says it can be sold, manufacturing will commit to providing the output capability somehow. How can a manufacturing executive say no? The problems magnify as we project beyond year two, into the third, fourth, and fifth years of a five-year business plan.

270

BUSINESS PLAN INACCURACIES

If all of the five-year plans that were projected five years ago actually had occurred, our economy would have fallen apart from lack of resources. Understanding this, manufacturing will rarely react in total to a five-year plan. In fact, none of the operating functions do. In many companies, any similarity between the actual annual financial plan and the detailed business plan made for the same year as recently as the prior year is coincidental. As a result, little emphasis is placed on the business plan. Many times it is treated like something that has to be done to satisfy upper levels of management but can be forgotten until it is time to make a plan again the following year. This is not to say the long-range planning effort is wasted, but rather to point out that exact dollars, percentages, and action plans contained in a long range plan rarely, if ever, occur exactly as envisioned by the planners. The long-range plan's chief value is the discipline it forces on each bus-ness unit to think through all aspects of its business in a framework other than the annual budgets. (Other chapters in this book focus on additional aspects of the importance of a good business planning process.)

This chapter assumes that sufficient effort is made to assure that the first year of a business plan is in close harmony with the financial plan that will also be prepared for that year. If follows that the manufacturing department must be in close harmony with the current year's financial plan. A certain amount of production must be generated and then reallocated into the profit-and-loss statement as a cost of goods sold or onto the balance sheet as inventory. Some businesses can state their general production objectives in physical units of production, some in dollars, some in direct labor hours, and still others in a combination of these denominators. This becomes the production plan that interacts with the business plan. To make things happen though, this production plan must be converted to the actual part numbers that must be produced. That is the role of the master schedule process.

IMPORTANCE OF THE MASTER SCHEDULE

The term master schedule is not as descriptive a term as the two words indicate by themselves. Mather and Plassl provide a definition that can serve as a starting point for further discussion. They say, "A master schedule is a statement of what will be made, how many will be made, and when they will be made. It is a production plan, not a sales plan. It must consider the total demands on a plant's resources, including finished product sales, spare (repair) part needs, and interplant (affiliate company) needs. It must also consider the capacity of the plant and its vendors to meet these needs. It provides the overall plan for each manufacturing facility's manufacturing operation. All planning for materials, manpower, plant, equipment, and financing for

the facility will be driven from the Master Schedule."[1]

Through 1973, very little has been written about the concept of master scheduling and its impact on manufacturing plant operations. A number of individual articles appeared on the subject, but then the American Production and Inventory Control Society (APICS) Training Guide was created and a start was made to pull the relevant factors together and discuss them in general but descriptive detail.[2] Since then, a number of other authors have added significantly to the available literature. Most of this literature discusses generalities and basic principles. By consolidating the experience of design and user involvement in several different Material Requirements Planning (MRP) systems together with the master schedule theories, it has been possible to design a computerized system to relate the master schedule planning process to the realities of the manufacturing environment. This chapter discusses the relevance of the master schedule in actualizing the business plan from the manufacturing viewpoint.

The elements of an on-going system are used to illustrate the implementation of principles and theories. Among the several valid approaches to implementing the concept of master scheduling, the author is suggesting one way of functionally integrating a business plan with the manufacturing plans.

THE MASTER SCHEDULE—OBJECT OR PROCESS?

For years, my actions concerning production planning were based on the belief that the master schedule was not the' sales forecast, but rather the production schedule of what was to be manufactured. When reviewing the original specifications for the system discussed herein, I discovered that the existing master schedule was basically a manually maintained, computer-sensitive forecast of part numbers for end products. The forecast was manual in the sense that future estimates were added to the file externally and were not the automatic by-product of updating the forecasts based on the most recent usage data. This practice of calling a forecast of end-product part numbers the master schedule was a contradiction of the theory.

One of the companies with which I had some experience had two different divisions under one roof. One was automotive oriented and it stated production targets in terms of units. Five production lines werre planned manually from a forecast maintained on a computer file by part number. Simply stated, the problem was to know when to stop and start the assembly of each part number on each line and to assure that the machining departments behind the assembly lines were producing the proper parts to support the scheduling decision.

The other division was orieinted to industrial brakes and clutches that were produced for stock. Production targets were stated in terms of standard hours based on a rule of thumb: ratio of sales dollars to standard hours. Production orders were stated on the basis of finished goods sales forecasts and heavily influenced by the existing shipping backlog as the parts neared the assembly areas. The forecast was maintained on a computer file and it was used as input to the MRP planning process.[3]

In both divisions, the forecast was available and computer sensitive. However, in the design effort, our search for a master schedule continued because the master schedule wasn't supposed to be the forecast. The existing theory and current writings strongly suggested it was supposed to be production "build" orders.

A change was made to the existing system to be able to utilize firm planned orders (FPO). Related to the planned order of MRP, FPOs are fixed in quantity, time, and order number, but no paper is released to the manufacturing floor. FPOs cannot be moved randomly over the planning horizon

by the MRP system as are the planned orders. The intention was to use the FPO as a part matching device for lower-level components in the bill of material. Part shortages against a valid order number could be ascertained without having to pull the parts from the storeroom. Until the change was made, one of the key virtues of the FPO had not been recognized. Once the FPO concept was implemented, it became obvious that the forecast was as much the master schedule as were the released and firm planned production orders. The "umbilical cord" that ties the forecast to the build plan is the firm planned order.

This becomes the basis for my thesis that the master schedule is not just the production build orders, not just the forecast, not just firm planned orders, but a combination of them, all framed within the boundaries of a capacity limitation, whether specified in units or hours. In other words, the master schedule is a process.

The balance of this chapter is concerned with identifying the role a production plan plays in tying the business plan to the master schedule, a brief review of the systems environment, basic concepts of master scheduling as a process, and a comparison of existing master scheduling theory with the concepts used in this system. By the end of the chapter, the reader should have an understanding of one way in which business planning can be integrated into practical use by the manufacturing function.

PRODUCTION PLAN VERSUS MASTER SCHEDULE

It is useful to establish a common understanding of the difference between production plans and master schedules. They both are handled somewhat differently depending on the industry, the type of product, and whether the product is sold from stock, assembled to customer order, or engineered to customer order. Ten different types of master schedules can be identified, as shown in Figure 1. From my experience, these master schedule types can be associated with one of three basic business types: continuous process, made-to-stock and/or assemble-to-order (production lots), and engineer-to-order.

Continuous Process

In the continuous process business, the production plan is usually stated in some form of units such as number of clutches per day or tons of metal per shift. Key equipment capacity constraints are usually the upper limit of production capacity. Current business conditions determine the number of units per time period that are to be produced. In many cases, production plans are determined by top management and strongly influenced by current business conditions and the requirements of the business plan.

These production plans are usually general and must be translated into specific part numbers. The master schedule, then, is based on part numbers and the master scheduler is responsible for maintaining this master schedule and helping to decide which of the specific part numbers that can be made should be made. He uses the production plan, the forecast, customer order backlog, material availability, and key equipment availability to help in the decision. The problem in this type of business is not so much what to build or determining what parts are needed but rather

Few major products built for stock
Many products built for stock
Few major units engineered and custom built to order
Many products assembled to-order.
Combinations of stocked and assembled-to-order products
Replacement parts
Affiliate plants
Products sold as is and used in higher level assemblies
Continuous or high volume production
Branch warehouses

FIGURE 1.   Ten different types of master schedules.

how to obtain scarce material or keep key machines running. MRP will be a big aid in facilitating master schedule changes but computerization of the master schedule will more than likely be a carryover of what had been done manually and previously called the build plan or schedule.

An example of a production plan for a continuous manufacturing process is shown in Figure 2 and could be the plan for air conditioner clutches being built for an automobile manufacturer. Two types of clutches are produced over dedicated facilities with some maximum upper limit of production. The marketing department provides the forecast of units that will be sold; for April, the total is 85,000. This means a minimum of 4,050 must be produced per day if a reduction of finished clutch inventory is not desired. Management has settled on 4,500 per day as the production plan. The master scheduler must decide what days the lines will be set to produce each of the two clutches. This decision will become the master schedule.

Make-To-Stock and/or Assemble-To-Order

In a make-to-stock production lot environment, the production plan is usually stated in number of units per day, actual hours required in the various departments, or standard hours required in various departments to produce some dollar amount of sales. This latter production plan is based on historical averages. An example is shown in Figure 3. Capacity constraints tend to be the number of hours that can be generated by key equipment and key equipment can vary depending on product mix. Assembly departments or the "production lines" rarely tend to be a constraint with their capacity generally sensitive to the number of people currently assigned to the assembly line. Again, these production plans are general and they must be translated into the part numbers for the actual product to be built. The role of the master scheduler is to release production orders at the top levels to

Days Per Month	21	20	21	17	22	21	. . .
Months	April	May	June	July	Aug.	Sept.	. . .
Big Car	65000	60000	75000	50000	50000	80000	. . .
Small Car	20000	20000	20000	15000	15000	25000	. . .
Total	85000	80000	95000	65000	65000	105000	. . .
Req. Units/Day	4050	4000	4524	3824	2955	5000	. . .
Production Plan	4500	4500	4500	4000	4000	5000	. . .

FIGURE 2. Compressor clutch-main line.

Days Per Month	21	20	21	17	22	21	. . . . .
Months	April	May	June	July	Aug.	Sept.	. . . . .
Sales Dollars (000)	2,000	2,100	2,100	2,200	2,200	2,250	. . . . .
Standard Hours Needed	40000	42000	42000	44000	44000	45000	. . . . .
Standard Hours Per Day	1905	2100	2000	2588	2000	2143	. . . . .
Production Plan	2000	2100	2100	2100	2100	2200	. . . . .
Dept. 814 (.45)	900	945	945	945	945	990	. . . . .
Dept. 815 (.35)	700	735	735	735	735	770	. . . . .
Dept. 816 (.15)	300	315	315	315	315	330	. . . . .
Dept. 817 (.05)	100	105	105	105	105	110	. . . . .

FIGURE 3. Industrial brakes and clutches.

utilize effectively the overall production plan that is based on a desired sales and/or stock position. The end-item forecast is his key criterion for firm planning assembly production orders and actual customer backlog is used as a fine-tuning mechanism to release or push the required assembly orders and their parts into the assembly department. In the assemble-to-order environment, the master schedule is not an actual finished product but rather a series of subassemblies that will be assembled and shipped upon receipt of a customer order. Billing targets also have a heavy influence on the final assembly schedule. MRP will be a big aid in handling master schedule changes and the integration of the firm planned orders using the computer will usually be a significant improvement in assuring matched sets of parts through a formal master schedule. A master schedule generated without directly considering *both* the forecast and the build schedule can generate shipments but not without a lot of grief and much excess inventory.

An example of a production plan for make-to-stock/assemble-to-order manufacturing process is shown in Figure 3. Management has decided that $2 million in sales is desired for April. An historical review indicates that, on the average, one standard hour yields approximately $50 in shipments. This means 40,000 standard hours are necessary. With 21 production days available, the total division production requirement is a minimum of 1,905 hours per day without depleting inventory. To build inventory in anticipation of a plant shutdown for one week in July, management has decided a production plan of 2,000 hours is appropriate. Historical ratios have been developed to show the percentage split of the division's total hour production among its four departments. The 2,000 hours are factored by these percentages and the production plan for this division, by department, is established. The master scheduler then plans the production of orders for specific part numbers to utilize this production plan. Capacity reports must be reviewed and the master schedule or available capacity is adjusted as necessary to match capacity by specific facility to the master schedule requirements.

Engineer-To-Order

In an engineer-to-order business, the lead time from receipt of order until components are needed in the assembly department is usually relatively long. Inventory control, MRP, and master scheduling are not usually problems in this type of business. The production plan results from a summation of the work to be done on orders already in the backlog. This plan is usually stated in terms of number of machines per month, dollar sales per month, or manufacturing hours needed per month. A master schedule is the customer order with its promise date. A bill of material will be created for required inventory parts and these items can be allocated early in the manufacturing departments. The problem of control in this type of business is oriented to keeping track of the special parts and clearing each phase of work through the major departments such as engineering, processing, machining, and assembly.

An example of an engineer-to-order production plan is shown in Figure 4. Usually, production plan constraints exist relative to skilled manpower and/or manufacturing space. Changes in capacity are not very flexible, and must be planned carefully. The production plan in the example shows a capacity in terms of manufacturing units and is constant at eight units for the first four months. A plan to increase production by two manufacturing units is scheduled for August. Two types of equipment are being engineered to order and each inspection machine is worth two manufacturing units while each layout machine (LOM) is worth one manufacturing unit. This is reflected in number of people required to produce each unit, the assembly space required, the manufacturing cost, and the selling price. Generally stated, marketing and production have decided that two inspection machine and four layout machines per month is a good allocation of resources when the manufacturing capacity is set at eight units. This becomes the production plan and marketing has a very important part in stating the master schedule by the way they promise delivery for each

Month	April		May		June		July		Aug.		Sept.		....
	Units Sold	Mfg. Units	Units Sold	Mfg. Units	Units Sold	Mfg. Units	Units Sold	Mfg. Units	Units Sold	Mfg. Units	Units Sold	Mfg. Units	....
56B INSPECT	1	2	2	4	2	4	1	2	2	4	0	—	....
76B INSPECT	1	2	0	—	0	—	1	2	1	2	2	4	....
48A LOM	1	1	2	2	4	4	2	2	2	2	0	—	....
72A LOM	3	3	2	2	0	—	1	1	2	2	3	3	....
TOTAL	8		8		8		7		10		7		....
MFG. UNIT CAPACITY	8		8		8		8		10		10		....

FIGURE 4. Layout and inspection machines.

MAJOR TYPE OF MASTER PRODUCTION SCHEDULE	TYPE OF BUSINESS CATEGORY*	PRODUCTION PLAN CRITERIA	MASTER SCHEDULE DATA
1. Few Major products built to stock	b	Units per day, standard hours per day. Actual hours related to sales. Key equipment capacity constraints.	Specific part numbers and options. Rought cut capacity required. Backlog, Forecast, billing targets.
2. Many products built for stock	b	Same as (1)	Same as (1)
3. Few major units engineered and custom built to order	c	Summation of orders already in backlog. Number of machines per month capacity. Dollar sale per month.	Customer order backlog. Forecast of key sub-assemblies in lieu of backlog.
4. Many products assembled to order	c	Same as (3)	Same as (3)
5. Combination of stock and	b & c	Varies as 1 & 3	Varies as 1 & 3
6. Replacement parts	a, b, c	Integrated as part of basic production plan for main business	Integrated as another component of forecast or backlog.
7. Affiliate Plants	a, b, c	Same as (6)	Same as (6)
8. Products sold as is and in higher level assemblies	b	Same as (1)	Same as (1)
9. Continuous or high volume production.	a	Number of units to be built based on current or anticipated business conditions. Key equipment.	Specific part numbers. Forecast, backlog, material and key equipment variability.
10. Branch Warehouses	a, b, c	Same as (6)	Same as (6)

*Type of Busines Category: (a) Continuous   (b)Make to Stock and/or assemble to order   (c) Engineer to order

FIGURE 5. Ten major types of master production schedules related to business category.

new order that is taken. Figure 4 shows that one more layout machine could be scheduled for July and one inspection machine and one layout machine or three layout machines for September.

Figure 5 shows the ten major types of master schedules categorized as to type of business. Each type also has its production plan criteria and basic data elements that form the master schedule. The examples are given only to review the considerations that are relevant when differentiating between a master schedule and a production plan. Each operating unit must define its type of business and incorporate its special needs as they are specified.

PRODUCTION PLAN AND MASTER SCHEDULE DIFFERENCES

To summarize the difference between the production plan and the master schedule, the first factor considered is that the production plan is developed based on a current financial plan. This is the original plan for the year's business or a revised version to reflect a change in the expected business level. In many cases, it is stated in terms that are not computer sensible because they are too general. There derives a need, then, to use the production plan as a guide and identify specific part numbers that will be built within that guide. These part numbers and their associated forecasts, backlogs, and production lot sizes become the master schedule. I have encountered a number of combinations of the ten master schedule types under one roof. This requires the master schedule process to be defined in general terms so that any of the types (or combinations thereof) can be incorporated into one planning group. This was a design consideration for the subject system and it can be used to plan manufacturing for any of the master schedule types listed in Figure 5.

The foregoing presented an overview of the theory that is relevant to discussing the master schedule process. It is appropriate at this point to discuss briefly the product diversity that is inherent in the systems environment. Then we can proceed to review the specific approaches used in the system.

PRODUCT TO BE MASTER SCHEDULED

The division involved is a medium-sized division of a very large multinational corporation. The principal product is precision measuring devices that range from very small machines selling for under $300 to very large, special-purpose machines with a sales price in excess of $400,000. The division has six distinct product lines with many models and sub-product lines. Three different kinds of inventory control and scheduling problems types exist, encompassing all of the master schedule types except continuous production lines and branch warehouses. Two of the product lines are made-to-stock type assemblies that have a number of standard subassemblies, but with many unique gauging problems that may require a unique fixture for each customer order. While 70% of the sales value of an order might be assembled from stock, the other 30% would be made to order and matched at assembly.

Two other of the product lines are large machine tool type equipment that involve model types varying in size and sophistication. Subassemblies and components are made for stock and then assembled and applied to customer orders. Option availabilty precludes manufacturing a complete saleable unit for stock. One of these two product lines is the heart of the division's business and must be planned and controlled well. Prior to MRP and the use of a master schedule, the approach had been to have enough of all parts available so that any combination of actual sales could be reacted to quickly. This was not always successful. In addition, this approach tied up significant dollars invested in excess inventory.

The final two product lines are the very large engineer-to-order special machines. Each machine involved a significant amount

Part No. 50015000						Rel Res 25			Ord Qty 30			Planner 1		Inv. Planning Code M		
BOH 0						Service 0			Lead Time 2					Unit Cost 1690		
Rel Orders 30						Service Interval 0			Mach Hrs/Pc 55							
FP Orders 60						Safety Stock 0			Assy Hrs/Pc 25							

Exception Messages

Period	Past due	1	2	3	4	5	6	7	8	9	10	11	12	13	14	15
Forecast/Service		10		5		20		15	5		40					40	
Bklg/Prod. Reqmts.	5	5	10					5									
On Order (Rel & FP)		30				30*						30*	(30)			(30)	
Planned Order Rel											30			30			
Projected Avail		20	20	15	15	25	25	10	5	5	−5	25	25	25	25	15	15
Projected Avail $	33800	33800	33800	25350	25350	42250	42250	42250	8450	8450	0	42250	42250	42250	42250	25350	25350

PEGGING

Rec Type	Due Date	Quantity Remaining	Quantity Received	Order No.	Parent (vendor) Part Number/Description
RES	PD	5	0	Cust. 1	Elgin Div.
MS	Per 1	10	0	Forecast	
RES	Per 1	5	0	Cust. 2	GE
ORD	Per 1	30	0	SO 1	Shop
RES	Per 2	4	0	Cust. 3	Bendix S.B.
RES	Per 2	6	0	Cust. 5	GM Pontiac
MS	Per 3	5	0	Forecast	
MS	Per 5	20	0	Forecast	
ORD	Per 5	30	0	SO 2	Shop
RES	Per 6	5	0	Cust. 4	Cummins

Abbreviations:
BOH: Balance on hand
REL: Released
FP: Final plan
RES: Reserved
ORD: Order
MS: Master schedule
SO: Shop order

FIGURE 6. Material requirements planning part status.

of engineering and many custom-made parts. Standard parts and assemblies are used where possible, but the units are generally long-lead time sales and inventory control and master schedule requirements are not as important as in the other four product lines. However, the technology in each of these product lines is somewhat standard and a master schedule is developed where appropriate. Bill of material structuring is potentially the key inventory control and scheduling factor along with service requirement considerations. Service requirements for critical parts are a very real concern in one of these lines.

Electronic assembly is an additional department that serves each of the six product lines as necessary and provides another master schedule variable. In fact, the variation in this division encompasses each of the master schedule variables shown in Figure 1 with the exception of a) continuous or high-volume production and j) branch warehouses.

Because the same inventory control department is responsible for controlling the parts for all of the product lines, an approach that is not uncommon in my experience, it was a design constraint to have the same MRP status report format for all product lines. It was also appropriate to have all master schedule items displayed on a different report but in the same relative format as the MRP status sheets. Figure 6 shows the MRP status format and Figure 7 shows the corresponding master schedule format for a master schedule item. Master schedule items are also shown in MRP status sheet format with its attendant indicative information and pegging display. Pegging is a display of detail supporting the numeric data shown in the heart of the MRP status report.

Part No.	BOH	Rel Res	Rel Ord	FP Ord	Safety Stock	Lt	Cum Lt	Cost	Option %	Assy Hrs. Pc.	Mach Hrs. Pc.
50015000	0	25	30	60	0	2	26	1690	0	25	55

Period	Past due	1	2	3	4	5	6	7	8	9	10	11	12	13	14	15	16	...
Forecast		10		5		20		15	5		40				40			...
Backlog	5	5	10				5											...
Orders		30				30*					30*							...
Avail	0	20	20	15	15	25	25	10	5	5	−5	−5	−5	−5	−45	−45	−45	...

50015001	6	4	4	4	6	0	0	4	26	15000	0	275	600

Period	Past due	1	2	3	4	5	6	7	8	9	10	11	12	13	14	15	16	...
Forecast		5	1			4	1			6	1			5				...
Backlog	1	3		1														...
Orders						4				6*								...
Avail	6	1	0	0	0	0	−1	−1	−1	−1	−2	−2	−2	−7	−7	−7	−7	...

⋮
5 per page

Abbreviations:
BOH: Balance on hand
CUM LT: Cumulative lead time
FP: Final plan
LT: Lead time
ORD: Order
REL: Released
RES: Reserved

FIGURE 7.   Master schedule.

First, Major Premise: The Master Schedule is a Planning Process

The master schedule is an action management tool to be utilized for controlling operations and is actualized through its role as input to the MRP system. Two other aspects are vital to a control loop; these involve initial planning and replanning after the results of action are evaluated.

In the subject system, the initial planning is accomplished each month in a master schedule meeting held separately for each of the six unique product lines. Present at each meeting are the master scheduler, the specific product manager, and the production and inventory control manager. The master scheduler is the former inventory control supervisor and understands the inventory control and product structure considerations well. The production and inventory control (P&IC) manager is also well versed in product line knowledge and himself was a former shop floor control supervisor. In this way, knowledge of shop operations and what can or cannot be reasonably accomplished is provided.

The product manager is accountable for all aspects of marketing his particular product area and can relate to the level of business that is required to meet division sales objectives and also relate to which specific part numbers should be planned to achieve his sales goals. He brings current quote information as well as future sales promotions or customer incentives that will be offered. In addition, the product manager is accountable for planned profit performance on his product line and thus has a vested interest in not only production but also in-process and finished inventory levels.

The master scheduling meeting is structured around a printout of all master schedule items for the product line in a form similar to Figure 7. In compliance with the definition of a master schedule a) the part number tells what is being made, b) the forecast line defines how many should be made, c) the backlog line indicates how many of the forecast have already been

sold, d) the order line indicates how many will be made and when, and e) the availability line indicates whether or not the forecast is being satisfied. If the availability line is running negative, then the forecast is not being satisfied. This would generally occur if the capacity constraints were being violated and adjustments into the future for the dating of the manufacturing lots had been made. The shop not being able to build at forecasted levels and times does not alleviate potential sales need but it does show the product managers where allowances may have to be made in customer promises. There are provisions for a rough cut capacity plan by having an estimate of the man-hours required to machine all of the parts used in a master schedule item and the number of man-hours used in assembly departments for each master schedule item. The division does not currently have standard hours for detail operations, so a detail capacity requirements plan is not possible.

The product manager is responsible for providing the forecast line on the master schedule report. The current customer backlog against that forecast is shown on the next line as an aid to evaluate performance against previous forecasts and to give indications of the future product mix. The backlog line is a memo figure only and is not used in any way for the available line calculations. The master scheduler and P&IC manager are responsible for the order line. These are production orders that should satisfy the forecast within reasonable limitations. Production orders are released within the planning lead time and firm planned orders are generated for each part to cover the cumulaive lead time. The system has released, firm planned, and planned orders. Using released orders and firm planned orders over the planning horizon, the effect of the forecast is blocked out through that point. Planned orders created by the MRP system are *not permitted* to slide in front of a released or firm planned order, regardless of the calculated need.

Rough cut capacity estimates are shown on a summary sheet that follows the master schedule detail report. These estimates are derived by accumulating the machining department time for the item through all of the levels in its bill of material structure. The same is done for assembly hours. These "machining hours per piece" and "assembly hours per piece" are multiplied by the number of units in the order line of the master schedule item. An estimate of the total hours required in the shop is time phased into the future.

Table 1 shows an example of four parts that make up the master schedule items for product code 260. The assembly and machining hours per piece were determined for each part and includes manufactured components and subassemblies from all levels of a specific parts bill of material structure. The released and firm planned order, the due date, and order quantity are listed next. The total hours required in assembly and machining departments are shown in the last column. These data are then dislayed by time period in a report similar in format to that shown in Figure 8.

There are some assumptions that need to be made with the resulting data, but in the hands of an experienced shop man, valid estimates of significant plant overloads or underloads can be picked out. Standard data by operation are not available in the division's data base so that a more definitive breakdown by work center that would come from capacity requirements planning is not available at this time. The data used for the rough cut capacity plan come from average actual times collected from accounting cost records.

If an overload exists, and the P&IC manager decides to cut the planned build, the resulting negative availability will show planned shortages against the forecast. This will be reviewed and dealt with at the next master schedule meeting. If a problem still exists between the product manager and the P&IC manager, then the director level in each department is brought into the picture. Any time that a director or the general manager wants to implement a particular policy relative to

Table 1. Product code 260

	MACHINING HOURS PER PIECE	ASSEMBLY HOURS PER PIECE	ORDERS	DATE	QUANTITY	TOTAL HOURS REQUIRED MACHINING	ASSEMBLY
Part 1	55	25	Order 1	Per 1	50	2,750	1,250
			Order 2	Per 5	50	2,750	1,250
			Order 3	Per 10	75	4,125	1,875
Part 2	600	275	Order 4	Per 2	5	3,000	1,375
			Order 5	Per 5	5	3,000	1,375
			Order 6	Per 6	5	3,000	1,375
			Order 7	Per 8	5	3,000	1,375
Part 3	300	100	Order 8	Per 1	15	4,500	1,500
			Order 9	Per 8	15	4,500	1,500
Part 4	100	100	Order 10	Per 3	30	3,000	3,000
			Order 11	Per 6	20	2,000	2,000
			Order 12	Per 9	20	2,000	2,000
						37,625	19,875

Department	Periods										
	1	2	3	4	5	6	7	8	9	10	Total
Machining	7250	3000	3000	0	5750	5000	0	7500	2000	4125	37625
Assembly	2750	1375	3000	0	2625	3375	0	2875	2000	1875	19875

FIGURE 8.   Master schedule summary report production hours (total product code 260).

production in a given product line, he would do so through active participation in the master schedule meeting or a review of the master schedule that has been established with appropriate guidance resulting.

Replanning, of course, occurs in a manner similar to that outlined for initial planning and it comes in the form of reviewing last month's decisions relative to the short-term planning horizon before new forecasts or firm planned orders are adjusted in the long term. Replanning can also occur with special meetings called during the month by either the marketing or manufacturing department relative to an unusual occurrence that requires immediate attention.

Second Major Premise: The Master Schedule Must Be Consumed

Because we believe that the master schedule is both the forecast and the build schedule, we also believe that both must be consumed dynamically. Oliver Wright discusses this concept by using the word "matching."[3] He appears to restrict his comments to an assemble-to-order environment. My contention is that forecasting is fundamental for any master schedule that is based on anything else but total known future demand, i.e., some element of forecasting is necessary within a planning horizon. A true engineer-to-order environment may have the least need for schedule consumption as long as the backlog remains heavy, but sooner or later, a forecast becomes necessary to plan for low-level parts when orders must be anticipated. If you do not insist on the idea that the forecast is not the master schedule and you employ appropriate use of the firm planned order, then consumption or matching of the master schedule can be accomplished by the marketing department by watching the forecast and availability numbers. A summation of the customer order backlog by part number keeps track of the marketing responsibilities for the master schedule and the availability line by part number keeps track of the manufacturing responsibilities for the master schedule.

The production lot is reduced by the number of pieces received into stock. Reduction is accomplished on the day of the receipt. The forecast is consumed by an issue from stock and it also occurs on the day of the issue. This means that the system is keeping track of the sales performance against forecast. If sales meets the forecast, the issues will reduce the current period to zero and then it will start on the forecast of the next period. The forecast is kept on a separate computer file called the master schedule file and is maintained by the master scheduler. The maintenance occurs as a result of the master schedule meeting mentioned previously. In Figure 9, if the forecast for period 1 and 2 was ten each and 13 were sold in the first period, during the next review the product manager must make a decision as to whether the seven now remaining in what was period 2 is a result of three units being sold ahead of forecast *or* three units over and above the original forecast of ten in period 1. If he believes that it was a normal ship ahead, then he does nothing and the system continues to plan to make seven available in period 2. If he believes it was an abnormal increase, then the master scheduler would be told to change the seven back to ten in the period 2 or add 3 more to some period in the future. Of course, if sales were three less than forecast in period 1, the quantity of 13 in period 2 would have to be analyzed in reverse fashion.

It should be noted that no effort is made to tie incoming customer orders to a particular forecast record or order lot. Too many variables can occur that would very quickly get the actual production lots applied out of synchronization with the actual customer order a unit or units of a given lot were reserved for. The backlog line on the master schedule sheet is used to keep track of the customer orders in-house that have been allocated out of a given forecast group. An issue of a master scheduled subassembly to the floor for final assembly or the shipment of a final assembly reduces the forecast and the backlog, thereby keeping the allocation in balance. Marketing can promise up to their forecast quantity without consultation, but when they want to prom-

BOH = 7

Period	Past due	1	2	3	4	5	6	7	8	9	10	11	...
Forecast		10	10	12	15	10	8	5	8	10	10	10	...
Backlog		9	7	4	1	0	0	0	1	0	0	1	...
Orders	20		40					40				40	...
Avail	27	17	47	35	20	10	2	37	29	19	9	39	...

After one period goes by and 13 are sold, 6 rec'd to stock

BOH = 0

Period	Past due	1	2	3	4	5	6	7	8	9	10	11	...
Forecast		7	12	15	10	8	5	8	10	10	10	10	...
Backlog		8	5	1	2	3	0	1	0	1	1	0	...
Orders	14	40					40				40		...
Avail	14	47	35	20	10	2	37	29	19	9	39	29	...

FIGURE 9. Forecasting.

ise more, they must check the part availability with production control. In most cases, enough units to cover more than the current period forecast are on a released production lot. If the forecast/production lots are being handled with discrete matching quantities, then the next production lot is usually close enough to move up. That is strictly the prerogative of the P&IC manager, however. If either the product manager or the P&IC manager are not satisfied with the efforts of the other, the issue can be bumped up to the director level.

Dick Ling of Arista Information Systems has been using a master schedule utilizing a direct consumption of production lots with incoming customer orders. That system made the assumption that the plan or forecast was discrete and could be identified with specific production lots that had been started to coincide with specific due dates. It is not clear what problems would be encountered on a product line where the production lot covered more than one period's forecast, or the quantities of the forecast were too large to keep track of each customer order as it was applied to the build lot, or the physical problems encountered in keeping the planned lot consistent numerically with the lot number actually applied to the order.

The *master schedule as a planning process* and the *master schedule must be consumed* are the two basic premises on which the system we are utilizing is based. In conclusion, I review the principles that have been established both here and in the literature and our particular systems reaction or incorporation of those principles.

REVIEW OF PRINCIPLE VERSUS SYSTEM PROVISION

In the training aid on master production scheduling produced by the American Production and Inventory Control Society (APICS) there is a specific attempt to ask and answer the question, What is a master production schedule?[4] That aid is used as a basis of comparison and the following points can be made:

1. *It (master schedule) determines the quantity per time period that is to be manufactured.* Our system determines the lot size and starting time period using time phased released and firm planned orders spread over the planning horizon for each master schedule part. This is basically a part matching device, and our assembly schedule then breaks down each lot size into the desired output per time period.

2. *It is not a sales forecast, i.e., what sales thinks it can sell, but a production plan, i.e., what manufacturing plans to produce.* We believe master scheduling is a process that includes the forecast as much a part of the process as a manufacturing build order. The forecast and the firm planned orders, their interaction visible through the available line, and an estimate of capacity requirements on a rough cut basis constitute the elements of that process.

3. *It is also a customer order backlog scheduling plan.* Because the planned production orders have been checked against capacity constraints and a positive availability line shows that the forecast is covered by manufacturing build orders, the order service function can schedule customer orders routinely to the limit of the forecast that has been made by time period. When negative availability is encountered or when more than the original forecast is desired, special negotiations must be held with the P&IC department. The current customer order backlog is shown at all times in very close proximity to the forecast on the master schedule report.

4. *It is a "finite" or "deterministic" loading concept and is the first stage of "capacity planning," in that it must allocate and utilize the available capacity or adjust capacity to load, in order to plan maximum productivity . . . In complex situations, the loading is done at a "gross" level . . . and may require additional 'dependent' loading and scheduling sub-systems to develop the detail necessary for complete control . . .* This is our rough cut capacity plan mentioned previously. This capacity plan is based on an estimate of machining hours per piece and assembly hours per piece for the master schedule production orders. The capacity constraint that is used as a target is the total number of hours per week to be generated in the machining and assembly departments. Although a system then can calculate time estimates by operation prior to the running of a job is being developed, no data are currently available to utilize as input to a capacity requirements planning program.

5. *It is a flexible plan that recognizes the fact that planning far enough out in time to deal with lead time requires considerable adjustment as the future periods come closer to the present.* Our plan is flexible, with time fences that are variable by product line. Firm planned orders are used to cover the planning horizon and when change or flexibility is required in the planning, the closer we are to today, the higher the level of management required to authorize a change. We have flexibility but we have also built in restraint.

6. *It is Management's entry point into, and therefore the management control of the production and inventory control system . . . It is important to recognize that master scheduling is the visible end result of a planning and decision-making effort that should include either management approval or management decisions, where tradeoffs, capacity, and/or delivery problems are detected.* Our approach is to do the routine things routinely. The forecast is the production goal. The rough cut capacity report and negative availability are signs for needed management intervention. The necessary management level will be alerted as deemed appropriate. As indicated previously, any upper management request will be implemented and evaluated for feasibility through the master schedule.

CONCLUSION

Because MRP is not a one-time statement of production objectives, its input is subject to relatively frequent changes to meet changing opportunities. The master schedule must be the steering wheel that permits the system to be driven around obstacles toward the desired objective. Holding that steering wheel or constraining it is the production plan and the business plan that dictate the environment in which the master schedule must function. These four ideas (the business plan, the production plan, the master schedule, and the assembly schedule or build plan) are all vital parts of a closed-loop manufacturing control system. Figure 10 shows their interrelation-

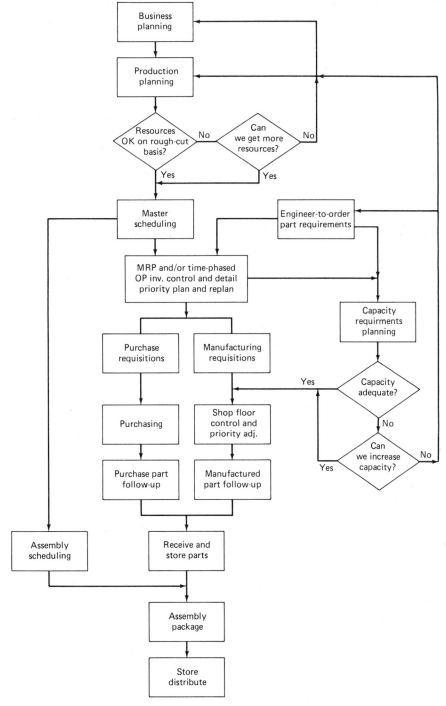

FIGURE 10.   Closed loop production and inventory management system.

ship at the beginning of the loop. The design and management of the master schedule is recognized today as one of the keys to the success or failure of an MRP-based manufacturing control system.

The definition of a master schedule says that it is a production plan, not a sales plan. The APICS training aid says, "It is not what sales thinks it can sell, but what Manufacturing plans to produce."

We say it is both and that master scheduling is a process linking the business and production plans with the build plan through the fundamental concept of the firm planned order. The firm planned order is the mechanism that gives manufacturing the ability to state their build plan and coordinate that plan with the marketing forecast through a computer. Through the firm planned order, the master schedule concept becomes a process, the process becomes a reality, and the reality

becomes the steering wheel for the production and inventory control system that resolves discrepancies between marketing wishes and manufacturing capabilities.

REFERENCES

1. Mather, Hal F. and Plossl, G.W., "The Master Production Schedule—Management's Handle on the Business," G.W. Plossl and Co, Inc., Decatur, Georgia, 1975.
2. Everdell, Romeyn, "Master Production Scheduling," APICS Training Aid
3. It is assumed the reader has a brief knowledge of MRP. An excellent in-depth study is available in Orlicky, Dr. Joseph, *Materials Requirements Planning*, McGraw-Hill, New York, 1975. An overview of the topic is provided in Wight, Oliver, *Production and Inventory Control in the Computer Age*, Cahners, Boston, 1974.
4. Everdell, ibid., p. 2.

25
Implementing an Effective Capital Expenditures Program

Earl A. Corriveau
Manufacturing Accounting Manager
Wang Laboratories

Because today's capital expenditures make the bed that the company must lie in tomorrow, today's decisions must be based on what tomorrow will be like. Recognizing the importance of efficient facilities, the author discusses the various steps in the implementation of a sound capital expenditures control program.

Effective planning of a company's capital expenditures involves a complex interaction of analysis and decisions regarding the future status of the economy, the industry, the company, and its objectives. It is better not to dwell on macroeconomic forecasting, but rather to emphasize its importance in capital programs because of the nature of the commitment regarding time, monetary constraints, and irreversibility. The major thrust of this chapter is to quantify and present data for effective capital expenditures management.

TEN COMMANDMENTS

In Joel Dean's "Measuring the Productivity of Capital,"[1] he puts forth ten components of capital expenditure management for an operational program.

1. *Creative search for profitable opportunities.*
2. *Long-Range capital plans.* Because today's capital expenditures make the bed the the company must lie in tomorrow, today's decisions must be based on what tomorrow will be like.

3. *Short-Range capital budget.* Listing by project and amount for annual capital budget:
   a. Review and evaluation of capital request with management's objective
   b. Determine demand for funds
   c. Approve as a budgeted item for potential acquisition during the year.
4. *Measurement of project worth.* Final justification of a capital expenditure based on its investment worth to the company.
5. *Screening and selection.* Compare a capital expenditure with rival projects:
   a. Supply of cash available
   b. Cost of money to the company
   c. Attractiveness of alternative investment opportunities.
6. *Control of authorized outlays.* Assure that actual expenditure conforms to specifications and that the outlay does not exceed the amount authorized.
7. *Post-mortems.* Post-completion audits to compare actual with projected earnings.

8. *Retirement and disposal.*
9. *Forms and procedures.* An effective system of capital-expenditure control must be implemented by specialized forms, written project analyses, and routines of approval that are tailored to the company's needs.
10. *Economics of capital budgeting.* Good estimates on the rate of return on capital expenditure projects require an understanding of the economic concepts that underlie sound investment decisions.

The elemental steps are listed in Table 1.

Table 1. Capital appropriation request (CAR) program

1. Goal of profitable opportunities
2. Requests to fall within predetermined parameters reflecting company's long-range capital plan
3. Short-range goal as determined by management's objectives and so budgeted
4. Measurement of project worth
5. Economics of capital budgeting
6. Screening and selection
7. Authorization and control of outlays
8. Post-mortems
9. Retirement and disposal
10. Forms and procedures

Centralization of a firm's capital appropriation request (CAR) program and its physical control system is preferred, although segregation of these functions is acceptable as long as the requirement for interactivity is recognized and fostered within the organization.

The capital appropriation request program interfaces with a physical control system for routine activities involving evaluation, decision making, and checks and balances of capital equipment program integrity. However, to be effective, the CAR program must also encompass the firm's investment concepts, which are conveyed to the program manager in the form of corporate goals and budgets. This allows the CAR program both to meas-

ure project worth effectively within established guidelines and to interact with the firm's physical control system, listed as items 7 through 10 in Table 1. The result is a permanent property program, based on the firm's financial objectives that authorize and control changes in capital (i.e., additions, disposals, transfers, and so on), while generating records substantiating accounting values as well as comparing actual to planned capital activity.

We will address a mechanism that achieves authorization and control after placing it in the perspective of general capital planning program concepts and theory.

GOALS AND PLANS

Corporate goals are based on product and market evaluations as determined by projections for the industry and the economy. Goals are directed at profitable opportunities identified in the evaluation process and become the basis for long- and short-term plans. It should be stressed that goals for profitable opportunities are based on profitability—the return on the company's resources—rather than profit on sales. Therefore, corporate goals require evaluation of a large range of investment objectives that include major physical assets and human resources planning and management.

Once the corporate goals are determined, either through a sophisticated or informal evaluation and presentation, a long-term plan can be developed. Normally, this type of planning covers a minimum of five years. It forces extraction from corporate goals of clearly stated assumptions and objectives required over the long term. It sets the parameters and measures for activity and proposals to achieve profitability for the designated time frame. The long-term plan is presented in many different ways, depending on the firm's philosophy. Presentations range in complexity from a concise position paper to a detailed package including projections of financial position using the firm's normal statement format. The latter method is preferred. However, presentation is secondary to conveying the objectives for activity and proposals.

The short-term plan is generally an annual plan broken down by month. It is based on and integrated with the long-term plan. The annual plan or budget is the tool by which operating and investment decisions are measured. An effective budget directs planning in three areas:

1. Operations
   Profit and loss statement
   a. Volume: Measure growth, expansion, product mix, and so on
   b. Costs: Internal controls
   c. Return on sales:

   $$\frac{\text{Net income}}{\text{Sales}} \quad \text{for measuring operating performance.}$$

2. Asset control
   Balance sheet and cost of manufacture
   a. Cost of manufacture interrelates operations with asset control
   b. Balance sheet: Line items are measured and analyzed to evaluate specific performance criteria (i.e., receivables → receivable days → ageing status and performance)
   c. Asset turn:
   $$\frac{\text{Sales}}{\text{Assets}} \quad \text{for measuring asset control.}$$
   d. Return on assets (or investment): asset turn × return on sales. Integrates operations and asset control into one measure.

3. Cash Flow
   Statement of cash flow sources and use of funds
   A. Sources of Funds
   1. Generated by operations through reinvestment of earnings, depreciation, and tax credits
   2. Projected changes in the balance sheet, which reflects actions to acquire funds by either reducing short- or long-term assets or increasing debt or equity from the financial market.

B. Use of funds
   1. Projected use of funds from actual commitments and projections in viewing operations
   2. Permanent property requirements/commitments as identified through asset control projections
   3. Commitments to the financial market (i.e., debt retirement)

The purpose of presenting details of the three financial areas to which budgeting should be addressed is to emphasize the interrelationship of these areas. Operations are highly dependent on cash flow, whereas both functions are affected by asset control. Asset control is concerned with minimizing assets required for effective operations, thereby minimizing funds required. It is also directed at long-term asset commitments and controls, specifically investment in permanent property or *capital*. It is this area of asset control to which we direct our attention, for decisions involving such investments are of major significance. They form the framework for future operating performance—profit and growth—while commiting the company to a position involving considerably greater risk (both in dollars and ability to retract or recover from an incorrect decision) than exists in daily operational decision making.

The permanent property program presented has numerous features common to many companies that emphasize asset control. However, this presentation is influenced by factors affecting the rapidly growing and ever-changing electronics industry. The subject matter is applicable to most industries and companies. It has become stressed increasingly by top management in companies within the electronics industry because of the necessity for sound planning at all organization levels.

MEASUREMENT OF PROJECT WORTH

Measuring worth evokes enormous controversy directed at identifying a single measure of profitability that will permit an objective evaluation and ranking of proposed projects. This subject has resulted in controversial articles and counterarticles among such luminaries as Joel Dean, Gordon and Shapiro, Modigliani and Miller, David Durand, Ezra Solomon, and numerous other academicians.

Four basic measures for measuring worth are recognized by these authors, although they do not agree on the relative validity of any particular method:

1. Payback method
2. Average book formula
3. Discounted cash flow
4. Present value method.

From a different perspective, in the *Theory of Financial Management*,[2] Ezra Solomon reviewed the most common standards that business has set for capital decision making. The concepts associated with the methods listed above are used in the business community, although in practice are not as sophisticated as presented by academicians. A fifth method, known as the discounted payback method, is discussed in relation to the shortcomings of the present value method.

Definition and evaluation of the four basic measures of project worth are presented with reference to a single example derived from the cash-flow analysis of a proposed project shown in Table 2. Results of each measurement method for the single project are presented in Table 3.

Payback Method

This measurement method simply involves computing the time required for the net after

Table 2. Net after tax cash flow

INVESTMENT		
Equipment	$250,000	
Freight	5,000	
Other	5,000	
Total	$260,000	

NET CASH FLOW	YEAR 1	YEAR 2
Annual savings		
Labor for production (attachment 1)[a]	$130,000	$130,000
Labor for inspection (attachment 2)[a]	100,000	120,000
Direct materials (attachment 3)[a]	60,000	140,000
Total savings	290,000	390,000
Less operating costs (attachment 4)[a]	70,000	60,000
Net savings	220,000	330,000
Less depreciation	50,000	40,000
Savings—profit before tax	170,000	290,000
Taxes	85,000	145,000
Less investment credit (260,000 × 10%)	26,000	—
Net taxes	59,000	145,000
Savings—profit after taxes	111,000	145,000
Add depreciation	50,000	40,000
Cash flow—annual	161,000	185,000
Cash flow—cumulative	161,000	346,000
Net cash status (investment less cash flow)	$ (99,000)	$ 86,000

Payback = 1-½ years[b]

[a]Attachments show detail calculations used in arriving at the numbers presented. The attachments are not included in this presentation.
[b]See Table 3.

tax cash flow from an investment to recover the initial capital outlay.

The advantages of this method are its emphasis on liquidity and its simplicity. By emphasizing liquidity, the measure is beneficial to financially weak firms. However, liquidity is also of import in highly solvent firms in technological industries in which obsolescence or flexibility is an ever-increasing consideration, because of the need for maintaining product and market position.

The concept of simplicity for this measure is dual. First, it is simple to calculate. Second, and more important, it is easy to understand. It is conducive to ease of communication from top management to line managers and other disciplines because it uses the common language of time. Payback is expressed in the same manner to the treasurer, who is concerned with funding the investment as it is to the line manager whose concern is efficiency and useful life of the investment.

The disadvantages of payback relate to time frame and value. It ignores cash flow beyond the payback period, thereby not recognizing cash flow after the total return of the investment. This is a serious drawback, especially in a mature industry, because alternative projects have different patterns of cash flow as well as length of inflow. These two factors are critical determinants of total return on an investment.

Payback does not recognize the time value of money. It incorrectly assumes that the value of cash received in future years is the same as that of the first year. This consideration poses numerous theoretical and practical considerations in investment policies.

Table 3. Overview of project worth measurement techniques

Investment $260,000

| YEAR | NET AFTER TAX CASH FLOW | | PRESENT VALUE 15% C OF C | DISCOUNTED NET AFTER TAX CASH FLOW |
	ANNUAL	CUMULATIVE		
1	$161,000	$161,000	0.86957	$140,000
2	185,000	346,000	0.75614	139,886
3	150,000	496,000	0.65752	98,628
4	75,000	571,000	0.57175	42,881
5	25,000	596,000	0.49718	12,430
	$596,000			$433,825

Return on Assets
$596,000 ÷ 5 = 119,200/260,000 = 45.87%

Discounted Cash Flow
Computation not shown (trial/error 55% − 58%) = 56.4%

Present Value Method
Present value as shown as discounted net after tax cash flow = $433,825

Payback Method
Year 1: 161,000 × 100% = $161,000
Year 2: 185,000 × 53.5% = 99,000
                                    $260,000
Payback = 1.53 years

Discounted Payback Method
Year 1: 140,000 × 100% = $140,000
Year 2: 139,886 × 85.8% = 120,000
                                    $260,000
Payback = 1.86 years

Average Book Formula

Dividing the average after tax inflow by the amount of the original investment results in the average book formula measurement. (see Table 3) Its advantages are simplicity of calculation combined with ease of comparing investment return against a predetermined financial guideline. The primary disadvantages of the method are that it ignores time value of money over the life of the asset (or inflows). It is also so financially oriented that the meaning of calculated returns is difficult to convey throughout the firm.

Discounted Cash Flow

This method identifies the rate of return that equates net after tax cash flow with the original amount invested. It is determined by finding the interest rate that discounts future cash inflows from the investment to a present value equal to the original cost of the investment. This method incorporates the time value of money into investment decisions and identifies the true rate of interest required for the life of the investment without incurring a loss. The significance of identifying the real rate of return cannot be stressed enough, as it is the measure that correctly quantifies the value of investment return patterns and time frames. The difference in interest rates as measured by average book formula and discounted cash flow is shown in Table 3. Discounted cash flow recognizes the greater value of cash inflows in early years as well as the diminishing amount of cash inflows (earning pattern) in later years.

Problems with discounted cash flow are that it ignores liquidity, assumes other projects are available that generate the same return, and it is both difficult to compute (requires trial-and-error calculations) and comprehend for different groups within the firm.

Present Value Method

This approach is similar in concept to discounted cash flow, while incorporating the firm's cost of capital into the calculation. The present value method requires the firm to determine its cost of capital. This cost, as a percentage rate, is then used in discounting net after tax cash flow to arrive at the total present value of the investment. When the present value exceeds the original cost of the investment, the project meets the acceptance criteria because the original investment will be exceeded by its inflow net of the firm's cost to acquire the investment.

The present value approach has all of the advantages of discounted cash flow as well as being easier to calculate. It integrates the firm's cost of capital into the computation, thereby eliminating the assumption of applying cash received from the investment at the same rate in another project. It has built in a minimum acceptable return for investment projects.

The disadvantages are similar to discounted cash flow. It ignores liquidity and is not readily understandable to the numerous disciplines involved in the capital-acquisition process.

In reviewing the traditionally recognized measurement methods, four factors have evolved as being integral to investment evaluation. They are liquidity, cost of capital, time value of money, and comprehension (ability of the measurement method to be used as a tool for effective dialog within the firm).

The present value method includes the key considerations of cost of capital and time value of money. However, it ignores liquidity. This consideration is emphasized by the payback method, which unfortunately ignores cost of capital and time value of money. Because of the current environment in which many firms are concerned with liquidity, another measurement method has evolved known as the discounted payback method.

Discounted Payback Method

Using the payback concept, this measurement integrates the firm's cost of capital into the calculation. The result is at present value of net after tax cash flow expressed as a unit of time. Discounted payback calculates the time required for net after tax cash flow at present value from an investment to recover the initial investment outlay.

The popularity of this measurement method is increasing because it satisfies the desire to measure liquidity while recognizing discounted value of future earnings as determined by cost of capital. Within the firm, ease of communication is established by presenting investment proposal measurement in the common language of time required for the investment to be paid back.

Table 3 shows how each of the methods presented would measure the project that appeared in Table 2. Although the project has high profitability, it does show advantages and disadvantages of these methods. Average book formula understates the rate of return because it ignores the cash inflow pattern of the project. Discounted cash flow is a better measure of rate of return, but it is difficult to compute and assumes other projects are available that generate the same return, which in this instance may be extremely optimistic. The present value method ignores liquidity and requires guidelines to be meaningful. Discounted payback is simply a more logical approach than the payback method because it incorporates cost of capital in the calculation. Its primary disadvantage of ignoring total return on investment is serious enough to disregard its use in mature industries where present value would be more applicable. In marginal and high-technology firms, discounted payback's emphasis on liquidity makes it preferable. What Table 3 does demonstrate is that discounted payback is a readily communicable measurement. Because each discipline in a firm can relate its objectives to

a time frame (treasurer, buyer, line manager, and so on). This method of communicaton is the most desirable. The other methods, percentages of dollars, must be related to some goal, and even then may not be meaningful to certain disciplines within the firm.

SCREENING AND SELECTION

Once a firm has established a measurement method by which it requires all investments to be evaluated, the purpose of screening and selection is more readily defined.

If the firm has selected discounted payback, it should have guidelines that limit the payback period for an investment to be considered. Proposed investments are then ranked from the shortest payback to those that fall just within the maximum allowable payback guideline. Introduction of available (or projected) funds for investment determines if the list of proposals is accepted or reduced to eliminate projects with longer paybacks in order to finalize a fundable capital budget.

The result of this exercise is a proposed capital budget based on funding ability, ranked in desirability by discounted payback. The budget ranking may be changed prior to finalization through management's evaluation of the attractiveness of the proposed investments.

Realistically, neither the capital budget nor evaluation of individual capital authorizations can be determined solely by cost justification as previously outlined. Nonfinancial factors may give certain investments high priority even though they do not meet financial guidelines. Examples include investments required to meet standards set by government regulations, replacing or upgrading equipment that is no longer efficient, capital required for R&D or marketing programs, and so on. Because of the nature of these investments, a firm may prefer to have such projects presented from outside the framework of the capital budget. The result is increased visibility to projects not justifiable within the firm's normal capital evaluation process.

AUTHORIZATION AND CONTROL OF CAPITAL

Restriction of capital equipment purchases by establishment of a formal authorization policy is basic to the success of a capital authorization and control program. Many firms have employed the capital appropriation request (CAR) successfully as the sole official authorization for additions to capital equipment, while using this vehicle to provide continuous control of activities involving acquisitions and capitalization of equipment.

Authorization

With an established authorization program, submission of a CAR becomes the only means by which capital equipment can be purchased. To accomplish this objective effectively, a standard form (Figure 1) is required, from which a request for capital is evaluated, processed, and authorized. The CAR form specifies the equipment to be purchased, amount to be spent, reason for the request, justification, and payback. This supplies responsible personnel with information to evaluate the proposal and provides a vehicle to grant approval in a concise manner.

The CAR form requires approval of personnel that may be categorized into three areas: line management, financial management, and executive. Line management initiates and justifies capital expenditures based on the firm's investment guidelines. Financial personnel review CARs to verify that they meet established budget and presentation criteria. The executive level approval is required and introduces an overview that encompasses both budget guidelines and policy while possibly introducing to the decision information not privy to lower management levels. The CAR flow is presented in greater detail in Table 4, showing information requirements and decision points.

Control

Capital equipment control requires integration of control procedures with the CAR program. Its effectiveness is based on documentation that relates all activity resulting from an appropriations approval to the original capital appropriation request. Figure 2 shows the documents resulting from activity of an approved appropriation with comments regarding discipline involvement and actions required. CAR control through documentation results in a central file containing documents used in acquiring the capital as well as a comprehensive reference of the firm's identication of the property for physical control once capitalized. The file is also extremely valuable for post-mortems. By centralizing all data pertinent to a capital acquisition, followup to compare actual with projected cost is simplified while serving as the starting point for audit of actual versus estimated profitability.

For effective cost control, all capital purchases should be made against a capitalization-in-process account. The accumulation of cost for a capital request occurs in this account until the equipment is deemed operational. Up to that point the equipment is *not* capital.

APPENDIX: DOCUMENTATION AND CONTROL

In his article "Rediscovering Asset Management," A. Howard Heeman[3] describes a proper system of asset management as one "whereby the progress of fixed assets is recorded from purchase to utilization to disposal. This requires a constant line of

REQUEST _____ TESTER _____

CAR NO. _____ 7256 _____   CAPITAL TAG NO. _____ 580359 _____

INVESTMENT REQUIRED

VENDOR	MODEL NO. & DESCRIPTION	QTY.	UNIT COST	TOTAL COST
AB Company	9999 — —	1	150,000	150,000
Electro, Inc.	8888 — —	2	30,000	60,000
Ekco Labs.	7777 — —	2	20,000	40,000
Misc. (including freight)		—	—	10,000
Total Value of Equipment Requested —				260,000

Delivery Date Required _____ 8/8/79 _____   Vendor Delivery Quote _____ 9/29/78 _____

REASON FOR REQUEST

Inability to maintain effective testing of current volume of critical part now used in product. Projected increase in volume, increasing percentage of tested failures as well as expectation of using more complex second generation parts are all factors contributing to the Tester Request.

JUSTIFICATION   FINANCIAL [X]   TECHNICAL [X]   OTHER [ ]

Financial — Cost reductions projected for inspection and production line labor. Eliminates need for a high volume purchased part.

Technical — See attached write up. Areas of concentration — 1. Present Equipment deficiencies, 2. Alternative actions, 3. Proposed solution, 4. Projected benefits of this proposal.

PAYBACK _____ 1-1/2 years _____   EST. USEFUL LIFE (ref. test) _____ 7 years _____

SIGNATURES: NAME   DATE   NAME   DATE

DEPT. MANAGER _____   OPERATING V.P. _____

ASSET ACCT. _____   FINANCIAL V.P. _____

DIV. MANAGER _____   PRESIDENT _____

CONTROLLER _____   BOARD OF DIR. _____

FIGURE 1. Capital appropriation request.

Table 4. Capital appropriation request flow

LINE MANAGEMENT	FINANCIAL	EXECUTIVE

1. Assist in establishing company plans and goals. Familiarity with corporate objectives.
2. Identify specific program as desirable for implementation.
3. Categorize program when submitting reason and justification under capital appropriation request:
   a. Profit
   b. Cost reduction
   c. Obsolete
      1. Product
      2. Equipment
   d. New products
   e. Capacity
   f. Engineering/redesign
   g. Operating efficiencies
   h. Standardize parts.
4. Review and receive approval of:
   a. Plant/cost accountant
   b. Division manager.
5. Submit to asset accounting
	1. Compare capital appropriations request with capital budget to determine if:
	   a. Item or project on CAR has been budgeted
	   b. Item or project on CAR falls within the guidelines or definition of a budgeted project or program.
	2. If either *(a)* or *(b)* are met and one CAR is readily understandable, the CAR is forwarded for executive approval with quantitative information on project annual budget, spending, and balance.
	3. If *(a)* or *(b)* are not met, asset accounting can:
	   a. Forward to executive with a suggested course of action adjusting budget.
	   b. Return to line management with a constructive critique.
		1. Final signature level required.
		2. Must receive from asset accounting in format so that project is readily understandable.
		3. Evaluate project based on data used in making the budget as well as any information that is not yet privy to lower management levels.

communication between operating personnel and the accounting department."

To emphasize the need for asset management, Heeman presents examples of capital overstatement with a general statement that "the typical gap between what the books show on an historical basis and what companies can actually account for on investigation is somewhere in the 10 to 15 percent range, according to many professional appraisers. On a national basis, that would mean that upwards of $80 billion of nonexistent assets are being carried on the books of American business."

Heeman attributes much of this situation to management's concentration of internal controls on operational activities at the expense of fixed-asset control. The resulting discrepan-

cies affect many areas of a business, including pricing decisions, expansion considerations, excessive insurance, taxes, and control of loss through theft.

The main text of *Mechanism Of An Effective Permanent Property Program* has presented a comprehensive outline of the subject. This appendix is directed at the specifics of documentation and control.

Documents: Forms and Flow

An effective capital appropriation request program is dependent on concise and consistent presentation of information required to evaluate, process, and authorize a capital expenditure. This is accomplished through standard

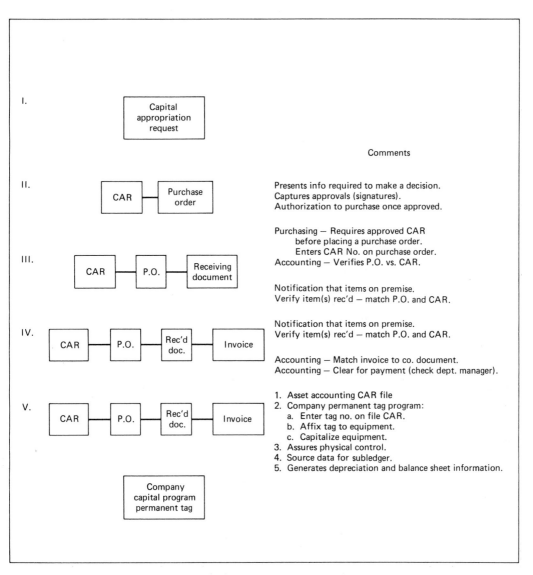

FIGURE 2.   CAR documentation—control.

forms, supplemented by effective procedures. Figure 1A presents a version of a capital appropriation request form. Table 1A shows a form that requires, in this example, a payback calculation. These forms are examples of two of the key sources of information for a CAR program. Their format and number should be tailored to the requirements of the individual firm's CAR program.

With standard forms, forms flow and procedures can be instituted to assure compliance with the program objectives. Table 2A pre-

REQUEST _____

CAR NO. _____   CAPITAL TAG NO. _____

EQUIPMENT REQUESTED:

VENDOR	MODEL NO. & DESCRIPTION	QTY.	UNIT COST	TOTAL COST

Total Value of Equipment Requested — Prime Material

Delivery Date Required _____   Vendor Delivery Quote _____

REASON FOR REQUEST

JUSTIFICATION   FINANCIAL ☐   TECHNICAL ☐   OTHER ☐

PAYBACK _____   EST. USEFUL LIFE (ref. test) _____

SIGNATURES: NAME   DATE   NAME   DATE

DEPT. MANAGER _____   OPERATING V.P. _____

ASSET ACCT. _____   FINANCIAL V.P. _____

DIV. MANAGER _____   PRESIDENT _____

CONTROLLER _____   BOARD OF DIR. _____

FIGURE 1A.   Capital appropriation request.

sents CAR documentation flow that is governed by procedures for approving the capital appropriation request.

The CAR is then submitted to the appropriate cost or plant accountant for review and critique. The accountant must evaluate the CAR content and presentation, and if necessary request additional information to complete the CAR to his satisfaction.

The CAR is presented to the department manager's superior, i.e., division manager. This individual should best be able to evaluate the request and determine if the information presented is complete and satisfactory.

The company property accountant receives the CAR and evaluates it based on company guidelines (i.e., budget). He also checks the company equipment listing to ascertain that equipment similar to that being requested is not at another company location. If identical equipment is located elsewhere in the company, he contacts the responsible person to determine if it is being used or is available in-house; the property accountant submits the CAR for required executive signature as specified by policy based on the value and/or nature of the equipment to be purchased. Authorizations on a CAR verify that all personnel required to approve an addition to capital have reviewed the request and are satisfied with the need for and financial effect of the request.

Documentation Procedure — Control

The capital appropriation request and document procedure establishes the flow of information essential to effective capital controls.

After a capital appropriation request is approved, a CAR number is assigned to the document, the original is kept by the property accountant, and copies are sent to the initiator and purchasing. This action informs the originator that he is authorized to buy the equipment and approves processing by the purchasing department of a pending capital equipment purchase requisition.

When purchasng receives the capital equipment purchase requisition, it identifies the requisition with the appropriate CAR. In generating the purchase order, a copy of which goes to the property accountant, the document will have the appropriate general ledger account, department number, and CAR number. The property accountant matches the purchase order with the CAR as both documents are identified numerically. By comparing the capital appropriation request and the purchase order, discrepancies between equipment authorized for purchase and the equipment actually purchased become immediately apparent. Cost disparities, likewise, become evident by similar comparisons. These comparisons permit followup, explanations, and approval of the differences, if acceptable.

Once equipment is received, a copy of the receiving document is forwarded to the property accountant to notify him that an addition to capital is on the premise. If there is no installation or modification required, the property accountant will tag the equipment with a

Table 1A. Net after tax cash flow

INVESTMENT
NET CASH FLOW
Annual savings
    Labor—production
    Labor—inspection
    Direct materials
        Total savings
    Less operating costs
        Net savings
    Less depreciation
        Savings—profit before tax
    Taxes
        Less investment credit
    Net taxes
    Savings—profit after taxes
        Add depreciation
    Cash flow—annual
    Cash flow—cumulative
    Net cash status (investment less cash flow)
Payback =

Table 2A. CAR documentation flow

SIGNATURE	PURPOSE
Supervisor	Identify need for capital and explain requirement in a manner that will allow for transfer of information to a standard form.
Department Manager	Fill out CAR form based on knowledge of the problem. Use input from knowledgeable sources: supervisor, accountant, and so on.
Cost/Plant Accountant	Must have completed knowledge of the capital being requested. Check math accuracy and evaluate completeness of information being presented. Satisfy himself that the CAR is well presented through his knowledge of the situation being highlighted.
Division Manager	Review the individual requirement requested on the capital application as well as the needs from an overview of the division's current and annual capital requirements and priorities. Prior to final approval, satisfies himself that the CAR is self explanatory to management not having the benefit of being on the scene daily.
Controller	Evaluate reason for CAR and justification from a layman's viewpoint of whether it imparts common sense. Detailed review of financial rationale and validity of data. Of primary interest to the controller are: 1. Payback 2. Cash flow See Table 1A.
Operating VP	Reviews division manager's approval with more knowledge of information of other company activities that may affect the CAR.
Financial VP	Reviews controller's area of evaluation with more knowledge of factors that may affect the CAR: availability of funds, and so on.
President	Total picture in evaluating CAR final approval.
Board of Directors	Required only in unusual circumstances.

PURCHASING

Note that from the division manager through the board of directors, there are minimum dollar amounts that must be projected to be spent that would determine what signature level is required.

---

serialized company equipment tag. The serialized tag number is recorded on the CAR and imputted, with all associated relevant information, to the capital equipment data base. Whenever additional equipment, installation, or modification is required to accomplish the CAR objectives, tagging will not occur until the equipment becomes operational.

Invoices for capital are routed to the property accountant. He compares each invoice with the capital appropriation request file, which includes an authorization (CAR), purchase order, and receiving document. If no discrepancy exists, he copies the invoice for his file and forwards the original for payment. When there is a discrepancy, the reason must be determined and appropriate action—invoice adjustment, approval for payment diffrential, and so on—must be taken. When changes in equipment or cost of equipment occur, documented approvals of changes to the original CAR must be recorded. By enforcing this procedure, a trail exists to enforce withholding requests due to situations such as equipment problems.

Figure 2A (which is the same as Figure 2) is reiterated to emphasize the importance of tracing the CAR documentation flow. It repre-

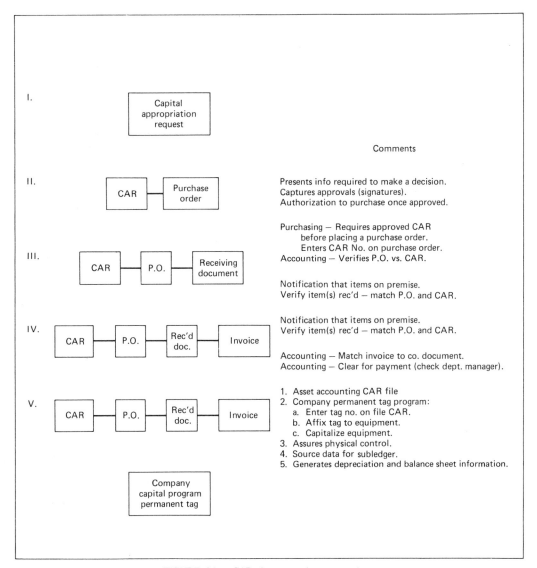

FIGURE 2A.   CAR documentation—control.

sents the development of a capital documentation file containing:

1. Capital appoprriation request.
    a. Equipment description and cost commitment
    b. Required signature approvals
    c. Capital appropriation request number.
    d. Tag number
2. Purchase order
3. Receiving document
4. Invoice
5. Authorized changes from the original CAR.

The capital documentation file centralizes data available for capital program efforts including measurement of project worth, control of capital outlays, post-mortems, and retirements and disposals. It also serves as a verification file for information presented through a firm's data processing capital reporting system.

In summary, the capital appropriations request and associated documentation provide a source of continuous control of activities involving acquisition and capitalization of capital equipment.

Control

Controls required to maintain asset management and integrity are both physical and reporting. They provide the framework for accounting personnel to control property transactions effectively through proper and routine identification, reporting, and physical inventory verification. Assignment of custodial and expense responsibility for property is made to the direct line executive superiors. A company asset accountant assists department managers in implementing physical control over property while maintaining property and depreciation schedules required to achieve the objectives of asset control.

Physical Controls

Equipment items are identified physically by a capital property tag number that is affixed to the equipment or engraved on items that cannot be tagged.

1. Capital Property Tags are serially numbered.
2. Tags are attached to property when capitalized.
3. Rental equipment is identified by a separate series of control numbers and by leased equipment tags.

Tags physically identify the equipment as the firm's property. The serial number on the tag is made part of the permanent property record and identifies the equipment on the company's property schedules and reports.

Departmental control is integral to physical control. An itemized list of company property is prepared by the company asset accountant for distribution to the appropriate department managers. They are required to compare this schedule with items physically present in the department, report, and with the company asset accountant, promptly resolve any discrepancies. When this procedure is followed, the central file of property records reflects the correct location of capital, and the time required for annual physical inventories is minimized.

Annual physical inventories of capital equipment are conducted to verify the existence and location of fixed assets and to effect physical control of property.

The responsibility for the conduct of physical inventories is vested in the controller/manager to assure that all property is inventoried and reports furnished, reconciling the physical inventory to property schedules.

Physical inventories of property should be required whenever 1) there is a change in department responsibility (splitting a department, combining two or more departments, and so on) or 2) the incoming department manager requires it. If the incoming manager accepts the existing list of property as his responsibility, the physical inventory at the time of change may be waived.

Reporting Controls

A central file of property records would be developed from the documentation flow. This file should be updated monthly from information submitted periodically (preferably monthly) by the company property accountant on property transaction schedules, to be used in computing depreciation and the preparation of various data processing schedules on property.

The property schedules prepared by data processing may include:

1. Item Lits: Gross value, reserve, net value
   a. Department/geographic location
   b. Tag number
   c. Equipment code (categories)

2. Additions: As in *a, b,* and *c,* above and in total.
3. Disposals: As in *a, b,* and *c,* above and in total.
4. Depreciation: As in *a, b,* and c, above and in total.
5. Amortization: As in *a, b,* and *c,* above and in total.
6. Transfers to: As in *a, b,* and *c,* above and in total.
7. Transfers from: As in *a, b,* and *c,* above and in total.
8. Special request reports: As in *a, b,* and *c,* above and in total.

Company ledger balances in the property and reserve accounts should be compared periodically (monthly) with the property schedules. Discrepancies are to be investigated and reconciled immediately.

The company asset accountant is responsible for the timely clearance of construction in process to assure that property accounts coincide with property installations and depreciation commences as soon as allowable. It should also be noted that by processing all capital purchased through a construction in process account, the asset accountant will be in a position to capitalize the resource under the correct general ledger capital account number.

Property Transactions

Based on the concepts of CAR and controls developed to this point, a method of handling property transactions is suggested through the remainder of this chapter.

Additions, transfers, and disposals of property are documented on a property transaction schedule and processed in accordance with established due dates. The information on the property schedule is used to update the central file of property records to reflect each type of transaction (additions, transfers, disposals, and so on). It may also be used for all activity on leasehold improvements.

It is essential that journal entries recording property transactions to the general ledger reflect the data reported on tabulated schedules of property transactions.

Additions. The cost of all additions to the property accounts are charged to a capitalization in Process Account as incurred. As soon as possible after an acquisition or completion, the item is tagged and a Property Transaction Schedule prepared. The following data for each addition would be entered:

1. Capital tag number or leased number tag for rental equipment.
2. Account number, i.e., general ledger account number
3. Plant code, department number and geographic location
4. Asset code
5. Acquisition date
6. Year's depreciation (or amortization). This is the life in years for depreciation or amortization purposes. Leasehold improvements are not amortized beyond the life of the lease.
7. Asset category code. To identify and group assets by type against a listing of appropriate useful lives.
8. Qualify for investment tax credit. The company asset accountant is responsible for identifying items that qualify for investment tax credit.
9. Identification. A description of the item, manufacturer's serial and model numbers, and company appropriation request.

Restorations. The costs of restoration are added to the book value of the original asset. Capitalization is effected through submission of a property transaction schedule. The depreciation method and tag number assigned to the restored asset corresponds to that of the original item. The proper current guideline life for tax and accounting purposes is assigned as if the items were new.

Late Charges or Credits. Late charges or credits to an asset included in the company's property records are processed on a property transaction schedule. Only changes greater than a predetermined amount are submitted for capitalization following initial capitalization of the original item.

The data center combines late charges or credits with the original item in the file of property records. Depreciation methods and estimated useful life assigned for investment

tax credit purposes are the same as for the original item and run from the initial capitalization date.

Transfers. Whenever a property item is to be moved from the department to which it is charged, the department manager initiating the move prepares a company property transfer ticket (Figure 3A) to authorize the move in order to maintain physical control. The timely

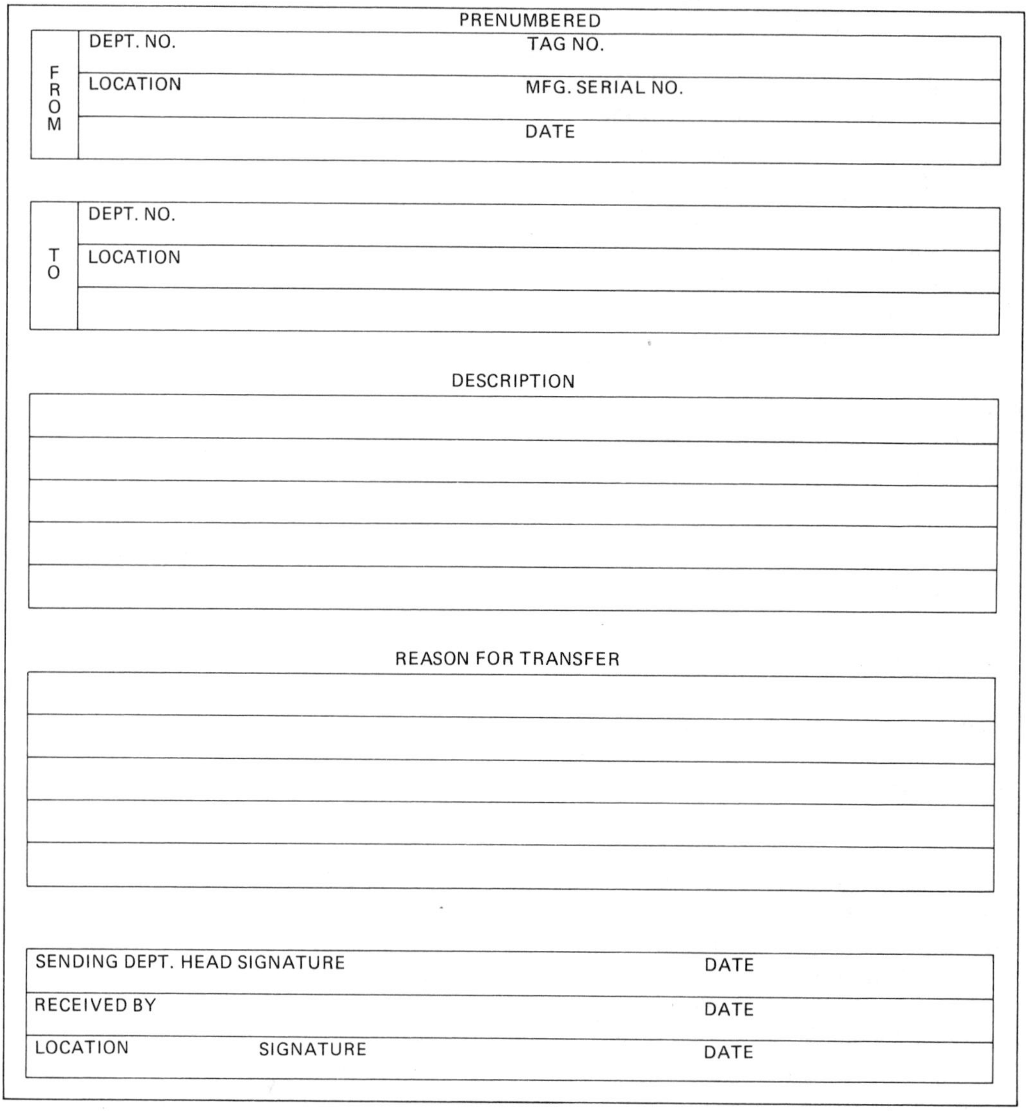

PRENUMBERED

FROM	DEPT. NO.	TAG NO.
	LOCATION	MFG. SERIAL NO.
		DATE

TO	DEPT. NO.	
	LOCATION	

DESCRIPTION

REASON FOR TRANSFER

SENDING DEPT. HEAD SIGNATURE		DATE
RECEIVED BY		DATE
LOCATION	SIGNATURE	DATE

FIGURE 3A. Property transfer ticket.

processing of transfer tickets is the responsibility of the company asset accountant.

Suggest that the property transfer ticket be a four-copy form, completed by the transferring department to show the following:

1. Date of transfer
2. Capital tag number
3. Description of item (including manufacturer's serial and model numbers)
4. From: department number, geographic code
5. To: department number, geographic code
6. Reason (transfer, repair, loan, and so on)
7. Department manager authorization.

Distribution of the four-copy form should be as follows:

1. Copy #1 attached to the equipment, where it remains until the transfer is completed.
2. Copy #2 retained by the transferring department.
3. Copies #3 and #4 are given to the company asset accountant who distributes copy #3 to the "receiving" department. He verifies receipt of the asset, signs the ticket to acknowledge receipt and returns it to the company asset accountant for matching with copy #4 previously retained.

The company asset accountant further documents and reports transfers through the preparation of the property transaction schedule.

All transfers of property are priced at net book value even when the remaining book value of the transferred asset is zero.

Transfers of leased equipment are also documented by use of property transfer tickets. In addition, the company asset accountant is responsible for notifying the purchasing department and accounts Payable of the transfer. These departments change their records to reflect the transfer to effect accuracy in their activities.

Disposals. Disposals of all property except for leasehold improvements, equipment leased to others, and real estate should be documented on a form such as an asset disposal authorization (Figure 4A).

The department manager responsible for the property initiates the request that is forwarded to the company asset accountant for approval prior to the movement of the asset.

After appropriate approvals are obtained on the facility disposal authorization the disposal may be effected. A property transaction schedule is completed to show the following: capital tag number, account number, department number/geographic location, and disposal code number, and proceeds.

Disposal codes, used to identify the various types of property for tax purposes are as follows:

CODE	TYPE OF DISPOSAL
1	Sold
2	Scrapped
3	Transferred to inventory—Surplus.
4	Transferred to capitalization in process—trade in.
5	Transferred to finished goods.
6	Contributions.

All entries to departmental expense/gain or loss on property disposals are based on monthly disposals prepared from a central file. Cumulative amounts must agree with the year-to-date amount shown on the general ledger.

Surplus, Scrap, and Idle Equipment. Each of the categories of equipment under this heading require detailed definition. Sign-off and transfer procedures, storage requirements, and dollar authorizations must be complied with in conjunction with the company's scrap and salvage procedures. These group's activities are measured on numerous variables including reclaimed products, dollars received for scrap, and so on.

The complexities of scrap and salvage will not be dealt with in this chapter.

DATE	DEPT.	LOCATION	COMPANY PROPERTY ACCOUNTANT		
ITEM DESCRIPTION			TAG NO.	ORIGINAL COST	BOOK VALUE
			CAP. DATE	RECOMMENDED ACTION — SURPLUS — SCRAP —— OTHER	
REASON FOR DISPOSAL					

APPROVALS

DEPARTMENT		FINANCIAL		EXECUTIVE	
		PLANT/COST. ACCT.	DATE	OPERATING V.P.	DATE
DEPT. MANAGER	DATE	CO. ASSET ACCT.	DATE	FINANCIAL V.P.	DATE
DIV. MANAGER	DATE	CONTROLLER	DATE	PRESIDENT	DATE

DISPOSING AUTHORITY

PURCHASER	EST. WORTH	PROCEEDS OR SALVAGE	PROCEEDS RECEIVED BY
			——— Cash ——— Check ——— Money Order

BIDS OBTAINED FROM (NAMES & ADDRESS)
1.
2.
3.

FINAL DISPOSITION
1. Sold   4. To finished goods
2. Scrapped   5. Traded
3. To inventory surplus   6. Contribution

FIGURE 4A. Facility disposal authorization.

Other. Design of a capital equipment reporting system requires collection of data (i.e., indices, latest cost, and so on) and a data base that will generate replacement cost information. This is of importance because of SEC replacement cost reporting requirements under ASR 190.

Development of capital equipment reports to complement operational programs that are directed at capacity planning. An example would be to integrate capital equipment (operational) data with a sophisticated MRP (material requirements planning) program that is capable of projecting future capacity requirements.

Finally, integrate capital equipment reporting with the firm's security program.

Conclusion

Through capture of an approved CAR and all documents generated from it, a file is built that contains all historical data from request to physical identification of the capital. This file ties the CAR activity to the company's physical control program through the *permanent capital tag*. Once so identified, the company's internal procedures regarding responsibility and acceptance of equipment, depreciation schedule and charges, documentation of movement, physical inventories, and other activities through disposal, scrap, and salvage can be monitored and controlled.

An effective capital program will result from proper integration of capital appropriation request and physical control programs with management's involvement in enforcing discipline required to achieve the benefits described for the company's asset control. These benefits are primarily improved accounting/reporting accuracy and reduction of the "asset gap" as described by A. Howard Heeman.

REFERENCES

1. Joel Dean, "Measuring the Productivity of Capital", *Harvard Business Review*, Jan.–Feb., 1954.
2. Ezra Solomon, *The Theory of Financial Management*, Columbia University Press, New York, 1967.
3. A. Howard Heeman, "Rediscovering Asset Management", *Quality*, June 1979.

SECTION VI
ASSURING PRODUCT QUALITY

26
Quality Management

John T. Hagan
Director of Quality Management
International Telephone and
Telephone Corporation

The most important goal of quality management is product quality improvement. The quality function is to assure that quality standards do not get eroded each time there are excessive pressures. In short, quality management must "tell it like it is."

Like the business plan itself, effective use of the quality management function can improve overall business performance and minimize exposure to unexpected and costly failures. Quality, like schedule and cost, is an important ingredient for each company operation. Quality management acts as a deterrent against product failure and also as a catalyst for improvement in each operating area. Through its own unique features and their subsequent execution, Quality management will enhance the value of the business plan and its implementation.

THE TWOFOLD FUNCTION OF QUALITY MANAGEMENT

Quality Management is a twofold function. First, it serves to provide protection from shipping products that will cause customer problems through its role as manager of product acceptance. This role begins with the marketing specification and continues through product design, design qualification testing, manufacturing planning, purchasing of supplies, production, and field operations, as applicable. It involves experience-based contributions to marketing, design engineering, purchasing, and manufacturing and the planning and conduct of necessary inspections and tests for each phase. Its objective is to assure satisfactory completion of each task and readiness for continuance into the next phase of operations.

The second function of quality management is to utilize the results of all product acceptance measurements as a measure of and contributor to overall performance through its role as manager of quality improvement. This role begins with the collection and analysis of all inspection and test data, continues through the clear identification of major product problems, and concludes with the permanent solution of these problems for current production and their prevention in new product developments. Within this concept, there are many opportunities for contributions to business growth and profits. The "obvious" problems in industry always receive management atten-

311

tion but there is a next level of major problems that can easily become a tolerated and hidden cost of doing business unless there is a function dedicated to permanent corrective action.

IDENTIFYING PRODUCT DEFICIENCIES AND SUGGESTING SOLUTIONS

The quality management function is not just another organization to help keep the product moving. There are plenty of people being paid for just that purpose. While quality management is expected to identify and contribute to the solution of problems, they are not responsible for solutions. If quality management is held accountable for problem solutions, or for product rejections and schedule delays, the shoe is on the wrong foot. This simply provides a crutch to the responsible organizations that, in turn, guarantee that they will never improve. They won't have to.

The quality manager needs to be a forceful and capable executive, conversant with all other executive functions. He can help the company face all issues squarely by being free to evaluate prime functions against their established standards of performance and assuring that the standards don't get eroded each time there are excessive pressures. His most important personal function is to "tell it like it is" so that a company can profit from its ongoing experience and never be condemned to repeat mistakes. His constant goal is quality improvement: "No matter where we are today in performance, we can do better tomorrow—if we are willing to learn from our experience."

THREE DETERRENTS TO EFFECTIVE QUALITY MANAGEMENT

Historically, there have been three deterrents to the effective utilization of the quality management function. The first is that too many managements are convinced that the "unexpected problems" that seriously affect this year's profits could *not* have been avoided. In a sense, they feel victimized as though by an unnatural occurrence. The second deterrent is that not enough managements understand and want to utilize a professional quality management function. They still have old-fashioned views of quality management as an inspection function. The third deterrent is the quality management profession itself, which has failed to convince American industry of its inherent value.

One well-known example of a costly, unexpected problem is the nuclear incident at Three Mile Island in Harrisburg, Pennsylvania in 1979. The Kemeny Report points out that the magnitude of the problem that developed could have been prevented. This incident is an affirmation of management's biggest mistake in the area of quality: assuming that things will actually happen according to the management plan. Management conveniently fails to realize that pressure on schedule and costs often leads to shortcuts that insidiously weaken the end results but remain hidden until problems develop, sometimes months or years later. Then they don't learn from the experience because the ultimate solution is usually replacement of the manager who "failed."

It seems anathema to management to have to pay for people to check the work of others just to be sure their plan is being implemented properly. In this regard, they can be very naive. They do not even recognize, let alone understand, the role of quality management as one of measuring performance and identifying improvement needs. The concept is too difficult to be accepted because each manager thinks he knows what he needs. The fact that most managers are not trained in quality systems leaves them free to decide for themselves. At best, some may see quality management as being necessary to help with today's shipping problems. At worst, they may see no need at all.

The quality profession has not fared too well, either. The basic concepts of statistical quality control, which were developed to optimize the mass-production process, are still struggling for acceptance—except by the Japanese, who have adopted them and used them beneficially in their post-World War II economic resurgence. The basic concept of quality management has never really been sold in the US. The quality managers of America have failed to provide the leadership required to make quality equal to schedule and cost. They have also failed as salesmen for quality and as educators of American management.

Most major setbacks to American industry are related to "quality of performance." The most notorious can be read about in the papers and business journals. Product recalls and project delays are no longer uncommon. Some setbacks are created by dissatisfied customers acting through warranty and product liability claims or by simply diminishing their orders. Other more pronounced, setbacks can be attributed to a miscalculation of an organization's ability to perform according to its promises, either internally to the general manager or externally to the customer.

Miscalculation of an organization's ability to perform is a problem that often ends up as an excuse for failure. Perhaps, by way of explanation, an overoptimistic view of past successes unwittingly leads to a credibility gap as related to actual performance. This can occur when actual performance is only measured by cost and schedule. When quality is not an integral part of the performance equation, expected schedules and cost may not be possible except at the expense of quality. Pressure to achieve the impossible will then cause risks to be taken that might not be considered if quality were part of the equation. Then an insidious problem begins. Looking at schedule and cost only is like looking at beauty that is skin-deep. It can be a trap.

All business leaders preach common sense. Why then do managers make decisions that in the light of exposed problems look like bad common sense? More often than not, it is because of pressures created by the sacredness of the numbers (cost and schedule). People feel fear when they do not have the answers that management wants. This makes them vulnerable to pressure. When this happens, it is more likely that data are generated to support the boss's position or desire rather than the other way around—a position taken from an honest evaluation of data. Then there are those bosses who deliberately carry things too far by worshipping at the shrine of expediency. The seeds of serious miscalculations are germinated by unwarranted pressures.

SETTING THE STAGE FOR EFFECTIVE QUALITY MANAGEMENT

Quality management is a function that has been developed, reconciled, and nurtured to combat the kind of setbacks to American industry that are related to quality of performance. Quality management can prevent or at least minimize the impact of poor performance and management miscalculations. Quality management is ready made for this real-life problem situation and offers additional benefits that no company should be without. Quality management can provide industry with a constant breath of fresh air based on the concept that, "If you plan to be honest, you don't need much preparation."

To ensure effective implementation of a quality management system, the president or general manager should set the stage by issuing a strong policy and making a clear personal commitment to his staff regarding its implementation. The policy should state that the company quality goal is genuine customer satisfaction and that each function is responsible for the quality of their work as it relates to the establishment of and conformance to product quality requirements and operating procedures. It should also state that it is the responsibility of quality management to measure performance against this responsibility.

The quality manager, for his part, can then be free to evaluate overall performance and influence its improvement through formal actions with other functions. Management will come to full recognition of the debilitating effect of grey areas of performance on the long-range health of the company and the genuine need for management standards of quality performance, in addition to the obvious standards of schedule and cost. Forceful pursuit of performance improvement will also make a positive contribution to another of industry's greatest challenges, the underdevelopment and underutilization of its most valuable resource, its young managers and other professional help. Quality management will help them to make a transition from today's level of quality performance or tolerance to the level of performance desired or needed to beat the competition.

A THOROUGH EVALUATION OF QUALITY NEEDS

Business planning time is an ideal time to look at the quality management needs of a company. It is a time when the growing quality reputation and competitive strength of the Japanese may come into sharp focus. The tremendous impact in dollars and reputation that product liabilities and recall programs are causing is another important factor to be considered. On the positive side, the opportunity to apply the principles of quality management to the administrative areas of the business—or to the entire service industry—could be an important consideration. If necessary quality management commitments cannot be justified at business planning times, they will be infinitely more difficult and more costly later on.

One last benefit of quality management can be seen in the relationship of business and society. In the social environment of the 1980s, an improved business financial position

through better product or service quality should sit pretty well with both the general public and the board of directors.

The role of quality management in business planning will be treated as it relates to major segments of the business plan.

QUALITY MANAGEMENT ENHANCING THE MARKETING PLAN

The effect of quality management on the marketing plan and strategy can be truly enhancing or it can be somewhere between slightly harmful to devastating. History has proven many times over that in good times and bad, the product with a reputation for quality will always sell. On the other hand, when products have a tarnished reputation, they take up an inordinate amount of marketing's energy and add to the difficulty of developing and keeping good salesmen. Any plan to increase market share cannot be successful without a concurrent plan to maintain or improve product quality. From a marketing viewpoint, then, it is important that quality management become an integral part of the company business plan and marketing's position should be one of support. Marketing can view quality management as an additional (free) resource to help them achieve their goals and objectives.

More specifically, marketing needs the involvement of quality management in several areas of activity, including product specifications, customer contracts, advertising literature, user documents, returned goods, field repairs, complaint handling, and distribution system. From a quality management point of view, it is also important that marketing establishes its responsibility clearly in the design and manufacturing phases of product development and life.

In preparing the initial definition (specification) and product plan for a new or revised product to be considered by a company, marketing always faces the danger that some important ingredient will be overlooked or miscalculated that would affect the real picture significantly, and possibly the decision to proceed, at this early stage. Possibilities range from inaccurately perceiving the needs and desires of the marketplace to a misconception about what a newly available supplier product or material can actually do. Also included will be failure to recognize design, processing, or environmental performance limitations. The most important omission of all would be failure to learn from your own detailed experience.

KNOWLEDGE OF CUSTOMER COMPLAINTS AND MANUFACTURING PROBLEMS

Normally, to minimize the risks inherent with early new product commitments, companies will almost always involve design engineering, manufacturing, and finance with marketing in the initial and all subsequent product planning activities. They will not normally involve quality management, who has the potential to come armed with the following major contributions:

1. Knowledge of past customer complaint patterns and problems, including major warranty and liability experience
2. Knowledge of in-house design and manufacturing problems
3. Knowledge of realistic new product introductory defect rates (scrap and rework costs) to prevent the initial profit and loss estimates from becoming overly optimistic

The difference between the knowledge presented by quality management and the others is that quality management is not emotionally involved and can, therefore, be more objective from an overall company point of view. This can be an important difference in any marginal situation.

Quality management can also be counted on to add important new questions to the planning agenda:

1. Are there any new or anticipated changes to government regulations and industry standards that may affect the design, manufacture, or use of these new products?
2. Has marketing carefully considered all possible uses, misuses, third-party applications, and so on, that could cause a customer problem with this product, most specifically in situations that could lead to personal injury or property damage?

Failure to consider any of the items described as potential contributions to the initial product plan by quality management can lead to a serious miscalculation of the new product's true potential to the future business of the company. While most businesses do not have many total disasters with new products, many of them have products that never seem to reach the full potential or vision that marketing originally had for them. Often, this is because they were conceived more in hope than in facts and there was no time or plan for corrective action. A wise marketing operation looks at history in the true light of these observations and makes certain that the quality management function gets the opportunity to help prevent any repeat of such history, most of which would become a reflection of poor marketing.

Winning the big contracts is an important part of any marketing strategy but sometimes the excitement of the win can serve to camouflage some of the small print in the contract, particularly as it might apply to product and process quality requirements. Problems created by such oversights can be costly but are not as likely to happen when a contracts administration function exists in the company organization. Contracts administration will normally involve most other functions, including quality management, in complete and thorough reviews of all contract details prior to commitment. In the absence of a contracts administration function, quality management can serve as a reliable substitute at least in the area of product requirements. Their qualification for this role comes from their need to "know the details" prior to final acceptance of product for delivery to the customer.

When preparing advertising literature, it is always good to put your best foot forward. Sometimes we have a tendency to exaggerate a bit when we present our best side. In advertising, we even pay people to help us stretch the point. No one would ever think of accusing a marketing department of not having good intentions in this regard. In fact, their motives are always in the right direction and, if the products listed never become involved in a problem, no harm will ever come. However, this is not always the case. Products do become involved with problems and when they do, everything about them is examined in fine detail. All possible misrepresentations will work against a company in the hands of its accusers.

The simplest and best way to prevent the problem of unintended "express warranties" and other problems with advertisements, catalogs, and sales brochures is to require a formal review by design engineering, quality management, and legal prior to issue. Design engineering should verify the technical content; Quality management the accuracy of quality characteristics and the overall clarity of presentation from the user viewpoint; and legal the proper presentation of liability commitments and transfers. As a group, all involved functions should address the need for and adequate inclusion of necessary cautions or warnings against improper use or application of product. This is an absolute necessity for liability protection when all product risks cannot be eliminated in design and manufacture.

QUALITY CONSIDERATIONS IMPORTANT IN PRODUCT LIABILITY PREVENTION

Even more important from a product liability prevention point of view is the content of user documents, which include all printed packaging materials and installation, operation and maintenance instructions, or manuals. These should be thoroughly reviewed by design engineering, quality management and legal if prepared by marketing or by marketing, quality management and legal if prepared by design engineering. Not only are cautions and warnings of paramount concern but also when telling a potential user about the product, assumptions must not be made. You cannot assume that the user has the skill level, training, or even the common sense necessary to use the product properly. Of course, there is a limit to how far one must go in this regard but it is better to be nearer the "idiot-proof" end than the other.

In some industries, customer service is an independent and major part of the business. When this is not so, you can almost always find customer service close to the heart of marketing. As a matter of fact, marketing personnel are often very protective of "their" customers—sometimes at the expense of overall business interests. By this, it is meant that some customer-caused and company-caused problems are handled completely by marketing and inadvertently may not get exposed for analysis and corrective action. It is not that marketing is against corrective action, it's just that their concern and enthusiasm for immediate customer satisfaction outweighs and completely overrides any other consideration. When this happens, even at times as a joint marketing/engineering venture, the net results are sometimes seen as slowly rising warranty costs, which almost always reflects more against manufacturing than its true cause.

One easy way to avoid the problem just described is to require a more significant role, preferably one of leadership, for quality management in the area of customer service. There is no substitution and resolution of product quality problems. The promotion of customer satisfaction should never be relegated to a system in which the involvement of too many company groups permits the mishandling of problems or the misinterpretation of responsibility. In industries where the customer is heavily involved (i.e., where resident or itinerant customer inspectors are involved with product acceptance), quality management is automatically involved. That is, quality management is given full responsibility for customer inspection liaison and ultimate acceptance of product. Why should it be any different with potential product problems after acceptance?

QUALITY FUNCTION WELL QUALIFIED TO SERVICE CUSTOMER PRODUCT PROBLEMS

With the experience of inspection and test, planned and conducted throughout each phase of product development, and the identification and resolution of problems along the way, quality management is eminently qualified to service customers where the possibility of a product problem exists. It is also an advantage to overall company interests that the provider of such service does not design, manufacture, or sell products—that is, does not have a vested interest. Marketing would do well to recognize the value and advantages of quality management operating on their behalf in this area and plan their actions accordingly. They might also be advised to involve quality management in programs to evaluate competitors' products.

Once established in a leadership role for customer service, quality management would be expected to establish and administer procedures for the handling of returned goods, field repairs, and customer complaints. In developing these procedures, the importance of maintaining direct customer communications through sales personnel must be preserved. Sales remains the point of contact but, when a problem is involved or suspected, sales initiates a documented flow of actions through quality management and subsequently through others as needed. Required field repairs would be organized utilizing qualified personnel from any area. Products to be returned would always be authorized through sales, evaluated by quality management, repaired or replaced,

and charged according to the responsibility established.

The handling of complaints is a very special and important procedure for any company. The only alternative to a clear policy to service customers' complaints is a gradual loss of business. Complaint handling should be swift and courteous. It should provide a fair settlement of claims. Careful handling of complaints will build loyal support for the company. In some cases, the complaint may be the tip of an iceberg in terms of a developing major problem. Swift action will go a long way towards minimizing the total cost of such problems. In addition to hardware problems, complaints also involve delivery problems, pricing mistakes, and other errors concerning items such as quantity, size, color, and so on. All are important. All require not only a settlement but some internal corrective action. Quality management should plan for and provide summary reports of results in the broad area of customer service. The credibility of marketing's business plan strategy will depend to some extent on the degree of progress in this area.

When distributors or representatives are an essential part of the business, quality management can often be called upon to provide some useful services. They can provide a monitoring or training service for necessary assembly operations, safety precautions, liability prevention, complaint handlings, warranty procedures, and problem communications. If the distribution system involves purchasing additional items for resale, quality management can provide a supplier quality control service. Sometimes they provide or assist in customer training programs. Whatever is needed by way of support from quality management should be considered carefully and built into the business plan.

In summary, the role of quality management in the marketing plan should be:

1. A clearly defined, contributing role for all new product developments and introductions.

2. Established responsibility and adequate budget for complaint handling, returned goods control, field repairs, and required service to distribution system.
3. Assurance of adequate control of customer contracts, sales literature, and user documents.

Proper utilization of the quality management function by marketing will make the plan more realistic, as opposed to optimistic, and it will assure a minimum of delay in new product introductions and a maximum possible improvement in customer satisfaction and market share.

QUALITY MANAGEMENT'S ROLE IN PRODUCT DESIGN AND DEVELOPMENT

If marketing is the lifeblood of a business, design engineering must provide the red corpuscles to give the blood its vitality. Without a steady flow of new product developments and applications, a company will be hard pressed to sustain any kind of growth pattern. The richness of the growth, however, will depend to a large degree on the "quality of design." That is, it will depend on the degree to which a product, manufactured in conformance to the design, truly satisfies the expectations of the customer. When a product design is marginal, it can have a devastating effect on product profit plans, whereas a product that is well designed can enhance its own reputation and profit potential.

Quality management has an important role to play during the design phase of product development. This role is aimed entirely at perfecting the design effort and preventing outright design deficiencies or errors that can be costly. They fulfill this objective through active participation in formal design reviews and qualification testing, and in providing service for the control of supplies, technical workmanship, equipment calibration, and configuration control. The extent to which quality

management's support is utilized may spell the difference between a mediocre and an outstanding design. It should be important, then, from an overall company viewpoint, that quality management be committed within the framework of the business plan to provide necessary design support.

Human nature is such that most chief engineers would not normally recognize the need for quality management help, or most other help, in perfecting their designs. Unfortunately, the kind of help that can be supplied by quality management is often seen in a negative and demeaning, rather than a constructive light. And yet, in the true light of less-than-satisfactory past designs, excess design costs, schedule delays because of design problems, and excessive design engineering assistance during the manufacturing phase, the history of industry says there is a universal opportunity for improvement. The progressive chief engineer who recognizes these facts will welcome and demand quality management involvement in the design effort.

PRODUCT QUALIFICATION TESTING— A GOOD STARTING POINT

A good starting point for discussion is product qualification testing, because this is an activity that may require a significant piece of the design manufacturing budget and verifies overall design accomplishment. Just like a final acceptance test is designed to verify that all manufacturing operations have been accomplished prior to shipment, a qualification test is intended to verify that all design actions have been successfully accomplished prior to the release of a product for full production. The business value of qualification testing is simply that the problems it causes to be discovered and resolved would be much more costly if not discovered until the manufacturing phase and worse yet, if not discovered until use by customers.

More specifically, qualification testing is the formal conduct of a series of tests on prototype or pilot run products, manufactured with production tooling, to provide assurance that the product as designed conforms to every one of its detail requirements. Requirements normally include the initial product specification (marketing- or customer-imposed), engineering drawings and specifications (design), and manufacturing process specifications that are an integral part of the design. In more detail, a typical qualification test program will include the following specific activities:

1. Inspection verification of qualification test samples for conformance to workmanship standards and complete design description
2. Verification of design configuration control
3. Functional testing to verify product performance under normal (ambient) conditions
4. Functional testing to verify product performance within specified environmental limits (environmental tests)
5. Special tests to verify the achievement of product safety requirements and, as applicable, reliability and maintainability requirements
6. Inspection and test to verify a product's ability to withstand specified transport and storage conditions.

In some companies, quality management is called upon to conduct the product qualification test program, with troubleshooting analysis support from design engineering. In others, the quality management role is one of monitoring and support to design engineering, including the documentation of results and preparation of the qualification test report. Regardless of role, the business plan should contain the plans, schedule, and budget for necessary qualification tests.

When specific customer contracts require qualification testing, the costs are usually recovered. For most commercial operations, however, product qualification cost is just another one-time cost to be spread over the life of a product. If the financial predictions for a new product are too marginal to allow the cost of proper qualification testing, the product is not viable. No poor profit situation has ever been saved by inadequate testing.

Once a product has been qualified, the need to requalify by repeating some or all of the qualification tests should be reviewed for each product year and after any major design change. The main reason for periodic requalification is that manufactured products usually do not continue to be identical to those that passed the qualification test. Many inconspicuous changes enter into supplies, processes, and the way that products are fabricated. These subtle changes may collectively cause a noticeable change in product performance in the future. The extent to which this can happen and cause a problem will vary widely for different product lines. Each company should know its own history in this regard and establish a plan, schedule, and budget for product requalification each year.

While the basic purpose of qualification testing is to provide assurance that all is right with the design of a product, actual practice at times reveals major weaknesses. Instead of minor design refinements, some programs are actually thrown into a tailspin as a result of major qualification test failures. One proven way to avoid such a costly experience and to maximize assurance of design success is the effective use of formal design reviews. Design reviews relate to qualification testing like in-process inspection and test relates to final acceptance of products. If you wait until final test to learn how good your product is, you have waited too long. Final test should verify that in-process controls are working; qualification test should verify that periodic design reviews have contributed to the accomplishment of a successful design.

The purpose and scope of a design review program is to establish a requirement for periodic reviews of design progress to assure 1) that all pertinent and significant company experience, both positive and negative, is being utilized; 2) that each company function that can contribute to the design development is being utilized sufficiently and in a timely manner throughout each phase of the design effort; 3) that all necessary disciplines and detailed coordination between design engineering and other functions are properly defined and being accomplished in acceptable time sequence; and 4) that the end results (a design that meets product cost and performance requirements) is being assessed continuously. The overall goal of design review is to achieve maximum design maturity and product value within the actual cost and schedule limitations that are imposed. Design engineering is required to involve and coordinate other functions in the design accomplishment.

DESIGN REVIEW OBJECTIVES

Design reviews should start with the original design concept, as an introduction from design engineering to the other involved functions, and continue until a complete product design review serves to release the design for qualification test samples (prototypes or pilot run). Within this framework, specific design review meetings are planned and scheduled. Within these meetings, the following specific design review objectives are considered:

1. To ensure maximum compliance with all product or contract technical requirements; and to control necessary specification changes or waivers
2. To ensure the early identification and achievement of reliability, maintainability, and product safety requirements or objectives; and to control technical tradeoffs from the viewpoint of optimization of program requirements and cost
3. To ensure successful design through the early identification of critical or new processes, materials, components, and testing or measurement requirements; and to ensure the involvement of those functions that will be required to develop or acquire new and improved capabilities
4. To ensure optimim setting of electrical

and mechanical tolerances consistent with required product performance, interchangeability requirements, and available manufacturing economies; and to identify critical parameters for mandatory inclusion in manufacturing, inspection, and test plans
5. To ensure the inclusion and control of the above objectives in any necessary subcontracts and the planning necessary for the timely integration of such items into end item equipment
6. To ensure the achievement of cost targets through the maximum use of existing or standard designs, tooling, materials, and manufacturing processes
7. To ensure the satisfaction of all internal and contractual data requirements within the bounds of schedule and cost constraints
8. To ensure a continuity of communication between functional areas throughout the design phase of product development.

If applicable design review efforts are planned, scheduled, and budgeted for all new product designs, qualification testing can be entered with a high degree of confidence. Major failures or surprises will be limited to state-of-the-art conditions, where prior knowledge is nonexistent. Overall design costs will have been minimized and the entire design effort will have been more effectively managed. There is no better way to start a production commitment.

While design reviews and qualification testing may offer a higher technical challenge, other quality management services to design engineering are equally as important. Making sure that engineering test and measurement equipment is calibrated, for example, will prevent the kind of problem that can be truly insidious. Consider what might happen if some key design decisions were based on inaccurate data. Production units could end up being biased towards one performance limit, making an entire lot appear marginal or, worse yet, the lot could be off the established performance requirement, resulting in false rejections. This kind of situation can be prevented by establishing the requirement for and planning to have all engineering equipment periodically checked against measurement standards that are traceable to the National Bureau of Standards.

In carrying out the day-to-day tasks of the typical design engineer, there can be considerable involvement with supplier parts, materials, and services and the services of laboratory and model shop technicians. It is normal for the design engineer to expect and trust that all such services or supplies will conform to the requirements established. He will not normally do much checking. When errors do occur, they will cause a discrepancy between what the designer describes in his notebook or preliminary drawings for the model and what actually exists. This type of error will almost always be difficult and costly to uncover but can be prevented easily with the utilization of inspection services planned for and provided by quality management.

Utilization of inspection services during the design phase can also be beneficial from the standpoint of configuration control. It is essential to the management of any product through its manufacturing, sales, and use phases that actual product configuration (change level) be identified and verified against product documentation at time of release to production and after each design change. Without such knowledge, some product problems could not be effectively identified and managed and product costs could not be tracked accurately. Ideally, configuration verification starts with the design documentation for prototype or pilot run models and continues through the entire life of a product. Inspection services during the design phase are ideally suited to support this need.

In addition to the stated role of quality management, design engineering should also consider other quality control functions as an integral part of their business planning effort. Design checking, for example, is an important

internal engineering control function applied to the drawing system to assure conformance to drafting procedures or policy and to prevent obvious drawing errors. Engineering support to manufacturing can be a significant effort in some companies. This can include management of change control board activities, participation in material review decisions, and liaison in support of problem identification and resolution. (These will be discussed more thoroughly in the Manufacturing section.) As required, commitments and budgets should be established.

MONITORING COST REDUCTION DESIGN CHANGES

Engineering will almost always be involved in cost reduction efforts for ongoing products. From a quality management viewpoint, caution should be exercised to ensure that all cost-reduction design changes be checked out thoroughly to be certain that the product will still perform to all requirements, especially environmental and manufacturing requirements. There is already too much sad history where cost-reduction changes, especially substitute parts or materials, ended up actually costing more in manufacturing or causing unexpected customer problems. A strong quality management role in the cost reduction program will prevent such mistakes from happening.

In summary, the impact of quality management in the design engineering Plan should be:

1. Schedule and budget for design reviews and qualification testing with a clearly defined role for quality management
2. Inspection and calibration services identified and included
3. Internal quality control responsibilities established and budgeted.

Proper utilization of the quality management function by design engineering will make their plan more realistic, as opposed to optimistic, and it will assure a minimum of design problems or marginal designs in manufactured products.

BEYOND MANUFACTURING INSPECTION PROCEDURES IN QUALITY MANAGEMENT

The quality management function has traditionally been associated with the manufacturing phase of product-oriented companies. It is here that most executives expect to find a quality function. More specifically, they envision some product inspections taking place mostly to prevent major problems from occurring in the field. In actuality, the role of quality management in the manufacturing phase, to be effective at all, must be much broader than a simple inspection program.

The overall aim of the quality management effort in manufacturing is the perfecting of the manufacturing process and the prevention of manufacturing deficiencies or errors that would reduce customer satisfaction or increase manufacturing costs. While it is not traditionally thought that quality management has such a broad and noble purpose in manufacturing, both the need and the opportunity exist in the world of industry. Quality management should start with the acquisition of equipment, continue through the purchasing and industrial engineering efforts, and include the training of employees. The extent to which quality management's support is utilized may spell the difference between a mediocre and an outstanding manufacturing effort. It should be important, then, from an overall company viewpoint, that quality management be committed within the framework of the business plan to provide necessary manufacturing support.

Excessive demands for schedule performance leave no room for a constructive attitude towards the contribution of quality management in the perfecting of the manufacturing process. In fact, the role of quality management is all too often looked upon as a negative contributor to schedule performance.

"Quality problems" are schedule-stoppers. And yet the prime objective of quality management is the manufacturing process, the prevention of product problems, is one of the best possible ways to assure schedule and productivity performance. The manufacturing manager who recognizes this truth will welcome and demand quality management involvement in the planning and execution of the manufacturing effort.

QUALITY PLANNING AT THE PLANNING PHASE OF NEW PRODUCTS

A good starting point for discussion is the planning phase for manufacture of a new product. As the plant layout, product flow, and manufacturing methods are being developed, clearly established plans for product inspection and test (product acceptance) should be developed concurrently. Where to inspect in the manufacturing process is an economic decision, a tradeoff between the higher cost of finding defects late in the process and the cost of additional inspections early in the process. The worst plan of all is *not* to think about what is likely to go wrong with products until just before you are ready to ship them. Those who do not learn from this kind of experience are doomed to repeat it.

QUALITY AS AN INTEGRAL PART OF THE MANUFACTURING PLAN

Inherent with the development of a product maufacturing plan, therefore, must be the establishment of specific plans for product acceptance—specific points within the manufacturing process where clearly defined inspections and tests will be performed. How much acceptance activity is needed depends upon the likelihood for error and the individual cost of foreseeable defect types. The amount of product acceptance needed is a dynamic affair—higher in the beginning of a new product before all the bugs or problems are discovered, lower as improved performance (fewer defects) is achieved. Even a 100% test program can be reduced in cost by varying the degree of testing for each parameter. The manufacturing manager should be in agreement with the product acceptance plan as conceived and view it as an asset to measure manufacturing performance and help it be improved.

PRODUCT ACCEPTANCE PLANS IN THE FABRICATION AND PROCESSING AREAS

Some areas of manufacturing do not change significantly with changing products. These are the fabrication and processing areas where the shape of the piece parts may be different but the basic manufacturing operations are the same. In these areas, the product acceptance plans would remain essentially the same, varying in scope more from the work being inspected (tooling, set-up, and so on) and the level of quality results achieved than from the nature of the products. From a business planning point of view, the thing to watch out for is the introduction of something new or different, such as a new machine or a modified process. In that case, additional inspections or tests should be planned for until the new situation is fully integrated into normal operations and the planned or expected result is achieved.

In American industry, there is a strong tendency to think that a majority of product defect problems are caused by the operators. It may be true that operators are personally involved in some of the unsatisfactory work but it is not likely to be true that they are the cause. One can never be sure until he has examined carefully that part of the job that is provided by management—operating instructions, training, tools, equipment, and materials. When any of these important needs of the operator are inadequate, defects are sure to result. Needless defects will also result from pressure to do quality work in a hurry.

MINIMIZING OPERATOR-INDUCED PRODUCT DEFECTS

One way to eliminate or at least minimize operator induced defects is to plan and budget for adequate work instructions, training, tools, gages, and so on. If the manufacturing planners think through the real needs of the operator and avoid assumptions regarding their role, they will not only prevent defects, they will also start building a positive quality attitude. In the same vein, it is important to specify in-process handling and storage needs and packaging requirements for shipment. An otherwise outstanding manufacturing effort can be seriously damaged by lack of adequate planning in these oft-neglected areas.

In addition to product acceptance and operator support plans, defect prevention in manufacturing can be further enhanced with the practice of certain disciplines prior to and during the production effort. Evaluating the capability of each production process is one such discipline. If one can measure the product dimensions or characteristics after a given operation or process, one can determine the process capability. It is simply a matter of preparing a frequency distribution of the results. This statistical picture will indicate immediately if an inherent problem exists—or it will show the normal variation of the results and the limits within which that normal variation will occur. If the tolerances on the product are outside the normal limits, there is no reason why a defect should ever be produced.

When process capabilities are ignored in the manufacturing planning phase, it is almost certain that problems will develop and the cause of such problems will not be easily known. The most serious ones will receive a lot of attention and everything but the basic process capability will be suspect. This frustrating and wasteful practice can be avoided completely by utilizing the simple discipline of knowing exactly what each process or operation is capable of producing. This knowledge is also useful to prevent the deterioration of profit margins with each major volume gain. Instead of the brute-force method with its ensuing losses, incremental volume increases can be planned carefully to maintain or improve margins.

CONTROL OF MATERIAL SUBSTITUTION DEFECTS AND/OR CHANGES

Another important discipline for the production process is the control of material substitutions and changes or deviations from the manufacturing plan. For some unknown reason, all the carefully thought out plans for the manufacturing process are thrown out the window whenever a serious obstacle occurs. Assumptions are made about substitutions or changes that would never be tolerated in the initial planning. A state of euphoria seems to develop about the output—so long as the schedule will be met.

DEVIATIONS FROM THE MANUFACTURING PLAN

Unfortunately for many manufacturing operations, unverified variations from the manufacturing plan result in serious problems. What adds to the mistake is the fact that the problems that do develop often occur after delivery to the customer. For example, a substitute bonding material may look great when the product is being shipped. But after some use or storage in a cold environment, it failed to hold up as expected. What is really needed here is a discipline that requires all variations from the plan to be approved formally and verified for capability the same as the original process. The secret is to anticipate such needs in the strategic plan for manufacturing and not let undue schedule pressures force mistakes that in the long run are more costly.

NONCONFORMING MATERIAL

There are two support activities to the production process that are best accomplished as a formal system: control of nonconforming ma-

terial and control of engineering changes. Whenever there is an inspection or test rejection, suspected nonconforming product exists. Unless an obvious rework (standard repair) or scrap decision is applicable, a formal evaluation (sometimes called a material review board) is needed 1) to determine the likely cause of the problem for corrective action; and 2) to determine the effect of the nonconformance on end-product performance for the purpose of disposition. Any decision to "use as is" or modify and "use as is," where the end product will not conform to requirements exactly, requires the concurrence of design engineering and quality management. In some cases, such as with the US government, "use as is" dispositions also require the concurrence of the customer. From a business management viewpoint, the most important requirement of material review should be corrective action. When disposition has first priority, problem recurrence can almost be guaranteed.

CONTROL OF ENGINEERING CHANGES

Engineering change control requires the close coordination of detailed production plans and schedules, inspection, and test plans and availability of needed supplies. For this reason, a formal change control board is often the best approach to ensure change implementation with a minimum of cost and disruption to production operations. Having appropriate manufacturing and other personnel working in a formal manner with design engineering will not only allow for the inclusion of each affected function's input to the implementation plan and schedule for engineering changes, it will also allow for change "reasons" to be challenged. From an overall company viewpoint, there are times when 1) a change proposed for ease of manufacture may be too costly from the design view; and 2) a design improvement change may not be justified in terms of manufacturing costs versus a small increase in performance improvement. Without a formal system, it is sometimes possible for narrow, parochial viewpoints to take precedence over the best interests of the company.

CONTROL OF UNAUTHORIZED WORK

One of the most difficult disciplines for a manufacturing manager to enforce is the control of unauthorized work—disciplining all manufacturing personnel to work exactly in accordance with the manufacturing plan or to cause the plan to be changed. Supervisors, engineers, and others often cause work to be done in an unauthorized manner in a sincere but blind attempt to help the company. By directing a different approach, they may think they are solving a problem or getting the job done better or faster, completely overlooking the fact that others are being paid to provide service as needed in an authorized way. Unauthorized work does not usually cause any actual harm, but on those occasions when it unwittingly causes or contributes to a new problem, its costs can be immeasurable—for the reason that the cause will be so difficult or impossible to discover. Tolerance of unauthorized work practices, therefore, can be dangerous to the growth of a business and should be condemned as part of the business strategy of manufacturing.

Inputs from quality management can be valuable in the purchase of new facilities or equipment. Not all capital investments have paid off exactly as expected. Some equipment purchases have never lived up to the stated or promised level of performance; some purchases have missed the opportunity to have built-in measurements for better control of output; and some installations have bombed out on schedule or cost because of "quality" problems. Most problems of this type can be prevented by including the quality management function as an integral member of the review team for major investments in manufacturing. Quality management's contributions can include evaluations or performance speecifications, identification of the benefits of built-in inspection features or supplementary inspection equipment, quality control evaluations of the equipment supplier, and support for major installations. For state-of-the-art investments, it may be necessary to point out the need for additional investments in state-of-the-art measurement techniques. The real problem to be avoided here is not to be lulled into believing that each investment of itself will provide a cure-all for the production problem or opportunity it is intended to satisfy. Quality management is trained to challenge every decision for its validity. Quality management's contributions will be enhanced by not being involved emotionally.

IMPORTANCE OF CALIBRATION AND MAINTENANCE

Business planning for manufacturing should recognize the importance of calibration and maintenance operations to the attainment of product quality requirements. A precisely planned and scheduled calibration of all measurement equipment and gages is normally the responsibility of the quality management function. A systematically executed calibration program provides confidence in the use of inspection and test data for acceptance decisions and as input to corrective action efforts. It also prevents most disparities between company and customer regarding exact product performance. Inadequate attention to or budget for equipment maintenance can cause serious quality deficiencies—from excess scrap and rework because of equipment breakdowns that could have been prevented to the develoment of marginal performance conditions that impact the basic capability of the equipment to produce an acceptable product consistently. A plan and budget for calibration and maintenance is an essential part of the manufacturing plan.

Before the manufacturing plan can be considered acceptable from a quality management viewpoint, there should be evidence of a commitment to quality as an ingredient equal to schedule and cost. Any gains in manufacturing objectives at the expense of quality are not gains to the company. Therefore, the responsibility for quality must be established clearly as an integral part of manufacturing strategies. The foreman must be made to realize that inadequate tools, untrained people, and so on, are not allowed as an excuse. Only then will he exert pressure on the support areas instead of tolerating and condoning their inefficiencies. As a key figure, he will then be acting as a catalyst in perfecting the manufacturing process. He should also be encouraged to remind his people everyday of their joint responsibility for quality, schedule, and cost. Vince Lombardi made champions of ordinary football players by stressing the fundamentals of their job each day.

One of the most destructive attributes of manufacturing operations in American industry towards quality is the well-known month-end crunch for shipments. It appears to be a special manufacturing emotion that somehow must be satisfied. Its omnipresence proves that schedule can become a built-in attitude that needs no triggering. The challenge to American industry for the 1980s will be to do the same for quality.

In summary, the role of quality management in the manufacturing plan should be:

1. A concurrent product acceptance plan, clearly integrating all inspections and tests with the manufacturing process
2. Assurance of adequate manufacturing capabilities, operator support plans, equipment controls and control of changes, nonconforming material, and variations to plan
3. Concurrent, planned support for all new manufacturing operations, including the installation and start-up of new facilities or equipment.

Proper utilization of the quality management function by manufacturing will make their plan more realistic, as opposed to optimistic, and it will assure a minimum of schedule delays and overruns resulting from product quality problems.

THE ROLE OF QUALITY IN MATERIALS MANAGEMENT

Quality is such an important ingredient of the materials management function that the role of quality management as it pertains to this area will be treated separately. For many manufacturing companies, the value of purchased supplies as a percentage of end-product price is 50% or better. Yet the investment in quality control of these supplies may range from meager to practically nothing.

It is paradoxical that some managements who skimp on their own quality control investments can be so trustful that the low-bid supplier will deliver perfect quality. Unfortunately, some managements have had to learn the hard way that unevaluated suppliers can be the cause of serious and costly problems. Problems can range from the new component that never quite performs as expected to the new material that does not hold up in situations that can become hazardous and subsequently lead to product liability litigation. In reality, problems with suppliers range from the most serious down to those that are just annoying. In no case, however, can they *not* be prevented. What is needed is a supplier quality program designed to meet the real needs of the company—in investment in prevention based on the actual facts of past and current supplier performance and realistic expectations based on detailed evaluations.

IMPORTANCE OF A SOUND SUPPLIER QUALITY PROGRAM

A supplier quality program begins with the establishment of clear-cut responsibilities. One of the principal causes of eroding quality levels in the supplier segment of American industry is that the purchasing organization is not held accountable for the conformance of supplies to exact requirements. When the quality of supplies becomes a problem, it is not uncommon to find them treated as a company problem with the emphasis placed more on fixes than causes. The worst case occurs when the quality management function is held accountable, while purchasing is free to proceed blindly towards the next major supplier problem. The first step needed to improve supplier quality is to place the responsibility for supplier product conformance to requirements in the hands of the buyer. This is the only way that a company will be able to profit from its supplier quality experience.

The next most important responsibility for supplier quality is in the hands of the people who define the quality requirements for supplies, namely the engineers from product design department. Experience in resolving supplier quality problems will often reveal that the communication between buyer and supplier is considerably lacking in technical depth and clarity. Each party has a completely different picture of exactly what the supplies are to look like or how they are to perform. This is an inevitable result whenever the purchasing company is too informal in establishing and communicating supplier product requirements. The only way to avoid such disparities is to make sure that each purchase order contains complete, accurate, and clear technical information.

After the purchasing and design engineering responsibilities for supplier quality are clearly established, the role of quality management can be more readily understood. Quality management can provide a service to purchasing that will assure the adequacy of the technical requirements from design engineering and then measure the performance of suppliers against these requirements. This service is usually provided in two ways. First, there is a detection system to keep existing supplier product defects out of the manufacturing operations. Second, there is a prevention system to minimize or eliminate defects from the purchasing program pipeline.

INCOMING MATERIALS INSPECTION

A supplier quality detection system is essentially composed of incoming inspection and test of all purchased products and a method for handling rejections. Each inspection or test of a supplied product should be performed to a documented plan to provide consistency of measures and a baseline for correlation should a problem develop. The inspection plan itself should be based on key characteristics of the purchased products as they may affect end-product performance. Fundamentally, the amount of inspection required is an economic tradeoff based on past experience and current expectations.

Whenever supplied products fail to pass incoming inspection, there is a need for documentation of the reasons for failure; disposition of the nonconforming material; and corrective action to prevent future occurrences. Normally, a defective material tag can be used to document the rejection for further processing. This same tag can also be used to document the disposition, which includes "return to supplier" or "use with modifications." For supplies that fail to meet requirements to be given the disposition of "use as is," the applicable requirements should be corrected to preclude future rejections. Regardless of disposition, the defective material tag can be used further to communicate a requirement for corrective action to the supplier. The long-range success of the supplier quality program will depend significantly on the investment in corrective action follow-up.

TECHNICAL REQUIREMENTS COMMUNICATED CLEARLY

The first step in preventing defects from entering the procurement system is to make sure that technical requirements are clearly established and communicated to the supplier. Quality management's role in the design engineering phase should help to assure that clearly defined requirements are established. Their further involvement in configuration control procedures should help to assure that only the latest requirements are available to purchasing for communication to suppliers. Sometimes, a further service is utilized to audit purchase orders as final assurance that the right requirements are actually being communicated.

The heart of the many serious disagreements and misunderstandings with suppliers lies in the clarity of the technical requirements as initially provided and then modified verbally between buyer and supplier personnel. To assure that all efforts going into the clear communication of technical requirements are never wasted, it is essential that the discipline of "no verbal changes" be installed resolutely and maintained throughout all purchasing operations.

SUPPLIER QUALITY RATING SYSTEM

Whenever long-range relations with suppliers is the norm, prevention of defects can be enhanced with a dynamic supplier quality rating system. The objective of a supplier quality rating system is to qualify each supplier for performance to requirements and then to track that performance in such a way that any serious slippage will be immediately noticeable. Normally, quality is only one characteristic of an overall supplier rating system, which is also concerned with schedule performance and financial stability. To avoid any one element from being discounted by the others, all rating systems should include veto power for each key element.

Qualification of a supplier for quality starts with the initial survey of basic capabilities that should always precede the first purchase order. Verification of capability through proven performance can then take place with inspection of the first lot of product. History can then be recorded with the use of a supplier history card to document the results of each delivery for a given part number or material. This history, which will normally include coppes of past defective material tags, can also be a resource for material review board (MRB) activities. Based on actual results, a rating can be established for each supplier, against which each current delivery is measured. Any failure to perform will change the rating from acceptable to question-

able. From there, depending on the corrective action response, the rating will return to acceptable or proceed to "unacceptable," at which point further business is cut off.

CHECKING THE FIRST LOT RECEIVED

In planning for supplier quality, the initial production lot received from a supplier represents a crucial point in the development of profitable relations. At this point, it is necessary to determine that the supplies will meet all quality requirements, including performance at the limits of all environmental expectations (worst-case conditions). This means that considerably more inspection and test is needed for the initial lot than for subsequent lots, where the need is merely to verify physical dimensions and ambient functional performance. Failure to plan for this need can lead to defects being discovered during customer use of products—the absolutely worst possible place from a business point of view. The quality management terminology for this more extensive evaluation of initial production is "first article inspection."

INCOMING INSPECTION SOMETIMES CONDUCTED AT SUPPLIER'S FACILITY

A supplier quality program can include other elements designed to minimize the cost of incoming inspection or to prevent defects in the pipeline. For example, incoming inspection may be conducted at the supplier's facility (source inspection). This is usually planned when duplication of the supplier's test equipment would be more costly than the benefits or when crucial characteristics of the supplier's end product would be impossible to inspect in the as-delivered condition (e.g., a hermetically sealed product). In other cases, contracting for supplier inspection and test data may allow for significantly less testing on arrival. The basis for this is the statistical correlation that can be achieved with a small sample when variable data is used.

In summary, the role of quality management in the materials management plan should be:

1. A concurrent plan for incoming inspection and test based on actual, current performance experience with suppliers
2. Assurance of adequate budget and commitment to systems for the control of supplier quality by purchasing and engineering
3. First article inspection plans and budget in support of all new or changing supplier business

Proper utilization of the quality management function by materials management can lead to less overall cost of purchased supplies, fewer schedule delays caused by nonconforming supplies, and an improved relationship with individual suppliers.

QUALITY ADMINISTRATION

Before discussing the quality section of the business plan, a clear explanation of the basic role of the quality management organization must be established. Unlike the older professions of marketing, product engineering, and manufacturing, the quality management profession is still not fully understood, accepted, and utilized by the chief executives of American industry. In Japan, because there was genuine interest and openness, quality management is a well-established, integrated entity—but in America the quality professionals are still struggling for their rightful niche in overall company operations.

American companies establish a quality management organization and a quality policy for a variety of reasons, ranging from mere enhancement of the corporate image to full recognition of the value of a quality management system to overall company performance. The average American manager has no real appreciation for how much easier his job can

be when he has an effective quality management system working on his behalf. Quality management is a people-oriented profession, aimed totally at getting others to perform better. A tough, interpersonal challenge to top management is to be constantly forgiving enough to encourage people to be honest about mistakes and results, and at the same time, demanding enough to encourage peak effort and performance. A credibility gap in this area would be dangerous to the company. Quality management can fill that gap.

PRODUCT ACCEPTANCE

When properly organized, quality management consists of two fundamental groups: product acceptance and quality engineering. Product acceptance (inspection and test) provides measurements of product within and at the end of each manufacturing process. The objective of these measurements is to confirm that product quality requirements have been met and product is ready for movement to the next operation or delivery to the customer, including any necessary liaison with customer inspection personnel. When acceptance cannot be secured, product acceptance provides the raw data for rejection, corrective action, and subsequent performance improvement.

QUALITY ENGINEERING

Quality engineering might be described briefly as applying the technology of quality systems to the specific technologies of a company's business. It is intended to supply the necessary engineering base to permit quality improvements to be achieved on product or service quality. Organizationally, quality engineering embodies activities of inspection and test planning, data analysis and corrective action, and the quality interface actions with marketing and design engineering. In this capacity, quality engineers are responsible for continued state-of-the-art improvements in documentation systems, statistical techniques, testing systems, failure analysis techniques, reliability programs, vendor quality systems, and others. Whenever in the business of quality improvement there is a need for product- or service-oriented engineering knowledge, there is a need for quality engineering.

The first job of quality engineering is quality planning—to provide a basic plan for the inspection and test of product throughout the manufacturing process, to place available inspection controls judiciously where they offer the most protection for the dollars spent, and to exert maximum influence on the planning of others in an effort to make conformance to requirements and prevention of errors an inherent part of each company operation. Visible evidence of the work of quality planning can be found in inspection and test plans, documentation systems, procedures for the control of quality (quality manual), and in the attitude of other planning groups with respect to the importance of quality as an ingredient equal to cost and schedule.

For companies that deal in products, quality engineering's contribution to product quality improvement will be directly related to its ability to effect corrective actions. Without corrective change, there can be no improvement. Opportunities for improvement begin with the first rejects, or nonconforming material, to be found during the production process. Quality engineers guide the product acceptance function in obtaining corrective action for obvious errors, perform failed product analyses to determine the causes of not-so-obvious errors, review and analyze product acceptance results periodically for presentation in a way that will support the need for improvement, organize and direct supplementary investigative efforts for more complex product problems, and require the commitment of responsible organizations to specific corrective actions. Experience in product problem identification and solution provides quality engineering with the qualifications for managing customer product problems and providing valid contributions to the marketing and design engineering phase of new products.

QUALITY MEASUREMENT AND CORRECTIVE ACTION

There are no paths to success in quality management that are not founded on basic quality measurements and corrective action. Investments in quality engineers will go for naught if it does not lead to improvement through permanent corrective actions. If the results of inspection and test are not used as inputs for improvement, the quality system in effect will merely be a sorting system. The "obvious" problems may be resolved but the "not-so-obvious" problems will become lost easily in the accepted cost of doing business. The true potential for performance improvement will be related directly to the company's basic capability to measure performance and to analyze performance results to discover those real, but often hidden, problems.

As a minimum, the end results of all key product acceptance efforts (such as receiving inspection, product inspection, and product testing) should be collected and reported as a trend. These trend charts will indicate clearly the current level of performance. The frequency of plotting can be daily, weekly, or monthly, depending entirely on the sensitivity of the measurement. Each key measurement (trend chart) should then be supplemented with a frequency distribution of defect types or causes. The object of the frequency distributions is to identify the most significant contributors to the situations being measured. Reorganization of the data in accordance with the Pareto principle* will show that only a few of the many contributing factors are responsible for most of the negative results.

DYNAMIC AND FLEXIBLE DATA-GATHERING SYSTEMS

The level of detail required for quality measurements can only come with experience. Also, it should be noted that data-gathering systems should be flexible and dynamic. As

*More formally known as Pareto's Principle of Maldistribution of Wealth. It is referred to in this case to point out that only a few operators are responsible for a large percentage of the defective production.

analyses are pursued in tracking down basic causes of problems, more or less data are needed from time to time. What is needed for today's problem may not be necessary (to the same level of detail) after the problem is solved. There is a proper general level of quality data needed for each company, supplemented as necessary for the pursuit of individual problem identification and analysis.

When a basic quality measurement system systematically identifies the most significant contributors to product deficiencies in each key measurement area, it is at the same time providing a strong inducement and justification for a formal corrective action system. Corrective action is needed to close the loop and complete the basic objective of quality management: to achieve overall performance improvement through the permanent elimination of problems affecting product quality.

Corrective action can be considered to be the total effort necessary to define significant problems, determine their cause, and accomplish their elimination. It is not just guessing at the causes or fixing just the symptoms. All operating functions share in the responsibility for corrective action, because all operating functions can affect product conformance to quality requirements directly or indirectly. A corrective action program should be a formal program in order that all investigation and improvement efforts be controlled to the extent necessary to assure utilization of the Pareto principle and to exclude uncoordinated actions that could adversely affect or camouflage the results. A corrective action system should be designed to work on the next most significant problems continuously from every phase of the company's operations. It should also ensure that each problem receives sufficient investigative and support efforts to bring it to a satisfactory conclusion.

CORRECTIVE ACTION MUST BE DOCUMENTED FOR EFFECTIVE TRACKING OF PROGRESS

To assure adequate control, items identified for corrective action should be cataloged into a documentation system officially. This system can be used for tracking, containing, and providing status of the complete corrective-action effort for each problem. One proven system establishes a numerical identifier for each separate problem and provides a problem folder to contain all pertinent documentation associated with each detail of the problem investigation. The folder can then be highlighted through use of a form to summarize each investigative or corrective action chronologically. The current status noted on these forms can then be used to prepare periodic summary reports of total corrective action status, or any part of it, at any given time.

An additional, available step in a truly effective corrective action system is the opportunity to pursue the correction of management systems or basic operating disciplines periodically, in an effort to prevent problems on a wholesale basis or to eliminate the atmosphere for error.

The objective of this approach would be to determine whether or not established management controls could have or should have prevented identified groups of problems. Inadequate or inadequately controlled management systems can create an environment in which problems are born or propagated. A periodic review and correction of identified management deficiencies is one way to prevent slippage back into the original conditions that permitted the problems to develop in the first place. When management controls are enforced rigidly or new management controls are created to prevent the propagation of newly discovered problems, overall management effectiveness is improved, problems are prevented on a wholesale basis, and performance improvements are guaranteed.

IN-PLANT AND OVERALL QUALITY MANAGEMENT REPORTING

An important communication responsibility of quality management is to establish and utilize necessary in-plant quality reports and an overall management quality report to communicate status, problems, and results to top management and associates. The in-plant reports are normally working level reports issued to various supervisors and engineers on a daily, weekly, or monthly basis as required to initiate specific actions, provide current status of performance, or as raw input for analysis. These reports are a natural outgrowth of using detailed quality data (inspection and test results) as a measure of performance and as input to corrective action.

The management quality report should be a synopsis of key distillations from the total purview of the quality management function. It should be organized to include significant problems and planned actions, major accomplishments and general status, such as overall performance trends, conformance to business plan goals, and new developments in government or the marketplace that could affect quality requirements in the future. As a management report, it should be factual and brief and it should highlight quality management performance.

SUCCESSFUL QUALITY MANAGERS AS GOOD EDUCATORS

Successful quality managers are all good educators. They have learned that quality, as an integral part of company operations, can best be instilled in individuals through education and continuous selling. To them, every quality report is an opportunity to educate and sell its readers on the benefits of quality. They also recognize that it is an important part of their job to educate others for the roles they must play in the overall company quality program. This opportunity can start with each new employee's indoctrination and continue into the many quality disciplines that must be maintained throughout all company operations. The mistake to be avoided here is assuming that people will read the quality procedures, understand them, and carry them out. The wise quality manager will plan and conduct quality education programs for other functions and thereby help to pave and earn his own way within the organization.

Quality improvement is not limited to products. The administrative or white-collar area of manufacturing companies, as well as the entire fast-growing service industry, have the same inherent possibility for human error and failure as any product-oriented system. For this reason, it is feasible and logical to apply the principles of quality management to achieve administrative quality improvement through performance measurements and corrective action. It is not uncommon to find a company-wide quality improvement program promoted and administered as an essential part of quality management.

Specific quality improvement programs may involve all company personnel in an overall program that includes personal commitment, goal setting, and error cause removal and recognition. Others can be found to have specific, limited application for improvement such as excess inventory, overdue receivables, or credit voucher causes. Still other approaches involve the application of participative management techniques, such as quality circles, an import from Japan. In each case, individual programs need to be well defined, adequately promoted, properly administered, and results measured. In the future, the opportunities for successful quality management may be greater in the administrative and service areas than they ever were in manufacturing areas.

PRODUCT SAFETY

As product liability claims and product recalls have been increasing in the United States, the need for product safety or liability prevention programs has become more pronounced. Product safety is an important area of responsibility within the quality management function. When a formal program is needed, the high cost of product recalls and liability claims will necessitate a high priority and a high level of management participation. The program will be aimed specifically at preventing that "first" product safety problem from ever happening. There is no room in any business plan for such a costly happening.

Fundamentally, a product safety program should be established to assure that adequate procedures exist and are enforced:

1. To identify inherent product hazards that could result in bodily injury or property damage and eliminate them from product design and manufacture.
2. To verify that marketing literature and user documents contain clearly written cautions or warnings associated with product use and foreseeable misuse and do not extend product performance warranties inadvertently.
3. To ensure that any suspected or confirmed product safety problem immediately results in notification and proper action by personnel assigned to act on safety problems.

One proven approach to fulfillment of the product safety responsibility is to organize a product safety review board comprising the managers from all key functions. They are held accountable to develop and execute necessary product safety disciplines, to assure compliance and applicable product safety laws or regulations, and to act on known or suspect product safety problems.

Another area of concern to many companies is the need to assure compliance with a growing set of applicable laws and regulations for the protection and improvement of the environment. Environmental quality is the title often given to the activities required by these laws and regulations. An environmental quality compliance manual can be the net result of appropriate studies and developments to assure that no laws are violated. Compliance to environmental requirements can be approached in a manner similar to the control of product quality and safety. Therefore, it is not uncommon to find environmental quality as a function of quality management.

When the quality management function itself is large or complex, it is sometimes necessary to utilize a quality audit program to assure that all quality management functions are being achieved successfully. Audits are conducted of each element of the quality management system (each procedure in the quality manual) and also of finished products ready for delivery. The results of such audits will measure the effectiveness of the quality program and clearly indicate where improvements are needed—an excellent input for quality business planning.

QUALITY MANAGEMENT AND PROFITABILITY

A crucial measurement of the effectiveness of quality management is its direct effect on profits. In order to meet this test of value and to improve direct communications with top management, the quality profession created and utilizes a measurement system known as the cost of quality, or simply quality costs. For the past decade, quality costs have been in vogue and have indeed improved the dialog between quality management and general management.

Simply stated, quality costs are a measure of all costs associated directly with the achievement of complete conformance to product quality requirements. They are *not* just the cost of quality management function. Specifically, quality costs are the total of 1) the cost of *appraising* product for conformance to requirements (inspection and test); 2) the costs incurred by *failure* to conform to product requirements (scrap, rework, and warranty costs); and 3) the investment cost of *preventing* product defects (includes most quality engineering efforts). Table 1 shows a detailed list of items that make up these prevention, appraisal, and failure costs.

The philosophy of use for quality costs is as follows:

1. Make every effort to drive failure costs to zero. Failure costs are normally the biggest element of quality cost and represent a total waste to the company. Reduction is achieved by using these

Table 1. Various cost factors

PREVENTION COSTS
Product design	— Formal design reviews
	— Design checking
	— Design support (reliability, safety, and so on)
Purchasing	— Supplier evaluations
	— Supplier rating system
	— Purchase order technical reviews
Manufacturing	— Process evaluations
	— Operator training
Quality administration	— Administrative labor and expenses
	— Quality (inspection and test) planning
	— Quality education
	— Quality audits

APPRAISAL COSTS
Product design	— Qualification tests
Purchasing	— Qualification of new supplies
	— Incoming inspection and test
	— Supplier source inspections
Manufacturing	— Production process proving
	— Product inspections and tests
	— Process control measurements
	— Setup inspections
	— Laboratory support
	— Storage, handling, and shipping audits
	— Maintenance and calibration (measurement equipment)

FAILURE COSTS
Production design	— Design problem investigations
	— Redesign efforts
	— Scrap and rework costs because of design problems
	— Warranty costs because of design problems
Purchasing	— Supplier product reject costs (disposition, replacement, and corrective action)
	— Supplier product rework costs
Manufacturing	— Rework and scrap costs because of manufacturing problems
	— Warranty costs because of manufacturing problems
	— Manufacturing reject costs (evaluation, disposition, and corrective action)
	— Substandard product losses
Quality administration	— Failure analysis and problem investigations
	— Reinspection and retest costs
	— Customer complaint investigations
	— Returned goods/field service
Overall company	— Warranty claim losses
	— Product liability losses
	— Penalties (underperformance)

measured costs to directly support the basic quality engineering effort of data analysis, problem identification, and corrective action.

2. Reduce appraisal costs according to actual results achieved by reducing the amount of inspection and test needed to assure control of each new level of performance achieved. This is accomplished through a combination of statistical and functional adjustments to the inspection and test plans.

3. Invest in prevention activities (quality disciplines) to the extend necessary to achieve and maintain improved levels of defect-free performance.

The reality of potential cost reduction achievement is based on the following premises:

1. Each defect, or failure to conform, has an assignable cause.
2. All causes of defects are discoverable and preventable.
3. Prevention is cheaper.

In essence, quality costs are used to help justify quality management actions and to outline the impact of quality management efforts, or lack of effort, on overall company costs and profitability. For this reason, the cost of quality should appear as a measured and planned-for improvement element of the financial section of the business plan.

QUALITY BUSINESS PLAN

The quality business plan can serve to summarize and bring into clear focus the overall objectives and responsibilities of the quality management function. Strategic planning for quality is as essential to the long-range health of a company as planning in any other business area. Companies will suffer losses if there is either too much or too little quality built into the plans and actions of other functions—based entirely on the expectations of the company's chief executive and its customers.

In essence, the quality plan should state the business goals of quality management, a summary of the actions necessary for their achievement, and the resources required for the role of the quality management organization. For the most part, the goals will reflect the support role of quality management in other functions' objectives and the action plans must include the parallel commitment of those other functions.

Typical goals for quality management in the marketing area might be specific support for the introduction of specified new products or increased market share for selected on-going products. For the product design area, goals might include design support and qualification testing of specified new designs, or support of selected design improvement cost-reduction projects. In manufacturing, quality management goals could be direct support of scrap and rework reductions, process improvements, new process introductions, and worker or process certification projects.

In the area of quality administration, there are unlimited opportunities for growth. Typical goals might be specific quality improvement projects (e.g., administrative quality improvement); conduct of major quality education projects; major efforts to upgrade specific quality system areas (e.g., inspection, process control, application of SQC, control of nonconforming material, formal corrective action, product safety, and so on); or development of new control programs (e.g., computer software quality improvement or customer communications improvement). Any weak area or newly discovered system problems would become an ideal goal for quality management planning.

Supporting each goal or objective in the quality business plan is the action plan for achievement. This is the most important part of the planning. It must be comprehensive and credible. It must include the actions committed to by the prime functions (marketing, engineering, manufacturing, and finance) as well as those actions to be accomplished by the quality management organization. It must also include a realistic schedule for implementation.

The last part of the quality business plan deals with the budget of the quality management organization: the manpower and other resources needed to *manage* the accomplishment of quality management responsibilities and business plan goals. Included in this part of the plan is a detailed expense budget, facility requirements, and a capital budget. Also included is a detailed manpower plan, including special new skills that are needed, such as software quality engineers or hybrid chip test engineers. Essentially, it is the quality manager's commitment to the resources he needs to do the things he is responsible for in accomplishing the overall mission of quality management.

More than any other function, quality management has to look at long-range goals. Unless the ingredient of quality is truly built into all company operations from the first concept of a new product to the ultimate satisfaction of its users, all of which may take many years, a company cannot be truly confident about the degree of actual customer satisfaction that will be achieved. In doing his business planning, therefore, the quality manager must:

1. Make a thorough analysis of his business (the quality goals of the company), his markets (those who have to be influenced to achieve them), and the competition (those who are competing for the resources of the company to meet their own parochial goals)
2. Establish a strategic direction for the long term (the ultimate integration of defect prevention in all operations)
3. Develop a business plan commitment for next year's performance that also serves as an important step towards implementing the long-term quality strategy.

REFERENCES

1. Hagan, J.T., *A Management Role for Quality Control*, AMA, 1968.
2. Juran, J.M. and Gryna, Frank M. Jr., *Quality Planning and Analysis*, McGraw-Hill, 1970.
3. Crosby, Philip B., *Quality is Free*, McGraw-Hill, 1979.
4. Feigenbaum, Dr. A.V., *Total Quality Control*, McGraw-Hill, 1961.
5. Groocock, J.M., *The Cost of Quality*, Pitman Publishing, 1974.

SECTION VII
COMPARING COMPANY RESULTS
WITH COMPETITORS

27
Industry Statistics as a Management Tool

George Rounds, CAE

While not perfect, a quality statistical program conducted by an industry's trade association can be a most useful management tool for comparing the company's results with those of the industry.

An intelligent knowledge of the essential facts pertinent to a corporation's internal and external environments is a basic necessity to competent management. Absence of that knowledge fosters unwise decisions leading to overproduction, excessive costs, misspent resources, and ultimately the demise of that corporation. The greater the amount of sound, relative information available to management, the better able that management is to control the destiny of the organization. Information on market trends, costs, labor, customers, economic impacts, international markets, finance, taxes, usage, supplies, and more are the foundation blocks to which management applies the mortar of its expertise to build a sound operating organization.

INFORMATION AS THE FOUNDATION FOR SOUND MANAGEMENT

Not only is it management's responsibility to gather as much information as possible before embarking on the decision making process, it is also management's responsibility to take every precaution to assure that the data gathered is the most reliable and currently possible. Before statistics are utilized by management, someone must examine the data generation process to evaluate its validity. All

too frequently, decisions are made from data that, for one reason or another, have been biased in the collection and analysis process. To be useful, the information must be as objective as possible. The sample used to create the information must be representative of the sector studied, even though based on only a sample of that sector. Projections from the data must be developed along established statistical principles. Ideally, the information base will be as close to 100% of the sector involved, but such conditions rarely prevail.

SOURCES OF INFORMATION

Quite obviously, the primary source of information for management is generated by the organization's *internal systems* covering daily, weekly, monthly, quarterly, and annual periods and such areas as sales, inventories, personnel, overhead, production costs, and efficiencies. These data are the most readily available and are vital to the management process. On an expanded basis, company data compiled and analyzed by an outside consultant can theoretically provide a more intense, objective view of an organization's operations without the biases frequently imposed by management.

339

Analysis of data from internal sources generated through a more thorough examination of a firm's own data is only the first step in taking an analytic look at an organization's performance. It is akin to trying to pitch horseshoes with one eye closed. You are able to guide the horseshoe directly toward the stake, but lack the depth perception needed to impart the proper loft, speed, and rotation so it will be a "ringer."

It's difficult enough to throw a ringer with two eyes. Why handicap oneself? The same is true of the information gathering and analysis process. Examination of corporate data alone is only part of the effort to place the organization into proper perspective. That data need to be placed alongside any and all appropriate data from every available source. Here wise management turns to information reflecting operations of a business sector or industry such as that provided by the United States Department of Commerce, financial analysts, or an industry group or association. Such comparisons will enable the manager to place his own operations into the broader perspective of his own industry sector, the overall market, and, where appropriate, dissimilar but parallel organizations. The latter can be useful where historical information on a new operation is lacking.

Useful information can be gleaned from an industry or organization that has a structure and operations similar enough to allow comparisons. Such might be the case of a retailer who brings to a new venture experience from a previous dissimilar but quite parallel business and, in effect, is comparing "apples to oranges" but with the understanding that the comparison is limited. The comparative knowledge is helpful in establishing operating goals but the extent of its usefulness is limited by the sheer dissimilarity of the information. Each industry or business operation is unique, and therefore any data must be treated with the knowledge of that uniqueness. For if all businesses were identical, there would be no need for managers, other than to input information to computers that would then run the business.

Company Data

While certainly the most available and current, company data are by its natural subject to bias toward the corporation. Even though great pains are taken to assure total objectivity in the data-gathering process, the simple fact that they are generated by and for management taints them with a measure of self-servitude. The form for the transmittal of the information was established by the management team that will ultimately need the information for decision making. Therefore the output from the data gathering may not totally provide what management *should* know. The "red flags" signaling deviation may not be present or may not be visible to the management that collected and developed the data.

If, however, the company data could be compared to the yardstick of external data that reflected a median or average operating practice, management would be more likely to spot deviations and could then dig deeper to find the causes of such variances. It is possible that the particular variance is peculiar to that operation, unique to that company, and that no corrective action is needed. It may also be that the variance is a sign of an oversight that could be costly if let go untended for too long. It is just such external yardsticks that consultants often apply to the company chart to measure the health of the firm against accepted industry practices. The sources of data most readily available to management for such comparisons are private institutions such as analysts and the academic realm; public, such as federal information sources; and quasi-public information such as industry trade groups. Each has strong points and weaknesses.

Depending on the depth and relevance of the data, management will be able to use it for comparison with company-generated data in such areas as:

1. Cost of production
2. Materials costs
3. Productivity
4. Transportation costs

5. Overhead costs
6. Debt burdens
7. Market penetration
8. Market trends
9. Price patterns (historical only)
10. Unit production ratios
11. User demand and use patterns
12. Payroll and benefit fluctuations.

The ability to overlay a company's data with other pertinent data depends on the format of the presentation and the source of the outside data. For truly accurate comparisons, the format must be similar. For example, an overlay of a firm's financial statement or balance sheets would match ideally line for line the items in a statistical review of that industry's operations. This will occur most often when the external data are generated by a trade association whose members are in the same business and whose operating methods, markets, and management structure are parallel. In such instances, management will be able to make specific comparisons of performance of the company versus industry averages or medians and thereby spot critical deviations in the company's operations.

Government Data

Depending on the sector of the business community in which management is operating, government data can be comprehensive, as in the case of heavy industries like steel, automotive, energy, or virtually useless, as in the case of the recreation industry, where government interest has only recently come to the fore. The size of an industry, however, is not a determinant of the validity of government information. Often, in the process of preparing for government action in a sector of the economy, even the smaller industries have been given close examination and some fairly reliable information has been generated from such an investigation.

The sources of the data should also be scrutinized if possible, for it is a common bureaucratic ploy to study the information prepared by another segment of government when developing the department's statistics. If the original data base is faulty, the resulting study will be equally wrong or more so. In addition, the gnomes of government are constantly being directed to compile statistical support data for a particular piece of legislation or proposed regulation. The data can be quite slanted in order to support that proposal without truly reflecting the real-life picture.

If, on the other hand, the government data have had the test of time as well as the test of applicability by the economic sector involved (a point that inquiry of others in the industry can establish), then the government data can be accepted as quite reliable. More often than not, the industry being dissected has been involved in the information-gathering and analysis process from the start, guiding the departmental agents to assure that reality is indeed reflected in the final statistical information.

Private Analysts

Like government sources, private analysts may very well provide accurate statistics on an industry, but they also can miss the mark substantially. This can occur because such analysts often depend on readily available sources of information such as government data in building their own data base for analysis. If the basic sources are inaccurate, then the resulting analysis will be out of phase with reality. But if the statistics have proven themselves over a period of time to be reliable, then the additional analysis provided by the outside analyst can be useful to management, as long as the sources are understood and the applicability of the information is clear.

Academia

In more than a few instances, notably where neither government nor industry has been able or willing to generate the appropriate information, the academic world has stepped in to fill the vacuum, often with a great deal of objectivity. The general independence of academia from government and industry allows the institutional analysts to collect and massage data as part of their educational process and to do so with a high degree of objectivity, avoiding the point-proving bent of some government programs and the vested interest nature of some industry programs. It can be admitted that there is a great deal of government-academic cooperation in today's environment; many institutions are dependent on government contracts to maintain their research departments. To this extent, the departments can be prone to limited prostitution to government demands, but the general attitude of university business research departments has been to maintain as high a degree of objectivity as possible.

Academic economic analysts can fall prey to their own insular status, lacking the hands-on knowledge of an industry. The traditional ivory tower of academia may place too much distance between the analysts and the facts. This is not the case where the information-gathering process has relied heavily on actual detailed data gathering from the participants in the industry, including interviews that augment the raw numerical data.

Finally, academic analysis programs may also suffer from a sophomoric handicap in which the maturity of experience in the business sector is lacking. Such faults can often be identified in the commentary that accompanies the hard data, rather than in the statistical information itself. When these shortcomings appear, they should serve as a clue to the user that there may be flaws in the data.

Trade Associations

It has been stated time and again both within and outside the courts that industry associations are not only in a position to collect and disseminate information on that industry, but have a responsibility to do so.

There is no conceivable reason why every businessman in the country is not entitled to know that facts of his industry. In absence of governmental action, there is *no* reason why an association should not gather such statistics so long as the facts are not misused to restrict competition. . . .Data of this character is invaluable.[1]

While not perfect, a quality statistical program conducted by an industry's trade association can be most useful to management. That utility can extend beyond the application to the industry members when the statistics become integral to the industry's efforts in government affairs.

In theory, an industry association is more closely attuned to the members' business and therefore in a better position to gather the right kind of information, to apply a more objective analysis to it, and to publish the results in a form most useful to the members of that industry. Not only are the gatherers more knowledgeable of the industry and therefore better able to catch and correct reporting errors, but the analysts can apply their in-depth knowledge of the industry and to its markets in asssembling the data.

At least that's the theory; it's not always the fact. Not all association statistical programs can be relied upon. A key to the measure of such programs is the degree of cooperation and involvement of the members of that industry. A high degree of cooperation in submitting information and structuring the program to fit the industry's needs lends credence to the data and enhance its usefulness to management. The opposite may also be true—insufficient input and ill-conceived analysis generates little more than paper, results in bad management decisions, and is a reflection on both those in charge of the program and the management maturity of the members. Almost without question, when you find a poor industry-sponsored statistical program, you will find a program manager that is not aware of the needs of his members; or is unable to structure a program of substance; or you will find members who lack the ability to see the value in timely and accurate reporting.

An organization that is responsive to its members' needs and abilities will fashion a statistical program that provides those members with the kind of data they need to conduct their businesses on a more profitable basis. Properly fashioned, an association statistical program can be one of the most valuable benefits the organization provides its members, enabling them not only to compare past performance of their company versus industry history but to draw projections from the data supplied and thus set their own management objectives more precisely.

TYPES OF ASSOCIATION DATA

There is almost no end to the types of data that a trade association can collect and provide for its members, with perhaps one singular exception: future prices. While the courts have supported the publication of pricing histories, they have stood fast in condemning programs that tend to smack of antitrust price agreements.

The ability of an association to draw information from its members is one of the justifications for the existence of such associations. Because they are composed of business entities representing a narrow segment of the economy, they are able to focus their information-gathering efforts on that sector and provide more in-depth analysis of the data. Further, most associations rely on the members to identify the informational needs of the industry and to shape the statistical program to fill those needs. A side benefit can be a higher degree of cooperation because the program is responsive to the management needs of the industry.

Unfortunately, this is not necessarily so. Often, the lack of business maturity in some industries blinds the association members to the need for cooperating with the data-gathering process, or corporate policy prohibits a company from submitting data to the pro-

gram. This latter point can be overcome by utilization of an outside fiduciary in the collection process to protect the individual corporate data, a ploy that sometimes is not always effective. More often than not, it is the absence of a perceived benefit on the part of the individual member that makes participation less than complete.

THE ASSOCIATION AS THIRD PARTY

In its position of being a service organization to the industry it represents, the association has the advantage of serving in a third-party capacity to assemble the information from its members (who are competitors) and analyze that information for dissemination in a secure form. The association also has the advantage over other organizations of being more cognizant of the industry's uniqueness and can tailor the statistical program to meet those particular conditions. Properly structured, a statistical program conducted by an industry association relieves the individual members of the potential of antitrust violations by providing a third-party conduit through which information normally considered to be trade-restrictive when exchanged by companies on a direct basis can be passed with greater anonymity and safety. However, the program must be properly structured to assure the confidentiality of individual corporate information and to provide the necessary objectivity and control to avoid the liability of antitrust.

One of the keys to remaining clear of antitrust involvement is to work only with historical information from which projections can be drawn in a general sense. Specific projections created by an association program could bias a market, however, against a particular manufacturer or segment of the manufacturing community and could expose not only the association but the participating companies to a sticky antitrust suit. An association program should not deal with future prices; in most instances, not with future production; and in some cases, not with future wage levels. The rule of thumb in all instances is that statistical reporting of *closed transactions* is not an antitrust violation.

CONFIDENTIALITY OF INFORMATION

As noted above, assurances of confidentiality of individual corporate data are necessary when seeking information from the industry members. The more highly competitive the industry, the more distrust prevails and the greater the need for absolute confidentiality of the data submitted. In some instances, this assurance can be provided by the association itself, although most participating members will insist on use of an outside objective fiduciary whose job it is to create a statistical report without risk of revealing the information of an individual company.

This applies not only to the security of individual company data, but calls for caution in the presentation of the final compiled aggregate data. An experienced analyst working in a fiduciary capacity is careful to avoid publication of data that could reveal a single company's shipments or profits unintentionally. This occurs where there is insufficient breadth of response to protect the individual companies that are reporting, or where one firm's data are so dominant in the report that an astute user would be able to segregate that company's specific data from the overall report. A reliable fiduciary will set specific parameters outside of which the data will not be published but only included in the summary data.

A case in point might be where a large number of companies are reporting data to a survey within which specific product categories are identified on a line basis. In the summary, no one firm's production stands out, but when broken down on a line item basis, that firm's data so dominate the category that publication of the total, despite the fact there is more than one firm in that category, would be revelatory.

Under present federal law, there are some protections provided to the confidential information submitted to industry statistical programs. Nonetheless, it is advisable for any association program to have a specific retention period for the raw data it collects. After a period of time, the data are destroyed, for there is the constant specter of a court subpoena for the source data that were used in creating a statistical report that may have had an impact on a manufacturer or segment of an industry. Thus, the data collected should be retained for only as long as is necessary to support the summary reports and to allow any necessary adjustments in the report. After that time has passed, the data should be destroyed. In considering submission of data to an association program, management should be satisfied that such protective measures are in place and are acted upon.

MEMBER INVOLVEMENT

Whether a company is a member of its industry's association or not, participation in the association's statistics program should be part of the management philosophy, regardless of the above noted risk. Without the maximum possible participation of industry, useful and comprehensive statistical programs are impossible. The involvement must be from the startup phase through development and into data submission. Beyond that, active involvement in a monitoring process is needed to assure the relevance of the data being generated and to assist in reshaping the program to meet fluctuations in the marketplace.

Ideally, a company would identify one member of its management team as the key contact with the association's statistical committee and department. Direct involvement through service on the statistical committee (or marketing committee, or whatever name it bears) affords management an opportunity to shape the program to reflect the industry properly and to provide the most usable information possible to management. It is also important that the persons directly involved in shaping the program have the authority and ability to place individual company objectives second to the more general objectives of the trade group to avoid skewing the information away from the median or average presentation. The individual also should have the full support of his management, including an agreement to participate in the reporting process, providing the process assures the confidentiality that is needed to protect the firm's own data.

At the same time, management should take steps to see that there is an individual who is responsible for preparing the information for submission to the program in the form called for. To leave this task to clerical personnel or support personnel is a direct comment on the importance management places on the program itself. The responsible person must have a clear concept of the kinds of information needed to create a valid report in the necessary format.

Involvement in the process of creating a statistical program by the members who will benefit from such a program will help align the information categories with normal company information reports and thus facilitate the reporting process. Nothing is more frustrating than to receive a reporting form that requires hours of additional data gathering and analysis by the reporting firm before it can be submitted to the fiduciary or the association's statistical department. Further, if the data program of the association does not reflect the categories and line items normally associated with the businesses being studied, the resulting report will be of little value. This can be avoided by direct involvement in the entire process by concerned industry members with the net result of enhanced participation by the members and a far better report at the end.

Participation in the reporting process should be voluntary, although there are some programs that make reporting a requirement of membership in the association. This requirement does have potential legal implications, but to date has appeared to stand the test of time. It may be a hindrance to membership, and should be studied carefully before being instituted. Generally, where there

are only a few corporations involved in an industry, it is easier to institute such a requirement without hurting membership in the organization. On the other hand, where the industry group comprises hundreds of smaller corporations, many of whom fail to recognize the value of the statistical program, making reporting a requisite of membership can seriously damage the degree of the association's penetration into the industry. This will affect other programs of the association, not to mention its financial resources.

It is possible, however, to restrict distribution of the completed reports to participating firms. This can be used as an inducement to other firms to participate in the reporting process. The more valuable the report to the industry members, the greater the desire to receive the data, and therefore, the higher the probability of participation by industry members. As an additional inducement to participation, an organization might consider a series of management seminars at which the statistical information prepared by the association is reviewed in more detail, perhaps by outside consultants and representatives of the fiduciary who prepared the data. Only participants would be able to gain a greater understanding of the data and thereby make better use of the data.

TYPES OF DATA GATHERING

By far the best method of assembling raw data for preparation of industry statistics is through direct and complete reporting by the industry members of the specific information on which the analysis is to be based. These data must, because of their potential revelatory nature, be held in strict confidence to prevent competitors' access to the data. Properly structured, such a data-gathering process will provide the most useful information in the best format for analysis.

While requesting comprehensive data may appear to place a burden on the company, consideration of proper reporting formats that match the company's own general data base will ease the process. The ideal situation would be to have the reporting companies agree to shape their data processing to an industry standard that would allow the anonymous submission of that data, in a computer-compatible format, to a collection agency that could then produce the statistical report in a format that would parallel the submitted data. Such a process would require a high degree of cooperation among the reporting companies to the extent that they would have to modify their own data processing to comply with the agreed-upon format. The end result could be faster and more useful information for the reporting companies.

In the absence of agreements to submit corporate data to the reporting process, an alternative method for generating broad industry statistics is through the estimating process. Though limited, it may be the only recourse available to an association. Here, individual members are asked to submit estimates of the total production, for instance, of a particular common product. These estimates are then averaged with elimination of those that appear to be radically low or high. The resulting average provides at least a guide to the scope of the market. It is far better to structure a reliable reporting program that uses empirical rather than intuitive data as a base, but it may not be possible in some industries.

LEGAL ASPECTS

Whenever a segment of the economy is involved in a collective effort relating to the market, it runs the risk of exposure to assertions of antitrust actions. This is not to say that every group program is suspect, but where that program deals with reports on the market or in discussions of costs and prices, care should be taken to structure such a program to minimize the potential of antitrust claims. There are several areas where managers should be wary as they relate to statistical programs.

First, the courts have upheld the right of associations to gather and disseminate infor-

mation on their industry so long as the process is open and fair and does not seek or imply to determine future production or prices. One of the foremost authorities on association law, George D. Webster, writing in *The Law of Associations*, cites a series of cases dealing with association statistical programs and points out that

> These cases illustrate several important aspects of statistical reporting: (1) Reports should deal primarily with past and closed transactions, although it has been observed that future forecasts of production involved few antitrust risks "in an industry that produces a nonstandardized consumer item, particularly if there is keen competition among a fairly large number of companies, if sales are increasing annually, and if market shares of the companies change from year to year." (2) Information concerning individual companies or transactions must not be disclosed to competitors. Confidentiality of individual company information must be maintained at all times. (3) Statistical information must be supplied to those who bargain with association members.[2]

Further, the Supreme Court, in the case of the Maple Flooring Manufacturers' Association v. the United States (268 U.S. 563), said:

> It is not, we think, open to question that the dissemination of pertinent information concerning any trade or business tends to stabilize that trade or business and to produce uniformity of price and trade practice. . . .But the natural effect of the acquisition of wide and more scientific knowledge of business conditions, on the minds of the individuals engaged in commerce, and its consequent effect in stabilizing production and price, can hardly be deemed a restraint of commerce, or, if so, it cannot, we think, be said to be an unreasonable restraint, or in any respect unlawful. . . .

. . .[t]rade associations/or combinations of persons or corporations which openly and fairly gather and disseminate information as to the cost of their product, the volume of production, the actual price which the product has brought in past transactions, stocks of merchandise on hand, approximate cost of transportation from the principal point of shipment to the points of consumption, as did these defendants, and who, as they did, meet and discuss such information and statistics without, however, reaching or attempting to reach any agreement or any concerted action with respect to prices or production or restraining competition, do not thereby engage in unlawful restraint of commerce.[3]

Thus a statistical program that does not seek to set future market conditions or reveal competitive information on a company's operations to other competitors, is not likely to subject the association or the participants to any action under the Sherman Anti-Trust Act.

While there is reference to the making of the statistical information generally available to all persons involved in that market segment, whether or not they report, there is no clear directive that all the data must be made available regularly. A common association practice is to provide limited summary information to the broad membership (in view of the fact that the members' dues were expended to conduct the program and they therefore can lay claim to some of the fruits of the expenditure), by summary reports in newsletters or association publications. This permits the entire membership to gain in limited sense from the trend data revealed in the statistics, but withholds from them the detailed information generated by the reports. Should a member persist in seeking more detailed information, it can be made available in the association offices for inspection. The member must be willing to make the effort to visit the statistical library of the association to obtain the data.

In any event, before a statistical program is instituted by an association, it would be wise to have the policies and practices of the program reviewed by counsel in light of both the Sherman Act and Federal Trade Commission regulations and policies.

As to whether the confidential information submitted to a trade organization for the preparation of aggregate statistics can wind up in the courts or in government files, Louis R. Sernoff, writing for the Chamber of Commerce of the United States of America, responds with a categorical yes.

Sernoff notes that "The FTC's authority to secure trade information submitted to an association was confirmed more than 20 years ago, as the agency challenged the acquisition of Rawlings Manufacturing Company by A. G. Spaulding & Bros. During the discovery stage of the its proceedings, the commission served a subpoena on Ernst & Ernst [now Ernst and Whinney], the accountants for the Athletic Goods Manufacturers Association, seeking, among other things, all of the individual company data they had received in the course of preparing aggregated sales 'census reports' for the association.

The matter went through United States District Court, which supported the position of Ernst & Whinney and the association that the FTC's power of subpoena did not apply in view of the fact that neither Ernst & Whinney nor the AGMA was a target of the proceedings. The appeals court reversed the ruling that held that even third-party data, if relative to the proceedings, could be considered evidence and were therefore subject to subpoena. Essentially, both the FTC and the Antitrust Division of the Justice Department have the legal ability to subpoena the raw data used to develop statistical reports when those data are relevant to determining market shares, market trends, and so on.

The Federal Trade Commission Improvements Act of 1980 provided some additional protection to confidential submissions. In Section 6(f) the commission is prevented from disclosing ". . . .any trade secret or any commercial or financial information which is obtained from a person and which is previleged or confidential." Further, in Section 21(b)(3)(C) the act provides that any information provided to the FTC as the result of a compulsory process or ". . . voluntarily in place of such compulsory process. . ." may not be disclosed other than to committees of Congress without the consent of the submitter. However, under Section 21(c)(3), persons who dispute the FTC's assertion that the data are not trade secrets can file an action in district court seeking an injunction against FTC to enjoin disclosure.

Mr. Sernoff concludes with the following advice.

> Thus, an association receiving sensitive statistical information from its members should not retain the individual company information any longer than necessary. . . .
> . . .Rather, the association's program should provide for disposition of all individual company statistical information, including that found in worksheets, as soon as cumulative data is compiled.[4]

Management, concerned with the confidentiality of the data it submits to its trade association, has the obligation and the right to receive evidence that its confidential data will be afforded the proper protection from action. If no such measures exist in the program, then management should insist that they be instituted immediately before reporting to the program.

George Webster concludes his discussion of statistical reporting for associations by noting the following:

> The following guidelines should be observed in conducting (association statistical) programs:
>
> 1. Participation in the program should be voluntary.
> 2. Nonmembers of the association should be allowed to participate in this associa-

tion program, even though some reasonable price differential may be charged.
> 3. Data collected should be of past transactions or activities.
> 4. Data should be collected by an independent (not connected with any one company) third party.
> 5. The confidentiality of an individual company's data must be preserved.
> 6. After data has been collected it should be compiled in composite form so as to conceal the identity of any company or of any specific transaction.
> 7. The data should be distributed in composite form.
> 8. Access to the composite data probably should be made available to all those with a valid business reason for the information.[5]

CONCLUSION

Given the vital need for management to have complete and accurate data available for proper decision making, management is obliged to investigate all possible sources of that data. In addition to the internal information of the company itself, information prepared by outside persons or agencies can be extremely valuable in providing industry-wide trends and information against which the manager can make comparisons of his own organization's performance.

In spite of potential legal risk connected with such cooperative ventures among competitors, the law has been supportive of the industry groups' right to collect such information and disseminate it, providing that 1) it deals in past and closed transactions and 2) concomitant actions are not taken to seek to determine future prices and supplies. A properly structured program can provide management with much of the data it needs, in the form it needs, and on the areas it needs to be better able to make sound management decisions. Structuring the program, whether it be a government, academic, or trade association is as much the responsibility of the individual company as is the need for that company to make the commitment to submit information to the program. By early involvement and full cooperation of all segments of an industry, the resulting information will be a truer picture of that industry's performance.

There is almost no limit to the kinds of data that can be developed, particularly through a third party that will assure the confidentiality of the data, with the sole exceptions of data dealing with future prices, supplies, and market shares where it can be shown that there was agreement to fix such areas.

REFERENCES

1. F. Jones, *Trade Associations Activities and the Law*, 47 (1922).
2. George D. Webster, *The Law of Associations*, p. 135 (1971).
3. Maple Flooring Manufacturers' Association v. the United States, 268 U.S. 563 (1925).
4. "Government Access to Confidential Data Gathered by Associations," Association Letter, Chamber of Commerce of the United States, June 1980.
5. Webster, op. cit., p. 139.

28
Analysis of Company Weaknesses
(A Case Example)

Thomas S. Dudick

This chapter demonstrates how a group of key executives can review the operating statement, make comparisons with industry statistics, and attempt to determine the reasons their company falls short of meeting the industry averages.

There is no conferral of degrees for the position of president, executive vice-president, or general manager. No college course and no series of case studies or seminars adequately provides the top executive with the type of practical information he needs to run his activity. In his position of key executive, however, he does have at his disposal the experts in various functional areas—whether it be sales, manufacturing, engineering, materials management, or finance. If these functional managers do not prove to be the experts he has assumed them to be, he will soon find out because he must rely upon them for the information he uses in making his decisions.

Although financial indicators can be a very helpful guide to a management interested in improving its competitive position, the analysis of such indicators in abstraction without the participation of the key members of management has only limited benefits.

TEAM PARTICIPATION

Team participation is mandatory if good results are to be achieved; it is necessary that key executives be fully aware of the strengths and weaknesses of their company in relation to the industry of which they are a part.

This chapter is devoted to demonstrating how a group of managers can review the operating statement, make comparisons with industry statistics, and attempt to determine the reasons their company falls short of meeting the industry averages.

MAKEUP OF THE TEAM

Table 1 shows the industry percentages for a five-year period. The last column shows the equivalent figures for the ABC Company for the most current year. The general manager of the company has called together the following executives whose titles and first names are:

General manager:	Don
Manufacturing manager:	Joe
Controller:	Jack
Personnel manager:	Bob
Sales manager:	Harry

General Manager: "Gentlemen, I have called you together so we can look at ourselves introspectively by comparing the results shown on our latest financial statement with the results for our industry as shown in Table 1 previously distributed to you.

"Through periodic meetings such as this, I hope to promulgate free and open discussion among ourselves as to:

Table 1. Financial ratio study: ABC Company compared to the industry

	INDUSTRY STATISTICS (%)					ABC	
	FOUR YEARS AGO	THREE YEARS AGO	TWO YEARS AGO	LAST YEAR	THIS YEAR	COMPANY, THIS YEAR	
Gross sales	103.7	103.8	103.9	103.8	104.0	104.8	"Clean up the
Less returns and allowances	3.7	3.8	3.9	3.8	4.0	4.8	'dirty' orders!"
Net sales	100.0	100.0	100.0	100.0	100.0	100.0	
Cost of goods sold							
Material	31.3	35.6	33.9	35.9	36.9	33.9	
Factory labor	13.8	12.1	12.6	9.1	9.0	14.0	"Automate!"
Factory overhead	17.7	16.4	17.2	16.2	14.6	16.0	"Establish budgets!"
Total	62.8	64.1	63.7	61.2	60.5	63.9	
Gross profit	37.2	35.9	36.3	38.8	39.5	36.1	
Selling expenses:							
Sales salaries and commissions	7.3	7.9	7.7	7.3	7.8	8.2	"Standardize sales
Travel expenses	1.5	1.2	1.2	1.4	1.2	1.3	compensation
Executive and office salaries	4.2	3.9	3.8	3.5	4.5	3.9	methods!"
Advertising	1.6	1.3	1.5	1.2	1.5	1.0	
Special promotions	2.1	2.1	2.8	2.6	2.7	3.1	
Total	16.7	16.4	17.0	16.0	17.7	17.5	
Product development	0.6	0.6	0.5	0.5	0.3	0.0	"Develop new products!"
Administrative expenses							
Executive salaries	2.1	2.4	2.6	2.2	2.2	2.2	"Oversophistication
Office salaries	2.4	2.2	1.8	2.4	2.8	2.7	of computer
Other expenses	5.2	4.9	4.7	5.2	4.4	5.6	operations!"
Total	9.7	9.5	9.1	9.8	9.4	10.5	
Other income	(1.2)	(0.9)	(0.7)	(0.5)	(0.9)	(0.3)	
Other expenses	1.0	0.8	0.7	0.8	0.2	0.2	
Pretax profit	10.4	9.5	9.9	12.3	12.2	8.2	"This is where the buck stops!"
Finished goods, days	19	16	18	17	16	18	"Stop overruns—stick to the schedule!"
Accounts receivable, days	38	41	39	44	48	52	"Issue credits promptly!"

1. Where our weak points are in relation to our competitors.
2. What we can do to overcome these weaknesses.

PRETAX PROFIT

"Let's begin by looking at the pretax profit. You will notice that figure is 8.2% of sales as compared with 12.2% for the industry. Prior to the time we began receiving the industry statistical reports, we thought this was reasonably good—we had some feeling of satisfaction with our performance as managers. The comparison in the exhibit you have in front of you points up the fact that we are not

quite as good as we have led ourselves to believe. With this as a background, let us look at the other items, a line at a time, in an effort to pinpoint some of our problems and possibly reach some meaningful conclusions.

RETURNS AND ALLOWANCES

"Let's look at returns and allowances. This seems to be the customary means of stating the amount of reduction of sales through rebates, defective products, and other reasons that we give credit to customers.

"Joe, as a manufacturing man, I ask you this question. We at the ABC Company show that 4.8%

of our sales are returns and allowances—compared with the industry average of 4.0%. The 0.8% may not sound large, but it is 80 cents out of every $100 multiplied by the dollars of gross sales. This becomes a significant number of dollars over a period of a year.

Controller: "Let me come to the defense of Joe. This is not quite as bad as it appears. If we inadvertently make a double billing or if we send out two shipments in error, we correct this in the returns and allowances account. Gross sales are thereby automatically reduced through this process. We have recently changed this practice. In the future, gross sales will be reduced directly rather than indirectly, and the items shown in returns and allowances will reflect only true allowances and returns."

General Manager: "I'm certainly glad you have changed the practice. I'd hate to think that a financial statement is being used as an accounting worksheet. If any other kinds of adjustments are being made in the same way, let's clean them up too."

Manufacturing Manager: "Some of the returns and allowances can be blamed on 'dirty orders.'"

Sales Manager: "What do you mean by dirty orders?"

Manufacturing Manager: "When an order comes in from the sales department marked 'same as last time,' we pull the order and it frequently turns out that it was not the same as last time, but two times ago. I suggest we prepare some instructions and do a better job of coordinating between sales and manufacturing so we know exactly what to make. This will also help our inventory turnover."

Sales Manager: "As far as asking you to make the order the same as last time, I am sure that is the best thing we can do because that is what the customer tells us. However, if we have problems in writing orders, I think we can specify what goes on them. It's only a matter of altering our approach."

Manufacturing Manager: "Suppose I do this, Harry. I'll have a list made up of all orders that are giving us problems. I'll have this ready for our next meeting so we can all work this out together."

General Manager: "We can do better than that. Would you make a photocopy as the order goes through production control? Bring these copies of all dirty orders to the next meeting so we can deal with specifics. Harry can't just write a memo to his salesmen asking them to write better orders—that's just too general an approach and it will accomplish little.

"So much for dirty orders. Let's move on to cost of goods sold. This is segregated into material, factory labor, and factory overhead. We don't usually have too many bouquets to pass out, but I think you are due one for material. Our material cost is lower than the average for the industry— 33.9% of sales as compared with 36.9% for the industry."

MATERIAL

Controller: "There is another factor to be considered before we hand out any bouquets. Our material costs are lower because our TV product line is concentrated more heavily on the table models and portables which have a relatively low material content in relation to sales value. Our competitors have more of the stylized, expensive wood cabinets in their lines which have a greater percentage of combination stereo-TV color sets. These have a larger material content and are, incidentally, more profitable. If Harry's salesmen would sell more of these we could increase the profit figure."

Personnel Manager: "I'm a little confused. Even if the table models and portables are less profitable, the material in them is less costly; so doesn't that compensate for the lower price? We sell a lot of them and we put out a good set."

Controller: "The markup on table models and portables is very low. Even though the material in a color TV-stereo combination is represented by more dollars, the selling price is even greater; so if we could sell more of them, we would come out with a better profit."

Sales Manager: "I'd like to sell more of the higher priced line but every time I send an order to the factory they goof it up. I got a complaint from a customer only last week that when he switched on the TV the stereo unit began to play. Apparently, our factory is geared up to make the simpler sets; and they do a good job on these—don't get me wrong. I just don't think the more exotic lines are our cup of tea.

Manufacturing Manager: "Now just a minute, Harry. Your salesmen send in a small order for combinations about once a month. We can't afford to keep together a group of people familiar with the intricacies of the more exotic items in our line—we have to use people from the lines we run day in and day out. If your department would go out and get some decent-sized orders, I would set up a special line and train people who would put out a quality product that you'd have no problem selling."

Sales Manager: "This is the old story of which came first. We can't sell the product if you can't produce it, and you can't produce it unless we can sell it.

General Manager: "Maybe we should do some soul searching in this area and develop a marketing program. Harry, why don't you give Joe an idea of the potential so he can develop some firm plans."

Manufacturing Manager: "Do you have any idea of what this potential really is? It's all well and good to say that we'll try to tap the potential, but I have been stung before. A few years ago, I set up a special line in anticipation of a heavy tape recorder business, but it never materialized and I was left holding the bag."

General Manager: "I remember the tape recorder problem—I was a party to it when I was sales manager. If you recall, that was about the time the cassette-type recorders became very popular. As a result, the conventional product we made took it on the chin. The same thing happened when tape recorders took the place of the wire recorders. We profited by that change; in fact that's how we got into the business.

"This is one of the things I hoped would come out of such a meeting as this one. It's obvious that we need to do a better job of forward planning and try not to repeat errors of the past. I see Joe's problem—he just can't have specially trained people available to run every small order that comes in the house. We need a plan; we need product selectivity so we can push more of the high profit items

rather than just the highly competitive ones. The three of us will have to get together in some extended sessions. We'll get some commitment on the part of the sales department in terms of units by product line as well as by dollars and gross margin.

"Then, armed with that type of information, we can get the opinion of the manufacturing department as to needs in terms of people, technology, equipment, and investment in inventory. We can't continue drifting in and out of product lines in a haphazard fashion.

"The next item I want to cover gentlemen, is factory labor. I'd like to hear about this from you, Bob, as personnel manager. As you can see, factory labor costs are running 14% of sales compared with 9% of industry. This is five points higher than our competition. What's the story?"

FACTORY LABOR COST

Personnel Manager: "I'm going to sound a little like a broken record. As you know, we're in an awfully tight labor market—the likes of which we haven't seen since the war. Another factor is turnover. It isn't only a matter of losing experienced people and hiring green replacements—we almost always have to hire these new people at higher rates than were paid to the ones we lost."

General Manager: "But we're in a distress area and have a very high level of unemployment."

Personnel Manager: "True, but the labor pool isn't made up of the type of employees we need. It's the male population that is largely in the ranks of unemployed. But as you know, we need women in our assembly operations for their manual dexterity—and we need inspectors who have a fairly good comprehension of the written word. These types are not available in the quantities we need."

"I do have one suggestion regarding turnover. We have to get closer to our employees so we can become aware of dissatisfactions before they look for other jobs. By the time we find out an employee is looking, it's too late."

Manufacturing Manager: "Who could disagree that we should get closer to our employees. But we could spend all our time wet-nursing 400 employees. There's always going to be some petty bickering that we can never resolve because of personality differences. Arbitrating these differences would take up too much time and accomplish little.

"The way you can make real inroads in the cost of factory labor—and I've been saying this for three years—is to automate some of the assembly operations. That's where a good deal of the cost is."

Controller: "That will require a good deal of capital money."

Manufacturing Manager: "Of course it will. But I didn't hear any objections from you when they built that new office building just to house your new computer—air conditioning and all—while my people sweat. There's a way to eliminate a good deal of employee dissatisfaction, Bob. Air condition the factory like our competitors are doing."

Controller: "But we were able to come up with some savings."

Manufacturing Manager: "You'll have to convince me of that. All I see is a lot more reports that I don't have time to read because of the unnecessary detail they show. I want the big picture, but your computer gives me all the nit-picking detail of what happened two days or more ago—something I can do without because I knew it from on-the-spot reports."

General Manager: "Joe and Jack, let's make the discussion of reports a subject of a separate meeting. Joe, suppose you get together copies of the reports you're criticizing and we'll get into them in greater depth.

"Regarding your recommendation for automation, I recall that you did talk about this before, and I have no doubt that you are right. However, as you know, the corporate office requires us to submit a request for appropriation with a calculation of payback—using the discounted cash-flow method. I know how you despise paperwork, but we'll have to do it."

Manufacturing Manager: "OK, I'll write something up and turn it over to Jack. I know that if I put in an automated conveyor line for $100,000 I can make payroll savings in excess of $40,000 per

year. After deducting depreciation and maintenance, there will be a net saving of $30,000 per year, or a payback of 3-⅓ years. If this isn't convincing enough and they want to use the discounted cash-flow method, I don't understand it—let Jack's computer do it."

FACTORY OVERHEAD

General Manager: "I'm sure Jack will be glad to help you once you give him the basic information. Let's move on to the factory overhead category. You may be able to throw some light on this one, Jack. Why is our overhead 16% of sales when the industry figures are only 14.6%?"

Controller: "I believe the major part of this difference is due to the way we handle depreciation. As you know, our equipment is quite new and we use accelerated depreciation in our costing. As far as I can tell, most of our larger competitors have equipment purchased 12 to 15 years ago when prices were lower.

General Manager: "You're probably right. There should be offsetting effects, though—our productivity should be higher for the newer equipment. We should check that."

Controller: "By the way Joe, when we justified purchase of the new equipment, one of the potential savings was a reduction in the number of maintenance men. We still have as many as we ever did. This is another reason the overhead is up."

Manufacturing Manager: "It just seems that everything has been going wrong. We had to use our maintenance crew for numerous building repairs—including preparatory work prior to building the new office building. By the way, why wasn't some of that maintenance capitalized since it was directly related to new construction?"

General Manager: "I do recall that you were to reduce your crew by five men if we purchased the new equipment. By the way, Jack, your departmental budget reports don't show budget figures by which we can compare the actual costs to see if they're in line. If you did include a budget based on the annual plan, we could spot these differences before too much time gets by. Let's discuss this after the meeting along with capitalization of maintenance costs when applicable.

SALES COMPENSATION

"Let's move into Harry's area now. You'll note that salesmen's salaries and commissions for the industry—for the entire five years—fall within a single percentage point. There is not a figure below 7% or one above 8%—which is surprising. In our case this cost is running at 8.2%. Are we paying the men too much? What's the story?"

Sales Manager: "As you know, Don, I inherited the sales organization. Some of the men are on compensation plans that include straight commission, salary and commission, salary and bonus, and salary only. One of my goals is to have the entire compensation plan uniform by next year.

"Along with this, you will notice that our executive office salaries are lower than industry. With the standardization of method of payment, I would like to restructure the sales organization to put more management into the field. The combined figure will probably not change but we will look better under salesmen's salaries and commissions and will be a bit higher under sales executives' and office salaries."

General Manager: "Sounds good to me. This should make the whole organization more effective.

ADVERTISING

"Let's focus on advertising next. We have spent about 1% of our sales dollar on this item—which is about 30% less than the rest of the industry. Would an increase in this figure result in added volume?"

Sales Manager: "I don't believe so. We haven't done too much in institutional advertising because we have no new product to advertise."

General Manager: "Other companies are glorifying their products through advertisements in national magazines."

Sales Manager: "That's because they have something new. You will see that we're spending a lot of money under special promotions. This is principally sales contests to motivate the salesmen. We do this because our product is at the cheaper end of the line and our men get gored with this sort of thing in a market where others are selling a broader line and glamorizing a variety of models.

"What I would like to do is take the money I am spending on sales contests and put it into product development where we are spending virtually nothing. This will be a greater inducement for our sales force. Of course this program will have to be long range. We have to plan on new products, techniques, and new designs for existing products."

NEW PRODUCTS

General Manager: "This interests me because it fits into the pattern. We have been talking about the fact that we are drifting into new products on a casual basis and not doing a good job because of lack of proper planning and coordination. What you are saying is that we need some specific product development. We can't tell what the outcome will be, but I can see the benefits of closer liaison among sales, production development, and manufacturing."

Sales Manager: "We can't do this for one or two years and then drop it—the program must go on according to a definite long-range plan."

ADMINISTRATIVE EXPENSES

General Manager: "We have already covered product development, so let's skip down to administrative expenses. Jack, I see that we are in good shape on executive salaries and office salaries but we're high on nonlabor expenses. We show 5.6% of sales—which is higher than our competitors in any of the five years. What are we doing here that puts us out of line?"

COMPUTER COSTS

Controller: "I guess this is mostly our computer rental. As you know, we're now putting out reports on sales by customer, by territory, and by product. We're also analyzing commissions by salesmen which we used to do manually. We're also giving the foremen a daily efficiency report by individual operation so they can nail down inefficiency by operator and by operations.

Manufacturing Manager: "We can do without these daily efficiency reports by operation. Each of my foremen gets a stack of paper one inch high showing a mass of detail. We receive the report two days after the fact. Even if we received it the next morning it would already be too late to take action on something that an operator has long since forgotten.

"I can tell how efficient my people are by the number of TV sets that come off the end of the line each hour. I can control poor workmanship by the number of reworks. As soon as we find someone is doing a poor soldering job, for example, we know the position on the line and take care of the problem immediately—without a stack of paper to tell us. As far as I'm concerned, you can cut out these reports and save the money."

General Manager: "Jack, I know that you and I went into this computer program with high hopes of improving efficiency and saving money. I'm wondering if we might not have been sold a bill of goods by that computer firm that would have us spend a dollar to get ten cents worth of information. Let's take a close look at this."

FINISHED GOODS

"The next topic is finished goods. I notice that we have an 18 days' supply compared with 16 days for the industry. As you know, this is money. Inventory represents assets that are not turned over. What is the story on getting this under control, Harry?"

Sales Manager: "My records show that the factory is overrunning production schedules. If they stick to the schedule I give them, we could be slightly under the industry figure."

General Manager: "Is this true, Joe?"

Manufacturing Manager: "Well, you know that when a line is running well—with very few de-

fects—it's much cheaper to keep it running because when we stop and start up again later, costs go up considerably."

Sales Manager: "What good is low cost inventory when you have to write it off a considerable amount at the end of the model year?"

General Manager: "Joe, this only reinforces my point. I think that it's imperative for you, Harry, and me to get together as soon as possible to do some down-to-earth planning. Let's set a definite date before the day is out."

ACCOUNTS RECEIVABLE

"The last item I want to cover is accounts receivable. As you can see, we have 52 days of outstanding receivables. Again, we're higher than industry averages. What can we do about this"?

Controller: "One of the reasons the receivables are so high is that it takes so long to process credits. I have one case where a customer won't pay a $5,000 bill because he says he is entitled to credit for $45 which hasn't been received."

"I suggest that the salesmen be allowed to approve credits for $50 or less. A credit still has to be processed and we have to find out why it is being requested, but this procedure would expedite collections.

Sales Manager: "If after the credit has been allowed and a study reveals that it really is the customer's fault, who is going to bear the cost of that credit? Will it be charged back to the sales department?"

Controller: "I don't think that is going to happen very often. The $50 that we might lose occasionally would be offset by savings in telephone calls, letter writing, and ill will."

General Manager: "I am a little concerned. I think we would have to institute a monitoring system to be sure that salesmen do not abuse this system."

Sales Manager: "I'll work this out with Jack, and we'll talk it over with you before I issue instructions to my sales people."

General Manager: "I hope this meeting has been as helpful to you as it has been to me. Just by way of summation, our discussions have highlighted the following areas which require our attention.

"We covered the subject of dirty orders which have been a source of confusion to our manufacturing people and have undoubtedly rankled some of our customers. This meeting permitted us to air the problem which we will explore further with a view toward taking corrective steps.

"We also talked about the problems of small orders and about increasing our volume in more profitable lines. Our approach will include a coordinated effort among sales, product development, and manufacturing to come up with a program for better selectivity in our product line."

"The sales compensation plan will be standardized and organizational shifts made in order to make out field sales effort more effective.

"Automation, as a means for reducing factory costs and coping with labor shortage problems, will be implemented in the foreseeable future.

"It's obvious, also, that we have other incongruities in our procedures which require further investigation. I refer to the possibility of overly detailed reports, the question as to whether or not we have overexpanded our computer facilities, and the problem of issuing credits to customers on a timely basis.

"I'm certain that future meetings of this type will put all these problems in proper focus and facilitate solutions. Thank you, gentlemen. I'll notify you of the date of our next meeting."

The foregoing describes a composite of actual happenings that can be brought out at a participatory management meeting. While use of meetings for problem solving is sometimes criticized because they can become a forum for the more vocal members of the group, a well-controlled discussion with specific objectives can be highly productive. The following guidelines will assure greater success.

1. *Establish a definite agenda of the topics to be covered.* In this case, the agenda consisted of explanations and solutions to specific out-of-line situations.
2. *Be alert to the opinions of those in other areas of responsibility.* These people are in a position to flush out deficiencies that might not otherwise be revealed by those directly responsible for the activity.
3. *Make a definite decision to take certain action.* If action cannot be taken, give specific reasons why it cannot. Should further investigation be required, make this known and set definite dates for accomplishment.

The ability to direct a group of executives in the pursuit of reasons for and solutions to problems is one of the marks of business leadership. Diagnosing a business through a team approach certainly calls for the exercise of leadership. As the example in this chapter demonstrates, one way such leadership can be achieved naturally and painlessly lies in framing the questions one wants first, then obtaining the benefit of the best-informed opinions in a frank and open group discussion.

SECTION VIII
PRODUCT COSTING AND PRICING

29
Improving Profitability
Through Realistic Pricing

Phillip J. Wingate
Vice-President (ret.)
E. I. Dupont De Nemours Co., Inc.

Pricing in a free economy is usually competitive, a circumstance borne out by the relatively narrow limits within which pricing decisions are made. The author discusses the factors that cause variations in these limits and provides illustrations.

In a sense, all pricing is competitive in the world of free enterprise because all goods and services have competition of some sort. Even when competing products differ greatly in appearance and other properties, as is the case when polyethylene film competes with brown paper as a wrapping material for vegetables at the grocery store, price is always a factor in determining which product will be used. So a firm, in setting prices, must not only consider direct competition from firms making essentially the same product, but indirect competition from other products that may provide only part of what the customer really wants.

PRICING DECISIONS MADE WITHIN RELATIVELY NARROW LIMITS.

One consequence of this broad reality is that pricing decisions are nearly always made within relatively narrow limits of a few percentage points, up or down, from some existing market price. Thus there is some truth to the claim that a relatively free market sets its own prices and a businessman should therefore not give too much attention to prices but

should center his attention on how to reduce costs and increase sales. This claim, however, is an exaggeration. For one thing, prices are important in determining what the sales volume will be. Second, any firm must set a price on its goods and services; it becomes a part of that competition that determines prices at any given moment.

Also, even when price decisions are made within the limits of a few percentage points, they can be vital to the success or failure of a firm because no other decisions are more quickly translated into profits or losses. If the firm raises prices by 1% and loses no sales, the benefits are easily calculated. Similarly, if it lowers prices and gains no additional business, the losses are equally clear and prompt. Of course, in actual practice a price increase is likely to reduce sales, in the future if not immediately, and a price cut is likely to increase sales. Calculation of the end result on profits in these cases is never a matter of simple arithmetic. The businessman must rely on judgment and experience, rather than the computer, to tell him if his decisions are good or bad.

361

Despite arguments to the contrary, it is necessary for a business manager to give much thought to pricing. And beyond all doubt, competitive pricing is a powerful factor in promoting the general welfare in a free society. All who wish to sell goods and services to their neighbors, near or distant, are forced by competitive pricing to look constantly for the most efficient processes for doing what the customer wants done.

COSTS AND PRICES

There is, of course, a relationship between costs and prices. No product will be sold for long in a free market unless the selling price is higher than the cost of manufacture. However, only the naive and inexperienced believe that a manufacturer can set his prices by the simple procedure of calculating his costs and adding a certain percentage to that cost to arrive at the selling price.

The choices on price, within that narrow range already mentioned, that are open to the seller are mostly not related to costs. The seller's "freedom" is centered in his profit margin. If his costs are too high, the market simply tells him that there is no place for him in that market.

In fact, in many cases the prices in a free market determine the costs as much as costs determine prices. This is true to some extent even in those businesses that are inherently monopolistic. Electric power and telephone companies cannot, for long periods of time, ignore the prices that are available to similar customers in other cities and areas of the country. A power company that continued to rely on obsolete and high-cost facilities would be certain to create public resentment that would, in time, punish the company severely. Consequently, managers of public monopolies must keep alert to developments in their fields and must pass on to their customers some part of the cost reductions made possible by new technologies.

Closer Costs and Prices for High-Volume Products

As a general thing, costs and prices tend to come closer together for products made in large volume than for those in which total sales are small. This is true because the large volumes may already have attracted a great number of competitors, who have reduced prices to obtain a share of the market, or because the early participants in the fields may have lowered prices to avoid attracting new competitors. Either way, the public benefits.

For example, the production of sulfuric acid in the United States is now in excess of 70 billion pounds per year. Selling prices usually are only 10% to 15% higher than the cost of manufacture, which has increased in recent years but at a rate far below the national rate of inflation. On the other hand, a specialty chemical produced at the rate of a few thousand pounds per year may sell at five or ten times the cost of manufacture. Very high profit margins, even for small volume products, will in time attract new competitors who will cut these prices. But some very small products, such as an eyeglass cleaner, may continue indefinitely to sell at 50 times the cost of manufacture. This is because the real contribution of the manufacturer lies not in his process for production, which may be a simple mixing of liquids, but in setting up a distribution system that is able to locate customers and sell to them.

Similarly, electronic connectors, which are now manufactured by the trillions, generally sell at a markup of only 5% 15% above cost of manufacture. However, a special electronic paste that sells only a few thousand pounds per year may have a markup of 60% or 70% above cost of manufacture.

PRICES AND QUALITY

Buyers like competitive pricing because it leads to lower prices. Sellers, for this same reason, like to relegate price to a secondary position and sell on the basis that they have superior quality rather than lower prices.

Because all the competitors in a field are likely to claim they have superior quality, it is obvious that in at least 50% of the cases these claims are empty puffery. But businessman A knows that if he can convince the customer that A's quality is superior to B and C, the customer may be willing to pay a premium price, or if the prices are the same, jump at the opportunity to buy from A.

Oddly enough, it is possible for A, B, and C all to make claims of superior quality and for all to be correct—but not for the same customer.

The products of A, B, and C are practically never identical. Even if all three are producing a commodity, such as sulfuric acid, their processes, end products, and raw materials are not identical. For most purposes, the three products may function in exactly the same manner but in some other application; even minor variations in composition may affect the result remarkably. The most "impure" product may be the one that is most effective.

The seller who is able to mesh the peculiarities of his product with the particular needs of his customer can do himself as well as his customer a real service. Of course, it is also possible that a trace impurity in a product may do great harm to a customer, even though the product passes all the established tests for high quality.

PRICES AND CONSISTENCY

Consistency in the quality of a product is a factor that the customer may be willing to pay a premium price for. The reactions of the public to different brands of gasoline illustrate both cases.

Oil companies know that the chemical composition of their gasoline varies from week to week or even day to day but they generally succeed in putting out a product that performs the same way in an automobile all the time. Consequently, most customers are unwilling to pay a premium price for consistency—when these customers are choosing among the better established oil companies. There are examples of customer loyalty to a given brand, but usually a difference of even a cent or two per gallon will send the automobile owner to the station across the street with the lower prices.

However, small oil companies that are not well known are generally forced to sell at lower prices even though the quality of their gasolines may be excellent — most of the time. Many automobile owners have learned by bitter experience that the lesser known gasolines may be wet or corrosive at times. Nevertheless, if the price is enough lower than the well-known brands, the new gasoline will find some buyers.

Product Consistency Commands Premium Prices

Consistency of product is always an important factor in the drug and medicine fields. Consistent high quality generally will command a substantial premium in price. In some quarters, it is popular to argue that there is no difference between the more expensive trademark drugs and the cheaper generic types. There is no simple answer to this claim because sometimes there is a significant difference and other times there is not.

But those who say that "aspirin is always aspirin" are making an oversimplification. Nothing is chemically 100% pure; there are always a few strange molecules in even the purest acetyl salicylic acid. The question is whether the strange molecules are significant in their effect. For many of the more complex drugs, this question is much harder to answer.

To complicate matters still more, the most careful manufacturers sometimes make mistakes that elude the quality control system. What then is this manufacturer entitled to ask the public to pay for superior quality and consistency? There is no quantitative answer.

The manufacturers of photographic films for the printing industry present another interesting case concerning consistency and quality. These manufacturers are all aware that their products are not identical even when they sell head to head. Photographic films are incredibly complex compositions that change in properties as they age. They vary in optical speed and many other properties important to printers. These printers follow practices that vary from shop to shop. But each individual printer tends to maintain his own consistency of product. Consequently, all manufacturers of photographic films claim that their products are first in consistency. How much of a premium price can this "greater" consistency command? It is an interesting fact that most suppliers conclude that they must sell at the going price for the product concerned, but some are forced to sell at lower prices. Nevertheless, it would be a mistake to conclude that a manufacturer selling at 10% below the going price was 10% more inconsistent than the bulk of his competitors. The relationship between price and consistency is not a quantitative one.

PRICE AND OFF-QUALITY MATERIAL

Most of the time, manufacturers cling steadfastly to the claim that their product is not only superior in quality but is consistently superior. However, at times their own testing shows clearly that they have made a substandard product and they realize that the customer's tests will show the same thing just as clearly. How should this substandard product be removed from the market?

Can it be reworked and made standard or can it best be sold at a lower price to some customer who can use it satisfactorily? The answer varies, of course, depending on the full set of circumstances. The measure of a good manager is his ability to decide when to do what.

Manufacturers of plastics and elastomeric products, such as synthetic rubber, face the problem continually because these materials are polymers that have more possibilities for mistakes than simpler materials. Sometimes

customers beg to be supplied with the low-priced, low-quality material that may work perfectly well in their application. The sales manager may even plead for the production of more off-quality material or for the labeling of standard material as "off-quality." The general manager who yields to such requests is operating on very tricky ground because he is feeding an insatiable appetite. Word of his behavior may soon reach his other customers who have been paying the full price for standard material.

PRICE AND PERFORMANCE

Finished products such as automobiles, television sets, and washing machines are sold partly on the basis of price, of course, but expected performance is more important to making the sale than a few percentage points in the price. Dealers in Chevrolets, Fords, Plymouths, and dozens of other foreign and domestic cars realize this as do their customers. A few dollars up or down will not be as decisive as the customer's idea of what kind of performance he can expect. This expectation of performance is based to only a small extent on what specific new features each car has. Mostly it is a matter of past performance by other cars of that make. A possible exception to all this concerns the miles per gallon performance which has become more and more important in recent years. Past performance no longer serves as a good guide to the customer who now relies heavily on claims posted by the manufacturer and determined by standardized road tests.

PRICES AND STYLE

Automobiles also illustrate the importance of style in determining what price the customer is willing to pay. Nothing is more difficult to quantify or even to define than style. Style is an appeal to esthetic values that vary from place to place, from time to time, and from one age group to another. It is partly whim and caprice but some inherent values, no matter how hard they are to define, seem to be involved.

The manager who is able to identify and assess these elements of style better than his or her competitors is an enormously valuable person to the firm involved. Some critics of free enterprise are offended by the high value often assigned to style, but they generally propose only to substitute their whims and caprices for those of the paying customer. The catering to style is clearly expensive but the free-enterprise system demands that style have its say in setting prices.

PRICES AND "VALUE-IN-USE"

As already mentioned, a new product may have no direct competition in kind but it permits the customer to do what he wants to have done in a quite different manner. In such cases, it was popular a few years ago to say that the price for the new product should be set by determining its "value-in-use." That is, how much does the new product save the customer, compared with his old procedure for doing whatever he was doing? This idea of "value-in-use" has a certain logic but it frequently fails to come up with useful numbers for prices because of false assumptions and an inability to assign quantitative values to factors that are inherently subjective. The numbers finally chosen can be put in the computer and processed mathematically but the result is no better than the assumptions.

For example, when the phthalocyanine blue and green pigments were invented they were quickly tried in printing inks and accepted by printers as superior products. They were brighter than the older pigments, more lightfast, and had many other desirable properties. But what was the "value-in-use" of phthalocyanine pigments? Should they be priced the same as the older pigments on a pound basis or on their greater covering power? And how much value should be assigned to their superior brightness and lightfastness? "Value-in-use" studies were no more able to answer these questions quantitatively than they were

able to give a quantitative value to the smoky taste of scotch whiskey when compared to bourbon. And if the exercise of "value-in-use" is futile in comparing two types of whiskey, it is even more so when asked to compare bourbon with beefsteak or hip boots.

When printed circuit boards and silicon chips began to replace wiring and tubes in computers and television sets, it was easy to see that the new technology gave cheaper end products. But these "value-in-use" studies did practically nothing to determine what the prices for printed circuit boards and silicon chips should be. Instead, the prices plunged as volume increased. Prices today are the result of thousands of decisions made by hundreds of competitors who were, since the beginning, competing with each other and not with the outmoded technology that they were replacing.

"Value-in-use" studies may indicate whether a given proposed price is in the ball park or not, but they do not tell whether the batter has hit a single, double, triple, or inside-the-park home run. There is no substitute for the intuitive judgment of experienced managers, followed by trials in the marketplace, when a firm is trying to decide what its price for a new product should be.

PRICES AND DISCOUNTS

When the consuming public concludes that the products of several competing companies are essentially the same in quality and consistency, it is just about inevitable that the prices of these competing firms will be the same. If company A tries to sell at a higher price than B and C, it will quickly start to lose sales and must come back to the prices of B and C. If A lowers its prices below B and C, then these two must come down in price or lose business to A. Other moves are possible, of course, in price competition involving A, B, and C. For example, if A lowers his prices but B and C believe that he has very limited capacity, they may elect to leave their prices at the old level, figuring that A cannot take much business from them. They will be better off with slightly lower volume but higher prices.

Even when a company concludes that it must, for any reason, sell its goods at lower prices than the competitors receive, this company will often publish list prices that are identical with the competitors' prices, but offer a discount of 5% or 10% to all customers. This discount is in reality, of course, a lower price but the myth of having the same prices as competitors may be useful to the morale of the selling force that likes to claim that its quality is the best.

If this discount is extremely successful in obtaining new business, it is not likely to last long for two reasons. First, competitors will respond with a discount of their own if they lose too much business. Second, the company initiating the discount will probably eliminate it as soon as this company approaches a volume close to capacity.

Certain other discounts, such as those for prompt payment of bills, are much more likely to become a permanent part of the marketplace. Prompt payment discounts promote an orderly settling of accounts and are useful to both the seller and buyer. However, on occasion these discounts have become price competition devices. Examples include granting large discount rates in excess of current interest rates and allowing prompt payment discounts even when payments are late.

Prompt payment discounts on late payments are a dangerous practice because they serve an insatiable appetite too much like the selling of standard goods at "off-quality" prices.

Promotional discounts, scheduled to last for only a brief period, are sometimes extended if they are very successful. If they succeed too well, they are almost certain to provoke retaliation of some sort—either in kind or a new promotion conceived by a competitor. One measure of a skilled sales manager is his ability to decide when a promotional discount has been of maximum value to his company and therefore should be ended.

A great many kinds of discounts, based on volume, freight, and other factors have been tried, as each company in a competitive situation seeks to exploit any natural advantage it has. For example, if company A sells most of its products to nearby customers while B and C and the other suppliers are much further away, then A may elect to allow a discount for all or part of the freight charges. If this discount is very successful in obtaining or holding business, then B and C are likely to respond in kind even though it costs them more to do so.

PRICE FIXING

It is illegal in the United States and many other countries for business competitors to reach agreement concerning what their prices will be. This, of course, has not stopped some businessmen from meeting to fix prices any more than the laws against burglary have stopped all those who have a yearning to pick up what is not theirs. Not even the fact that price fixing is seldom, if ever, effective for very long has eliminated attempts at price fixing and they can be expected to occur in the future.

Nevertheless, the laws against price fixing are very valuable because these laws make it more difficult than would otherwise be the case, for the price fixing attempts to succeed for even brief periods of time. With the laws in place, price fixing meetings must take place in secret and the threats made to enforce any agreements must be veiled and ambiguous.

Why are price fixing attempts so appealing? The answer is complex but naivete is surely a factor in most cases.

Most businessmen know that they are in special jeopardy whenever they change prices either up or down and seek some special protection at the expense of their customers. They want the gain that can come from change without running the risk of loss. This is naive.

If businessman A, acting on his own as required by law, raises prices he knows that B and C may leave theirs unchanged for a while, and thereby pick up part of his business. It is a part of the risk A must take in reaching for higher prices. On the other hand, if A lowers prices, hoping to take business from B and C, he knows that B and C may lower theirs immediately so that A, B, and C all lose, but the customers gain. Even worse, from A's point of view, B and C may leave their prices unchanged and depend on quality advantages, real or imaginary, for holding their business even at prices higher than A is now charging. A is the only loser.

It seems to A, in his lonely anxiety, that any change he makes is likely to do him harm but he is under pressure to make changes anyway. So if he is naive and fails to think it all through, the thought occurs to him that the dilemma can be solved by getting together with B and C and having them all agree to raise their prices the same amounts. Thus the conspiring begins.

Conspiring soon ends, because it always carries with it the seed of its own destruction. This seed is the dissatisfaction of each conspirator with the share alloted to him. Having broken the law, the conspirators will not hesitate to cheat each other whenever they think they see an opportunity, which usually is every week or even every day.

A is not satisfied with his share of the business and he knows that a lower price is one of the most effective ways to gain new business. So he goes to a major customer and offers him a "hidden" discount for a larger share of the business. However, when the representative of B learns that he has lost the business he asks the customer why and eventually learns the answer. The purchasing agent may be a friend of B and tell him openly about the new discount, or if he has promised not to do that he may "carelessly" leave on his desk an invoice showing the hidden discount.

Anyway, A learns why he has lost the business and he responds somehow. He may simply and openly cut the price or he may use some other device to take business from B at another location. Or he may pull some other trick on C who then decides to get even with both A and B. And so it goes. Pretty soon the illegal agreement has so many holes in it that it is clearly worthless and the conspirators must meet again secretly to make a new one. But this second one deteriorates even faster than the first.

The electrical conspiracy of the 1960s was a perfect example of the futility of price fixing. There was excess capacity among the manufacturers and prices had gone down so much that returns on investment were generally quite low. The conspiracies that sprang up attempted to aid all suppliers at the expense of all customers, but the greed of the conspirators came to the rescue of the customers. An agreement on price and share of market would not last a week. By the end of a month, the agreement was being violated in so many places that free enterprise was always present whether it was welcome or not.

So the conspirators met frequently, even regularly at one time, but always to no avail because each time they solemnly vowed not to cheat each other and each time quickly broke their vows. When supplier A lost an account because of a lower price granted by B then A quickly took that information to B's other customers and the race was on. Soon everyone in the industry knew about the conspiracy and eventually the United States Department of Justice had enough information to prosecute many of those involved.

Price fixing has a better chance of lasting for a while, of course, if only two conspirators are involved. If the conspiracy is highly successful and prices and returns on investment remain high, then a third competitor is certain to be attracted to the field. And next a fourth, followed by a fifth.

Price fixing on an international basis, in countries where it is not illegal, can succeed but even here certain conditions must exist. The most important of these conditions is that demand for the product must exceed supply and in such circumstances prices inevitably go up anyway, without a conspiracy. Prices being set by the oil cartel will collapse as soon as some members of the cartel are selling less oil than they wish to sell. This will not happen, of course, until alternate sources of energy are developed by the cartel's customers and the demand for oil becomes at least a little less than the cartel, individually and collectively, wishes to sell.

SUMMARY

Competitive pricing is not an exact science. It is mostly a matter of starting with the current situation and modifying it by trial and error, as directed by experience, intuition, and whim.

The price is never entirely satisfactory to sellers and when it is nearly so, it is certain to change because new competitors will be drawn into this attractive field. This new competition will bring about prices that are less satisfactory to the sellers but more nearly satisfactory to the buyers.

The system of competitive pricing has a lot of lost motion in it and many inequities are always present, but the system is fluid and keeps changing under the pressures created by the self-interest of individual buyers and sellers. Because self-interest is a universal human characteristic, it gives a voice to the many—not to just a few—in the setting of prices.

30
Impact of Capacity Levels on Product Unit Cost

D. Gordon Gibson
Manager
Ernst & Whinney

The unit manufacturing cost, which is influenced by the capacity level, could lead to misleading product cost/selling price relationships if the incorrect capacity level has been used. The author discusses five methods for arriving at capacities and demonstrates the impact on unit costs for each of the methods.

When accountants allocate indirect overhead costs to products, a major consideration is the selection of an appropriate volume of production or capacity level. Capacity level refers to the total amount of some appropriate unit of activity (direct labor hours, direct labor dollars, machine hours, and so on) that will be divided into the indirect costs to arrive at a unit cost for product costing. In selecting an appropriate capacity level, the accountant should use an approach that is acceptable under generally accepted accounting principles (GAAP) and to the Internal Revenue Service, while at the same time providing management with a realistic measure of idle or unused capacity costs.

It is the measurement and treatment of unused capacity costs that present the accountant with a problem. Many contend that the indirect overhead costs of plant and equipment should be applied to the goods produced only to the extent that those facilities were used in the production of goods. For example, if a plant was expected to produce 10,000 units

and produced only 5,000 units, then only half the cost of plant and equipment was applicable to goods produced while the remainder was spent maintaining unused capacity. Therefore, this portion of the cost should not be applied to the cost of goods produced, but instead be treated as a period cost.

DIFFICULTY OF MEASURING IDLE FACILITY COSTS

GAAP provides, under some circumstances, for idle facility costs to be treated as a current period charge rather than as a part of the cost of production. However, idle facility costs are not defined. The accountant is left to decide whether the facility must be completely idle "in mothballs" or if portions of the expense attributable to underutilization can be considered idle facility costs. If the concept of treating the cost of unutilized capacity as a charge to the current period is acceptable, then the accountant must next select an appropriate basis for effectively measuring the capacity of the plant and equipment.

Deciding on the appropriate volume of production or capacity level is not an easy task. There appears to be no real agreement as to which concept of capacity level is most appropriate. Actual/expected capacity, normal capacity, practical capacity, and theoretical capacity are some of the more common approaches in use. In addition to the capacity levels just mentioned, I would like to introduce another type of capacity level called *rate of return capacity*. Rate of return capacity is based on the idea that the capacity level chosen should be coordinated with manage-

ment's profit objectives. Preferably, the capacity level chosen should be based on the level of capacity needed to produce a desired rate of return on the company's investment in plant and equipment. When a company is considering a new investment in plant and equipment, its decision is often based on the investment's rate of return. To determine the rate of return, it is necessary to prepare estimates of sales, costs, and volume. This required an evaluation of the number of units the plant was capable of producing and what volume of production and sales would be needed to obtain a satisfactory return. However, these same companies, once the invest-

Table 1. Impact of using alternate production volumes to allocate fixed production costs

	ACTUAL/ EXPECTED CAPACITY	NORMAL CAPACITY	PRACTICAL CAPACITY	THEORETICAL CAPACITY	RATE OF RETURN CAPACITY
I. Units					
Beginning inventory	30,000	30,000	30,000	30,000	30,000
Manufactured	160,000	160,000	160,000	160,000	160,000
Subtotal	190,000	190,000	190,000	190,000	190,000
Sold	150,000	150,000	150,000	150,000	150,000
Ending inventory	40,000	40,000	40,000	40,000	40,000
II. Operating results					
Sales ($5.00 per unit)	$750,000	$750,000	$750,000	$750,000	$750,000
Cost of goods sold					
Standard cost of goods sold					
Variable costs ($1.50 per unit)	225,000	225,000	225,000	225,000	225,000
Fixed costs[a]	375,000	333,000	199,500	166,500	300,000
Period costs					
Actual	400,000	400,000	400,000	400,000	400,000
Fixed costs absorbed[b]	(400,000)	(355,200)	(212,800)	(177,600)	(320,000)
Total cost of sales	600,000	602,800	611,700	613,900	605,000
Gross Margin	150,000	147,200	138,300	136,100	145,000
General expenses	145,000	145,000	145,000	145,000	145,000
Profit (loss) before income taxes	5,000	2,200	(6,700)	(8,900)	-0-
Federal income taxes (50%)	2,500	1,100	-0-	-0-	-0-
Net profit (loss)	$ 2,500	$ 1,100	$ (6,700)	$ (8,900)	$ -0-
Basis for standard fixed cost per unit					
Total cost	$400,000	$400,000	$400,000	$400,000	$400,000
Standard production volume	160,000	180,000	300,000	360,000	200,000
Unit cost	$2.50	$2.22	$1.33	$1.11	$2.00

[a]Standard fixed cost per unit × Units Sold.
[b]Standard fixed cost per unit × Units Manufactured.

ment is made, will then use some other capacity level to measure capacity cost. From the many cost-accounting systems that I have had the opportunity to review, it appears that few companies, if any, use a capacity level based on rate of return.

Before we begin to discuss the different types of capacity levels in detail, it should be understood that the level chosen will have an impact on reported profits. Table 1 shows the profit results for each of the capacity levels to be discussed where there has been a change in the number of units in inventory (before consideration of lower of cost or market). If there had been no change in inventory, which is rare, the results from all methods would be the same.

Actual/Expected Capacity

This approach allocates production cost to products based on the expected actual capacity for the coming year. It attempts to charge products with the actual expenses expected to be incurred. Actual costs not absorbed during the year might be treated as a period cost (if not significant) or allocated to the goods produced. This approach is often used when there is disagreement on what is normal production. Many accountants feel that this is not an acceptable approach because it does not recognize the cost of unutilized capacity as a period cost and instead allocates a portion of that cost to units in inventory. Also, it does not provide management with information telling them what is the minimum capacity level that must be achieved to meet desired profit objectives. As shown in Table 1, profits can be overstated because of the capitalization in inventory of unused capacity costs.

Using actual production appears acceptable only when the actual production results in management reaching or exceeding its return on investment goals. When this happens, there is little interest in determining the cost of unused capacity.

Normal Capacity

Normal capacity appears to be the most widely used basis and is acceptable to the IRS. It is ordinarily based upon the historic experience of the plant. There are a number of variations on how to arrive at what is normal capacity. For example, it can be the highest level of production actually attained or it could be an average of several prior years' production. Usually, it is an average of more than one year's experience. The key to this level of activity is that it is an activity level that the company actually experienced.

Once the normal capacity level has been established, it will not change from year to year except in those years where there have been significant increases or decreases in the investment in plant and equipment that change the facilities' actual rate of production materially. Normally, at the end of each year the allocated expenses will differ from the actual expenses incurred. This can be caused by spending differences from budget or the actual capacity level. The amount not absorbed can be treated as a period cost as shown in Table 1.

The primary difficulty I have with this approach is it tends to lose sight of the original profit objectives of the capital investment. Table 2 shows the profit objectives of the capital investment. Table 2 shows the profit that would be obtained if the production level for each approach used in Table 1 were obtained and all units produced were also sold. Table 2, assuming management wished to earn a 20% return on invested assets, shows a case where normal production does not achieve that result. Therefore, any unabsorbed capacity variances that would result from using this approach are developed from a capacity level that is too low. If the level (standard) is not desirable, then how can the variance be meaningful or provide a reasonable estimate of capacity usage? Normal capacity becomes acceptable only when the desired capacity is reached or exceeded.

Table 2. Results of achieving standard production volume

	ACTUAL/ EXPECTED CAPACITY	NORMAL CAPACITY	PRACTICAL CAPACITY	THEORETICAL CAPACITY	RATE OF RETURN CAPACITY
I. Units					
Beginning inventory	30,000	30,000	30,000	30,000	30,000
Manufactured	160,000	180,000	300,000	360,000	200,000
Subtotal	190,000	210,000	330,000	390,000	230,000
Sold	150,000	170,000	290,000	350,000	190,000
Ending inventory	40,000	40,000	40,000	40,000	40,000
II. Operating results					
Sales ($5.00 per unit)	$750,000	$850,000	$1,450,000	$1,750,000	$950,000
Cost of goods sold					
Standard cost of goods sold					
Variable costs ($1.50 per unit)	225,000	255,000	435,000	525,000	285,000
Fixed costs[a]	375,000	377,400	385,700	388,500	380,000
Period costs					
Actual	400,000	400,000	400,000	400,000	400,000
Fixed costs absorbed[b]	(400,000)	(400,000)	(400,000)	(400,000)	(400,000)
Total cost of sales	600,000	632,400	820,700	913,500	665,000
Gross Margin	150,000	217,600	629,300	836,500	285,000
General expenses	145,000	145,000	145,000	145,000	145,000
Profit (loss) before income taxes	5,000	72,600	484,300	691,500	140,000
Federal income taxes (50%)	2,500	36,300	242,150	345,750	70,000
Net profit (loss)	$ 2,500	$ 36,300	$ 242,150	$ 345,750	$ 70,000
Total assets	$350,000	$350,000	$ 350,000	$ 350,000	$350,000
Return on assets	1%	10%	69%	99%	20%
Standard fixed cost per unit	$2.50	$2.22	$1.33	$1.11	$2.00

[a]Standard fixed cost per unit × units sold.
[b]Standard fixed cost per unit × units manufactured.

Practical Capacity

Practical capacity was found to be used by a number of companies. It is the level of utilization that can be actually sustained over normal operating conditions and hours. It is often arrived at by taking the theoretical maximum rate and reducing it for expected and unavoidable operating delays such as maintenance, repairs, setups, and operator personal time. For example, if the plant was scheduled to be run two shifts a day, five days a week, this level of capacity, less normal interruptions, would be the level used. In Tables 1 and 2, practical capacity was assumed to be 300,000 units over a two-shift operation. A capacity level based on practical capacity is changed only when the scheduled plant hours are changed and/or when equipment capacity is increased or decreased within the plant's scheduled hours of operation. Changes in operating costs and market conditions will have no effect on capacity level.

While practical capacity has been found to be used by a number of companies, it does not appear to be a satisfactory method unless the plant is actually operating at or very near this level. If the plant never reaches practical capacity, there is the question of whether management ever expected or needed to operate at this level in order to achieve its profit objectives. For example, management sometimes finds it more economical to provide for more capacity than is actually needed. If an investment decision were based on practical capacity where there was limited flexibility in increasing the scheduled hours, there would be very little margin for error in the investment calculations. Lower selling prices or higher costs could not be offset by increased production because the rate of return was already based on the maximum capacity that could be sustained. This means that a realistic and conservative investment calculation should provide for more plant capacity than is needed to obtain an acceptable rate of return. Therefore, it would appear that practical capacity is not a realistic measure of unused capacity if the investment in plant and equipment was not based on practical capacity and management did not expect to operate at this level.

As indicated in Table 2, this method could result in lower unit costs that are not realistic in relation to selling prices. This will result in lower inventory costs and understatement of profits as shown in Table 1 if this level of capacity is not reached.

Theoretical Capacity

This is the maximum output for which a plant is designed if it can be operated continuously without interruption. There is no allowance for down time or other normal interruptions. Because this level of activity cannot be sustained indefinitely, it is not considered an acceptable basis for allocating costs to production. It is also unlikely that a capital investment would be undertaken based on the need to achieve theoretical maximum capacity.

For example, Table 1 assumes that the plant could produce theoretically 180,000 units a year per shift (or 360,000 units in two shifts). Table 2 calculates the profit and rate of return on assets if that number of units could be produced and sold. The high rate of return on assets indicates the leverage effect. Also, it is not a realistic measure of capacity. It sets goals that will not be attained; any capacity variances have little or no value.

Rate of Return Capacity

When predetermined rates are used based on a certain activity level, any resulting variance from that activity level (capacity or volume variance) is supposed to indicate to management how effectively they are using the plant's capacity. The activity level standard, as with other standards, should be desirable, realistic, and meaningful. Using the rate of return for making a capital investment decision appears to satisfy these requirements and is consistent with management's objectives. If management's goal is to have a 20% return on investment, it would seem preferable to use the activity level upon which this investment is based rather than use a normal activity level that yields only a 10% return on assets or use a practical capacity level that would yield a higher return but could not be attained.

To evaluate new capital investment, management must predict the annual net cash inflow from the project and predict the number of years the annual net cash flow is expected to continue. The cash flow for each year is then discounted, using the appropriate present value tables, to arrive at the expected rate of return. Predicting the annual net cash inflow involves an extensive study that includes estimating sales, production levels, and operating costs. Based on these estimates, most new ventures will probably have an uneven cash flow over the early years of the project. This is because of plant startup problems and time needed to build sales volume. Thus the estimated production levels used is the investment analysis would vary from year to year over the life of the investment. Eventually if everything goes as expected, a maximum production volume will be attained.

This maximum production volume should be the capacity level used for calculating the standard rates for fixed costs. Using this capacity level will result in a portion of the fixed costs being written off as a period cost rather than carried in inventory in those years the maximum production volume required by the investment was not attained. The fixed costs written off can be considered unused capacity or idle facility costs because an effective level of volume has been established in line with management profit objectives and it is a volume management expects to attain.

The estimated maximum production volume used in the investment study is the initial capacity level that should be used. However, the likelihood of events going as estimated would be unusual. Additional costs and changes in selling prices would all contribute to deviations from the plan, which could have an impact on the level of production needed to meet the investment rate of return. If prices fall, because of greater automation by competitors, management must consider the acquisition of more modern equipment.

BENEFITS OF USING RATE OF RETURN CAPACITY

Using rate of return means that management must evaluate operations constantly to decide how the plant capacity can be used effectively. This can result in decisions on new product lines, pricing, and operating costs. Comparing rate of return with capacity level would also indicate when a plant can no longer be operated economically, thus forcing management to look for alternative investments while disposing of uneconomical operations. For example, if the rate of return capacity needed was greater than practical capacity, management would first have to determine if the scheduled plant hours can be increased (e.g., third shift). If they cannot justify an increase in the scheduled hours, it would mean the plant has reached an operating capacity that is not realistic. As explained earlier, under theoretical capacity actual levels greater than practical capacity, for the scheduled hours, cannot be sustained over an extended period of time. Therefore, management cannot achieve the desired rate of return by increasing the volume of production because there is not sufficient unused capacity. Its only alternatives are price increases, reductions in operating costs, or increases in operating efficiencies. If these alternatives are not feasible, then management should consider other investment alternatives.

With capacity levels based on rate of return, resulting capacity variances will be more meaningful. Underabsorbed capacity indicates that other steps must be taken to offset this variance. However, it should be noted that achieving the expected capacity level does not necessarily mean the rate of return will be attained. Lower prices, changes in sales mix and other variances from budget must also be considered.

ALTERNATE BASIS FOR RATE OF RETURN

An alternate approach that would appear to be effective with existing plants would be to base capacity levels on the rate of return earned on assets. This ratio is calculated by dividing the sum of net profits after taxes plus interest expenses by total assets as shown in Table 2. (Table 2 assumes no interest expense). Total assets include cash, receivables, inventories, and other assets as well as the investment in plant and equipment. For a division within a company, total assets might include only inventory and fixed assets because these are readily identifiable. This ratio is an indicator of how the company is managing its resources and is useful when comparing efficiency of operations over a number of years or with the efficiency of other firms in the same industry. Often, management sets certain desirable ratios that plant managers must try to attain. If the rate of return standard has been established, it makes sense to determine the volume or capacity level needed to reach that rate of return standard. Variances below that capacity level can then be considered idle facility cost.

This approach, like the other methods of determining capacity level, would require re-evaluation each year based on changing operating and marketing conditions. Changes in total assets would also have an impact on the capacity volume needed to attain the desired rate of return.

SUMMARY

In summary, it appears that if management is to control capacity cost effectively, it should use a capacity level in line with its profit objectives. Capacity variances should be meaningful. By using rate of return as a guide in setting capacity levels, management will be evaluating the capital investment constantly based on the original criteria for that investment. Using rate of return will also result in inventory costs that will bear a reasonable relationship to the selling prices that can be obtained when those goods are sold.

31
The Learning Curve—A
Tool For Improving Performance

Raymond B. Jordan

Administrator
Cost Systems and Studies (ret.)
General Electric Company

The learning curve is based on the concept that whenever the total production of units doubles, the cumulative average cost per unit declines by a constant percentage. The author explains how this concept can be implemented.

INTRODUCTION

Since the mid-1930s, the aircraft companies, particularly the airframe manufacturers, have made extensive use of a technique known as the *theory of the learning curve*. This new technique, however, did not become widespread until the reliability of its application was verified by several government-sponsored projects investigating the actual cost trend of World War II production.

The learning curve has now become an accepted tool in industry for projecting shop loads, determining manpower requirements, and negotiating subcontracts. The armed forces, especially the Air Force, now use the technique to determine the reasonableness of quotations from prime contractors.

BASIC THEORY

We all recognize that the more often we repeat an operation, the more proficient we become, whether we are practicing the piano or running a milling machine. The theory of

the learning curve holds that this proficiency increases steadily and is expressed by the following rule:

Whenever the total quantity of units produced doubles, the cumulative average cost per unit declines by a constant percentage.

This constant percentage identifies the degree of cost decline or learning experienced. Table 1 is a simple illustration of a 90%

Table 1. Illustration of a 90% learning curve

CUMULATIVE PRODUCTION	CUMULATIVE AVERAGE HOURS PER UNIT	RATIO TO PREVIOUS CUMULATIVE AVERAGE
1	100.0 hours	—
2	90.00	90%
4	81.0	90%
8	72.9	90%
16	65.6	90%
32	59.0	90%
64	53.1	90%
128	47.8	90%

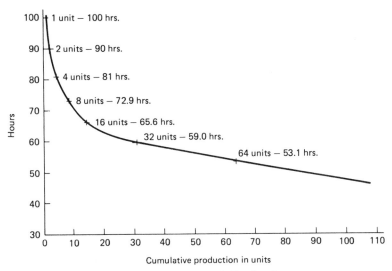

FIGURE 1. Graphic illustration of 90% learning curve.

learning curve. Note that as the quantity doubles, the new cumulative average hours per unit are 90% of the previous cumulative average hours. Hours have been used as a basis for this simple illustration, but factory cost or selling price applies equally as well.

Figure 1 shows the 90% sample from Table

1 plotted on ordinary graph paper. Here the cumulative average hours per unit are shown on the vertical axis and the cumulative units produced are shown on the horizontal axis. Note that the decline in average hours is fairly rapid at first, but as the quantity continues to double, the difference in hours between suc-

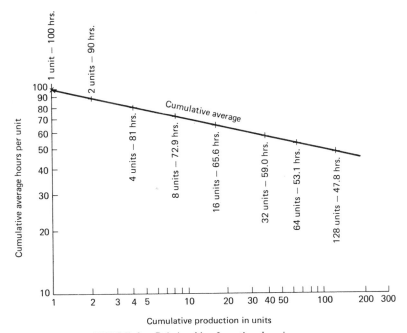

FIGURE 2. Relationships for other learning curves.

cessive units becomes ever smaller until it approaches zero.

Just how fast does cost decline take place whenever production doubles? Using the 90% illustration from Table 1, the calculation is as follows:

2 units @ 90 hrs. cumulative average	180 total hours
Subtract 1 unit @ 100 hours	100
Hours required to produce second unit	80 hours

This leads to the conclusion that, in a 90% learning curve, whenever production of a unit is doubled, the average value of the additional block or 100% increase in production is 80% of the previous cumulative average. Figure 2 shows this relationship for other learning curves. As can be seen from Figure 2, a 50% learning curve would require making the next block for nothing. In general, a learning curve below 70% is impractical. By now you can see that a learning percentage of 100% would indicate no learning at all, while a percentage in excess of 100% would indicate that costs were increasing, which is otherwise known as *reverse learning*.

Table 2. Relationship between 100% block increase and previous cumulative average

LEARNING PERCENT	RATIO OF 100% BLOCK INCREASE TO PREVIOUS CUMULATIVE AVERAGE
95%	90%
90	80
85	70
80	60
75	50
70	40
65	30
60	20
55	10
50	0

Figure 2 is a plot of the data from Table 1 using log-log graph paper. Plotting of the data on log-log paper results in a straight line. Later you will see that this relationship is very helpful in performing learning curve calculations.

Figure 1 showed an example of a 90% learning curve plotted upon ordinary graph paper. It was noted that as production continued to increase, the curve tended to level out so that eventually it became parallel to the horizontal axis wherein the difference in cost

Table 3. Difference in hours per unit—90% learning

CUMULATIVE PRODUCTION	CUMULATIVE AVERAGE HOURS	QUANTITY	PER BLOCK AVERAGE PER UNIT	BLOCK REDUCTION
1	100.0 hours	1	100.0 hours	—
2	90.0	1	80.0	20.0 hours
4	81.0	2	72.0	8.0
8	72.9	4	64.8	7.2
16	65.6	8	58.3	6.5
32	59.0	16	52.4	5.9
64	53.1	32	47.2	5.2
128	47.8	64	42.5	4.7
256	43.0	128	38.2	4.3
512	38.7	256	34.4	3.8
1,024	34.8	512	30.9	3.5
2,028	31.3	1,024	27.8	3.1
4,096	28.2	2,048	25.1	2.7

between successive units approaches zero. The rate of reduction in cost between blocks as production doubles is an interesting study. Table 3, for example, describes this phenomenon.

Theoretically, because the learning curve is a geometric progression, cost would still be declining at infinity, but the difference between units would be impossible to measure. For all practical purposes, learning ceases by the time 5,000 units are reached. In Table 3, although the average of the last block has declined by 2.7 hours from the previous block, the difference between units 4,095 and 4,096 is only 0.8 hours. We will learn later, however, that learning continues only while there is a motivating power such as a dynamic cost-reduction program.

LEARNING EXPLAINED

The word "learning" as applied to the decline in cost or hours of a product as production increases is actually incorrect. "Experience" is probably a more correct description although "cost progress" is used by some authors. Now let us examine the various factors that contribute to the decline in cost as production increases shown in Table 4.

Table 4. Factors influencing learning

1. Improved proficiency of the operator as production increased
2. Reductions in manufacturing losses
3. Stabilization of design resulting in fewer design changes
4. Increases in lot size
5. Improvement in special tooling
6. An adequate cost-reduction and value-analysis program
7. Changing from daywork to piecework as an employee payment system
8. Changing from manual to automatic machinery as production warrants.

WHAT LEARNING CAN BE EXPECTED

In the various illustrations in this text, a 90% learning curve has been used. This is not to imply that this is the optimum learning rate. There is no rule of thumb by which learning rates may be selected. For many years the airframe manufacturers, who were the pioneers in the development of learning theory, have talked of an 80% curve. Examination of results published by various study groups, however, does not support this theory. For example, a study by the Rand Corporation[1] showing the results of 12 post–World War II fighter aircraft listed a range from 67.3% to 91.1%.

In many instances, learning results are influenced by the degree of preparation by industrial engineering crews before production of a new product begins. If a poor job is done, leading to excessive starting costs and manufacturing problems, a high degree of learning will result. If a good job of preplanning is done, leading to lower starting costs and few manufacturing problems, a rate might result that, to the casual observer, would indicate poor performance. The average unit cost over a long period would show, however, that the poorer slope experienced the lowest cost.

THE MATHEMATICS OF THE LEARNING CURVE

The path of the learning curve represents the path of a geometric series or progression wherein each point is determined by multiplying the previous point by a constant factor as represented by Table 1 and Figure 1. The plotted learning curve from Figure 1 is a hyperbola with the following formula:

$$Y = KX^{-N}$$

where Y = the cumulative average cost (or hours) for X units
K = the value of the first unit (theoretical or actual)

N = the exponent representing the rate of learning which is equivalent to the tangent of the angle which the learning curve on a log-log paper makes with the horizontal axis.

The Formula for N

The formula used for the logarithmic plot in Figure 2 is represented by the following formula:

$$\log Y = \log K - N \log X$$

all variables are as described previously.

Manipulation of this formula at a doubling point results in a formula for N as follows:

$$N = \frac{\log \text{ (learning percent)}}{\log 2}$$

To derive the value of N for a 90% curve,

$$N = \frac{\log 0.9}{\log 2} = \frac{9.95424 - 10}{0.30103} = -$$

$$\frac{0.4576}{0.30103} = -0.1520$$

Values for N for a wide range of curves are shown in Table 5.

The Conversion Factor

If the cumulative average value (Y) for X units equal X^{-N}, assuming the value for the first unit is one, it follows that the extended value would be $(X)(X^{-N})$.

Because we add exponents when we multiply, we can simplify this result as follows:

$$Y \text{ (extended value)} = X^{1-N}$$

Under differential calculus, any individual unit would have a value represented by the first derivative of the foregoing equation. Thus to find the value of the Xth unit when the cumulative average value for X units in known, we take the first derivative as follows:

$$\frac{dy}{dx} = (1-N) (X^{-N})$$

But we already know that X^{-N} is the cumulative average value for X units. Thus we can conclude that by subtracting the value for N for any learning curve from 1 we arrive at a handy factor for the last unit. A wide range of values for the conversion factor $1-N$ is shown in Table 5.

We will find later that multiplying the factor by the cumulative average value for X units will give us the value for the Xth unit. Likewise, if we are given the value for the Xth unit we may find the cumulative average value by dividing by $1-N$.

Table 5. Values for the conversion factor 1—N

LEARNING %	SLOPE N	1 − N
70%	0.5146	0.4854
71	0.4942	0.5058
72	0.4739	0.5261
73	0.4541	0.5459
74	0.4345	0.5655
75	0.4150	0.5850
76	0.3959	0.6041
77	0.3771	0.6229
78	0.3585	0.6415
79	0.3401	0.6599
80	0.3219	0.6781
81	0.3041	0.6959
82	0.2863	0.7137
83	0.2688	0.7312
84	0.2516	0.7484
85	0.2345	0.7655
86	0.2176	0.7824
87	0.2009	0.7991
88	0.1845	0.8155
89	0.1681	0.8319
90	0.1520	0.8480
91	0.1361	0.8639
92	0.1204	0.8796
93	0.1047	0.8953
94	0.0892	0.9108
95	0.0740	0.9260
96	0.0589	0.9411
97	0.0439	0.9561

The Cumulative Average Factors

Assuming that the value of the first unit is one in the basic equation, solving for different values for X will result in factors that when applied to the theoretical value (or actual) of the first unit, will bring learning-curve calculations within the range of a desk calculator. If the cumulative average value is known, the theoretical value of the first unit (a necessary calculation in learning-curve extrapolation) may be obtained by dividing by the factor. For those who do not like to divide, the reciprocal of the factor may be used for multiplication. Values for factors for a range of learning rates are shown in Table 6 along with reciprocals.

For purposes of illustration, we will determine the cumulative average factor for 100 units in order to show the reader how to derive factors not shown in Table 6.

$$\text{Factor (100)} = 100^{-0.152} = (\log 100)\,(0.152) = -0.304$$

Because this is a negative logarithm, we must convert to positive by subtracting from 10.

$$\text{Factor (100)} = \text{antilog } 9.696 - 10 = 0.4966$$

which checks with the value in the table.

The Percent Additional Factor

A little used factor, but one that can be helpful in extrapolating learning curves based upon historical data, is the *percent additional factor*. In using the formula, the factor is applied to the cumulative average of all historical data. Selection of the factor is based upon the ratio of the desired quantity to the previous cumulative average quality. It is presumed that the user has a knowledge of the learning rate. The formula is as follows:

$$F = \frac{(1.0+P)^{1+N}-1.0}{P}$$

where

F = the factor
P = the ratio of the desired quantity to the previous cumulative quantity
$1+N$ = the conversion or last unit factor shown in Table 5.

Table 6. Mathematical factors 90% learning

QUANTITY	Y	K	PERCENT ADDITIONAL	FACTOR
25	0.6131	1.6311	25%	0.8333
50	0.5518	1.8122	50	0.8207
75	0.5188	1.9276	75	0.8098
100	0.4966	2.0135	100	0.8000
125	0.4800	2.0832	125	0.7913
150	0.4670	2.1415	150	0.7833
175	0.4561	2.1925	175	0.7761
200	0.4470	2.2372	200	0.7693
225	0.4390	2.2779	225	0.7631
250	0.4321	2.3144	250	0.7573
275	0.4258	2.3485	275	0.7518
300	0.4203	2.3794	300	0.7467
325	0.4151	2.4089	325	0.7418
350	0.4105	2.4358	350	0.7372
375	0.4062	2.4618	375	0.7329
400	0.4023	2.4858	400	0.7287
425	0.3985	2.5091	425	0.7248
450	0.3952	2.5307	450	0.7210
475	0.3919	2.5519	475	0.7174
500	0.3889	2.5715	500	0.7139
525	0.3859	2.5910	525	0.7106
550	0.3833	2.6090	550	0.7074
575	0.3806	2.6271	575	0.7043
600	0.3783	2.6438	600	0.7013

To derive the percent additional factor for 100 units when a total of 200 units have already been produced, the additional percent is 50% and the value for $1+N$ for a 90% curve is 0.848.

$$F(50\%) = \frac{(1+0.5)^{0.848}-1}{0.5} =$$

$$\frac{0.41035}{0.5} = 0.8207$$

A wide range of factors for a 90% curve are included in Table 6.

LIMITATIONS OF THE LEARNING CURVE

The theory of the learning curve can be applied adequately to a new line of apparatus or a line that has been in operation for some time but has not reached the end of learning.

It cannot be applied to any products that have been mass-produced for a number of years and can be assumed to have reached the point on the curve where the difference between successive units approaches zero.

New products that represent an old product with specific design changes may be applied to learning theory, but it will be necessary to determine the point on the learning curve that applies to both products. A practical application of this type will be shown later.

Apparatus with a long cycle, such as three years for the manufacture of a large steam turbine, generally are not adaptable to learning-curve calculations because learning is lost between units and frequently there is excessive employee turnover.

Shipbuilding construction would appear to be in the class of long-cycle apparatus. There are individual segments of ships, however, such as bulkheads and panels that are used throughout the ship, which could experience learning.

Home building construction, such as the building of a large quantity of homes in a new development, should experience learning providing there are only a few crews involved.

Mass-produced items, such as television sets and refrigerators, should experience learning on the first 5,000 units (or thereabouts). By that time, all methods have been established and there is very little opportunity for cost improvement without disturbing the production setup. It should be remembered, however, that the major contribution to learning after starting costs have been liquidated and peak production reached is a dynamic cost-reduction program. This means that the door is always open to learning if management decisions regarding cost reduction and value analysis can be made.

COST ELEMENTS AND THE LEARNING CURVE

Both material and labor costs are readily adaptable to learning-curve calculations. Materials, because they generally include the vendors' fixed charges (which bear no relation to volume), generally do not experience a steep slope. In making labor calculations, either hours or dollars are applicable. Because it is necessary to reflect the ravages of inflation, however, it is best to use hours in any calculations extending beyond the current year. This allows the results to be adjusted to reflect the expected labor rates for the proper year.

Although opinion is divided, overhead, because it reflects the impact of the entire business volume rather than the product being estimated, does not lend itself to learning-curve calculations. Once the labor calculations have been completed, the proper overhead rates may be applied reflecting the business volume that will be experienced in each year.

APPLICATIONS OF THE LEARNING CURVE

The application of the learning theory is almost unlimited. A few industrial applications now in use are as follows:

1. Setting selling prices for future production
2. Projecting labor loads in the factory
3. Determining manpower and facilities requirements
4. Control of shop labor
5. Determining realistic prices for subcontracted items
6. Estimating starting load costs of a new product
7. Examination of training programs of new employees to eliminate incompetent workers
8. Make-or-buy decisions.

Unlimited savings can result from use of the applications listed above even though limited to but a few applications.

Setting Selling Prices

Example One: In the defense industries, it frequently becomes necessary to establish selling prices for products to be manufactured

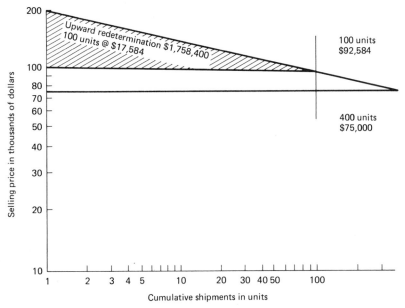

FIGURE 3. Price redetermination.

under some form of redetermination contract with retroactive redetermination at, for example, 25% of shipments. This form of pricing is especially adaptable to the first production contract following completion of development.

Consider the case wherein the contract includes 400 units at an average price of $75,000 per unit with retroactive redetermination at the end of the first 100 units shipped. Figure 3 illustrates the amount of upward redetermination that will take place following shipment of the 100th unit.

Using the factors from Table 6, the theoretical value of unit one is $75,000 times 2.4858 or $186,435. The first 100 units should have a value of $92,584, which is obtained by multiplying 186,435 by the factor for the cumulative average value for 100 units (0.4966).

Thus:

Learning curve value	$92,584
Contract price	75,000
Upward redetermination 100 units at	$17,584 or $17,758,400

This represents upward redetermination of approximately 23.5% which would place the

contractor in an unfavorable position with the Pentagon.

The contractor can reduce redetermination problems to a minimum by use of the learning curve. In this case, it is recommended that the contract be split into blocks of 50 engines each.

The value of unit one has already been determined ($186,435). From the tables:

MULTIPLY EACH BY $186,435	CUMULATIVE UNIT	CUMULATIVE AVERAGE VALUE
0.5518	50	$102,875
0.4966	100	92,584
0.4670	150	87,065
0.4470	200	83,336
0.4321	250	80,559
0.4203	300	78,359
0.4105	350	76,532
0.4023	400	75,000

The value of each block is then obtained by use of a desk calculator as follows:

First 50 units	$102,875
100 units at $92,584	9,258,400
50 units at $102,875	5,143,750
Total value of units 51–100	4,114,650
$\frac{4,114,650}{50}$	$ 82,293

By following the above method through each block, the quotation to the Pentagon would be as follows:

INDIVIDUAL BLOCKS		CUMULATIVE AVERAGE	
		UNITS	PRICE
First 50 units	$102,875	50	$102,875
Next 50 units	82,293	100	92,584
Next 50 units	76,027	150	87,065
Next 50 units	72,149	200	83,336
Next 50 units	69,451	250	80,559
Next 50 units	67,359	300	78,359
Next 50 units	65,570	350	76,532
Final 50 units	64,276	400	75,000

In order to remove the implication of extreme mathematical accuracy, it would be advisable to round off all figures to the nearest five dollars.

Example Two: A major design change often poses a problem in negotiating prices. Consider the case wherein a design change takes place at the end of 200 units. It will be necessary to determine at this point 1) the value of the parts common to both designs and 2) the value of the parts peculiar only to the design change.

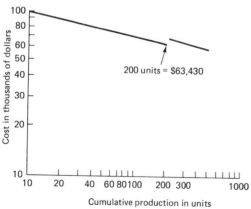

FIGURE 4. Design changes and selling prices.

In the example in Figure 4, the first 200 units of the superseded design had a cumulative average cost of approximately $63,430 which can be read from the chart or computed mathematically as follows:

First 10 units	$100,000	(from the chart)
Value of first unit	$141,900	(100,000 × 1.4190 from Figure 3)
200 unit average	$ 63,430	(141,900 × 0.4470 from Figure 3)

The value of parts common to both designs is $60,000. The first 100 sets of parts common only to the new design are expected to cost $5,000. Required: Expected cost of first 200 units of the new design.

Common Parts:

First 200 units	$ 60,000 (basic assumption)
Value of first unit	134,230 (60,000 × 2.2372)
Cumulative average — 400 units	54,000 (134,230 × 0.4023)
400 units at $54,000	21,600,000
200 units at 60,000	12,000,000
Total cost of next 200 units	9,600,000
Cost per unit	48,000

Design Change:

First 100 units	$ 5,000 (basic assumption)
Value of first unit	10,070 (5,000 × 2.0135)
First 200 units	4,500 (10,070 × 0.4470)

Summary:

First 200 units of old design	$60,000
Add cost of first unit	10,030
Approximate cost — first 200	70,070 (Beginning point on chart for new design)

First 200 new design	$48,000 (common parts only)
design change	4,500
Average cost — first 200	52,500
Cumulative — first 400	$54,000 (common parts only)
design change	4,500
Cumulative — 400 units	58,500 (to establish second point on chart)

Because the first 200 sets of design change parts are at the beginning of the curve where cost decreases faster than the common parts, the resulting curve is not parallel to the old curve. As production continues to increase, however, the curve bends until it is again parallel. The chart and computations also indicate that the new design is a cost reduction after liquidation of starting costs.

As an alternate, the percent additional factors may be used in computing the cost of the individual blocks. Thus:

Under old design:	
previously manufactured	− 200 units
next block	200 units
ratio	100%
From Figure 3:	100% additional factor is 80%
Next block:	60,000 × 0.8 = $48,000.

Contract Cancellation Problems. The price redetermination problem shown here illustrates the steps that can be taken when a contract is canceled after a portion of the units have been shipped. When a cancellation occurs, we are concerned with 1) the establishment of a new price for the units already shipped and 2) recovery of the work-in-process inventory.

The second item does not concern itself with learning curves. In the case of the first item, using the price redetermination example, if the contract is cancelled after delivery of 50 units, the price should be reset at $102,-

875 each rather than the average of $75,000 for the 400 units originally contracted.

Projecting Labor Loads

The study of learning theory has revealed that a certain amount of cost reduction can be expected solely from learning or experience without the need for specific cost-reduction projects. When applied to labor loads or manpower requirements when building up a new line of apparatus to capacity, it reveals that increases in production can be expected from experience alone rather than adding people to the payroll. In fact, if the production buildup is slow enough, all of the increases in production could be obtained from reduced costs. An increase in employees is required when building up production to capacity only when production buildup rates exceed the expected learning experience.

Consider the hypothetical case where first shipments to customers are to take place in January. With a 13-week cycle, it is necessary to put the shipments for the first week in January in the pipeline during the first week of October. The shipments for the second week of January would have to be started in the second week of October, and so on, building up to a rate of 25 units per week. By assuming that the first 100 units averaged 100 hours each on a 90% learning curve, the hours required for each unit per week can be determined.

If the first 100 units average 100 hours on a 90% curve, unit one will be 201.35 hours (using Table 6).

The cumulative average hours for each unit to be shipped would first be calculated. Because of the odd quantities, the factors used in this calculation are not shown in Table 6. Next the individual blocks would be computed. It is suggested that the reader who owns a hand calculator with the power function (Y^X) perform the calculations to determine the odd factors included in this example as a check against the accuracy of the author.

CUMULATIVE SHIPMENTS	MULTIPLY BY 201.35	CUMULATIVE AVERAGE HOURS	INDIVIDUAL BLOCKS QUANTITY	INDIVIDUAL BLOCKS AVERAGE HOURS
5	0.7830	157.7	5	157.7
11	0.6946	139.9	6	125.1
18	0.6445	129.8	7	113.9
26	0.6095	122.7	8	106.7
35	0.5826	117.3	9	101.7
45	0.5607	112.9	10	97.5
56	0.5424	109.2	11	94.1
68	0.5266	106.0	12	91.1
81	0.5128	103.3	13	89.2
95	0.5005	100.8	14	86.3
110	0.4895	98.6	15	84.7
126	0.4795	96.5	16	82.1
143	0.4704	94.7	17	81.5
161	0.4620	93.0	18	79.5
180	0.4542	91.5	19	78.8
200	0.4470	90.0	20	76.5
221	0.4403	88.6	21	75.3
243	0.4340	87.4	22	74.3
266	0.4280	86.2	23	73.5
290	0.4224	85.1	24	72.9
315	0.4172	84.0	25	71.2

With a manufacturing cycle of 13 weeks, the five units to be shipped during the first week of January must be started in the shop during the first week of October. Likewise, the six units to be shipped during the second week of January must be started during the second week of October. Assume that the cost of each unit will be spread evenly over the 13-week cycle.

Thus, labor input for the first week of October would be 5 units at 157.7 divided by 13 or 60.6. The second week would be:

5 units at 157.7 divided by 13	60.6
6 units at 125.1 divided by 13	57.8
Total second week	118.4

Continue each week as above.

Total input hours are then summarized as follows:

MONTH	WEEK	TOTAL HOURS
October	1	60.6
	2	118.4
	3	179.7
	4	245.5
November	1	315.8
	2	390.8
	3	470.5
	4	554.6
December	1	643.3
	2	736.5
	3	834.0
	4	935.8
	5	1041.8

Continue on as far into the future as required.

Determining Manpower Requirements

From the previous example, the number of hours required per week have already been determined. Using a 40-hour week as normal, the following would be the employee requirements:

MONTH	WEEK	HOURS REQUIRED	EMPLOYEES
October	1	60.6 hours	2
	2	118.4	3
	3	179.7	5
	4	245.5	7
November	1	315.8	8
	2	390.8	10
	3	470.5	12
	4	554.6	14
December	1	643.3	16
	2	736.5	19
	3	334.0	21
	4	936.8	24
	5	1,041.8	26

Continue as required.

At the point where the required schedule of 25 units per week has been reached, further progress on the learning curve without an increase in output will necessitate a slight layoff. The alternative is for the marketing organization to secure sales to meet the increase in production resulting from learning.

Control of Shop Labor

For shop labor control, the estimated labor hours contained in Projecting Labor Loads may be used. As an alternative, an achievable labor standard may be set as a base from which to measure labor variance as a percentage of standard.

Using 5 hours per unit per week as standard, the following variances can be set as controls.

WEEK	UNITS IN PROCESS	STANDARD	EXPECTED HOURS	VARIANCE	V%
1	5	25.0 hours	60.6 hours	35.6 hours	142%
2	11	55.0	118.4	63.4	115
3	18	90.0	179.7	89.7	100
4	26	130.0	245.5	115.5	89
5	35	175.0	315.8	140.8	80
6	45	225.0	390.8	165.8	74
7	56	280.0	470.5	190.5	68
8	68	340.0	554.6	214.6	63
9	81	405.0	643.3	238.3	59
10	95	475.0	736.5	261.5	55

The ratio of raw material content to selling price will play an important part in selecting the appropriate learning percentage for determining a reasonable price for a repeat order. If possible, the breakdown of the vendor's selling price by elements should be obtained.

Nonrecurring items such as special tools should also be removed from the price of the previous order before proceeding with calculations.

Problem One: A quantity of 225 pcs of part X is required from the PDQ Company. Previous purchase history is as follows:

Purchase order 12345
dated 3/26/56   75 pcs. at $125.00 each

Part X is principally a machined component, with no assembly. We select 90% as the applicable learning percentage.

PURCHASING

One of the most fruitful applications of the learning theory concerns its use in determining the reasonableness of a vendor's quotation on nonstandard items on which the vendor has had experience by means of a previous order. Single-source procurement of special fabrications often places the customer at a disadvantage in negotiating prices for orders beyond the initial quantity because the vendor is aware that the customer no longer is in a position to develop new sources with their duplication of starting costs, tools, and so on.

Previous orders	75 pcs.
New order	225 pcs.
Ratio	300%

We select 300% as the proper factor on a 90% learning percentage. This factor (from the tables) is 0.7467

$$\$125 \times 0.7467 = \$93.34$$

Problem Two: A quantity of 1875 pcs. of part Y is required from the QED Corporation. Previous history is as follows:

Purchase order 10369 dated 6/20/55	500 pcs. at $175.00 each
Purchase order 10635 dated 2/20/56	750 pcs. at $150.00 each

Because only 90% factors have been included in Table 6, 90% will be used for this problem.

Previous order 10369	500 pcs. at $175.00	$87,500
10635	750 pcs. at 150.00	112,500
Cumulative average	1250 pcs.	160.00 $200,000

Previous orders (cumulative):   1,250
New orders: 1,875
Ratio: 150%

Factor for 150% on an 90% learning curve = 0.7833

$$160 \times 0.7833 = \$125.33$$

The application of learning theory should be a tool for negotiating prices. It should be used as a basis for a mutual understanding between the buyer and the vendor concerning what constitutes a reasonable price. It should not be used to sway the vendor into unreasonable reduction in price.

The estimating of starting load costs and the examination of training progress on new employees can be factored from the example on determining manpower requirements. Make-or-buy decisions involve the calculation of learning curves on both the vendor's prices and the cost of internal manufacture to determine whether to purchase or manufacture.

THE LEARNING CURVE ON LOG-LOG PAPER

Thus far we have experimented with learning-curve calculations using the handy mathematical factors that bring learning-curve calculations within the grasp of anyone who has an electronic desk calculator. Earlier we learned that the learning curve on log-log paper is a straight line when we plot the cumulative average. Plotting on log-log paper is an excellent tool for doing approximations. The problem with log-log paper is that the results are very difficult to read and therefore are inclined to be inaccurate compared with the results involving mathematical factors (which imply a mathematical accuracy that probably does not exist).

Consider the problem of being given that the cumulative average value of the first 50 units on a 90% curve is 55 hours. Required is a log-log plot that shows both the cumulative average and individual unit curves that allows us to make many calculations for units to be produced beyond the first 50.

We already have one point on the cumulative average line. Because two points make a straight light, we can obtain the second point by taking 90% of 55 which, by definition, will give us the cumulative average value for 100 units. If we want more accuracy by obtaining a third point, we may multiply again by 90 to obtain the value at 200 units. We can now join the three points and extend the line back to unit one which will give us its theoretical value. We can extend the line to the right as far as we desire.

We now have a working curve on log-log paper, but we will have difficulty reading it because, in its present form, finding the value of units 51–100, for example, would require the following steps:

1. Multiply 100 times its cumulative average
2. Subtract 50 times its average
3. Divide the result by 50.

The log-log plot can be made instantly readable by constructing the individual unit curve. We already know that any point on the individual unit line is 84.8% of the cumulative average value at that point. Using this conversion factor, we determine two points at 50 and 100 units, respectively, and draw the individual line. We extend the line to the left only as far as unit ten from which we draw a smooth curve back to the first unit. (Note: the conversion factor $1-N$ does not apply until after the first ten units.)

Figure 5 is a sample log-log plot using the given data and making the mathematical calculations for the value at the 100th unit and the corresponding values on the individual unit curve. The value for units 51–100 may be approximated by taking the midpoint.

DETERMINING ACTUAL LEARNING

Thus far we have been concerned with learning-curve calculations using a 90% learning rate. Proper use of the learning theory, however, dictates that a business should be pre-

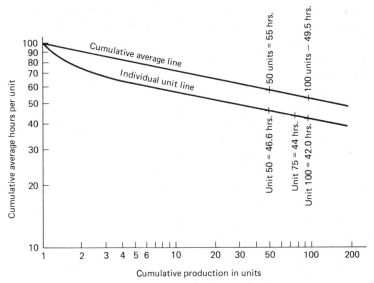

FIGURE 5.   Determining individual units.

pared to measure its own historical progress before assuming calculations that will commit the business to a cost performance it may find difficult to meet. The use of learning rates based upon hearsay or someone else's experience is dangerous.

The remainder of this chapter will be devoted to the various methods through which a business may measure its historical performance. The following methods will be discussed:

1. The scattergram method using triangulation
2. The scattergram method using two points representing the doubling principle
3. The two-point formula
4. Long-linear least squares regression analysis

Given: experience in the manufacture of Product X is as follows:

First 75 pcs.	125.2 hours per piece
Next 150	84.3 hours per piece
Next 200	66.5 hours per piece
Next 300	60.0 hours per piece

The Scattergram Method Using Triangulation

The first step in plotting the data on log-log paper is to determine the plot point for each lot. The rule of thumb in plotting learning results dictates that the first lot is plotted at the 1/3 point while all subsequent lots are plotted at the midpoint. We are using hours for the example, thus eliminating the need for deescalation to a base year. Rearrangement of the data to include plot points results in the following:

Table 7. Scattergram plot points

LOT	CUMULATIVE QUANTITY	PLOT POINT	HOURS
75	—	25	125.2 per piece
150	225	150	84.3
200	425	325	66.5
300	725	575	60.0

In the next step, the data are plotted on three-cycle log-log paper. The scattergram method is also known as the "eyeball" method in that, once the data have been plotted, we must draw a line (called the line of regression) equidistant between the two points. Under the least-squares theory, we are attempting to draw a line such that the sum of the squares of the distances from the points to the line will be the lowest attainable.

Once the line is drawn, we proceed to measure its slope. Under the triangulation method, we place a right triangle on the plot with one leg resting upon a straight edge or ruler and the hypotenuse resting on the line of regression. Keeping the ruler stationary (which is very important), we slide the triangle to the left until it crosses any vertical log-log line at the beginning of a cycle (one, ten, 100, or 1000). The horizontal reading at the point where the triangle intersects the vertical two (20 or 200 depending upon the cycle selected) represents the degree of learning. For example, if the triangle crosses the vertical line at a horizontal reading of 9, a 90% curve has been experienced.

Figure 6 is a plot of the data from Table 7. Note that the triangle crosses between 8.6 and 8.8, perhaps closer to 8.6. From this we can conclude that we have experienced an 86% learning curve.

Scattergram Using Two Points Representing the Doubling Principle

Under this method, we read the approximate value at one point on the line of regression, then the corresponding point at twice the quantity. This is in keeping with the principle that when production is doubled, the cost or hours at the doubled quantity differs from the cost or hours at the base point by the learning percent. Although we have drawn the individual unit curve, we must remember that the unit and cumulative average curves are parallel to each other beyond the tenth unit, their difference being represented by the conversion factor.

Reading the plot in Figure 7, it appears that the hours at unit 100 are approximately 89 while the hours at unit 200 we would guess at being 77. The learning rate is 77 divided by 89 or 86.5%. This compares favorably with the 86% we are derived using the triangulation method.

The Two-Point Formula

The two-point formula allows the measurement of learning based upon the measurement

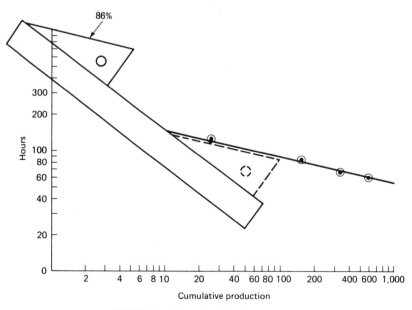

FIGURE 6. Measuring learning progress.

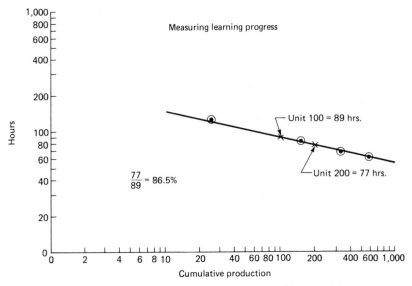

FIGURE 7. Measuring learning progress with doubling principle.

between two points, which does not represent a doubled quantity. Under this formula, we arrive at a value for N, the slope coefficient or exponent, which must be converted to the learning percent by a rearrangement of the formula for N shown in The Mathematics of the Learning Curve.

$$N = \frac{\log\left(\dfrac{\text{Cost } 2}{\text{Cost } 1}\right)}{\log\left(\dfrac{\text{Qty } 2}{\text{Qty } 1}\right)}$$

$$\log(\text{learning } \%) = (\log 2)(N)$$

For an example we will take two of the points from our problem.

PLOT POINT	HOURS
25	125.2 hours
150	84.3 hours

$$N = \frac{\log\left(\dfrac{84.3}{125.2}\right)}{\log\left(\dfrac{150}{25}\right)} = \frac{\log 0.6733}{\log 6} =$$

$$\frac{9.8282 - 10}{0.7782} = \frac{-0.1718}{0.7782} = -0.2208$$

$$\log (\text{learning } \%) = (-0.2208) (\log 2) =$$
$$(-0.2208) (0.3010) = -0.0665$$

Because this is a negative logarithm, we must convert to positive by subtracting from 10.

$$\log (\text{learning } \%) = -0.0665 = 9.9335 - 10$$

$$\log (\text{learning } \%) = 86\% \text{ (antilog)}$$

In view of the answers obtained by triangulation and the doubling concept, this answer appears reasonable.

Scientific Log-Linear Regression Analysis

Under this concept, we will be fitting the data in Table 7 to the log-linear version of the learning curve, $\log Y = \log K - N\log X$ using the method of least squares.

We will be concerned with determining the value for N that will allow us to determine the learning percent using the variation of the formula for N as we did in the previous exercise. Under the method of least squares, we will be substituting logarithmic values for X and Y using the following columns:

$\log X$; $\log Y$; $(\log X)(\log Y)$; $(\log X)^2$

The formula for N:

$$N =$$

$$\frac{T\Sigma(\log X)(\log Y) - (\Sigma\log X)(\Sigma\log Y)}{T\Sigma(\log X)^2 - (\Sigma X)^2}$$

where T = the number of points or observations

$\Sigma (\log X)(\log Y)$ = the sum of col 3

$\Sigma \log X$ = the sum of col 1

$\Sigma \log Y$ = the sum of col 2

$\Sigma (\log X)^2$ = the sum of col 4

Col 4 = the square of col 1

$(\Sigma X)^2$ = the square of the sum of col 1

PLOT POINTS X	HOURS Y	COL 1 LOG X	COL 2 LOG Y	COL 3 (LOG X)(LOG Y)	COL 4 (LOG X)^2
25	125.2	1.3979	2.0976	2.9322	1.9541
150	84.3	2.1761	1.9258	4.1907	4.7354
325	66.5	2.5119	1.8228	4.5787	6.3096
575	60.0	2.7597	1.7782	4.9073	7.6159
		8.8456	7.6244	16.6089	20.6150

$$T = 4 \quad (\Sigma X)^2 = 78.2446$$

$$N = \frac{(4)(16.6089) - (8.8456)(7.6244)}{(4)(20.6150) - 78.2446}$$

$$N = \frac{66.4356 - 67.4424}{82.4600 - 78.2446}$$

$$N = \frac{-1.0068}{4.2154}$$

$$N = -0.2388$$

Note: the value for N must always be negative, signifying that learning is taking place. If N is positive, reverse learning has taken place.

$$\log (\text{learning } \%) =$$
$$(-0.2388)(0.3010) = -0.0719$$

$$\log (\text{learning } \%) = 9.9281 - 10$$

$$\text{Learning } \% = 84.8\% \text{ (antilog)}$$

REFERENCE

1. Rand Corporation, *Cost–Quality Relationships in the Aircraft Industry* (July 1, 1956).

SECTION IX
IMPROVING PROFIT
PERFORMANCE

32
Coordination of Key Functions
for Greater Efficiency in Manufacturing

W. T. O'Neill

Executive Vice President

Newport News Shipbuilding and Dry Dock Company

The success or failure of a company will depend on how well the manufacturing department manages the resources under its scope of responsibility. This, in turn, is dependent upon the degree of coordination between the manufacturing operation and the various support functions within the company.

The long-range planning process enables a company to focus on the game plan and the various plays needed to insure that all functions of a company will concentrate on the achievement of its objectives.

The success or failure of a company will significantly depend on how well the manufacturing department manages the resources under its scope of responsibility. These resources, generally consisting of the bulk of the firm's land, plant, and equipment, its raw-material inventory, work-in-process inventory, and a shared part of finished goods inventory often represent most of the asset value of the balance sheet.

Only a relatively small part of the manufacturing manager's responsibilities are custodial. He must use these assets in a manner that produces salable products to specifications, on schedule, and at costs that meet the company's profit objectives. In performing this mission, the magnitude and span of the manufacturing manager's responsibilities are at least equal to that of other key management executives. For example, manufacturing usually is responsible for the largest part of the costs of operating the business. It is responsible for selecting, costing, and if approved, installing new plant and equipment. The manufacturing manager is responsible for maintaining a skilled workforce and balancing workloads and capacities to run the operational part of the business to full effectiveness. He is responsible for seeing that the total facility is adequately supplied with utility, security, and maintenance services. Finally, he is responsible for compliance with a number of growing regulations concerning employee and environmental welfare.

Although most of the manufacturing manager's time will be devoted to input/output responsibilities, they are basically routine functions; a leading executive manager constantly will be aware of his responsibilities to improve return on investment, increase cash flow, and reduce exposures to inventory and other financial write-offs. To do this, the manager must have an unrelenting demand for performance excellence from his functional managers. It is, however, a team's excellent performance that is needed to extract the highest potential from the manufacturing organization, and this team effort does not act in a vacuum. The manufacturing team is part of the company team, with each department working to make the firm's overall objectives become realities.

For the purposes of this chapter, manufacturing is considered to include production, product engineering, materials/production control management, plant engineering, quality control, and industrial engineering.

Even for a company producing only a few products, the process by which manufacturing plans are developed and implemented requires the manufacturing manager to have a detailed knowledge of the plans and objectives of all other company functions.

Among the functions with which the manufacturing manager must coordinate his plans are such internal divisions as:

- Marketing
- Finance
- Employee Relations
- Research and Development
- Legal

Examples of the main elements of functional business plans of other departments that a manufacturing manager usually has to consider in developing the manufacturing plan are:

Marketing

Sales volume, number of units of production
Competitive analysis
service levels
quality, warranties
customer support

Finance

Cash flow
Unit costs
Profit assurance
Cost reduction

Employee Relations

Employment
Union contract
EEOC, OSHA, and other government mandated laws

Research and Development

New products
Approved vendor sources

Legal

Product liability
Workmen's compensation
Old age discrimination
Environmental Protection Agency

The reason that all managers must be aware of the plans of other departments is to assure that they work as a team in the development of objectives and supporting actions. A coordinated, cooperative plan will lead to continued team efforts during the execution of the plan.

PLANNING CYCLE

The manufacturing manager's planning cycle starts when he receives information from the marketing department concerning the units of production by product that the company expects to sell over the plan life. At this point, the financial department furnishes the target costs of the company products. Later as the requirements to achieve the sales and cost objectives are being worked out, the restraints or assistance from other departments will be introduced and adjustments, if necessary, will be made by the manufacturing or other managers.

Manufacturing department objectives that will support the marketing and financial objectives can then be established.

DEFINITIONS—OBJECTIVES, GOALS, STRATEGIES, AND ALTERNATIVES

It is appropriate at this time to define certain terms which are common in long-range planning. These are objectives, goals, strategies, and alternative strategies.

An objective is an element of the business plan that must be achieved. For the manufacturing manager, objectives may involve such things as getting a new process on line, meeting a cost reduction target, improving yield or quality, or improving the delivery service level to a given figure. Agreement to meet an objective must be obtained from each manager as early as possible in the planning process. Weak commitments from any of the managers will destroy the unity of the team and consequently the business plan itself.

A goal on the other hand is a hoped-for but not guaranteed target of achievement. It is an important concept in that it gives a general direction to the company's efforts. An objective is a shorter-term measurable event which a manager must achieve to insure that a company will realize its long-term development.

The term *strategy* connotes a useful concept in business planning. Strategies describe the ways in which an objective will be accomplished. If successful, a strategy will lead to the achievement of an objective.

For example, if an improvement in customer service level objective is required to support a marketing objective, manufacturing should have a strategy to achieve the objective. To improve customer service, the strategy may involve branch warehousing, a change in routing, and an increase in inventory levels. In many cases, more than one strategy may be available. Thus various strategies leading to a given end result can be compared to determine which will be the most practical.

Along with the alternate strategy review, the planner can identify and test the seriousness of events that may prevent the strategy from being successful.

In the above example, an increase in inventory may not be possible because of limits on product shelf life, or it may not be possible to open a branch warehouse in time to meet the marketing department's schedule to support its faster order delivery objective. By identifying problems associated with strategies, it is possible to test the validity of the plan objectives and consequently the plan itself.

As the implementation of the primary strategy is underway, unforeseen events may come up that make it ineffective. As the objective must be achieved, a sound business plan will have alternative strategies to put to use if the primary strategy is not producing the anticipated result.

The situation could also be reversed as opportunities for profitability over the original objective become apparent. Sales of a new product could be greater than originally budgeted, requiring more production. An alternate plan should be available to exploit this positive situation.

Examples of how the manufacturing department's objectives interface with those of other departments are described in the next section.

MARKETING DIVISION PLAN COORDINATION

The main data manufacturing requires from the marketing department is a forecast of units of production required to meet sales objectives.

The manufacturing manager uses this information to determine:

- The utilization of existing facilities
- Whether new plant and equipment are required
- The utilization and fit of the present work force
- The types of raw materials, parts, and components needed and the likely availability of material sources

- Whether storage facilities for raw materials, parts and components, work in process, and finished goods are adequate for space and environmental requirements
- Whether special quality control procedures or certificates are required, such as meeting certain industrial codes, compliance with military specifications, Underwriters Laboratory approval, and many others encountered in the industrial world

While it is desirable to have as accurate a forecast of sales volume and mix as possible, it would be unusual to get an exact sales plan by product mix and size over the plan life. The importance of the forecast is that it establishes a reference plan for the company to work from. The more difficult it is to forecast accurately, the more attention should be given to the exercise including the testing of the assumptions which formed the basis of the forecast. In the absence of a firm number, likely ranges of sales can be calculated, probabilities of achievement estimated, and contingencies identified.

Plant Utilization

The first test by the manufacturing manager of the marketing plan is to determine whether there is sufficient capacity to produce the volume and mix required by the marketing plan.

In many industries, this can be a complex task particularly when different products are run on the same equipment. In some instances, an increase in volume, or the addition of a new product, may economically permit greater automation in the manufacturing of new and existing components. When a decrease in volume occurs, the excess capacity may be absorbed by returning previously subcontracted work to in-house manufacturing.

In process industries, it is common to have more than one product being run through the same equipment at different rates. Certain products may require a costly changeover and

equipment clean-up to prevent contamination from previous runs. Products may require continuous operation because of product specification or the cost of temporary shutdowns. For complex utilization studies, the manufacturing manager will find it useful to enlist the assistance of the systems department to develop computerized models of the plant operation so that the various combinations of product requirement runs can be tested for capacity and minimum costs.

Trade-offs of longer runs and higher storage costs for in-process or finished goods can be compared to changeover costs and the least cost method selected. It is the manufacturing manager's responsibility to obtain the maximum financial benefit from the assets under his control within the circumstances of the business plan.

To a lesser degree, the same complexities of determining plant utilization can exist in plants that specialize in machining and assembling operations. The plan product mix may overutilize certain machine centers and idle others. Tooling design requirements and lead times in obtaining them must be considered part of the utilization study. Similarly, for the assembly lines, new jigs and fixtures may be required or work stations modified or designed to produce the desired products.

For this type of manufacturing, computerized simulation of the product processes also will be useful in determining under- and overloaded production centers. The plant utilization will provide information needed for the manufacturing capital expenditures program, subcontracting, or a scheduling plan to relieve burdened work centers.

Capacity to produce the marketing forecasted products is not only a question of having sufficient plant and equipment. Obviously, it is necessary to staff the facility with enough employees of a certain skill to man and support product output. A recruitment and training program may be in order to staff up to appropriate levels.

Obsolete plant, high labor costs, shortage of local sources of labor, need to get nearer to markets or raw material suppliers are common reasons to open a new facility on a site away from present locations. Recruitment and training of personnel for the new facility will take time. This should be factored into the plan.

Hazardous Materials

The marketing plan may include products that are composed of hazardous materials. The manufacturing manager should be knowledgeable about local, state, and federal rules and regulations pertaining to the handling and storage of raw materials and the allowable means of disposing of waste materials.

Materials may require special storage facilities with such things as humidity and temperature controls, heavy floor loading, or for liquids, tankage made of specialty metals.

Quality Control

The trend in quality control is toward higher standards and additional documentation. Increased company exposure to monetary claims because of potential product liability and other government laws for consumer protection are the significant driving forces causing this trend.

The marketing plan may require higher-quality standards because of new products or the extension of existing products into uses requiring performances beyond current levels.

The manufacturing manager should be aware of the exposures and extended uses of production. Higher-order testing and instrumentation may be needed; quality control procedures may have to be rewritten to higher standards; or ASME/Underwriters Laboratory or other code certification may be required. For government sales, products may have to perform to special standards. The manufacturing manager's plan should include information on quality control requirements as applicable.

Competitive Analysis

Most marketing departments will analyze company strengths and weaknesses against those of major competitors. The purpose of this analysis is to identify which products, services, or operations can be improved to maintain or gain a competitive advantage.

Some common items of comparison that affect the manufacturing manager are:

Service levels affecting delivery of products to customers. Here an analysis of the elements of order-turnaround time can reveal potential savings in time.

Quality, warranties.   Competitors may have quality features that have customer appeal or offer better warranties. A study of test data and/or an improvement in product design would be called for to extend product warranty or to support a marketing performance claim.

Customer support.   Competitors may have a better record of customer support. The manufacturing manager can help by increasing inventories of replacement parts, training service personnel, and helping to prepare maintenance manuals.

FINANCIAL DIVISION PLAN COORDINATION

The manufacturing department's performance will significantly affect the financial objectives of the company.

Cash Flow

An important responsibility of the financial department is the effective management of cash flows into and out of the company. The activities of manufacturing directly affect cash flow, and it is essential that the manufacturing manager be aware of cash limitations for capital expenditures, major maintenance, inventories, and other asset items under his responsibility.

Cash flow objectives will vary from company to company and from time to time within a company, usually depending upon economic conditions or investment philosophy. Manufacturing management should work closely with the finance department on cash requirements. Trade-offs and alternates can be considered so that financial and production objectives can be met.

Unit Costs

The financial department and manufacturing share a joint responsibility for establishing acceptable unit costs. The purchasing department is required to forecast price levels for purchased materials using available economic forecasts. Errors in price level forecasts will be offset if an assumption is made that cost increases can be passed on in concurrent price increases. The exercise has the benefit of signaling which material prices are likely to become excessive and of permitting a value analysis search for substitute materials to be initiated.

Labor costs in manhour terms can be reviewed, with allowances made for efficiency gains either through methods improvement or capital investment. The determination of wage rates are generally the responsibility of the employee relations department.

Overhead rates are calculated by the financial department from data received from all departments. It is a cost element that is accelerating well beyond basic labor costs in many industries. The rapid escalation is due to increases in fringe benefits from government mandated programs as well as union pressure for inflation protection and for increased job security, hospitalization, and pension benefits. Depreciation expenses increase as old equipment is replaced with new equipment purchased at inflated prices.

Energy is often a source of needless waste and resultant unnecessary cost. Every manufacturing company should have a comprehensive energy management plan as one of its objectives. An individual should be identified as having the responsibility for coordinating the efforts of the company. The plan should include provisions for energy conservation, alternate sources, and, as economics permit, the replacement of relatively high energy-using equipment with equipment of lower requirements.

Many companies have obtained savings in electricity by installing computerized energy management programs. Others have supplemented large combined heating and process steam plants with smaller units to give a spot steam supply to specific processes during periods when the main boiler produces steam in excess of requirements. In-plant electricity generation can be used to replace or supplement utility supplied power during periods of low requirements, or to keep demand curves within acceptable limits. Companies with a significant supply of waste materials have solved their trash disposal problems and have satisfied some steam and electrical power needs by installing waste disposal incinerators that have steam and electric generating capability. Waste heat from foundry operations, chemical processes, and other operations can often be recovered for economic secondary use. The manufacturing manager should be alert to these and other opportunities for energy conservation and savings.

Profit Assurance

A *profit assurance plan* is a compilation of specific short-range actions developed to anticipate and respond to business conditions that are significantly changed from those planned for years 1 and 2 in the business plan. The purpose of these plans is to insure achievement of income objectives under adverse business conditions. The establishment of trigger points at which time some or all of the profit assurance plan is implemented is a feature of the exercise.

A profit assurance plan trigger point may not always be keyed to the profit and loss statement. For example, it may also cover potential deferral or cancellation of capital and other investment type projects to maintain a given asset-to-sales ratio or cash flow objective.

The manufacturing manager is a key participant in establishing the profit assurance plan. He should not confuse it with the cost reduction plan, which is developed routinely to lower unit cost base lines. An example of a trigger point for a profit assurance plan would be implementation commencing with a significant shortfall in order input for a given product. In this case, the manager could defer a capital expenditure, reallocate manpower, restructure an organization, or shelve an industrial engineering project associated with the problem product. Subcontracted work could be brought inhouse or the company could do subcontracting work for other firms to make use of idled facilities.

Cost Improvement

The financial department is usually responsible for compiling, verifying, and reporting on the results of the unit's cost reduction program. Although the controller is generally considered to be the custodian of the company's assets, actually manufacturing is the true custodian of the bulk of asset and manpower resources as well as materials usage and energy consumption. Manufacturing, therefore, usually contributes the largest monetary volume to the cost reduction program.

The financial department measures the effect of cost improvement and incorporates it with other cost of sales data to determine which manufacturing cost elements have changed and the magnitude of such changes.

A detailed analysis of the differences in costs performed jointly by the financial and manufacturing departments will provide information for recommendations to reprice, identifying cost elements that require special attention for further cost reduction, value analysis, or extra marketing emphasis to increase volume.

The information can also be used to identify products or product lines that are marginally profitable and are likely candidates for product pruning.

EMPLOYEE RELATIONS DIVISION PLAN COORDINATION

The manufacturing plan will be influenced by the actions of the employee relations department. The manufacturing plan may require a significant buildup in labor in an existing plant or for the establishment of a new facility in another location.

The employee relations department is in the best position to advise the manufacturing manager on the available labor pool and skill mix in a given locality. If the skills are not available, employee relations can advise on the likelihood of attracting the needed skills and a competitive compensation package.

If the skills are not available anywhere, the employee relations department can be of service in setting up and managing training programs and in selecting candidates who are likely to be trainable. Employee relations will also be knowledgeable about state and federally financed programs that may be applicable and desirable for the company.

Union Negotiations

If the company is unionized, it is likely that one or more labor contracts will be negotiated over the plan life. The manufacturing manager and the employee relations manager should review the present contracts and make predictions as to the likely thrust of union demands. An increase in night shift premium may increase costs to a point where it would be more economical to increase capacity so that a shift can be knocked off. An extra holiday, for which many companies pay a premium at double time, may be treated in like manner.

The manufacturing manager should alert the employee relations manager of contract clauses that should be modified for competitive and productivity improvements. There are always opportunities to trade off these changes for other management concessions that may be unavoidable.

Strike Plan

Employee relations and manufacturing management can read the mood of union employees and predict the likelihood of a strike. If the probability of a strike is high, the company should prepare a strike contingency plan. Depending on the type of manufacturing operations, the company may wish to continue manufacturing with salaried personnel, to subcontract, to build up inventory in branch warehouses, or to use other means of continuing to serve customers and improve the company's bargaining position.

All reports and information on management strategies with respect to union relations should be highly confidential. For example, strike plans should not be included as part of the business plan. The business plan has a restricted, but wide enough circulation to make strict confidentiality difficult. If the strike plan is in writing at all, distribution should be limited on a need-to-know basis.

Government Regulations

Government mandated programs such as EEOC, OSHA, and EPA (discussed in more detail under Legal Department) are certain to become more of a burden on management despite recent administration statements on reducing government control over the private sector.

Significant capital funds may be required to comply with EPA regulations; extra employment and training may be necessary to comply with EEOC affirmative action requirements; or a skilled staff of safety engineers and industrial hygienists may be required to comply with OSHA and EPA regulations. The trend is toward heavy fines and criminal intent citations by regulatory agencies, even though a company may have an outstanding safety and environmental record.

It is beyond the scope of this section to discuss these laws and their potential impact. It is important that the manufacturing manager be aware of actual regulations, proposed regu-

lations, and trends in government mandated programs and to consider them when developing a supporting plan.

RESEARCH AND DEVELOPMENT DIVISION PLAN COORDINATION

The manufacturing manager should have an early association with research and development plans to insure that new products are producible at the lowest possible cost and that the development and introduction schedule provides sufficient lead time for manufacturing.

Product Engineering

In some companies, particularly high-technology companies, R&D pursues a program of somewhat pure research to develop a product, but leaves the translation of the product from the laboratory to the production stage to another engineering division oftern referred to as product engineering. In other words, R&D works with concepts and ideas that are summarized into a set of general specifications. From the specifications, product engineering develops a set of working drawings, materials, and quality specifications. Product engineering should be in close liaison with R&D to insure a smooth transition from concepts to product design.

R&D and Productivity

The use of the company's R&D department as a force to improve manufacturing productivity should be considered. It can be the most significant source for productivity improvement, yielding gains beyond traditional industrial engineering methods. The manufacturing manager should work with R&D on processes and equipment improvement projects that will lower costs. For example, for one consumer products company a new detergent product was scaled up from a laboratory to a pilot plant operation and then to a large-scale production processing unit. The specifications called for narrow tolerances of the various chemicals in the finished product, which were met in the production unit only with reduced flow rates and unanticipated recycling of off-spec materials. Presented with the problem, R&D made minor formula and specification changes that allowed the production rate to increase to predicted levels without affecting the performance of the product. This experience prompted the company to review all major products for improved production by adjusting formulas and specifications. The company was able to significantly reduce material and production costs in a number of cases.

The ability of the computer and integrated circuit manufacturers to reduce costs through research is legendary, but as the detergent example shows, the opportunities for cost improvement through R&D is not unique to high technology, hardware producing companies.

Vendor Approval

R&D will usually provide a list of approved vendors from whom materials can be purchased that will meet product specifications. This should be a cooperative selection between R&D and the purchasing department. Purchasing can supply information on vendors concerning performance on quality, service, and delivery to insure that all factors are being considered in the selection process.

LEGAL DIVISION PLAN COORDINATION

Product liability laws have the potential for substantial claims against the company. The legal department can provide the manufacturing manager with information on regulation changes, the result of court cases, and claims against the company. The legal department can advise on the compilation of quality documentations, product batch control data, or other information that would be of value in defending the company's position against future claims.

Prominent among laws that could involve the manufacturing manager in legal matters are those concerned with Workmen's Compensation, Equal Employment Opportunity Commission (EEOC), Occupational Safety and Health Administration (OSHA), Environmental Protection Agency (EPA), Employee Retirement Income Security Act (ERISA), and old age discrimination.

Accurate accident reports and prompt referral of injured employees to a company sponsored or approved medical examination will go a long way toward protecting the company against unreasonable claims.

Compliance with the affirmative action regulations of EEOC may require a review of minority participation at various levels of skills and management. Depending on the nature of the operations, an affirmative action plan could have a significant effect on the company's training and selection processes. Similarly, recent government interest in expanding directed opportunities for economic improvement to small and disadvantaged persons adds a further complication to vendor selection. Prime contractors and subcontractors on government sponsored procurements are especially subject to compliance with regulations on these programs.

As previously discussed, the regulations of the Occupational Safety and Health Administration should also be considered a potential compliance requirement during the life of the business.

For old age discrimination and ERISA, the manufacturing manager must be sure that he or she is on sound legal ground if it is necessary to give older employees less work or to modify pension rights in the case of plant shutdowns or permanent layoffs.

The above information may not appear in the manufacturing plan as specific items but the manager should take them into consideration when developing strategies for the accomplishment of his or her objectives.

ORGANIZING FOR BUSINESS PLANNING

So far in this chapter the need for the manufacturing manager to know the objectives and services of other functional divisions has been discussed. There are several approaches as to how communications between divisions can be carried out.

One technique is to have a single person or team designated as the business plan coordinator. The company president furnishes to the functional managers the broad goals to be accomplished over the plan life. Each manager develops an independent set of objectives to meet the plan requirements. These are submitted to the coordinator who reviews, reconciles differences, and prepares a draft plan for managerial review and modification.

Another technique is to have the president write a broad overview of the economic, environmental, and political influences on the business over the plan life along with desired key financial and marketing objectives. The functional managers then develop individual objectives. Reconciliation is accomplished through meetings and exchange of draft functional plans.

Still another technique is to prepare a planning guide that outlines the procedures and forms to be used in preparing the plan. The functional managers follow the guide in preparing their plans under the supervision of a business plan coordinator. This latter method is helpful when a company first starts long-range planning or when it desires to have a formal, consistent format. A formal format has the advantage of requiring less effort for updating and making year-to-year comparisons simpler.

For companies with mature long-range planning programs, the most common preference is for a combination of a consistent format, a business plan corrdinator, and frequent contacts among functional managers. The consistent format lends itself to computer modeling so that several alternate conditions can be tested. The coordinator is in a position to keep the preparation on schedule and to apprise participants of the latest developments. Frequent meetings allow for an interchange of ideas, thus sharpening the plan's content and feasibility.

MANUFACTURING FUNCTIONAL PLAN

The remainder of this chapter will discuss the preparation of the manufacturing long-range functional plan and the relationship of the various manufacturing department operational objectives to the manufacturing plan.

The manufacturing functional plan is prepared in a manner that supports the company business plan. It consists of a mission statement in which the manufacturing manager states the principal mission to be achieved over the planning period, and the role each function will fulfill in achieving the plan objectives.

Each department within the manufacturing function uses the mission to set functional objectives and the strategies that are to be carried out in order to meet the company business plan objectives and strategies.

The mission statement is a brief, clear explanation of where the division is at present and where it is heading. A sample mission statement for a large job order shop could be as follows:

It is the mission of the manufacturing division to provide industry leadership in the processing of orders and to manufacture to customer requirements on schedule within cost estimates. All divisional activities will be dedicated to maintaining this leadership. The division is also committed to expand its heavy machinery capability to meet the marketing forecast of an annual 15 percent compounded growth in this work.

Another company may be in a high-technology market. For such a company, the manufacturing mission could have as part of its statement:

The manufacturing division is to produce a full line of xxxxxxxxx in accordance with marketing forecasts within cost targets. The division will work closely with R&D in order to anticipate new developments and to be ready to produce them on schedule, and with a minimum of inventory obsolescence.

As a final example, consider a fast growing consumer products company with a number of new products and expanding markets. The manufacturing mission statement could read:

The mission of the manufacturing division is to expand production, warehousing, and the distribution system to meet the marketing forecasts as stated.

Each of the mission statements could contain other items considered to be of equal importance. This would be especially true of complex, multi-industry companies.

The statement, in general, should define what the division is currently doing and what are the major considerations that will guide the company in the future. Here are some hypothetical situations in which the above mission statements would apply.

In the first example, a competitive edge in turnaround and cost is currently enjoyed by the company. The mission is to maintain this advantage and, concurrently, expand the company's production base for large machined products. The situation is typical of many companies in the highly competitive field of machinery and metal fabrication.

In the second example, the company maintains leadership by the constant introduction of improvements through superior R&D. Manufacturing must keep ahead of these developments in providing facilities and, at the same time, hold down inventories that are subject to sudden technological obsolescence. The semiconductor, computer, microprocessor, telecom, and other electronics specialties are industries in this category.

In the last example, the manufacturing manager is faced with an explosive marketing situation where the advantage to the company over competition is to get on the market quickly with good customer service. Recent business history abounds with such situations in electronic products, consumer hard goods, personal care and household products.

Once the mission is established and understood by the manufacturing division functional managers, the objectives that state exactly what must be achieved by each manager can be identified. One cannot overemphasize the need for all managers to understand that objectives must be achieved. They cannot be regarded as goals or targets that would be nice to reach. In many cases, objective achievement may require substantial sacrifices on the part of managers. Before a commitment is made, a manager must clearly understand that whatever it takes to make the objective (within the bounds of the law, and business and moral ethics, of course) must be done.

Objectives should support the overall plan and manufacturing plan mission. For purposes of establishing lead responsibility for the accomplishment of an objective, they should be listed by function, followed by the strategies that the various supporting departments are required to carry out.

It is not necessary to include all the details of objectives and strategies in the business plan. Clearly worded statements with key events and planned progress is all that is usually necessary. The business plan text should be as concise as possible for continuing use as a quick reference to company-wide coordinated actions and as a benchmark for comparisons of actual to planned progress.

The objectives and strategies may be supported in considerable detail by supplementary information covering each segment of the plan.

For example, for a high-technology company, the success of the business plan may depend on a build-up of the company's engineering capability. To insure credibility to the plan, the engineering manager should provide an estimate of manpower requirements by project and by type of engineering discipline, and the level of technical and clerical support. A timetable of hires, training, and assignment would be part of the engineering manager's manpower plan. This part of the plan would be developed in conjunction with the personnel department as the party responsible for recruitment and in many cases training of new employees. The personnel department in turn would add an engineering recruitment segment to their plan in which they would identify the means which would be employed to meet the engineering objective. The plan may have a stepped-up college recruitment effort, help wanted advertising, and in-company training and promotion programs.

This example illustrates the interdependency of the various functions within the company particularly with respect to one function informing another of a necessary contribution. Through this means alternate strategies for meeting the engineering manpower objective will surface. The personnel department in analyzing the engineering manpower situation may determine that the turnover rate is excessive and recommend ways to improve employee retention. Personnel may be aware of lower manpower needs in other departments or divisions of a parent corporation, which could be a source of experienced manpower rather than new hires.

The personnel department because of its knowledge of job markets and available manpower resources may advise engineering that they cannot guarantee a reasonable chance of success for the recruitment program. As the engineering buildup is presumed to be necessary to the success of the company plan and is therefore classified as an objective, the engineering manager will have to explore other strategies to get the work done. The manager may elect to subcontract engineering design to engineering firms that specialize in this type of work, or if possible, to university research departments.

If the subcontracting of a significant amount of work is necessary, the department must get organized to operate the program. This usually means more careful preparation of specifications and an examination of the format in which the data is furnished to and received from the subcontractor, particularly if the information is to be used without editing by purchasing and production. It may be necessary to change company procedures to accommodate the subcontractor's methods or to require that the subcontractor furnish information in a prescribed manner.

If the volume warrants, one or more engineering personnel may have to be assigned to the administration of the subcontracting program.

Besides the manpower plan, engineering should include a schedule in their business plan segment itemizing the major projects to be worked on over the plan life. The schedule will briefly describe the project and break it down into measurable units of work which are planned to be completed in a given timeframe. The end point of each is classified as the completion of a key event. At each end point, it is usual to evaluate the results to date and to determine whether it is necessary to make modifications.

In the company business plan, the above engineering objectives and strategies should be described in concise statements. An example of a product engineering plan follows. A similar format can be used for other manufacturing departments.

PRODUCT ENGINEERING OBJECTIVE AND STRATEGIES

Objective

To support the introduction of new products as specified by the five year marketing forecast, whereby an increase in engineering capability equivalent to 100 engineers of various disciplines and 50 technical, drafting, and clerical personnel will be required.

Strategies (required to meet this objective)

Turnover. Fifty clerical, technical and engineering personnel were hired in 19__, but 20 out of the total workforce have resigned or retired, leaving a net increase of 30. An improvement in motivation and opportunity for advancement is required to stabilize our engineering workforce.

Working conditions. Most engineering work areas require refurbishing and modernization. Improvement is now in progress and will be completed next year.

Training. Training programs for draftsmen and technicians will be expanded. The designer apprentice program will be reinforced to help increase the designer role.

Computer-aided design. This will be expanded to improve engineering productivity. A good start on computer aided design has been made with the programs in structural and piping design. Programs are in process to improve these systems. Other programs to extend computer aided design to electrical systems and mechanical systems are under development. This activity has allowed the division to move personnel to new work and has reduced overall manpower requirements. The program will be continued throughout the planning period.

University contacts with cooperative working arrangements are to be cultivated to help with the workload and to enhance engineering recruitment. Recent contacts with the engineering department at XYZ University have resulted in helping in the recruitment of graduates. The company is participating in a cooperative work/study program at three state universities. The company will participate to the fullest extent possible, opening up opportunities to recruit graduates and to use the universities' engineering capabilities for work on our programs.

Experienced engineering recruitment. Engineering and technical personnel recruitment will be conducted by the personnel department. Newspaper ads will be placed in major Sunday editions of cities with engineering labor pools. In areas with known large concentrations of engineers and technicians, temporary local recruiting offices will be established.

Use of design consulting firms. Recruitment shortfalls will be made up by the use of engineering design firms. A survey of available sources has been made. A list of qualified companies has been made, and the purchasing department has requested a schedule of billing rates. As needed, the assistance of these firms will be phased into our design efforts.

As for other functional plans, the business plan need only show an exhibit listing the individual items in the product engineering program with key milestone dates shown. A brief summary of strategies could follow, itemized by project with the detail available in a comprehensive work plan for each project.

The work plans would be the main reference for projects and would carry considerable detail including progress reports as the work continued.

MATERIALS/PRODUCTION CONTROL MANAGEMENT PLAN

In most companies, materials account for approximately half or more of the cost of sales. Furthermore, many industries are confronted with the possibility of fewer available sources of materials, increasing dependence on foreign supplies, or competition for certain scarce materials. Further complicating the situation will be a trend toward more complex product structures and a demand on the materials management function to find reliable sources of supply with manageable lead times.

Another challenge to materials management will be to use the explosive advances in data processing to improve the materials management function. Improvement applications will range from materials requirements forecasting, paperwork processing, and the traceability of specific parts and manufactured components from engineering concepts and original specification to the arrival of the finished product at the customer's door. Indeed, some management science thinkers view this growing information processing ability as the third industrial revolution.

PLANT ENGINEERING MANAGEMENT PLAN

The plant engineer's responsibilities traditionally have included the operation of the plant's power, heat, light, water, and waste disposal facilities and the replacement, expansion, and maintenance of the entire physical plant. While these traditional responsibilities have not changed, the management liabilities in carrying out its functions recently have been greatly increased for the plant engineer. This change in emphasis is due to a number of factors.

First, there is a large and still growing number of regulations regarding the environment and plant safety promulgated by a number of local, state, and federal agencies. Failure to comply with many of these regulations can bring heavy fines, forced shutdowns of manufacturing units, and, if some administrators have their way, personal liability for responsible employees, including fines and jail sentences.

In most companies the plant engineer is responsible for the modification of facilities to comply with environmental regulations. Many companies have an environmental engineering function reporting to the plant engineer. Its main duty is to specify facility design modifications to existing equipment to meet environmental regulations, or to make sure that facility additions are in compliance. This function may also monitor effluents, sample

air quality, and perform other tests to insure that the plant remains within specified regulatory limits. It also collects data and prepares the documents necessary to obtain permits from regulatory agencies to carry on with applicable processes.

Second, the plant engineer has always been a key participant in the employee safety program. However, prior to the establishment of the Occupational Safety and Health Administration, the plant engineer had only to interface with plant safety engineers. Although he may not deal directly with OSHA inspectors, the plant engineer will be responsible for the design and installation of devices to insure that all facilities comply with OSHA regulations. OSHA inspections could result in citations for alleged unsafe equipment or practices. For equipment citations, it is the plant engineer who must rectify the condition. Obviously where employee safety is involved, the corrective action should be taken immediately, provided the citation is valid and it is deemed prudent to do so.

In some cases, an OSHA inspector will note an unsafe condition on one machine only even though similar conditions are present on other machines not cited. The plant engineer should examine all citations to determine whether this condition exists on other equipment and include these items in his correction program. An employee injury either caused by the item on any machine cited or not, or as a contributing factor, could result in heavy fines or legal action against the company and its officers.

Third, as the responsible agents, plant engineers have always been alert to increasing demand for and the costs of utilities. Costs of utilities and other energy sources and uncertain supplies place an increasingly heavy responsibility on the plant engineer. As mentioned previously in this chapter, every company regardless of size should have an energy management program. This program can be best administered by plant engineering. For most plants, the potential savings can support at least a full-time engineer.

Fourth, the plant engineer must work closely with the purchasing department to insure a supply of fuel for power plant and other operations requiring gasoline, diesel, coal, and fuel oil, propane, and other fossil energy sources. Natural gas and electricity supplies are a special case. With a slow down in power plant construction and increasing regulations of both fossil-fuel and nuclear power plants, the availability of a constant supply of power could become less reliable over the life of the business plan. The plant engineer should be in contact with the power company as to their capacity plans for purchased power as well as construction plans for other significant power users in the service area. Through liaison with the power companies, the plant engineer should know when the supplying power plant is scheduled for shutdown maintenance and arrange to be notified of scheduled or emergency shutdowns. Of course, information regarding power requirements should flow both ways, and the plant engineer should notify the power company of any unusual circumstances regarding power requirements. A similar liaison should be established with gas suppliers, particularly if the plant is subject to interrupted service.

With respect to the capital program requirements, the plant engineer may recommend an increase in electrical generating capability if already in place, or provision of supplemental electrical power generation. Users of natural gas may need to add alternate fuel capability and/or increased storage capacity for propane.

Any of the above could affect the business plan enough to merit detailed discussion in the long-range plan, particularly if the unit is a subsidiary or division of a major corporation. Otherwise, the problems can be summarized in the company plan with separate comprehensive plans to support the summary.

As part of the more traditional function of plant engineering, the maintenance of plant and equipment and the management of the company capital expenditure programs, the plant engineer works closely with marketing, finance, material and production control, industrial engineering, and in the case of a new process, research and development and product engineering in establishing capital requirements for plant and equipment. Some companies will show only the gross capital spending amount per year as part of the plan financial data. Others prefer to include a schedule listing the major projects with the expenditures indicated year by year. Regardless of the amount of detail shown in the five year plan, the plant engineer should have a comprehensive report backing up the summary information. As major projects usually run over a year, or are phased to capacity requirements, they should be scheduled in concert with a long-range facility plan that will indicate a logical allocation of space to insure an orderly approach for equipment changes and additions.

QUALITY CONTROL FUNCTIONAL PLAN

The quality control function is enjoying a renaissance in importance as a means to lower costs. The concept of "gold in the mine" formalized through sample inspection and defect prevention by Professor Juran in the 1950s has evolved into concepts centered around defect prevention programs as refined by Phillip B. Crosby. Mr. Crosby's experience in using the quality function as a potent force for profit improvement at International Telephone and Telegraph is proof of its effectiveness. The interest in these programs has intensified as U.S. industries' traditional competitive advantage by being the world's most productive economy narrows or disappears compared to continuing Japanese and Western European gains.

The success of these foreign industries is considered to be significantly due to an intense attention to quality principles, and to dedicated management-labor teamwork to make a part so that it meets product specification the first time without unnecessary modification or rework.

Manufacturing management should be aware of the productivity improvements inherent in evolving quality control management techniques; and if deficient, develop programs to take advantage of them.

INDUSTRIAL ENGINEERING FUNCTIONAL PLAN

Industrial engineering, although considered to be a supportive function, continues to be a potent force in manufacturing management. Old techniques such as labor standards application continue to provide a reliable benchmark for measuring performance and predetermining labor costs. Recently some predetermined labor standard systems have been simplified and computerized. Standards can be accurately and quickly applied to work by nonindustrial engineers using the computer and these systems.

Other techniques such as process simulation models and linear programming can be readily applied to complex manufacturing processes, material handling, and other systems through direct access to large computers through terminals or by the use of dedicated minicomputers. Labor process sheets, specifications, and other data can be stored for rapid reproduction or modification in a computer data base. Cash flow and rate of return for proposed capital expenditures can be quickly calculated by using computers. A major advantage of using the computer is the ability to try a number of alternative proposals to solve a given problem and to quickly identify the best solution.

As part of this plan, the manufacturing manager should ensure that industrial engineering is using the latest processing techniques to reduce routine operations.

MEASURING PROGRESS

As mentioned previously in this chapter, the success of the plan depends on each functional manager's realization that all objectives must be accomplished as stated and as scheduled. Therefore, there should be a procedure to measure actual progress against objectives and supporting strategies. A recommended technique is to have each functional manager prepare a list of objectives and supporting strategies against which to measure progress. A time schedule identifying start and completion dates is also developed and progress measured against the schedule.

A business plan is usally prepared each year dropping off the prior year and adding one more to the end. Although objectives may extend beyond the first year, performance against objectives in the current year will give an indication of future results. If delinquencies in meeting the schedule occur, appropriate action can be taken to recover. A realistic appraisal of progress may show that the objective cannot be attained. The company may wish to substitute an alternate or in an extreme case trigger the profit assurance plan.

SUMMARY

In this chapter, the interdependence of various company functions and their effect on the manufacturing business plan have been explained. Objectives, goals, and strategies have been defined and the importance of meeting objectives emphasized. As events unforeseen at the time the plan was prepared can either enhance or upset the plan objectives, the concepts of alternate strategies and profit assurance supplementary programs were introduced.

Through discussion and example, the manufacturing manager was encouraged to be alert for applications of research and development and quality assurance assistance in cost reduction. Opportunities for operational improvement from computer-aided design/computer-aided manufacturing, word processing, and computer capabilities will grow, and the manufacturing manager should be knowledgeable about applications.

Some manufacturing functions such as plant engineering and quality control will have expanding roles in protecting the company from possible violations of environmental, product liability, EEOC, and OSHA laws and regulations.

Lastly, it was pointed out that progress must be monitored and achievements against objective milestones reported so that appropriate action may be taken if delinquencies are indicated.

33
Improving Operating Performance through Use of Operations Budgets

Hugo Swan
Vice-President of Operations
Clausing Corporation

The author cautions against using budgetary controls as a substitute for other operational controls and describes the steps required in an intelligently prepared budget.

OPERATIONS BUDGETING

Operations budgets are an excellent cost control tool when properly used. The purpose of this chapter is to familiarize the reader with operations budgets, their uses, limitations, preparations, and relationships with other operating controls for improving operating performances.

Definitions and Importance

A budget is a plan or target for income or spending for the various elements of a business, governmental unit, bank, hospital, school, or other organization. Budgetary control is the organization's use of a budget or budgets to monitor performance.

A budget usually extends for one year; a long-range plan covers several years and includes strategies for:

1. Entering new markets and retaining or expanding old markets

2. Improving existing products and developing new ones
3. Making long-range make-or-buy decisions
4. Investing in new plant and equipment
5. Developing new suppliers
6. Developing the organization to implement the long-range plan
7. Providing the requisite funds

The length of period for a budget is usually one year, broken into monthly or quarterly detail. This plan should fit into the long-range plan and be a part of its implementation. The budget period should also coincide with the fiscal year to permit comparisons of results with the budget estimates.

Preparation of a budget is a planning process that should cause an organization to analyze its objectives and the resources needed to attain these objectives. Frequently, however, budgets are based on history with adjustments for changes in activity levels without sufficient thought given to whether previous objectives are still valid and how much the need for resources has really changed. This might be termed incremental budgeting.

Preparation of a budget should start with a definition or redefinition of an organization's goals and objectives. A goal of a 10% pretax profit should be accompanied by specific objectives that must be attained to realize this goal. The importance of intelligently prepared budgets lies in the analytical process in each department and function. If the analysis is thorough, the budgeting process can be an extremely valuable management tool forcing immediate attention to all phases of an organization's operation. If the analysis is haphazard, the budgeting process probably will be nothing more than a time-consuming exercise.

PURPOSE OF BUDGETS

Heckert and Wilson (*Business, Budgeting, and Control*) list the purposes of budgeting as:

Planning

1. To base action on investigation, study, and research.
2. To enlist the assistance of the entire organization in determining the most profitable course.
3. To serve as a declaration of policies.
4. To define objectives.
5. To stabilize employment.
6. To make more effective use of physical equipment.

Coordination

1. To coordinate human effort within the business structure.
2. To relate the activity of the business to the general trend of economic conditions.
3. To direct capital and effort to the most profitable channels by means of a balanced and unified program.
4. To reveal weaknesses in the organization.

Control

1. To control specific operations or expenditures.
2. To prevent waste.

Added to the above purposes are the following:

3. To recognize when the budgetary plan needs modification and trigger management actions.
4. To recognize how well various managers are conforming to budgets.

Communications

1. To foster vertical communications up and down the organizational ladder.
2. To foster interdepartmental horizontal communications and cooperation.

USES AND LIMITATIONS

Some uses of operations budgets were described previously as purposes of budgets. Some additional uses include:

To plan for the unexpected. For example, one medium-sized manufacturing company embarked on a new venture of importing and marketing material handling machinery with much enthusiasm and a few misgivings. To appease some cautious members on the board of directors, the company prepared three two-year quarterly budgets for the following activity levels:

1. *Most optimistic sales level.* This budget was prepared to determine the maximum amount of funds that might be needed for the new venture.
2. *Expected sales level.* This budget was prepared in conjunction with the establishment of burden rates and most of the planning for the new venture.
3. *Lowest acceptable sales level.* If this level were unattainable, the company planned to discontinue the venture and

limit its losses. Unfortunately, an unanticipated recession prevented sales from rising to this level. Despite expectations of strong sales in the future, the company sold this division to a conglomerate and thereby minimized its losses. This was a difficult decision to make because of the expected satisfactory future. Without the lowest-acceptable-sales-level plan, the decision might not have been triggered in time to prevent huge losses that would have jeopardized the parent company before the division started to make money.

To measure whether planned improvements achieve expected benefits. This will be discussed later in this chapter.

Budgeting controls have definite limitations that require the use of other controls. For example, several years ago a chemical company with a large maintenance budget was purchased by a conglomerate that believed in the superiority of budgetary controls. A recent analysis of why the chemical company's profits had been deteriorating showed that a comprehensive maintenance control system had been discontinued because of an improperly prepared budget. Failure to schedule repair jobs and measure maintenance productivity led to a general decline in worker pace and a gradual deterioration in plant and equipment.

Because budgetary controls are measurements of performance only, they should be used in conjunction with:

1. Inventory control
2. Production planning, scheduling, and control
3. Quality control
4. Daily efficiency reporting and control
5. Absenteeism and tardiness reporting and control
6. Equipment utilization planning and control
7. Sales activity planning and control
8. Early warning systems of warranty problems.

This need for other management controls will be discussed in more detail later in this chapter.

TYPES OF BUDGETS

Budgets are used for planning and controlling all elements of an organization's income and expenditures and include:

Income budgets

1. *Sales budgets.* All other budgets and plans for a manufacturing or merchandising organization usually are based upon this plan of what is forecast to be sold.
2. *Revenue budgets.* These take the place of sales budgets for governmental units.
3. *Revenue and reimbursement budgets.* These take the place of sales budgets in the health care industry.

Manufacturing production budgets

1. *Materials budgets.* These are usually purchasing plans based on a master schedule (prepared from the sales forecast) that may level seasonal loads and adjust inventories to suit forecast business conditions.
2. *Labor budgets.* These are based on the staffing needed to achieve the master schedule.
3. *Manufacturing overhead budgets.* These are plans for manufacturing expenses needed to achieve the master schedule. They should be broken down into fixed and variable overhead budgets when variable budgeting is used.

Operating expense budgets for nonmanufacturing organizations.
These both differ and resemble manufacturing expense budgets. For example, a city's snow removal budget could be variable, based upon the number of days snow exceeds a specified number of inches. In many cases, however, such budgets are fixed based on revenue allocations.

Administrative budgets.

1. Selling and marketing expense budgets.
2. General and administrative expense budgets.

Capital budgets. These are targeted spendings for the fiscal period of capital items such as plant and equipment.

Research and development budgets. These are targeted spendings for the fiscal period for research and development of new products, materials, and processes.

Job cost budgets. These are expected costs of sales for products that are unique to a customer rather than being built to stock.

Cash budgets (forecasts). This type of budget involves cash-flow forecast to determine whether sufficient funds will be availabe when needed to support all of the other budgets.

Budgets are also classified by their flexibility of adjustment to meet changing conditions. This classification grades budgets as fixed, flexible, or stepped.

A fixed budget is established for a fixed activity level of an organization. This is satisfactory only when the level can be predicted with reasonable certainty, such as in a municipality where tax and other revenues can be established in advance. In such cases, however:

1. If an expected federal grant or some other form of revenue is not forthcoming, the expense budgets normally must be changed to reflect changes in revenue.
2. Even in such cases, variable expense budgets may be desirable in certain areas, such as snow removal, which has variable expenditures based upon snowfalls.

A flexible (variable) budget is one that can be adjusted within limits to reflect varying activity levels. These are used primarily for sales budgets, direct materials, direct labor, and variable expenses. In manufacturing firms, flexible budgets are more satisfactory than fixed budgets because of the seasonality of activity and other difficulties in predicting activity levels accurately. Flexible budgets frequently are set by analyzing revenues and expenses for 10% and 15% on either side of the expected activity level.

Where changes in activity levels are sufficient to cause changes in the number of shifts or other adjustments in supervisory and fixed costs, a stepped budget should be used to recognize when such adjustments should be made. The stepped budget usually is flexible with steps as shown in Figure 1.

A technique for forcing managers to examine their functions and operations thoroughly is called *zero-base budgeting*. Peter A. Pyhrr, the father of zero-base budgeting, defined it

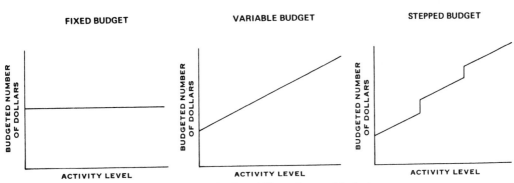

FIGURE 1. Fixed, variable, and stepped budgets

as "an operating, planning and budgeting process which requires each manager to justify his entire budget request in detail from scratch (hence zero-base) and shifts the burden of proof to each manager to justify why he should spend any money at all." The zero-base budgeting process is rarely used in manufacturing budgets, because labor standards, material standards, and indirect labor staffing tables can be effective in justifying budgets. The zero-base budgeting process is used for identifying selling, general, administrative, and manufacturing support budgets.

This process consists of the following steps:

1. Activities are identified in decision packages.

2. Packages are ranked in cost/benefit order.

3. Funds are allocated to the higest ranked packages.

In traditional budgeting, the focus is on justifying new incremental programs and assuming that existing activities are necessary. In most organizations it is easier to start a function or a program than to stop it when its value or purpose ceases. In zero-base budgeting, all programs and service, old and new, compete for the same resources. Table 1 shows a typical form used for preparing an activity's decision package, which displays the following information:

Table 1. Decision Package.

Objective No._____   Date_____

ACTIVITY (OR OBJECTIVE) NAME BUDGET DIVISION ADMINISTRATION LEVEL NO. 1 OF 2	DEPARTMENT CONTROLLER'S DIVISION BUDGET	PREPARED ABC APPROVED	RANK

PURPOSE OF ACTIVITY Basic secretarial and statistical typing support to Division	RESOURCES REQUIRED*	CURRENT YEAR	BUDGET YEAR
	Personnel	1	1
	Labor $	11,111	12,000
DESCRIPTION OF ACTIVITY Provide secretarial and basic typing support to Manager and all other members of Division. Provide statistical typing of budget analysis reports and budget documents. Maintain division files and supply cabinets.	Outside services $	0	0
	Other $	400	500
	Total $	11,511	12,500

ALTERNATIVE WAYS OF PERFORMING WORK ON PROGRAM AND COSTS

Share workload for basic typing and secretarial support with another Division.
Require one budget analyst or the statistical clerk to perform statistical typing as an added duty.
Retain "Kelly Girl" statistical typist during quarterly peak load periods @ $8.00 per hour.

ADVANTAGES OF RETAINING ACTIVITY

Provides fast, accurate typing of reports and correspondence of many kinds. Deadlines for Friday Management Committee meetings (for review of departmental budget proposals) are met.

CONSEQUENCES IF ACTIVITY IS ELIMINATED

Productivity of entire Division would be seriously impaired. Division workload would need to be cut and remaining workload accomplished on an extended schedule.

1. Activity name
2. Purpose of activity
3. Description of the activity's recommended approach
4. Alternative approaches
5. Advantages of retaining the activity
6. Consequences if the activity is eliminated
7. Resources required
8. Activity rank or priority.

Table 2 displays a typical form used for ranking priorities.

Zero-base budgeting frequently generates a large number of decision packages. Methods for controlling this volume should be established at the system design stage. Some methods include:

1. Consolidate decision packages having similar objectives.
2. Establish as mandatory those packages that cannot be altered or eliminated because of contractual or other arrangements.
3. Use computers to speed the paperwork and the consolidations.
4. Stagger the departments using the zero-base budgeting process so that it occurs every second or third year.
5. Direct management's attention to key decision points.

The general requirements for the successful implementation of zero-base budgeting are:

1. A strong commitment of top management

Table 2. Priority Ranking.

Date_____

Department CONTROLLER'S	Division BUDGET				Prepared DEF (CONTROLLER)		Page 1	
					Approved DEF		of 1	
ACTIVITY					CURRENT YEAR		BUDGET YEAR	
Rank	Name and Description	Level No. of No.		Org. Obj.No.	Personnel	$ (000)	Personnel	$ (000)	Cumulative $ (000)
1	PERSONNEL AND OPERATING BUDGET ADMINISTRATION	1(A)	3(B)		1	14.3	1	15.5	15.5
2	CAPITAL BUDGET ADMINISTRATION	1	3		2	28.8	2	31.5	47.0
3	BUDGET DIVISION ADMINISTRATION	1	2		1	11.5	1	12.5	59.5
4	PERSONNEL AND OPERATING BUDGET ADMINISTRATION	2	3		3	46.2	3	46.5	106.0
5	CAPITAL BUDGET ADMINISTRATION	2	3		1	17.1	1	18.5	124.5
6	BUDGET DIVISION ADMINISTRATION	2	2		1	23.8	1	26.0	150.5
7	CAPITAL BUDGET ADMINISTRATION	3	3	76-4	0	0	1	21.5	172.0
8	PERSONNEL AND OPERATING BUDGET ADMINISTRATION	3	3	76-7	0	0	1	15.0	187.0
		Totals			9	141.7	11	187.0	

Notes: (A) This activity has been number 1 of the activities submitted by the Personnel and Operating Budget Administration.

(B) Three activities have been submitted by the Personnel and Operating Budget Administration.

2. An effective system design to meet the needs of the individual organization
3. Sufficient funds
4. Knowledgeable people
5. Effective system management.

In theory, zero-base budgeting is an excellent management tool for periodically analyzing all programs and services and adjusting them as needed. In actual practice, benefits frequently fall short of potentials because of insufficient analysis and a desire by department managers to protect their bailiwicks. For example, one utility that introduced zero-base budgeting found that each manager had added 10% to the previous year's budget and then had explained the increase with zero-base techniques. Management subsequently cut each budget 7% across the board and thereby switched to historical budgeting rather than zero-base.

It requires tough-minded management, substantial effort, and proper attitudes to make zero-base budgeting work. Where it is made to work, it is a powerful management analysis and control tool.

PREPARATION OF OPERATIONS BUDGETS

ORGANIZATION FOR BUDGETING

Responsibility for coordinating budget preparation should be assigned to a budget executive. He may be the controller in a small firm or he may have a staff of assistants in a large firm. He generally reports to the controller, although the vice-president of planning doubles as the budget executive and reports directly to the chief executive officer in a few firms.

The following conditions are essential to a successful budgeting program:

1. The chief executive must back the program fully.
2. The accounting system must be adequate to support the program. The chart of accounts should be broken down by lines of authority and responsbility.
3. The budget executive must motivate people to prepare budgets honestly and accurately.
4. The individual responsibile for conforming to a budget should prepare the budget estimates.
5. Each budget must be realistic with attainable goals.
6. A budget should be prepared for all areas of the operation.
7. Budget revisions should be prepared as needed on a timely basis.
8. People should be given sufficient time, assistance, and training to prepare their budgets.
9. A budget committee, consisting of the chief executive officer, executives of the organization's various divisions, and the budget executive, should be established to:

a. Promulgate budget policies.
b. Translate the company's long-range plans into the next period's budget preparation policies
c. Review individual budget estimates and recommend revisions
d. Approve budgets and revisions
e. Monitor conformance to budgets and recommend appropriate actions
f. Recognize when outside conditions require a complete budget review and revision.

This committee can be a valuable aid to the chief executive officer in communicating policies, monitoring organizational and divisional performances, and in recognizing when changes of organizational directions are needed.

Table 3 shows who normally should be responsible for preparing various types of manufacturing budgets. Table 3 also shows who might be expected to assist in the budget preparation. The method for calculating each line item of the budget will be discussed in a later section.

Table 3. Responsibility for Budget Plans.

BUDGET PLAN OR FORECAST	DEPARTMENT RESPONSIBLE	
	PREFERRED	OTHER
Sales orders and shipments	Sales	Accounting, Material Control
Inventories:		
Finished goods:		
(If levels are set by market conditions)	Sales, Material Control	Accounting
(If levels are set by production conditions)	Material Control	Accounting
Work in process	Material Control	Accounting
Raw materials	Material Control	Accounting, Purchasing
Production requirements:		
Units	Material Control	
Direct labor hours	Department Foremen	Material Control, Industrial Engineering
Indirect labor hours	Department Foreman	Industrial Engineering
Direct materials	Material Control	
Other direct manufacturing expenses	Department Foremen	Industrial Engineering, Accounting
Other indirect manufacturing expenses	Department Foremen	Industrial Engineering, Accounting
Allocation of indirect manufacturing expenses	Industrial Engineering	Accounting
Purchases	Purchasing	Material Control
Selling, General, and Administrative:		
Executive	Accounting	
General office	Accounting	
Data processing	Department Head	
Industrial relations	Department Head	
Sales	Department Head	
Marketing	Department Head	
Research and development	Department Head	
Capital improvements	Manufacturing Engineering	Department head, Production, Accounting, Purchasing
Costs of goods—manufactured	Accounting	
—sold	Accounting	
Other income and expenses	Accounting	
Prepaid expenses and accruals	Accounting	
Accounts receivable	Accounting	
Accounts payable	Accounting	
Payroll	Accounting	
Long- and short-term loans payable	Accounting	
Interest payable	Accounting	
Profit and loss	Accounting	
Balance sheet	Accounting	
Cash	Accounting	
Consolidation of all budgets	Budget Officer	Chief Financial Executive

SALES FORECASTS AND BUDGETS

Sales forecasts should be prepared annually and updated periodically to ensure that the following are kept current:

1. Medium-range make-or-buy decisions
2. Facility, equipment, and capital budget planning
3. Staff planning in conjunction with the master production plan
4. Master production scheduling in some industries
5. Long-lead-time purchasing.
6. Preparation of the sales department budget
7. Activity levels for preparing operations budgets in conjunction with the master production plan.

The accuracy of these sales forecasts affects the accuracy of all subsequent planning and budgeting. Because forecasts rarely are completely accurate, periodic reviews and revisions of the forecast and subsequent updating of plans are very important but frequently ignored or haphazardly executed.

These forecasts may be by units or dollars of individual products, or by sales dollars to customers or markets. Units of individual products provide better detail for facilities planning and preparation of operations budgets. These forecasts should consider:

1. Seasonal fluctuations
2. The business climate and leading economic indicators
3. Market strategies
4. Historical performance
5. Market and share-of-market trends
6. Inflationary trends.

Normally, marketing is responsible for preparing sales forecasts with guidance from top management and, in larger companies, from economists or econometric analysts.

After the sales forecast in units has been prepared, it should be converted to sales dollars by month for each product line or division measured by the books of account. This sales forecast is normally set for the expected level of activity. A few organizations prepare three-level forecasts and budgets to plan cash needs under the most optimistic and pessimistic conditions and also to make contingency plans for the unexpected, as discussed earlier. Sometimes these three-level forecasts and budgets are prepared for activity levels 10 or 15% on either side of expected level for use in establishing formulas for variable budgets.

THE PRODUCTION PLAN

The production plan is based upon the sales forecast and includes:

1. A master production plan that frequently attempts to level fluctuations and seasonality in the sales forecast. Present difficulties in recruitment, union contracts, and unemployment insurance laws make direct labor almost a fixed cost and thereby force managements to consider alternatives other than seasonal layoffs
2. A facilities and equipment utilization plan to implement the master production plan
3. A staffing plan to implement the master production plan
4. An inventory plan, which reflects expected changes in inventory expected to result from implementing the master production plan and the dictates of market requirements
5. A purchasing plan.

The master production plan may be stated in terms of units, tons, some other measurement of production, or dollars. The use of computerized material requirements planning programs makes a detailed master production plan easier to prepare than by manual methods, which frequently use historical percentages to save time and effort. In either case, recognition of changes in production methods and conditions is essential.

FACILITIES AND STAFFING PLANS

Facilities and staffing plans, based upon the production plan, should be prepared for each department. In job-shop manufacturing plants, it is rarely possible to determine the exact equipment and staffing that will be needed a year in the future. Here historical profiles of facilities and staffing usage are frequently used. In many types of manufacturing companies, sales forecasts and production plans frequently can be converted into standard labor or machine hours for preparing direct labor and facilities plans.

Facilities plans should show the hours of expected utilization and setup. If new equipment is to be added, the plan should show when the equipment is to be added, the expected utilization, and setup time. If the plan shows that facilities will be overloaded at specific times, it should be adjusted for load-leveling or subcontracting.

The staffing plan should be based upon the production plan and should conform to the facilities plan. It should be based upon staffing tables for direct and indirect labor, supervision, and technical and clerical personnel. For flexible and stepped budgets, these staffing plans should be prepared for appropriate levels of activity and should indicate fixed and variable staffing. Table 4 shows a typical staffing plan.

To determine direct labor staffing requirements when standard hours for the period are known, the following factors should be considered:

1. Efficiency
2. Direct labor diversion to indirect tasks or idle time
3. Absenteeism, vacations, and holidays.

Indirect labor staffing requirements also should consider absenteeism and vacations. Many companies use labor pools to cover absenteeism and vacations. Some use summer help to replace people on vacation. In the case where no labor pool exists and absenteeism averages 7% in a 47-person department, three extra people should be hired to compensate for absenteeism.

Table 4. Personnel Requirements.

| DEPARTMENT NUMBER | 31 | DEPARTMENT NAME | PRESSROOM | PREPARED BY _____ | | DATE _____ |

LEVEL OF ACTIVITY   56,000 total direct labor hours @ 81%* effectiveness

| | SHIFTS AND NUMBER OF PEOPLE | | | TYPE OF BUDGET | | |
POSITION	1ST	2ND	TOTAL	FIXED	VARIABLE	STEPPED
Press Operator	20	15	35		35	
Press Setup Person	3	3	6	2	4	
Material Handler	2	2	4		4	
Custodian	1	1	2	1	—	1
# Total hourly	26	21	47	3	43	1
Supervision	1	1	2	1	—	1
Total	27	22	49	4	43	2

*Calculated at 90% direct labor utilization and 90% direct labor efficiency (90% × 90% = 81%).

Production plan (expected level) requires 56,700 press hours.

Press utilization = $\dfrac{56{,}000 \text{ press hours}}{24 \text{ presses} \times 4{,}000 \text{ hours/press}}$ = 59%.

#Assumes that the labor pool will make up for absenteeism.

An example of the value of labor budgeting occurred in a small automotive supplier that was losing $50,000 a year. When they hired a management consulting firm to help them install a budgetary control system, the consultant assisted them in preparing a staffing plan and found the company had twice as many workers as needed for the planned activity level. The resulting reduction in staff by one-half caused a momentary drop in production, but one week later, production returned to its original level. The company made a $35,000 profit the next year. Minimum staffing and expense, however, do not necessarily mean maximum profits. One automatic components supplier found that changing from five to three automatic screw machines per operator increased machine utilization, schedule conformance, and profits signficantly. A stamping shop increased machine utilization and profits by raising their pay scale for die repair people to the prevailing wage for the area. This change enabled them to reduce turnover of skilled labor.

RELATIONSHIP BETWEEN LABOR STANDARDS, INCENTIVES, AND BUDGETS

A labor standard is an estimate of how long it will take a worker to perform a task. Engineered labor standards frequently are based upon the concept of a normal employee producing a fair day's work at a pace which can be sustained all day long. These standards are then adjusted for normal delays, personal time, and fatigue where applicable.

Labor standards are used to:

1. Estimate costs for sales proposal purposes
2. Plan staffing and equipment needs
3. Measure machine and labor loads
4. Measure labor efficiency and calculate efficiency variances
5. Prepare standard costs
6. Calculate incentive wage payments
7. Trigger variable budgets.

Standards used for costing need not be those used for other purposes, but some companies do not have an industrial engineering department large enough to prepare labor standards and keep them current. A rule of thumb is that one full-time industrial engineer is needed to prepare and maintain labor standards for every 100 workers. Care should be exercised in applying this rule because individual companies may have different requirements. Because labor standards are frequently inaccurate and productivity varies daily, actual productivity must be measured and compared with budgeted productivity. This comparison is the efficiency variance to be discussed later. Where a significant efficiency variance is expected, it should be recognized in the budget and in product cost estimates.

Managements have devised numerous incentive plans to spur labor productivity. Most are based upon produced units per hour or allowed time per unit. Some plans are individual-oriented; others, group-oriented. The individual incentive is also based on work standards for each operation in a plant. The individual is paid a bonus on the basis of the improvement of the standards. (Piece work is a variation of this method.) The advantages of individual incentives are:

1. The incentive is close to the individual, and his effort determines his productivity and earnings.
2. The workers understand the plan.
3. It is flexible. As products or processes are added or deleted, the standards and payments can easily be adjusted.

The disadvantages of individual incentives are:

1. The objectives of labor and management can easily oppose each other. Whereas management wants increased production, labor wants more pay without necessarily increasing production. It is more to labor's advantage to attack

and loosen the standards than in a measured day work system.

2. To the end of loosening standards, labor will work to thwart the time-study man or whoever sets the standards.
3. Because of the difficulty of setting uniformly tight standards on variable environment jobs, earnings will vary among workers and from one period to another. This may cause resentment.
4. Generally speaking, nonproduction employees do not participate in such incentives, yet they have an important bearing on productivity.
5. Administrative expense of the plan is generally high.
6. Management must plan well for the usual premium to be earned by the worker.
7. Product quality may suffer.
8. There is no incentive for workers to suggest methods improvements.

Overall incentives are based on a composite measure of labor productivity for a plant, department, or product group.

The advantages of group incentives are:

1. The earned-hour standards may be established through the same work-measurement techniques used for individual incentive or by other methods.
2. Cooperative effort is stimulated; the workers understand that their collective efforts affect their earnings; and their performance can be posted daily so that they are informed of their current earnings position.
3. Adjustments easily can be made in the standards as operations are added, modified, or deleted.
4. Earnings ratios will not vary among workers in a department or plant.
5. Nonproduction employees may be included in the group and receive incentive earnings for contributing to productivity, as the productive workers may have many of these nonproductive tasks

included in their work assignments, thereby reducing the total manpower and payroll.

6. Division of the proportion of hours earned in excess of actual hours on a 75–25, 67–33, or similar basis is more frequently attainable with a large group than with individual incentives.

The disadvantages of group incentives are:

1. As with individual incentives, labor will make attacks on the standards to loosen them.
2. When two or more men are performing similar operations, the faster man may slow his gait to match the productivity of the slower worker.
3. Standards may not be policed by management representatives quite so carefully as when individual incentives are used, on the theory that the effect of a loose standard created by a methods or tooling change is "watered down" by the number of people who share in any deviation.
4. There is no incentive for the workers to suggest methods improvements.

Numerous other systems exist, including productivity incentives and profit sharing. The effect of a plan on motivating people and in improving direct and indirect labor efficiency should be estimated and allowed for in the budgets. When a plan has been in effect for several years, it is relatively easy to recognize its effects on the budget.

Preparing a budget with a new labor incentive plan is more difficult. It is important to estimate and budget for the plan's effects on:

1. *Product quality.* Frequently, incentive plans have an adverse effect on product quality, particularly when quality control is poor and the plan makes no distinction between good production and scrap. One woodworking company recently substituted a group incentive sys-

tem for a piece rate system because of difficulties in obtaining product quality under the old system. Acceptable production soon doubled.

2. *Downtime.* When workers' pay is based upon efficiency, they are much quicker to recognize and report real and imagined delays.

3. *Improper production reporting.* Numerous examples exist of workers inflating their incentive plan by overreporting production or reporting wrong part numbers with looser standards.

   Many managements accept this condition, but some employ production count auditors. Others add special timekeepers to obtain accurate shop reporting.

4. *Efficiency.* If a new incentive plan is successful in improving efficiency, the effect of this increase on indirect staffing and other departmental cost elements should be recognized and budgeted.

5. *Incentive systems require greater administrative costs.*

RELATIONSHIP BETWEEN BUDGETS AND BURDEN RATES

Manufacturing burden (or overhead) rates generally are applied to direct labor costs to include a wide variety of factory expenses when calculating the value of inventories and costs of sales. Table 5 shows some methods for estimating expenses when preparing both burden rates and budgets. Table 5 also lists items that may be included in burden costs.

Table 6 shows some indirect department costs that must be allocated to direct departments when calculating burden rates. These costs usually are budgeted for each indirect department and usually not allocated to the direct departments for budgetary control purposes. An exception to this rule occurs when

the direct department supervisor exercises control over an indirect department's costs in his department, such as material handling, manufacturing engineering, custodial, or timekeeping costs.

Budgets and burden rates should be prepared simultaneously and should tie together. Budgetary control reports may report to each supervisor only those budgets and actual costs of those elements over which he exercises control. When companies report all department costs to a supervisor, budgets and standard burden costs should usually be identical.

BUDGETS FOR EXPECTED VARIANCES

Many plants should but do not enter expected variances into budgets, burden rates, or cost estimates for sales proposals. The following list contains types of variances and circumstances under which budgeting of expected variances should be considered:

1. *Material usage variance when material usage standards are known to be tight.*

2. *Material price variance when an expected inflation rate has been added to the material cost standard.* In such cases, a favorable variance might be budgeted in the first month of the fiscal year, gradually decreasing each month to zero by mid-fiscal year. Thereafter, a gradually increasing unfavorable variance might be budgeted to the end of the fiscal year. The total of these budgeted variances for all 12 months should be zero. Some companies separate material price variances into original price variances from targets and subsequent price changes caused by inflation. This separation is useful when a company has a policy of passing cost increases on to customers through frequent price increases.

3. *Direct labor efficiency variance when labor standards are known to be tight.*

Table 5. Suggested Methods for Expense Estimation and Charging.

The following descriptions are general. Detailed analysis will be required of certain accounts to establish if the expense should be charged directly or allocated to a department or cost center. Likewise, similar determinations will be required to isolate manufacturing from sales, general and administrative expenses. The four classifications of expenses are intended as general guides pending detailed analysis.

DESCRIPTION	CHARGE	ALLOCATION OF AN IND. DEPT. CHARGE	INCLUDED IN MFG. BURDEN AND BUDGETS	INCLUDED IN SALES, GENERAL, AND ADMIN.	BASIS FOR COMPUTATION
Material, labor and burden variances (1)	X		X		Engineering estimates
Salesmen salaries and commissions	X			X	Salaries—manning tables. Commissions—Sales Forecasts
Supervision	X	X (2) (3)	X	X	Manning tables
Technical and engineering	X	X (2)	X	X	Manning tables
Clerical	X	X	X	X	Manning tables
Set-up and machine change	X		X		Manning tables and engineering estimates
Reset up and set-up servicing	X		X		Manning tables and engineering estimates
Tryout and experimental	X		X		Engineering estimates
Salvage	X	X	X		Manning tables
Other indirect labor	X	X	X		Manning tables
Lost production time	X			X	Engineering estimates
Fringe benefits		X	X	X	Proportion to manning table data based on analysis of historical data
Supplies—office	X		X	X	Estimate on basis of historical data
Supplies—manufacturing	X		X		Engineering estimated based on planned production levels
Telephone and telegraph	X	X (2)	X	X	Analysis of historical distribution budgeted to planned activity levels
Water		X (2)	X		Correlation of historical costs to production levels, allocated by engineering estimates of consumption, and budgeted to planned activity levels
Electricity		X (2)	X	X	Correlation of historical costs to production levels, allocated by engineering estimates of consumption, and budgeted to planned activity levels
Fuel	X	X (2)	X	X	Correlation of historical costs to production levels, allocated by engineering estimates of consumption, and budgeted to planned activity levels
Freight	X		X	X	Estimate on the basis of historical data and future plans
Purchased services	X	X	X	X	Analysis of future plans and present contracts
Rent	X	X (2)		X	Analysis of future plans and present contracts

Table 5. Suggested Methods for Expense Estimation and Charging—Continued

DESCRIPTION	CHARGE	ALLOCATION OF AN IND. DEPT. CHARGE	INCLUDED IN MFG. BURDEN AND BUDGETS	INCLUDED IN SALES, GENERAL, AND ADMIN.	BASIS FOR COMPUTATION
Insurance	X	X (2)	X	X	Analysis of premium costs, allocated on basis of value or space depending on the type of insurance
Depreciation—buildings	X	X (2)	X	X	Analysis of present and planned depreciation charges distributed by area
Depreciation—machinery and equipment	X		X	X	Analysis of present and planned depreciation charges by department and cost center
Depreciation—tools, dies, etc.	X	X	X	X	Analysis of present and planned charges by department and cost center
Property taxes	X	X (2)	X	X	Correlation of estimated taxes to buildings and allocation based on area
Taxes N.O.C.	X		X	X	Analysis of estimated taxes
Employees' expenses	X		X	X	Estimates of budgeted expenses based on historical data
Postage	X			X	Estimates of budgeted expenses based on historical data
Publication, dues and subscriptions	X	X (2)	X	X	Analysis and estimates
Professional services	X		X	X	Planned costs by analysis
Patent	X			X	Planned costs by analysis
Outside commissions	X			X	Budgeted on basis of sales forecasts, correlated to planned activity levels
Miscellaneous	X	X (2)	X	X	Budgeted on basis of historical data, correlated to planned activity levels

Notes:

(1)—Explains expected differences from standard

(2)—Indirect department cost elements are allocated to direct departments for manufacturing burden rate purposes, but these cost elements are usually budgeted to the indirect department because its supervision usually has control over them. Other cost elements, such as fringe benefits, will frequently be allocated on budgets.

(3)—An "X" in the charge and allocation columns denotes a charge or an allocation.

Table 6. Suggested Methods for Allocation of Service Department Expenses for Burden Rates.

DESCRIPTION	BASIS OF ALLOCATION
Quality control:	
In plant	Charge directly to department.
General service	Allocate to departments on the basis of engineering usage estimates.
Other	Allocate to departments in proportion to the sum of in-plant and general service quality control.
Inspection:	
In plant	Charge directly to department.
Other	Allocate to department in proportion to in-plant inspection.
Technical department	Charge directly to departments on the basis of engineering usage estimates.
Warehouse:	
In plant warehouses	Charge directly to using department (rod, tube, etc.).
Sales oriented functions	Not included in burden rates, develop pricing basis depending on production usage.
General overhead	Distribute to in-plant warehouses and sales oriented functions in proportion to dollars or labor or expense or inventory or on engineering usage estimates.
Research and development	Excluded from manufacturing burden.
General plant (occupancy)	Depending on nature of expenses, allocate to all departments on basis of area.
Process engineering	Allocate on basis of engineering usage estimates (to departments or product lines) or in proportion to direct labor.
Tool control:	
Tool cribs	Charge directly to using department.
Other	Allocate on basis of engineering usage estimates.
Tool and die design	Allocate on basis of engineering usage estimate.
Tool room:	
Sharpening and grinding	Charge directly to using departments.
Main tool room	Allocate on basis of engineering usage estimates.
Building services:	
In plant	Charge directly to using departments.
Other	Allocate in proportion to occupancy costs.
Material handling:	
In plant	Charge directly to using departments.
Other	Allocate on basis of engineering usage estimates.
Maintenance control	Allocate as general overhead to the maintenance department, and then reallocate with maintenance (see the next item).
Plant engineering—technical support	Allocate on basis of engineering usage estimates.
Power plant	Allocate on basis of engineering usage estimates.
Standards and methods	Allocate on basis of engineering usage estimates or in proportion to total departmental labor.
Project engineering	Allocate on basis of engineering usage estimates.
Engineering administration	Allocate in proportion to number of personnel supervised.

Stationery
Allocate in proportion to usage estimates.

Table 6. Suggested Methods for Allocation of Service Department Expenses for Burden Rates—Continued

DESCRIPTION	BASIS OF ALLOCATION
Factory clerks:	
In plant	Charge directly to using department.
Other	Allocate in proportion to in-plant factory clerks.
Receiving	Allocate in proportion to direct labor.
Material burden	When used, this includes the costs of purchasing, receiving, receiving inspection, and material storage. Allocate in proportion to direct material pounds or dollars.

When piece-rate incentives are used, there is no labor efficiency variance.

4. *Direct labor guarantee variance.* When workers on incentives fall below a certain productivity level, they are frequently paid a base rate. The difference between this cost per piece and the piece rate labor cost is the direct labor guarantee variance.

5. *Direct labor rate variance.* Here again the total budgeted variance would be zero for the year. Individual months, however, might reflect contractual obligations in the budgeted variance. Because a supervisor rarely controls the pay rate of hourly workers, reporting of this variance on budgetary control reports frequently is meaningless, unless lower paid workers can be used for the same tasks as higher paid workers.

6. *Scrap variance.* This should be budgeted only when a scrap percentage is built into standard costs and then only to reflect expected monthly differences from the scrap costs targets.

7. *Burden volume variance.* Such a variance may occur for several reasons, such as:

    a. No scheduled work because of seasonality, decreases in customer demands, or excess capacity.

    b. No operators

    c. Tooling problems

    d. Machine breakdowns

    e. No instructions

    f. Waiting for work

It may be desirable to recognize some or all of these reasons and prepare reasonable targets for each department's budgets.

8. *Burden efficiency variance.* If a labor efficiency variance is budgeted, the burden efficiency variance should also be budgeted.

RECOGNITION OF IMPROVEMENTS

One of the biggest problems with most organizations' budgets is that they are prepared annually and recognize only volume of business changes but not methods and equipment changes. Failure to recognize change in budgets can work against a company. For instance, a foreman in a department assembling brass plumbing fixtures once recommended a change that cut his direct labor requirement in half. His budget was based on direct labor hours, so it too was cut in half rather than changed to reflect the methods improvement. With half as much material handling labor, custodial labor, and supplies for the same production requirements, his department could not produce as before and he was criticized unjustly.

One way to recognize change is to measure department performance against current labor standards while valuing inventory with accounting standards established at the beginning of the year. The difference in the standards can be measured as a methods-change variance. If a company has an improvement program that should result in savings during the fiscal year, these savings can be budgeted as a methods-change variance and compared with actual savings when the standards are revised to reflect the methods change. This method of change recognition also applies to material standards.

Companies frequently budget a period's improvements without definite plans of how these improvements will be obtained. Specific improvement programs should be identified with specific responsibilities and schedules for each task, improvement savings and costs, and estimated effects upon the budget. Improvement program controls are needed to augment budgetary controls, or else these improvements probably will not occur.

Budget analysts should be reviewing changes constantly in material standards, labor standards, and factory costs with industrial engineers and department foremen. Whenever changes are significant, budgets should be changed immediately. Without such changes, budgets lose their value as a cost-control tool. By showing such changes as material-change, methods-change, and overhead change variances, the budget variances still can be reconciled.

Frequently organizations make large investments in capital equipment based on certain forecast paybacks and then never measure whether they have achieved these paybacks. An excellent way of making such measurements is to adjust budgets to reflect expectations when equipment becomes operative.

RECOGNITION OF INFLATION

Until the last decade, inflation has not been considered significant in preparing monthly budgets. Companies generally added a certain percentage for inflation and expected to have favorable burden spending and purchase price variances in the early months of a fiscal year and unfavorable variances in the later months. Labor rate variances have been treated in a similar manner after analyzing contracted increases and expected cost-of-living increases.

In double-digit inflationary times, a company might consider adjusting the budget on a monthly basis for burden spending variances, purchase price variances, labor rate variances, and other variances affected by inflation. Such attention probably is too sophisticated for small companies, but it attunes the budget more nearly to actual conditions and makes large company budgets more believable.

OPERATIONS BUDGET PREPARATION

Table 5 suggests a basis for computation of each budget line item. Once computed, budget triggers must be established for flexible and stepped budgets. The budget trigger for a stepped budget normally is the number of shifts. Budget triggers for flexible budgets relate to some production measurement such as scheduled production, actual production, and standard hours or dollars of production. Budget triggers are used only to adjust variable line items and not fixed items, such as for depreciation or occupancy cost budgets.

After the budget trigger has been determined, a formula must be established for each variable line item. For example, if standard labor dollars of production is the budget trigger for a department's material handling budget and the budget formula is one dollar of material handling labor for every nine standard labor dollars of production, $10,080 standard labor dollars of production would produce a budget of $1,120 for material handling labor. The equipment depreciation budgeted would remain the same because depreciation is a fixed expense.

Selling, marketing, general, and administrative budgets should be prepared in a manner similar to that for operations budgets.

JOB COST BUDGETS

Job cost budgets are frequently prepared for job shop products such as a special machine tool. Experience has shown that the accuracy of using job costs budgets to predict annual costs tends to increase with the detail considered in the budget preparation. These budgets are usually prepared prior to making a customer proposal. Their uses include:

1. Comparing actual engineering, direct hourly, and purchased labor; purchased materials and services; and installation labor with budgeted costs
2. Forecasting profits and cash requirements
3. Feedbacks to cost estimating on where forecast and actual costs differ.

Job cost budgets are used with but do not supersede departmental budgets.

INVENTORY AND PURCHASING BUDGETS

One of the most difficult determinations in industry is the proper size of inventories. Sales usually wants a large balanced inventory so that everything can be sold or shipped immediately. Manufacturing prefers long production runs, which provide increased labor efficiency and unbalanced inventories. Accounting wants inventories held to a minimum to reduce investments in inventories, reduce borrowings, and improve the organization's cash position. Moreover, high interest rates drive inventory carrying costs up dramatically.

Experience has shown that proper application of production and inventory control principles usually will optimize inventories. Some of these principles are:

1. *Establish realistic customer service levels.* Customer service level is a term used to describe the percentage of customer orders that a company wants to fill or has historically filled from stock. Customer service levels have a significant effect upon the size of safety stocks needed to cover demand fluctuations. For example, customer service

levels in the following table increase the safety stock sizes (Q) in multiples.

APPROXIMATE CUSTOMER SERVICE LEVEL	SAFETY STOCK SIZE
69%	Q
85%	2Q
94%	3Q
98%	4Q
99%	5Q
Almost 100%	6Q

Q depends upon the fluctuations in usage and production lead times. If demand and lead times have been proven to be constant, Q becomes zero, because no safety stock is needed to cover variations. Conversely, if the fluctuation varies significantly, Q can become quite large compared to the average demand. The capability of shipping 97.7% of customer demands doubles inventory sizes over the capability of 84.1%. Improving from 84.1% to 99.9% triples the size.

2. *Use proper reordering techniques.* For example, use bill of material explosions of needs (material requirements planning) for dependent-demand items rather than reorder-point-quantity triggers. One company's inventory increased 56% in one year with no change in sales volume when it implemented a computerized system improperly using reorder-point quantities for dependent demand items. Because the inventory growth was in components rather than finished products, customer service levels did not improve with the larger inventory. The company is presently changing its inventory control system.

3. *Prepare realistic production and purchasing schedules.* Machine tool companies are notorious for preparing production schedules that exceed man-

ufacturing capacities. The result is that purchased materials are frequently received and paid for long before they can be used.

4. *Know your work center loads.* One company implemented a machine load system and found a nine-month backlog in front of a bottleneck machine. Using alternate equipment and redeploying people, the company eliminated the backlog in two months and reduced its inventory from $4,000,000 to $3,000,-000 in one year's time. It later found it could reduce the work force by 10% and improve on-time shipments.

5. *Keep accurate inventory records.* Companies with out-of-balance inventories usually have inaccurate inventory records that have caused improper purchasing and production ordering.

6. *Maintain a sound cost system.* Companies that think they are making a profit frequently find book-to-physical inventory write-down at inventory time is so great that the expected profits are really losses.

CASH FORECASTS

The cash forecast is sometimes the *cash-flow forecast* or the *cash budget*. Because it is not usually used as a control tool over internal expenditures or sales, it is really a forecast and not a budget.

The purposes for cash forecasts are to:

1. Make certain an organization has sufficient cash to meet oblications in a timely manner.
2. Determine when borrowing is needed to provide more cash.
3. Identify excess cash and the length of time it may be invested in the short- or long-term money markets.

The two methods of preparing a cash forecast are the cash receipts and disbursement method and the adjusted income method. Because it is difficult to forecast exactly when transactions will occur, considerable detail is needed to compare actual against expected transactions and prepare forecast revisions in a timely manner. The following are specific problems in cash-flow forecasting:

1. In companies with poor production and inventory control systems, shipments and invoices frequently are later than forecast.
2. The lag between collections and sales is erratic.
3. Vendor performance in deliveries and billing cannot be predicted with accuracy.
4. Timing errors of a few days for large receipts and disbursements can cause large errors in forecasting cash needs.

The cash receipts and disbursement method uses considerable detail from the operating budgets. This detail is valuable in comparing actual with forecasted cash flow and in making forecast revisions.

The adjusted income method adjusts the net profit (loss) on the forecast operating statement by eliminating all noncash income and expenses (such as depreciation) and adjusting for all forecast balance sheet changes involving cash. Because this method usually is not accompanied by transaction details, weaknesses include:

1. Analysis of forecast errors and subsequent forecast correction is difficult.
2. On long-lead-time products, expenditures may occur in one or more periods prior to when the product is sold. It may be difficult to adjust the expenditures to the proper periods without product sales details.
3. The variations in the daily cash requirements may be greater than the range indicated in the beginning and ending cash forecasts. The absence of details

makes daily cash requirement fluctuations difficult to project.

HOW TO IMPROVE OPERATING PERFORMANCE

Previous parts of this chapter have described operations budgets and their preparation. This part describes how to use budgets in conjunction with other controls to improve operating performance.

BUDGETARY PERFORMANCE REPORTS

Budgetary performance reports should be prepared for all significant levels of authority and responsibility. They include both this month's performance and year-to-date performance. The latter is a better indicator of conformance to budget for line items that fluctuate widely from month to month, such as departmental maintenance costs incurred. Figure 2 is an example of such a report.

The major problems with budgetary performance reports as a management control tool are:

1. The normal monthly reporting is too infrequent to be a precise control tool. Managers wishing good controls must keep duplicate manual controls if on-line inquiry is not available.
2. The writing of a requisition to purchasing is not recognized as a committed expenditure in most systems until the item is received, invoiced, and the expense distributed to the proper account. Governmental accounting systems frequently encumber such requisitions to recognize the expense commitment. In the absence of an encumbrance system and on-line inquiry, managers must keep manual records to recognize the commitment.
3. Budgetary controls should not be a substitute for other operating controls, as discussed later.

COST CENTER

No.	Name

Month__________

Year__________

ACCOUNT		THIS MONTH				YEAR TO DATE				PRIOR YEAR
No.	Name	Budget	Actual	Variance	%	Budget	Actual	Variance	%	Actual

FIGURE 2. Budget performance report.

PUTTING BUDGETARY CONTROLS TO WORK

The fact that budgetary controls should not be used as a substitute for other operational controls is emphasized throughout this chapter. This part of the chapter discusses how budgetary controls should be used to augment and monitor the effectiveness of other controls over operating performance.

Sales Forecasting and Budgetary Control

Monthly monitoring of the conformance of sales dollars to the sales forecast provides top management with an indication of the overall accuracy of the sales forecast. Other controls should exist, however, to provide warnings of the need to revise forecasts for sales of individual products, for market or customer activity levels, or for specific geographic areas or sales outlets. Recognition of when to change the sales forecast is important for:

1. Controlling inventory levels
2. Adjusting staffing levels and deploying personnel
3. Directing marketing and sales efforts.

Inventory Controls and Budgetary Controls

Monthly monitoring of actual versus budgeted inventory sizes provides top management with an indication of how well middle management is conforming to the inventory plan or budget. As discussed earlier, the following inventory control techniques, however, are needed to optimize the inventory size (which may or may not be the size specified by the inventory budget):

1. Establish realistic customer service levels.
2. Use proper inventory reordering techniques. Entering production orders into the master schedule from sales forecasts, from time-phased reorders, from reorder point quantities, from customer orders, and by material requirements planning are proper techniques under certain circumstances.
3. Establish data integrity over on-hand, on-order, committed, and available inventories. Breakdowns of inventory data integrity cause frequent inabilities to produce and ship on schedule. For example, a company in the capital goods industry recently experienced a 10% write-down of book-to-physical inventory and a 6% write-up of the inventory control records. At the same time, its actual shipments were running two months late. A review showed that completed components frequently were not recorded into stores, on-hand inventories were not cycle-counted, and production counts were highly distorted. Furthermore, the inventory control and accounting systems were not fed exactly the same transaction data.
4. Use proper production control techniques (discussed later) to keep work-in-process inventories optimized.

Quality Control and Budgetary Controls

Too frequently, quality control and inspection functions are trimmed at budget preparation time to levels that cause subsequent quality problems. The money saved can be an illusion if scrap and rework costs escalate. For example, one bearing manufacturer employed an unprincipled management consultant to assist in reducing costs. The consultant advised reducing the inspectors from seven to one. The resulting deterioration in product quality caused the company to lose sales and turned marginal profits into substantial losses. It took the company several years to recover.

Conversely, quality cannot be inspected into a product. Quality must be engineered in by the design and manufacturing engineers. Quality control and inspection serve the functions of preventing inferior products from reaching customer, monitoring quality trends, and recommending quality improvements. Quality control and inspection activities should be reviewed frequently to ensure adequacy. Scrap and rework budgetary controls are one measure of this effectiveness.

Production Counts and Budgetary Controls

Frequently, companies try to save money by having workers or foremen report production counts. There is no room in their budgets for special production counters, combination timekeeper-counters, or combination dispatcher-counters. Experience has proven that production people and foremen rarely report counts, part numbers, and operation numbers accurately. They are under more pressure regarding efficiency and quality. Workers on incentive plans usually are very inaccurate in reporting production.

Most companies with incentive plans have found that it pays to add special count checkers. The added cost of the checkers frequently is more than offset by accurate reporting of efficiencies, more production for the same incentive payments, and better production counts for relieving shop loads, determining when an operation has been completed (for machine tear-down and new setup purposes), and production expediting.

One mass producer of pipe fittings established a computerized method of checking production count accuracy and found 50% of the counts in error. A company producing relatively larger volumes of machine tools was able to reduce count errors from 30% to virtually zero. Both companies had labor incentive programs; their costs for production count checkers were quickly recovered in accurate incentive payments and improved data integrity in their computers.

Production Control and Budgetary Controls

The production schedule sets the level of departmental activity, which directly or indirectly triggers the variable budgeted amounts in flexible budgets. The budgetary control reports show how successful an organization has been in conforming to budgets. Good production control techniques improve effectiveness in keeping costs down in areas of idle time, direct labor diverted to indirect, inefficiencies because of workers' fears of running out of work, overtime, and work-in-process levels. A few of these techniques are:

1. *Capacity planning.* Monthly capacity utilization plans by work center show percentages of idle capacity available to handle additional sales. An increasing number of companies are translating this available capacity into products to be pushed by sales and marketing in order to arrive at an optimum product mix.

   Conversely, when certain types of capacities are oversold, management has time to increase capacity or arrange for subcontractors.

2. *Staff planning.* Conversion of work center capacity plans into staff plans for direct and indirect labor provides management with information on hiring, training, and medium-range staff deployment needs.

3. *Master scheduling.* When master schedules are prepared, extended, or revised, the level of plant activity specified by these schedules can be checked against the expected level to make certain there are no discrepancies.

4. *Input/output control.* This is a technique of watching that the queues of work ahead of work centers are under control. Where the queues are so short that workers are idle or inefficient, more shop orders are released or the workers

are deployed elsewhere. If the queue is so long that prduct manufacturing lead times and work in process are likely to increase beyond desirable levels, some combination of the following may be used to reduce queues: restriction of orders placed in the shop, overtime, extra shifts, and subcontracting.

5. *Work center loading.* This technique looks at work center loads for past-due work and weekly loads for the next two to four weeks. It is used in conjunction with input/output control to determine whether queues are likely to expand or contract without employing input/output control techniques.

6. *Direct labor skills loading.* This technique examines direct labor skills loads for past-due work and weekly loads for the next two to four weeks. The better systems separate loads already available for processing at a work center from scheduled work which has not yet arrived at the work center. Because loads have a tendency to ripple through job shops, it is helpful to have a pool of multiskilled workers to move along with the ripples.

Tool Control and Budgetary Control

When budgets are established for a manufacturing department, the setup labor usually is calculated and expressed as a ratio to the variable budget trigger. Certain tool control techniques are useful in some industries for keeping setup costs within budgets. These techniques include:

1. *Last piece tool and die inspection.* At the end of each production run, tools, fixtures, and dies should be inspected to determine whether they need reworking

before the next production run. Frequently, the last production piece is attached to the tooling to aid this decision without holding up tear-down for the next setup.

2. *Tool repair scheduling.* When the need to repair or sharpen a tool has been established, production control should schedule the repair to be completed prior to the next production run.

3. *Toolroom loading.* Very simple toolroom loading techniques can be established to show weekly toolroom loads. One company found that it was not meeting production schedules because new tool orders overloaded both tool design and the toolroom. The company installed a simple system based on estimates of the magnitude of the job and accepted tool orders to capacity. A methods engineer ordering a new tool that would create an overload condition was given the option of withdrawing another unstarted order or the one he was submitting. In two months, the tool design and the toolroom conformed to schedules and stopped delaying production schedules.

Cost Accounting and Budgetary Control

The cost accounting system must have data integrity to provide accurate actual costs for comparison with budgeted costs. If the cost system lacks credibility, the budgetary control system loses effectiveness. Management frequently has been surprised when the cost system fails to evaluate inventories properly. Book-to-physical inventory write-down have often changed an expected annual profit into a loss.

34
Overcoming The Computer Programming Problem

Kit Grindley
Director
Urwick Dynamics Limited
London, England

Mr. Grindley points out that hardware is no longer the cost problem that it has been in the past, with the tenfold reduction that has occurred. Further cost reductions are surely on the way with the availability of the desktop computer. The real problem, according to the author, is software. The problem in England (as well as the United States) is a shortage of programming skills. This chapter outlines a highly successful method that has been implemented to remedy this condition.

Computers installed by medium-sized companies 20 years ago typically cost 800,000 of today's pounds. The present cost of an equivalent machine is about £60,000 more than a tenfold reduction. The desktop computer has arrived and further cost reductions are promised. There are some who predict that the computer will soon come free with the desk. The barrier restraining automation is no longer the cost of the hardware, it is the provision of something called software. Isaac Auerbach gave us a clue in the early 1950s when he was asked, "What will a computer do for my business?" "When you switch it on," he replied, "it will make a little light and a little heat."

THE PROGRAMMING PROBLEM

Computers will do nothing until someone writes the programs for them to carry out. These programs are the software component in automation. And programmers today are in desperately short supply. The National Computing Centre recently reported a shortage of 20,000 programmers in Britain rising by 2,000 per annum. The special Neddy working party on computers reported last year that two out of three users are experiencing a "severe" or "very severe" shortage of programming staff. A survey of major issues facing DP managers today, carried out by Urwick Dynamics, showed staff shortage to be the top of the list for all those interviewed. Staff retention was second, with a turnover of 25% per annum being typical for the industry. The story is borne out by the number of advertisements appearing in the computer press. Forty to 50 pages of vacancies appear each week, with salaries up to £6,000 pa for minimal experiences. Yet many of those who advertise for staff receive no replies at all.

The cause of programmer shortage is our unwillingness, from the early days right up to the present time, to employ other than high-ability and experienced staff. In the late 1950s and early 1960s, when computers were just starting, there was a good reason for this strategy. Programming was a difficult task, involving complex logical problems and the pioneering of techniques for processing data. But when the pioneering days were over we persisted through the 1970s in employing university graduates as programmers, preferably with two or three years' experience.

The attraction of this sort of recruit is clear. First, they are esaily able to pick up fresh problems, new programming languages, and different machines to become productive very quickly with a minimum of supervision and instruction. This was important with the technology developing so fast. Even more important, it was seen as the only way of meeting pressure from users to get their systems going quickly. Faced wtih the problem of installing hardware that could do nothing until it was programmed, it has naturally enough been a continual story of trying to write programs as fast as possible. For 20 years we have not had the time to sit back and think about how to do the job, to train people in these methods, and to bring on the less able. To a great extent, this strategy is self-perpetuating. By relying on very able, experienced staff who are self-sufficient, we can cope with a minimum of management and supervision. But without good programming managers and supervisors we cannot introduce trainees effectively and are forced to rely on further supplies of able, experienced people.

Although the recruitment and training of less able newcomers has been neglected, we find enormous progress has been made with what appeared to be an alternative solution to the programmer problem: deskilling the job. Easy-to-use programming languages have been produced, together with a large number of programming aids. These aids consist of already written programs that can be used by programmers and incorporated in their work, provided we are prepared to accept the limitations of standard solutions. Unfortunately these two approaches—using high-ability staff and deskilling the job—have combined to disastrous effect on our efforts to produce computer software. Deskilling is demotivating. The university graduate thrives on the challenge of writing his first programs, but after a while he finds the routine and repetitive aspects of the deskilled work tedious and boring. One of the paradoxes of automation is that what appears to be a serious understaffing of programmers is in fact a symptom of persistent overstaffing. The following serious problems, faced in nearly all companies employing computers, are the result:

Professional Self-Indulgence

Routine programming lacks long-term job satisfaction for the able graduate programmer. In an effort to retain their staff, many DP managers are forced to introduce the latest hardware devices. "I recommended the installation of a real-time machine to boost morale," confided one manager. The practice of having the latest equipment in order to recruit good programmers is now so general that it has become the accepted thing and seems in many cases to need no further justification. But using the latest equipment involves pioneering the technology. This may be professionally satisfying for the data processing staff but is normally not what the company is in business for. It leads to criticism from users that the DP department is pursuing technical objectives rather than contributing to business results.

High Staff Turnover

The dilemma facing the DP manager is that he has a choice of two evils. If he does not provide technical challenges for his programmers constantly, morale in the department falls. On the other hand, if he provides interesting programming work on the latest equipment, his programmers develop skills and experience that are very marketable. It seems that either way, with so many job opportunities, his staff are going to leave. Staff turnover of 25% is common today.

Unmaintainable Programs

Programming work falls into two categories, developing new programs and altering existing programs to keep them in line with business developments. Writing new programs provides job interest for able people. But the unpopularity of improving programs that other people have written has become notorious. "I lost two excellent programmers last year," said a DP manager in a recent interview. "But it was my own fault. I had no new development work for them and put them on maintenance for six months." The dislike highly able people have of altering programs written by others is serious. The problem is made worse by the "ingenious" way such programmers write the programs in the first place. They are very hard for others to understand. There are many organizations today who are prevented from doing the things they want because they cannot alter their computer programs.

The Peter Principle

The career progression of programmers provides an interesting example of the Peter Principle of promoting staff to their level of incompetence. In order to retain staff who are threatening to leave from their lack of job interest, promotion is frequently offered. Programmers have only two basic promotion opportunities in most companies: programming manager or systems analyst. The able programmer does not necessarily make a good manager or analyst, however. Too often the results of such "staff retention" promotions are doubly serious; we lose good programmers and thus worsen the shortage, and get poor managers or analysts in exchange.

Salaries Out-Of-Line

It is to be expected that staff in short supply throughout the world are able to command high salaries. In fact the salaries paid to programmers to retain them, or to attract them from other companies are so high that most organizations have difficulty accommodating their salary grading systems. "Artificial" management and specialist positions have to be created so that market rates can be paid.

Freelancers

Faced with the boredom of continuing in the same job and the strong and steady demand for programmers, many high-ability staff leave and become freelancers. Selling their services, often the stumbling block for freelancers in other professions, is not difficult in such a buoyant market. Programmers in their early 20s and with as little as three years' experience are able to charge rates of £60 per day and more. But to get the software produced, it seems that DP managers are prepared to pay. A recent discussion revealed that one installation had a standard strength of 20 programmers. "But I've only got 12 at present," said the manager. Further discussion showed that in fact he hadn't got any. All 12 were freelancers supplied by programming agencies. In fact, he had given up trying to recruit staff on a permanent basis. His problems had shifted to trying to select the best agencies:

User Discontent

Where the shoe really pinches from the DP manager's point of view is the discontent this staff shortage generates among users of DP systems. It is becoming harder and harder to satisfy the needs of users for new systems and improvements to existing ones. Some 12 years ago one company set up a computer steering committee, with the main objective of "selling" the idea of using their computer to the production, marketing, and other departments. This was done very successfully. Having automated many of the company's systems, however the DP department is now facing acute programmer shortage. The old steering committee still meets, but it has changed its name. It is now called the computer priorities committee, and has the job of "rationing" work among users who are clamoring for systems improvements.

A NEW APPROACH TO PROGRAMMER TRAINING

The following case history is the study of a company where the programmer shortage became such a threat to its continued prosperity that the managing director decided to take a hand.

The company manufactures pharmaceuticals in Oxfordshire. They installed their first computer in 1967. They successfully transferred the accounting, production, and inventory control systems onto the machine over a period of five years. Since then, they improved their systems and also installed some up-to-date hardware with user-operated terminals employing screens for entering data and getting information. Their experience was that eight programmers could cope with the volume of systems development and maintenance work.

Two years ago, however, they were down to three because of high staff turnover. They advertised twice for experienced staff in the computer press, offering salaries comparable with their existing programmers. On the first occasion, they received two replies. One was from someone with no experience. The other was from an experienced programmer, who eventually declined the job, deciding he did not want to move to the district. The second time they advertised, they received no replies at all.

The computer systems formed a vital part of the company's operations. Some changes were required to the order processing system urgently to enable the company to expand its exports. The DP manager was unable to make these changes, because the three programmers he had were fully tied up programming other important systems. He proposed subcontracting the work to an outside software house. The managing director refused to authorize

this, however, because they were having difficulty maintaining another system that they had previously subcontracted to outsiders. The DP manager was in fact quite pleased to have his proposal turned down, because the employment of outsiders at higher rates than his own staff were getting only had the effect of worsening morale inside his own department. Failure to meet target dates, inability to cope with users' requests for changes, and bad feelings created by making "special cases" of the programmers in order to get their salaries up were long-standing problems in the company. Exasperated by this latest frustration, the managing director decided to investigate the running of the DP department. His analysis was as follows:

1. The company did not have the same management control over the DP department as it had over the rest of the company.
2. Staff turnover averaged 28% over the last three years compared with a 4% company average.
3. Paradoxically, automation had created some redundancies in the firm and put a number of jobs at risk, but there was a severe and continuous shortage of staff in the programming department. The trade union had objected to the advertisements for programmers to be recruited from outside when the other staff in the company were likely to lose their jobs.
4. The attitude in the DP department gave rise to concern. There was a "we/they" atmosphere vis-á-vis the rest of the company, little understanding existed of what the company did, and motivation mainly centered around building ingenious systems instead of contributing to the making and selling of pharmaceuticals. Job advertisements and programmer salaries in other companies appeared to be the main topics of conversation.

5. Present policies for overcoming the staffing problem (external recruitment of graduates with two or three years' experience and the use of subcontractors as a stopgap) provided no evidence that the company could rely on developing the computer systems it needed in the future. This presented the biggest single threat to the continuing prosperity of the company.

The managing director proposed that they should change their policy and recruit and train programmers from clerical and shop floor workers. Urwick Dynamics were working as consultants with this company and were asked to advise on the possibility of implementing this policy successfully. They had recruited and trained internal personnel as programmers on a number of previous occasions and had developed a special retraining scheme for the purpose. They were able to say from experience what the two main difficulties in implementing the policy would be.

The first concerns attitudes. The tradition of using graduate programmers, usually mathematicians, has now become deeply engrained. This affects the attitudes of three groups of people. The clerks and shop floor workers believe they will not be able to do programming work; they are in some awe of the mystique that has grown up around computers and in many cases are understandably reluctant to apply for the job. Another group consists of the existing programmers. They are somewhat resentful of untrained and less qualified people being brought in to do their job. If these recruits are successful, it detracts to some extent from the feelings of importance and security that come from being difficult to replace. More important, however, is the tradition that programmers work to a great extent on their own and are largely self-sufficient; they are generally against having to work with a trainee and having constantly to spend time telling him what to do. Finally, there is the attitude of the DP manager himself. He is used to employing a group of able,

technically self-sufficient programmers. It is clearly going to be very different managing mixed ability teams, planning for training, and "nursing" newcomers through their first programs. He is understandably anxious whether he can "deliver the goods" using mixed ability teams.

The second problem area is concerned with providing suitable training for internal recruits. In February last year the Neddy working party on computers, referred to earlier, reported that training facilities and courses provided in Britain were "completely inadequate." The fact is, there is hardly any programmer training provided of the type required. One of the most surprising things about traditional programmer training is the almost total reliance placed on a short instruction course. About four weeks is allowed to learn the basic vocabulary of a computer language, and from then on the trainee is on his own. Able graduates can cope—more or less. But however talented, they spend a long time learning programming techniques in practice—and reinvent the wheel many times on the way. For less able people, and the sort of internal recruits that this MD had in mind, this four-week "language" course is totally inadequate. The remainder of this chapter describes how the Urwick retraining scheme was used in this pharmaceutical company to overcome the two problem areas just outlined—and what happened as a result.

Stage I: Encouraging Candidates

We have already talked about the understandable reluctance of internal staff to consider themselves for programming work. A number of companies who have tried internal recruitment have been put off by the lack of people coming forward. The objective of this stage is to overcome this reluctance and to get people to apply for the job. It was decided to recruit from one of the factories, the despatch department and the accounts department. In all, 218 staff people were involved. An advertisement was agreed upon with the personnel department and with union approval, inviting people to come to short discussion sessions on job opportunities within the computer department. This advertisement was posted on the notice board. Two sessions were held in the canteen, lasting about 15 minutes each—and were well attended. During the discussion, a one-day computer course was described and those present invited to attend. It was emphasized that those attending the course would learn how computers worked, what the job of writing programs entailed and, most important, that no intelligence test would be involved.

Stage II: Selection

Selection was carried out in two phases. First, the one-day course was held. In the event, 16 people decided to attend. During the day, the way computers process data was described. Six verbs in a computer language were explained and those on the course then wrote eight small programs. These exercises were used to illustrate the duties of a programmer. After the course ended, the exercises were marked. On the basis of these marks seven people were selected as potential programmers. The second phase involved interviewing the candidates, discussion with unions and management, and making the final selection of trainees. It is important that all candidates are interviewed, not just those who have done well in the exercise. In this way all are given the opportunity to discuss the job; people usually select themselves. Those who found the work appealing and who did well were keen to go on. Others were happy to say that programming wasn't for them.

Two points to note. In addition to being off-putting, intelligence tests and other aptitude tests are not suitable for this sort of recruitment. Very few of the candidates will have a high standard of formal education. Some will have "O" levels, others will have left school at about 15. And those above 30 will be decidedly rusty, whatever their educa-

tional attainments. The best way to see if someone can write program is to give him some programs to write. This approach is also appreciated by the candidates, who see its relevance and find it helps them to decide whether they want to go on. Second, the unions were very concerned about the way in which the candidates were picked. They insisted that selection was carried out by independent outsiders.

Six people were finally selected to go forward for training. Only one had any "A" levels. The best performer in the programming exercises had left school at 15 and was a finished goods examiner. Two were clerks, one from the despatch department, and the rest from the shop floor. Four of the six were women. The average age was 27, the oldest being 35.

Stage III: Training Course

Formal training is not the most important part of internal recruitment. The real training takes place on the job during a programming apprenticeship (which is described later). Before anyone can begin an apprenticeship, however, they have to learn certain basics: how to talk to the computer in a programming language, how computer records are organized, and the various processes that the machine performs. The company faced two problems. First, where could this formal training be carried out? The trainees needed to be away from their workplace to be able to concentrate on learning, but not too far away because they all lived locally. Some had family responsibilities, which made a residential course out of the question. Local hotels offered suitable facilities, but in the end the local sports club was chosen (virtually unused during the week) on grounds of economy.

The main problem, however, was how to teach people, unaccustomed or unreceptive to classroom methods of instruction. How long a course could they take; "how will you get them to sit down?" as the personnel manager put it. The answer was to avoid lectures altogether. Each trainee was given a computer terminal and, with the aid of the instructor, began to write a program in the first hour of the first day of the course. This method proved very successful. The complexity of programming was approached gradually in a number of small steps; instead of teaching principles, techniques were introduced as solutions to actual problems being faced by the trainee at the time. Compare, for example, teaching principles of performing range tests on data with solving the problem, "How can we check these 'hours worked' are reasonable?" As a trainee added some instructions to his program through the terminal, they were immediately tested by the computer. If they were wrong, it was apparent right away. This learning by mistakes approach contrasts with traditional teaching, which encourages the writing of quite large amounts of program before getting any feedback. Diagnosing mistakes this late in the day is unnecessarily complex. Most important, building programs piece by piece on a computer terminal motivates the trainees to achieve results. The training course lasted four weeks. By the end of this period, each of the trainees selected had written a payroll program that read data from clock cards, calculated employee's pay, and printed payslips. They each had a program under their belts and were gaining in confidence every day.

Stage IV: Programming Apprenticeship

The most important part of a programmer's career is the first six months. It is also the most neglected. During this time he will learn habits and form attitudes that will stay for life. But it is almost universally the case that programmers are largely left to fend for themselves after a short language course. People of high ability survive; they learn the techniques for themselves, some good, some bad. This

"in at the deep end" approach was clearly not on for these recruits, however, and the company arranged a six-month apprenticeship for the trainees. The main technique used was "program review." Periodically all the apprentices went through a review of their work in groups and different approaches to logical structure, coding, testing, and documentation were discussed. In this way, good practice and techniques were acquired, through the consideration of alternative ways of solving the actual problems they were facing at the time.

The difficulty in arranging programming apprenticeships is providing the master programmer who will look after the apprentices. The number of experienced programmers in this company was so low that it was impossible for them to provide time to review the newcomers' work. Even where time can be spared, it is still difficult to find the right sort of person to do this work. Few experienced programmers have rationalized their approach into teachable techniques. Even fewer want to be bothered with nursing trainees. In this case a trained instructor was employed part-time to review the apprentice's work.

The results achieved were as follows:

Recruitment pool	218
Candidates attending selection course	16
Candidates selected	6
Candidates completing training course	6
Candidates completing apprenticeship	6

These figures are fairly typical. It seems that an average pool of clerks and shop floor workers will provide 2 to 3% of their number as programmers from the first campaign. A second campaign seems to provide a further 2 to 3% because the others are encouraged to come forward by the success of their colleagues. Most important, all those selected on the one-day computer appreciation course usually complete the training and become successful programmers.

The quality of work turned out by these internal recruits was the most pleasing result. During their apprenticeship, each person wrote and tested a number of programs that were then used operationally by the company. These programs were of high quality when judged by the low number of faults discovered after becoming operational, and the ease with which they could be understood by other programmers and altered subsequently.

This was not surprising during the apprenticeship because the programs were heavily scrutinized by the instructor and the other trainees during "program reviews." What was particularly pleasing was that this quality did not fall when the trainees had later to stand on their own. The data processing manager admitted that their work compared more than favorably with graduate programmers: "Not so elegant perhaps—they don't treat each new job as an intellectual challenge. But they produce really serviceable programs."

Staff turnover dropped dramatically. It is early to judge, but after a year none of the recruits shows signs of leaving. It would be a major decision for them to move. "If you live at the end of the road you think twice about changing your job." Compared with the graduates, who found programming boring and resented its routine nature when the challenge of learning how to do it was over, these staff experienced "job enrichement." Said one, "For the first time since I've been at work I couldn't believe it was five o'clock." Other

advantages arose from having a mixed ability team. Not everyone was a high flyer seeking promotion; a sharing of work took place with people contributing their particular abilities where they were best suited. Maintenance was no longer a dirty word; some of the newcomers actually preferred altering existing programs to writing new ones. And the managing director was delighted with the success of his scheme. As time passed it was clear that management was regaining control of the programming department. "It's a new feeling," he said.

Urwick Dynamics has now retrained a number of clerks and shop floor workers as computer programmers. Experience with the scheme in general can be summarized as follows:

1. About 5% of any internal recruitment pool will make excellent programmers, if the right selection and training methods are used.
2. Traditional intelligence and aptitude tests are unsuitable and should be replaced by short program exercises.
3. Traditional classroom teaching methods should be replaced by trial and error learning using terminals connected to a computer.
4. Programming skills should be taught. A six-month apprenticeship employing program review sessions produces excellent results.

35
Gaining A Competitive Edge Through Participative Management of Overhead

Thomas G. Hardy
McKinsey & Company, Inc.
and
John E. Neuman
Dewey, Ballantine,
Bushby, Palmer & Wood
(Formerly of McKinsey &
Company, Inc.)

In most companies, those responsible for providing overhead services have little or no communication with the users of these services. As a result, services are frequently requested without regard to the cost involved in creating them, while the suppliers often create services without regard for their actual need or benefit to the company.

"We must reduce our cost of doing business!" This statement and dozens like it are heard almost every day in boardroom across the country and around the world. And who can argue with it? Even in the best of times, ways of cutting costs should be seriously, if not vigorously, pursued. In today's economy, however, reducing the cost of doing business is more than just a laudable goal; the strategic position of a company, indeed its very survival, may well depend on it.

Overhead activities and expenditures represent big costs that have grown enormously in recent years. For example, between 1950 and 1980 the number of nonproduction workers in manufacturing industries increased nine times as fast as that of production workers. Nonproduction employees now account for at least 40% of all payroll costs. This is not an isolated case. It has become quite usual for the cost of overhead to outpace the cost of other

444

activities. In many instances, overhead even outpaces revenue.

The irony in all of this is that many of the activities and expenditures that constitute overhead are of little real value to companies. In this respect, the large sums of money budgeted for them represent a potentially wasteful use of funds. These funds could be used to strengthen a company's financial and competitive position. In many cases, they are being spent on unnecessary overhead activities and services.

Why is it that many companies find it so difficult to manage overhead and make cuts that last? One reason may lie in the corporate structure itself. For example, in most companies suppliers of overhead products or services have little or no communcation with the people who receive items such as reports, analyses, and memos. As a result, managers often request services without regard to the cost involved in creating them, while suppliers often create services without regard for their actual need or benefit to the company.

Human factors also play an important role in maintaining high overhead costs. Professionals who are hired to manage service departments (data processing, accounting, or engineering, for example) may suffer from what is commonly known as "excessive professionalism." Such a condition is characterized by a desire to compare favorably with the leading professionals in one's chosen area of expertise. Whole departments may be geared to pursuing the latest technical advances in a particular field, regardless of their value or benefit to the company. This often leads to performance of services that have no relevance whatsoever to the company's business.

Another factor that works against effective overhead control is that many companies do not create an atmosphere that is conducive to meaningful and lasting cost reduction. Managers are rewarded more for towing the line, than for exhibiting cost-effective behavior. Eliminating unnecessary services or activities may in fact lead to the question, "Why didn't you do that last year?" In addition, reducing overhead often means reducing staff, a prospect that can haunt even the most cost-conscious managers. Staff reduction might mean eliminating the jobs of close friends or acquaintances, which is not a pleasant task. Furthermore, managers accustomed to empire building look upon staff reductions as a lowering of their own personal importance and prestige, and so may avoid it at all costs. (In fact, managers may even create projects just to keep from letting people go.)

Given all these difficulties, what can be done to control overhead?

TRADITIONAL APPROACHES TO CUTTING OVERHEAD

To most senior executives, the word "overhead" conjures up the image of hundreds of people performing a vast range of activities. They know that many of these activities may be unnecessary. Yet few companies attempt to tackle the problem of overhead reduction in a systematic and comprehensive manner because the thought of evaluating each and every end product (report, analysis, meeting, and so on) and service (advice, training, and so on) can seem overwhelming, if not downright impossible. Instead, it becomes easier to cut costs in a more or less random fashion. The edict goes out to cut the budget 10% across the board, or a directive is issued to keep the budget the same as it was during the previous year.

The problem with this approach is that managers are given no help in distinguishing between activities that are truly necessary and those that are not. Quite often, cost items that are large but difficult to justify in terms of immediate payback (advertising, training programs, research and development) suffer the most from such random cuts, despite the fact that they may be absolutely essential to the company's future growth. In addition, the whole process of across-the-board cutting is often perceived as a temporary exercise in corporate belt tightening: doing without or doing with less until the crisis of cost consciousness blows over. The result is a company-wide expectation that services cut or reduced eventually will be restored. Too often this expectation becomes a self-fulfilling prophecy; in no time at all activities and expenditures that were axed from the budget are reinstated.

The across-the-board method of cutting overhead is just one of many widely employed traditional approaches. The most common ones include zero-base budgeting, flexible budgeting, bracket budgeting, ad hoc project team efforts, and annual cost-reduction campaigns. While programs based on these approaches may be applied with some degree of success, quite often they are riddled with serious drawbacks. For example, most programs based on traditional approaches concentrate on improving employee efficiency (that is, the way overhead tasks are performed) rather than evaluating and reducing the amount of overhead that employees actually produce. Experience has shown that the results of programs directed solely at improving employee efficiency are usually limited and short lived. Such efforts may be exacerbated further by the fact that most traditional approaches:

1. Deal with each major company function in relative isolation
2. Fail to use top managerial talent to guide the cost-reduction program
3. Take a long time to complete (enthusiasm for the process often waning well before the program ends)
4. Fail to provide strategies for dealing with available human resources.

This last point is of particular importance, because a successful cost-reduction program often means the elimination of jobs. With this comes the responsibility to minimize the anxiety and strain on individual employees. The fear created by the prospect of unemployment may cause valued employees to seek jobs elsewhere, long before the results of the program are obtained. Unless a company is fully prepared to deal with this potential problem, a cost-reduction program can turn into a nightmare.

Traditional approaches to cutting overhead exhibit other major drawbacks as well. For example, many programs set their cost-reduction sights too low, not allowing for the fact that some departments can reduce costs more than others. Other programs assume value in end products automatically (reports, analyses, or services) even though the need for them may have long since disappeared. Still other cost-reduction programs address departments on a selective basis, creating resistance, resentment, even paranoia among those departments targeted for cost reduction. Moreover, when cost-reduction programs are run entirely by consultants (as many programs are), employee resentment may set in. Employees tend to view consultants as outsiders who lack the requisite knowledge and experience to make decisions on running the business. Such a view can create a tense working environment that distracts managers from the task of identifying good cost-reduction opportunities.

MANAGING OVERHEAD SUCCESSFULLY

Given the drawbacks of traditional cost-reduction methods, can overhead be managed successfully? Yes, it can. In fact, a major, well-documented overhead improvement process exists that not only avoids the numerous drawbacks of traditional methods, but actually results in substantial and permanent cost reductions. The process, often referred to as *overhead value analysis* (OVA) or *activity value analysis* (AVA), is not a technique as such, but rather an application of powerful, common-sense principles that together form the basis for sound and effective overhead management.

Principle 1: Sound overhead management focuses on end products and services (that is, the results of work actually being done) rather than on the people who produce these items.

In an OVA program, the emphasis is on eliminating and/or reducing unnecessary work. The intent is not to get people to work harder (it's already assumed that each department is operating at a reasonable level of efficiency), but simply to find ways of reducing work output. Roughly two-thirds of all savings in an average OVA program comes from the reduction of output. (Internal efficiencies such as streamlining account for only one-third of the savings.)

Principle 2: The value of end products and services must be determined by both suppliers and receivers.

In an OVA program, managers who produce end products and services as well as managers who receive or benefit from those items are jointly responsible for identifying which end products and services to cut. This places the burden of overhead reduction squarely on the shoulders of those best able to assess the cost and value of individual overhead items. In addition, by getting suppliers and receivers to agree on which items to cut, there is less likelihood that these activities and expenditures will creep back once the program comes to an end.

Principle 3: A stretch target for cost-reduction ensures thorough analysis and innovative thinking.

In order to challenge conventional overhead activities and thinking, managers participating in an OVA program must stretch their own thinking and be comfortable suggesting brand new ways of doing things. An overhead reduction approach that requires "unrealistic" reduction levels creates an environment for, indeed legitimizes, an absolutely thorough analysis of current end products and activities and innovative thinking about them. Therefore, not only do the managers assigned to an OVA program think through 100% of their overhead functions, but they must come up with ideas that reduce workload and expenses by 40 percent. Ultimately, top management decides which ideas to implement. Rarely is the entire 40% reduction achieved. However, such an overreach target insures that every possible way of reducing a department's output of end products and services is uncovered and examined.

Principle 4: A bottom-up approach, in which primary reliance for the idea generation is placed on line managers, can help a program develop hundreds, even thousands, of quality cost-reduction ideas.

The greatest number of overhead activities take place at the lower levels of management. Only line managers who are thoroughly familiar with the details of these activities can offer meaningful ways to eliminate or reduce them. The OVA process starts at the bottom and works its way upward. Ideas generated by line managers are evaluated and refined by each higher level of management. The result is a large number of high-benefit/low-risk cost-reduction ideas that are ready for immediate implementation.

Principle 5: The success of any overhead reduction program depends on top management being totally committed and visibly involved in the process.

An OVA program is managed by the company's own management at all levels. While outside consultants may act as advisors, they do not run the program, nor do they make any substantive judgments about specific cost-reduction ideas. Therefore, the success of OVA depends upon the level of commitment communicated by senior management to the entire organization and the quality of the management team assigned to run the program. Senior management must be willing to free the best people to take charge of the program. Indeed, a willingness to make available the best managers is in itself an indication of commitment to the program.

Principle 6: A comprehensive human resource plan can make an overhead reduction program even more effective by dealing efficiently and humanely with employees whose jobs are ultimately eliminated.

A key attribute to the OVA process is that, in addition to the mainstream program, it provides a parallel program responsible for manpower redeployment. This program is designed to minimize terminations by developing strategies for redeploying and retraining employees freed by the OVA process. It also develops support services (job counseling, résumé preparation, and so on) for those employees who are terminated.

Principle 7: The more extensive the program, the greater the need for careful, ongoing communication among participants and among the organization as a whole.

The activities associated with any comprehensive overhead reduction program are new to everyone: people need training and tasks need explaining. Ongoing communication throughout a program can help people better understand the process and the part they play in it. Such communication can also deal with the job-threatening aspects of a program by underscoring the company's commitment to the redeployment of freed personnel. By allaying fears, a company can encourage the active and enthusiastic participation of its employees. Recognizing the need for effective communication, the OVA process provides for a full-time communications coordinator.

Principle 8: Regardless of the program, all approved cost-reduction ideas must be consistent with company strategy.

In the OVA process, senior management, acting as part of the program's organizational structure, has the important task of measuring all cost-reduction ideas against the long-term interests and goals of the company before the ideas are approved.

Principle 9: Sound overhead management focuses on all indirect activities, including those that cross departmental lines.

Cross-company expenditures and services (employee expense accounts, company cars, telephone service, conventions) often are rife with cost-reduction opportunities. However, because they do not belong to any one department, many of these opportunities may be overlooked. In the OVA process, a manager is assigned the explicit task of evaluating cross-company costs and recommending cost-reduction ideas.

Principle 10: Ideally, an overhead reduction program should be accomplished in a relatively short period of time.

If a program takes too long to complete, a great deal of uncertainty, insecurity, and disruption may set in. By design, OVA is a short-term program. From the initial stages to the implementation of cost-reduction ideas, the entire process typically takes only four to five months. Moreover, unless the organiza-

tion exceed approximately $200 million in sales, all departments should go through the project simultaneously. The advantages of synergy and a shorter total elapsed time are considerable.

The ten principles listed above represent sound overhead management practice. Ironically, when it comes to traditional approaches to cost reduction (zero-base budgeting, flexible budgeting, and so on) few, if any, of these principles actually are put to use. Any traditional approach can be modified and strenghtened by including one or more of these principles in its program. However, when all ten are applied together, they become the foundation of a particularly powerful and effective cost-reduction program known as overhead value analysis (OVA).

THE RESULTS OF OVA

OVA is a well-tested, well-documented program. The benefits derived from such a program include:

1. Permanent cost reduction
2. Elimination of unnecessary functions
3. Increased productivity
4. Meaningful redeployment of freed manpower
5. Creation of an information base that encourages more efficient indirect cost management in the future
6. Upgrading of management sensitivity and skills in dealing with future overhead activities and expenses.

When the OVA process is properly managed—which includes highly visible involvement from senior management—the results are clearly impressive. It is not unusual for an industrial or consumer goods company to have overhead expenses equal 25% of total costs when OVA is applied. In financial institutions and insurance companies, OVA has been applied to all areas of the company. While gross savings vary from company to company, a typical company can expect an overall reduction in overhead of 17% (see Figure 1). In addition, within any given company, savings varies by department. For example, one company in which 144 departments participated in the program realized an average of 20.4% in savings per department. The savings by department varied from 4% to 48% (see Figure 2).

OVA Has Led To Substantial Savings In Virtually Every Situation

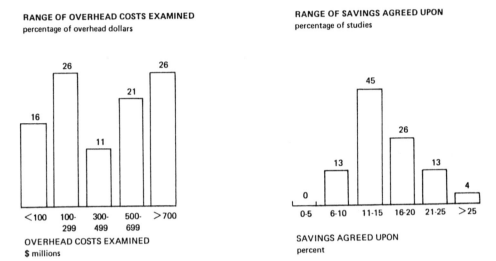

FIGURE 1.   Overhead reduction with OVA

Overhead Value Analysis yields tailored reductions in each unit

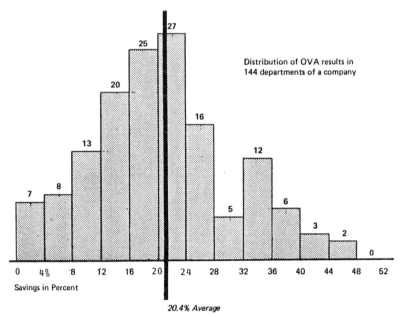

FIGURE 2.   Savings by department with OVA

Over the years, OVA has been adapted and implemented by hundreds of companies representing almost every kind of industry (see Figure 3). In terms of cost reductions and savings, the results have been consistent regardless of the industry involved, and surprisingly, regardless of whether other approaches have been used in the past.

The savings generated by an OVA program can translate into millions of dollars. More important, such savings improve a company's strength and competitive position by permanently lowering its overall cost of doing business.

THE OVA PROCESS

OVA is a process whereby managers themselves value the end products and services they produce or request in relation to the cost of producing them. The end products of each department and the activities required to generate those end products are clearly laid out. Then each end product and activity is scrutinized carefully to see if it can be eliminated, reduced, or streamlined. Potential cost savings are weighed against the risks of elimination or reduction, with each manager affected by the end product or activity offering opinions. Ultimately, top management makes the final decisions as to which end products and activities will be changed, but in effect managers at all levels affected by any change have participated in the process. This bottom-up approach helps to bring to the surface quality cost-reduction ideas. It also helps build a managerial consensus that paves the way for acceptance of the more difficult decisions, while limiting resistance to the analytical process itself.

OVA has been broadly adapted and implemented

	UNITED STATES AND CANADA	EUROPE	LATIN AMERICA	AUSTRALIA AND JAPAN
Airlines	2	2	2	2
Automotive		6		
Banking	6	10		
Chemicals	2	7	1	
Construction	3	6		1
Communications	2	1	1	
Electronics, Appliances	10	11	5	4
Food and Beverages	5	3		2
Food Chains (Retail)	3	2		1
Insurance	4	4	1	
Machinery	2	6	1	1
Metal and Mining		3	1	1
Office Machinery	3	1	1	2
Other Services	5	6	1	3
Pharmaceuticals	3	4		
Precision Equipment	1	2		
Textiles	1	1	0	0
Miscellaneous*	3	10	1	2

* Miscellaneous category includes paints, ball bearings, shipbuilding, rubber, glass, diversified companies and government

FIGURE 3. Wide applicability of OVA

PROGRAM PHASES

The OVA process incorporates the principles of sound overhead management into a formal program consisting of five distinct phases, plus a preparatory phase known as Phase O. What follows is a brief description of each program phase.

Phase 0

Each OVA program is designed to meet the specific needs and goals of the company employing it. The purpose of Phase 0 is to finalize program design (including the job securities policy and communications strategies) and to select and train the management team that will run the program. To facilitate analysis, the company is divided into overhead departments known as OVA units. Each OVA unit develops its own baseline budget, a breakdown of the total costs, personnel and nonpersonnel, involved in running one unit for one year. Once a unit's baseline budget is determined, a cost-reduction target (40% of the baseline budget) can be set.

Phase I

The purpose of Phase I is to separate each OVA unit in a way that reveals the results and costs in that unit. In Phase I, which takes approximately three weeks to complete, a data base of information is created that:

1. *Describes the missions of an OVA unit.* A mission is a statement of purpose that answers the question "Why does this unit exist?"
2. *Identifies each activity that supports a mission.* Activities answer the question "How is a mission accomplished?" One mission may rely on several activities being performed. Logically, each activity should support its mission. In addition, all activities listed must be mutually exclusive, with no overlap.
3. *Identifies the end products and services that result from activities.* End products and services answer the questions "What does a unit produce?" and "What are the outputs?" End products are any tangible outputs or services (such as reports, analysis, meetings, and advice). The receivers of each end product are also identified.
4. *Allocates costs to each end product.* Total end-product costs should equal the total cost of resources (the baseline budget) for that unit. Costs of end products are then aggregated for each activity and mission.

In addition, a top-management person or subcommittee is assigned the task of identifying cross-company services and policies (activities that cross departmental lines) that have cost-reduction potential. Expenditures for the corporate image, management perquisites, and building maintenance are just a few examples of these kinds of costs.

Phase II

The second phase of the program requires about six weeks to complete and involves the development and evaluation of specific cost-reduction ideas for each OVA unit. (Cross-company cost-reduction ideas also are generated during Phase II.) All missions, activities, and end products contained in the Phase I data base are analyzed to determine which ones can actually be eliminated, reduced, or streamlined without serious risk to the company. The goal is to reduce by at least 40% the cost of each OVA unit's baseline budget. Cost-reduction recommendations must represent a broad spectrum of quality ideas. In general, it is less risky, and therefore more desirable, to propose many small cuts rather than a few large ones. Unit managers, assigned by top management to head each OVA unit, assess the relative risks and benefits of each idea, as do all receivers who might be affected by the idea. In the end, the unit manager reconciles all comments and evaluations and put together a final list of cost-reduction ideas. This list then is submitted to the next higher manager, possibly a division head, for consideration.

Next higher managers review all ideas. They make sure that the total of each unit's ideas adds up to a 40% cost reduction. They may decide to add new ideas of their own. They cannot, however, delete an idea; once an idea is in the system, it stays until top management makes a final decision. Frequently, next higher managers are called upon to resolve differences between suppliers and receivers. At the end of Phase II, these managers prepare a revised list of ideas and submit them to top management.

Phase III

During Phase III, senior managers review and assess all cost-reduction ideas from their own vantage points. They may refine some of these ideas or generate new ones. The final step in Phase III occurs when senior managers present a revised list of ideas to the program's steering committee for approval. (A list of cross-company cost-reduction ideas also is submitted to the steering committee.) This committee, which oversees the entire program and is made up of top-management personnel, receives all recommendations and makes the final decisions. The estimated time for the completion of Phase III is three to four weeks.

Phase IV

During the Phase IV of the program, the implementation plan is developed. The steering committee sends all *approved* cost-reduction ideas back to the appropriate unit managers for implementation planning. Each implementation plan must describe in detail the following information:

1. A description of the approved idea
2. The specific steps required to implement the idea
3. All individuals responsible for implementation
4. A specific timetable for completion of each step of the implementation process
5. The reduction in the unit's budget stemming from each idea implemented.

Each implementation plan then is submitted to the appropriate level of management for approval. The estimated time for the completion of Phase IV is two to three weeks.

Phase V

During Phase V, actual implementation of approved ideas takes place. Unit managers are responsible for implementing ideas and submitting periodic progress reports to senior management.

Parallel Programs

In addition to the program phases outlined above, there are two parallel programs that play a key role in the OVA process.

The first parallel program deals with manpower planning. A Human Resources Planning Committee is assigned the task of developing strategies for dealing with freed human resources.

The second parallel program deals with communications. A communications coordinator is assigned several tasks, including:

1. Assisting senior management in making visible to the organization their commitment to the program's success.
2. Helping to communicate program objectives, including the steps taken to minimize the impact on employees
3. Helping to rally support for the program from all levels of management
4. Gathering feedback from employees on a regular basis.

Together, these two parallel programs support the efforts of the mainstream program and help insure its success.

Although the driving principles of OVA are relatively straightforward, no company should engage in an OVA program unless it is fully committed to organizing and carrying out the detailed and complex tasks such a program entails. If a company *is* willing to make such a commitment, there is no doubt that it soon will realize lasting cost reductions and an overall improvement in its competitive position. However, in order to understand what commitment to the program really means, let's take a look at how Fall River Industries carried out its overhead analysis program.

FALL RIVER INDUSTRIES: A CASE STUDY

Fall River Industries (FRI) is a chemical manufacturing company that does about $200 million dollars in annual sales. Located in Fall River, Massachusetts, FRI is made up of three main divisions: Fall River Chemicals, a supplier of bulk chemicals to industry; Chemline, Inc., a consumer products division that manufactures and distributes detergents and cleaning solvents; and FRI International, the division that sells and distributes FRI products around the world. Together, these divisions employ about 1,000 indirect workers.

FRI decided to undertake an OVA program in order to improve its competitive cost position and its chances to become a leader in the chemical industry. Previous studies had shown that indirect activities and expenditures at FRI were growing at an alarming rate. (Administrative expenses alone had been increasing at a greater rate than income for over five years.) If FRI were to become a leader in the industry, it was imperative that all nonessential activities and services be identified and eliminated. Top management felt that a permanent and significant reduction in overhead costs would have a favorable impact on FRI's overall financial position, allowing it to mount a more aggressive marketing campaign.

Leland Phillips, FRI's chief executive officer, considered a number of traditional approaches to overhead reduction, but decided on OVA as the program most advantageous to his company's needs. Two features in particular sold him on OVA:

1. The program would be carried out by FRI's own managers—the people who knew the most about the business.
2. All recommendations for cuts in services and activities would be made by the actual managers involved—both suppliers and receivers.

Phillips hired a consulting firm to set up the program and coach and advise the FRI managers. But FRI management was expected to make all of the actual cost-reduction decisions. After all, it was FRI's program.

FRI'S OVA PROGRAM

Phase 0: Preparing For the Program

Leland Phillips realized the complexities involved in running an OVA program, so he decided to pick his best people to form the OVA management team. At the top of the management team was the Steering Committee. Although the Steering Committee would only work part time, it had overall responsibility for the program's success. The Steering Committee consisted of Phillips along with five direct-reporting Senior Managers, each selected on the basis of commitment to the program, ability to implement cost-reduction ideas, and a willingness to be visibly involved in the process. The tasks of the Steering Committee included:

1. Establishing the overall scope of the program
2. Approving the overall design of the program
3. Approving cost-reduction ideas and all plans for implementation.

Perhaps the most important task assigned to the Steering Committee was the appointment of an Advisory Task Force (ATF). This task force actually ran the OVA program on a day-to-tday basis. Unlike the Steering Committee, ATF members served full time for the duration of the program.

The Steering Committee at FRI selected six highly talented and respected "Impossible-to-free-up" managers* to serve on its ATF (approximately one ATF member for eveyr 200 workers covered by the study and one ATF member for cross-company analysis). These managers represented a cross section of company functions. In addition, the most competent and respected of the six, Bruce Carbine (senior vice-president of manufacturing and engineering), was selected as OVA director.

His job was to direct the ATF and serve as liason between it and the Steering Committee (see Figure 4).

The first item on the agenda for Bruce Carbine and the ATF was to set up OVA units tailored to the specific organizational needs of FRI. Each unit was designed to represent one or more related deartments within the company. For example, the research and development (R&D) department, which was relatively large, was formed into two OVA units. Purchasing was formed into three separate units because FRI had three separate purchasing departments. In total, 35 OVA units were established, each representing 20 to 40 employees. In addition, the ATF recommended (with line management approval) an OVA Unit Manager for each OVA unit. Typically, the Unit Man-

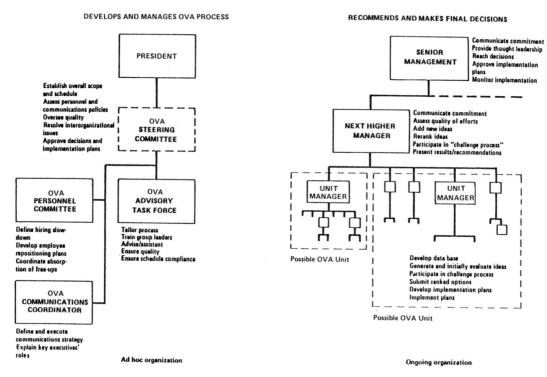

FIGURE 4.   OVA program organization

*The more difficult these managers are to free up, the more likely it is that the right people have been chosen. Their selection should be viewed as a key management development investment because these managers will know more about the company's inner workings than any other person oce the OVA program is over.

ager was chosen from among department heads. In the case of R&D, however, two Unit Managers were needed. Bill Murray, the head of the department, became the manger of one of the units. Larry Johnson, a key supervisor in the department, was chosen for the other unit. Johnson was chosen because of his ability to communicate well with other staff members.

The consulting firm was responsible for training the ATF to conduct the OVA program. (A major part of this training involved the preparation of baseline budgets for each of the 35 OVA nunits.) In turn, the ATF was responsible for training the Unit Managers. The official kickoff of the OVA program began with the training session for Unit Managers that took place at the Fall River Motor Lodge. Bruce Carbine and the ATF conducted the training session, which lasted the entire day. Carbine schedules Leland Phillips to address the gathering. Phillips welcomed everyone to the meeting and then went on to explain the purpose of the OVA program and what he hoped it would accomplish at FRI. Phillips introduced the 35 Unit Managers to the program's Steering Committee and ATF. The he turned the meeting back to Carbine.

During the morning session, Carbine's presentation dealt with the following program areas:

1. The role of the Steering Committee
2. The role of the ATF members (including the Director)
3. The role of Unit Managers
4. An overview of Phases I through V
5. A detailed description of Phase I, with particular emphasis on Unit Manager responsibilities.

Carbine ended the morning session with a description of the two parallel programs that would be initiated simultaneously with the main program.

The first was known as the Manpower Redeployment Program, and it came under the aegis of the Human Resources Planning Com-

mittee appointed by the Steering Committee. It was no secret that a truly successful OVA program would eliminate a great deal of nonessential work and probably a number of jobs as well. The Human Resource Planning Committee was set up to create strategies for dealing with this prospect. Its objectives included:

1. Defining overall personnel job security policies
2. Identifying transfer or retraining opportunities
3. Taking full advantage of natural attrition by instituting, for example, a meaningful companywide hiring, transfer, and promotion slowdown (or freeze, in the case of some departments) as soon as the OVA program began.

The second parallel program involved communications. In a complex, company-wide OVA program, good communication among participants and within the company in general is absolutely essential. The Steering Committee, thereore, set up an OVA Communications Coordinator whose job was to define and implement communications strategies. Basic communications objectives included:

1. Maximizing understanding of the program (why the program is being done, how it fits into company strategy and priorities, and why it is designed as it is)
2. Enlisting full employee cooperation and participation
3. Dispelling rumors, particularly as they might relate to job layoffs*
4. Obtaining feedback from employees throughout each phase of the program.

In addition, the Communications Coordinator was assigned the task of issuing special bulletins relating to the start-up and imple-

---

*One such rumor common to many programs involves the 40% cost-reduction target. If not explained carefully, employees may misinterpret this as a 40% cut in personnel.

mentation of each program phase. These bulletins were prepared under the guidance of the ATF.

By the time Bruce Carbine had finished his morning speech, the entire audience had a clear understanding of how the OVA program would work, how it was organized, what it was designed to accomplish, and how freed employees would be accommodated.

The afternoon meeting was an actual work session designed to train unit managers to handle their Phase I responsibilities. Each member of the ATF was assigned eight to ten unit managers who they would be responsible for training and then supervising during the entire program. In almost all cases, the ATF member was from a different division or job function than the Unit Managers they were assigned. Bruce Carbine was responsible for only two Unit Managers. Because he was also the OVA Director, he needed to have most of his time available for dealing with the Advisory Task Force and the Steering Committee. However, by having some Unit Manager assignments, Carbine was able to experience each detail of the OVA process firsthand.

The consultant team was present during the work session, but they kept a low profile. They restricted their activities to answering questions that ATF members were unable to answer and, in general, seeing that the program was explained accurately.

By the end of the work session, the Unit Managers had a good idea of what they would be doing during Phase I. Before leaving, they were all given a schedule of the entire program, including commencement and completion dates for each program phase (see Figures 5 and 6). Phase I was to begin the next day. The communications coordinator planned to write and distribute a special information bulletin for all employees explaining the program, including comments by Leland Phillips and Bruce Carbine, and announcing its kickoff. He also arranged a lead story to appear in *Fall River News*, the company's house organ.

Phase I: Developing the Data Base

The first step phase of the program was made up of the following three steps:

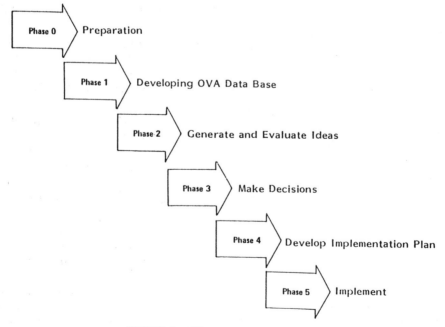

FIGURE 5. OVA as a multiphase process

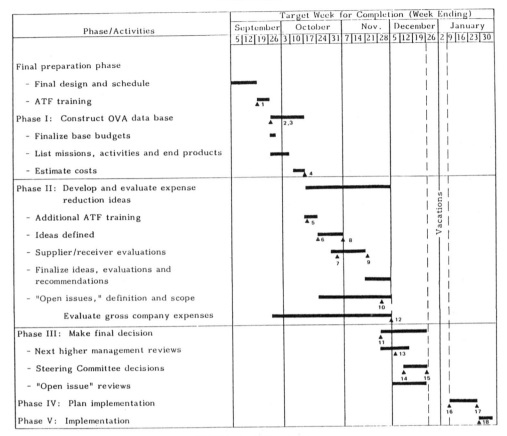

OVA Schedule   *Fall River Industries*

FIGURE 6.   OVA schedule

Step 1: Finalizing the Baseline Budget.

The baseline budget for each OVA unit was equal to the total of all costs (manpower plus expenses) for that unit for one year. The costs are total gross costs ignoring any charges to other units as a result of the company's cross-charging system. Finalizing the budget means getting each Unit Manager to agree on the items and figures that the ATF had prepared for his or her group during their training session (Phase 0). For example, in the case of one of the purchasing units, the baseline budget was finalized at $1.1 million. (Martha Stewart, the Unit Manager, and the ATF both agreed on this sum.) This figure became the starting point from which Stewart computer her unit's cost-reduction target—

40% of 1.1 million, or $440,000 (see Figure 7).

Step 2: Defining Mission, Activities, and End Products.

The purpose of Phase I is to see how a unit's resources are currently being utilized and to establish a data base that stimulates new ways of looking at what a unit does, why, and at what cost. To this end, each unit was responsible for dividng its work into missions, activities, and end products.

Missions describe *why* a department or unit exists. Usually, one unit will have three to five missions.

Activities describe *how* a unit fulfills its missions. Usually there are no more than five or six activities for each mission.

WORK SHEET 1A
BASELINE BUDGET

Fall River Industries

Unit: _____ Date: _____

Unit Leader: _____ Task Force Review: _____ Date: _____

DEPARTMENT NUMBER	#	#	#	#	#	TOTAL UNIT
DESCRIPTION						
Exempt Comp. – Current						
– Open						
Total Exempt Comp.						
Nonexempt Comp. – Current						
– Open						
Total Nonexempt Comp.						
Other Comp.						
NHM Allocation						
Total Comp.						
Other Expenses						
Exp. Code Description						
Subtotal						
Additions/(Exclusions)						
Total Other Expenses						
OVA Baseline Budget						
40% Cost-Reduction Target						
Headcount (FTE)						
Exempt – Current						
– Open						
Total						
Non-Exempt – Current						
– Open						
Total						
NHM Allocation						
Grand Total						

Exhibit G

FIGURE 7.   OVA baseline budget worksheet

End products are *what* activity supplies or produces. Usually there are no more than five or six end products for each activity.

Many Unit Managers found it difficult to describe missions, activities, and end products. Quite often their descriptions were too general to be useful. In order to formulate clear-cut descriptions of missions, activities, and end products, each Unit Manager was encouraged to think through the specific goals and functions of his or her unit. Frequently, descriptions would go through several revisions until they could be stated in clear, concise language.

Missions were described as briefly and specifically as possible. For example, *Purchase petroleum products* was an acceptable way to describe a mission. *Improve purchasing organization*, however, was too general and therefore not acceptable. Once all missions were identified, Unit Managers were responsible for describing the major activities that supported each mission. The following are some of the activities that were essential to support mission 1, *Purchasing petroleum products*.

1.1 Solicit bids; negotiate pricing and terms

1.2 Insure continuity of supplies through inventory control

1.3 Study and analyze market trends and present buying recommendations.

Unit Managers made a practice of going over each list of activities with key unit members to make sure all basic activities were included.

Finally, every Unit Manager was responsible for listing the end product(s) of each activity. End products could be tangible items, such as forms or reports, or they could be intangible, such as briefings or counsel. The following are some of the end products produced by activity:

1.1.1 Bid requests
1.1.2 Quotations
1.1.3 Vendor meetings
1.1.4 Bid analyses
1.1.5 Letters of acceptance
1.1.6 Notifications to mills and offices.

Occasionally, Unit Managers would list an end product that was, in reality, two or three end products lumped together. For example, Martha Stewart's purchasing unit identified one end product as *Purchase orders of various kinds*. Upon closer examination, however, Stewart realized that her unit produced three kinds of purchase orders: those sent by telecommunications (such as computer to computer), those sent by mail, and those that were based on once-a-year purchase orders but were actually release orders. *Purchase orders to vendors of various kinds* divided into three separate and distinct end products. Together these three end products would generate a great many more cost-reduction ideas that the one end product from which they originated.

Missions, activities, and end products for each unit were listed on Worksheet 1B and then reviewed with the appropriate ATF member (see Figure 8). If necessary, the Unit Manager and his or her ATF member would rework the list, taking the time to think through each mission activity and end product.

Step 3: Allocating Costs to End Products. Each Unit Manager was responsible for allocating the cost of all personnel and nonpersonnel expenses to end products, activities, and missions. Thus a dollar figure for each end product, activity, and mission was determined (to an accuracy of plus or minus 20%). In allocating costs, unit managers were instructed by their ATF members to accomplish the following:

1. Estimate the time each employee spent on end products
2. Allocate personnel costs by Full-Time Equivalent (FTE)*
3. Assign major line items to specific end products
4. Spread costs of all remaining expense items (travel, supplies, and so on) across end products.

Costs then were aggregated for each activity and mission.** The results were written in the appropriate spaces on Worksheet 1B (see Figure 8). The total of end-product costs had to equal the unit's baseline budget.

Once Worksheet 1B was completed, each Unit Manager met with his or her ATF member and next higher manager to review, in detail, all cost allocations from Phase I. Upon agreement of the dollar figures for end products, activities, and missions, each unit's data base was complete. This data base identified a unit's overhead costs with a fair degree of accuracy. In addition, it would now serve as a springboard from which to launch quality cost-reduction ideas.

Cross-Company Costs

While unit managers were working on Phase I, Bruce Carbine (with the advice of the Steering Committee) appointed Peter Berk, an ATF member, to develop cost-reduction ideas for cross-company services and expenditures (cost that did not belong and exclusively to any one department or OVA unit). The cross-company analysis would last for several phases and would be handled somewhat differently than the mainstream process. Berk handled the job in the following way: Working with Carbine and other ATF members, Berk compiled a master list of all cross-company expenditures (by cost code) and serv-

ices. His list included such items as employee expense accounts, conventions, telephones, and management perquisites.

Next, Berk screened the list for areas that seemed particularly ripe for cost reduction. For example, one such area was the preparation of Division Review Reports. Each division at FRI (Industrial Products, Consumer Products, and International) prepared weekly, biweekly, and monthly reports dealing with operations problems and strategies. The total cost for preparation and distribution came to about $150,000 per year per division. Berk arrived at this figure by analyzing the Phase I end products of each OVA unit. He also discovered that the monthly report was, in effect, a summary of the weekly and biweekly reports. Upon further investigation, he found out that the receivers of the reports (top management at FRI Corporate Division) were not in the habit of reading the weekly and biweekly reports because they knew that the monthlies would fill them in on what they had missed. This led Berk to develop a simple cost-reduction recommendation:

Do away with all weekly and biweekly division reports. Set up a mechanism for reporting *important* information on an as-necessary basis so that 30 days need not transpire before such information is made known.

Berk estimated that his recommendation, if instituted, would realize a savings of $89,000 per division, or almost 60% of the current cost of the report.

Peter Berk continued to generate cross-company cost-reduction ideas, relying on experts within the company (traffic and quality control engineers, scientists in R&D, accountants, lawyers, and so on) for information and advice. In Phase II, he consolidated his ideas by ranking them in order of attractiveness (potential savings versus potential risks). Next, he reviewed each one with the appropriate managers. Then, during Phase III of the program, Berk submitted his cost-reduction

---

*In general, end products totaled no less than O.1 FTE.

**Some unit managers found it easier to cost our activities first and then allocate the costs to each end product.

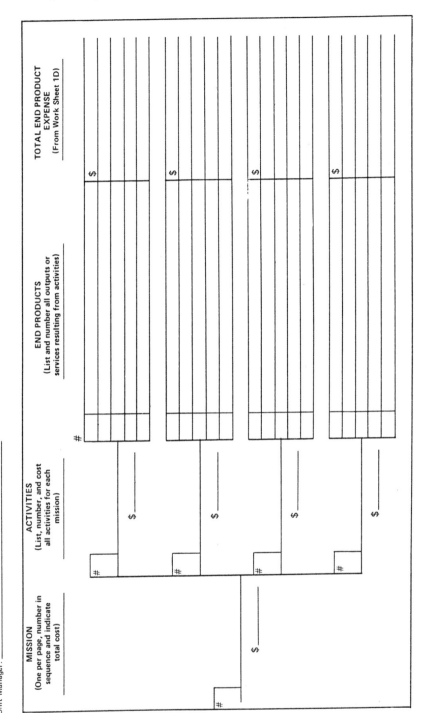

FIGURE 8. OVA missions activity worksheet

ideas to the OVA Steering Committee. The Steering Committee decided which cost-reduction ideas should be implemented and then in Phase IV passed them back to Berk so that he could formulate plans for implementation. Once these plans were approved by the Steering Committee, Phase V began and all of Peter Berk's approved ideas were implemented.

Phase II: Generating and Evaluating Cost-Reduction Ideas

During Phase I, Bruce Carbine and the entire ATF played a dual role in the OVA process. They were responsible for guiding each Unit Manager in the development of an accurate and meaningful data base, while at the same time preparing and finalizing the design for Phase II. The ATF spent some of its time developing the forms, procedures, and schedule for the second phase. They even conducted a dry run of Phase II (with ATF members assuming the roles of Unit Managers) in order to determine just how well their design would work. This role-playing exercise helped the ATF to identify and correct deficiencies in the Phase II design.

The purpose of Phase II is to generate a large number of quality cost-reduction ideas. To this end, the ATF retained the skills of a creativity specialist (a professor from the school of business) from a local university. The specialist's job was to train the ATF in techniques that would encourage and enhance creative thinking among program participants, ultimately leading to the development of hundreds of top-quality cost-reduction ideas. ATF members would, in turn, train Unit Managers in these techniques.

Phase II officially began with a kickoff breakfast and all-day training session. Leland Phillips addressed the assembled Unit Managers and congratulated them for accomplishing Phase I on schedule. Then, working in small groups, ATF members trained the Unit Managers in creative thinking techniques, as well as the procedures necessary for carrying out

Phase II. Next Higher Managers also sat in on this training session because they would become involved in the process at the end of Phase II.

The second phase of the OVA program was scheduled to last six weeks and consisted of five major steps.

Step 1: Generating an Initial Set of Ideas. Each Unit Manager was assigned the task of generating an initial set of cost-reduction ideas that would reduce the unit's baseline budget by at least 40 percent. In order to accomplish this task, every single mission, activity, and end product had to be analyzed. Brainstorming sessions were held in which Unit Managers and key personnel considered as many ideas as possible. Two categories of ideas were generated during these sessions: *demand reduction* and *streamlining*.

Demand-reduction ideas concentrated on the legitimacy of *end products* and *services*; that is, whether or not they were really necessary. Demand reduction could be accomplished in several ways:

1. Reducing the content, quality, frequency, or quantity of an end product or service
2. Eliminating the end product or service entirely
3. Substituting or combining one end product with another
4. Deferring an end product or service until it becomes absolutely necessary to produce.

The following are examples of the types of questions designed to uncover demand-reduction opportunities:

1. Do we need such precise cost figures in this area?
2. Why do we need regional sales meetings this often?
3. How many (and which) foreign office visits can be eliminated?
4. Can this report be prepared as necessary, instead of once a week?

In the end, each unit manager chose the demand-reduction idea or ideas that were most appropriate for the end product or service being analyzed.

Streamlining ideas concentrated on improving the efficiency with which units carried out their activities. Streamlining could be accomplished in several ways.

1. Combining activities
2. Automating or de-automating activities
3. Balancing workloads
4. Changing procedures or work plans
5. Increasing or decreasing skill levels to allow more cost-effective use of manpower
6. Standardizing activities
7. Centralizing or decentralizing activities.

The following are examples of questions designed to uncover streamlining opportunities:

1. Can we computerize vendor requests?
2. Can the purchase of petroleum products be combined with the purchase of other raw materials?
3. Can we standardize our order forms?
4. Can we purchase for all divisions centrally?
5. Can an administrative assistant place purchasing orders instead of the higher paid purchasing agent?

As with demand reduction, each Unit Manager chose the streamlining approach most appropriate for the activity being analyzed. To help unit managers develop cost-reduction ideas, Worksheet 2A was created as a kind of thought-starter (see Figure 9). When completed, Worksheet 2A briefly described each idea and how it would be accomplished through demand reduction or streamlining. It also allows for a rough estimate of net savings and risk (low, medium, or high), should the idea be implemented. Each Unit Manager put together the best quality ideas (usually of low risk) that added up to at least a 40%

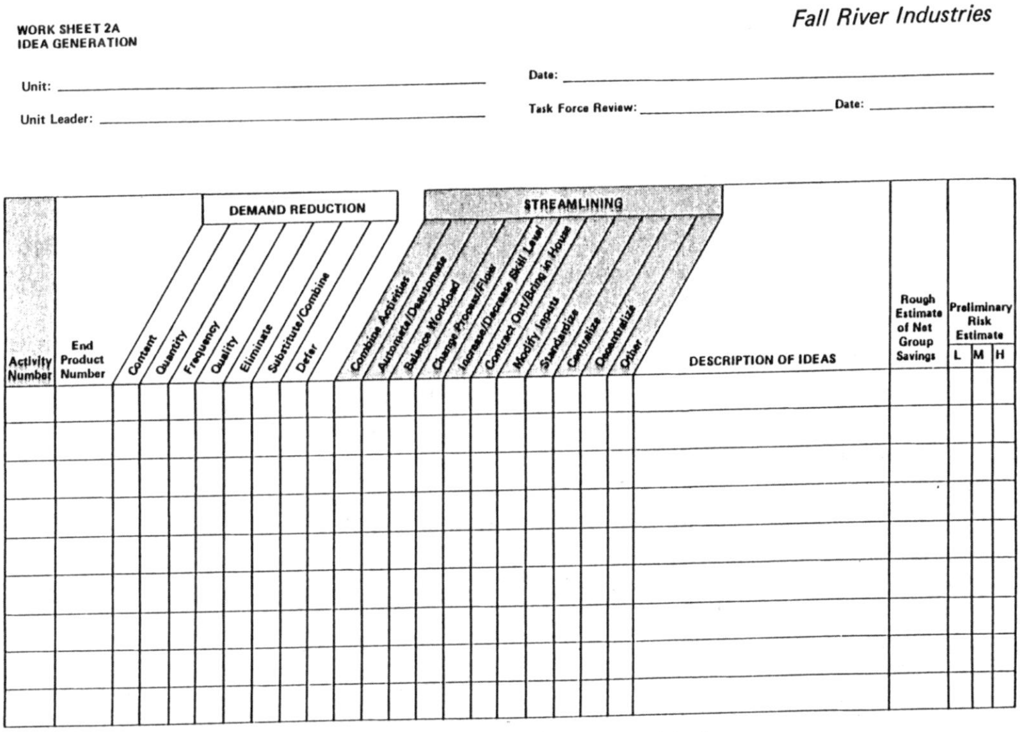
WORK SHEET 2A
IDEA GENERATION
Fall River Industries
Unit:
Unit Leader:
Date:
Task Force Review:
Date:
Activity Number
End Product Number
DEMAND REDUCTION
Content
Quantity
Frequency
Quality
Eliminate
Substitute/Combine
Defer
STREAMLINING
Combine Activities
Automate/Deautomate
Balance Workload
Change Process/Flow
Increase/Decrease Skill Level
Contract Out/Bring in House
Modify Inputs
Standardize
Centralize
Decentralize
Other
DESCRIPTION OF IDEAS
Rough Estimate of Net Group Savings
Preliminary Risk Estimate
L
M
H

FIGURE 9. OVA thought-starter worksheet

reduction in that unit's costs. Then the Unit Manager reviewed the ideas with his or her ATF member. Bruce Carbine, in his role as an ATF *member*, reviewed all of Martha Stewart's ideas for reducing purchasing costs.

Carbine was interested particularly in the quality of ideas generated by Stewart's unit. To help improve quality, Carbine used the following guidelines:

1. Have all missions, activities, and end products been examined?
2. Could less drastic measures be employed to achieve the same cost reduction?
3. Are there too many streamlining ideas and not enough demand reduction?
4. Do any ideas overlap, or are they so similar that the 40% target really has not been reached?
5. Have any attractive, low-risk ideas been overlooked or not included because the 40% target has been reached already?
6. Is the preliminary assessment of risk appropriate?
7. Do cost reductions represent an actual reduction in workload or is the same workload being done with a reduced staff?
8. Is each idea implementable and going to yield a net workload or expense reduction?

He and Stewart agreed on most of the ideas; one or two, however, were discarded and replaced by new ones suggested by Carbine and Stewart's next higher manager, Gene Barney, vice-president in charge of Corporate Planning. Barney was also a member of the Steering Committee, and Carbine invited him to sit in on the meeting. Barney, Carbine, and Stewart worked together refining and revising ideas. For example, one of Stewart's cost-reduction ideas was to use one vendor as the sole source of refined petroleum products. Barney, however, thought the idea was too risky. Carbine agreed. They worked out a modification by identifying those refined pe-

troleum products that could be obtained through one vendor at little or no risk to the company.

In the end, Martha Stewart left Bruce Carbine's office with a preliminary list of quality cost-reduction ideas that were slightly more than a 40% reduction in her unit's baseline budget.

Step 2: Refining the Initial Set of Ideas. Step 2 involved a detail description and refinement of each cost-reduction idea. To this end, Unit Managers were required to fill out Worksheet 2B, The Idea Summary (see Figure 10). Worksheet 2B was the key OVA form. Once an idea was recorded on this form, it could not be deleted. The idea was in the system permanently and would pass through each higher level of management until it reached the OVA Steering Committee. Along the way, managers would make recommendations, but only the Steering Committee could decide whether or not to implement an idea.

Worksheet 2B provided space for the following information:

1. *Idea description.* Each idea had to be stated clearly, completely, and specifically. Generalities were to be avoided.
2. *Estimated savings.* This figure had to be broken down to annualized personnel and nonpersonnel cost savings (plus or minus 10% accuracy).

In addition, on the left side of the worksheet, the unit manager was expected to add important information that would bear on a decision about the idea, including the following points:

1. *Identification of other benefits.* Additional benefits, meaning those other than cost savings, include increased morale, better training opportunities, and faster access to information.

It was important to list as many additional benefits as possible. Often this category provided the Steering Committee with the justifi-

WORK SHEET 2B
IDEA SUMMARY

Fall River Industries

Unit: _____   Date: _____

Unit Leader: _____   Task Force Review: _____ Date: _____

Idea Number (Unit #/Sequence #):   Idea Name: End Product Number:

Idea Description

UNIT MANAGER EVALUATION

Other benefits

ESTIMATED SAVINGS (COST)

	OVA Unit		Receiver/Other Units
	_____	Man - Years	_____
$	_____	Personnel	$ _____
$	_____	Other	$ _____
$	_____	Net Unit	$ _____
		Net Company	
		$ _____	

RISK

☐ Low ☐
☐ Medium ☐
☐ High ☐

RECEIVER AND OTHER UNIT EVALUATIONS

Other benefits

Adverse consequences (Quantity, if possible)

Adverse consequences (Quantify, if possible)

Implementation considerations and costs (if any)

Receiver, Demander Name	Initial	Go	No Go	Further Study
_____	_____	☐	☐	☐
_____	_____	☐	☐	☐
_____	_____	☐	☐	☐
_____	_____	☐	☐	☐

Recommendation

	UL	NHM
Go	☐	☐
No Go	☐	☐
Further Study	☐	☐

Total Savings { Net Company $ _____
              { Net Unit $ _____

FIGURE 10. OVA idea summary worksheet

cation it needed to implement an otherwise risky idea.

2. *Identification of adverse consequences.* Keep in mind that at this stage of the process, only the Unit Manager (supplier) was expressing the benefit and consequences of ideas. Therefore, the analysis was far from complete. However, in refining an idea, any adverse consequences as viewed by the "supplier" were described in such terms as Disruption of internal operations and control, reduced employee morale, unfavorable community reactions, inadequate customer service, and adverse impact on vendors.

Unit Managers were advised to quantify adverse consequences whenever possible, such as "one-week delay every three months in issuing quarterly report" or "an additional staff person needed to handle new filing procedure."

3. *Assessment of risk to FRI.* The risk of each idea was assessed as low, medium, or high. Risk assessment proved to be a tricky business. Many factors had to be considered, including the likelihood of an adverse consequence, the degree to which a decision is reversible (the easier it is to reverse a decision, the lower the risk), and the impact of cost-reduction ideas on more than one category of adverse consequences.

The consultant team proved extremely helpful in this area by providing the ATF (and, through them, each Unit Manager) with suggested guidelines for assessing the risk value of adverse consequences (see Figure 11).

4. *Implementation considerations and costs.* This section of the worksheet was used to indicate special factors that might affect the decision to implement a cost-reduction idea. These factors include capital investment (such

RISK LEVEL

Category of Adverse Consequences	Elements To Consider	Low	Medium	High
Disruption of internal operations and control	– Effects on department or group – Effects on company – Information for decision making	– Minor impact on management control department or group level – Negligible impact on management's control of company – Disruption is short term – Information in files or on internal forms somewhat less accurate and up to date	– Management's ability to exercise control at department or group level impaired – Small, but noticeable, impact on management's ability to control company-wide operations – Occasional confusion or inaccuracy results from incomplete or inaccurate data	– Management unable to exercise necessary control at department or group level – Senior management's ability to take action on company operations noticeably reduced – Documents or important information often incorrect or missing
Direct adverse effect on financial results	– Revenue level and growth – Cash flow – Expenses – Taxes – Investment required	– Cost reduction generates profit improvement that outweighs negative impact on other financial measures	– Cost reduction marginally outweighs adverse financial impact considering both amount and timing of likely cash flows	– Highly questionable trade-off between serving and adverse financial effect, either short versus long term or between financial measures
Inadequate customer service	– Image of the company and its representatives – Existing/potential customers – Competitive standards	– Negligible increase in customer complaints – Negligible impact on service levels	– Modest increase in customer complaints – Activity with customer impact occasionally inferior to competitive standards	– Substantial increase in customer complaints – Customer relationships jeopardized – Ability to obtain new customers impaired – Overall service level below competitive standards
Reduced employee morale	– Physical environment – Income and fringe benefits – Esprit – Turnover – Grievances – Productivity	– Small number of employees irritated for a few weeks	– Significant number of employees upset over period of several months – Minor increase in employee complaints	– Substantial lowering of morale over extended period of time – Significant increase in turnover – Significant decrease in productivity – Significant increase in employee complaints
Unfavorable community/governmental reaction	– Specific communities – Community and business press – Legality – Regulatory bodies	– Small interest groups irritated - by action that affects only them – Unfavorable action quickly forgotten	– Significant segment of the general public upset – Some letter writing to company, press, and/or government units	– Influential community groups bring substantial citizens and/or political pressure – Significant "bad press" – Adverse reaction over period of several months – Exposure to regulatory action (actions in clear violation will not be considered)
Disruption of vendor relations or timely supply of required goods and services	– Stability/reliability of source of supply – Purchasing cost-effectiveness – Importance of vendor – Importance of goods or services purchased	– Minor vendors irritated for short period – Some reduction in capability to tract or product requirements and prices for minor inputs	– Major vendors upset for several months – Costs for minor inputs not closely controllable	– Ability to negotiate or enforce major purchase agreements – Occasional difficulty in meeting time/quality specifications – Relationships with major vendors strained

FIGURE 11. Guidelines for assessing risk level of adverse consequences

as word processors), one-time expenses (such as computer programming), significant action steps, including preconditions (such as management training), and the time required to implement a decision.

Once the initial set of cost-reduction ideas were refined and recorded, it was time to begin the first major review.

Step 3: Reviewing Ideas With Next Higher Manager and ATF Member.

At this point in the process, each Unit Manager went back to his or her Next Higher Manager and ATF member so that they could jointly review each of the Idea Summaries prepared on Worksheet 2B. The purpose of this review was to insure:

1. A clear expression of ideas
2. Overall attainment of the 40% reduction
3. Appropriate preliminary risk assessments
4. Identification of appropriate receivers for the joint evaluation process
5. Grouping of similar ideas for ease of review by receivers or affected demanders
6. All "other benefits" and "adverse consequences".

Step 4: Conducting the Joint Evaluation Process with Receivers.

One of the important principles of an OVA program is that cost-reduction ideas are evaluated by both suppliers and receivers. Up to this point, the FRI program had only involved suppliers' (Unit Managers') evaluations. Now the opportunity had arrived for receivers of services and end products to comment on the proposed cost-reduction ideas.* Ultimately, this process would help to refine existing ideas and generate new ones.

The joint evaluation process was carried out by different units in different ways. There

*If the end product or service had many receivers, a sample would be used. In the case of receivers outside the company, perhaps a surrogate would be appointed.

were three basic options, depending on the complexity and controversial nature of the idea.

1. Unit Managers could telephone receivers and record their comments on the right side of Worksheet 2B (see Figure 10). A copy of the worksheet would then be sent to the receiver. This option was employed most of the time.
2. Worksheet 2B could be sent to the receiver, who would then fill out the right side and return it to the originating Unit Manager. If there were any disagreements, a meeting would be set up to resolve them.
3. A meeting could be set up between both parties right at the beginning so that they could discuss the idea together. This proved particularly useful when the proposed idea was complex or controversial.

The evaluation process is designed not simply to test the feasibility of an idea, but to modify and improve cost-reduction ideas and generate new ideas that make sense. Receivers are responsible for contributing to the creative as well as testing side of the process.

The only ideas that were exempted from the joint evaluation process were those that only affected internal end products (for example, vendor meetings) or streamlining ideas that did not affect end products or services in other departments or areas.

Regardless of the option chosen for conducting a joint evaluation, all receivers commented on benefits, adverse consequences, risks, and the cost impact on their organization (whether an increase or a decrease) for each cost-reduction idea submitted to them. In addition, the receiver indicated a recommendation of *Go* (OK), *No-Go* (not OK), or *Further Study* (analyze further) for each idea. The Further Study category had to be backed up with details on exactly what needed to be understood in order to make a decision (what should be studied, how it should be analyzed, by whom, and by when).

Once all comments from the receivers were recorded, Unit Managers were in a good position to make their own final recommendations. Usually, a Unit Manager's decision was in agreement with the receiver's recommendation. (To the greatest extent possible, agreement is sought.) However, this was not a requirement of the program. In fact, every Unit Manager wound up recommending at least two or three cost-reduction ideas for implementation that were rejected flatly by the receivers, and vice versa. (In these cases, of course, the Steering Committee had to give careful consideration to the additional benefits, adverse consequences, and overall strategic needs in order to make the final Go, No-Go, or Further Study decision.)

Step 5: Finalizing Recommendations and Grouping Cost-Reduction Ideas. Unit Managers were required to go over each idea to make sure that all information requested on Worksheet 2B was included and that they were certain about their final recommendations. In many instances, Unit Managers called on their next higher managers to help in making decisions. Unit Managers also checked to see that the 40% target was achieved. Finally, Unit Managers were asked to summarize their ideas and group them from most attractive to least attractive, recognizing disagreements between themselves and receivers or themselves and Higher Managers if and when they existed (see Figure 12).

Upon completion of all Idea Summary worksheets (Figure 10), each Unit Manager met with his or her ATF member to review

WORK SHEET 2C
IDEA EVALUATION

Fall River Industries

Unit: _____

Unit Manager: _____

Date: _____

Task Force Review: _____ Date: _____

Recommendation Category		Number of Ideas	Net Group Savings			Savings/Costs In Other Areas	Net Corporate Savings
			Personnel Expenses	Nonpersonnel Expenses	Total	Total	Total
GO	Agreement						
	Controversy						
FURTHER STUDY							
NO GO	Agreement						
	Controversy						
TOTAL							

Baseline Budget

40%

FIGURE 12. OVA idea evaluation worksheet

the unit's entire package of ideas. At the end of Phase II, the ideas were submitted to the appropriate next higher manager for further review.

Using one of the purchasing units as an example, Martha Stewart submitted her unit's Idea Summaries to Bruce Carbine (her ATF member) for review. Where necessary, changes were made in the description of the idea or the cost-saving estimate. In certain cases, the adverse consequences and risk were reassessed and, if necessary, recommendations were changed. After receiving Carbine's input, Stewart submitted her purchasing unit's ideas to Gene Barney (her next higher manager) for review, and Phase II came to an end.

Extended Idea Generation. During the course of Phase II, each unit developed an average of 32 cost-reduction ideas related specifically to the functions of that unit. However, it was realized that the process itself was likely to generate cost-reduction ideas that crossed departmental lines. Therefore, Unit Managers were assigned the additional task of keeping track of ideas that were not necessarily related to their own unit but were of definite value to the company. These ideas fell into four separate categories:

1. *Suggestions for other groups.* Such ideas were routed to the appropriate unit managers.
2. *Revenue-producing ideas.* These ideas were routed to the Unit Manager's ATF member.
3. *Cross-company cost-reduction ideas.* These ideas were routed to Peter Berk, who was carrying out the cross-company costs analysis.
4. *Open issues.* These ideas included broad issues that affected the performance of the company but were beyond the scope of an OVA program. Some examples include overall organizational structure, strategy weaknesses, cash management looseness, pricing anomalies. At FRI, open issues ideas were routed to the ATF. Worksheet 2D was used to describe these ideas (see Figure 13).

Phase III: Reviewing Ideas and Making Final Decisions

The OVA program was now going full speed ahead, and senior management was quite pleased with the level of involvement and commitment exhibited by all personnel. Leland Phillips issued a "Letter from the President" congratulating Unit Managers and ATF members on the successful completion of Phase II. In addition, the Communications Coordinator placed another article in the *Fall River News* that summarized the program to date and outlined the upcoming phases.

Phase III demanded the direct involvement of senior management and the program's Steering Committee. During this phase, senior managers would:

1. Review the package of cost-reduction ideas of each OVA unit assigned to them
2. Prepare presentations of ideas to be made before the Steering Committee.

The ATF began designing Phase III of the program while Phase II was still in progress. Their job during Phase III would be to act as counselors to senior management, guiding them through the important and sometimes politically delicate process of identifying those cost-reduction ideas that should be implemented. As part of their preparation for Phase III, the ATF:

1. Developed review criteria to help senior managers examine each package of cost-reduction ideas properly and prepare for Steering Committee presentations
2. Developed a detailed procedure for making presentations to the Steering Committee, which included:

WORK SHEET 2D
EXTENDED IDEA GENERATION

Fall River Industries

Unit: _____   Date: _____

Unit Leader: _____   Task Force Review: _____ Date: _____

ATF USE ONLY
DISPOSITION: • Other Unit #   ☐
               • Revenue-Generating Project   ☐
               • Longer Payback Project   ☐
               • Corporate wide or Policy Issue   ☐

Name (Optional)	Department
Department(s) or Function(s) Affected by Idea	
Estimated Savings From Implementation of Idea	

Explanation of Idea

FIGURE 13.   OVA extended idea generation worksheet

a. What a presentation would consist of

b. Who would be involved in making a presentation

c. Who else would attend

d. Where presentations would be made

e. When presentations would be made.

3. Developed review criteria to help the Steering Committee make its final decisions as to which ideas to recommend for implementation.

Leland Phillips then sent out a memo to senior management personnel (Steering Committee members and those senior managers who would be making presentations to the Steering Committee) outlining Phase III procedures as designed and developed by the ATF.

Phase III began formally with a kickoff dinner and training session. Bruce Carbine and the ATF were on hand to explain Phase III in detail and answer any questions the Steering Committee or other senior managers might have on the roles they would be playing. The third phase of the program was scheduled to last about four weeks, and it began with a senior management review of all cost-reduction ideas.

Senior Management Review. Senior management review refers to the process by which the senior managers who would eventually make presentations to the Steering Committee examined each unit's entire package of cost-reduction ideas. (Sequentially, this occurred after next higher managers conducted their reviews at the end of Phase II.) Within two days after the kickoff dinner, senior managers had copies of each unit's ideas (in the form of Worksheets 2B and 2C; see Figures 10 and 12). Senior management's primary review responsibilities included:

1. Checking the quality of each idea and making sure it represented clear thinking
2. Resolving differences between and among suppliers, receivers, and ATF members with regard to *Go, No-Go,* and *Further Study* recommendations, wherever possible
3. Making sure each cost-reduction package included the maximum number of *Go* ideas possible
4. Where appropriate, combining ideas or adding new ones (In no case, however, were any ideas to be eliminated—no matter how risky!)
5. Checking to make sure that the 40% cost-reduction target had been reached
6. Ordering, reworking or rethinking ideas in cases where quality was poor.

When the review process was over, each unit's list of cost-reduction ideas had been strengthened and refined. They were now ready to be presented to the Steering Committee for final action. The Steering Committee received, in advance, each package of ideas with summaries attached. In this way, they could familiarize themselves with the relative merits of each idea prior to the actual presentation, and thereby insure the efficiency of the final decision-making meeting.

Steering Committee Presentations. Over a one-week period, all cost-reduction ideas from the 35 units were presented formally to the Steering Committee. The ATF arranged for certain units to be grouped together, so that only eight presentations were made. The time allotted each presentation ranged from one to three hours depending on size, complexity, and degree of unresolved controversy. Only two people were allowed to make presentations on behalf of a group: the

senior manager presenting the ideas, and one other person (usually a Next Higher Manager selected by the senior manager who could answer detailed questions posed by the Steering Committee).

Each idea was presented in the form of Worksheet 2B, so that all Steering Committee members could see the full range of qualifiers that affected the idea (see Figure 10). When multiple 2Bs existed for a given idea (when a number of receivers were involved), a summary 2B was presented. A *decision risk analysis matrix* guided committee members as they made their decisions (see Figure 14). All ideas that fell into white areas on the matrix were not discussed at all unless individual Steering Committee members had questions. For example, a low-risk idea recommended *Go* by all reviewers almost always was accepted without discussion; a high-risk idea recommended *No-Go* by all reviewers almost always was rejected without discussion. Ideas that fell into shaded areas required more intensive review and discussion.

Phase III and The Purchasing Unit. At the beginning of Phase III, Martha Stewart presented her unit's package of cost-reduction ideas to Stanford Lasker, a vice-president of Chemline. Lasker was the senior manager assigned to the three purchasing units. (R&D and labor relations also reported to him.) After reviewing Stewart's ideas carefully, Lasker made a couple of important refinements. He changed the wording of three or four ideas descriptions so that the Steering Committee would have a better understanding of what was being proposed. He also challenged Stewart on two of her *No-Go* recommendations, convincing her to change one of them to CO_A Overall, Lasker was impressed with the job Stewart had done and with the way she was able to express her ideas, so he invited her to join him in presenting her unit's cost-reduction ideas to the Steering Committee. (It was a bit unusual, though certainly not without precedent, for a Unit Manager to be

Fall River Industries

Unit_____

DECISION RISK ANALYSIS

	DECISION CATEGORY				
Risk Category	Go Agreement	Go Disagreement	Further Study	No Go Disagreement	No Go Agreement
Low					
Medium					
High					
Total $ (%)					

NOTE: Shaded areas require discussion before the Steering Committee (subject to change)

FIGURE 14. OVA decision risk analysis worksheet

involved in a Steering Committee presentation. However, in this case it was highly warranted.)

At the appointed time, Lasker and Stewart walked into the Steering Committee meeting room, and Lasker began the presentation. Using slides and charts, he reviewed the purchasing unit's baseline budget and cost-reduction target (in dollars). He also added a brief description of how purchasing was organized. Next, he showed a breakdown of all the cost-reduction ideas in terms of savings:

1. All *Go* recommendations represented 21% in savings. (Where there was supplier/receiver/Next Higher Manager agreement, *Go* recommendations represented 16% in savings; where there was disagreement, *Go* represented 5% in savings.)
2. All *No-Go* recommendations represented 17% in savings. (Where there was supplier/receiver/Next Higher Manager agreement, *No-Go* recommendations represented 14% in savings; where there was disagreement, *No-Go* represented 3% in savings.)
3. All *Further Study* recommendations represented 6% in savings.
4. The total net savings of all cost-reduction ideas equaled 44%, 4% above the target.

Lasker then proceeded to explain the *Go* savings by category (raw material purchasing, capital, and construction purchasing), including the actual cost-reduction ideas within each category. Both he and Stewart fielded tough questions related to ideas the committee perceived as risky. In the end, however, they made out quite well: The Steering Committee accepted cost-reduction ideas that added up to a whopping 24% savings for that purchasing unit. In addition, all the *Go* ideas were accepted. Two *No-Go* ideas were accepted, one *No-Go* idea was assigned to *Further Study*, and two of the *Further Study* ideas were dropped because they were not considered worth studying further.

At the end of Phase III, the Steering Committee notified all presenters of the results of their deliberations. Each cost-reduction idea presented to the committee was categorized as either *Go, No-Go,* or *Further Study. No Go* ideas would be filed away. (Some of these ideas would prove useful in the future, if and when company conditions or strategies changed.)

Open Issues and Cross-Company Costs. During Phase III, the Steering Committee also considered cost-reduction ideas related to open issues and cross-company costs. In the case of open issues, various ATF members presented ideas that had been gathered from among the 35 Unit Managers or that had been gleaned from the suggestions sent in by employees. Phillip Berk presented the ideas related to cross-company costs. (He had been working on them since the beginning of Phase I.)

The Steering Committee spent the last day of Phase III making final decisions on cost reductions in both of these areas and scoping and approving special studies of some of the most promising and critical open issues.

Phase III and The Purchasing Unit. At the beginning of Phase III, Martha Stewart presented her unit's package of cost-reduction ideas to Stanford Lasker, a vice-president of Chemline. Lasker was the senior manager assigned to the three purchasing units. (R&D and labor relations also reported to him.) After reviewing Stewart's ideas carefully, Lasker made a couple of important refinements. He changed the wording of three or four ideas descriptions so that the Steering Committee would have a better understanding of what was being proposed. He also challenged Stewart on two of her *No-Go* recommendations, convincing her to change one of them

to CO_A Overall, Lasker was impressed with the job Stewart had done and with the way she was able to express her ideas, so he invited her to join him in presenting her unit's cost-reduction ideas to the Steering Committee. (It was a bit unusual, though certainly not without precedent, for a Unit Manager to be involved in a Steering Committee presentation. However, in this case it was highly warranted.)

At the appointed time, Lasker and Stewart walked into the Steering Committee meeting room, and Lasker began the presentation. Using slides and charts, he reviewed the purchasing unit's baseline budget and cost-reduction target (in dollars). He also added a brief description of how purchasing was organized. Next, he showed a breakdown of all the cost-reduction ideas in terms of savings:

1. All *Go* recommendations represented 21% in savings. (Where there was supplier/receiver/Next Higher Manager agreement, *Go* recommendations represented 16% in savings; where there was disagreement, *Go* represented 5% in savings.)
2. All *No-Go* recommendations represented 17% in savings. (Where there was supplier/receiver/Next Higher Manager agreement, *No-Go* recommendations represented 14% in savings; where there was disagreement, *No-Go* represented 3% in savings.)
3. All *Further Study* recommendations represented 6% in savings.
4. The total net savings of all cost-reduction ideas equaled 44%, 4% above the target.

Lasker then proceeded to explain the *Go* savings by category (raw material purchasing, capital, and construction purchasing), including the actual cost-reduction ideas within each category. Both he and Stewart fielded tough questions related to ideas the committee perceived as risky. In the end, however, they made out quite well: The Steering Committee accepted cost-reduction ideas that added up to a whopping 24% savings for that purchasing unit. In addition, all the *Go* ideas were accepted. Two *No-Go* ideas were accepted, one *No-Go* idea was assigned to *Further Study*, and two of the *Further Study* ideas were dropped because they were not considered worth studying further.

At the end of Phase III, the Steering Committee notified all presenters of the results of their deliberations. Each cost-reduction idea presented to the committee was categorized as either *Go, No-Go,* or *Further Study. No Go* ideas would be filed away. (Some of these ideas would prove useful in the future, if and when company conditions or strategies changed.)

Open Issues and Cross-Company Costs. During Phase III, the Steering Committee also considered cost-reduction ideas related to open issues and cross-company costs. In the case of open issues, various ATF members presented ideas that had been gathered from among the 35 Unit Managers or that had been gleaned from the suggestions sent in by employees. Phillip Berk presented the ideas related to cross-company costs. (He had been working on them since the beginning of Phase I.)

The Steering Committee spent the last day of Phase III making final decisions on cost reductions in both of these areas and scoping and approving special studies of some of the most promising and critical open issues.

Phase IV: Planning the Implementation of Approved Cost-Reduction Ideas

During Phase IV, each *Go* and *Further Study* cost-reduction idea was sent to the appropriate line or staff manager for the purpose of implementation planning. Such planning involved four basic steps:

1. Analysis of capturability
2. Development of program action plans
3. Coordination of action plans with the Human Resources Planning Committee
4. Integrating savings into the budget.

The preparatory work for Phase IV had actually begun at the end of Phase II. At that time, the ATF (in conjunction with the consulting team) had designed and developed the procedures, activities, and forms that would be necessary to carry out Phase IV. They also put together a detailed schedule of the entire phase. This schedule was important particularly because Phase IV was the point at which primary responsibility for carrying out the program began to shift away from the ad hoc OVA team (Steering Committee, ATF, and so on) and back to line and staff management. By Phase IV, line and staff management would have total responsibility for carrying out each implementation plan, with senior management overseeing the process; the role of the ad hoc OVA team would, for the most part, be over.

Finally, during Phase III, Leland Phillips sent a memo to department heads, Steering Committee presenters, and Unit Managers outlining the Phase IV schedule and delineating the roles and responsibilities of the key personnel who would be involved. The memo also described, in detail, the four basic steps that made up the process known as implementation planning.

Step 1: Analysis of Capturability. Each cost-reduction idea represented a potential savings in man-years. The purpose of capturability analysis was to realize or capture all savings by figuring out the fractional man-years that each idea actually saved. The total man-years saved (within each unit) then could be used to restructure the way in which departments functioned.

It was the job of the senior managers to oversee the entire process. The actual analyses were conducted by Next Higher Managers and, in some cases, Unit Managers. The capturability analysis was done mathematically and required some creative thinking. It involved the use of Worksheets 4A and 4B (see Figures 15 and 16)

Worksheet 4A listed all *Go* ideas. Then, for each idea, the following information was filled in:

1. Estimated man-year savings (from Worksheet 2B; see Figure 10)
2. Estimated man-year savings by position, grade, or personnel category
3. Special considerations that might affect the capturability of the personnel savings
4. The total personnel savings, by category, in terms of whole man-years saved.

Worksheet 4A (Figure 15), for example, shows that the cost-reduction ideas listed would free two Clerical 5 positions.

The capturability of man-years often implies the capturability of related nonpersonnel expenses, such as telephones and supplies. The remainder of the captured savings that come in the form of nonpersonnel are listed separately. Worksheet 4A also allowed space for these savings to be listed.

Worksheet 4B (Figure 16) was designed for developing ideas that would help capture the man-year savings left over from Worksheet 4A. Ideas for capturability included:

1. Consolidating workloads
2. Changing work content to downgrade/upgrade required skill level

Fall River Industries

WORKSHEET 4A: EXPENSE CAPTURABILITY

Department __Operations Support__   Department Head __Joe Smith__   Department Number __81201__

NO.	DESCRIPTION (COST REDUCTION IDEA)	M-Y FROM FORM 2B	Supervisor	Financial Analyst	Admin. 11	Admin. 9	Clerical 6	Clerical 5		NON-PERSONNEL EXPENSES DESCRIPTION	$K	COMMENTS
F40-01	Produce report X annually instead of quarterly	1.4		.4			.6	.4				
F40-03	Eliminate quarterly status report	1.1			.1			1.0		External Contract	1.5	Must cancel external printing contract
F40-15	Sample branch reports for errors rather than exhaustive check	.4					.4					
F40-23	Reduce phone followup on exceptions and assign to clerical	.1	.1				.1	.1				
F40-24	Eliminate report Y	.8						.8		Supplies	.4	
F40-27	Eliminate branch visits	.2	.2							Travel	.6	
F40-35	Automate quarterly exception analysis	1.0		.4	.1	.2		.3				One-time programming cost of $5.0
	Totals	5.0	.3	.8	.3	.6	.5	2.5			2.5	
	Whole Man-Years							2.0				
	Fractional Man-Years	3.0	.3	.8	.3	.6	.5	.5				

Note: List man-years to nearest tenth.

FIGURE 15. OVA expense capturability worksheet

3. Accepting as one full position something that is close to a full position (for example, 0.8 or 0.9 man-year)
4. Transferring work to another related group to capture time that has been freed there
5. Using part-time employees where feasible.

Figure 16, for example, shows how a financial analyst position was saved by having a supervisor pick up a small remaining fraction of his or her work.

Step 2: Development of Program Action Plans. Worksheet 4C was used to develop program action plans for each and every approved cost-reduction idea (see Figure 17). Line managers were directly responsible for

carrying out this part of Phase IV, although all plans had to be approved by higher management before being implemented. The action plan for each idea consisted of five separate items:

1. The idea number (for reference)
2. The specific action steps required to carry out the plan
3. The personnel directly responsible for implementing the plan
4. The time frame for the plan
5. The reductions expected for the year (in terms of personnel and dollars).

A "plan for resolution" also was developed for each *Further Study* idea. In addition, Next Higher Managers were responsible for developing plans to replace noncapturable workload

WORKSHEET 4B: HEADCOUNT CAPTURABILITY   *Fall River Industries*

Department: __Operations Support__   Department Head: ___Joe Smith_____   Department Number: ___81201___

IDEAS FOR CAPTURING FRACTIONAL MAN-YEARS / FRACTIONAL MAN-YEARS (FROM WORKSHEET 4A)	MAN-YEARS BY POSITION, GRADE OR PERSONNEL CATEGORY							
	Supervisor	Financial Analyst	Admin. 11	Admin. 9	Clerical 6	Clerical 5		
	.3	.8	.3	.6	.5	.5		
Consolidate workload of Clerical 5 into job of Clerical 6.					.5	.5		
Have supervisor pick up remaining work of financial analyst.	.2	.2						
Have quality control check of monthly report W done by Adm. 9 in R.C. A-102; transfer workload out of R.C.				.1				
Upgrade work from Admin. 9 position to Admin. 11			.3	.3				
Total Whole Man-Years Capturable on Worksheet 4B	–	1.0	–	1.0	–	1.0		
Total Whole Man-Years From Worksheet 4A						2.0		
Grand Total Capturable Man-Years	–	1.0	–	1.0	–	3.0		

FIGURE 16.   OVA headcount capturability worksheet

Department: __Operating Support__   Department Head: ___Joe Smith_____   Department Number: __81201___

IDEA NO.	ACTION STEPS REQUIRED	RESPONSIBILITY	TIMING Start	TIMING Finish	Headcount	Expense Code	$000 Amount
F40-63	Combine departments 123 and 456.						
	o Develop new organization charts and position descriptions; redesign work flow.	Van Allen	1/25/81	2/15/81	--	--	--
	o Cross-train manager of 123 to take over responsibility from combined departments.	Van Allen	1/25/81	3/1/81	--	--	--
	o Find new office space and arrange movement of both departments to same location.	Jones	1/25/81	3/1/81	--	239	(2.0)
	o Formal combination of departments resulting in reduction by 1 manager and 1 secretary. (Total $.7/week)	Smith	--	3/15/81	2.0	011 012 019 Total	14.7 7.3 6.7 28.7
F40-67	Automate tracking for system Z.						
	o Conduct feasibility study	White	1/31/81	3/15/81			
	o Review with Division Head and obtain approval for go-ahead.	White/VanAllen/ Smith		3/31/81			
	o Develop policy recommendations and detailed implementation plans. (one-time programming cost of $13K)	White/VanAllen	6/15/81	7/20/81	--	224	(13.0)
	o Obtain Group Head approval.	Smith		5/3/81			
	o Implementation results in reduction of staff by 3 clerks, grade 6. (Total .9/week)	Van Allen	6/6/81	8/11/81	3.0	011 019 Total	15.4 4.4 19.8
F40-78	Reduce staff by one administrative assistant.	Smith		1/31/80	1.0	011 019 Total	9.0 2.0 11.0

FIGURE 17.   OVA action plan worksheet

reductions with work deemed valuable to the department or company. (For example, during the months of March and April the uncapturable 0.3 man-year in purchasing raw materials might be used to research the potential of synthetic substitutes.)

Step 3: Coordination of Plans With the Human Resources Planning Committee (HRPC).

As the action plans for all ideas were developed, it was time to involve the HRPC in the mainstream program.* Each unit submitted to the HRPC a list of positions that would be eliminated as a result of the implementation of cost-reduction ideas. The list included the names of employees that were

*The Human Resources Planning Committee was organized during Phase 0 and had been busily at work during Phases I, II, and III, assembling a data base that would enable it to develop options for manpower redeployment/reduction.

selected based on HRPC guidelines, their job descriptions, and the dates they were expected to be free. This information, along with the list of vacant positions (because of the hiring, transfer, and promotion slowdown in effect since Phase 0) enabled the HRPC to make its final recommendations to the Steering Committee regarding manpower redeployment. At this point, the Steering Committee may suggest a switch in overall implementation timing to facilitate a more orderly redeployment or retraining of freed-up personnel.

Step 4: Integrating Savings Into The Budget:

This last step in the implementation planning process was perhaps the most critical in that it reflected OVA's reason for being. In Step 4, the actual savings generated by the hundreds of approved cost-reduction ideas finally were integrated into the budget. Each Unit Manager was responsible for filling out Worksheet 4D, which identified each action plan, listed its total cost savings for the year, and contained a breakdown of those savings by month (see Figure 18). With the submission to the company controller of Worksheet 4D for all action plans, Phase IV came to an end.

Phase V: Implementing Cost-Reduction Plans

As each program action plan was approved by the Steering Committee and other senior managers, it was returned to the appropriate staff or line manager for implementation. Thus began Phase V, also known as the action phase of the program.

Phase V was the culmination of roughly four months of hard work and determined effort on the part of dozens of Fall River employees, from top management on down. During Phase V, ideas that were once merely adjectives and nouns became action verbs and states of being, as hundreds of cost-reduction strategies were put into effect. It was truly an exciting and gratifying experience for all those who participated in the program.

Staff and line managers were responsible for submitting a quarterly progress report on each implementation plan. These reports were reviewed by senior management and the Steering Committee, which met periodically (monthly, at first, and then quarterly). The most valuable elements of each report were incorporated into the company's ongoing planning and budgeting process. In addition, audits of the entire program were conducted at six- and 12-month intervals. Here, too, the results were incorporated into the company's future plans.

After initiating all approved cost-reduction plans, line and staff managers had one more task to fulfill: They had to make sure that all

Worksheet 4D

Department Operating Support

STATUS OF OVA COST REDUCTION PROGRAMS
$ in 000's

Fall River Industries

PROG. #	IDENTIFICATION Program/Responsibility			TOTAL YEAR	Jan.	Feb.	Mar.	Apr.	May	June	July	Aug.	Sept.	Oct.	Nov.	Dec.
F40-63	Combine Depts. 123 & 456	Planned Reduction	$	26.7		(2.0)	1.4	2.8	2.8	3.5	2.8	2.8	3.5	2.8	2.8	3.5
			#			---	1.0	2.0	2.0	2.0	2.0	2.0	2.0	2.0	2.0	2.0
		Actual	$													
			#													
		Var. to Plan	$													
			#													
F40-67	Automate Tracking for System Z	Planned Reduction	$	6.8							(13.0)	3.6	4.5	3.6	3.6	4.5
			#									3.0	3.0	3.0	3.0	3.0
		Actual	$													
			#													
		Var. to Plan	$													
			#													
F40-78	Eliminate Admin. Assistant	Planned Reduction	$	24.0		2.0	2.5	2.0	2.0	2.5	2.0	2.0	2.5	2.0	2.0	2.5
			#			1.0	1.0	1.0	1.0	1.0	1.0	1.0	1.0	1.0	1.0	1.0
		Actual	$													
			#													
		Var. to Plan	$													
			#													
		Planned Reduction	$													
			#													
		Actual	$													
			#													
		Var. to Plan	$													
			#													
		Planned Reduction	$													
			#													
		Actual	$													
			#													
		Var. to Plan	$													
			#													
Total OVA Impact		Planned Reduction	$													
			#													
		Actual	$													
			#													
		Var. to Plan	$													
			#													
Actual Department Results		Budget	$													
			#													
		Actual	$													
			#													
		Var. to Budget	$													
			#													

FIGURE 18. Status of OVA cost reduction programs

ideas committed to *Further Study* were reclassified *Go* or *No-Go* within the time allotted. (*Further Study* ideas were dealt with at the regular meetings of the Steering Committee.) Those ideas reclassified as *Go* would be put into effect immediately by the appropriate manager.

FRI's OVA program was a great success, primarily because of the commitment of FRI's top management. Statistically, the final results more than justified the company's involvement in the program:

1. Each of the 35 units involved generated an average of 25 *Go* ideas.
2. Each unit averaged a cost-reduction savings of 18% and $7,000 per idea.
3. The grand total net savings was $6.3 million, and since company operating income was running at 15% of total revenue, the program yielded a 21% jump in operating income.
4. Valuable human and financial resources were able to be reallocated to needed areas.
5. Prices were able to be trimmed.
6. The company became more competitive.

In addition, the OVA process itself was instrumental in creating a climate of cost consciousness at FRI, as well as building an *esprit de corps* among the management team and improving their evaluation skills. As a result of OVA, FRI was well on its way to becoming a leader in the chemical industry.

The Manpower Redeployment Program

Substantial reduction in overhead costs, of necessity, means the elimination of jobs and the possible displacement of large numbers of employees. Employers are often frightened by the prospect of facing such an eventuality, especially because traditional planning and budgeting approaches make no provision for dealing with freed human resources. An OVA

program, however, tackles this problem head-on by establishing an HRPC well before the main program begins. The purpose of this committee is to:

1. Define personnel policy
2. Identify transfer and retraining opportunities
3. Develop strategies for the redeployment and/or reduction of personnel as quickly and humanely as possible
4. Advise the Steering Committee on all personnel-related issues
5. Insure the EEO requirements and age discrimination laws are followed (to the maximum extent possible) as employees are redeployed and/or retrained.

An equally important responsibility of the HRPC is to maintain high morale among the workforce while the program is in progress. This is done by supplying the Communications Coordinator with accurate personnel policy guidelines so the Coordinator, in turn, can assure workers that, for example:

1. There will be no mass layoffs.
2. There will be ample opportunity for redeployment, transfer, and, if necessary, retraining (at company expense).
3. Every effort will be made to take advantage of natural attrition and early retirement.

The Manpower Redeployment Program complements the main program and is accomplished in three stages.

Stage 1: Early Planning (before the main program begins).

In Phase I of the Manpower Redeployment Program, the Steering Committee appoints the members of the HRPC. These members, who will work mostly part-time on this assignment, would be drawn not just from personnel functions but also from key line management positions. This lends realism to the planning effort and assists in gaining commitment in the line to the committee's policies and procedures. The Planning Committee then begins the task of assembling a basic data base that allows them to analyze the supply-and-demand outlook for all personnel for the coming year. The committee gathers or develops a projection of personnel needs by job category and skills required, along with an estimate of projected retirements and natural turnover. Together, this information provides a base that matches supply of employees to demand for employees.

Another goal of the Committee during Phase I is to develop a company policy regarding hiring, promotions, transfers, and recruiting while the OVA program is under way. In the United States, the usual policy adopted is a major slowdown in hiring, transfers, and promotions that begins before the formal kickoff of the OVA program. Procedures also are developed to govern exceptions to the policy should they become necessary.

Stage 2: Personnel Planning During the Mainstream Program. As the results of the mainstream program begin to pour in, the Human Resources Planning Committee continues to build and revise its data base. Estimates are made on positions likely to be eliminated and personnel likely to be freed. The committee concentrates on the development of a portfolio of manpower redeployment options. Basic strategies and tactics are devised, along with suggested actions for carrying them out (see Figure 19*). Once this planning stage had been completed, the committee is in a position to select the strategies most likely to be successful.

As the portfolio of redeployment options is assembled, the Planning Committee examines potential problem areas, such as groups or departments that might be eliminating more

jobs than anticipated. The committee also develops guidelines to help Unit Managers identify excess personnel.

At the end of the second stage, the Steering Committee finalizes the portfolio of redeployment options and strategies and establishes guidelines for carrying them out within each unit. A training session is held to instruct Unit Managers on how to deal with excessed personnel.

In addition, a temporary talent bank may be set up (for six months or more) to facilitate the reassignment of excessed personnel. Department managers are required to draw on talent bank members before hiring from outside the company.** Ontplacement services such as job counseling and reésumé preparation, also are developed to help workers who will be laid off.

Stage 3: Implementation. During the implementation stage, management actually begins to work with the people who have been identified as excess.

1. Redeployment options are put into action.
2. Outplacement services are activated.
3. The talent bank is put into operation.

Moreover, the implementation of the Manpower Redeployment Program is monitored carefully to make sure that:

1. Each department is implementing the program at the right pace, one designed to achieve optimal manageability, morale, and economic benefits
2. No one group (women, minorities, and so on) is excessed more than any other group (this may necessitate the shifting of workers in order to achieve balance).

---

*Although Figure 19 indicates the basic redeployment options available, considerable innovation, modification, or tailoring may be necessary within the context of a company's particular situation (culture, history, style, growth and so on) and overall strategy.

**Although some companies prefer not to set up a talent bank, others have found that by restricting such a bank to solid performers, the system works quite well. (On occasion, even employees *not* excessed by the program will seek to use the bank, in order to get their careers moving again.)

Fall River Industries

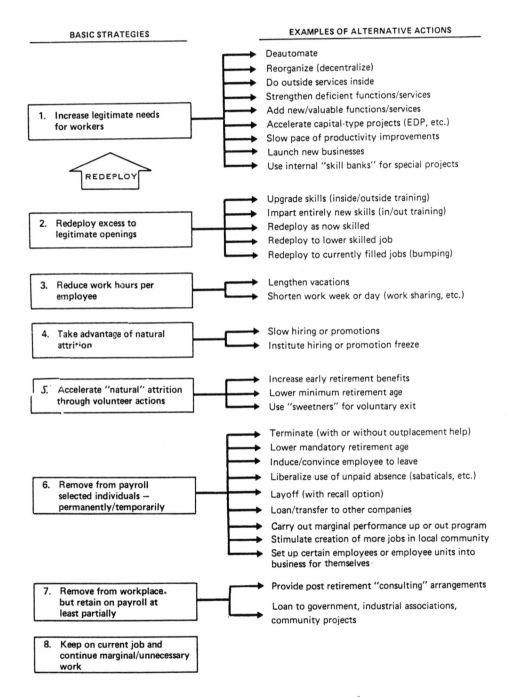

BASIC STRATEGIES

EXAMPLES OF ALTERNATIVE ACTIONS

Deautomate
Reorganize (decentralize)
Do outside services inside
Strengthen deficient functions/services

1. Increase legitimate needs for workers

Add new/valuable functions/services
Accelerate capital-type projects (EDP, etc.)
Slow pace of productivity improvements
Launch new businesses
Use internal "skill banks" for special projects

REDEPLOY

2. Redeploy excess to legitimate openings

Upgrade skills (inside/outside training)
Impart entirely new skills (in/out training)
Redeploy as now skilled
Redeploy to lower skilled job
Redeploy to currently filled jobs (bumping)

3. Reduce work hours per employee

Lengthen vacations
Shorten work week or day (work sharing, etc.)

4. Take advantage of natural attrition

Slow hiring or promotions
Institute hiring or promotion freeze

5. Accelerate "natural" attrition through volunteer actions

Increase early retirement benefits
Lower minimum retirement age
Use "sweeteners" for voluntary exit

6. Remove from payroll selected individuals — permanently/temporarily

Terminate (with or without outplacement help)
Lower mandatory retirement age
Induce/convince employee to leave
Liberalize use of unpaid absence (sabaticals, etc.)
Layoff (with recall option)
Loan/transfer to other companies
Carry out marginal performance up or out program
Stimulate creation of more jobs in local community
Set up certain employees or employee units into business for themselves

7. Remove from workplace, but retain on payroll at least partially

Provide post retirement "consulting" arrangements
Loan to government, industrial associations, community projects

8. Keep on current job and continue marginal/unnecessary work

FIGURE 19.   Options for excess personnel

The HRPC continues to monitor the implementation of its program until all workers have been dealt with satisfactorily. It should be pointed out that in most companies, cost-reduction savings have been realized without many (and in some cases no) terminations. Typically, for every 100 positions deleted by the OVA process, some 30 to 50 may be vacant already because of previously initiated hiring, transfer, and promotion slowdown; another 30 to 50 are taken care of by all of the other portfolio options listed in Figure 19 (short of termination/layoffs); a final zero to 15 are laid off or terminated with effective outplacement assistance. Normal turnover, combined with in-house transfers, staff retraining, and reductions in new hires, usually has accomplished the task with a minimum of discomfort. This fact underscores the important contribution that a well-managed Human Resources Planning Committee makes to the success of the main OVA program.

Communications

FRI employed about 1,000 people in indirect positions. Of that number, only about 50 or so were part of the OVA management team (Steering Committee, ATF, Unit Managers, and so on). The remaining 950 employees (including all levels of management) generally were not involved in the process, although they did submit ideas. They were, however, quite aware of the fact that a cost-reduction study was being conducted and that it had as its goal a 40% cut in overhead activities and expenditures. Therefore, in order to keep the company informed properly and accurately of the OVA process and to avoid anxiety, false rumors, and other difficulties that might arise because of a lack of understanding, the Steering Committee appointed an OVA Communications Coordinator. This person was responsible for creating a communications

network that would, on a regular basis, disseminate program policies and information (as determined by the ATF), among all non-OVA employees. The basic communication objectives included:

1. Maximizing employee understanding of the program
2. Gaining employee support
3. Keeping morale high
4. Making top management's commitment visible
5. Obtaining feedback from employees throughout all phases of the program.

In addition, the Communications Coordinator, under the guidance of the ATF, kept all OVA participants and senior management informed on the progress of each program phase.

The potential audience identified by the Communications Coordinator as needing to receive information included:

1. Line management: board of directors, senior management, staff executives
2. Program management: Steering Committee, ATF next higher managers, Unit Managers
3. All employees, whether participating or not
4. Union management, as appropriate
5. Direct business relations: vendors, customers
6. Nonparticipating subsidiaries
7. Shareholders
8. Media
9. Government agencies
10. General public (including the local community).

In order to get information to these various audiences, the Communications Coordinator developed such vehicles for communication as:

1. Regular program bulletins released at prearranged intervals
2. Special messages from top management
3. Memorandums from program management
4. Training manuals
5. Informal breakfast and lunch meetings, including senior executives with small groups of Unit Managers
6. Question-and-answer forums, either written or oral
7. Major meetings of employee groupings (by unit, by phase, and so on)
8. Press releases
9. Articles in the internal newspaper
10. Videotapes of the president's kickoff remarks for dissemination to distant locations.

The Communications Coordinator also developed a communications timetable for each phase of the program, including Phase 0. The information contained in each timetable was guided by the ATF, approved by the Steering Committee and included:

1. Dates for releasing information
2. Vehicle for delivering information
3. Information required
4. Person or group needing information
5. Person or group preparing information
6. Person approving information.

Finally, the Communications Coordinator was responsible for setting up and monitoring feedback mechanisms that would allow the program to benefit from employees' and participants' comments, questions, and suggestions. Formal feedback mechanisms included written forms (that did not have to be signed), a phone number for people to call, and direct questioning of ATF members on a regularly scheduled basis.

Informal feedback mechanisms included special breakfasts and lunches with senior ex-

ecutives at which participants were asked to comment on various aspects of the program.

Once the OVA program officially began at FRI, the Communications Coordinator was responsible for drafting and delivering all messages and information on time, as specified in each program timetable.*

By carefully planning its communications network and seeing to it that it was well organized, FRI provided a unifying link between management commitment and employee participation that helped keep its OVA program running smoothly.

THE BENEFITS OF AN OVA PROGRAM

An OVA program allows a company to make substantial cuts in overhead—cuts that really last. Moreover, the results of such a program can be achieved rapidly. The program increases productivity by eliminating unnecessary outputs. In the process, a company's cost competitiveness is greatly strengthened. With overhead reduced and under control, financial and human resources can be reallocated in a way that supports strategic plans and priorities. In this respect, an OVA program can have a permanent impact on a company's future growth and development. There are many other benefits to be derived from such a program.

1. Planning, budgeting, and evaluation skills among managers are significantly improved.
2. Management increases its cost-benefit sensitivity.
3. A comprehensive data base is created to help assess future organizational structure and product profitability.
4. Detailed contingency plans (in the form of cost-reduction ideas) that are not implemented are always on file.

---

*The ATF reviewed (and in some cases prepared) each item before distribution.

5. Numerous spinoff ideas (in the form of open issues) are generated for further study.*

6. Suppliers and receivers of a service or activity get a better understanding of each other's functions.

7. An *esprit de corps* is developed among program participants.

8. The ongoing planning and budgeting process can be upgraded intelligently as a result of the lessons learned during OVA, as can the skills that the management team has developed.**

9. The ATF members have accelerated their professional development.

DETERMINING WHETHER THE OVA PROGRAM IS FOR YOU

With all the benefits to be derived from an OVA program, it would seem foolish for a company *not* to embark on such a course of action immediately. Yet the real foolishness would lie in jumping on the bandwagon too quickly, without given the whole matter w great deal of thought and consideration. The program described in this chapter is detailed and complex, involving many people filling out many forms and making many decisions, all in a relatively short period of time. If conducted without proper preparation and commitment, this type of program can be dangerous to morale, management credibility, and retention of key personnel. Without

*The very process of conducting such an extensive OVA program allows the ATF director and other key personnel to gain insight into organizational problems not directly related to cost. For example, a shortage of experienced plant foremen might be noticed during the program. At the end of the program, the ATF issues a series of white papers that (1) identifies each problem, (2) cites evidence, and (3) offers possible solutions.

**For example, the Phase I data base is frequently maintained as an excellent planning tool, mini-OVAS are run on all proposals for new systems that exceed a threshold amount, and the supplier/receiver evaluations are used where changes in service or end-product quality or cost are contemplated.

proper preparation, it would be better not to attempt it at all.

Of course, a company can aim to achieve much less and therefore need not launch an OVA program all at once. It can choose instead to apply the principles of OVA selectively, in a less comprehensive manner. By aiming for a more modest level of overhead improvement, risks are reduced. However, if a company does decide to establish an entire OVA program, there is no time to sit back and take it easy. Success is assured only if top management is willing to:

1. Make a total commitment to the program and be visibly involved on a day-to-day basis

2. Free several of its best people, full time, to run the program and to coach and assist all active participants

3. Demand from the managers thorough preprogram preparation and planning

4. Establish effective parallel programs dealing with manpower redeployment and ongoing communications so that top management is ready for success

5. Demand from each program unit quality cost-reduction ideas that add up to 40% of its baseline budget and that challenge everything, including sacred cows, historically "hands off" functions, and pet prjects

6. Set a time schedule for completion of the program and stick to it

7. Implement each and every approved cost-reduction plan so that all identified savings are actually realized.

Finally, the successful outcome of an OVA program depends on the caliber of the management team assembled to run it. The team must be willing to take ownership of the program from the very start. It must be capable of dealing with the rigors of conducting and implementing such an extensive plan of action. The responsibilities are great, but so too are the potential rewards. And they are there to be claimed by any quality management team ready to make the necessary commitment.

DEFINITIONS OF TERMS

The following list defines the terms used in the WORKSMART! process.

Activities   The tasks performed in carrying out a mission, resulting in one or more outputs—the HOW

Advisory Task Force (ATF)   Personnel trained in OVA procedures used to help Unit Managers analyze and evaluate their own areas effectively

Baseline Budget   The budget adjusted for an OVA unit

End Products   The outputs, both hard copy and non-hard copy, of an OVA unit that result from its activities (for example, reports, documents, advice, visits—the WHAT)

Missions   The main purposes (charter) of the unit; the reasons for its existence—the WHY

Next Higher Manager (NHM)   The manager to whom one or more OVA Unit Managers report. The NHM may also be a Division or Unit Manager; in these cases he or she will have dual responsibilities

Outputs   Products and services of an OVA unit

Receivers   Any customer, department, or organization that receives end products from an OVA unit

Services   The non-hard copy outputs of an OVA unit—the WHAT

Steering Committee   Top management personnel responsible for overseeing the entire OVA program

Unit   The selected unit in which the OVA process is carried out. It is often the same as an existing department, but it can include several small departments or be a portion of a larger one

Unit Manager   An appointed manager or key staff person who is responsible primarily for the OVA process in a unit

BIBLIOGRAPHY

Controlling Inventories

Bierman, Harold, Bonini, Charles P., and Hausman, Warren H. *Quantitative analysis for business decisions.* Richard D. Irwin, Inc., Homewood, Ill. 5th edition. Chapters 17-19. 1977.

Carter, Albert G. *Computing inventory return on investment.* Management Accounting, July 1973, Page 43.

Chase, Richard B. and Aquilano, Nicholas J. *Production and operations management.* Homewood, Ill. Richard D. Irwin, Inc., 1977.

Deakin, Edward B. *Finding optimal order quantity when quality discounts are offered.* Cost and Management, May-June 1975. Page 40.

Dudick, Thomas S. and Ross H. Cornell. *Inventory control for the financial executive.* John Wiley & Sons, New York. 1979.

Deakin, Edward B. *Finding optimal order quantity when quantity discounts are offered.* Cost and Management, May-June, 1975. Page 40.

Janson, Robert L. *Production control desk book.* Englewood Cliffs, NJ. 1975. Chapter 5.

Lambert, Douglas M and LaLonde, Bernard J. *Inventory carrying costs.* Management Accounting, August, 1976. Page 31.

Pattinson, W. Richard. *Excess and obsolete inventory control.* Management Accounting, June 1974. Page 35.

Shycon, Harvey N. and Sprague, Christopher R. *Put a price tag on your customer servicing levels.* Harvard Business Review, July-August 1975. Page 71.

Costing and Pricing Products

Deakin, Michael D. *Pricing for return on investment.* Management Accounting, December, 1975. Page 43.

Dudick, Thomas S. *Cost controls for industry.* Englewood Cliffs, NJ 1976. 2nd edition. Chapter 9.

Fremgen, James M. Accounting for managerial analysis, Homewood, Ill. Richard D. Irwin, 1976. 3rd Edition. Chapter 15.

Fuss, Norman H. *How to raise prices judiciously to meet today's conditions.* Harvard Business Review, May-June 1975. Page 10.

Hampel, Robert E. Pricing policies and profitability. Management Accounting, July 1977. Page 53.

Shillinglaw, Gordon, *Managerial cost accounting.* Homewood, Ill. 4th Ed. Richard D. Irwin 1977.

Wells, M. C. *Justifying price discrimination.* The Australian Accountant, July 1976, Pages 338-42.

Financial Controls

Cammann, C. *Effects of the use of control systems.* Accounting, Organizations and Society, Volume 2, 1977. Pages 301-14.

Cammann C., and Nadler, D. *Fit control systems to your managerial style.* Harvard Business Review, Volume 54. 1976. Pages 65-72.

DeWelt, Robert L. *Labor measurement and control.* Management Accounting October 1976. Page 26.

Dudick, Thomas S. *Profile for profitability: Using cost control and profitability analysis.* New York: John Wiley & Sons, 1972.

Fox, Harold. *The marketing controller as planner.* Managerial Planning, July-August 1974. Page 33.

Goodman, Sam R. *Techniques of profitability analysis.* New York, John Wiley & Sons. 1970.

Grinnell, D. Jacque. *Activity levels and the disposition of volume variances.* Management Accounting, August 1975. Page 29.

Hathaway, Bruce R. *Controlling new facilities costs.* Management Accounting April 1975. Page 47.

Horngren, Charles T. *Cost Accounting: a managerial emphasis:* 4th Edition. Englewood Cliffs, NJ 1977.

Matz, Adolf and Usry, Milton F. *Cost accounting: Planning and control.* 6th Edition. Cincinnati, Ohio: South-Western Publishing Co. 1976

Sisco, Anthony F. *Overhead variance analysis and corrective action.* Management Accounting, October, 1973. Page 45.

Seed, Allen H. *Utilizing the funds statement.* Management Accounting May 1976.

Forecasting and Budgeting

Bierman, Harold and Smidt, Seymour. *The capital budgeting decision.* 4th Ed. New York: Macmillan Co. 1975.

Cheek, Logan M. *Zero-base budgeting comes of age.* American Management Assn. 1977.

Dudick, Thomas S. *Zero-base budgeting in industry.* Management Accounting. May, 1978.

Makridakis, S. and Wheelwright, S.C. *Interactive forecasting.* Palo Alto, California: The Scientific Press, 1977.

Mason, R. D. *Statistical techniques in business and economics.* 4th Edition, Homewood, Illinois: Richard D. Irwin, Inc. 1978

Mehler, Edmund -W. *Capital budgeting: theory and practice.* Management Accounting, September 1976. Page 32.

Pindyck, R. S. and Rubinfeld, D. L. *Econometric models and economic forecasts.* New York: McGraw-Hill, 1976.

Pyhrr, Peter A. *Zero-base Budgeting.* New York: John Wiley & Sons. 1975.

Watson, Spencer C. *A vote for R & D profit centers.* Management Accounting. April 1975, Page 50.

Welsch, Glenn A. *Budgeting: profit planning and control.*. Englewood Cliffs, NJ Prentice-Hall 1976.

Information Systems

Alter, Steven L. *How effective managers use information systems.* Harvard Business Review. November-December, 1976. Page 97.

Axelson, Charles F. *How to avoid the pitfalls of information systems development.* Financial Executive, April, 1976. Page 25.

Anthony, Robert N. and Dearden, John. *Management control systems.* Homewood, Illinois. Richard D. Irwin, Inc. 1976.

Joslin, Edward O and Bassler, Richard A. *Management data processing.* Alexandria: College Readings, 1976.

Martin, R. K. *The financial executive and the computer: the continuing struggle.* Financial Executive, March 1977, Page 26.

Murdick, Robert G and Ross, Joel E. *Information systems for modern management.* Englewood Cliffs, NJ: Prentice-Hall, 1975.

Turney, Peter B. *Transfer pricing management information systems. Management information systems quarterly.* Volume 1, No. 1, March 1977.

Marketing and Marketing Strategy

Bogart, Leo *Mass advertising.* Cambridge, Mass. Harvard Business Review, September-October 1976, p. 107.

Buzby, Stephen L., and Heitger, Lester E. *Profit contribution by market segment.* Management Accounting, Nov. 1976, page 42.

Clewett, Richard M., and Stasch, Stanley F. *Shifting role for the product manager.* Harvard Business Review, Cambridge. January-February 1975, page 65.

Goodman, Sam R. *Sales reports that lead to action* Financial Executive, June 1973, page 20.

Minkin, Jerome M. *Developing the marketing budget.* Handbook of Modern Marketing, New York: McGraw-Hill Book Co., page 70.

Mullins, Peter L. *Integrating marketing and financial concepts in product line evaluations.* Financial Executive, 1972, page 32.

Spiegel, Reed S. *The accountant, the marketing manager and profit.* Management Accounting, January, 1974. Page 18.

Stevens, Ross *Product line cash income, a reliable yardstick.* Management Management Accoutting, January, 1974. Page 18.

Stevens, Ross *Product line cash income, a reliable yardstick.* Management Management Accounting, November 1974 Page 46.

Mergers and Acquisitions

Cheek, Logan M. *Corporate expansion: predicting profitability.* Financial Executive. March 1975, Page 38.

Heath, John *Valuation factors and techniques in mergers and acquisitions.* Financial Executive, April 1972, Page 34.

Levinson, Harry. *A psychologist diagnoses merger failures.* Harvard Business Review. January-February 1975 Page 41.

Seed, Allen H. *Why corporate marriages fail.* Financial Executive, December 1974, Page 56.

Organization and Planning

Alderfer, C. P. *Existence, relatedness, and growth: Human needs in organizational settings.* New York: Free Press, 1972.

Alderfer, C. P. Boundary relations and organizational diagnosis. In H. Meltzer and F. R. Wickert (eds.), *Humanizing organizational behavior.* Springfield, Ill.: Charles Thomas, 1976.

Alderfer, C. P. and Smith, K. Studying intergroup relations in organization. Working paper, Yale University, School of Organization and Management, 1980.

Ansoff, H. Igor *The State of Practice in Planning Systems.* Sloan Management Review, Winter, 1977. p. 1.

Argenti, John. Systematic corporate planning, New York: John Wiley & Sons, 1974.

Argyris, C. *Integrating the individual and the organization.* New York: John Wiley & Sons, 1964.

Argyris, C. Problems and new directions for industrial psychology. In M. D. Dunnette (Ed.), *Handbook of industrial and organizational psychology.* Chicago: Rand McNally, 1976.

Brickner, William H., and Cope, Donald M. *The planning process.* Cambridge, Mass.: Winthrop Publishers, Inc. 1977.

Business Week, Texas Instruments Shows U. S. Business How to Survive in the 1980's. September 18, 1978.

Cammann, C. Effects of the use of control systems. *Accounting, Organization, and Society,* 1976, 1(4), 301-313.

Cammann, C. and Nadler, D. A. Fit control systems to your managerial style. *Harvard Business Review,* 1976, 54(1), 65-72.

Davis, L. and Lawrence, P. R. *Matrix organizations.* Reading, Mass.: Addison-Wesley, 1977.

Deci, E. L. *Intrinsic motivation.* New York: Plenum, 1975.

Frost, C. F., Wakeley, J. H. and Ruh, R. A. *The Scanlon Plan for organizational development:* Identity, participation, and equity. Lansing, MI: Michigan State University Press, 1974.

Galbraith, J. R. *Designing complex organizations.* Reading, Mass.: Addison-Wesley, 1973.

Golembiewski, R. T. and McConkie, M. The centrality of interpersonal trust in group processes. In G. L. Cooper (Ed.) *Theories of group processes.* New York: John Wiley and Sons, 1975.

Hackman, J. R. Work redesign. In J. R. Hackman and J. L. Suttle (Ed.), *Improving life at work.* Santa Monica: Goodyear, 1977.

Hackman, J. R. and Lawler, E. E. Employee reactions to job characteristics. *Journal of Applied Psychology,* 1971, 55(3), 259-286.

Hackman, J. R. and Oldham, C. R. *Work redesign.* Reading, Mass.: Addison-Wesley, 1980.

Herrick, N. Q. and Maccoby, M. Humanizing work: A priority goal of the 1970's. In L. E. Davis and A. B. Cherns (Eds.), *The quality of working life* (Vol. 1). New York: Free Press, 1975.

Katz, D. and Kahn, R. L. *The social psychology of organizations* (2nd ed.). New York: John Wiley & Sons, 1978.

Lawler, E. E., III *Motivation in work organizations.* Monterey, Calif.: Brooks/Cole, 1973.

Lawler, E. E. and Rhode, J. G. *Information and control in organizations.* Pacific Palisades, Calif.: Goodyear, 1976.

Nadler, D. A., Cammann, C. and Mirvis, P. H. Developing a feedback system for work units: A field experience in structural change. *Journal of Applied Behavioral Science,* 1980, 16(1).

Staw, B. M. *Intrinsic and extrinsic motivation.* Morristown, NJ: General Learning Press, 1976.

Planning and Strategy

Ansoff, H. Igor. *The state of practice in planning systems.* Sloan Management Review, Winter 1977. Page 1.

Argenti, *John Systematic Corporate planning.* New York: John Wiley & Sons. 1974.

Brickner, William H. and Cope, Donald M. *The planning process.* Cambridge, Mass. Winthrop Publishers, Inc. 1977.

Gillmore, Frank. *Formulating strategies in smaller companies.* Harvard Business Review. May-June 1971 Page 71.

Haner, F. T. *Business policy, planning and strategy.* Cambridge, Mass. Winthrop Publishers, Inc. 1976.

Lorange, Peter and Vancil, Richard F. *Strategic planning systems,* Englewood Cliffs, NJ. 1977.

Mintzberg, Henry. *Strategy making in three modes.* California Management Review. Winter 1973. Page 44.

Naylor, Thomas H and Gattis, Daniel R. *Corporate planning models.* California Management Review, Summer 1976. Page 69.

Nelson, William G. *The use of the economic forecasting staff.* Financial Executive. September 1976, page 69.

Product Life and Product Research

Cook, Leslie G. *How to make R & D more productive.* Harvard Business Review, July-August, 1966. Page 145.

Dearden, John. *Budgeting and accounting for R & D costs.* Financial Executive, November 1963. Page 20.

Farley, John, John Howard, L. Winston Ring: *Consumer Behavior, Theory and Application.* Allyn & Bacon, Inc., Boston, 1974.

Harness, Edward G.: *Some basic beliefs about marketing.* Address to the Conference Board 1976 Marketing Conference.

King, Stephen. *Developing new products.* John Wiley and Sons, New York, 1973, pages 2-6.

Kotler, Philip *Phasing out weak products,* Harvard Business Review. March-April, 1965.

Kotler Philip *Marketing management.* Second Edition. Prentice-Hall, Englewood Cliffs, NJ 1972. Chapter 12. Pages 429-438.

Luck, David J. *Product policy and strategy*. Prentice-Hall. Englewood Cliffs, NJ, 1972 Chapters 2, 6, 7 Pages 10-21, 61-79.

Nielsen, A. C. *The life cycle of grocery brands*. The Nielsen Researcher, No. 1, 1968.

Potischman, Ernest *How to breathe new life into your old brand*. Advertising Age, July 16, 1973. Pages 39-44.

Thompson, Paul, Gene W. Dalton *Are R & D organizations obsolete?* Harvard Business Review November-December, 1976 Page 105.

Watson, Spencer C. *A vote for R & D profit centers*. Management Accounting. April, 1975 Page 50.

Index